CALL of CTHULHU

Horror Roleplaying in the Worlds of H. P. Lovecraft

Howard
Phillips
Lovecraft

Author,
Scholar,
Gentleman

Born 1890
Died 1937

CALL of CTHULHU

EDITION 5.6

Horror Roleplaying in the Worlds of H. P. Lovecraft

Sandy Petersen
majority of 1983 text

&

Lynn Willis
most of current text

additional text and information
Keith Herber, Kevin Ross, Mark Morrison, William Hamblin, Scott David Aniolowski, Michael Tice, Shannon Appel, Eric Rowe, Bruce Ballon, William G. Dunn, Sam Johnson, Brian M. Sammons, Jan Engan, and friends

cover painting John T. Snyder

section illustrations & sidebar decorations Paul Carrick

additional illustrations
Gene Day, Tom Sullivan, Lori Deitrick, Gus DiZerega, Chris Marrinan, Dreyfus, Lisa A. Free, Earl Geier, John T. Snyder, Tony Ackland, Drashi Khendup

project, editorial Lynn Willis

design, layout Shannon Appel

editress, copy reading Janice Sellers

sales, support, promotions Dustin Wright

Chaosium Inc.
1999

Clear Credit

Keith Herber wrote the *Necronomicon* chapter, Mythos Prehistory, H. P. Lovecraft and the Cthulhu Mythos, The Edge of Darkness, Prehistory of the Cthulhu Mythos, and (with Kevin Ross) Books of the Cthulhu Mythos. Mark Morrison (with Lynn Willis) wrote Dead Man Stomp. Les Brooks created the ready-to-play investigators and compiled sample gear and prices. Kevin Ross tracked down many quotes and sources, and added material and statistics. Scott Aniolowski concentrated on monster descriptions and statistics. Long ago Bill Dunn wrote the Guide to Sanity Losses. William Hamblin wrote three Sadowsky episodes here summarized as "In Rerum Supernatura." Michael Tice, Eric Rowe, and Shannon Appel assembled much of the present Sanity information. Shannon Appel also constructed the Alien Technology section, using some inventions from past supplements, and did revisionary work on Deities, Creatures, and Mythos Prehistory. Bruce Ballon, Chaosium's psychiatric consultant, updated the Sanity chapter and wrote the Dangerousness Criteria example, the timeline, and the summaries of drugs and treatments. Jan Engan contributed the occult book summaries. Brian Sammons created the two-part Mythos tomes table. Sam Johnson wrote the tournament notes for the keeper's chapter, more stats for the weapon table, and about research modifiers in the keeper's toolkit section.

Thanks to Alexis G. Diaz, whose questions provoked 5th edition, and to John Tarnowski.

Playtesters

Utah playtesters for the first edition of Call of Cthulhu were Steve Marsh, James Memmot, Wade Round, Paul Work, Scott Clegg, Marc Hutchison, Bill Hamblin, and Eric Petersen. Chaosium playtesters were Al Dewey (keeper), and in alphabetical order Yurek Chodak, Allan Dalcher, Charlotte Coulon, Al Dewey, Bruce Dresselhaus, Jerry Epperson, Sherman Kahn, Ken Kaufer, Charlie Krank, Fred Malmburg, Hal Moe, Steve Perrin, Rory Root, Greg Stafford, Anders Swenson, and Lynn Willis.

Acknowledgments

Thanks are also due to the original authors (especially Steve Perrin) and play group connected with the 1978 roleplaying game *RuneQuest*, now owned by Hasbro, from which the mechanics of Call of Cthulhu were adapted via the intermediary and out-of-print *Basic Roleplaying*. Mark Morrison has remarked that when he wishes to see how some problem of physical action is handled in a game, he turns first to *RuneQuest*. He is not the only one.

Sandy Petersen, who authored the original Cthulhu rules, labored long and to great effect on his game's behalf. He still exercises strong influence on the game through his thoughtful forebearance and in his agreeable notions of rules economy. Everywhere his words have been weighed and mined.

Table of Contents

Foreword

Welcome to Call of Cthulhu! If you have ever been enthralled by a ghost story or spellbound at a horror movie, you are in for a treat. Part the veil that separates frail humanity from the terror that lurks beyond space and time. Investigate forgotten ruins, haunted woods, and nameless menaces.

Enter the world of Call of Cthulhu.

This game was first published in 1981. At that time, three major national awards were issued in the United States for excellence in game design. Call of Cthulhu won all three. It spawned foreign language editions in Finnish, French, German, Hungarian, Italian, Japanese, Polish, and Spanish. Supplements to this game have won more than fifty major awards, in the U.S. and internationally. In 1996, Call of Cthulhu was chosen for the Origins Hall of Fame, gaming's most prestigious award.

My introduction to H. P. Lovecraft was as a child, when I found a tattered book of stories, printed for the use of servicemen during World War II. I read that book in bed that night, and become entranced forever. If you, too, love Lovecraft's stories, you can now experience the Cthulhu Mythos in a new way. What would you have done in the place of Lovecraft's intrepid heroes? Could you have solved the sinister Whateley mystery? Would you have been able to save the world from the nightmare of the deep ones? Could you face shoggoths without going mad? Now you can find out!

— Sandy Petersen.

Dedication

To my father, who introduced me to Lovecraft and to
science fiction in general. From one of his books I read
my first Lovecraftian story, "Pickman's Model."
Thanks, Dad. — S. P.

Additional Acknowledgements

At one time or another, Mythos material has been adapted from many individual scenarios and articles, a tradition stemming from the original circle of writers encouraged by Lovecraft himself. After most of two decades, it is a hopeless task to try to indicate who accomplished what. We gratefully thank all the scenarists and contributors from the initial supplement, *Shadows of Yog-Sothoth*, through to early 1998. In alphabetical order they are Chris Adamas, Jamie Anderson, Marion Anderson, Phil Anderson, Scott Aniolowski, Sandy Antunes, Shannon Appel, Bruce Ballon, Ugo Bardi, William A. Barton, Mark Beardsley, Fred Behrendt, Andre Bishop, Michael Blum, Gustaf Bjorsten, Sean Branney, Russell Bullman, Bernard Caleo, James Cambias, K. L. Campbell-Robson, John Carnahan, Yurek Chodak, Stacy Clark, Harry Cleaver, Jacqueline Clegg, John Scott Clegg, Morgan Conrad, Peter Corless, Matthew J. Costello, Alan K. Crandall, Peter Dannseys, Gregory W. Detwiler, Michael DeWolfe, Larry DiTillio, Ralph Dula, William G. Dunn, Chris Dykins, Chaz Engan, E. C. Fallworth, Phil Frances, D. H. Frew, Geoff Gillan, Ed Gore, Mark Grundy, Owen Guthrie, Nick Haggar, David Hallet, William James Hamblin III, David A. Hargrave, Mark Harmon, Steve Hatherly, Bob Heggie, Erik Herber, Tony Hickie, Herbert Hike, Kathy Ho, Susan Hutchinson, Marc Hutchison, L. N. Isinwyll, Kevin W. Jacklin, Peter F. Jeffery, Sam Johnson, Drashi Khendup, Steve Kluskens, J. Todd Kingrea, Charlie Krank, Michael LaBossiere, Richard T. Launius, Michael Lay, Nigel Leather, Christian Lehmann, Andrew Leman, Thomas Ligotti, Jean Lishman, Penelope Love, Toivo Luick, Doug Lyons, Michael MacDonald, Barbara Manui, Wesley Martin, Randy McCall, Paul McConnell, Robert McLaughlin, Kurt Miller, John B. Monroe, Mark Morrison, Scott Nicholson, Gary O'Connell, Jeff Okamoto, Mark Pettigrew, Thomas W. Phinney, Glenn Rahman, Steven C. Rasmussen, Kevin Ross, Liam Routt, Eric Rowe, Marcus L. Rowland, Gregory Rucka, Brian M. Sammons, Justin Schmid, Cyndy Schneider, Janice Sellers, Sam Shirley, John Sullivan, Gary Sumpter, Neal Sutton, Lucya Szachnowski, Michael Szymanski, G.W. Thomas, Michael Tice, Richard L. Tierney, John Tynes, Justin Tynes, Fred Van Lente, Russell Waters, Richard Watts, Chris Williams, M. B. Willner, Ian Winterton, Jay J. Wiseman, Elizabeth A. Wolcott, Todd A. Woods, William A. Workman, Benjamin Wright.

THE CALL OF CTHULHU

*(Found Among the Papers of the Late
Francis Wayland Thurston, of Boston)*

by H. P. Lovecraft

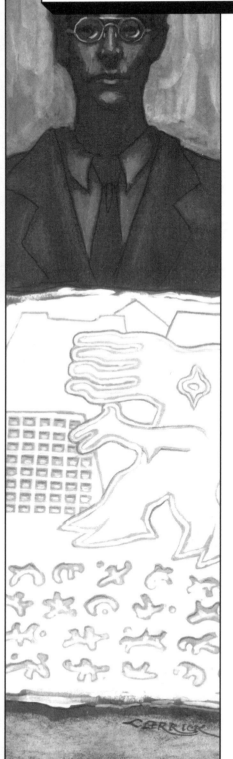

"Of such great powers or beings there may be conceivably a survival . . . a survival of a hugely remote period when . . . consciousness was manifested, perhaps, in shapes and forms long since withdrawn before the tide of advancing humanity . . . forms of which poetry and legend alone have caught a flying memory and called them gods, monsters, mythical beings of all sorts and kinds . . . ."
— Algernon Blackwood

I.
The Horror in Clay.

The most merciful thing in the world, I think, is the inability of the human mind to correlate all its contents. We live on a placid island of ignorance in the midst of black seas of infinity, and it was not meant that we should voyage far. The sciences, each straining in its own direction, have hitherto harmed us little; but some day the piecing together of dissociated knowledge will open up such terrifying vistas of reality, and of our frightful position therein, that we shall either go mad from the revelation or flee from the deadly light into the peace and safety of a new dark age.

Theosophists have guessed at the awesome grandeur of the cosmic cycle wherein our world and human race form transient incidents. They have hinted at strange survivals in terms which would freeze the blood if not masked by a bland optimism. But it is not from them that there came the single glimpse of forbidden aeons which chills me when I think of it and maddens me when I dream of it. That glimpse, like all dread glimpses of truth, flashed out from an accidental piecing together of separated things—in this case an old newspaper item and the notes of a dead professor. I hope that no one else will accomplish this piecing out; certainly, if I live, I shall never knowingly supply a link in so hideous a chain. I think that the professor, too, intended to keep silent regarding the part he knew, and that he would have destroyed his notes had not sudden death seized him.

My knowledge of the thing began in the winter of 1926-27 with the death of my grand-uncle George Gammell Angell, Professor Emeritus of Semitic Languages in Brown University, Providence, Rhode Island. Professor Angell was widely known as an authority on ancient inscriptions, and had frequently been resorted to by the heads of prominent museums; so that his passing at the age of ninety-two may be recalled by many. Locally, interest was intensified by the obscurity of the cause of death. The professor had been stricken whilst returning from the Newport boat; falling suddenly, as witnesses said, after having been jostled by a nautical-looking Negro who had come from one of the queer dark courts on the precipitous hillside which formed a short cut from the waterfront to the deceased's home in Williams Street. Physicians were unable to find any visible disorder, but concluded after perplexed debate that some obscure lesion of the heart, induced by the brisk ascent of so steep a hill by so elderly a man, was responsible for the end. At the time I saw no reason to dissent from this dictum, but latterly I am inclined to wonder—and more than wonder.

As my grand-uncle's heir and executor, for he died a childless widower, I was expected to go over his papers with some thoroughness; and for that purpose moved his entire set of files and boxes to my quarters in Boston. Much of the material which I correlated will be later published by the American Archaeological Society, but there was one box which I found exceedingly puzzling, and which I felt much averse from shewing to other eyes. It had been locked, and I did not find the key till it occurred to me to examine the personal ring which the professor carried always in his pocket. Then indeed I succeeded in opening it, but when I did so seemed only to be confronted by a greater and more closely locked barrier. For what could be the meaning of the queer clay bas-relief and the disjointed jottings, ramblings, and cuttings which I found? Had my uncle, in his latter years, become credulous of the most superficial impostures? I resolved to search out the eccentric sculptor responsible for this apparent disturbance of an old man's peace of mind.

The bas-relief was a rough rectangle less than an inch thick and about five by six inches in area; obviously of modern origin. Its designs, however, were far from modern in atmosphere and suggestion; for although the vagaries of cubism and futurism are many and wild, they do not often reproduce that cryptic regularity which lurks in prehistoric writing. And writing of some kind the bulk of these designs seemed certainly to be; though my memory, despite much familiarity with the papers and collections of my uncle, failed in any way to identify this particular species, or even to hint at its remotest affiliations.

Above these apparent hieroglyphics was a figure of evidently pictorial intent, though its impressionistic execution forbade a very clear idea of its nature. It seemed to be a sort of monster, or symbol representing a monster, of a form which only a diseased fancy could conceive. If I say that my somewhat extravagant imagination yielded simultaneous pictures of an octopus, a dragon, and a human caricature, I shall not be unfaithful to the spirit of the thing. A pulpy, tentacled head surmounted a grotesque and scaly body with rudimentary wings; but it was the *general outline* of the whole which made it most shockingly frightful. Behind the figure was a vague suggestion of a Cyclopean architectural background.

The writing accompanying this oddity was, aside from a stack of press cuttings, in Professor Angell's most recent hand; and made no pretense to literary style. What seemed to be the main document was headed "CTHULHU CULT" in characters painstakingly printed to avoid the erroneous reading of a word so unheard-of. This manuscript was divided into two sections, the first of which was headed "1925—Dream and Dream Work of H. A. Wilcox, 7 Thomas St., Providence, R.I.", and the second, "Narrative of Inspector John R. Legrasse, 121 Bienville St., New Orleans, La., at 1908 A.A.S. Mtg.—Notes on Same, & Prof. Webb's Acct." The other manuscript papers were all brief notes, some of them accounts of the queer dreams of different persons, some of them citations from theosophical books and magazines (notably W. Scott Elliot's *Atlantis and the Lost Lemuria*), and the rest comments on long-surviving secret societies and hidden cults, with references to passages in such mythological and anthropological source-books as Frazer's *Golden Bough* and Miss Murray's *Witch-Cult in Western Europe*. The cuttings largely alluded to outré mental illnesses and outbreaks of group folly or mania in the spring of 1925.

The first half of the principal manuscript told a very peculiar tale. It appears that on March 1st, 1925, a thin, dark young man of neurotic and excited aspect had called upon Professor Angell bearing the singular clay bas-relief, which was then exceedingly damp and fresh. His card bore the name of Henry Anthony Wilcox, and my uncle had recognised him as the youngest son of an excellent family slightly known to him, who had latterly been studying sculpture at the Rhode Island School of Design and living alone at the Fleur-de-Lys Building near that institution. Wilcox was a precocious youth of known genius but great eccentricity, and had from childhood excited attention through the strange stories and odd dreams he was in the habit of relating. He called himself "psychically hypersensitive", but the staid folk of the ancient commercial city dismissed him as merely "queer". Never mingling much with his kind, he had dropped gradually from social visibility, and was now known only to a small group of aesthetes from other towns. Even the Providence Art Club, anxious to preserve its conservatism, had found him quite hopeless.

On the occasion of the visit, ran the professor's manuscript, the sculptor abruptly asked for the benefit of his host's archaeological knowledge in identifying the hieroglyphics on the bas-relief. He spoke in a dreamy, stilted manner which suggested pose and alienated sympathy; and my uncle shewed some sharpness in replying, for the conspicuous freshness of the tablet implied kinship with anything but archaeology. Young Wilcox's rejoinder, which impressed my uncle enough to make him recall and record it verbatim, was of a fantastically poetic cast which must have typified his whole conversation, and which I have since found highly characteristic of him. He said, "It is new, indeed, for I made it last night in a dream of strange cities; and dreams are older than brooding Tyre, or the contemplative Sphinx, or garden-girdled Babylon."

It was then that he began that rambling tale which suddenly played upon a sleeping memory and won the fevered interest of my uncle. There had been a slight earthquake tremor the night before, the most considerable felt in New England for some years; and Wilcox's imagination had been keenly affected. Upon retiring, he had had an unprecedented dream of great Cyclopean cities of titan blocks and sky-flung monoliths, all dripping with green ooze and sinister with latent horror. Hieroglyphics had covered the walls and pillars, and from some undetermined point below had come a voice that was not a voice; a chaotic sensation which only fancy could transmute into sound, but which he attempted to render by the almost unpronounceable jumble of letters, "*Cthulhu fhtagn*".

This verbal jumble was the key to the recollection which excited and disturbed Professor Angell. He questioned the sculptor with scientific minuteness; and studied with almost frantic intensity the bas-relief on which the youth had found himself working, chilled and clad only in his night-clothes, when waking had stolen bewilderingly over him. My uncle blamed his old age, Wilcox afterward said, for his slowness in recognising both hieroglyphics and pictorial design.

Many of his questions seemed highly out-of-place to his visitor, especially those which tried to connect the latter with strange cults or societies; and Wilcox could not understand the repeated promises of silence which he was offered in exchange for an admission of membership in some widespread mystical or paganly religious body. When Professor Angell became convinced that the sculptor was indeed ignorant of any cult or system of cryptic lore, he besieged his visitor with demands for future reports of dreams. This bore regular fruit, for after the first interview the manuscript records daily calls of the young man, during which he related startling fragments of nocturnal imagery whose burden was always some terrible Cyclopean vista of dark and dripping stone, with a subterrene voice or intelligence shouting monotonously in enigmatical sense-impacts uninscribable save as gibberish. The two sounds most frequently repeated are those rendered by the letters "*Cthulhu*" and "*R'lyeh*".

On March 23rd, the manuscript continued, Wilcox failed to appear; and inquiries at his quarters revealed that he had been stricken with an obscure sort of fever and taken to the home of his family in Waterman Street. He had cried out in the night, arousing several other artists in the building, and had manifested since then only alternations of unconsciousness and delirium. My uncle at once telephoned the family, and from that time forward kept close watch of the case; calling often at the Thayer Street office of Dr. Tobey, whom he learned to be in charge. The youth's febrile mind, apparently, was dwelling on strange things; and the doctor shuddered now and then as he spoke of them. They included not only a repetition of what he had formerly dreamed, but touched wildly on a gigantic thing "miles high" which walked or lumbered about. He at no time fully described this object, but occasional frantic words, as repeated by Dr. Tobey, convinced the professor that it must be identical with the nameless monstrosity he had sought to depict in his dream-sculpture. Reference to this object, the doctor added, was invariably a prelude to the young man's subsidence into lethargy. His temperature, oddly enough, was not greatly above normal; but his whole condition was otherwise such as to suggest true fever rather than mental disorder.

On April 2nd at about 3 p.m. every trace of Wilcox's malady suddenly ceased. He sat upright in bed, astonished to find himself at home and completely ignorant of what had happened in dream or reality since the night of March 22nd. Pronounced well by his physician, he returned to his quarters in three days; but to Professor Angell he was of no further assistance. All traces of strange dreaming had vanished with his recovery, and my uncle kept no record of his night-thoughts after a week of pointless and irrelevant accounts of thoroughly usual visions.

Here the first part of the manuscript ended, but references to certain of the scattered notes gave me much material for thought—so much, in fact, that only the ingrained scepticism then forming my philosophy can account for my continued distrust of the artist. The notes in question were those descriptive of the dreams of various persons covering the same period as that in which young Wilcox had had his strange visitations. My uncle, it seems, had quickly instituted a prodigiously far-flung body of inquiries amongst nearly all the friends whom he could question without impertinence, asking for nightly reports of their dreams, and the dates of any notable visions for some time past. The reception of his request seems to have been varied; but he must, at the very least, have received more responses than any ordinary man could have handled without a secretary. This original correspondence was not preserved, but his notes formed a thorough and really significant digest. Average people in society and business—New England's traditional "salt of the earth"—gave an almost completely negative result, though scattered cases of uneasy but formless nocturnal impressions appear here and there, always between March 23rd and April 2nd—the period of young Wilcox's delirium. Scientific men were little more affected, though four cases of vague description suggest fugitive glimpses of strange landscapes, and in one case there is mentioned a dread of something abnormal.

It was from the artists and poets that the pertinent answers came, and I know that panic would have broken loose had they been able to compare notes. As it was, lacking their original letters, I half suspected the compiler of having asked leading questions, or of having edited the correspondence in corroboration of what he had latently resolved to see. That is why I continued to feel that Wilcox, somehow cognisant of the old data which my uncle had possessed, had been imposing on the veteran scientist. These responses from aesthetes told a disturbing tale. From February 28th to April 2nd a large proportion of them had dreamed very bizarre things, the intensity of the dreams being immeasurably the stronger during the period of the sculptor's delirium. Over a fourth of those who reported anything, reported scenes and half-sounds not unlike those which Wilcox had described; and some of the dreamers confessed acute fear of the gigantic nameless thing visible toward the last. One case, which the note describes with emphasis, was very sad. The subject, a widely known architect with leanings toward theosophy and occultism, went violently insane on the date of young Wilcox's seizure, and expired several months later after incessant screamings to be saved from some escaped denizen of hell. Had my uncle referred to these cases

by name instead of merely by number, I should have attempted some corroboration and personal investigation; but as it was, I succeeded in tracing down only a few. All of these, however, bore out the notes in full. I have often wondered if all the objects of the professor's questioning felt as puzzled as did this fraction. It is well that no explanation shall ever reach them.

The press cuttings, as I have intimated, touched on cases of panic, mania, and eccentricity during the given period. Professor Angell must have employed a cutting bureau, for the number of extracts was tremendous and the sources scattered throughout the globe. Here was a nocturnal suicide in London, where a lone sleeper had leaped from a window after a shocking cry. Here likewise a rambling letter to the editor of a paper in South America, where a fanatic deduces a dire future from visions he has seen. A despatch from California describes a theosophist colony as donning white robes en masse for some "glorious fulfillment" which never arrives, whilst items from India speak guardedly of serious native unrest toward the end of March. Voodoo orgies multiply in Hayti, and African outposts report ominous mutterings. American officers in the Philippines find certain tribes bothersome at this time, and New York policemen are mobbed by hysterical Levantines on the night of March 22-23. The west of Ireland, too, is full of wild rumour and legendry, and a fantastic painter named Ardois-Bonnot hangs a blasphemous "Dream Landscape" in the Paris spring salon of 1926. And so numerous are the recorded troubles in insane asylums, that only a miracle can have stopped the medical fraternity from noting strange parallelisms and drawing mystified conclusions. A weird bunch of cuttings, all told; and I can at this date scarcely envisage the callous rationalism with which I set them aside. But I was then convinced that young Wilcox had known of the older matters mentioned by the professor.

II.

The Tale of Inspector Legrasse.

The older matters which had made the sculptor's dream and bas-relief so significant to my uncle formed the subject of the second half of his long manuscript. Once before, it appears, Professor Angell had seen the hellish outlines of the nameless monstrosity, puzzled over the unknown hieroglyphics, and heard the ominous syllables which can be rendered only as "*Cthulhu*"; and all this in so stirring and horrible a connexion that it is small wonder he pursued young Wilcox with queries and demands for data.

This earlier experience had come in 1908, seventeen years before, when the American Archaeological Society held its annual meeting in St. Louis. Professor Angell, as befitted one of his authority and attainments, had had a prominent part in all the deliberations; and was one of the first to be approached by the several outsiders who took advantage of the convocation to offer questions for correct answering and problems for expert solution.

The chief of these outsiders, and in a short time the focus of interest for the entire meeting, was a commonplace-looking middle-aged man who had travelled all the way from New Orleans for certain special information unobtainable from any local source. His name was John Raymond Legrasse, and he was by profession an Inspector of Police. With him he bore the subject of his visit, a grotesque, repulsive, and apparently very ancient stone statuette whose origin he was at a loss to determine. It must not be fancied that Inspector Legrasse had the least interest in archaeology. On the contrary, his wish for enlightenment was prompted by purely professional considerations. The statuette, idol, fetish, or whatever it was, had been captured some months before in the wooded swamps south of New Orleans during a raid on a supposed voodoo meeting; and so singular and hideous were the rites connected with it, that the police could not but realise that they had stumbled on a dark cult totally unknown to them, and infinitely more diabolic than even the blackest of the African voodoo circles. Of its origin, apart from the erratic and unbelievable tales extorted from the captured members, absolutely nothing was to be discovered; hence the anxiety of the police for any antiquarian lore which might help them to place the frightful symbol, and through it track down the cult to its fountain-head.

Inspector Legrasse was scarcely prepared for the sensation which his offering created. One sight of the thing had been enough to throw the assembled men of science into a state of tense excitement, and they lost no time in crowding around him to gaze at the diminutive figure whose utter strangeness and air of genuinely abysmal antiquity hinted so potently at unopened and archaic vistas. No recognised school of sculpture had animated this terrible object, yet centuries and even thousands of years seemed recorded in its dim and greenish surface of unplaceable stone.

The figure, which was finally passed slowly from man to man for close and careful study, was between seven and eight inches in height, and of exquisitely artistic workmanship. It represented a monster of vaguely anthropoid outline, but with an octopus-like head whose face was a mass of feelers, a scaly, rubbery-looking body, prodigious claws on hind and fore feet, and long, nar-

row wings behind. This thing, which seemed instinct with a fearsome and unnatural malignancy, was of a somewhat bloated corpulence, and squatted evilly on a rectangular block or pedestal covered with undecipherable characters. The tips of the wings touched the back edge of the block, the seat occupied the centre, whilst the long, curved claws of the doubled-up, crouching hind legs gripped the front edge and extended a quarter of the way down toward the bottom of the pedestal. The cephalopod head was bent forward, so that the ends of the facial feelers brushed the backs of huge fore paws which clasped the croucher's elevated knees. The aspect of the whole was abnormally life-like, and the more subtly fearful because its source was so totally unknown. Its vast, awesome, and incalculable age was unmistakable; yet not one link did it shew with any known type of art belonging to civilisation's youth—or indeed to any other time. Totally separate and apart, its very material was a mystery; for the soapy, greenish-black stone with its golden or iridescent flecks and striations resembled nothing familiar to geology or mineralogy. The characters along the base were equally baffling; and no member present, despite a representation of half the world's expert learning in this field, could form the least notion of even their remotest linguistic kinship. They, like the subject and material, belonged to something horribly remote and distinct from mankind as we know it; something frightfully suggestive of old and unhallowed cycles of life in which our world and our conceptions have no part.

And yet, as the members severally shook their heads and confessed defeat at the Inspector's problem, there was one man in that gathering who suspected a touch of bizarre familiarity in the monstrous shape and writing, and who presently told with some diffidence of the odd trifle he knew. This person was the late William Channing Webb, Professor of Anthropology in Princeton University, and an explorer of no slight note. Professor Webb had been engaged, forty-eight years before, in a tour of Greenland and Iceland in search of some Runic inscriptions which he failed to unearth; and whilst high up on the West Greenland coast had encountered a singular tribe or cult of degenerate Esquimaux whose religion, a curious form of devil-worship, chilled him with its deliberate bloodthirstiness and repulsiveness. It was a faith of which other Esquimaux knew little, and which they mentioned only with shudders, saying that it had come down from horribly ancient aeons before ever the world was made. Besides nameless rites and human sacrifices there were certain queer hereditary rituals addressed to a supreme elder devil or *tornasuk*; and of this Professor Webb had taken a careful phonetic copy from an aged angekok or wizard-priest, expressing the sounds in Roman letters as best he knew how. But just now of prime significance was the fetish which this cult had cherished, and around which they danced when the aurora leaped high over the ice cliffs. It was, the professor stated, a very crude bas-relief of stone, comprising a hideous picture and some cryptic writing. And so far as he could tell, it was a rough parallel in all essential features of the bestial thing now lying before the meeting.

This data, received with suspense and astonishment by the assembled members, proved doubly exciting to Inspector Legrasse; and he began at once to ply his informant with questions. Having noted and copied an oral ritual among the swamp cult-worshippers his men had arrested, he besought the professor to remember as best he might the syllables taken down amongst the diabolist Esquimaux. There then followed an exhaustive comparison of details, and a moment of really awed silence when both detective and scientist agreed on the virtual identity of the phrase common to two hellish rituals so many worlds of distance apart. What, in substance, both the Esquimaux wizards and the Louisiana swamp-priests had chanted to their kindred idols was something very like this—the word-divisions being guessed at from traditional breaks in the phrase as chanted aloud:

"Ph'nglui mglw'nafh Cthulhu R'lyeh wgah'nagl fhtagn."

Legrasse had one point in advance of Professor Webb, for several among his mongrel prisoners had repeated to him what older celebrants had told them the words meant. This text, as given, ran something like this:

"In his house at R'lyeh dead Cthulhu waits dreaming."

And now, in response to a general and urgent demand, Inspector Legrasse related as fully as possible his experience with the swamp worshippers; telling a story to which I could see my uncle attached profound significance. It savoured of the wildest dreams of mythmaker and theosophist, and disclosed an astonishing degree of cosmic imagination among such half-castes and pariahs as might be least expected to possess it.

On November 1st, 1907, there had come to the New Orleans police a frantic summons from the swamp and lagoon country to the south. The squatters there, mostly primitive but good-natured descendants of Lafitte's men, were in the grip of stark terror from an unknown thing which had stolen upon them in the night. It was voodoo, apparently, but voodoo of a more terrible sort than they had ever known; and some of their women and children had disappeared since the malevolent tom-tom had begun its incessant beating far within the black haunted woods where no dweller ventured. There were insane shouts and harrowing screams, soul-chilling chants and dancing devil-flames; and, the frightened messenger added, the people could stand it no more.

So a body of twenty police, filling two carriages and an automobile, had set out in the late afternoon with the shivering squatter as a guide. At the end of the passable road they alighted, and for miles splashed on in silence through the terrible cypress woods where day never came. Ugly roots and malignant hanging nooses of Spanish moss beset them, and now and then a pile of dank stones or fragment of a rotting wall intensified by its hint of morbid habitation a depression which every malformed tree and every fungous islet combined to create. At length the squatter settlement, a miserable huddle of huts, hove in sight; and hysterical dwellers ran out to cluster around the group of bobbing lanterns. The muffled beat of tom-toms was now faintly audible far, far ahead; and a curdling shriek came at infrequent intervals when the wind shifted. A reddish glare, too, seemed to filter through pale undergrowth beyond the endless avenues of forest night. Reluctant even to be left alone again, each one of the cowed squatters refused point-blank to advance another inch toward the scene of unholy worship, so Inspector Legrasse and his nineteen colleagues plunged on unguided into black arcades of horror that none of them had ever trod before.

The region now entered by the police was one of traditionally evil repute, substantially unknown and untraversed by white men. There were legends of a hidden lake unglimpsed by mortal sight, in which dwelt a huge, formless white polypous thing with luminous eyes; and squatters whispered that bat-winged devils flew up out of caverns in inner earth to worship it at midnight. They said it had been there before d'Iberville, before La Salle, before the Indians, and before even the wholesome beasts and birds of the woods. It was nightmare itself, and to see it was to die. But it made men dream, and so they knew enough to keep away. The present voodoo orgy was, indeed, on the merest fringe of this abhorred area, but that location was bad enough; hence perhaps the very place of the worship had terrified the squatters more than the shocking sounds and incidents.

Only poetry or madness could do justice to the noises heard by Legrasse's men as they ploughed on through the black morass toward the red glare and muffled tom-toms. There are vocal qualities peculiar to men, and vocal qualities peculiar to beasts; and it is terrible to hear the one when the source should yield the other. Animal fury and orgiastic license here whipped themselves to daemoniac heights by howls and squawking ecstacies that tore and reverberated through those nighted woods like pestilential tempests from the gulfs of hell. Now and then the less organized ululation would cease, and from what seemed a well-drilled chorus of hoarse voices would rise in sing-song chant that hideous phrase or ritual: *"Ph'nglui mglw'nafh Cthulhu R'lyeh wgah'nagl fhtagn."*

Then the men, having reached a spot where the trees were thinner, came suddenly in sight of the spectacle itself. Four of them reeled, one fainted, and two were shaken into a frantic cry which the mad cacophony of the orgy fortunately deadened. Legrasse dashed swamp water on the face of the fainting man, and all stood trembling and nearly hypnotised with horror.

In a natural glade of the swamp stood a grassy island of perhaps an acre's extent, clear of trees and tolerably dry. On this now leaped and twisted a more indescribable horde of human abnormality than any but a Sime or an Angarola could paint. Void of clothing, this hybrid spawn were braying, bellowing, and writhing about a monstrous ring-shaped bonfire; in the centre of which, revealed by occasional rifts in the curtain of flame, stood a great granite monolith some eight feet in height; on top of which, incongruous in its diminutiveness, rested the noxious carven statuette. From a wide circle of ten scaffolds set up at regular intervals with the flame-girt monolith as a centre hung, head downward, the oddly marred bodies of the helpless squatters who had disappeared. It was inside this circle that the ring of worshippers jumped and roared, the general direction of the mass motion being from left to right in endless Bacchanal between the ring of bodies and the ring of fire.

It may have been only imagination and it may have been only echoes which induced one of the men, an excitable Spaniard, to fancy he heard antiphonal responses to the ritual from some far and unillumined spot deeper within the wood of ancient legendry and horror. This man, Joseph D. Galvez, I later met and questioned; and he proved distractingly imaginative. He indeed went so far as to hint of the faint beating of great wings, and of a glimpse of shining eyes and a mountainous white bulk beyond the remotest trees—but I suppose he had been hearing too much native superstition.

Actually, the horrified pause of the men was of comparatively brief duration. Duty came first; and although there must have been nearly a hundred mongrel celebrants in the throng, the police relied on their firearms and plunged determinedly into the nauseous rout. For five minutes the resultant din and chaos were beyond description. Wild blows were struck, shots were fired, and escapes were made; but in the end Legrasse was able to count some forty-seven sullen prisoners,

whom he forced to dress in haste and fall into line between two rows of policemen. Five of the worshippers lay dead, and two severely wounded ones were carried away on improvised stretchers by their fellow-prisoners. The image on the monolith, of course, was carefully removed and carried back by Legrasse.

Examined at headquarters after a trip of intense strain and weariness, the prisoners all proved to be men of a very low, mixed-blooded, and mentally aberrant type. Most were seamen, and a sprinkling of Negroes and mulattoes, largely West Indians or Brava Portuguese from the Cape Verde Islands, gave a colouring of voodooism to the heterogeneous cult. But before many questions were asked, it became manifest that something far deeper and older than Negro fetichism was involved. Degraded and ignorant as they were, the creatures held with surprising consistency to the central idea of their loathsome faith.

They worshipped, so they said, the Great Old Ones who lived ages before there were any men, and who came to the young world out of the sky. Those Old Ones were gone now, inside the earth and under the sea; but their dead bodies had told their secrets in dreams to the first men, who formed a cult which had never died. This was that cult, and the prisoners said it had always existed and always would exist, hidden in distant wastes and dark places all over the world until the time when the great priest Cthulhu, from his dark house in the mighty city of R'lyeh under the waters, should rise and bring the earth again beneath his sway. Some day he would call, when the stars were ready, and the secret cult would always be waiting to liberate him.

Meanwhile no more must be told. There was a secret which even torture could not extract. Mankind was not absolutely alone among the conscious things of earth, for shapes came out of the dark to visit the faithful few. But these were not the Great Old Ones. No man had ever seen the Old Ones. The carven idol was great Cthulhu, but none might say whether or not the others were precisely like him. No one could read the old writing now, but things were told by word of mouth. The chanted ritual was not the secret—that was never spoken aloud, only whispered. The chant meant only this: "In his house at R'lyeh dead Cthulhu waits dreaming."

Only two of the prisoners were found sane enough to be hanged, and the rest were committed to various institutions. All denied a part in the ritual murders, and averred that the killing had been done by Black Winged Ones which had come to them from their immemorial meeting-place in the haunted wood. But of those mysterious allies no coherent account could ever be gained. What the police did extract, came mainly from the immensely aged mestizo named Castro, who claimed to have sailed to strange ports and talked with undying leaders of the cult in the mountains of China.

Old Castro remembered bits of hideous legend that paled the speculations of theosophists and made man and the world seem recent and transient indeed. There had been aeons when other Things ruled on the earth, and They had had great cities. Remains of Them, he said the deathless Chinamen had told him, were still to be found as Cyclopean stones on islands in the Pacific. They all died vast epochs of time before men came, but there were arts which could revive Them when the stars had come round again to the right positions in the cycle of eternity. They had, indeed, come themselves from the stars, and brought Their images with Them.

These Great Old Ones, Castro continued, were not composed altogether of flesh and blood. They had shape—for did not this star-fashioned image prove it?—but that shape was not made of matter. When the stars were right, They could plunge from world to world through the sky; but when the stars were wrong, They could not live. But although They no longer lived, They would never really die. They all lay in stone houses in Their great city of R'lyeh, preserved by the spells of mighty Cthulhu for a glorious resurrection when the stars and the earth might once more be ready for Them. But at that time some force from outside must serve to liberate Their bodies. The spells that preserved Them intact likewise prevented Them from making an initial move, and They could only lie awake in the dark and think whilst uncounted millions of years rolled by. They knew all that was occurring in the universe, for Their mode of speech was transmitted thought. Even now They talked in Their tombs. When, after infinities of chaos, the first men came, the Great Old Ones spoke to the sensitive among them by moulding their dreams; for only thus could Their language reach the fleshly minds of mammals.

Then, whispered Castro, those first men formed the cult around small idols which the Great Ones shewed them; idols brought in dim eras from dark stars. That cult would never die till the stars came right again, and the secret priests would take great Cthulhu from His tomb to revive His subjects and resume His rule of earth. The time would be easy to know, for then mankind would have become as the Great Old Ones; free and wild and beyond good and evil, with laws and morals thrown aside and all men shouting and killing and revelling in joy. Then the liberated Old Ones would teach them new ways to shout and kill and revel and enjoy themselves, and all the earth would flame with a holocaust of ecstasy and freedom. Meanwhile the cult, by appropriate rites, must keep alive the memory of those ancient ways and shadow forth the prophecy of their return.

In the elder time chosen men had talked with the entombed Old Ones in dreams, but then something happened. The great stone city R'lyeh, with its monoliths and sepulchres, had sunk beneath the waves; and the deep waters, full of the one primal mystery through which not even thought can pass, had cut off the spectral intercourse. But memory never died, and the high-priests said that the city would rise again when the stars were right. Then came out of the earth the black spirits of earth, mouldy and shadowy, and full of dim rumours picked up in caverns beneath forgotten sea-bottoms. But of them old Castro dared not speak much. He cut himself off hurriedly, and no amount of persuasion or subtlety could elicit more in this direction. The *size* of the Old Ones, too, he curiously declined to mention. Of the cult, he said that he thought the centre lay amid the pathless desert of Arabia, where Irem, the City of Pillars, dreams hidden and untouched. It was not allied to the European witch-cult, and was virtually unknown beyond its members. No book had ever really hinted of it, though the deathless Chinamen said that there were double meanings in the *Necronomicon* of the mad Arab Abdul Alhazred which the initiated might read as they chose, especially the much-discussed couplet:

> "That is not dead which can eternal lie,
> And with strange aeons even death may die."

Legrasse, deeply impressed and not a little bewildered, had inquired in vain concerning the historic affiliations of the cult. Castro, apparently, had told the truth when he said that it was wholly secret. The authorities at Tulane University could shed no light upon either cult or image, and now the detective had come to the highest authorities in the country and met with no more than the Greenland tale of Professor Webb.

The feverish interest aroused at the meeting by Legrasse's tale, corroborated as it was by the statuette, is echoed in the subsequent correspondence of those who attended; although scant mention occurs in the formal publications of the society. Caution is the first care of those accustomed to face occasional charlatanry and imposture. Legrasse for some time lent the image to Professor Webb, but at the latter's death it was returned to him and remains in his possession, where I viewed it not long ago. It is truly a terrible thing, and unmistakably akin to the dream-sculpture of young Wilcox.

That my uncle was excited by the tale of the sculptor I did not wonder, for what thoughts must arise upon hearing, after a knowledge of what Legrasse had learned of the cult, of a sensitive young man who had *dreamed* not only the figure and exact hieroglyphics of the swamp-found image and the Greenland devil tablet, but had come *in his dreams* upon at least three of the precise words of the formula uttered alike by Esquimau diabolists and mongrel Louisianans? Professor Angell's instant start on an investigation of the utmost thoroughness was eminently natural; though privately I suspected young Wilcox of having heard of the cult in some indirect way, and of having invented a series of dreams to heighten and continue the mystery at my uncle's expense. The dream-narratives and cuttings collected by the professor were, of course, strong corroboration; but the rationalism of my mind and the extravagance of the whole subject led me to adopt what I thought the most sensible conclusions. So, after thoroughly studying the manuscript again and correlating the theosophical and anthropological notes with the cult narrative of Legrasse, I made a trip to Providence to see the sculptor and give him the rebuke I thought proper for so boldly imposing upon a learned and aged man.

Wilcox still lived alone in the Fleur-de-Lys Building in Thomas Street, a hideous Victorian imitation of seventeenth-century Breton architecture which flaunts its stuccoed front amidst the lovely colonial houses on the ancient hill, and under the very shadow of the finest Georgian steeple in America, I found him at work in his rooms, and at once conceded from the specimens scattered about that his genius is indeed profound and authentic. He will, I believe, some time be heard from as one of the great decadents; for he has crystallised in clay and will one day mirror in marble those nightmares and phantasies which Arthur Machen evokes in prose, and Clark Ashton Smith makes visible in verse and in painting.

Dark, frail, and somewhat unkempt in aspect, he turned languidly at my knock and asked me my business without rising. When I told him who I was, he displayed some interest; for my uncle had excited his curiosity in probing his strange dreams, yet had never explained the reason for the study. I did not enlarge his knowledge in this regard, but sought with some subtlety to draw him out. In a short time I became convinced of his absolute sincerity, for he spoke of the dreams in a manner none could mistake. They and their subconscious residuum had influenced his art profoundly, and he shewed me a morbid statue whose contours almost made me shake with the potency of its black suggestion. He could not recall having seen the original of this thing except in his own dream bas-relief, but the outlines had formed themselves insensibly under his hands. It was, no doubt, the giant shape he had raved of in delirium. That he really knew nothing of the hidden

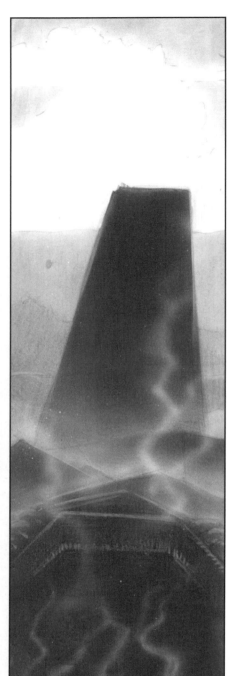

cult, save from what my uncle's relentless catechism had let fall, he soon made clear; and again I strove to think of some way in which he could possibly have received the weird impressions.

He talked of his dreams in a strangely poetic fashion; making me see with terrible vividness the damp Cyclopean city of slimy green stone—whose *geometry*, he oddly said, was *all wrong*—and hear with frightened expectancy the ceaseless, half-mental calling from underground: "*Cthulhu fhtagn*", "*Cthulhu fhtagn*". These words had formed part of that dread ritual which told of dead Cthulhu's dream-vigil in his stone vault at R'lyeh, and I felt deeply moved despite my rational beliefs. Wilcox, I was sure, had heard of the cult in some casual way, and had soon forgotten it amidst the mass of his equally weird reading and imagining. Later, by virtue of its sheer impressiveness, it had found subconscious expression in dreams, in the bas-relief, and in the terrible statue I now beheld; so that his imposture upon my uncle had been a very innocent one. The youth was of a type, at once slightly affected and slightly ill-mannered, which I could never like, but I was willing enough now to admit both his genius and his honesty. I took leave of him amicably, and wish him all the success his talent promises.

The matter of the cult still remained to fascinate me, and at times I had visions of personal fame from researches into its origin and connexions. I visited New Orleans, talked with Legrasse and others of that old-time raiding-party, saw the frightful image, and even questioned such of the mongrel prisoners as still survived. Old Castro, unfortunately, had been dead for some years. What I now heard so graphically at first-hand, though it was really no more than a detailed confirmation of what my uncle had written, excited me afresh; for I felt sure that I was on the track of a very real, very secret, and very ancient religion whose discovery would make me an anthropologist of note. My attitude was still one of absolute materialism, *as I wish it still were*, and I discounted with almost inexplicable perversity the coincidence of the dream notes and odd cuttings collected by Professor Angell.

One thing I began to suspect, and which I now fear I *know*, is that my uncle's death was far from natural. He fell on a narrow hill street leading up from an ancient waterfront swarming with foreign mongrels, after a careless push from a Negro sailor. I did not forget the mixed blood and marine pursuits of the cult-members in Louisiana, and would not be surprised to learn of secret methods and rites and beliefs. Legrasse and his men, it is true, have been let alone; but in Norway a certain seaman who saw things is dead. Might not the deeper inquiries of my uncle after encountering the sculptor's data have come to sinister ears? I think Professor Angell died because he knew too much, or because he was likely to learn too much. Whether I shall go as he did remains to be seen, for I have learned much now.

III.

The Madness from the Sea.

If heaven ever wishes to grant me a boon, it will be a total effacing of the results of a mere chance which fixed my eye on a certain stray piece of shelf-paper. It was nothing on which I would naturally have stumbled in the course of my daily round, for it was an old number of an Australian journal, the *Sydney Bulletin* for April 18, 1925. It had escaped even the cutting bureau which had at the time of its issuance been avidly collecting material for my uncle's research.

I had largely given over my inquiries into what Professor Angell called the "Cthulhu Cult", and was visiting a learned friend in Paterson, New Jersey; the curator of a local museum and a mineralogist of note. Examining one day the reserve specimens roughly set on the storage shelves in a rear room of the museum, my eye was caught by an odd picture in one of the old papers spread beneath the stones. It was the *Sydney Bulletin* I have mentioned, for my friend had wide affiliations in all conceivable foreign parts; and the picture was a half-tone cut of a hideous stone image almost identical with that which Legrasse had found in the swamp.

Eagerly clearing the sheet of its precious contents, I scanned the item in detail; and was disappointed to find it of only moderate length. What it suggested, however, was of portentous significance to my flagging quest; and I carefully tore it out for immediate action. It read as follows:

MYSTERY DERELICT FOUND AT SEA

Vigilant Arrives With Helpless Armed New Zealand Yacht in Tow.
One Survivor and Dead Man Found Aboard. Tale of Desperate Battle and Deaths at Sea.
Rescued Seaman Refuses Particulars of Strange Experience.
Odd Idol Found in His Possession. Inquiry to Follow.

The Morrison Co.'s freighter *Vigilant*, bound from Valparaiso, arrived this morning at its wharf in Darling Harbour, having in tow the battled and disabled but heavily armed steam yacht *Alert* of Dunedin, N.Z., which was sighted April 12th in S. Latitude 34° 21', W. Longitude 152° 17' with one living and one dead man aboard.

The *Vigilant* left Valparaiso March 25th, and on April 2nd was driven considerably south of her course by exceptionally heavy storms and monster waves. On April 12th the derelict was sighted; and though apparently deserted, was found upon boarding to contain one survivor in a half-delirious condition and one man who had evidently been dead for more than a week. The living man was clutching a horrible stone idol of unknown origin, about a foot in height, regarding whose nature authorities at Sydney University, the Royal Society, and the Museum in College Street all profess complete bafflement, and which the survivor says he found in the cabin of the yacht, in a small carved shrine of common pattern.

This man, after recovering his senses, told an exceedingly strange story of piracy and slaughter. He is Gustaf Johansen, a Norwegian of some intelligence, and had been second mate of the two-masted schooner *Emma* of Auckland, which sailed for Callao February 20th with a complement of eleven men. The *Emma*, he says, was delayed and thrown widely south of her course by the great storm of March 1st, and on March 22nd, in S. Latitude 49° 51' W. Longitude 128° 34', encountered the *Alert*, manned by a queer and evil-looking crew of Kanakas and half-castes. Being ordered peremptorily to turn back, Capt. Collins refused; whereupon the strange crew began to fire savagely and without warning upon the schooner with a peculiarly heavy battery of brass cannon forming part of the yacht's equipment. The *Emma*'s men shewed fight, says the survivor, and though the schooner began to sink from shots beneath the waterline they managed to heave alongside their enemy and board her, grappling with the savage crew on the yacht's deck, and being forced to kill them all, the number being slightly superior, because of their particularly abhorrent and desperate though rather clumsy mode of fighting.

Three of the *Emma*'s men, including Capt. Collins and First Mate Green, were killed; and the remaining eight under Second Mate Johansen proceeded to navigate the captured yacht, going ahead in their original direction to see if any reason for their ordering back had existed. The next day, it appears, they raised and landed on a small island, although none is known to exist in that part of the ocean; and six of the men somehow died ashore, though Johansen is queerly reticent about this part of his story, and speaks only of their falling into a rock chasm. Later, it seems, he and one companion boarded the yacht and tried to manage her, but were beaten about by the storm of April 2nd. From that time till his rescue on the 12th the man remembers little, and he does not even recall when William Briden, his companion, died. Briden's death reveals no apparent cause, and was probably due to excitement or exposure. Cable advices from Dunedin report that the *Alert* was well known there as an island trader, and bore an evil reputation along the waterfront. It was owned by a curious group of half-castes whose frequent meetings and night trips to the woods attracted no little curiosity; and it had set sail in great haste just after the storm and earth tremors of March 1st. Our Auckland correspondent gives the *Emma* and her crew an excellent reputation, and Johansen is described as a sober and worthy man. The admiralty will institute an inquiry on the whole matter beginning tomorrow, at which every effort will be made to induce Johansen to speak more freely than he has done hitherto.

This was all, together with the picture of the hellish image; but what a train of ideas it started in my mind! Here were new treasuries of data on the Cthulhu Cult, and evidence that it had strange interests at sea as well as on land. What motive prompted the hybrid crew to order back the *Emma* as they sailed about with their hideous idol? What was the unknown island on which six of the *Emma*'s crew had died, and about which the mate Johansen was so secretive? What had the vice-admiralty's investigation brought out, and what was known of the noxious cult in Dunedin? And most marvellous of all, what deep and more than natural linkage of dates was this which gave a malign and now undeniable significance to the various turns of events so carefully noted by my uncle?

March 1st—our February 28th according to the International Date Line—the earthquake and storm had come. From Dunedin the *Alert* and her noisome crew had darted eagerly forth as if imperiously summoned, and on the other side of the earth poets and artists had begun to dream of a strange, dank Cyclopean city whilst a young sculptor had moulded in his sleep the form of the dreaded Cthulhu. March 23rd the crew of the *Emma* landed on an unknown island and left six men dead; and on that date the dreams of sensitive men assumed a heightened vividness and darkened with

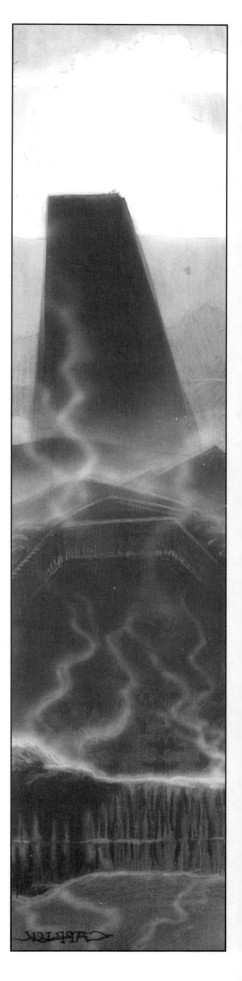

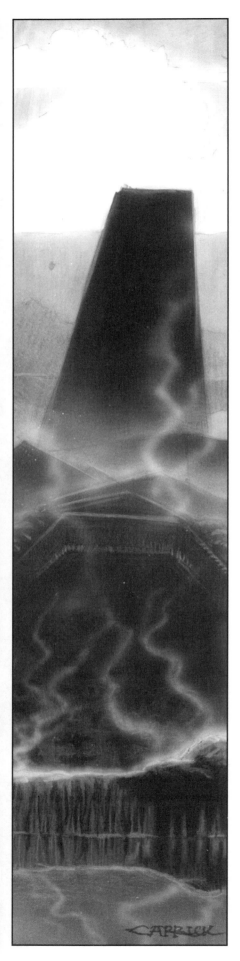

dread of a giant monster's malign pursuit, whilst an architect had gone mad and a sculptor had lapsed suddenly into delirium! And what of this storm of April 2nd—the date on which all dreams of the dank city ceased, and Wilcox emerged unharmed from the bondage of strange fever? What of all this—and of those hints of old Castro about the sunken, star-born Old Ones and their coming reign; their faithful cult *and their mastery of dreams?* Was I tottering on the brink of cosmic horrors beyond man's power to bear? If so, they must be horrors of the mind alone, for in some way the second of April had put a stop to whatever monstrous menace had begun its siege of mankind's soul.

That evening, after a day of hurried cabling and arranging, I bade my host adieu and took a train for San Francisco. In less than a month I was in Dunedin; where, however, I found that little was known of the strange cult-members who had lingered in the old sea-taverns. Waterfront scum was far too common for special mention; though there was vague talk about one inland trip these mongrels had made, during which faint drumming and red flame were noted on the distant hills. In Auckland I learned that Johansen had returned *with yellow hair turned white* after a perfunctory and inconclusive questioning at Sydney, and had thereafter sold his cottage in West Street and sailed with his wife to his old home in Oslo. Of his stirring experience he would tell his friends no more than he had told the admiralty officials, and all they could do was to give me his Oslo address.

After that I went to Sydney and talked profitlessly with seamen and members of the vice-admiralty court. I saw the *Alert*, now sold and in commercial use, at Circular Quay in Sydney Cove, but gained nothing from its non-committal bulk. The crouching image with its cuttlefish head, dragon body, scaly wings, and hieroglyphed pedestal, was preserved in the Museum at Hyde Park; and I studied it long and well, finding it a thing of balefully exquisite workmanship, and with the same utter mystery, terrible antiquity, and unearthly strangeness of material which I had noted in Legrasse's smaller specimen. Geologists, the curator told me, had found it a monstrous puzzle; for they vowed that the world held no rock like it. Then I thought with a shudder of what Old Castro had told Legrasse about the Great Ones; "They had come from the stars, and had brought Their images with Them."

Shaken with such a mental revolution as I had never before known, I now resolved to visit Mate Johansen in Oslo. Sailing for London, I reembarked at once for the Norwegian capital; and one autumn day landed at the trim wharves in the shadow of the Egeberg. Johansen's address, I discovered, lay in the Old Town of King Harold Haardrada, which kept alive the name of Oslo during all the centuries that the greater city masqueraded as "Christiana". I made the brief trip by taxicab, and knocked with palpitant heart at the door of a neat and ancient building with plastered front. A sad-faced woman in black answered my summons, and I was stung with disappointment when she told me in halting English that Gustaf Johansen was no more.

He had not long survived his return, said his wife, for the doings at sea in 1925 had broken him. He had told her no more than he had told the public, but had left a long manuscript—of "technical matters" as he said—written in English, evidently in order to safeguard her from the peril of casual perusal. During a walk through a narrow lane near the Gothenburg dock, a bundle of papers falling from an attic window had knocked him down. Two Lascar sailors at once helped him to his feet, but before the ambulance could reach him he was dead. Physicians found no adequate cause for the end, and laid it to heart trouble and a weakened constitution.

I now felt gnawing at my vitals that dark terror which will never leave me till I, too, am at rest; "accidentally" or otherwise. Persuading the widow that my connexion with her husband's "technical matters" was sufficient to entitle me to his manuscript, I bore the document away and began to read it on the London boat. It was a simple, rambling thing—a naive sailor's effort at a post-facto diary—and strove to recall day by day that last awful voyage. I cannot attempt to transcribe it verbatim in all its cloudiness and redundance, but I will tell its gist enough to shew why the sound of the water against the vessel's sides became so unendurable to me that I stopped my ears with cotton.

Johansen, thank God, did not know quite all, even though he saw the city and the Thing, but I shall never sleep calmly again when I think of the horrors that lurk ceaselessly behind life in time and in space, and of those unhallowed blasphemies from elder stars which dream beneath the sea, known and favoured by a nightmare cult ready and eager to loose them on the world whenever another earthquake shall heave their monstrous stone city again to the sun and air.

Johansen's voyage had begun just as he told it to the vice-admiralty. The *Emma*, in ballast, had cleared Auckland on February 20th, and had felt the full force of that earthquake-born tempest which must have heaved up from the sea-bottom the horrors that filled men's dreams. Once more under control, the ship was making good progress when held up by the *Alert* on March 22nd, and I could feel the mate's regret as he wrote of her bombardment and sinking. Of the swarthy cult-fiends on the Alert he speaks with significant horror. There was some peculiarly abominable quality about them which made their destruction seem almost a duty, and Johansen shews ingenuous wonder at the charge of ruthlessness brought against his party during the proceedings of the court of inquiry. Then, driven ahead by curiosity in their captured yacht under Johansen's command, the men sight a great stone pillar sticking out of the sea, and in S. Latitude 47° 9', W. Longitude 126° 43' come upon a coast-line of mingled mud, ooze, and weedy Cyclopean masonry which can be nothing less than the tangible substance of earth's supreme terror—the nightmare corpse-city of R'lyeh, that was built in measureless aeons behind history by the vast, loathsome shapes that seeped down from the dark stars. There lay great Cthulhu and his hordes, hidden in green slimy vaults and sending out at last, after cycles incalculable, the thoughts that spread fear to the dreams of the sensitive and called imperiously to the faithful to come on a pilgrimage of liberation and restoration. All this Johansen did not suspect, but God knows he soon saw enough!

I suppose that only a single mountain-top, the hideous monolith-crowned citadel whereon great Cthulhu was buried, actually emerged from the waters. When I think of the *extent* of all that may be brooding down there I almost wish to kill myself forthwith. Johansen and his men were awed by the cosmetic majesty of this dripping Babylon of elder daemons, and must have guessed without guidance that it was nothing of this or of any sane planet. Awe at the unbelievable size of the greenish stone blocks, at the dizzying height of the great carven monolith, and at the stupefying identity of the colossal statues and bas-reliefs with the queer image found in the shrine on the *Alert*, is poignantly visible in every line of the mate's frightened description.

Without knowing what futurism is like, Johansen achieved something very close to it when he spoke of the city; for instead of describing any definite structure or building, he dwells only on broad impressions of vast angles and stone surfaces—surfaces too great to belong to any thing right or proper for this earth, and impious with horrible images and hieroglyphs. I mention his talk about *angles* because it suggests something Wilcox had told me of his awful dreams. He said that the *geometry* of the dream-place he saw was abnormal, non-Euclidean, and loathsomely redolent of spheres and dimensions apart from ours. Now an unlettered seaman felt the same thing whilst gazing at the terrible reality.

Johansen and his men landed at a sloping mud-bank on this monstrous Acropolis, and clambered slipperily up over titan oozy blocks which could have been no mortal staircase. The very sun of heaven seemed distorted when viewed through the polarising miasma welling out from this sea-soaked perversion, and twisted menace and suspense lurked leeringly in those crazily elusive angles of carven rock where a second glance shewed concavity after the first shewed convexity.

Something very like fright had come over all the explorers before anything more definite than rock and ooze and weed was seen. Each would have fled had he not feared the scorn of the others, and it was only half-heartedly that they searched—vainly, as it proved—for some portable souvenir to bear away.

It was Rodriguez the Portuguese who climbed up the foot of the monolith and shouted of what he had found. The rest followed him, and looked curiously at the immense carved door with the now familiar squid-dragon bas-relief. It was, Johansen said, like a great barn-door; and they all felt that it was a door because of the ornate lintel, threshold, and jambs around it, though they could not decide whether it lay flat like a trap-door or slantwise like an outside cellar-door. As Wilcox would have said, the geometry of the place was all wrong. One could not be sure that the sea and the ground were horizontal, hence the relative position of everything else seemed phantasmally variable.

Briden pushed at the stone in several places without result. Then Donovan felt over it delicately around the edge, pressing each point separately as he went. He climbed interminably along the grotesque stone moulding—that is, one would call it climbing if the thing was not after all horizontal—and the men wondered how any door in the universe could be so vast. Then, very softly and slowly, the acre-great panel began to give inward at the top; and they saw that it was balanced. Donovan slid or somehow propelled himself down or along the jamb and rejoined his fellows, and everyone watched the queer recession of the monstrously carven portal. In this phantasy of prismatic distortion it moved anomalously in a diagonal way, so that all the rules of matter and perspective seemed upset.

The aperture was black with a darkness almost material. That tenebrousness was indeed a *positive quality*; for it obscured such parts of the inner walls as ought to have been revealed, and actually burst forth like smoke from its aeon-long imprisonment, visibly darkening the sun as it slunk away into the shrunken and gibbous sky on flapping membraneous wings. The odour rising from the newly opened depths was intolerable, and at length the quick-eared Hawkins thought he heard a nasty, slopping sound down there. Everyone listened, and everyone was listening still when It lumbered slobberingly into sight and gropingly squeezed Its gelatinous green immensity through the black doorway into the tainted outside air of that poison city of madness.

Poor Johansen's handwriting almost gave out when he wrote of this. Of the six men who never reached the ship, he thinks two perished of pure fright in that accursed instant. The Thing cannot be described—there is no language for such abysms of shrieking and immemorial lunacy,

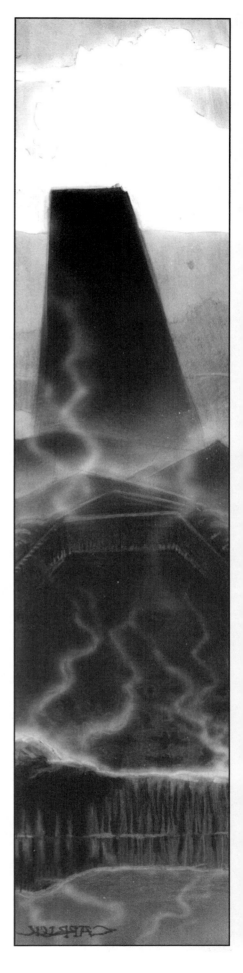

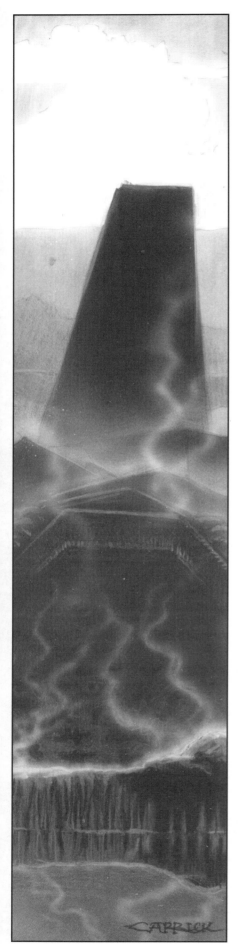

such eldritch contradictions of all matter, force, and cosmic order. A mountain walked or stumbled. God! What wonder that across the earth a great architect went mad, and poor Wilcox raved with fever in that telepathic instant? The Thing of the idols, the green, sticky spawn of the stars, had awaked to claim his own. The stars were right again, and what an age-old cult had failed to do by design, a band of innocent sailors had done by accident. After vigintillions of years great Cthulhu was loose again, and ravening for delight.

Three men were swept up by the flabby claws before anybody turned. God rest them, if there be any rest in the universe. They were Donovan, Guerrera, and Ångstrom. Parker slipped as the other three were plunging frenziedly over endless vistas of green-crusted rock to the boat, and Johansen swears he was swallowed up by an angle of masonry which shouldn't have been there; an angle which was acute, but behaved as if it were obtuse. So only Briden and Johansen reached the boat, and pulled desperately for the *Alert* as the mountainous monstrosity flopped down the slimy stones and hesitated floundering at the edge of the water.

Steam had not been suffered to go down entirely, despite the departure of all hands for the shore; and it was the work of only a few moments of feverish rushing up and down between wheel and engines to get the *Alert* under way. Slowly, amidst the distorted horrors of that indescribable scene, she began to churn the lethal waters; whilst on the masonry of that charnel shore that was not of earth the titan Thing from the stars slavered and gibbered like Polypheme cursing the fleeing ship of Odysseus. Then, bolder than the storied Cyclops, great Cthulhu slid greasily into the water and began to pursue with vast wave-raising strokes of cosmic potency. Briden looked back and went mad, laughing shrilly as he kept on laughing at intervals till death found him one night in the cabin whilst Johansen was wandering deliriously.

But Johansen had not given out yet. Knowing that the Thing could surely overtake the *Alert* until steam was fully up, he resolved on a desperate chance; and, setting the engine for full speed, ran lightning-like on deck and reversed the wheel. There was a mighty eddying and foaming in the noisome brine, and as the steam mounted higher and higher the brave Norwegian drove his vessel head on against the pursuing jelly which rose above the unclean froth like the stern of a daemon galleon. The awful squid-head with writhing feelers came nearly up to the bowsprit of the sturdy yacht, but Johansen drove on relentlessly. There was a bursting as of an exploding bladder, a slushy nastiness as of a cloven sunfish, a stench as of a thousand opened graves, and a sound that the chronicler could not put on paper. For an instant the ship was befouled by an acrid and blinding green cloud, and then there was only a venomous seething astern; where—God in heaven!—the scattered plasticity of that nameless sky-spawn was nebulously *recombining* in its hateful original form, whilst its distance widened every second as the *Alert* gained impetus from its mounting steam.

That was all. After that Johansen only brooded over the idol in the cabin and attended to a few matters of food for himself and the laughing maniac by his side. He did not try to navigate after the first bold flight, for the reaction had taken something out of his soul. Then came the storm of April 2nd, and a gathering of the clouds about his consciousness. There is a sense of spectral whirling through liquid gulfs of infinity, of dizzying rides through reeling universes on a comet's tail, and of hysterical plunges from the pit to the moon and from the moon back again to the pit, all livened by a cachinnating chorus of the distorted, hilarious elder gods and the green, bat-winged mocking imps of Tartarus.

Out of that dream came rescue—the *Vigilant*, the vice-admiralty court, the streets of Dunedin, and the long voyage back home to the old house by the Egeberg. He could not tell— they would think him mad. He would write of what he knew before death came, but his wife must not guess. Death would be a boon if only it could blot out the memories.

That was the document I read, and now I have placed it in the tin box beside the bas-relief and the papers of Professor Angell. With it shall go this record of mine—this test of my own sanity, wherein is pieced together that which I hope may never be pieced together again. I have looked upon all that the universe has to hold of horror, and even the skies of spring and the flowers of summer must ever afterward be poison to me. But I do not think my life will be long. As my uncle went, as poor Johansen went, so I shall go. I know too much, and the cult still lives.

Cthulhu still lives, too, I suppose, again in that chasm of stone which has shielded him since the sun was young. His accursed city is sunken once more, for the *Vigilant* sailed over the spot after the April storm; but his ministers on earth still bellow and prance and slay around idol-capped monoliths in lonely places. He must have been trapped by the sinking whilst within his black abyss, or else the world would by now be screaming with fright and frenzy. Who knows the end? What has risen may sink, and what has sunk may rise. Loathsomeness waits and dreams in the deep, and decay spreads over the tottering cities of men. A time will come—but I must not and cannot think! Let me pray that, if I do not survive this manuscript, my executors may put caution before audacity and see that it meets no other eye. ■

Investigator Sheets, Half-Size

See pp. 279-282 for full-size sheets

CALL OF CTHULHU
Horror Role-Playing

1920s Investigator's Sheet

1920s

Player's Name _____

Investigator Name _____
Occupation _____
Colleges, Degrees _____
Birthplace _____
Mental Disorders _____
Sex _____ Age _____

Characteristics & Rolls

STR ___	DEX ___	INT ___	Idea ___
CON ___	APP ___	POW ___	Luck ___
SIZ ___	SAN ___	EDU ___	Know ___
99-Cthulhu Mythos			Damage Bonus

Sanity Points
Insane 0 1 2 3 4 5 6 7 8 9 10 11 12 13 14
15 16 17 18 19 20 21 22 23 24 25 26 27 28 29 30 31
32 33 34 35 36 37 38 39 40 41 42 43 44 45 46 47 48
49 50 51 52 53 54 55 56 57 58 59 60 61 62 63 64 65
66 67 68 69 70 71 72 73 74 75 76 77 78 79 80 81 82
83 84 85 86 87 88 89 90 91 92 93 94 95 96 97 98 99

Magic Points
Unconscious 0 1 2 3
4 5 6 7 8 9 10 11
12 13 14 15 16 17 18 19
20 21 22 23 24 25 26 27
28 29 30 31 32 33 34 35
36 37 38 39 40 41 42 43

Hit Points
Dead -2 -1 0 1 2 3
4 5 6 7 8 9 10 11
12 13 14 15 16 17 18 19
20 21 22 23 24 25 26 27
28 29 30 31 32 33 34 35
36 37 38 39 40 41 42 43

Investigator Skills

Accounting (10%)
Anthropology (01%)
Archaeology (01%)
Art (05%):

Astronomy (01%)
Bargain (05%)
Biology (01%)
Chemistry (01%)
Climb (40%)
Conceal (15%)
Craft (05%):

Credit Rating (15%)
Cthulhu Mythos (00)
Disguise (01%)
Dodge (DEX x2)
Drive Auto (20%)
Electr. Repair (10%)
Fast Talk (05%)
First Aid (30%)
Geology (01%)
Hide (10%)
History (20%)
Jump (25%)

Law (05%)
Library Use (25%)
Listen (25%)
Locksmith (01%)
Martial Arts (01%)
Mech. Repair (20%)
Medicine (05%)
Natural History (10%)
Navigate (10%)
Occult (05%)
Opr. Hvy. Mch. (01%)
Other Language (01%):

Own Language (EDUx5%):

Persuade (15%)
Pharmacy (01%)
Photography (10%)
Physics (01%)
Pilot (01%):

Psychoanalysis (01%)
Psychology (05%)
Ride (05%)

Sneak (10%)
Spot Hidden (25%)
Swim (25%)
Throw (25%)
Track (10%)

Firearms
Handgun (20%)
Machine Gun (15%)
Rifle (25%)
Shotgun (30%)
SMG (15%)

Weapons

	melee	%	damage	hnd	rng	#att	hp		firearm	%	damage	malf	rng	#att	shots	hp
☐	Fist (50%)		1D3+db	1	0'	1	n/a	☐								
☐	Grapple (25%)		special	2	0'	1	n/a	☐								
☐	Head (10%)		1D4+db	0	0'	1	n/a	☐								
☐	Kick (25%)		1D6+db	0	0'	1	n/a	☐								

Personal Data

Investigator Name _____
Residence _____
Personal Description _____

Family & Friends _____

Episodes of Insanity _____

Wounds & Injuries _____

Marks & Scars _____

Investigator History

Income & Savings
Income _____
Cash on Hand _____
Savings _____
Personal Property _____
Real Estate _____

Adventuring Gear & Possessions

Mythos Tomes Read

Entities Encountered

Magical Artifacts / Spells Known
Artifacts _____
Spells _____

INTRODUCTION

Distinguishing the Mythos; keepers
and investigators; the purpose of play;
what to expect; dice and play aids;
sources and references.

Call of Cthulhu is a horror roleplaying game based upon the writings of Howard Phillips Lovecraft and a few others. Lovecraft wrote during the 1920s and 1930s, and he became a cult figure before dying in 1937. Since then his stature as an author has grown, and now he is generally recognized as the major American horror-story writer of the twentieth century. His fiction ranges from pure science fiction to gothic horror. His non-fiction includes a history of Quebec, the commentary *Supernatural Horror in Literature*, and a gigantic correspondence (five volumes of his letters have been issued by Arkham House publishers).

Author-publisher August Derleth coined the term "Cthulhu Mythos", but the commonality of plot and suggestion behind the term remains an enduring monument to Lovecraft. A series of his stories share as elements certain diabolical entities (especially the Great Old Ones) and books of arcane lore and great power, first among them the ghastly *Necronomicon*. The Cthulhu Mythos is named after a god-like entity, Cthulhu (kuh-THOO-loo is the easiest, though not the best way to say it). Many Great Old Ones, Cthulhu included, are prophesied to wake and to lay waste to the world "when the stars are right".

These tales fired the imagination of other authors, mostly protégés and friends of Lovecraft, and soon they were adding to his mythology. Today, Cthulhu stories are still being written by heirs to Lovecraft's literary legacy.

This game continues the tradition. Young writers from around the world have contributed to or independently written well over a hundred new books of scenarios and other supplements. Besides English, translations and original new supplements also appear in French, German, Japanese, Italian, Polish, and Spanish.

In imitation of Lovecraft, who also wrote excellent tales of horror unconnected with the Mythos, not all Call of Cthulhu scenarios need explore the Mythos: plenty of scope for horrible motive and despicable deed exists apart from it.

The Roots Of Play

Each Cthulhu game needs two types of players. Most take the part of characters who attempt to solve some mystery or to resolve some situation. (The rules call these characters "investigators" because that is what they do, not because they are professional investigators—player characters can have all kinds of occupations.) One player becomes the keeper—the Keeper of Arcane Lore. He or she chooses the scenario or creates the plot, sets the stage, describes the scene, portrays the people whom the investigators meet,

and helps resolve the action. Since the keeper must make extra preparation, players often rotate the duty of keeper.

The game is an evolving interaction between players (in the guise of characters unraveling a mystery) and the keeper, who presents the world in which the mystery occurs. Play is mostly talking: some situation or encounter is outlined, and then the players tell the keeper what they, in the guise of their investigators, intend to do. Using the rules to keep matters consistent and fair, the keeper then tells them if they can do what they proposed, and the steps they must follow. If the proposal is impossible, the keeper narrates what happens instead. Roll dice to resolve encounters. Dice keep everybody honest, add drama, and promote surprises, dismal defeats, and hair's-breadth escapes.

The game rules make the game world understandable, define what can and cannot be done, and offer an objective determination of success and failure.

PLAYERS

Unless acting as keeper, each player takes on one or more investigator personas. During the game, the player attempts to speak and act in terms of those personalities. It is often more fun to create investigators entirely different from the real-life player: a tough private eye, perhaps, or a rude taxi driver, or a tuxedo-clad millionaire dilettante.

A player might play two or even three investigators at a time, but how many investigators are allowed in play at any one time is something for the keeper to decide. The usual custom is to play one investigator.

A player has a duty to roleplay an investigator within the limits of the investigator's personality and abilities. That is the point of roleplaying. Try to know as little or as much as the investigator would in life: the skill rolls the keeper requests will be of great help in doing this. Try to develop the investigator's personality well enough that other players can imagine what he or she would do in a specific situation. "Good old Al," they'll say, "we knew he'd do that."

Call of Cthulhu promotes interesting roleplaying, because play frequently hinges on difficult choices: were you right, for instance, in burning down a farmhouse full of cultists, when in the eyes of the law your actions were murderous? Operating within the limits of their investigators presses the imaginations of all players, and is an important part of the game.

THE KEEPER

The player who acts as keeper becomes the game moderator. Perhaps using a published scenario, or creating one of his or her own, the keeper knows the entire plot of the story and presents it during play, incidentally taking the parts of all of the monsters, spooks, and sinister or ordinary people that the investigators meet. The keeper has the responsibility for preparing a scenario without bias. He or she must make the opposition smart and mean, or there will be little challenge for the players, and they will be bored.

The keeper needs to understand the game in order to be able to answer player questions and to be able to present the material fairly. To be a keeper, read the rules on creating investigators, the game system, and sanity, and then go on to read about magic and the Mythos. You'll find individual monster and spell descriptions in the reference section. Those entries can be consulted, and do not need to be read through and memorized. (That would be quite a feat!) Skim the keeper's lore chapter.

Then choose one of the short scenarios from this book. Read it, then invite some friends over. Have them roll up investigators together (be sure to photocopy enough investigator sheets first). Or photocopy the ready-made investigators at the back of this book, and let them each choose one—all they need are 60 more points of skills.

Summarize the rules for the players, and supply a photocopy of the game tables at the back of this book. When you're set to play, don't worry about making mistakes the first time around. It is your privilege to make mistakes. While you are learning how to invent your own scenarios, use the ones in this book or consult one of the many scenario supplement books available. Often printed scenario thoroughness and extra information can be welcome.

As you need, consult the reference and resources sections, or read pertinent sections in the keeper's lore chapter.

With the purchase of this book and some dice, you have everything needed to play the game.

PURPOSE OF PLAY

The purpose of horror roleplaying is to have a good time. Right down to pounding hearts and sweating brows, it's part of human nature to find pleasure in being scared, as long as being scared is not for real. For some, the relaxation after the scare is the most important result. For others, it is the scare itself. Call of Cthulhu is a vehicle for alternately scaring and then reassuring players.

The game is also a way to portray Lovecraft's dark philosophy of a humanity which can exist but not surpass, and for Lovecraft's now-dense, now-archaic language unwinding like pages from one of those ancient books of magic he described. We even can find as much pleasure in lampooning his ideas and motifs as in taking them at face value, for Lovecraft laughed about himself and wrote stories which satirized his friends. All the time, however, he continued to write with increasing conviction and depth. As you play Call of Cthulhu, your enjoyment also will deepen.

Cooperation

Gaming is social. Roleplaying brings together a number of people in order to form a communal fantasy often more verdant and imaginative than one person could ever create.

Working together enhances investigator survival. For instance, an expedition into some ghoul-haunted ruin would be in trouble if the investigators were unwilling to give each other First Aid, or unwilling to warn each other. Whether deceitful or angelic, make clear to the other players the essential character of your investigator, so that their investigators have honest chances to react. Whether or not investigators cooperate, the players should. Investigators may be played as nice people, as brutes, or however the players wish, but most of the entertainment of roleplaying is in the perceivable ingenuity of players' roleplaying.

There also needs to be cooperation between players and the keeper. Though the keeper masterminds the world and sets up and runs the details, the game remains a game for him or her as well, and every keeper likes to have fun.

If the investigators do exciting things stylishly and memorably, keeper and players alike have won. Bad roleplaying is the only real loss possible. If a mission fails, perhaps it can be returned to some other time. Or perhaps there's a new mission which needs attention. But the point of the game is to roleplay.

What This Game Covers

The parts of the Cthulhu Mythos originated by Lovecraft himself define this game. Certain concepts and creations by some of Lovecraft's friends are also used, and since original publication the circle of inclusion has gradually widened, in imitation of his own widening circle of correspondents. The Cthulhu Mythos transcends all time and space, but certain arcane books may be yet unwritten or unpublished in other centuries.

Most Call of Cthulhu scenarios are set in the United States, in the 1920s or the present day. The latter half of the 1920s and the first half of the next decade were Lovecraft's most productive period. Some players enjoy a slightly more genteel epoch: 1890s games are usually in England. Others find the 1920s too strange, too plodding, and too lacking in firepower, and move games forward into the 1990s, where bullet holes can aid the airconditioning. Supplements exist for each era. The eras are distinguished when the rulesbook refers to historical information, but one era is not better than another. Set play when you wish. Make a new era.

Historical settings are as real as possible. The world and the United States were very different in the 1890s and 1920s from now, and behaviors most find repugnant today then were ordinary and acceptable. Racism, xenophobia, religious bias, and sexual discrimination as we now perceive them were then normal parts of life, and often loudly espoused. Local, state, and federal laws systematically supported segregation and discrimination of every sort, and social forces of great power underwrote that legislation.

Scenario authors can choose to ignore social history as not germane, or decide to incorporate specific elements into their plots. Both sorts of approaches have been published. To preclude information about earlier eras (or about this one) dishonors the memory of those who prized freedom, fairness, and opportunity, perhaps long before we were born.

THE HEAD WAS TERRIBLE BECAUSE OF THE MOUTH

Expectations & Play

Call of Cthulhu differs in feel and motivation from other roleplaying games. In many such games, player-characters can directly confront and attempt to destroy obstacles and opponents. This strategy typically leads to disaster in Cthulhu scenarios. The majority of other-world monstrosities are so terrible and often so invulnerable that choosing open combat almost guarantees a gruesome end for an investigator. Even the merest glimpse of some of the more macabre horrors can send one into screaming insanity. What can a player do, then?

ACCUMULATE INFORMATION

First, the investigators should determine what they are up against. This may involve going to the library, speaking with local residents, trying to obtain journals and diaries of those

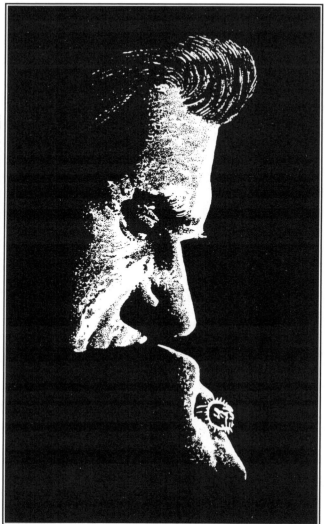

involved, and weighing reports of the problem, perhaps with the help of arcane books. To save time, split up the group and look in different places, as long as it seems safe.

Often newspapers and diaries have pertinent information. Libraries, newspaper files, state and local records of births and deaths, historical societies, hospitals and schools, individual doctors and lawyers, ministers and priests, and private organizations like chambers of commerce—among others!—may offer information which proves lifesaving in retrospect. Don't worry too much about choosing the right place to look: listen closely to your keeper, who'll be dropping clues.

Many times published scenarios include quotations, excerpts, statements, or letters which are given to the players to study and interpret. These materials always contain clues or potentially useful information—or they would not be handed out.

Question local inhabitants carefully and try to befriend the nonplayer-characters whom your investigators meet. Consider what they have to say. Even if they know nothing now, they may be of help in the future. As detectives of the supernatural, investigators should proceed cautiously and try to make allies. Anything could be out there.

AT THE SCENE

At the scene of an investigation or disturbance, the investigators should comb the area for clues, looking in desks and dressers, inspecting the clothing and belongings of victims, and attempting to arrive at a realistic picture of what happened. If important information is to be found, the keeper will be patient with player queries and rolls. If nothing is to be found, then the keeper so advises the players. However, the way that such queries and responses are phrased may be significant.

Take precautions and stay together where danger has been: something as bad or worse might return. If that Something does return, and there is no easy way to handle It, do not hesitate to run. Your feet are your friends. Your investigator can always return later.

MAKE A PLAN

When you understand the situation, make a plan to deal with the problem. Novice players should not assume that the danger is too much to face—any competent keeper will try to match the dangers to the party's capabilities, unless he or she has already clearly warned of the over-match.

If disaster occurs and eldritch horrors overwhelm the party, those who can should flee and leave the scenario as "a story better left untold!" If the keeper consents, the players might attempt the same scenario later on, when they feel more confident and their investigators are better able to handle themselves. Of course, the keeper is within his rights to beef up the monsters and dangers of the scenario. After all, the horror has had that much more time to grow.

USE YOUR HEAD

The cheapest and safest way to emerge victorious is to use brain power. In many published scenarios, a way exists for

"THE CHEAPEST AND SAFEST WAY TO EMERGE VICTORIOUS IS TO USE BRAIN POWER."

the investigators to solve or dispel the problem with little or no physical combat, though Sanity may need risking.

As a rule of thumb, pursue physical combat against creatures who have already made physical attacks. Otherwise rely on repeating the words from the manuscript, breaking the mirror that the tracks lead through, melting down the dire statuette, and so on. If the investigators find out that a grisly demon inhabits the old rickety mine shaft, they need not climb down it again and get eaten or struck permanently insane. They could set fire to the mine supports, dynamite the shaft, or pour concrete into the opening, thus burying the threat, perhaps forever.

DIFFERENT INVESTIGATORS

Are any investigators specialists? One handy sort is the wise old professor who knows foreign languages, reads arcane manuscripts, and pieces together Sanity-blasting spells able to send the Elder Horrors back whence they came. He or she is typically of little use if a fight develops, and generally has low Sanity points, due to intensive study of the Mythos.

An opposite sort is the tough operator able to fight well with fists or guns. He or she should leave the eldritch aspects of the Mythos to others and remain a bodyguard and scout. He or she can be helpful with police and gangsters.

Still another sort is the investigator who can do things. He or she drives very well, maybe pilots an airplane, has good mechanical and electrical repair skills, and might be a wizard with locks. Yet another sort could be the street-wise investigator who knows the floaters and drifters of a city, and who has a tongue glib enough to keep good relations with them.

Many types could be proposed. No one investigator can learn to do everything or be prepared for all eventualities. But they can act in balanced groups and approach adventures in ways that compensate for individual deficiencies.

MULTIPLE INVESTIGATORS

Knowing that no one can do everything certainly argues for as many investigators as possible on a case, but the keeper will be reluctant to deal with hordes of investigators scurrying about, looking under everything and asking dozens of questions at the same time.

Though some players find it distasteful to roleplay more than one investigator at a time, others can play two or three investigators without much trouble. If the keeper is willing and if you wish to, take two investigators per player. This widens the pool of skills and experiences, and keeps a player in the action if one investigator goes insane or is seriously injured. And if (as never should be done if danger threatens) the investigator team splits up—"You guys guard the plane, while we look in the cave!"—then one investigator belonging to the same player can be in each place, again with the benefit of keeping everyone in the game. That's why they bothered to come in the first place.

AVOID GUNFIGHTS

Every group of players has its own feel and customs. If gangsters and foreign spies are common features in a campaign, all the investigators probably carry concealed weapons for self-defense. The number of devastating weapons floating about in the 1990s practically demands sidearms. On the other hand, in a campaign in which the investigators devote most of their time to studying the grislier mysteries of the Cthulhu Mythos, the only use for a gun may be to shoot oneself if in danger of permanent madness.

By all means have lots of firearms. But do not rely on firearms. Most powerful monsters are not harmed by gunfire, explosions, and such. They are genuinely alien creatures from vaults of space-time very different from ours. If the plan is to shoot 'em until they die, that plan will not work. Try another plan first.

Volleys of gunfire tend to attract police, the state militia, G-men, and everyone with a stake in law and order. If the investigators happen to assassinate the local priest of Yog-Sothoth without first convincing the police of the necessity, they will certainly be questioned and arrested, almost certainly be convicted, and probably end up on death row.

Further, observant keepers will notice that if the investigators' response to difficulties is to shoot their way out. Many will react accordingly. Three or four gun-slinging worshipers of Yig could well prove more than the investigators would like to handle. In Call of Cthulhu, as in the real world, guns are lethal. Avoid them.

Playing Aids

Dice; Important Rolls

People new to roleplaying may never have seen dice with other than six sides. A variety of them can be found at most game stores and hobby shops.

For the most part Call of Cthulhu calls for three dice roll results—abbreviated as D100, D8, and D6—to judge the success of a skill use, to indicate how many hit points were lost to an attack or accident, to generate investigators, etc. The dice from which these rolls derive also can give D20, D10, D4, D3, and D2 results.

The letter D stands for the word die or dice. The number after the D stands for the range of random numbers sought: D8 generates the random numbers 1 through 8, for instance, while D100 generates the numbers 1-100. For convenience, players normally use their own dice.

D100 (PERCENTILE DICE)

Percentile dice (as the abbreviation D100 means) usually consist of two 10-sided dice of different colors, rolled at the same time. Most such dice are numbered 1, 2, 3, 4, 5, 6, 7, 8, 9, 0. When rolled, read the top numbers on such dice to get the result.

Read the die of one color consistently as the tens-column, and the other as the ones column: thus a result of 2-3 reads as 23, a result of 0-1 reads as 1, and a result of 1-0 reads as 10. A result of 0-0 reads as 100.

Call of Cthulhu Terms

BASE CHANCE: percentage chance that an untrained investigator can successfully use a skill. Some skills cannot be picked up quickly by untrained characters, and thus have a 1% base chance. On the other hand almost everyone has a good chance of successfully using skills such as Climb, and so such skills have larger base chances.

CHARACTERISTIC: eight characteristics are rolled for each investigator—Strength, Constitution, Size, Intelligence, Power, Dexterity, Appearance, and Education. Sanity derives from Power. Characteristics determine a character's fundamental capacities. They do not much affect the ability to learn a skill or to effectively use a skill.

CHECK, EXPERIENCE CHECK, SKILL CHECK: when an investigator successfully uses a skill and the keeper says something like "You get a check," then mark the box on the investigator sheet that is next to the skill. Roll for improvement when the keeper advises. Skills improve in 1D10-point increments. Improvement usually waits until the end of an adventure.

COMBAT ROUND, ROUND: the elastic unit of game time against which character movement, weapon use, and skill use are compared. Actions in a round are resolved in DEX-rank order, highest to lowest.

CTHULHU: *kuh-THOO-loo in Chaosium-ese*. His obscene gigantic bulk lies sleeping in dread drowned R'lyeh, to rise again "when the stars are right". One of the Great Old Ones. Cthulhu's earthly cultists are many. He was created in tales by H. P. Lovecraft, and since has been present or been intimated in hundreds or thousands of stories by other authors. The Lovecraft story at the front of this book, "The Call of Cthulhu", best summarizes him.

CTHULHU MYTHOS: the gods, entities, monsters, and fiendish knowledge of the greater universe. In contrast to what normal humans find comfortable to believe, the Cthulhu Mythos represents the secret horrifying truth about all things.

DAMAGE: in the game, attacks and accidents are said to *do damage*—that is, to create wounds or injuries. The game usually shows this by subtracting hit points from those who suffer accidents or successful attacks.

DAMAGE BONUS: a modifier for hand-to-hand attacks.

FAINTING: an optional temporary insanity. It's now out of style to faint, but Lovecraft's characters fainted regularly. If your investigator is too tough to faint, perhaps he or she can rescue investigators who aren't.

FIRST AID: this skill and the Medicine skill can restore 1D3 hit points to an injured character. See also Healing.

FUMBLE: a D100 result of 00 is an automatic failure, usually the most catastrophic result possible to the situation.

GREAT OLD ONES: the demi-deities of the Cthulhu Mythos. They are uniformly heedless, arrogant, and supremely evil, but they have awesome powers, and some

humans can be tempted into their worship. Occasionally, they may be encountered by investigators. For aiding their return to our world or for opening the way to our world, they promise much to their human worshippers. Cf. Outer Gods.

HAND-TO-HAND: a fighting mode or a weapon attack powered by muscle, such as a sword. Personal attacks such as Fist/Punch are also hand-to-hand attacks.

HEALING: a successful use of the First Aid skill can *immediately* restore 1D3 hit points. All characters also naturally heal, restoring hit points at the rate of 1D3 per game week. Under a doctor's care, a successful Medicine roll also can restore 1D3 hit points. Optimally, therefore, a character could have 3D3 hit points restored in one week.

HIT POINTS: the average of a character's CON and SIZ. Hit points can be checked off to indicate a wound or injury. No play effect occurs at the loss of a few points. Unconsciousness arrives when 2 or fewer hit points are left. A character begins to die at 0 hit points.

HORROR: fear and repugnance intermixed, a feeling which perceives not just a threat but a quality of intense wrongness or perversity about the threat, yielding a sense of evil. As a genre, Lovecraft called supernatural horror "the literature of cosmic fear" and said that "no better evidence of its tenacious vigour can be cited than the impulse which now and then drives writers of totally opposite leanings to try their hands at it . . . as if to discharge from their minds certain phantasmal shapes which would otherwise haunt them."

IMPALE: a D100 result which is one-fifth or less of a character's chance to hit with the attack. An impale represents a particularly successful attack, and consequently two damage rolls for that attack are made. Most keepers accept the idea as inherent in a skill roll—one-fifth or less of a skill represents a fine performance, and it should earn some extra reward.

INSANITY, INDEFINITE: when an investigator loses 20% or more of his or her current Sanity points within an hour of game time, the result is insanity as the keeper sees fit. Keeper and player should discuss how to play the investigator.

INSANITY, PERMANENT: if an investigator's current Sanity points reach zero, he or she is deeply insane for a period of months or years, and perhaps institutionalized. Keeper and player should discuss how to play the investigator.

INSANITY, TEMPORARY: if an investigator loses 5 or more Sanity points as the consequence of a single Sanity roll, he or she has suffered major emotional trauma. The player must roll D100. If the result is equal to or less than INT x5, the investigator fully understands what has been seen, and goes insane for a period of minutes or hours.

INVESTIGATOR: a game term for *player character*.

KEEPER: the person who runs the game. He or she knows the secrets of the plot, describes the situations and non-player characters, and determines what skills and rolls to apply.

MAGIC POINTS: magic points represent the fluctuating expression of characteristic Power. They are used in casting and resisting spells. Magic points are inherent to humans and other intelligences. Reaching 0 magic points, a character falls unconscious, and remains unconscious until one magic point regenerates. That takes (24 divided by POW) hours. Magic points regenerate entirely in 24 hours.

MEDICINE: a skill. Immediately restores 1D3 hit points to an injured or sick character and doubles natural healing while under a physician's care, such as in a hospital.

NECRONOMICON: written in the eighth century, with the Arabic title *Kitab Al-Azif*. The most powerful book about the Cthulhu Mythos, it contains many spells, describes otherworldly places, and relates dreadful secrets. It is said to push readers into madness. See also pages 88 and 101.

OCCUPATION: shows what an investigator does for a living but never determines how an investigator acts. In creating an investigator, an investigator gets EDU x20 occupation points.

OUTER GODS: the rulers of the universe, so blind to all but themselves and so whimsical and terrible that they are like natural forces. Only Nyarlathotep, their messenger, seems much swayed by intelligence, purpose, or perception.

PARRY: against hand-to-hand attacks, a character may try one parry per round, to block or divert an intended blow. Determine success of the parry by an attack roll for the weapon. State the target of the parry at the beginning of the round.

PERCENTAGE: most die rolls in the game are D100 (percentage) rolls. Skills are expressed as percentages. Investigator skill percentages never rise above 99%. A roll of 00 is an automatic failure.

PERCENTILE: in game usage, any of 100 equal divisions that make up the whole. Percentiles may be added or subtracted from each other: thus *subtracting ten percentiles* from 60% yields 50%, while *subtracting ten percent* from 60% yields 54%.

PERSONAL ATTACK: Fist/Punch, Kick, Head Butt, or Grapple. An unarmed human can make one of these four hand-to-hand attacks per combat round. The Martial Arts skill can double the damage done with these attacks.

PERSONAL INTEREST: while creating an investigator, the player can apply INT x10 skill points to any skills he or she desires.

PSYCHIATRIC DRUGS: in the present day, as long as the investigator can get and take the prescribed psychiatric drugs, the player can avoid roleplaying the *symptoms* of the mental illness distressing the investigator. Psychiatric drugs do not give immunity to further Sanity loss. Stopping taking psychiatric drugs can bring back the illness slowly enough that the investigator doesn't notice.

PSYCHOANALYSIS: a therapeutic skill which can palliate temporary insanity for a while. Over time, it can help restore Sanity points to patients.

RESISTANCE TABLE: a table which establishes target numbers for D100 rolls, allowing percentile rolls in order to resolve matches of one characteristic against another. See the Game System chapter, page 49.

SAN: characteristic originally equals POW x5. Maximum SAN almost never changes, but can if POW changes.

SANITY: every character is sane, regardless of the number of Sanity points, unless 0 Sanity points has been reached, or unless the keeper has announced that a state of temporary insanity or indefinite insanity has been reached by the character because of mental trauma. See insanity, above.

SANITY POINTS: *current Sanity points* are the number of points shown in the investigator sheet's Sanity Points box. This number begins as equal to the SAN characteristic, but can fluctuate. *Maximum Sanity points* equal 99 minus whatever percentiles of the Cthulhu Mythos skill the investigator has. Sanity points can decline or be increased, but they do not routinely regenerate as do magic points and hit points.

SANITY ROLL: a D100 roll. A success is equal to or less than current Sanity points. A success may cost nominal Sanity points, or none at all. A failure always costs more, and leads toward temporary or indefinite insanity.

SCENARIO, ADVENTURE, STORY: an organized and plotted narrative devised for roleplaying, one which includes the sequence of events, character statistics, special rules and spells, and other descriptions which investigators may find useful, interesting, or evocative.

SKILL: in the game, a defined body of knowledge, technique, or physical ability, especially pertaining to investigators and the skills available to them. Many non-player characters list skills unknown to investigators—such skills are not game components, and are for keeper information only; they are unavailable to investigators.

SKILL ROLL: a D100 roll. A success is equal to or less than the character's skill percentage. A failure is higher than the character's skill percentage.

SPOT RULE: in the rules chapter, several pages are devoted to minor rules covering special situations. Spot rules include those for combat, firearms, and injuries from fires, drowning, etc.

SUCCESS: a successful D100 roll is a result equal to or less than the target number. A D100 result of 01 is always a success and the best result possible. See also Fumble.

UNCONSCIOUS: a character who reaches 0 magic points or who has 2 or fewer hit points left goes unconscious. So does a character who loses half or more of his hit points from a single wound or blow and whose player cannot then roll CON or less on 1D20. Unconsciousness lasts from one combat round up to the time needed to regenerate 1 magic point or 2 hit points, as applicable. A successful First Aid or Medicine roll may return a character to consciousness. ∎

Silhouette of a Dark Young.

D8 (EIGHT-SIDED DIE)

This single die has eight sides, each side numbered once 1, 2, 3, 4, 5, 6, 7, 8. Read the top number on the die.

D6 (SIX-SIDED DIE)

This sort is what people normally think of as dice. The D6 has six sides, and is numbered 1, 2, 3, 4, 5, 6. Read the top number on the die.

D4 (FOUR-SIDED DIE)

Some have four sides, some eight. Read the top number for the eight-sided variety; for the four-sided version, read the vertical number at the base.

OTHER ROLLS

Occasionally players may also want to make D20, D10, D5, or D3 rolls. These rolls can be simulated with the D100, D8, or D6 dice. D20 and D4 dice are available and are more satisfactory.

- For D20, roll one of the 10-sided dice and one six-sided die. If the D6 result is 1, 2, 3 the result is the face amount of the 10-sided die (0 counts as 10). If the D6 result is 4, 5, 6 add ten to the face amount of the 10-sided die.

- For a D10 roll, roll one of the percentile dice.

- For D5, roll one 10-sided die and divide the result by two: thus 1, 2 = 1, and 9, 0 = 5.

- For D4, roll D8 and divide the result by two: thus 1, 2 = 1, and 7, 8 = 4; or roll D6 and ignore 5, 6.

- For D3, roll D6 and divide the result by two: thus 1, 2 = 1, and 5, 6 = 3.

- For D2, roll D6 and divide the result by three: thus 1, 2, 3 = 1 and 4, 5, 6 = 2.

VARIATIONS

Sometimes a dice notation in the rules or in a scenario is preceded by a number: it tells the reader that more than one such die should be rolled, and that their results should be added together. For instance, 2D6 means that two 6-sided dice should be rolled and totaled. If you don't have enough dice to roll all at once, roll the one you have for the requisite number of times and total the results.

Sometimes additions are shown to die rolls. You might see 1D6+1, for instance. This means that the number following the plus sign should be added to the result of the D6 roll. For 1D6+1 the final result must be 2, 3, 4, 5, 6, or 7.

A notation may require that different dice, etc., be rolled at one time. If a monster claws for 1D6+1+2D4 damage, find the power of the actual attack by rolling the three requested dice, totaling the results, and adding one. The notation +db appended to attack damage reminds the keeper to add the actual damage bonus of the creature, since the statistic for the species gives the average.

Investigator Sheet

Players should record their investigators on investigator sheets, found near the back of this book, and ready to photocopy. There are versions for the 1890s, the 1920s, and today. The investigator sheet holds all the data needed for investigators to tackle mysteries. The next chapter explains how to fill out this sheet.

Figures; Playing Position

Call of Cthulhu can be played verbally, without figures or paraphernalia other than dice and investigator sheets. Others find that figures, tokens, or markers give focus to the action, and help in weaving together player imaginations. Arranging the investigators in a marching order shows who can believably whisper to each other and who must shout, or it can show who is at the rear to attempt to listen for pursuers, or it can show who must first risk being entangled in a snare, and so forth. You must decide what expression of the game you more enjoy.

Using figures stresses questions such as whether fields of fire are open, or whether an investigator might give First Aid to another in this round or must wait until the next. These markers provoke questions like "What does the flashlight show?" and "Where is the elephant?" They bring position and physical nature into the game in styles some find intrusive. Pieces of cardboard, pennies, tokens from other games, or lead figures can be used interchangeably, as keeper and players find pleasing.

Props can lend drama or end up looking silly. Some players cannot believe that a styrofoam block is anything other than a styrofoam block. Others enjoy and compliment each other on using model railroad accessories, cake decorations, weird things from hardware bins, dollhouse pieces, broken chunks from discarded toys, or the leftovers from a plastic model kit, and say that they give otherwise dull situations intriguing possibilities for deployment, tactics, and use of particular skills.

Game figures—miniatures—are lead statuettes about an inch high, cast with bases for stability. They are purchasable at many game and hobby stores, or can be ordered by mail. Many people employ economical plastic figures. These are not intended for roleplaying, but are useful all the same. No one has every figure that an adventure might demand. Substitution is common.

Whether or not dimensional models are used, keepers often sketch out the area of activity on a sheet of paper and note the scale. When the action shifts to combat rounds, then some keepers turn to miniature figures and sketch out the arena again, at that smaller scale.

Players may find graph paper an aid in mapping ruins or old buildings. ■

To the right: *The first of several scenes scattered throughout this book, displaying locations evocative of the horrors of the Mythos and the normalcy of 1920s life.*

Resources for the Game

For game questions, information concerning titles currently in print, to learn about upcoming titles, to be baffled along with us when a title crashes off the schedule, or to offer comments, please write to Chaosium Inc., 950-A 56th Street, Oakland CA 94608, or email us at chaosium@chaosium.com. Please do not telephone game questions.

Updated monthly, the Chaosium web site is at www.chaosium.com. Refer there first to learn what is currently in print or about titles on the active schedule.

CORE RULES

The *Call of Cthulhu* rules, the *1920s Investigator's Companion*, the *Creature Companion*, and the forthcoming *Keeper's Companion* are the most important books for the game.

GAME SUPPLEMENTS

For the Call of Cthulhu game, Chaosium regularly publishes books of scenarios such as *Unseen Masters*, campaign books such as *Beyond the Mountains of Madness*, background books such as *The Black Chamber*, and topical books such as *Encyclopedia Cthulhiana*. At any one time, between 20-30 such titles are in print.

THE MYTHOS COLLECTABLE CARD GAME

Available from local hobby stores or by mail-order from Chaosium. Start with the Standard Game Set, then explore the world of the 1920's, Miskatonic University, the Dreamlands (delve beyond the wall of sleep), and New Aeon (the Mythos in the present day).

HOW TO ORDER

Wizard's Attic now fulfills all Chaosium mail, email, and telephone orders. Emailing is fully encrypted and secure. Order all items through Wizard's Attic: write to 950 56th Street, Oakland CA 94608, order by phone at 1-800-213-1493, or go online at www.wizards-attic.com.

WHAT'S AT WIZARD'S ATTIC?

For the seriously demented, an ever-changing selection from a Miskatonic University cloissone pin to a $100 statuette of Great Cthulhu to miniature figures, T-shirts, and background CDs for the game. Also find books by Clark Ashton Smith and Brian Lumley, S. T. Joshi's Lovecraft biography, etc. To make sure of sizes, colors, etc., call first, 10–4 Pacific time weekdays only. Carries 30–50 Cthulhu-related items at any one time.

MINIATURE FIGURES

All Call of Cthulhu miniature figures produced by RAFM Co., Inc., are carried by Wizard's Attic. For pictures, see RAFM's web site at www.rafm.com. Packs released include many favorite monsters (there is a very large, very heavy metal Cthulhu, for instance) as well as superb investigator and cultist figures dressed for different climates and variously equipped.

WEB PAGES, NEWSGROUPS

Our web page at www.chaosium.com carries current information about Chaosium, its publications, color images of book covers, descriptions of books, announcements of new releases, and so on. It is linked to Wizard's Attic, and to more than a hundred Cthulhoid sites.

CALL OF CTHULHU SUPPLEMENTS

Our web page www.chaosium.com carries current information on the dozens of game supplements available now. For a selection of them, see page 262.

CALL OF CTHULHU FICTION

We publish four to six titles a year concerning the Cthulhu Mythos and associated topics or authors. Many of these books are introduced by Robert M. Price, and they often include an appropriate story by H. P. Lovecraft. Prices vary. Dimensions are 5.375" by 8.375". The fiction is in various lengths, from 192 pages to more than 600. See our web site for current availability.

Cthulhu's Heirs—a variety of original Cthulhu Mythos short stories.

Made in Goatswood—new tales set in Ramsey Campbell's Severn Valley universe, featuring the insects from Shaggai, Nodens, Eihort, and more.

The Disciples of Cthulhu 2nd ed.—unavailable for more than twenty years; includes Wade, Campbell, Bertin, Lumley, and Leiber.

The Dunwich Cycle—includes two of Machen's best, a Derleth, Indick, HPL, and five more.

The Cthulhu Cycle—thirteen stories of the time when the stars come right. One of the most popular titles.

The Hastur Cycle 2nd ed.—fine horror from Chambers and Machen to Karl Edward Wagner and Ramsey Campbell.

The Necronomicon—tales of, quotations from, and provocative essays concerning Abdul al-Hazred's sanity-shaking book. A Chaosium best-seller.

The Nyarlathotep Cycle—fifteen stories about the God of a Thousand Forms, including Lovecraft, Bloch, Carter, Derleth, Howard, Myers, etc.

Singers of Strange Songs—original stories celebrating Brian Lumley and his Guest of Honor appearance at NecronomiCon. Includes two rare tales by Lumley.

The Xothic Legend Cycle—the complete Mythos fiction of Lin Carter, including "Terror Out of Time".

The Scroll of Thoth—the collected Simon Magus Mythos fiction by Richard L. Tierney.

The Innsmouth Cycle—"Shadow Over Innsmouth", Dunsany, Chambers, Irvin S. Cobb, two by James Wade, Stephen Mark Rainey, John S. Glasby, eight more stories and poems.

The Complete Pegana—Dunsany's finest writing relates the cruel and vivid world of Pegana and the gods who rule it. Full texts of *The Gods of Pegana*, *Time and the Gods*, and "Beyond the Fields We Know". Never before published as a single book.

Nightmare's Disciple—a new novel stuffed with brilliant scenes. A Mythos-worshipping serial killer is on the loose.

Encyclopedia Cthulhiana—An A-to-Z of the Cthulhu Mythos. This new edition is much more comprehensive than the first edition. Full of systematic information.

The Ithaqua Cycle—starts with Blackwood's trailblazing "Wendigo"; includes three selections by August Derleth and a stunner by Stephen Mark Rainey.

Tales Out of Innsmouth—a second Innsmouth collection, nearly all new stories.

The Antarktos Cycle—the Mythos in the polar regions. Poe, Lovecraft's "At the Mountains of Madness", a novel from John Taine, a long unpublished tale from Colin Wilson, and four more stories.

OTHER PUBLICATIONS

Fortean Times, "a monthly magazine of news, reviews, and research on strange phenomena and experiences, curiosities, prodigies and portents." Sensible, amusing, brash. Strives for editorial honesty. For subscriptions, see their web site at www.forteantimes.com.

Cryptozoology Review, 137 Atlas Avenue, Toronto, Ontario, Canada M6C 3P4. Write for subscription information. As the title indicates, unknown species, remnants, anomalous survivors, etc. Looking for information on those dinosaurs perhaps still existing in the deep jungles of the Congo? — look here.

Strange Magazine, P.O. Box 2246, Rockville, MD 20847. Mysteries, curiosities, often well written essays. See their web site at www.strangemag.com for some good reading. Paper publication bi-annually.

General gaming magazines such as *Dragon*, *Pyramid*, or *Games Monthly* review Cthulhu supplements, though the reviews are frequently a year behind publication. *The Unspeakable Oath* is an excellent magazine devoted to Cthulhu and connected matters (Pagan Publishing, 4542 18th Street, Apt. 4, Seattle, WA 98105). *Lovecraft Studies* has a literary orientation; *Crypt of Cthulhu* combines articles and fiction; *Cthulhu Codex* is mostly original Mythos fiction. For these last three, contact Necronomicon Press, 101 Lockwood Street, West Warwick, RI 02893.

CALL OF CTHULHU IN LANGUAGES OTHER THAN ENGLISH

Other-language editions include translated Chaosium titles and new titles original to the language.

Finnish—concerning *Cthulhun Kutsu*, ask TK-Kustannus Oy, Fredrikinkatu 14 1 2-3, 00120 Helsinki, Finland.

French—concerning *L'Appel de Cthulhu*, ask Jeux Descartes, 1 rue du Colonel Pierre Avia, 75503 Paris, Cedex 15, France.

German—concerning *Auf Cthulhus Spur,* ask Pegasus Spiele, Dieselstrasse 1, 61169, Friedberg, Germany.

Hungarian—concerning *Cthulhu Hivasa*, ask Latomas Kerekedelmi, Szolgaltats Betiti Tarasag, 8000 Szikesfehirvar, Radnsti tir 1, Hungary.

Italian—concerning *Il Richiamo di Cthulhu*, ask Stratelibri s.r.l., Via Paisiello no. 4, 20131 Milano, Italy.

Japanese—ask Hobby Japan Co., Ltd., 5-26-5 Sendagaya, Shibuya-ku, Tokyo 151, Japan.

Polish—concerning *Zew Cthulhu,* ask Wydawnictowo MAG, Jacek Rodek, 00-657 Warszawa, Poland.

Spanish—concerning *La Llamada de Cthulhu,* ask La Factoria de Ideas, Plaza, 15, 29043 Madrid, Spain.

GUIDELINES

Prospective contributors should consult our web site for guidelines. We do not accept solicited fiction. If requesting guidelines by mail, please include a postal address. The guidelines contain a release form. Artists may send representative photocopies to the Art File care of Chaosium Inc, 950-A 56th St., Oakland, CA 94608.

WHOLESALE ORDERS, DEALERS

Scores of national and international distributors carry English-language Call of Cthulhu titles. For retailer and distributor location and terms, contact ChaosiumSouthwest Sales & Marketing at (512)-336-8269 (voice) or (512)-336-8309 (fax).

DICE

Most towns include a store which stocks gaming supplies. Check the Yellow Pages under Games, Hobbies, or Dice. U.S. customers might also write to suppliers such as Koplow Games, 369 Congress St., Boston, MA 02210 who can refer you to local retailers.

LOVECRAFT EDITIONS

The most reliable texts are those edited by S. T. Joshi and published by Arkham House, P.O. Box 546, Sauk City, WI 53585. Joshi's text retrieves Lovecraft's inimitable spelling and punctuation. *The Dunwich Horror and Others*, *At the Mountains of Madness*, and *Dagon and Other Macabre Tales* contain all of HPL's important tales. Several more volumes hold peripheral material, and there are also five volumes of his letters. All the books are in hardback.

LOOKING FOR A PARTICULAR BOOK?

Local used bookstores are your quickest bet. Contact information for specialist booksellers appears in genre magazines such as *Locus*. If online, try www.bibliofind.com, www.interloc.com, www.abebooks.com, www.amazon.com, etc. ■

**For Ready-To-Play
Investigators
See p. 274**

CREATING YOUR

1. Determine Characteristics

Find a blank investigator sheet. Be sure it is for the right era of play. Write your name in the space on the side.

- Roll 3D6 once each for the characteristics STR, CON, POW, DEX, and APP. Enter the results on the investigator sheet, in the appropriate spaces. Use a pencil. Write lightly enough that you can erase.

- Roll 2D6+6 once each for SIZ and INT. Enter the results.

- Roll 3D6+3 for the characteristic EDU. Enter the result.

- SAN equals POW x5. Write in that amount.

These numbers are your investigator's skeleton. Be alert for ways to flesh out your investigator by explaining the numbers you rolled.

If you want to roll up someone representative of a particular profession, see the notes under "Alternate Ways" on p. 37.

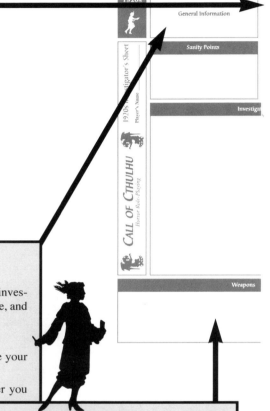

6. Determine Additional Background

At some time—it needn't be now—fill in other information on the front side of the investigator sheet. Under the investigator name, write in colleges and degrees if appropriate, and a birthplace.

- Marks, scars, and mental disorders may come in the course of play.

- Be sure your name is on the left side of the sheet, not at the top. The top is where your investigator's name goes.

- The minimum age for an investigator is EDU+6 years. For each ten years older you make your investigator than that, add a point of EDU and allot an additional 20 occupation points. With maturity comes mortality: for each ten years above age 40, subtract your choice of 1 STR, 1 CON, 1 DEX, or 1 APP.

The back of the investigator's sheet is mostly self-explanatory. See the About Investigators chapter, "Reverse Side of the Sheet" (p. 44).

5. Determine Weapons

The Hand-to-Hand Weapons box contains four personal attacks: information about their attacks is found on the Weapons Table, on pp. 58-59. Unless the investigator's damage bonus is zero, enter it after each weapon's attack damage in the Hand-to-Hand Weapons box (for instance 1D3+1D4 for the Fist/Punch skill).

Swords and fists are hand-to-hand weapons; pistols and shotguns are firearms.

Firearms may be era-dependent. For instance, no M16 assault rifles exist in the 1920s.

If allotting skill points to firearms, add the points to the appropriate firearm classes (on the front of the investigator sheet) as well as to the particular weapon. For instance, adding 20 points to .38 Revolver means that weapon is written in as 40% in the Firearms box, that Handgun rises to 40% in the firearms classes just above the Firearms box, and that skill with other handguns (if the investigator obtains them) also rises by twenty percentiles.

INVESTIGATOR YEARLY INCOME AND PROPERTY

Select the appropriate era of play—1890s, 1920s, or Present.

For the 1890s, roll 1D10: a result of 1 = $500 + room & board, 2 = $1000, 3 = $1500; 4 = $2000, 5 = $2500, 6 = $3000, 7 = $4000, 8 = $5000, 9 = $5000, 10 = $10,000.

For the 1920s, roll 1D10: a result of 1 = $1500 + room & board, 2 = $2500, 3 + 4 = $3500, 5 = $4500, $6 = 5500, 7 = $6500, 8 = $7500, 9 = $10,000, 10 = $20,000.

For the Present, roll 1D10: a result of 1 = $15,000, 2 = $25,000, 3 = $35,000, 4 = $45,000, 5 = $55,000, 6 = $75,000, 7 = $100,000, 8 = $200,000, 9 = $300,000, 10 = $500,000.

The investigator also has property and other assets of value equal to five times yearly income: an investigator in the Present who makes $55,000 has $225,000 in assets. One tenth of that is banked as cash. Another one tenth is in stocks and bonds, convertible in 30 days. The remainder is in old books, a house, or whatever seems appropriate to the character.

INVESTIGATOR

SEE ALSO

Skills: p. 60
Weapons: p. 58
Occupations: p. 40

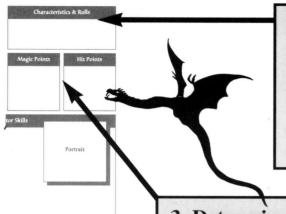

2. Determine Characteristic Rolls

- In the characteristics box, multiply INT x5 for *Idea*, POW x5 for *Luck*, and EDU x5 for *Know*, and enter the results.

- Add STR to SIZ, and find the die roll in the Damage Bonus Table nearby. Write in the result for Damage Bonus. The roll may be positive or negative; if none, write in *none*.

- Enter the number 99 for *99 minus Cthulhu Mythos*. If your investigator gains points in that skill, lower this number by a like amount.

3. Determine Derived Characteristic Points

The *Hit Points* box is directly below the Characteristics & Rolls Box. Add CON + SIZ and divide by 2: round up any fraction. Circle the resulting number in the hit points box. If your investigator loses hit points, mark them off with pencil slashes, which can be erased as the investigator regains hit points. The circled number represents the investigator's maximum hit points.

In the *Magic Points* box, circle that number equal to POW. If your investigator loses magic points, mark them off with pencil slashes, then erase the slashes as the investigator regains magic points. The circled number is the maximum magic points regenerated.

In the *Sanity Points* box, circle that number equal to SAN. Sanity points rise and fall; use pencil slashes to show their present number. Unless POW changes, SAN will not change. As the investigator accumulates Cthulhu Mythos skill points, black out an equal number of Sanity points, starting with 99 and working down. Blacked out Sanity points are a ceiling into which current Sanity points cannot be increased.

DAMAGE BONUSES

STR+SIZ	DB
2 to 12	-1D6
13 to 16	-1D4
17 to 24	+0
25 to 32	+1D4
33 to 40	+1D6
41 to 56	+2D6
57 to 72	+3D6
73 to 88	+4D6

For each +16 or fraction thereof, +1D6 more

4. Determine Occupation & Skills

A. Find the proper era in the Investigator Yearly Income and Property box nearby, and roll 1D10: your investigator has that much money and property. Enter the amounts in the Cash and Property box on the back of the investigator sheet.

B. Choose an occupation that you find befitting the investigator's characteristics and income. Choose from the *Sample Occupations* listed in the About Investigators chapter, or consult with your keeper and create a new occupation. If you want a specific occupation for which the characteristics are already tuned, see the "Alternate Ways" box on p. 37, and apply one of those methods. Then return here.

Multiply the investigator's EDU by 20, and allot those points only to the eight or so skills listed for the occupation. The skills are found on the front of the investigator sheet. You can have up to 99 points per skill.

Hand-to-hand and firearm values are found on the Weapons Table, in the Game System chapter. Write in the pertinent data in the boxes at the bottom of the investigator sheet front.

C. Multiply the investigator's INT x10. These are personal interest points, and can increase any skill except Cthulhu Mythos. Add these points to any printed base chances printed on the investigator sheet, and any amounts already in the blanks to the right of the skills. Total the amount for each skill.

Allot every point; points unallocated are lost.

Weapon skills are found in the Hand-to-Hand and Firearms boxes just below Skills.

Not all skills need to be given points. A single skill of 70% or 80% may be much more valuable than two skills of 35% or 40% each.

ABOUT INVESTIGATORS

Wherein we set the context of their creation and consider elements important to all characters in the game, as well as the persistent question of investigator backgrounds.

The players take the parts of "investigators" in the game, roles so-called because much of the game consists of searching for and evaluating clues and evidence. It is an accident of alphabetization that the first skill on the alphabetical list of game skills is Accounting, yet it is also telling that the first skill is not something like Aikido or Attack (the first attack skill on the skills list is all the way down to the F's, Fist/Punch). Investigators are not fighting machines. The single extraordinary thing about most investigators is what they come to know.

Beneath the surface appearances of the world, they find a truth of a terrifying sort. The world and universe are insane and horrible. Physical law is not uniform. It varies across the universe. Humans have evolved in a cosmic billiards pocket where the full natural law is somehow abbreviated. It is the Mythos creatures who are "more", and it is humans who are "less". Beyond, the cosmic gaming table extends through all time and space, and across it worlds careen and incomprehensible forces roam and raven.

Those other worlds and other beings are very different. A few of the incredibly powerful things that live elsewhere have come to Earth to stay. The Cthulhu Mythos chapter contains more about them.

Humans who come to admire or understand this alien Mythos are progressively changed by it (in game terms, they accumulate Cthulhu Mythos points). In substituting new truths for what they once believed, they start a process which progressively corrupts their mental balance, and they gradually abandon themselves and society. Friend or enemy, all go mad. (Thus in the game, as Cthulhu Mythos rises, maximum Sanity decreases.)

Ultimately, investigators come to define their own limits, realizing that individual people are unlikely to dispel the danger and strength of the Mythos. They may volunteer to sacrifice themselves, as do soldiers in war, or to retire from active struggle, as veterans. They do not betray the effort—they pass on the burden to those younger and now stronger, as life always has.

In its ambitions, Call of Cthulhu offers parallels to life. In it, for instance, death is a serious threat, and the player characters are not superhuman. Investigators have problems of emotions as well as sixgun-style showdowns. Many of the skills (like Accounting) useful to civilization are present and are important in the game—but they do not augment one's ability to fight and loot. The game is set historically, not in a fantasy out of time. Its societies have many more elements than tavern-hut-castle. Societies have their own interests and priorities, and have ways of dealing with people who cause too much damage, attract too much attention, or are clear and present dangers.

Like anything else, roleplaying is easier to do the more you do it. Always have some idea of your investigator's personality and character before you start, but also allow the events of his or her life to help shape the investigator and allow him or her to grow. Allow yourself different roles for different investigators. Choose from your investigators those most appropriate to an adventure. Then let the action help define their personalities. Always create investigators whom you can enthusiastically roleplay.

Developing an investigator also depends upon the characteristics and skills which he or she has, and those will be discussed below. But the real play in the game is in clothing these numbers with imagination.

Characteristics

We refer solely to investigators during this and the next several chapters, but these remarks apply to every human character important enough to develop, as keepers will understand.

To create an investigator, roll the characteristics first. A characteristic is one of nine numbers which summarize investigators. Other matters being equal, it is always better to have higher characteristics than to have lower ones. These numbers may be likened to skeleton and muscles: our bodies are of different sizes and proportions, but all humans have heads, hearts, and so forth. In the game, each characteristic stands for a general aspect of an investigator—his or her intelligence, dexterity, and so on. These identified quantities help determine the relative value and capability of investigators, and suggest ways for them to act and react during roleplaying.

A player makes random rolls for characteristics for the same sort of reason that tennis players use a tennis net—context creates meaning.

Characteristics rarely increase after being rolled, because investigators are created as adults and have finished growing. Characteristics do occasionally decrease as a consequence of magical or physical injury. Though a suggestion is included for each characteristic, the effect of 0 or a low value in a characteristic is mostly left for the keeper to describe. It should be suitable to the current situation and apt in tone—horrible, grievous, or funny. Such a loss is always a blow to the investigator. As an identity rounds into a full personality, every player shares in the pleasure, and the meshing of the various investigators takes on life and becomes good drama.

STR (STRENGTH)

Strength measures the muscle power of investigators. Use it to judge how much they can lift, or push or pull, or how tightly they can cling to something. This characteristic is important in determining the damage investigators do in hand-to-hand combat. Reduced to Strength 0, an investigator is an invalid, unable to leave his or her bed.

CON (CONSTITUTION)

This compares health, vigor, and vitality. Constitution also helps calculate how well investigators resist drowning or suffocation. Poisons and diseases may directly challenge investigator Constitutions. High-CON investigators often have higher hit points, the better to resist injury and attack.

Serious physical injury or magical attack might lower CON. If Constitution reaches 0, the investigator dies.

SIZ (SIZE)

The characteristic SIZ averages height and weight into one number. To see over something, to squeeze through a small opening, or even to judge whose head might be sticking up out of the grass, use Size. Size helps determine hit points and the damage bonus. One might decrease SIZ to indicate loss of several limbs, though lowering DEX is more often the solution. Presumably if investigators lose all SIZ, they disappear—goodness knows to where.

INT (INTELLIGENCE)

Intelligence represents how well investigators learn, remember, and analyze, and of how aware they are of that which is around them. To help describe different circumstances, keepers multiply INT times various numerals and then call for D100 rolls equal to or less than the products. INT x5—the Idea roll—is especially popular. For more about it, see further below.

Difficult concepts, plans, or inspired guesses have lower chances to be derived, and hence get lower multipliers, down to INT x2 or INT x1. Such rolls can establish whether or not an investigator makes a deduction or links information, avoiding the question of the player deducing (for instance) that the presence of a volcano argues that a world has a molten core.

An investigator without INT is a babbling, drooling idiot.

Intelligence determines the number of personal interest skill points allotted to a new investigator, and also how quickly an investigator can learn a Cthulhu Mythos spell.

If the amount of Intelligence seems to contradict a characteristic rolled later, that's another chance for roleplaying: an investigator with high EDU and low INT, for instance, might be a pedantic teacher or a sideshow performer, someone who knows facts but not their meanings. Conversely, high INT and low EDU might mean ignorance—a farm boy or poor immigrant, new to the Big City—but this person would not be dull-witted.

POW (POWER)

Power indicates force of will. The higher the POW, the higher the aptitude for magic. Power does not quantify leadership, which is a matter for roleplaying. The amount of Power or the number of magic points (they derive from Power) measure resistance to magical or hypnotic attack. An investigator without POW is zombie-like and unable to use magic. Unless stated otherwise, lost POW is lost permanently.

POW x5 is the Luck roll, about which see further below. That amount also equals a character's initial SAN characteristic. Magic points, unlike Power, are spent and regenerated. The POW of ordinary characters rarely changes.

One who is adroit in the magic of the Cthulhu Mythos may be able to increase personal POW. Keepers especially are referred to the boxed text titled How Sorcerers Get That Way, on p. 95, near the end of the Magic chapter.

DEX (DEXTERITY)

Investigators with higher Dexterity scores are quicker, nimbler, and more physically flexible. A keeper might call for a DEX roll in order to grab a support to keep from falling, to stay upright in high winds or on ice, to accomplish some delicate task, or to take something without being noticed. As with the other characteristics, the difficulty of the roll depends on the multiplier which the keeper selects for the characteristic. An investigator without DEX is uncoordinated, unable to perform physical tasks without also receiving a successful Luck roll.

In combat, the character with the higher DEX hits or fires first, and thus may be able to disarm or disable an opponent before the foe can attack.

DEX x2 determines the starting percentage of investigator Dodge skills.

APP (APPEARANCE)

Appearance shows attractiveness and friendliness. Some multiple of APP might be useful in social encounters, or when trying to make an initial impression on a member of the opposite sex, perhaps in conjunction with a Fast Talk or Bargain roll. Appearance is a surface characteristic, however: initial impressions are not necessarily lasting. APP measures what one sees in the mirror, not ongoing personal leadership or charisma. An investigator without APP is appallingly ugly, provoking comment and shock everywhere.

EDU (EDUCATION)

Education measures formal and factual knowledge possessed by the investigator, as well as the number of years it took him or her to learn that material. EDU measures information, not intelligent use of information. EDU partly determines how many skill points an investigator has. And EDU x5 is the Know roll, about which see further below. EDU x5 also represents the investigator's starting percentage with the skill Own Language.

An investigator without EDU would be like a newborn baby, or an amnesiac without knowledge of the world, probably curious and credulous.

An EDU score of 12 suggests a high school graduate. More than that indicates a person with some college years. EDU greater than 16 indicates some graduate-level work or degree. An investigator with a high Education may not be schooled, but still might be studious and observant.

See also the spread for Creating Your Investigator, on pp. 34-35.

SAN (SANITY)

Find Sanity by multiplying POW x5. Sanity is derived, but it is crucial to investigators and central to the idea of this game. An entire chapter in this section is devoted to Sanity: it distinguishes between the SAN characteristic, Sanity points, and maximum Sanity. Sanity points fluctuate. Characteristic SAN does not change.

An investigator's maximum of Sanity points is never more than 99. Sanity points of 99 represent the strongest possible mind, one capable of deflecting or lessening even extreme emotional shocks. On the other hand, 30 Sanity

SCENE: A GRAVEYARD (1)

points would indicate a more fragile mind, one which might be driven into temporary or permanent madness. Most Mythos monsters and some natural events cost Sanity points to encounter, and Mythos spells cost Sanity points to learn and to cast.

An investigator's Sanity points are never more than 99 minus current Cthulhu Mythos percentiles. Up to that maximum, it is possible to regain Sanity points lost, or even to increase Sanity points above the original total, but that process is slow.

Characteristic Rolls

Keepers are encouraged to use characteristic rolls to decide matters which are not appropriate as skill rolls, or ones for which all investigators should be able to receive rolls.

CHANGES IN CHARACTERISTIC VALUES

If the deriving characteristic changes, the Idea, Luck, or Know roll changes immediately as well. Similarly, hit points and the damage bonus change if the characteristics related to them change.

Magic points might not change immediately. If excess points existed, they would have to be spent before maximum magic points need equal a new, lower POW.

IDEA ROLL (INT X5)

The Idea roll represents hunches and the ability to interpret the obvious. When no skill roll seems appropriate, this roll might show understanding of a concept or the ability to solve a pressing intellectual problem. The Idea roll is specially handy to show awareness: did the investigator observe and understand what he or she saw? Would a normal person have become aware of a particular feeling about a gathering or a place? Is anything out of place on that hill?

Save the Spot Hidden skill for specific clues or items not immediately noticeable. Employ the Psychology skill when dealing with individuals.

LUCK ROLL (POW X5)

Did the investigator bring along some particular piece of gear? Is he or she the one the dimensional shambler decides to attack? Did the investigator step on the floorboard which breaks, or the one that squeaks? The Luck roll is a quick way to get an answer.

Luck is the ability to be in the right place at the right time: this roll is often called for in emergency situations, especially when the keeper desires higher percentage chances for the investigators, more than might result from, say, calling for Jump or Dodge rolls.

KNOW ROLL (EDU X5)

All people know bits of information about different topics. The Know roll represents what's stored in the brain's intellectual attic, calculated as the percentage chance that the investigator's education supplied the information.

The investigator might know what happens if one puts sulfuric acid into water or water into sulfuric acid (without ever studying Chemistry), or be able to remember the geography of Tibet (without a Navigate roll), or know how many legs arachnids have (and possess only a point of Biology).

Identification of present-day earthly languages is an excellent use for the Know roll.

Since no one knows everything, the Know roll never exceeds 99 even though an investigator might have EDU 21.

DAMAGE BONUS (STR + SIZ, SEE TABLE)

All physical beings have a damage bonus. The term is confusing, because the 'bonus' may actually turn out to be a reduction, but the idea is simple: larger, stronger creatures on average do more physical damage than lesser, weaker brethren.

To determine a damage bonus, add STR to SIZ, and find the total in the Damage Bonus Table (p. 35). Each range of results correlates with a stated die or dice roll. In hand-to-hand combat, add the indicated roll to all the character's blows, whether using a natural weapon such as a fist or a man-made weapon such as a club or knife, and whether striking a foe or some object (such as a door).

■ For thrown objects, add half the thrower's damage bonus to the injury or damage it does.

■ Do not add damage bonuses to firearms attacks, or to other attacks which are independent of Strength and Size.

■ Keepers should not routinely add damage bonuses to Bite attacks.

■ For simplicity's sake, keepers might ignore damage bonuses for characters they run. Individual or average damage bonuses for creatures are always given in the rules.

HIT POINTS (AV. OF CON + SIZ)

All physical beings have hit points. Figure hit points by adding CON plus SIZ, and dividing the total by two. Round up any fraction.

When an investigator is injured or wounded, use a pencil to mark off the number of hit points lost on the hit point section of the investigator sheet. Always apply the hit point loss before any loss to CON. Lost hit points return naturally at the rate of 1D3 hit points per game week. The First Aid or Medicine skills can immediately restore 1D3 hit points as emergency treatment.

■ When hit points reach two or less, characters go unconscious, and no longer influence the game.

■ When hit points reach zero or lower, the character dies unless hit points can be raised to at least +1 by the end of the following round. See the First Aid and Medicine skills, pp. 66 and 68.

MAGIC POINTS (MAX. = POW)

Investigator magic points equal investigator POW. Magic points might be spent casting spells or fighting off malign influences. Magic points naturally regenerate: all can return in 24 hours. Prorate the return of partial losses.

Sample Occupations

An occupation is a way to explain the skills that a character has. Any number of occupations exist. Those important in Lovecraft's stories are asterisked. The occupations presented here offer some ideas about character formation. If creating a new occupation, it is best to confine the number of skills to eight or fewer, or the notion behind an occupation, that of concentrated skills, quickly becomes pointless.

Most occupations can be applied to the three eras without change, but Hackers and Spokespersons exist only in our interesting times.

*ANTIQUARIAN—Art, Bargain, Craft, History, Library Use, Other Language, Spot Hidden, any one other skill as a personal or era specialty.

ARTIST—Art, Craft, Fast Talk, History, Photography, Psychology, Spot Hidden, any one other skill as a personal or era specialty.

ATHLETE—Climb, Dodge, Jump, Martial Arts, Ride, Swim, Throw, any one other skill as a personal or era specialty.

*AUTHOR—History, Library Use, Occult, Other Language, Own Language, Persuade, Psychology, any one other skill as a personal or era specialty.

CLERGYMAN—Accounting, History, Library Use, Listen, Other Language, Persuade, Psychology, any one other skill as a personal or era specialty.

CRIMINAL—Bargain, Disguise, Fast Talk, Handgun, Locksmith, Sneak, Spot Hidden, any one other skill as a personal or era specialty.

*DILETTANTE—Art, Craft, Credit Rating, Other Language, Ride, Shotgun, any two other skills as personal or era specialties.

*DOCTOR OF MEDICINE—Biology, Credit Rating, First Aid, Latin, Medicine, Pharmacy, Psychoanalysis, Psychology, any one other skill as a personal or era specialty.

DRIFTER—Bargain, Fast Talk, Hide, Listen, Natural History, Psychology, Sneak, any one other skill as a personal or era specialty.

ENGINEER—Chemistry, Electrical Repair, Geology, Library Use, Mechanical Repair, Operate Heavy Machine, Physics, any one other skill as a personal or era specialty.

ENTERTAINER—Art, Credit Rating, Disguise, Dodge, Fast Talk, Listen, Psychology, any one other skill as a personal or era specialty.

FARMER / FORESTER—Craft, Electrical Repair, First Aid, Mechanical Repair, Natural History, Operate Heavy Machine, Track, any one other skill as a personal or era specialty.

HACKER / CONSULTANT—Computer Use, Electrical Repair, Electronics, Fast Talk, Library Use, Other Language, Physics, any one other skill as a personal specialty.

*JOURNALIST—Fast Talk, History, Library Use, Own Language, Persuade, Photography, Psychology, any one other skill as a personal or era specialty.

LAWYER—Bargain, Credit Rating, Fast Talk, Law, Library use, Persuade, Psychology, any one other skill as a personal or era specialty.

MILITARY OFFICER—Accounting, Bargain, Credit Rating, Law, Navigate, Persuade, Psychology, any one other skill as a personal or era specialty.

MISSIONARY—Art, Craft, First Aid, Mechanical Repair, Medicine, Natural History, Persuade, any one other skill as a personal or era specialty.

MUSICIAN—Art, Bargain, Craft, Fast Talk, Listen, Persuade, Psychology, any one other skill as a personal or era specialty.

PARAPSYCHOLOGIST—Anthropology, History, Library Use, Occult, Other Language, Photography, Psychology, any one other skill as a personal or era specialty.

PILOT—Astronomy, Electrical Repair, Mechanical Repair, Navigate, Operate Heavy Machine, Physics, Pilot, any one other skill as a personal or era specialty.

*POLICE DETECTIVE—Bargain, Fast Talk, Law, Listen, Persuade, Psychology, Spot Hidden, any one other skill as a personal or era specialty.

POLICEMAN—Dodge, Fast Talk, First Aid, Grapple, Law, Psychology, and any two of the following as a personal specialty: Bargain, Drive Automobile, Martial Arts, Ride, or Spot Hidden.

PRIVATE INVESTIGATOR—Bargain, Fast Talk, Law, Library Use, Locksmith, Photography, Psychology, and any one other skill as a personal or era specialty.

*PROFESSOR—Bargain, Credit Rating, Library Use, Other Language, Persuade, Psychology, and any two of the following as a personal specialty: Anthropology, Archaeology, Astronomy, Biology, Chemistry, Electronics, Geology, History, Law, Medicine, Natural History, or Physics.

SOLDIER—Dodge, First Aid, Hide, Listen, Mechanical Repair, Rifle, Sneak, any one other skill as a personal or era specialty.

SPOKESPERSON—Credit Rating, Disguise, Dodge, Fast Talk, Persuade, Psychology, any one other skill as a personal or era specialty.

TRIBAL MEMBER—Bargain, Listen, Natural History, Occult, Spot Hidden, Swim, Throw, any one other skill as a personal or era specialty.

ZEALOT—Conceal, Hide, Library Use, Persuade, Psychology, any two of the following (Chemistry, Electrical Repair, Law, Pharmacy, Rifle), and any one other skill as a personal or era specialty. ■

Should an investigator's magic points reach zero, he or she is emotionally drained, and faints until one magic point regenerates.

Should POW decrease, magic points would not diminish until spent, whereupon they would return only to the new maximum. Should POW increase, magic points would begin a pro rata increase immediately.

Background

The numbers for the characteristics (and the numbers derivable from the characteristics) make up the basis of the investigator. Most of the ideas and abilities which make the investigator interesting and fun to play are a matter of choice, not dice roll results.

Examine the investigator sheet to see the scope of useful background. All of history is available for ideas.

SEX OF THE INVESTIGATOR

The investigator can be male or female. No game rule distinguishes between male and female; neither sex has advantage or disadvantage. Some published scenarios may consider the effect of sex in specific societies, but keepers are free to ignore that if they wish.

NAME AND AGE

The name of the investigator is whatever the player finds entertaining or evocative. The age chosen may be influenced by changing the investigator's EDU—see Creating Your Investigator on pp. 34-35.

COLLEGES, DEGREES

The player can enter any degrees or colleges desired. Any degrees entered or colleges reported should be compatible with the investigator's EDU, unless the intent of the entry is that the investigator is a fool or a fraud. Either sort of investigator would be enjoyable to roleplay.

BIRTHPLACE

Choose the investigator's nation of birth. No game penalty or advantage exists for one country or culture over another. The choice made, however, leads to other deductions: for instance, while an investigator born in the United States of America has a good chance of English as his or her own language, an investigator born in Quebec might learn French at infancy, one born in Arizona might have Spanish or Navajo, and one born in San Francisco might speak Cantonese.

MARKS, SCARS, MENTAL DISORDERS

If something significant to the investigator's background story produced body changes or mutilations or emotional scaring, that could be entered here. There are no game penalties for such matters unless the investigator has suffered great loss, such as an arm, a leg, or an eye. Consult with the keeper for such cases.

THE PICTURE

If you like, draw in or have a friend draw in your investigator's face, or photocopy a likely face from a magazine or book and paste it in. It's a useful way to introduce him or her to the other players. Even a small picture can say a lot. Film stars from the 1920s and 1930s seem to be particularly apt, no matter what the era.

If you don't want a picture here, the space can hold notes or material for later transcription to the back of the sheet.

Skills And Occupations

Space for the skills fills about two thirds of the front side of the investigator sheet. The use of and increase of investigator skills is of corresponding interest.

A skill in Call of Cthulhu is a somewhat arbitrary range of ability and comprehension whose very fuzziness of definition lends its use to a variety of situations. Thus someone with a doctorate in Biology has good understanding of the biological sciences. By extension, he or she also knows of the leading theoreticians and experimenters in the field, in what journals they publish, and where they teach or work. "Does my investigator Sam know any biologists at Miskatonic University?" asks the player. The keeper ponders, and calls for a Luck roll. It succeeds. "Yes," he replies, "you know Miller, he's a parasitologist. Maybe he can identify that creature you've found."

Even more extended connections between skill and need are frequently made. On the whole, the skills encompass much of the range of human achievement, or at least that spectrum of achievement useful for roleplaying.

OCCUPATIONS

An investigator's occupation shows how he or she has spent time in the past. That past reflects in the skills held in the present. Choose an occupation because you like the skills it offers—don't take the occupation too seriously. No character classes exist in Call of Cthulhu.

Some occupations are typically Lovecraftian: Antiquarian, Author, Dilettante, Doctor of Medicine, Journalist, Police Detective, and Professor. They are asterisked in the list of sample occupations. Other occupations are not those of Lovecraft heroes, but may interest particular players.

An occupation ties together a cluster of skills. In the sample occupations, for instance, "antiquarian" encom-

Psychiatrist

A doctor of medicine can be a psychiatrist. Calculate his or her value as a therapist as 1/2 of Medicine plus 1/2 of Psychoanalysis. Unlike a psychoanalyst, the psychiatrist prescribes drugs and has hospital standing.

The psychiatrist diagnoses mental disorders and administers treatment. He or she also can identify medical conditions masquerading as mental disorders. See pp. 78-81 for more information.

Notes on Occupations

These entries correspond to some of the investigator occupations listed nearby. They might help define new investigators or other characters. Some have more history or sociology in them than description, but that may help orient you as well. Though a few might more likely occur in one era than another, most of these stereotypes pass easily between eras. If you wish, you may combine elements of two sketches to form a more interesting or more complex investigator.

These are average people. If you need statistics immediately, choose from among the sample ready-to-play investigators at the back of this book. Most of the entries below have been cast in male form, since earlier eras would demand the masculine form, but the probability of female equivalents is also given.

SELECTED OCCUPATIONS

ANTIQUARIAN — he revels in the timeless excellence of design and execution, and in the power of ancient lore, the most Lovecraft-like occupation. The antiquarian rarely deals in what he loves. More often, an independent income allows him to sharpen and define his pleasure in things old and obscure. He has an appreciative eye and a swift mind, and frequently finds mordant or contemptuous humor in the foolishness of the ignorant, the pompous, and the greedy — or are those perceptions clues to his own mental instability? Occasionally female, though usually too obsessive and voyeuristic to be of that sex.

ARTIST — he is self-absorbed with his own visions, but is blessed with a talent that lets him express himself. Often he also has a crafty entrepreneurial streak. Usually a painter or sculptor but, by the 1990s, academic infusions have so enwrapped the fine arts that technique has become less important than concept or the ability to write a grant proposal. Talented or not, the artist's ego must be hardy and strong to surmount initial obstacles and to keep him working if success arrives. This occupation is equally available to males and females.

AUTHOR — as distinct from the journalist, the author uses words to define and explore the conditions of human life, and especially the range of human emotions. It is said that an author does not so much write as rewrite; his labors are solitary and his rewards solipsistic: only a relative handful make much money in the 1990s, though in previous eras the trade once provided livable wages. The work habits of authors vary widely. Typically an author withdraws during periods of intense creation. The author who is constantly expansive and sociable is written-out, or perhaps had no talent to start with. May be male or female.

DILETTANTE — the dilettante has so much money that specialists are needed to take care of it. He or she is well educated, though not systematically educated or necessarily accomplished in anything. Money frees the dilettante to be eccentric and outspoken. He or she has had plenty of time to learn how to be charming and sophisticated; what else has been done with that time betrays the dilettante's true character. Lacking financial compulsion, his or her family relations are sometimes very odd. Can be male or female.

DOCTOR OF MEDICINE — perhaps a general practitioner, a surgeon or other specialist, a psychiatrist, or (especially in the 1890s and 1920s) an independent medical researcher. Apart from personal goals, three aims — helping patients, gaining money and prestige, and promoting a more rational and wiser society — are common to the occupation. Doctors tend to be self-sufficient sorts for whom families become adjuncts to respectability. A successful practice requires dedication and much time. May be male or female. By the 1990s, female physicians are no longer unusual.

DRIFTER — as opposed to someone who is poverty-stricken, the drifter's wandering life is chosen, perhaps compensating for social, philosophical, sexual, or economic lacks. The drifter takes jobs, sometimes for months, but he is disposed to solve problems with the answer of mobility and isolation, not comfort and intimacy. The life of the road might seem especially American, but the same sort of life is chosen wherever travel itself is not systematically dangerous. Because the road can be perilous and is without organized protection, the drifter is often male.

ENTERTAINER — this occupation might include dancer, singer, juggler, athlete, musician, or anyone else who earns a living in front of an audience. These people love to be seen, love to show what they do best, and love the consequent applause. These proclivities can be observed in children as young as age three or four, but the talent that reaps success may lie fallow for years. Show-business families make excellent incubators. May be male or female. This profession is not often respectable in the 1890s, but the money which Hollywood stars make in the 1920s changes most minds, and by the 1990s such a background is generally felt to be an advantage.

JOURNALIST — uses words to report and comment upon topics and incidents of the day, writing as many words in a day as an author may in a week. Journalists work for newspapers, magazines, and radio and television news services. The best report, but keep themselves independent of the corruption and self-serving they witness. That reality overwhelms the worst, who eventually forfeit any sensibility except the power of their words. Nearly always male in earlier eras, interchangeably male or female by the 1990s.

MISSIONARY — has accepted the call to spread the word of God. May be independent of all except his or her own vision, or may be backed by some organization to do just that—and in that case has demonstrated some ability to perform such duties. The clear-sighted missionary is able to focus on the humanity of converts and does not confuse alien customs with human souls, so that questions of dress, behavior, or diet do not become paramount. Where morality leaves off and religion begins is by no means clear. This occupation requires settled emotions and a sense of humor. The successful missionary remains personally humble and exalts god. Christian and Islamic proselytizers are encountered worldwide in all the eras, as are certain other sects, and as are Buddhist and Hindu teachers in the 1920s and the present. The missionary is of either sex.

PARAPSYCHOLOGIST—prestigious universities grant no degrees for parapsychology. Standards in the field are based entirely upon personal reputation, and so the most acceptable representatives tend to hold degrees in related areas—physics, psychology, or medicine. Who chooses this study is unusually sympathetic to the notion of invisible mystical powers, and in validating that belief to the satisfaction of physical scientists. This would represent an unusual cohabitation of faith and doubt—the parapsychologist may have difficulty separating the conflicting desires. A person uninterested in observation, experiment, and proof is not a scientist, though he or she may be an occultist.

POLICE DETECTIVE—though 1990s detectives may attend police science classes, take a degree, and undergo special training and endless civil service exams, police detectives of every era are grounded in their experiences as junior officers and ordinary patrolmen. Police routine and discipline becomes vital to self-identification as well as an ongoing source of frustration as the detective is tempted by extralegal shortcuts to successful arrests. The police detective may be a manager who coordinates staff in some important investigation, but rarely has the luxury of concentrating on a single case. In the United States, his responsibilities at any one time may number in the dozens or hundreds of open cases. The detective's crucial function is to marshal enough evidence to allow an arrest, in turn leading to a successful criminal prosecution. Detectives everywhere sort truth from lies by evidence and reconstruction. The offices of detective and prosecutor are everywhere separate, so that the evidence may be weighed independently before trial. More recently in the United States, women have become detectives, but the profession before then was almost exclusively male.

PRIVATE EYE—in most places the private investigator is licensed by the police and must be privately bonded as well, guarantees of minimal honesty. Proven malfeasance costs him his license and puts him out of business. The private eye usually acts in non-police situations: he gathers information and evidence for private clients in impending civil cases, tracks down fleeing spouses or business partners, or acts as an agent for private defense attorneys in criminal cases. In detective classics, the private eye is hired to handle some ordinary civil or private matter (such as a cheating spouse), and then is drawn into the investigation of a murder or series of murders as the case unfolds. Like any professional, the private eye separates his personal feelings from the job at hand, and cheerfully works for the guilty and innocent alike, as long as his fee is paid. The private investigator is usually shown to have been a member of a police force in the past, using those connections to his advantage in the present. Usually he is not prosperous and never has known much money, but his private code and keen awareness purifiy his manners. Depending on state or on local law, police experience may not be necessary. A higher proportion of women act as private eyes than as police detectives.

PROFESSOR—for the most part the occupation indicates a Ph.D. That rank can earn tenure at universities around the world. He is qualified to teach and to perform competent research, and has a discernible academic reputation in his area of expertise. He may be an absolute idiot in other fields, of course, and such contradictory investigators are fun to play. Unless they are of independent means, and have taken leave of their universities, professor-investigators tend to be tethered close to home by their ongoing responsibilities to school and students. Indiana Jones was lucky to have a department head who would allow extended absences—your investigator may not have such an understanding boss. A small minority of female scholars existed in each era, but even in the 1990s male bastions such as Engineering exist in which female academics are rare.

TRIBAL MEMBER—in the sense of family allegiance, at least, tribalism is everywhere. In a tribe the primacy of kinship and custom is self-evident. A tribal group is relatively small. In place of a blanket of law and general individual rights, the tribal personality defers to personal honor. Allegiance to the group shines from within. Praise, vengeance, gifts, and glory—all must be personal to him or her, and if leaders or enemies are to be treated as men of honor, they too must be personally known in some way. The notion of "exile" has real power in such a setting. In the United States, the concept of the tribe as a mutual frame of mind developed during the 1960s, and the notion of the urban tribe or even a tribal nation has become more and more synonymous with the sullen friction between the new paganism and active Christian fundamentalism.

ZEALOT—intense and vision-driven, scorning an easy life, the zealot agitates for a better life for humanity or for some advantage for the group imagined to be the most worthwhile part of humanity. Some promote their beliefs through violence, but the peaceable majority will be just as implacable. All dream of the vindication of their beliefs. The zealot is not typically young or old, and a good chance exists for a female counterpart to the male. ∎

To the left and above: silhouettes of two mi-go, the mysterious fungi from Yuggoth.

passes Art, Bargain, History, Law, Library Use, Other Language, Spot Hidden, and one other skill of the player's choice (to reflect something special about the past). Some occupations include no free choices, others have two.

SKILL POINTS

Having chosen an occupation, the player multiplies the investigator's EDU x20 and allocates the resulting total as percentiles among those skills listed for the occupation. All the skills do not need to have points given to them, but points undistributed are lost. Definitions of all the skills are found in the Rules & Skills chapter, pp. 60-68.

Add to these allotted points those pre-printed on the investigator sheet alongside the skills. For instance, allotting 25 percentiles to Throw, we see 25% printed beside the skill: the player should total the two numbers and write in 50% as the current amount for the skill.

No skill is ever higher than 99%. Cthulhu Mythos excepted, a higher skill percentage is always better.

PERSONAL INTERESTS

Investigators also have hobbies and do things other than for money. Multiply INT x10 and allot the points to any skill or skills, except Cthulhu Mythos.

WEAPONS

Even if your investigator takes no weapons, he or she has significant base chances with many weapons. Consider his or her character and past. Few people in any era are actually expert with weapons, though often they have passing acquaintance with them. Except in a few occupations like Soldier, additional points for weapons would have to come out of personal interest points.

Reverse Side of the Sheet

An investigator with skills and numbers in place can be played, but much about him or her is still unknown. Those questions may not have been asked and need not be answered, but they should be kept in mind as possibilities, and recorded on the back of the investigator sheet when it seems amusing or pertinent.

INVESTIGATOR INCOME

Income may or may not be important in your play. Take dollar signs with a grain of salt. Many keepers never mention money or personal property, and rarely do published scenarios raise the subject. Only in campaigns does earning and spending hold much interest or intent.

The Creating Your Investigator spread includes a way to establish investigator income. Some keepers may choose to change those amounts to fit their individual styles of play.

The amount of income can show how bad or good the investigator is at the chosen career, or how dissatisfied he or she is with it, as it might in real life.

DEEP BACKGROUND

Background ideas need not be amazing. The unusual flows out of the ordinary, and in the process gains meaning, context, and depth. Start with the ordinary, and the miraculous will follow.

For instance, is the investigator in love? Betrothed? Married? Are there children? Lost loves? Were there tragedies?

What schools were attended? What friendships formed?

Did the investigator have military experience? When? Where? What happened? Who were friends? Were medals earned or mentions made in dispatches?

Who are the investigator's family? What is their origin? Gradually come to know fathers, mothers, siblings, aunts, uncles, cousins, etc., living or dead.

What is the investigator like? A little time spent going over the investigator sheet can yield insights. Comb the characteristics and skills for hints and contradictions. Is she or he quiet, rowdy, lusty, stuffy, respectable, brilliant, erratic, mystical, charitable, money-grubbing, short, dark, tall, pale, good-looking, ugly, plain, dowdy, elegant, punctilious, frenzied, chivalric, nervous, intellectual, brawny, muscle-bound, vigorous, mousy, courteous, impulsive, excitable, foolish, bald, bearded, thin, crippled, hairy, sleek, or something entirely different? As you find the words to express your ideas, write them down on the back of the investigator sheet.

ULTIMATE FATE

Perhaps your investigator becomes a leader during games —a famous author or a renowned occultist or perhaps he is just a private eye no better than he ought to be. Perhaps he or she is a top specialist, to whom everyone comes begging when that vital job comes up.

Many games and jobs involve thwarting the malign purposes of the Great Old Ones and Outer Gods. Such challenges may bring a long, rich life, or one as short and dramatic as a falling star. It depends upon fate and upon the player's attention and care.

Investigators played incautiously will surely die or go insane. The situation is not so different from real life, except that in the game an investigator who stands against evil and does his or her best will always earn respect. ■

Creating Harvey Walters

Here begins the story of how Harvey Walters, the noted 1920s New York journalist, mystic, and psychic investigator, comes to be. The player takes up a fresh investigator sheet, a pencil, and three six-sided dice, and then opens the rulesbook to p. 34.

CHARACTERISTICS

STR (Strength): the roll is 3D6. The player rolled a 4, nearly the worst possible result. In consequence, the new investigator is an exceptional weakling. But the player is not dismayed: Call of Cthulhu is an unusual game—the stars yet may be right.

DEX (Dexterity): the roll is 3D6. The roll result is a 12, high average, and the investigator's Dodge is 24%. Given good Dexterity despite low Strength, the investigator might want to learn skills which show off that ability—or perhaps he or she will just be a good dancer or a good typist.

INT (Intelligence): the roll is 2D6+6. The INT result is 17, an excellent score. This investigator may be someone to reckon with. Her curiosity piqued, the player smiles and rolls the next characteristic.

CON (Constitution): the roll is 3D6. The result is 14, another good score. This investigator's hardiness helps compensate for the terrible STR score.

APP (Appearance): the roll is 3D6. The result is 17, another outstanding score. Whatever other flaws arise, this investigator's personality sparkles.

POW (Power): the roll is 3D6, and the result is a 9. No one with POW 9 is destined for greatness in the magical arts. Nor should someone with a Luck roll of 45% count on luck to extricate himself or herself from a tight situation.

SIZ (Size): the roll is 2D6+6, and the result is a 16. As soon as the dice stopped moving, she started thinking of her new investigator as male. At SIZ 16, he is hefty, if weak. Perhaps he is overweight, or perhaps an injury has left him partly paralyzed. The mere bare numbers of the characteristics may suggest personality. Roleplaying begins in explaining unusual combinations of characteristics. A first name comes to mind. She has never had an investigator named Harvey, but it seems to fit. For now, the investigator is Harvey.

SAN (Sanity): the multiplier is 5x POW, a result of 45 for Harvey. Not a terrible score, but less than average. Perhaps he is nervous and high-strung, or he has undergone a shattering mystical experience already.

EDU (Education): the roll is 3D6+3, and a 16 comes up, a good score, high enough that it makes Harvey a college graduate. His player decides that Harvey has an Master of Arts degree, though that title has no game function. Harvey speaks English at 80%. His player wants Harvey to be youngish, and does not age him, so he remains age 22 (EDU+6 years).

Idea Roll: with an INT of 17, Harvey's x5 Idea roll is 85%. He is quite clever, and stands a high chance of coming up with workable plans.

Luck Roll: with a POW of 9, Harvey's x5 Luck roll is 45%. He is slightly more often unlucky than lucky. He should depend on ideas and knowledge, and not hope for the best from a roll of the dice.

Know Roll: with an EDU of 16, Harvey's x5 Know roll is 80%. He worked hard in school and learned a lot.

Damage Bonus: the sum of Harvey's STR+SIZ is 4+16=20. His bonus is zero.

Hit Points: the sum of Harvey's CON+SIZ is 14+16=30. Divided by 2, he has 15 hit points, a good score. Harvey is not a fighter, though. With his brains and charm, he can often talk his way out of difficulties.

Magic Points: these equal POW. Harvey has 9. At this point Harvey's last name comes to his player: Walters, because the *wall* sound reminds her of *wallflower*, and because *Walters* rhymes with *falters*, which she thinks a nervous guy like Harvey may do.

BACKGROUND

Harvey is a 1920s character. Rolling on the Investigator Income Table, his player gets a 2, putting $2500 in Harvey's pocket and another $2500 in the bank. (The keeper cruelly rules that the rest of Harvey's property is in his inheritance, unavailable until his parents die.) Even with adequate money for a time, Harvey sharpens a pencil and wisely starts looking for a job.

CHOOSING SKILLS

Harvey Walters is to be a journalist, and his player states that he has joined *Enigma Magazine*, which looks into mysteries of the occult.

Harvey has EDU 16, and multiplied times 20 yields 320 points to add to his base chances. His player may add occupation points only to the skills listed for the occupation Journalist. Since there are rarely more than eight skills listed for an occupation, each can get an average of 40 points.

Personal Data
Investigator Name: Harvey Walters
Residence: Boston, MA
Personal Description: Overweight, with a pale complexion, intelligent features & a sparkling personality.
Family & Friends:
Father: Quinten Walters Jr.
Mother: Rebecca Walters (deceased)
Elder Brother: Quinten Walters III

Episodes of Insanity

Wounds & Injuries

Marks & Scars

Investigator History
3/15/1902: Born, Boston MA
6/1/1916: Saw mother's ghost
1919-1924: Student at M.U.
05/1924: Hired by Enigma magazine.

Income & Savings
Income: $5,500
Cash on Hand: $2,750
Savings: $2,750
Personal Property: Occult Library
Real Estate

Adventuring Gear & Possessions
Camera
DKroom Gear
Arch. Equip.
Camping Gear

Mythos Tomes Read

Entities Encountered
Mother's Ghost

Magical Artifacts / Spells Known
Artifacts   Spells

Harvey's present skill in Own Language (English) is already 80% (EDU x5), so she decides not to add points to that score. She chooses that he learns Latin: it has a base chance of 01%, and she adds 49 of his 320 points for Latin 50%. Now he is at home in a language encountered in Mythos researches; 271 occupation points remain.

Next, she adds 60 to his Fast Talk rating, raising it to 65%, and increases Persuade by 50, for a total of 55%. To evaluate the people he questions, his player adds 55 to make a 60% Psychology. As an investigative reporter, Harvey is well equipped to ask questions and get honest answers. With Persuade, he can change minds and make allies. Now 106 occupation points remain. Every reporter needs to collect evidence. His player puts 20 points into Photography for 30% total, since seeing is believing in the 1920s. Now

86 occupation points are left. Journalists are permitted two skills as personal specialties: she chooses Archaeology and adds 79 points to that for 80%, and 7 points for Law, for a total of 12% in that skill. Harvey's player now has spent all of his Journalist occupation points. He has good communication skills, useful for a reporter, and is expert in a Mythos-related skill, Archaeology.

Harvey's INT is 17, so his personal interest points total 17 x10 or 170 points. These can be spent as the player desires. Harvey's player spends 59 points for Pilot Aircraft 60% ("Because it sounds exciting") and, since she is an experienced Call of Cthulhu player, she adds 40 points to Library Use, raising it to 65%. There are 71 personal interest points left, and these she splits up for their potential tactical advantage, adding 20 for Listen 45%, 25 for Occult 30% (this low score may be a weakness in Harvey's job), 15 for Bargain 20%, and 11 for Credit Rating 26% (another weakness for a person who must make person-to-person contact all the time). All of Harvey's points have been spent.

Harvey's player did not choose to increase his weapons skills, though she might have. Harvey is a 1920s intellectual, not the sort to carry a gun. If anything is unrealistic about him, it might be the choice of Archaeology instead of a higher Credit Rating that might gain him entrance to upper class homes and functions. The Archaeology choice clearly anticipates game situations.

Harvey has other skill points, preprinted on the investigator sheet and even more points tucked away as base chances in the weapons tables, all part of his human inheritance.

She gives him 5% Ballroom Dancing under the Art skill. Her early idea about his Dexterity didn't survive, but she salvages this much. Harvey is ready to play. She will continue to accumulate ideas about him. She ignores the chance to age Harvey: he makes an interesting young man now, but aged by ten or twenty years he would be relatively ordinary.

Harvey's player must decide what he will look like. Satisfied with Harvey's unique characteristics and skills, she finds him easy to visualize. She is so pleased with how Harvey turned out that she commissions a fine portrait of Harvey on the front of the character sheet. Sometimes she photocopies a picture of some 1930s film star and pastes that in—other players immediately understand the sorts of investigators she intends.

DEEPER BACKGROUND

Harvey Walter's player decides that Harvey attended Miskatonic University, and that he graduated with a M.A. in Journalism. She also decides that Harvey is brave. She already knows that he has an engaging personality, but is delicate physically and emotionally. She has not yet decided what Harvey's low STR means, but for the moment will play him as physically lazy, always scheming to get someone else to lift the box or change the flat tire.

She thinks Harvey's grandfather made great profits during the Civil War, but that his father and elder brother have since gambled away much of it, or spent it on mysterious projects they refuse to discuss.

This is enough. Roleplaying Harvey in the future will add more information, and that accumulation over time is much of the fun. ■

RULES AND SKILLS

Movement; game time; percentile dice rolls; injury and healing; combat; using and improving skills; spot rules for injuries; firearms; definition of game skills.

Rules transform play into a game. With rules, each player or each side is treated equally and each participant has the same hypothetical chance to share in the victory. In Call of Cthulhu the players form one side, while the keeper plays all the other parts as well as that of Nature herself. The game is not zero-sum. Everyone wins when good roleplaying occurs.

Rules define the limits of what the game is prepared to handle, including the sorts of characters and actions important to the game. New players understand this point acutely: their "Who shall I be?" gets to the center of roleplaying in a sentence. Every rule limits itself because it would be foolish to use rules to describe all situations. Where rules join, common sense smooths the seams.

Movement

Rates of movement vary by species. Individual rates for many forms of life are found in the Creatures, Beasts and Monsters, and Deities chapters, They are the Move entries. Humans move at up to eight units per combat round, a maximum representing a sustainable rate of movement.

This number represents an average ability to move, one not pretending to represent effort in 100-yard dashes or in cross-country marathons. Since all humans move at the same game-rate maximum, no Move entry exists on the investigator sheet. Exact distances and rates are rarely important in the game. If the keeper wishes, each unit nominally stretches a yard to several yards, depending on the situation. If distance and rate become important in the game, the keeper can provide specific measurements, or better yet answer the question in game terms: "You can get there in one combat round."

Movement rates are proportional to each other. Animals, supernatural creatures, and vehicles may be faster or slower than humans. Proportionality makes races between them simple to resolve and reasonably accurate in result. Subtract the higher from the lower to find who opens up a lead or closes in. Thus a tiger (Move 10) gains not less than two units per round on its human prey, or leaves human hunters on foot further behind by not less than two units per round.

Movement need not be represented by tokens or figures on a table. The keeper can set the scene, and statements of intent can be general. If no physical position is kept, the keeper uses Luck rolls or some other semi random way to determine which investigator is near or far, touching or untouched, and so forth.

HANDLING MOVEMENT

If the species movement rates differ, the gap between pursuer and pursued closes or opens by that many units per round, until capture or escape.

In a long race, the keeper may also begin to ask for CON rolls in order to find out who is exhausted first.

Between opponents of the same species, roll CON against CON, DEX against DEX, Swim against Swim, etc., on the Resistance Table, as the keeper finds appropriate.

If wounded or maimed, an investigator may have to move more slowly, at a rate set by the keeper.

Game Time

Combats and encounters which are potentially combative are played out in combat rounds, about which see under the Combat section, further below; see p. 53.

Occasionally a rule requires a longer span of time. For instance, finding information in a library might take a game day. Natural healing is always said to occur in game weeks. Magic points regenerate in 24 game hours.

Game time is fictional: it has nothing to do with real time. Game time is also variable. It passes at whatever rate the keeper says. Keepers routinely expand and contract time as well as space, in order to maintain a lively narrative. As storytellers, that is their province. When nothing is happening, the keeper may simply remark, "Several days pass." He or she can make a year pass in the same number of syllables.

Players rarely get more than one try at any skill roll in a reasonable amount of game time. That amount of time varies, depending on the skill and the situation. Riding a horse that is galloping out of control may demand several Ride rolls in a minute or two of game time, while someone struggling to comprehend the dull and enormous *Codex Vobiscum* may get a Latin roll only every week or so.

SKILL TIME

The use of a skill can also mark the passing of time. Though fighting skills can be repeated round after round, a skill which summarizes a process may represent the passage of hours or days of game time.

The frequency with which a particular skill roll can be attempted correlates with the length of game time the keeper thinks adequate to the job. A Library Use roll customarily represents four hours or more of persistent application, while a simple job like opening a jammed door might take 15 minutes with Mechanical Repair. Without a complication such as a monster breathing down your neck a simple Mechanical Repair job could be attempted many times in a day.

Actions

An action can automatically succeed in an ordinary situation, but resolve a crisis such as an attack with a die roll. Most such rolls are made with D100. Percentile dice are fundamental to the game. Other sorts of dice usually help determine characteristics or the damage done by an attack.

AUTOMATIC ACTIONS

Routine physical and intellectual actions in routine circumstances always succeed. There is no need to roll dice to walk or run, to talk or see or hear, nor is there reason to roll dice for any ordinary use of a skill. But the routine may become extraordinary in a moment.

EXTRAORDINARY CIRCUMSTANCES

Attempting to perform ordinary actions or to use skills under dangerous conditions, under critical scrutiny, or in ways that demand concentration requires resolution with dice.

Skills such as Pilot Aircraft, Climb, and Shotgun—those inherently dramatic or downright dangerous—are routinely rolled for whenever used.

The keeper determines when and what the needed roll is. It may be a skill roll, a characteristics roll (perhaps modified for special conditions), or a characteristics match-up on the Resistance Table.

D100 Rolls

To determine an investigator's success with a skill or characteristics roll, the player usually rolls D100. The keeper rolls for non-player characters. If the result equals or is less than the investigator's percentile level, the action succeeded. Otherwise, the act failed. (Exception: a result of 00 is always a failure.) Failing, the keeper usually rules that some time must pass before another try can be made. The keeper determines the appropriate interval.

Example: while flying over the Rockies, Harvey's airplane runs into turbulence. Desperately he struggles with the controls, trying to stay in the air. His Pilot Aircraft skill is 60%. For Harvey to succeed, his player must roll 60 or less on D100.

Resistance Table Rolls

To pit characteristics against one another, use the Resistance Table. Find the number equal to the active or attacking characteristic at the top of a file. Then find the passive or defending characteristic number at the left of a rank. The number where the rank and the file meet represents the highest D100 result at which the active characteristic can be a success.

The same or different characteristics can be matched on the Resistance Table. Were an investigator to try to lift a friend to safety, it might be appropriate to pit the lifter's STR against his friend's SIZ, for instance.

Example: to continue to shadow a suspect, Harvey Walters needs to open a tight-fitting door. It is stuck with a force of STR 6. Poor Harvey has only STR 4. Tracing the intersection of the two lines on the Resistance Table, we see that Harvey has a 40% chance to open the door. His player must roll 40 or less on D100.

Rewards Of Experience

A great pleasure of roleplaying is participating in the advancement of an investigator from humble beginnings. Increases of skills percentiles are particularly noticeable, since the more a skill is used, the better an investigator becomes at it. As investigators solve mysteries, overcome challenges, and improve skills, players remember the circumstances of the changes, and savor them.

THE SKILL CHECK

Investigator sheets record skill (experience) checks. When an investigator successfully uses a skill in play, the keeper may prompt the player to check the box beside that skill on the investigator sheet. This gives the investigator a chance to learn from his or her experience.

No matter how many times a skill is used successfully in an adventure, only one check per skill is made until the keeper calls for experience rolls. Then only one roll can be made per check to see if the investigator improves. Typically these experience rolls are made in concluding a scenario or after several episodes.

When the keeper calls for experience rolls, examine the investigator sheet to see which skills have been checked as successes. For each skill check, the player rolls D100.

■ If the result is higher than the current skill number, then the investigator improves in that skill: roll 1D10, and immediately add the result to the current skill points.

About the Resistance Table

This formula determines a Resistance Table chance:

Base Chance of Success = 50%

plus Active Characteristic x5

minus Passive Characteristic x5

Though the printed Resistance Table has only 31 on an axis, the dimensions may be extended as far as desired. The results are valid.

To mentally calculate one's position on the table, subtract the smaller amount from the larger amount and multiply the difference by 5: then either add or subtract that result from 50 for the percentage chance. Whether you add or subtract depends only upon whether the larger number is the active or the passive force.

The Resistance Table

Active Characteristic

Passive Characteristic

	1	2	3	4	5	6	7	8	9	10	11	12	13	14	15	16	17	18	19	20	21	22	23	24	25	26	27	28	29	30	31
1	50	55	60	65	70	75	80	85	90	95	—	—	—	—	—	—	—	—	—	—	—	—	—	—	—	—	—	—	—	—	—
2	45	50	55	60	65	70	75	80	85	90	95	—	—	—	—	—	—	—	—	—	—	—	—	—	—	—	—	—	—	—	—
3	40	45	50	55	60	65	70	75	80	85	90	95	—	—	—	—	—	—	—	—	—	—	—	—	—	—	—	—	—	—	—
4	35	40	45	50	55	60	65	70	75	80	85	90	95	—	—	—	—	—	—	—	—	—	—	—	—	—	—	—	—	—	—
5	30	35	40	45	50	55	60	65	70	75	80	85	90	95	—	—	—	—	—	—	—	—	—	—	—	—	—	—	—	—	—
6	25	30	35	40	45	50	55	60	65	70	75	80	85	90	95	—	—	—	—	—	—	—	—	—	—	—	—	—	—	—	—
7	20	25	30	35	40	45	50	55	60	65	70	75	80	85	90	95	—	—	—	—	—	—	—	—	—	—	—	—	—	—	—
8	15	20	25	30	35	40	45	50	55	60	65	70	75	80	85	90	95	—	—	—	—	—	—	—	—	—	—	—	—	—	—
9	10	15	20	25	30	35	40	45	50	55	60	65	70	75	80	85	90	95	—	—	—	—	—	—	—	—	—	—	—	—	—
10	05	10	15	20	25	30	35	40	45	50	55	60	65	70	75	80	85	90	95	—	—	—	—	—	—	—	—	—	—	—	—
11	—	05	10	15	20	25	30	35	40	45	50	55	60	65	70	75	80	85	90	95	—	—	—	—	—	—	—	—	—	—	—
12	—	—	05	10	15	20	25	30	35	40	45	50	55	60	65	70	75	80	85	90	95	—	—	—	—	—	—	—	—	—	—
13	—	—	—	05	10	15	20	25	30	35	40	45	50	55	60	65	70	75	80	85	90	95	—	—	—	—	—	—	—	—	—
14	—	—	—	—	05	10	15	20	25	30	35	40	45	50	55	60	65	70	75	80	85	90	95	—	—	—	—	—	—	—	—
15	—	—	—	—	—	05	10	15	20	25	30	35	40	45	50	55	60	65	70	75	80	85	90	95	—	—	—	—	—	—	—
16	—	—	—	—	—	—	05	10	15	20	25	30	35	40	45	50	55	60	65	70	75	80	85	90	95	—	—	—	—	—	—
17	—	—	—	—	—	—	—	05	10	15	20	25	30	35	40	45	50	55	60	65	70	75	80	85	90	95	—	—	—	—	—
18	—	—	—	—	—	—	—	—	05	10	15	20	25	30	35	40	45	50	55	60	65	70	75	80	85	90	95	—	—	—	—
19	—	—	—	—	—	—	—	—	—	05	10	15	20	25	30	35	40	45	50	55	60	65	70	75	80	85	90	95	—	—	—
20	—	—	—	—	—	—	—	—	—	—	05	10	15	20	25	30	35	40	45	50	55	60	65	70	75	80	85	90	95	—	—
21	—	—	—	—	—	—	—	—	—	—	—	05	10	15	20	25	30	35	40	45	50	55	60	65	70	75	80	85	90	95	—
22	—	—	—	—	—	—	—	—	—	—	—	—	05	10	15	20	25	30	35	40	45	50	55	60	65	70	75	80	85	90	95
23	—	—	—	—	—	—	—	—	—	—	—	—	—	05	10	15	20	25	30	35	40	45	50	55	60	65	70	75	80	85	90
24	—	—	—	—	—	—	—	—	—	—	—	—	—	—	05	10	15	20	25	30	35	40	45	50	55	60	65	70	75	80	85
25	—	—	—	—	—	—	—	—	—	—	—	—	—	—	—	05	10	15	20	25	30	35	40	45	50	55	60	65	70	75	80
26	—	—	—	—	—	—	—	—	—	—	—	—	—	—	—	—	05	10	15	20	25	30	35	40	45	50	55	60	65	70	75
27	—	—	—	—	—	—	—	—	—	—	—	—	—	—	—	—	—	05	10	15	20	25	30	35	40	45	50	55	60	65	70
28	—	—	—	—	—	—	—	—	—	—	—	—	—	—	—	—	—	—	05	10	15	20	25	30	35	40	45	50	55	60	65
29	—	—	—	—	—	—	—	—	—	—	—	—	—	—	—	—	—	—	—	05	10	15	20	25	30	35	40	45	50	55	60
30	—	—	—	—	—	—	—	—	—	—	—	—	—	—	—	—	—	—	—	—	05	10	15	20	25	30	35	40	45	50	55
31	—	—	—	—	—	—	—	—	—	—	—	—	—	—	—	—	—	—	—	—	—	05	10	15	20	25	30	35	40	45	50

Range of Automatic Success (upper right area)

Range of Automatic Failure (lower left area)

For success, roll 1D100 equal to or less than the indicated number.

- If the player rolls equal to or less than the investigator's skill level, then the investigator hasn't learned from the experience, and the skill amount does not change.

Repeat the procedure for all the skill checks, then erase all checks on the investigator sheet. The Cthulhu Mythos skill never receives a skill check, and no box for such a check exists on the investigator sheet. Not improving a skill has no other consequence.

Succeeding at something poorly known is hard, but if successful then the investigator learns from the experience. Conversely, being expert at something guarantees success most of the time, but that high skill leaves the investigator unlikely to learn something new. It gets progressively harder to add percentiles to a skill.

Example: Harvey, on assignment from Enigma, *covers a fancy dress ball put on by the occult Order of the Silver Twilight. To impress his dance partner, he expounds upon Archaeology. The skill roll succeeds, but the keeper allows no skill check, since Harvey has not learned anything. If he had correctly identified an ancient pottery fragment, that might be different. Later, Harvey sees three men in tuxedos slip out through the service entrance. He decides to Sneak after them. His player rolls 07 on D100 against Harvey's Sneak, a success. The keeper tells her to check that skill, since the keeper knows that Harvey's action had serious consequences if it failed.*

90% ABILITY

If in the course of play an investigator attains 90% or more ability in a skill, he or she adds 2D6 points to current Sanity points. This reward represents the discipline and self-esteem gained in mastering a skill. The Cthulhu Mythos skill is an exception to this.

Physical Injury

Hit points measure the relative health of investigators, and the amount of injury they can absorb. Losing hit points indicates the relative physical harm done by attack or injury. An attack is that sum of damage done by a single opponent in a related sequence of combat rounds. An injury is damage taken in an accident or as a consequence of natural force, such as a hurricane.

With exceptions, physical harm is inflicted by physical cause, such as falling from a height or being shot. An investigator's attacks are said to do damage; an investigator who has been attacked successfully is said to take damage or, more precisely, to lose hit points.

When an investigator is injured or wounded, subtract the loss from the amount currently shown on the investigator sheet. Unless a keeper decrees otherwise, or unless losing half or more of current hit points from a single attack, an injured investigator functions normally until lowered to

2 hit points or fewer, and then goes unconscious or dies, depending on the loss. This cut-off point is an abstraction: it keeps investigators in play, and eases bookkeeping.

Descriptions of injuries should be appropriate to the type of damage received, and dramatized. Thus the investigator is not merely shot but shot in one or the other arm, the fall does not merely cost hit points but the ankle is sprained, or a lump is raised on the back of the skull. The keeper may rule that actions such as climbing a ladder have become difficult or impossible because of a previous injury.

STUN

A knock-out attack, electrical shock, fall, or other injury may incidentally stun an investigator for up to 1D6 combat rounds. Stunned, the investigator may parry or Dodge, but not otherwise act. The keeper indicates when a stun occurs, perhaps as a result of a special or critical hit. Being stunned may or may not include losing hit points.

SHOCK

If, from a single wound, an investigator loses hit points equal to half or more of his or her current hit points, the player must roll the investigator's CON x5 or less on D100 or the investigator falls unconscious.

UNCONSCIOUSNESS

When an investigator has 1 or 2 hit points left, he or she automatically falls unconscious, and no longer actively participates in the game. Though living, he or she will not wake until hit points rise to 3 or more. The keeper may privately determine an alternative length of unconsciousness.

Time may heal the wound enough that the investigator can stagger away, or he or she may be helped by a successful First Aid or Medicine roll.

DEATH

When an investigator's hit points drop to zero or negative, he or she dies at the end of the following combat round. During those few seconds a friend might intervene. See the Healing section below for the potential result.

The loss of a well-loved friend is a sorrowful occasion. It calls for consolation during play, and acknowledgment and recognition when play is over.

Healing

All living creatures heal naturally. In the game, an investigator regenerates 1D3 hit points per game week until all hit points have returned. Thus it takes three to seven game weeks to replace naturally seven hit points. First Aid and Medicine skills can speed recovery.

Possessing three or more hit points, an investigator moves and operates without penalty, except that with so few hit points even moderate injury is likely to be deadly.

FIRST AID, MEDICINE

A success with one or the other skill immediately restores 1D3 hit points due to a single attack or injury. Conceivably

Spot Rules for Injuries

Besides intentional assault, lots of ways exist to be injured. All injuries cost hit points, which usually regenerate over time. More rarely, an injury may cost hit points and CON or APP; such an injury is one from which full recovery never occurs. The loss of a limb is an example.

ACID

Damage from acid is a function of the molarity (relative dilution) of the acid, a spectrum too complex to explain here. For game purposes, only significant contact is of interest, such as the immersion of a hand or arm.

■ Weak acids cost 1D3-1 hit points per round.

■ Strong acids cost 1D4 hit points per round.

■ Very strong acids cost 1D6 hit points per round.

DROWNING, SUFFOCATION

Apply this rule to drowning or failed swimming rolls, and use the same procedure for strangulation or to dramatize the effect of a cloud of gas containing no oxygen.

If the investigator is unable to breathe, the player attempts a D100 roll of CON x10 or less during the first combat round. In the second round, the roll lowers to CON x9. In the third round, the roll becomes CON x8, and so on, until reach CON x1. It stays at that multiplier thereafter.

A surprised character has had no time to prepare by inhaling, so the keeper chooses a lower multiplier with which to begin. CON x6 is often appropriate.

If a roll fails, the character has inhaled a medium which cannot be breathed or has begun to suffer serious injury to the respiratory system or brain. He or she loses 1D6 hit points. In each round following, the victim automatically loses another 1D6 hit points. Continue the rolls until escape, rescue, or death.

EXPLOSION

Explosions do a combination of shock and projectile damage. Calculate the effect of an explosion in terms of the power of the blast and of the radius of effect in yards.

Rated explosions decrease in damage by 1D6 per each additional stated radius of effect from the point of explosion. Thus a stick of dynamite does 5D6 damage in the first two yards, 4D6 in yards 3-4, 3D6 in yards 5-6, and so on. An anti-personnel round from an Abrams tank gun does 15D6 in the first four yard radius, 14D6 in yards 5-8, 13D6 in yards 9-12, and so on.

To reflect the damage, subtract hit points from each target equal to the total of the damage rolled. Roll separately for each target.

To change the strength of a blast: doubling the charge increases the damage and the radius of effect by half again, and halving the same charge decreases the damage done and the radius of effect by one third.

FALLING

Freely dropping from a height costs 1D6 hit points per ten feet of fall, or fraction over the first ten feet. With a successful Jump roll when leaping, the investigator thereupon loses 1D6 fewer hit points. This is a bonus for being prepared.

FIRE

Fires threatening investigators should be tailored by the keeper. Many classes and causes of fires exist. Burn temperatures range from about 400°F to thousands of degrees. Fire size can vary from a match or a torch to a block-square inferno. As well as from direct burns, injury or death often comes from asphyxiation or inhalation of toxic gases.

Burn damage more than half of an investigator's hit points may cost APP or CON as well as hit points.

■ A hand-held flaming torch does 1D6 damage each round it is thrust against a target. The target gets a Luck roll to prevent hair and clothes from burning. If they burn, the victim continues to lose 1D6 hit points per round without added application of the torch. Use a Luck or First Aid roll to put out the fire, or perhaps a Sanity roll to stifle panic.

■ A large bonfire does 1D6+2 damage each round. The target's hair and clothes are engulfed as well.

■ An average-sized room in flames does 1D6+2 hit points each round to each person trapped inside. A Luck roll must succeed each round for each character, or begin asphyxiation rolls as per the drowning spot rule.

■ Larger fires are special cases, to be described individually. Death should always threaten.

POISON

Every poison has a numerical rating. The higher the rating, the more deadly and speedy the poison. A poison rating is indicated by the abbreviation POT, for potency.

Use the Resistance Table to match the poison's potency rating against the target's CON. The poison is the attacking force. If the poison overcomes the target's CON, then something bad happens. Commonly, the victim loses hit points equal to the poison's POT.

If the poison fails to overcome the victim's CON, the results are less serious. Perhaps half-POT in hit points are lost, or no damage at all may occur. The keeper must judge by the poison and its application.

The Sample Poisons Table presumes the fiction of a "standard dose", roughly equal to a single bite or application. The keeper should adjust the entries to account for conditions of play. Only the keeper can determine whether a dose is sufficient for death. Faster-acting poisons begin to work within a combat round or two. Death from cyanide may occur within a minute. Many poisons are slow, so poisoners must be subtle. The symptoms noted are only a few of those possible. ■

the same investigator might receive several First Aids or Medicines for wounds or injuries inflicted by separate attacks or accidents.

Investigators treated with First Aid heal at the natural rate and so add a second 1D3 hit points at the end of that game week. Investigators treated with Medicine heal at 2D3 hit points per game week, including the first week: the total recovery for the first week of Medicine's application (including initial emergency treatment) would be 3D3 hit points.

Each treatment is specific to one injury. Medicine supersedes natural healing. Once it is applied, all injuries heal at the Medicine rate, but Medicine must be applied each week, or the rate returns to natural healing.

Hit points cannot be restored past the average of SIZ + CON.

BACK FROM DEATH

If, before the end of the combat round following the round in which he or she died, a dead investigator can be treated successfully by either First Aid or Medicine, and if the treatment increases the dead investigator's current hit points to at least +1, then he or she was near death but not dead, and has returned to life.

INJURY AND HEALING: AN EXAMPLE

To escape a menacing cultist, Harvey successfully Jumps through an open window. He crashes to the ground 15 feet below, to receive 2D6 hit points for the fall minus 1D6 for the jump (for which he successfully prepared). His net loss is 6 hit points. Since he had 15, that loss was not enough to put him in shock. Groggy, Harvey staggers across the street, toward safety. He has 9 hit points.

A car rounds the corner and skids into our hero. Harvey loses 5 more hit points to the new impact, leaving him with 4, a loss of more than half. The keeper calls for a CON x5 roll. The player rolls 71, higher than Harvey's CON. The investigator falls to the pavement, out cold.

The driver of the car applies First Aid, restoring 2 hit points and raising Harvey to 6 hit points. Since Harvey was already injured, the keeper decides that Harvey does not regain consciousness. The driver stuffs him into the roadster's rumbleseat and rushes to St. Mary's hospital, in Arkham.

There an intern treats Harvey for shock, contusions, a slight concussion, an ankle fracture, and two broken ribs. The journalist has already been treated with First Aid for the auto accident. The intern does use Medicine to heal 2 hit points of those lost in the jump from the window, so that Harvey now has 8 hit points. The keeper decides that Harvey regains consciousness.

He stays in the hospital. Since the Medicine skill supersedes the natural healing rate, Harvey regains 2D3 hit

points at the end of a week. His hit points rise to 12. He leaves the hospital. He will continue to heal at the natural rate of 1D3 per week. If a doctor continued direct treatment, he would heal at the 2D3 rate.

At the end of the second week Harvey adds 2 more hit points, and is once more at 15 hit points at the end of the third week.

For the purposes of the game, Harvey Walters is completely healed. For purposes of playing Harvey, his player records a small crescent-shaped scar on one hand from a slight wound sustained from the fall.

Combat

We distinguish between hand-to-hand melee attacks and those made using firearms. Hand-to-hand includes Fencing Foil, Fist/Punch, Fighting Knife, and Club. Firearm includes Handgun, Shotgun, and Rifle.

A victim may lose hit points when successfully attacked. The amount varies: weapons inflict different amounts of damage, and nearly all damages given allow a range of results. Adding to uncertainty, some creatures are armored, modifying the hit points lost, and other rules may alter the initial results of attacks.

A variety of weapons make up the table on pp. 58-59. Any weapon is admissible in this game. The ones included in the table are common or exemplary, showing how other, similar attacks might be made. The keeper may restrict ownership of some weapons.

Later subsections discuss problems peculiar to hand-to-hand weapons and firearms.

THE COMBAT ROUND

Fights occur in combat rounds, each round lasting several to a dozen or so seconds. A combat round is a deliberately

Sample Poisons

poison	speed of effect	POT	symptoms
amanita	6-24 hours	15	violent stomach pains, vomiting, jaundice
arsenic	1/2 to 24 hours	16	burning pain, vomiting, violent diarrhea
belladonna	2 hours-2 days	16	rapid heartbeat, impaired vision, convulsions
black widow	2-8 hours	7	chills, sweating, nausea
chloral hydrate	1-3 minutes	17	unconsciousness for 1 hour; each added dose increases effect by 1 hour plus a 10% chance of respiratory failure.
chloroform	1 round	15	unconsciousness, depressed respiration
cobra	15-60 minutes	16	convulsions, respiratory failure
curare	1 round	25	muscular paralysis, respiratory failure
cyanide	1-15 minutes	20	dizziness, convulsions, fainting
rattlesnake	15-60 minutes	10	vomiting, violent spasms, yellowish vision
Rohypnal, etc.	15-30 minutes	18	odorless, tasteless, unconscious for 4-8 hours
scorpion	24-48 hours	9	intense pain, weakness, hemorrhaging
sleeping pills	10-30 minutes	6	normal sleep; each additional dose increases the chance for respiratory failure by 5%.
strychnine	10-20 minutes	20	violent muscle contractions, asphyxiation

Spot Rules for Combat

ARMOR

Some creatures have armor listed in their statistics, representing tough hide, a thick layer of muscles and fat, or an extraterrene body. Humans have worn a variety of body armors, from boiled leather to bullet-stopping vests. How much and what sort of damage armor stops is for ingenious investigators to explore.

Armor is not lost if one attack penetrates it. Armor has a lot of surface area, and bullet holes and knife holes are small. The chance of penetrating armor in the same place twice is too small to consider.

To account for armor in the game, subtract the listed hit point factor from the damage actually rolled.

Sample Armors

Armor	Damage Stopped
Heavy Leather Jacket	1 H.P.
WWI Helmet	2 H.P.
1" Hardwood	3 H.P.
Elephant Skin	4 H.P.
Present U.S. Helmet	5 H.P.
Heavy Kevlar Vest	8 H.P.
6" Concrete	9 H.P.
Military Body Armor	12 H.P.
1.5" Bulletproof Glass	15 H.P.
2" Steel Plate	19 H.P.
Large Sand Bag	20 H.P.

DODGE

Keepers, every investigator has this skill. Along with the Luck roll it can be the roll of last resort in a time of danger. Remember to call for it.

IMPALES

An impale result can be achieved by pointed hand-to-hand weapons and by all firearms. Blunt weapons and personal attacks cannot perform impales.

If an attacker gets a D100 result equal to or less than one fifth of his skill maximum for the attack, then an impale occurs. This means that the thrusting weapon or bullet chanced to strike a vital area, drove deeply through arteries, or slashed crucial tendons or muscles. Example: Harvey has Handgun at 20%. Dividing 20 by 5 yields 4, so if his player rolls 01, 02, 03, or 04 on D100, Harvey's shot would impale the target.

■ An impale does more damage. Roll for damage twice, not once, and total the results to determine impale damage. For instance, a .22 bullet does 1D6 damage, but an *impaling* .22 bullet does 2D6 damage. In theory, a .22 automatic could impale three times in one round, doing 6D6 damage.

■ Some Mythos creatures are immune to impales.

■ If a hand-to-hand weapon impales, it sticks in the body of the foe. In the next combat round, the attacker must pull it free by means of a D100 roll equal to or less than his skill with the weapon. An impale does no extra damage when removed.

THE PARRY

A parry is the blocking of or the diversion of a hand-to-hand attack. It does not work against firearms. The parry skill always equals the skill percentage held by the defender in the weapon or object being used for the parry. A parry is always defensive. A parry does no damage to the attacker.

One parry per participant can be attempted during a combat round. The player states which potential attacker will be parried. If the defender is knocked out or stunned before the attack occurs, then the parry is foregone. If the attack does not occur, the parry is foregone.

An object used to parry absorbs all damage from a parried blow. If the damage exceeds the object's hit points, the object breaks and the defender absorbs any damage exceeding the object's hit points.

■ Personal attacks can parry each other.

■ An edged or impaling hand-to-hand weapon can be parried with most other hand-to-hand weapons and with rifles and shotguns. Personal attacks cannot parry weapon attacks without risking normal damage, but if the range is touch and the person parrying has the higher DEX, he or she could Grapple for a weapon, yielding the effect of a parry. See below.

■ Foils, rapiers, and most swords and sabers can attack and parry in the same round.

■ Rifles, shotguns, and the largest submachine guns can parry, but cannot fire and parry in the same round. When a firearm's hit points are exceeded in a parry, it no longer fires but does not break.

■ Two successful Grapples can in effect parry an attack, one to establish contact and the next to grab the weapon or weapon hand.

■ A character can both parry and Dodge in the same round.

■ Bullets cannot be parried.

SURPRISE

In the first round of a surprise attack, halve the DEX ranks of the defenders. Those with unready guns would get at most one shot. For extreme surprise, allow no defender attacks in the first round. Defenders can still parry or Dodge attacks coming from the front or sides.

continued next page

elastic unit of time in which everyone wishing to act and capable of action has a chance to complete at least one action. An investigator's equality of opportunity is much more important than that the combat round represent a precise amount of real-world time. If an inequality becomes apparent, let the keeper devise a satisfactory compromise and continue playing.

When every investigator and other character has had an opportunity to act, the combat round is over and the next can begin.

DEXTERITY AND THE ORDER OF ATTACK

Who gets the first opportunity to attack? In a fight, this can be nearly as important as a successful attack. Determine order of attack by ranking combatant DEX from highest to lowest. If two or more investigators have the same DEX, the lowest D100 roll goes first.

■ If hand-to-hand weapons and firearms are being used in the same general encounter, then aimed and ready firearms shoot once in DEX order before any hand-to-hand fighting takes place. (It is relatively quicker to pull a trigger than to swing a club or sword, hit, and recover.)

■ After these first shots, rank the pertinent DEXs again. Include all who are performing automatic actions, using some version of a characteristic, using a skill, or casting a spell.

■ In this second DEX cycle now also include (a) those making hand-to-hand attacks, (b) those firing who needed either to draw their pistols or to shoulder their rifles or shotguns, and (c) those firing for a second time in the round. All these actions occur in DEX order.

■ A gun rated at *three* shots in a round fires once more, at half the shooter's Dexterity, in the last part of the round.

In a few seconds, firearms can launch two or three times the number of attacks possible to hand-to-hand weapons, and automatic weapons up to thirty times as many. But plotted scenarios rarely call for running gun battles. Beware of gunfights: they're signs that the investigators have made bad choices.

Hand-to-hand Fighting

Any hand-to-hand weapon can be used in Call of Cthulhu. The possibilities are so numerous and often so strange that it is pointless to write them up as skills. Everyone can perform Fist/Punch, Head Butt, Kick, and Grapple. These four personal attacks are discussed later, among the skills.

Most hand-to-hand weapons can perform one attack and one parry per combat round. Personal attacks have limited parries. Knives without crossguards cannot parry. See Parry in the Spot Rules For Combat on the facing page.

In attacking, a hand-to-hand weapon never does damage to itself. Add full damage bonuses to these weapons' attacks except when thrown: thrown weapons get halved damage bonuses.

CLUBS, BLUNT INSTRUMENTS

Clubs include the policeman's nightstick, the criminal's blackjack, handy branches and rocks, and fireplace pokers. These weapons are too dissimilar in size, weight, and material to share in a general skill increase, and so are individual skills, such as Large Club, Small Club, and Blackjack. Their values are shown on the Weapons Table.

Things like blackjacks and rocks cannot be used to parry. A thundering big club might do 1D10 damage, but

More Spot Rules for Combat

DIMNESS, DARKNESS, INVISIBILITY

If something cannot be seen, there's little chance to hit it, to find it, or to notice it. If the interest of the game situation demands that the investigators nevertheless act, then the keeper lowers relevant skills by at least half in moonlight, or makes their successful use a function of some low multiplier of POW. If the intention of the darkness is that the investigators will find it difficult to act in it, then the keeper lowers skill thresholds to 01. Some tasks, such as reading a map, are plainly impossible without sight.

KNOCK-OUT ATTACKS

Use this rule to render a target unconscious rather than to do physical harm. The player or keeper should state the intention before making the attack. Perform knock-out attacks only with Fist/Punch, Kick, Grapple, Head Butt, clubs, or other blunt instruments.

Roll for damage as in an ordinary attack, but match the result against the target's hit points on the Resistance Table. A success knocks the target unconscious for several minutes, and the target takes one third of the damage originally rolled (round down any fraction). If the attack succeeds but the Resistance Table roll does not, then there is no knock-out, and the target takes full rolled damage.

■ Knock-out attacks work against humans, but not against most creatures of the Mythos.

■ At the keeper's option, knock-outs may work against deep ones, ghouls, serpent people, and other humanoids.

A successful First Aid or Medicine roll immediately wakes a victim of a knock-out attack.

PARTIAL CONCEALMENT

A target partially concealed should not normally reduce the attacker's chance to hit or the observer's chance to notice the target. If the target does seem difficult to notice, allow a Spot Hidden roll or an Idea roll to locate it.

THROWN OBJECTS

If a character throws an object, add half of his or her damage bonus to the damage done. See also the Throw skill.

TWO WEAPONS

In a combat round, a hand-to-hand weapon might be held in each hand, but only one attack and one parry could be made in the round. See also "Two Handguns" in the Spot Rules for Firearms.

Spot Rules for Firearms

AUTOMATIC WEAPONS, BURSTS

Fully automatic weapons, such as Thompson submachine guns, may fire a burst (multiple shots) on the shooter's DEX rank. For each shot fired in a burst, raise the attacker's chance to hit by 5 percentiles. No matter how many shots are fired, the shooter's chance cannot more than double.

Roll D100 once for all the shots fired against a single target. If the attack roll is a success, roll an appropriate die to determine the number of hits: thus if eight shots are fired, roll 1D8 to determine the number of hits. Per target, only the first bullet impales if an impaling hit is rolled. Some keepers ask that bursts occur only in quantities easy to roll, such as 6s, 8s, 10s, and so on.

■ If multiple target are spread across a field of fire, the shooter's chance to hit does not change: the opportunity exists to hit each target at normal chance, and each target is rolled for separately. The shooter allots how many bullets head toward each target.

■ If a single target or multiple targets are within a narrow cone of fire, such as a group coming down a hallway or tunnel, increase the shooter's chance to hit, but never more than double the chance to hit.

In either situation, the keeper's description should include the information necessary to allow a player to choose the best tactic.

BIG TARGETS

Big things are easier to hit. For monsters of SIZ 30 or more, every 10 SIZ above SIZ 30 adds 5 percentiles to an attacker's base chance to hit with bullet, thrown object, or shotgun round. Point-blank and extended range modifiers apply.

CHOOSING A SHOTGUN

Commonly, shotguns come with multiple single-shot barrels, with one barrel fed by pump action, and with one barrel fed by semi-automatic action. In the 1890s, most shotguns are double-barreled, and in the present day nearly all are pump-action or semi-automatic.

A double-barreled shotgun may fire both barrels simultaneously at DEX in one round, one barrel at DEX and at half DEX in the same round, or one barrel each in different rounds. Depending on gauge, a pump-action fires once or twice in a round. Any semi-automatic fires once or twice in a round.

EXTENDED RANGE

A character may fire at up to double a weapon's base range at half-normal chance to hit. He or she may fire at up to triple the weapon's base range at one quarter of normal chance to hit, quadruple at one eighth chance to hit, and so on. At such extreme ranges, damage done may be lessened as the bullet slows.

LOADED REVOLVERS

When revolvers were common, a common safety practice was to leave empty the chamber under the hammer, on the theory that if five bullets did not stop some malefactor, the sixth was unlikely to do so. A fully loaded revolver may sometimes go off accidentally. Resolve the situation with a Luck roll.

MALFUNCTION NUMBERS, JAMS

If a firearm skill roll is equal to or higher than the weapon's malfunction number (*mal* on the Weapons Table), the weapon cannot fire.

■ If the weapon is a revolver, bolt-action rifle, or double-barreled shotgun, the problem is a dud round.

■ If the weapon is automatic, semi-automatic, pump-action, or lever-action, then the malfunction is a jam.

Fixing a jam takes 1D6 combat rounds plus a successful Mechanical Repair roll or a skill roll for the jammed firearm. The owner can keep trying until succeeding, or until ruining the gun on a D100 result of 96-00.

POINT-BLANK FIRE

Point-blank is that distance equal to or less than the shooter's DEX in feet. The shooter's chance to hit is doubled at point-blank range. The damage done is unchanged.

PRECISION AIM, LASER & TELESCOPIC SIGHTS

The shooter braces the weapon or takes other care in bringing the weapon to bear, shooting just once in a round at half normal DEX rank. The effect is to double the point-blank and base ranges for the firearm.

RELOADING FIREARMS

Allow one combat round to load two shells into any handgun, rifle, or shotgun. Allow one round to exchange a clip. Allow two rounds to change a machine gun belt.

In a round, it is possible to put one round in a chamber and get off that shot at half DEX rank.

TWO HANDGUNS

One person can hold and fire two handguns during a combat round. Use the unaimed shots rule below.

UNAIMED SHOTS

The shots-per-round entries for firearms assume that a shooter has an earnest desire to hit a target, and thus aims with care. As a general guide, unaimed fire allows twice the number of attacks per round listed for the weapon on the Weapons Table. Reduce the shooter's chance to hit to one fifth of normal. If there is more than one target, determine randomly who gets hit. Impales occur normally. But given laser sight aid and training, and Handgun 60% and above, increase the chance to hit to normal. ■

would require a wielder of at least STR 13. Clubs never *impale* (see Impales among the Spot Rules For Combat). The base chance for Small Club or Large Club could be extended to barroom chairs, hall trees, and other small furniture, if the keeper prefers. Clubs and other blunt instruments can be used to make *knock-out attacks*.

FOILS, RAPIERS

Foil and rapier are similar skills, and a skill increase with one increases the rest. Treat most sword-canes as sharpened foils. Foils and rapiers can impale.

KNIVES

Bowie knives, butcher knives, hunting knives, dirks, daggers, switchblades, and kitchen knives have big enough blades to be significant weapons. An increase in skill with one increases skill most of the others. Knives can impale.

PERSONAL ATTACKS

Fist/Punch, Head Butt, Kick, and Grapple are personal attacks, meaning each can be made by a person who is otherwise unarmed. All people know these attacks. Each personal attack is used individually, and ability in each increases individually through experience. Each personal attack is discussed in the skills section. Grapple especially is a complex skill and deserves close study.

■ With a successful Martial Arts skill roll, double the rolled damage done by a successful personal attack.

■ A knock-out attack can lessen physical damage to a target. See the spot rules for combat.

■ In general, a personal attack can be parried by any hand-to-hand weapon or personal attack. Only a Grapple can parry another Grapple.

■ As an option, some keepers may recognize the effect of a human Bite attack. It does no hit points of damage, but might break a human Grapple if a POW against POW Resistance Table roll favors the biter.

SWORDS, SABERS

A great variety of such weapons exist, some one-handed and some requiring two hands. A skill increase with one does not increase the rest. Some of these weapons can impale, but others were designed as slashing weapons for cavalry use and parrying, and are relatively blunt-tipped— these latter cannot impale.

Using Firearms

The five firearm skills are Handgun, Machine Gun, Rifle, Shotgun, and Submachine Gun. All investigators start with modest ability in each skill, except that submachine guns do not exist in the 1890s. These skills appear in the skills section of this chapter, starting on p. 60.

See the nearby box, Spot Rules For Firearms, to learn more about employing firearms.

An investigator may fire any small arm and have some chance to hit. If loading and firing antique firearms, the keeper may also require a successful History roll to do it properly.

An increase in ability with a particular weapon improves the general skill. For example, improving with a .45 Revolver also improves the chance to hit with a .22 Revolver because they are both Handguns. Make the changes on the investigator sheet in the Investigator Skills section as well as the two weapons lists at the bottom of the sheet.

■ Not all firearms to which a single skill applies have the same base chance. A weapon such as the .44 Magnum revolver is heavy and clumsy, enough to have a slightly lower base chance.

■ Base ranges appear on the Weapons Table.

■ An investigator can parry hand-to-hand attacks with any rifle, shotgun, or large submachine gun. But these weapons are not designed to take a hammering: if the gun's hit points are exceeded by a single blow, the weapon no longer can fire.

A SHORT COMBAT EXAMPLE

While searching the old Crowninshield Manor near Arkham, Harvey Walters encounters a prowler. The burglar hears Harvey coming and has his revolver ready when Harvey enters the library. Having heard a suspicious noise, Harvey is carrying a chair leg, but has not raised the club to swing.

The burglar's .32 revolver allows him to fire first since Harvey carries a hand-to-hand weapon. The burglar's handgun skill is 25%. That is doubled for point-blank range, but then halved again for the moonlit night, remaining 25%. The burglar misses when the keeper rolls a 72.

Harvey now lashes out with the chair leg, also at 25% as per Small Club on the Weapons Table. Harvey's player rolls 84, no hit.

Accessories for Firearms

TELESCOPIC & LASER SIGHTS

For rifles equipped with telescopic sights, double the base range. If both telescopic sights and precision aim apply, quadruple the rifle's base range. Laser sights quadruple the base range without requiring the precision aim modifier.

SUPPRESSORS (SILENCERS)

A silencer is a long, thick tube filled with baffles. It can be machined to attach to the muzzle of a firearm in order to muffle the sound of its shots. In doing so, it slows each bullet's velocity and halves the weapon's range. A silencer is made to order. It wears out completely after D100+10 bullets have been fired through it. The more powerful the cartridge, the more quickly the silencer wears out. A silencer cannot be attached to a shotgun or to a heavy machine gun, but a small automatic gun such as an Uzi can be silenced.

Silencers are illegal almost everywhere by the 1920s and up to the present, and by local jurisdictions in the 1890s.

Weapons Table

	base chance, or starting skill	damage done	base range	attacks per round	bullets in gun	HPs resistance	era $ cost	mal	common in era
HAND—TO—HAND WEAPONS									
Fencing Foil*, sharpened	20	1D6+1+db	touch	1	—	10	4/6/70	—	all
Sword Cane*	20	1D6+db	touch	1	—	10	10/25/100	—	all
Rapier / Heavy Epee*	10	1D6+1+db	touch	1	—	15	6/20/150	—	all
Cavalier Sabre	15	1D8+1+db	touch	1	—	20	15/30/75	—	all
Cavalry Lance*	10	1D8+1+1D6**	touch	1	—	15	15/25/150	—	all
Wood Axe	20	1D8+2+db**	touch	1	—	15	3/5/10	—	all
Hatchet / Sickle	20	1D6+1+db	touch	1	—	12	2/3/9	—	all
Fighting Knife* (dirk, etc.)	25	1D4+2+db	touch	1	—	15	1/2/15	—	all
Butcher Knife*	25	1D6+db	touch	1	—	12	1/2/7	—	all
Small Knife* (switchblade, etc.)	25	1D4+db	touch	1	—	9	.50/2/6	—	all
Blackjack (cosh, life-preserver)	40	1D8+db	touch	1	—	4	.60/2/15	—	all
Large Club / Cricket Bat / Poker	25	1D8+db	touch	1	—	20	1/3/35	—	all
Small Club / Nightstick	25	1D6+db	touch	1	—	15	1/3/35	—	all
Garrote	15	strangle***	touch	1	—	1	.20/.50/3	—	all
Bullwhip	05	1D3 or grapple	10 feet	1	—	4	2/5/50	—	1890s, 1920s
War Boomerang	Throw %	1D8	see Throw rule	1/2	—	8	1/2/40	—	rare
Thrown Rock	Throw %	1D4	see Throw rule	1	—	—	—	—	all
Thrown Spear	Throw %	1D8+1	see Throw rule	1/2	—	15	1/1/25	—	rare
Quoit	25	1D6+1+1/2 db	Throw%	1	—	15	.05	—	all
Burning Torch	10+cloth. fire %	1D6	touch	1	—	15	.05	—	all
Taser (dart)†	20	stun	DEX in feet (max 14)	1	varies	8	400	95	present
Taser (contact)	Fist / Punch %	stun	touch	1	varies	7	200	97	present
Mace†	DEX x5	stun 2D10 mins	1/2 DEX in feet	1	25 squirts	4	10	00	present
Live Wire, 110-Volt Charge	Elec. Repair %	1D8 + stun	touch	1	—	6, fuse box	—	—	1920s, present
Live Wire, 220-Volt Charge	Elec. Repair %	2D8 + stun	touch	1	—	6, fuse box	—	—	present
Chainsaw††	20%	2D8	touch	1	—	20	$300	97	present
HANDGUNS*									
Flintlock Pistol	20	1D6+1	10 yards	1/4	1	8	15/30/300	95	rare
.22 Short Automatic	20	1D6	10 yards	3	6	6	25/190	00	1920s, present
.25 Derringer (1B)	20	1D6	3 yards	1	1	5	4/12/55	00	1890s,1920s
.32 or 7.65mm Revolver	20	1D8	15 yards	3	6	10	6/15/200	00	all
.32 or 7.65mm Automatic	20	1D8	15 yards	3	8	8	20/350	99	1920s, present
.357 Magnum Revolver	20	1D8+1D4	20 yards	1	6	11	425	00	present
.38 or 9mm Revolver	20	1D10	15 yards	2	6	10	8/25/200	00	all
.38 Automatic	20	1D10	15 yards	2	6	8	30/375	99	1920s, present
Glock 17 9mm Auto	20	1D10	20 yards	3	17	8	500	98	present
Model P08 Luger	20	1D10	20 yards	2	8	9	75/600	99	1920s, present
.41 Revolver	20	1D10	15 yards	1	6	10	20	00	1890s
.44 Magnum Revolver	15	2D6+2	30 yards	1	6	12	475	00	present
.45 Revolver	20	1D10+2	15 yards	1	6	10	10/30/300	00	all
.45 Automatic	20	1D10+2	15 yards	1	7	8	40/375	00	1920s, present
IMI Desert Eagle	20	2D6+2	30 yards	1	7	9	650	94	present
RIFLES, see also assault rifles*									
.58 Springfield Rifle Musket	25	1D10+4	60 yards	1/4	1	12	10/25/325	95	rare
.22 Bolt-Action Rifle	25	1D6+2	30 yards	1	6	9	10/13/70	99	all
.30 Lever-Action Carbine	25	2D6	50 yards	1	6	8	12/19/150	98	all
.45 Martini-Henry Rifle	25	1D8+1D6+3	80 yards	1/3	1	12	15/5/275	00	1890s
Col. Moran's Air Rifle‹	15	2D6+1	20 yards	1/3	1	7	200	88	1890s
Garand M1, M2 Rifle	25	2D6+2	110 yards	1/2	8	11	400	00	WW2, later
SKS Carbine	25	2D6+1	90 yards	2	10	10	500	97	present
.303 Lee-Enfield	25	2D6+4	110 yards	1/2	10	12	25/50/300	00	all
.30-06 Bolt-Action Rifle	25	2D6+4	110 yards	1/2	5	12	30/75/175	00	all
.30-06 Semi-Automatic Rifle	25	2D6+4	130 yards	1	5	12	275	00	present
.444 Marlin Rifle	25	1D8+1D6+4	90 yards	1	5	12	400	98	present
Elephant Gun (2B)	15	3D6+4	100 yards	1 or 2	2	12	100/400/1800	00	all
SHOTGUNS*									
20-gauge Shotgun (2B)	30	2D6/1D6/1D3	10/20/50 yds	1 or 2	2	12	25/35/rare	00	1890s,1920s
16-gauge Shotgun (2B)	30	2D6+2/1D6+1/1D4	10/20/50 yds	1 or 2	2	12	30/40/rare	00	1890s,1920s
12-gauge Shotgun (2B)	30	4D6/2D6/1D6	10/20/50 yds	1 or 2	2	12	30/40/rare	00	1890s,1920s
12-gauge Shotgun (pump)	30	4D6/2D6/1D6	10/20/50 yds	1	5	10	75/45/100	00	1920s, present
12-gauge Shotgun (semi-auto)	30	4D6/2D6/1D6	10/20/50 yds	2	5	10	75/45/100	00	present
12-gauge Shotgun (2B, sawed off)	30	4D6/1D6	5/10 yds	1 or 2	2	14	15/NA/NA	00	1920s
10-gauge Shotgun (2B)	30	4D6+2/2D6+1/1D6	10/20/50 yds	1 or 2	2	12	35/rare/rare	00	1890s
12-gauge Bellini M3 (folding stock)	30	4D6/2D6/1D6	10/20/50 yds	2	7	14	895	00	present
12-gauge SPAS (folding stock)	30	4D6/2D6/1D6	10/20/50 yds	1	8	6	600	98	present

	base chance	damage	range	attacks	bullets	HPs	cost	mal	eras
ASSAULT RIFLES									
AK-47 or AKM	25	2D6+1	90 yards	2 or burst	30	12	200	00	present
AK-74	25	2D8	120 yards	2 or burst	30	12	1000	97	present
Barrett Model 82	25	2D10+4	210 yards	1	11	12	3000	96	present
FN FAL	25	2D6+3	100 yards	1 or burst	20	11	1500	97	present
Galil AR	25	2D6+3	110 yards	1 or burst	20	12	2000	98	present
M16A2	25	2D8	130 yards	1 or burst of 3	30	11	NA	97	present
Steyr AUG	25	2D6	120 yards	1 or burst	30	12	1100	99	present
Beretta M70/90	25	2D6	120 yards	1/3/burst	30	12	2800	99	present
SUBMACHINE GUNS									
Thompson	15	1D10+2	20 yards	1 or burst	20/30/50	8	NA/NA	96	1920s
Heckler & Koch MP5	15	1D10	45 yards	2 or burst	15/30	10	NA	97	present
Ingram MAC-11	15	1D8	20 yards	3 or burst	32	6	750	96	present
Skorpion SMG	15	1D8	20 yards	3 or burst	20	6	NA	96	present
Uzi SMG	15	1D10	40 yards	2 or burst	32	8	1000	98	present
MACHINE GUNS									
Model 1882 Gatling Gun	15	2D6+4	100 yards	burst	200	20	1000/200/6500	96	1890s
Browning Aut. Rifle M1918	15	2D6+4	90 yards	1/2 or burst	20	11	NA/800	00	1920s
.30 Browning M1917A1, belt-fed	15	2D6+3	150 yards	burst	250	12	—/3000/NA	96	1920s
Maschinengewehr-42 7.92mm, belt-fed	15	2D6+4	200 yards	burst	300	18	rare	00	WWII
FN Minimi, 5.56mm, clip/belt	15	2D8	130 yards	burst	30/200	11	NA	99	present
EXPLOSIVES, HEAVY WEAPONS, MISC.									
Molotov Cocktail	Throw %	2D6 + luck to burn	thrown	1/2	1 only	1	NA/NA	95	1920s, present
Signal Pistol (Flare Gun)	25	1D10+1D3 burn	10	1/2	1	11	10/15/75	00	all
M79 Grenade Launcher	25	3D6 / 2y	20	1/3	1	12	NA	99	present
Dynamite Stick	Throw %	5D6 / 2y	thrown	1/2	1 only	1	1/2/5	99	all
Blasting Cap	Elec. Repair %	2D6 / 1y	NA	NA	one use	3	$20/box	00	all
Pipe Bomb	Elec. Repair %	4D6 / 3y	in place	one use	1 only	3	NA/NA/NA	95	all
Plastique (C-4), 4 oz.	Elec. Repair %	6D6 / 3y	in place	one use	1 only	15	NA	99	present
Hand Grenade	Throw %	4D6 / 4y	thrown	1/2	1 only	8	NA/NA	99	1920s, present
81mm Mortar	01	6D6 / 6y	500 yards	2	separate	10	NA	00	present
75mm Field Gun	01	10D6 / 2y	500 yards	1/4	separate	40	3000/1500/—	99	1920s, present
120mm Tank Gun, stabilized	01	15D6 / 4y	2000 yards	1	separate	35	NA	00	present
Ship-mounted 5-inch Rifle, stblzd.	01	12D6/4y	3000 yards	2	auto-mgzn	50	NA	98	present
AP Mine	Conceal% + Luck roll	4D6 / 5y	in place	in place	one use	9	NA/NA	99	1920s, present
Claymore Mine	luck roll	6D6+6/3D6+2/1D6	10/25/50 yds	in place	one use	12	NA	99	present
Flamethrower	05	2D6 + shock	25 yards	1	at least 10	6	NA/NA	93	1920s, present
GE Mini-Gun****	15	2D6+4	400 yards	33	4000	14	NA	98	present
LAW*****	15	8D6/1y	150 yards	1	1	10	NA	98	present
Jungle Hunting Bow	01	1D6 + db	30 yards	1	1	6	NA	90	1890s

+db—plus damage bonus, which varies by individual.

special—see the grapple rules in the skills section for the possibilities.

stun—may parry, but may not act for 1 or 1D6 rounds, or as the keeper indicates; POW x1 not to be temporarily blinded.

Col. Moran's Air Rifle—uses compressed air rather than explosive propellant, achieving relatively silent operation.

1B, 2B—1 barrel, 2 barrels.

1/2, 1/3—can be accurately fired every second/third round.

1 or 2—one or both barrels firable in same round.

*—this weapon or class of weapon can impale.

**—the listed damage bonus assumes the impetus of the horse.

***—use rulesbook drowning procedure to determine hit point loss or death.

****—gatling style heavy machine gun, often mounted in helicopters. Hand-firing such a weapon takes minimum STR 16 and SIZ 16.

*****—Light Anti-tank Weapon, disposable.

†—do not use the point-blank range rule for this weapon.

††—An impale severs a random limb.

Burst—burst capability unavailable to civilians; prices reflect gray-market.

NA—unavailable in auto-fire configuration or at all. Autofire is illegal to own. Converter kit may be available.

mal—Malfunction Number—with any attack die roll result equal to or higher than the firing weapon's malfunction number, the shooter does not merely miss—his or her weapon does not fire. If the weapon is a revolver, break-open gun, or bolt-action rifle, the problem is merely a dud round. If the weapon is lever-action, the malfunction is a jam. Fixing a jam takes 1D6 combat rounds plus a successful Mechanical Repair roll or appropriate firearm skill roll (e.g., one's Rifle skill could fix a jammed rifle). The user can keep trying until succeeding or else destroying the mechanism on a Mechanical Repair result of 96-00.

Shotgun solid slugs—10-gauge 1D10+8, 12-gauge 1D10+6, 16-gauge 1D10+5, 20-gauge 1D10+4; base ranges 50 yards; slugs can impale.

Rare—perhaps obsolete, a fine specimen for collectors, or perhaps illegal.

Era Cost—present-day prices reflect collectors' market, 1920s prices do not.

2yds, 3yds, etc.—damage radius of explosion in yards; damage done in each yard beyond radius decreases by 1D6 per yard.

Claymore Mine—the weapon has a cone of fire; allow nominal 120-degree effect.

At his DEX 10, the burglar fires again. The keeper rolls another miss. Since a .32 fires three times in a round, the burglar gets a third shot at half DEX (DEX 5). This time the keeper rolls 00, a malfunction. For a revolver, the keeper knows that the malfunction is caused by a dud round. But he reports only what happens—that the hammer makes a loud click, but that the gun does not go off.

Harvey's player exclaims that the prowler must be out of bullets—a hasty assumption that the keeper sees no reason to correct. The keeper says that the gunman is surprised that his weapon did not fire, and that he forfeits his first shot in the new combat round.

Harvey believes that he has the advantage. He swings his chair leg and the player rolls 01—a hit! A light club does 1D6 damage. Harvey's player rolls a 4. (Harvey has no damage bonus.)

The keeper says that the gunman screams in pain. Because the D100 result was so low, he also rules that Harvey smashed down on the man's gun hand, sending the revolver skating across the floor and into the darkness.

At the beginning of the third round, Harvey has the advantage since his DEX is higher and the fight now is between hand-to-hand weapons. This time Harvey misses on a result of 22, since his skill too is halved for the darkness. The keeper decides that the burglar wants to escape from this mysterious expert fighter. The burglar flees into the night.

Harvey's triumph is dimmed when he sees that the .32 contains four bullets, but the keeper applauds the reporter's valor and grants a skill check. A week or two later, when the keeper asks the players to make their skill checks, Harvey rises in Small Club (Chair Leg) to 32%.

Skill Definitions

Definitions of skills have to be general summaries of intent and coverage. Unforeseen circumstances provoke new uses and interpretations of skills. Discuss special applications with your keeper.

Following each skill name is the base chance for the skill in parentheses.

Skills represent what is known to an era. Skill percentiles are not proportions of what is hypothetically knowable. If they were able to stack their respective knowledge on a table like poker chips and measure the difference, a physicist of 60% in 2002 knows much more than a physicist of 90% skill in 1902.

In general, a skill level of 50% is high enough to let a character eke out a living from it. If an investigator rises high in a skill, player and keeper could confer about a new profession, and increased income from it.

ACCOUNTING (10%)

Grants understanding of accountancy procedures, and reveals the financial functioning of a business or person. Inspecting the books, one might detect cheated employees, siphoned-off funds, payment of bribes or blackmail, and whether or not the financial condition is better or worse than claimed. Looking through old accounts, one could see how money was gained or lost in the past (grain, slave-trading, whiskey-running, etc.) and to whom and for what payment was made.

ANTHROPOLOGY (01%)

Enables the user to identify and understand an individual's way of life from his behavior. If the skill-user observes another culture from within for a time, or works from accurate records concerning an extinct culture, he or she may make simple predictions about that culture's ways and morals, even though the evidence may be incomplete. Studying the culture for a month or more, the anthropologist begins to understand how the culture functions and, in combination with Psychology, may predict the actions and beliefs of representatives. Essentially useful only with existing human cultures.

ARCHAEOLOGY (01%)

Allows dating and identification of artifacts from past cultures and the detecting of fakes. Having thoroughly inspected a site, the user might deduce the purposes and way of life of those who left the remains. Anthropology might aid in this. Archaeology also help identify written forms of extinct human languages.

ART (05%)

Specify song, some musical instrument, painting, cooking, etc.—any non-literary art which a creative person might seriously pursue through life. With a success, the performance or creation is pleasing and the audience is satisfied. Failure indicates that the artist was off-key or inexpressive. Lovecraft's artists invoke the traditional muses, but the keeper might allow wider definitions of "art". The points where Art ends and Craft begins vary with each keeper.

The investigator sheet contains blank spaces for different versions of this skill. The player should note the style or medium: opera singer, oil painter, etc.

ASTRONOMY (01%)

The user knows or knows how to find out which stars and planets are overhead at a particular day or hour of day or night, when eclipses and meteor showers occur, and the names of important stars, and something of current perceptions about life on other worlds, the existence or the formation of galaxies, and so on. An academic might be able to calculate orbits, discuss stellar life cycles, and (in the present) have a specialty such as infrared astronomy or long-baseline interferometry.

BARGAIN (05%)

The skill of obtaining something for an agreeable price. The bargainer must state the price at which he or she wishes to purchase the item and, for each 2% difference between that price and the asking price, he or she must subtract 1 percentile from his Bargain skill. The seller will not take a loss, no matter how good the bargaining. The keeper usually determines the bottom-line amount secretly.

Example: Harvey Walters purchases a shotgun in Germany, to take with him while he investigates the disappearance of his manservant, Kurt, in the old ruins nearby. (Kurt failed a Sneak roll and was caught by the Inhabitant.) The elderly shopkeeper asks $100 American for the weapon, and Harvey is on a limited budget. Harvey offers the shopkeeper $70, and his player makes a D100 roll. Harvey has Bargain 20%, but he wants the gun for 30% less than normal, so his chance for success is reduced by 15 percentiles to only 05%. The player rolls 22—a failure. Harvey then offers $80, increasing his chances to 10%. The player rolls 02, a success.

By implication, use this skill in any negotiation which features an exchange of value. Combination rolls with Credit Rating, Fast Talk, or Persuade might help in bargaining.

A simple bargain may be struck in a few minutes. A complex contract might take weeks, and Bargain might then work in combination with Law.

BIOLOGY (01%)

The science of life, including botany, cytology, ecology, genetics, histology, microbiology, physiology, zoology, and so on. The investigator's understanding reflects the era of play. With this skill one might develop a vaccine against some hideous Mythos bacterium, or isolate the hallucinogenic properties of some jungle plant.

CHEMISTRY (01%)

A study of the composition of substances, the effects of temperature, energy, and pressure upon them, and how they affect one another. With chemistry, one might create or extract complex chemical compounds, including simple explosives, poisons, gases, and acids, requiring at least a day or so with the proper equipment and chemicals. The user could also analyze an unknown substance, given proper equipment and reagents.

CLIMB (40%)

A Climb roll must be attempted every 10 to 30 vertical feet, depending on the difficulty of the climb as the keeper perceives it. Conditions such as firmness of surface, wind, visibility, rain, etc., may be factors.

If an investigator needs to climb quietly, match the player's D100 roll against both Climb and Sneak. If succeeding in Climb but failing in Sneak, he or she climbed successfully, but made noise. If the Climb failed but the Sneak succeeded, he or she fell, but did not attract attention.

COMPUTER USE (01%)

This skill is not needed to use microcomputers nor to run ordinary commercial software. Special manipulations of a microcomputer system may require this roll.

A skill for the present day, Computer Use allows the investigator to program in various computer languages to achieve his or her end: perhaps write new programs, retrieve and analyze obscure data, break into a secured system, explore a complicated network, or detect or exploit intrusions, back doors, and viruses.

Each application of the skill takes half a day or more, and perhaps more than one successful roll. The keeper must judge the actual requirements and results, and should probably make secret Computer Use rolls at times. Once inside a network, Library Use might be employed also.

CONCEAL (15%)

Allows the visual covering up, secreting, or masking of an object or objects, perhaps with debris, cloth, or other intervening or illusion-promoting materials, perhaps by making a secret panel or false compartment, or perhaps by repainting or otherwise changing an item's characteristics to escape detection.

With it, a person might be secreted from sight, but could not be disguised to evade even a cursory inspection. Larger objects of any sort should be increasingly hard to conceal. Things larger than elephants should not be concealed by one person, though they might be by a group.

Compare with the Hide skill.

CRAFT (05%)

A craft is a specialized skill for making and repairing practical things or for creating pleasing effects. It requires manual dexterity or artful application. As an occupation, a craft typically provides more income than laboring, but not as much as a profession.

A multitude of crafts exist, from house painter to liontamer to safecracker. Particularize a craft on the investigator sheet, in the same general fashion as for Art: for instance, *Craft (Cobbler)*, *Craft (Barber)*, or *Craft (Blow Vacuum Tube)*.

Making or repairing something typically requires equipment and time, to be determined by the keeper if necessary. With a very low result, a craftsman might make an exceptionally fine item. With a failing roll, the item might break on its first use, or fail to fit into some larger whole. A successful Craft roll might provide information about an item, such as where or when it might have been made, reveal some point of history or technique concerning it, or who might have made it.

CREDIT RATING (15%)

Narrowly, how prosperous and confident the investigator seems to be. This is the investigator's chance to panhandle or get a loan from a bank or business, and it is also the chance for the investigator to pass a bad check or to bluff past a demand for credentials.

In small towns, or in narrow societies such as Edwardian England, everyone knows everyone, and Credit Rating amounts to an index of personal reputation as well as monetary worth. Thus Credit Rating might ebb and flow because of scandal or personal behavior, while the loss or accumulation of money effected minor change or no change. As appropriate, the keeper may cause a character to make clear such distinctions.

Skills & Base Chances

skill	base chance
Accounting	10%
Anthropology	01%
Archaeology	01%
Art	05%
Astronomy	01%
Bargain	05%
Biology	01%
Chemistry	01%
Climb	40%
Computer Use	01%
Conceal	15%
Craft	05%
Credit Rating	15%
Cthulhu Mythos	00%
Disguise	01%
Dodge	DEX x2%
Drive Auto/Horses	20%
Electrical Repair	10%
Electronics	01%
Fast Talk	05%
First Aid	30%

Fist/Punch	50%
Geology	01%
Grapple	25%
Handgun	20%
Head Butt	10%
Hide	10%
History	20%
Jump	25%
Kick	25%
Law	05%
Library Use	25%
Listen	25%
Locksmith	01%
Machine Gun	15%
Martial Arts	01%
Mechanical Repair	20%
Medicine	05%
Natural History	10%
Navigate	10%
Occult	05%
Operate Heavy Machine	01%
Other Language	01%

Own Language	EDU x5%
Persuade	15%
Pharmacy	01%
Photography	10%
Physics	01%
Pilot	01%
Psychoanalysis	01%
Psychology	05%
Ride	05%
Rifle	25%
Shotgun	30%
Sneak	10%
Spot Hidden	25%
Submachine Gun	15%
Swim	25%
Throw	25%
Track	10%

NOTES ON SKILLS

Computer Use and Electronics available in the 1990s only.

No submachine guns were available for sale in the 1890s.

The Weapons Table lists dozens of attack and weapon skills.

In the 1890s, Psychoanalysis is unavailable as a skill for the Doctor of Medicine occupation.

In the 1890s, Pilot is Pilot Balloon or Pilot Boat only. In the 1920s, it is Pilot Balloon / Dirigible / Aircraft /Boat. In the 1990s, it is Pilot Civil Prop / Civil Jet / Airliner / Jet Fighter / Helicopter / Balloon / Dirigible / Boat.

In the 1890s Drive Horses starts at 20%. In other eras Drive Car starts at 20%.

WHAT ARE THE MOST USEFUL SKILLS?

The answer depends on the play style of keepers and players. For printed scenarios, however, several of the following are likely to be rolled for in a session.

Cthulhu Mythos—central to the game, but the more you rise in it, the more your mental stability shrinks. Every character is a prisoner of this skill.

Library Use—invaluable for locating evidence, clues, and background, but of no use at all in deciding what to do with them.

Spot Hidden—handy for noticing clues, lurking cultists, and objects of all sorts.

Other Language—Mythos tomes and other evidence are often not written in English. If you don't know the language, can you find someone who can translate?

Bargain / Fast Talk—quickly talk your way past, deceive, or make a deal with almost anyone. Persuade takes time.

Credit Rating (1890s) / Computer Use (today)—important skills in very different eras.

Firearm / Melee Weapon—muscle to deal with henchmen and madmen is handy. Of no value against the supernatural.

An academic skill such as Astronomy or Physics—one or two may be useful, but which ones?

First Aid / Medicine—emergency treatment keeps investigators alive, and knowledgeable treatment heals better.

Psychology / Psychoanalysis—the former offers insight into the motives of others, and the latter offers vital first aid or extended therapy for those suffering severe emotional shocks.

TRAINING

Given enough money, someone will teach anything. The existence of training makes game sense only in campaigns, where the same players and characters meet regularly and understand each other.

Without good reason, one should not go to school and learn more than 1D10 points in a skill per six months of game time. The keeper decides if multiple courses can be taken, and how to judge if the investigator's class participation is satisfactory. An experience check comes automatically upon successfully completing a segment of training, but too many adventures in a semester will invalidate classroom work or practice for that term.

At the keeper's option, the learning rate for a skill might be increased or the learning interval shortened if the investigator has access to a renowned teacher. Such access should come as a reward for an outstanding deed or after great perseverance, since many compete for the favor of the famous.

Player and keeper may arrange self-study of any academic subject. The investigator must study for six months, then the player tries to roll D100 equal to or less than the investigator's (INT + POW) x2%. Succeeding, he or she gets 1D10 points in the subject.

Combat skills such as Fencing Foil are so little used that schools represent the only way to learn them.

STARTING A SKILL FROM ZERO

In previous editions, seventeen skills began at 00%. This was sometimes confusing and also unrealistic, since most people know a little about everything, or should have the chance to make a lucky guess. Cthulhu Mythos excepted, if you have 00% skills on old character sheets, change them to 01%. ■

CTHULHU MYTHOS (00%)

This skill differs from the others in the game. No starting investigator may take points in Cthulhu Mythos either with occupation points or with personal interest points. There is no check box for Cthulhu Mythos on the investigator sheet, because successful use of the skill does not offer an increase in the investigator's percentiles in the skill.

Instead, points in Cthulhu Mythos are gained by encounters with the Mythos which result in insanity, by optional insane insights into the true nature of the universe, and by reading forbidden books and other Mythos writings. On occasion, witnessing some ceremony or participating in some event might prompt a keeper to award Cthulhu Mythos points as well, but that is up to the keeper.

A few Mythos points may be useful, but investigators do not want many of them, because 99 minus an investigator's Cthulhu Mythos points represents the maximum Sanity points possible to an investigator. As Mythos points proliferate, they crowd out Sanity points, and leave the investigator vulnerable. See Sanity, p. 69, for more about this.

The Cthulhu Mythos skill does have useful applications. Whenever spoor or other evidence of Mythos monsters is found, a successful D100 roll against this skill allows the investigator to identify the entity, deduce something about its behavior, or guess at some property it may possess. A successful Mythos roll also might allow an investigator to remember some fact concerning the Mythos, identify a spell by seeing it cast, remember that a particular spell or kind of information may be in a particular Mythos tome, or achieve some other task.

No human, even one with 99% Cthulhu Mythos, ever approaches complete knowledge of the Mythos. It is fair to say that not even Great Old Ones do. Their 100% scores represent convenient comparisons against what humans can achieve, not a thorough plumbing of the mysteries of the Mythos. Perhaps the Outer Gods know it all, if they bother to think about such things. But only gods can cope with infinity. The cruel darkness of the Mythos extends forever. Seeming mastery of its puzzles is temporary, local, and illusory.

DISGUISE (01%)

The user changes posture, costume, and/or voice in order to seem another person or another sort of person. Theatrical makeup may help. Dim lighting definitely helps. Increase the chance for detection if the disguise involves significant differences in sex, age, size, or language. To look like a specific person, as opposed to a particular *kind* of person, halve the Disguise skill percentage—this sort of illusion is best maintained by distance.

A successful Spot Hidden or a Psychology roll might lead an observer to suspect someone in disguise. A successful Fast Talk roll by the player of the disguised character lowers the success chance for either of those skills by 10 percentiles.

Though explaining die results is the province of the keeper, a low and successful D100 result might give the disguised character some ability to issue convincing orders or to pass inspection by intimates. A failed Disguise roll causes onlookers to notice uncharacteristic behavior or expression. A very high failure, from 90 to 00, declares in effect, "This person is suspicious! Investigate immediately!"

DODGE (DEX x2%)

Allows an investigator instinctively to evade blows, thrown missiles, attacks from ambush, and so forth. A character attempting Dodge in a combat round may also parry, but not attack. Dodge can increase through experience, like other skills. If an attack can be seen, a character can try to dodge it. Against guns, a defender can try to dodge only the first bullet fired at him in a round.

DRIVE AUTOMOBILE / HORSES (20%)

Anyone with this skill can drive a car or light truck, make ordinary maneuvers, and cope with ordinary vehicle problems. If the investigator wants to lose a pursuer or trail someone, both participants might attempt Driving rolls until one fails and the other succeeds. For more complicated chases, consult the optional auto chase rules, p. 250. Dangerous maneuvers always call for Drive rolls.

In the 1890s, this skill is Drive Horses, with equivalent benefits and dangers. This represents a one-horse buggy or cart, or a two- or four-horse wagon or coach. Those of that era who wish Drive Automobile start at 01%. Investigators of later eras similarly would begin Drive Horses at 01%.

ELECTRICAL REPAIR (10%)

Enables the investigator to repair or reconfigure electrical equipment such as auto ignitions, electric motors, fuse boxes, and burglar alarms. In the present-day, has little to do with Electronics. To fix an electrical device may require special parts or tools. Jobs in the 1920s may call for this skill and for Mechanical Repair in combination.

ELECTRONICS (01%)

For trouble-shooting and repairing electronic equipment. Allows simple new electronic devices to be made. This is a skill for the present day—use Physics and Electrical Repair for electronic developments in the 1890s and 1920s. Unlike the Electrical Repair skill, parts needed for Electronics work cannot be jury-rigged: they are designed for precise jobs. Without the right microchip or circuit board, the skill user is out of luck.

FAST TALK (05%)

Causes the target to agree with the user for a short time. Without reflecting, the target signs the paper, allows the trespass, lends the automobile, or whatever else within reason is asked. Given a little more time to think and the benefit of a successful Idea roll, the target comes to his or her senses, and the Fast Talk loses effect.

Example: Count von Samme succeeds with a Fast Talk pitch, and Harvey goes upstairs to find a fountain pen with which to sign the Count's fraudulent contract. As he rummages around, Harvey is absent from the Count long enough to begin to think for himself. The keeper asks for an Idea roll. It succeeds. Harvey comes to his senses and returns determined not to sign. The Count must renew his pitch some other time, or change tactics and attempt to Persuade Harvey.

In a few game minutes, Fast Talk may pass off suspect goods as valuable, false facts as reliable, and fine items as not worth bothering about. In contrast, Persuade and Bargain may take hours or days to conclude. Fast Talk is quick to take effect, but it can be used at most on a handful of people. Fast Talk will not work on targets whose minds are made up; use Persuade instead.

FIRST AID (30%)

The percentage chance of awakening an unconscious or stunned comrade, setting a broken limb, treating burn damage, resuscitating a drowning victim, etc. First Aid has no effect on diseases or subtle physical ailments, nor on poisonings unless the keeper allows the roll. Treated with First Aid, an investigator's healing rate stays at 1D3 points per week. (Moved to a hospital and successfully treated with Medicine, that rate rises to 2D3 per week.)

Failure in applying First Aid requires that the user wait some reasonable amount of time to try again (something new, presumably, since what was done didn't work), but another practicioner could make an attempt in the next round.

■ A success with this skill allows the user immediately to heal 1D3 hit points of a single attack or injury. Thus an investigator suffering multiple gunshot wounds might receive First Aid for each, as long as they were not incurred in the same combat round.

■ In the same or the succeeding combat round, an investigator who has just died may be returned to life if the emergency treatment raises hit points to at least +1.

■ A success with First Aid immediately awakens any victim of a knock-out attack and, if the keeper wishes, anyone unconscious for other reasons.

Once a character has had First Aid successfully applied to an injury, further applications either of First Aid or of Medicine have no effect on that injury. A new injury would be treated independently. An application of the skill takes a combat round, or as the keeper determines. See also Medicine.

FIST/PUNCH (50%)

A self-explanatory skill, which might be depicted as a closed fist, a karate chop, a roundhouse punch, a violent slap, etc. One can use Fist/Punch to parry Kick and Head Butt, Martial Arts can add to the skill's impact, and the knock-out rule applies to it.

GEOLOGY (01%)

Enables an investigator to tell the approximate age of rock strata, recognize fossil types, distinguish minerals and crystals, locate promising sites for drilling or mining, evaluate soils, and anticipate volcanism, seismic events, avalanches, and other such phenomena. Sherlock Holmes was expert in London-area soils, and could trace a man's movements by studying the dirt on his boots.

GRAPPLE (25%)

A Grapple is a special personal attack, frequently chosen to subdue an opponent without harming him. This attack may be parried by a countering successful Grapple or other attack by the target, but only in the first round of attack.

If a Grapple attack succeeds in the first round and is not neutralized, then the attacker holds the target and may thereafter exercise one of several options.

■ Immobilize the target by overcoming the target's STR with his or her own STR, using the Resistance Table. With a success, the target is held fast indefinitely, until the grappler attempts another action.

■ Knock down the target. If used, this option automatically succeeds.

■ Knock out the target in the first or a later round: see the knock-out rule, p. 55.

■ Disarm the target. With successful Grapples in consecutive rounds, an investigator could Grapple to prevent a hand-to-hand attack in the first round and then seize the weapon or weapon hand in the second round.

■ Physically injure the target. The opponent already must be successfully grappled. Then the grappler must receive a second successful Grapple roll in that round, or a successful Grapple in some later round. Success costs the target 1D6 hit points plus the attacker's damage bonus. Harm in subsequent rounds requires a new Grapple success in those rounds, and the amount of injury done remains the same.

■ Strangle the target. Beginning in the round in which the intention is stated, the target begins to asphyxiate as per the Drowning rules. This continues in subsequent rounds. The attacker needs no further Grapple rolls.

In either injury-making Grapple, the victim can escape only by a successful STR match on the Resistance Table. Combine STRs if two people are attacking.

HANDGUN (20%)

Use for all pistol-like firearms when firing discrete shots. For machine pistols (MAC-11, Uzi, etc.), in the present day, use the Submachine Gun skill when firing bursts. The rate-of-fire difference between handguns is partly from recoil and time needed to take new aim on the target, and partly from the difference in mechanism between a revolver and a semi-automatic.

Properly loading and firing a black-powder handgun may, at the keeper's option, require a successful History roll as well.

HEAD BUTT (10%)

The essential barroom brawl skill, Head Butt is applied to the belly of an opponent, or else to his temple, crown, nose, chin, or back of the head. This personal attack can be made in cramped surroundings. It is surprisingly quick and of demoralizing intensity. One cannot parry with Head Butt, but Martial Arts can add to its effect. The knock-out rule can be applied to it.

HIDE (10%)

As opposed to Conceal, Hide concerns the individual user's ability to escape detection in an unprepared position. Use this skill only in a pursuit situation, or when under surveillance or patrol. It lets the user choose objects, bushes, deep shadows, etc., in which to lurk for a while. Some sort of cover must be present. In an area being watched, the user can move while hiding. Figure the chance for successful movement by halving the Hide skill amount.

HISTORY (20%)

Enables an investigator to remember the significance of a country, city, region, or person, as pertinent. Lessen the chance if the facts are obscure. A successful History roll might be used to help identify tools, techniques, or ideas familiar to ancestors, but little known today.

JUMP (25%)

With a success, the investigator can leap up vertically and grab to his or her own height, safely leap down vertically to his or her own height, jump horizontally from a standing start across a gap for a distance equal to the jumper's own height, or run and then jump horizontally to a distance of twice the jumper's own height. If falling from a height, a successful Jump prepares for the fall, subtracting 1D6 hit points from those lost to the injury.

KICK (25%)

Whether a straight forward kick to the groin or the jaw, an elegant karate-style flying kick, or a kick with both legs while lying on a floor, a Kick is powerful enough to do damage wherever it lands. A Kick may parry and Martial Arts may add to its effectiveness, but do not apply the knock-out rule to Kick except in rare circumstances.

LAW (05%)

Represents the chance of knowing pertinent law, precedent, legal maneuver, or court procedure. The practice of law as a profession can lead to great rewards and political office, but it requires intense application over many years. A high Credit Rating is crucial to it. No other profession is so easily sullied by the bizarre behavior common to investigators. In the United States, one's practice of law must be sanctioned by the State Bar of a particular commonwealth or state. In another country, halve the chance for success with this skill, unless the character has spent 30-INT months studying that nation's law.

LIBRARY USE (25%)

In many ways this is the most important skill in the game. Library Use enables an investigator to find a given book, newspaper, or reference in a library or collection of documents, assuming that the item is there. Each use of this skill marks four hours of continuous search. An investigator rarely gets more than two tries per day.

This skill can locate a locked case or rare-book special collection, but Fast Talk, Persuade, Bargain, Credit Rating, a bribe, or special credentials might be needed to get at the books.

LISTEN (25%)

Measures the ability of an investigator to interpret and understand sound, including overheard conversations, mutters behind a closed door, and whispered words in a cafe. The keeper may use it to determine the course of an impending encounter: was your investigator awakened by that crackling twig? By extension, a high Listen can indicate general awareness in a character.

LOCKSMITH (01%)

The user may repair locks, make keys, or open locks with the aid of skeleton keys, picks, and other tools. Especially difficult locks may lower the chance for success. A locksmith can open car doors, hot-wire autos, jimmy library windows, figure out Chinese puzzle boxes, and penetrate ordinary commercial alarm systems. Sophisticated safes, vaults, and other serious defensive systems are beyond this skill. Keepers might combine Locksmith with DEX or POW rolls to cover a variety of surreptitious situations.

MACHINE GUN (15%)

Use this skill whenever firing bursts from a bipod or tripod mounted weapon. If single shots are fired from a bipod, use the Rifle skill if it is higher. The differences between assault rifle, submachine gun, and light machine gun are tenuous today.

MARTIAL ARTS (01%)

Use in combination with an attack with Fist/Punch, Head Butt, Kick, or Grapple. If the attack roll is equal to or less than the attacker's Martial Arts percentage, the attack does double damage: thus Fist/Punch would do 2D3 plus normal damage bonus. Martial Arts doubles the damage done if the attack strikes home, but do not double any damage bonus.

■ A person with Martial Arts may choose which attack to parry just before that attack, and does not need to make a parry statement at the beginning of the round.

■ Even with Martial Arts, bullets and other projectiles cannot be parried.

People develop martial arts to compensate for forcible disarmament: judo, aikijutsu, aikido, capoera, karate, savat, tae kyun or tae kwon do, white crane kung fu, 7 straws praying mantis kung fu, etc. Choose one or invent a new one. In earlier days, these schools were secret and their techniques jealously guarded. Outside their cultures, martial arts are little known until the present era.

MECHANICAL REPAIR (20%)

This allows the investigator to repair a broken machine, or to create a new one. Basic carpentry and plumbing projects can be performed. Special tools or parts may be required.

This skill can open common household locks, but nothing more advanced. See the Locksmith skill. Mechanical Repair is a companion skill to Electrical Repair, and both may be necessary to fix complex devices such as an auto or an aircraft.

MEDICINE (05%)

The user diagnoses and treats accidents, injuries, diseases, poisonings, etc., and makes public health recommendations. If an era has no good treatment for a malady, the effort is limited, uncertain, or inconclusive. Failure in application requires that the user wait some amount of time to try again, but another practicioner could make his or her attempt in the next round.

- In an emergency, the successful user of Medicine can immediately restore 1D3 hit points, once per wound or injury.

- In the same or the succeeding combat round, an investigator who has just died may be returned to life if hit points rise to at least +1.

- An investigator successfully treated with Medicine heals at 2D3 hit points per game week, including the first week.

- Including any emergency treatment, the total recovery for the first week of Medicine's application could be 3D3 hit points.

- A success with Medicine immediately awakens any victim of a knock-out attack and anyone unconscious for other reasons.

- The keeper may rule that a medical condition is not treatable. See also First Aid.

NATURAL HISTORY (10%)

Originally the study of plant and animal life in its environment. By the nineteenth century this study had long separated into many academic disciplines. As a game skill it

SCENE: A GRAVEYARD (III)

represents the traditional knowledge and personal observation of farmers, fishermen, inspired amateurs, and hobbyists. It identifies species, habits, and habitats in a general way and is able to guess at what may be important to a particular species. Natural History information may or may not be accurate—this is the region of appreciation, judgment, tradition, and enthusiasm. Use Natural History to judge horseflesh at a county fair, or to decide whether a butterfly collection is excellent or just excellently framed.

NAVIGATE (10%)

Allows the user to find his or her way in storms or clear weather, in day or at night. Those of higher skill are familiar with the astronomical tables, charts, instruments, and satellite location gear as they exist in the era of play. Roll results for such a skill should be kept secret, a matter for the investigators to attempt and then to witness the results. One could also use this skill to measure and map an area, whether an island of many square miles or the interior of a single room.

OCCULT (05%)

The user recognizes occult paraphernalia, words, and concepts, and identifies grimoires of magic and occult codes when he sees them. The occultist is familiar with the families of secret knowledge passed down from Egypt and Sumer, from the Medieval and Renaissance West, and perhaps from Asia and Africa as well.

Comprehending certain books may provide percentiles of Occult. Some occult books are noted in the Magic chapter, p. 84. This skill does not apply to spells, books, and magic of the Cthulhu Mythos, but occult concepts are often adopted by worshipers of the Great Old Ones.

OPERATE HEAVY MACHINE (01%)

Required to drive and operate a tank, backhoe, steam shovel, or other large-scale construction machine. Once the skill is known, no skill roll is needed except for difficult or dangerous tasks, or bad or dangerous conditions. For very different sorts of machines, the keeper may decide to lower an investigator's nominal skill if the problems encountered are mostly unfamiliar ones: someone used to running a bulldozer, for instance, will not be quickly competent with the steam turbines in a ship's engine room.

OTHER LANGUAGE (01%)

Specify the language. An individual can know any number of languages. The skill represents the user's chance to understand, speak, read, and write in a language other than his or her own. Ancient or unknown languages comparable to Aklo should not be chosen, but ordinary earthly languages may be. Occasionally the keeper may determine that a number of separate complex points exist in a document or speech, and call for several such language rolls, one for each point. Similarly, the keeper may momentarily reduce a user's skill in a language if archaic speech or writing in that language is encountered. A single successful Other Language roll normally comprehends an entire book.

If an investigator has several points in a particular Other Language, he or she grasps the gist of normal conversation. A character needs INT x5 or better points in a second language to pass for a native speaker. Blank spaces exist for other languages on the investigator sheet.

To identify an unknown present-day human language, use a Know roll. To identify an extinct human language, use an Archeology roll. To identify an alien language, use a Cthulhu Mythos or possibly an Occult roll.

OWN LANGUAGE (EDU x5%)

Specify the language. In infancy and early childhood, most humans use a single language. For most people in the United States, that tongue is some dialect of English. The tongue chosen by the player for the investigator's Own Language automatically starts at EDU x5: thereafter the investigator understands, speaks, reads, and writes at that percentage or higher.

Normally no skill roll is necessary to use Own Language. If a document is extremely difficult to read, or in an archaic dialect, the keeper may reduce the user's skill chance in that situation.

Authors typically have high Own Language skills.

PERSUADE (15%)

Use Persuade to convince a target about a particular idea, concept, or belief. (Like Fast Talk, Persuade may be employed without reference to truth.) Unlike Fast Talk, Persuade's effect lingers indefinitely and insidiously, for years perhaps, until events or another Persuade turn the target's mind in another direction. The successful application of Persuade might take an hour to several days, depending on what's being attempted.

PHARMACY (01%)

The user recognizes, compounds, and perhaps dispenses a wide variety of drugs and potions, natural and man-made, and understands side effects and contra-indications. He or she has a good practical knowledge of poisons and antidotes, and can use Pharmacy as a first-aid skill in cases of poisoning. The skill grants no ability to diagnose diseases nor the right to prescribe medicines.

PHOTOGRAPHY (10%)

Covers both still and motion photography. This skill allows one to take clear pictures, develop them properly, and perhaps enhance half-hidden detail. Failures are blurred or do not show what was desired. In the present day, the skill extends to cover video cameras, video playback equipment, and digital photography.

PHYSICS (01%)

Grants theoretical understanding of pressure, materials, motion, magnetism, electricity, optics, radioactivity, and related phenomena, and some ability to construct experimental devices to test ideas. The degree of knowledge depends on the era of use. Practical devices such as automobiles are not the province of physicists, but experimen-

tal devices may be, perhaps in conjunction with Electronics or Mechanical Repair.

PILOT (01%)

The air/water equivalent of Drive Automobile, this is the maneuver skill for flying or floating craft. An investigator might have several versions of this skill in the spaces on the investigator sheet. Each starts at 01%.

■ Pilot Aircraft skills change by era. Pilot Boat does not change, and does not distinguish between sail and motor craft. Bad weather, bad visibility, and damage apply to air and water craft.

■ A skill user of less than 15% knows just enough to get into trouble. He or she can sail or fly on a calm day with good visibility, but needs Luck rolls for take-offs and landings, dockings, changing sails, judging wind and current, etc. Keepers must require Pilot rolls for storms, navigation by instrument, low visibility, and other difficult situations.

PILOT AIRCRAFT: understands and is increasingly competent with a general class of aircraft named below. Upon any landing, even under the best conditions, a Pilot roll must be made. If conditions are good, double the chance for success. If conditions are bad, the pilot lands at his or her normal chance. A failure may represent damage to the craft, which must be repaired before the next takeoff. Pilot and passengers may walk away or need Luck rolls to avoid serious injury. A result of 00 is a memorable disaster, with at least the death of the pilot.

■ Each class of aircraft counts as a different skill, and should be listed independently, or as the keeper sees fit: 1890s, Pilot Balloon only; 1920s, Pilot Balloon/ Dirigible/ Civil Prop only; in the present day, Pilot Civil Prop, Pilot Civil Jet, Pilot Airliner, Pilot Jet Fighter, Pilot Helicopter.

PILOT BOAT: understands the behavior of small motor and sailing craft in wind, storms, and tides, and can read wave and wind action to suggest hidden obstacles and approaching storms. In a wind, novice sailors will find docking a rowboat difficult.

PSYCHOANALYSIS (01%)

Enables the user to staunch temporary and indefinite insanity for a day or so. If the condition persists beyond that period, the unfortunate person relapses, and only time heals the insanity. This emergency treatment takes up to an hour to perform, and can be applied just once per incident of insanity, no matter how many analysts are available.

■ Treatment by a psychotherapist can add Sanity points during indefinite insanity. See Sanity, p. 76.

■ Psychoanalysis cannot increase a person's Sanity points beyond POW x5, nor above 99-Cthulhu Mythos.

The skill refers to the range of emotional therapies, not just to Freudian procedures. Formal psychotherapy was little-known in the 1890s, though some procedures are as old as humanity. Sometimes it was looked on as a fraudulent study even in the 1920s. The common term then for an analyst or scholar of emotional disorders was *alienist*. In the present day, a combination of therapies has evolved, and this skill now could be justly named Psychiatric Treatment.

PSYCHOLOGY (05%)

A skill common to all humans, it allows the user to study an individual and form an idea of his or her motives and character. In general, the keeper should make the rolls for this skill and keep the results secret, announcing only the information, true or false, that the user gained by employing it. Players should not expect that this skill penetrates skillful deceit unless the person's confidence somehow has been shaken.

RIDE (05%)

Intended to apply to saddle horses, donkeys, or mules. A camel might be ridden successfully at a lowered percentage chance. The skill grants knowledge of basic care of the riding animal, riding gear, and how to handle the steed at the gallop or on difficult terrain.

Should a steed unexpectedly rear or stumble, the rider's chance of remaining mounted equals his or her Ride. If an investigator falls from a mount, either because the animal has collapsed, fallen, or died, or because a Ride roll failed, he or she loses 1D6 hit points in the accident. A successful Jump roll saves 1D6 hit points.

Wielding a weapon effectively while riding takes both a weapon skill and a Ride skill in excess of 50%. The keeper might apply modifiers to reflect a particular situation.

RIFLE (25%)

The user can fire any type of rifle, whether lever-action, bolt-action, or semi-automatic. When a military assault rifle fires a single shot or burst, use this skill. When a shotgun fires a rifled slug, use this skill.

Shots per round mostly vary because of the weapon's action and recoil, and the subsequent time needed to reacquire the target.

At the keeper's option, use of a black-powder rifle requires a History roll as well to load and fire it properly. At the keeper's option, combine Rifle and Shotgun as a single skill, differentiating only between pellet and slug ammunition.

SHOTGUN (30%)

With this skill any scatter-gun can be fired. Since the load expands in a spreading pattern, the user's chance to hit does not decrease with range, but the damage done does. At ranges from 10-20 yards, 1D3 close-together targets can be hit with one round, and from 20-50 yards, 1D6 such targets can be hit. The keeper decides whether the targets are close enough for this rule.

Double-barreled shotguns can be sawed off, for purposes of concealment and portability. In the United States, such weapons are illegal by the 1920s.

If firing a rifled slug, use the Rifle skill. At the keeper's option, combine Rifle and Shotgun as a single skill, differentiating only between pellet and slug ammo.

SNEAK (10%)

The art of moving quietly, without alerting those who might hear. Used in combination with Hide, the investigator makes a single D100 roll, the result of which is matched against the investigator's percentages in both skills. Use this combination when silent movement is necessary. See also Hide.

SPOT HIDDEN (25%)

This skill allows the user to spot a secret door or compartment, notice a hidden intruder, find an inconspicuous clue, recognize a repainted automobile, become aware of ambushers, notice a bulging pocket, or anything similar. This is an important skill in the game.

SUBMACHINE GUN (15%)

When firing any machine pistol or submachine gun, use this skill. Present-day machine pistols, such as the Skorpion, may be so small that the Handgun skill should be used when firing single shots from them. No submachine guns exist in the 1890s.

SWIM (25%)

The ability to float and to move through water or other liquid. Only roll Swim in times of crisis or danger when the keeper thinks it appropriate. A failing Swim roll starts the drowning procedure. Someone drowning may receive a Swim roll attempt each round—with a success, he or she reaches the surface and breathes. With a second success, he or she can begin to move through the water. If the second Swim roll fails, drowning begins again.

THROW (25%)

To hit a target with an object, or to hit a target with the right part of the object thrown (such as the blade of a knife or hatchet), use Throw. A palm-sized object of reasonable balance can be hurled three yards for each STR point exceeding the object's SIZ. An object designed to be thrown can be hurled up to six yards for each STR point in excess of the object's SIZ, and perhaps bounce on for more. Keepers must choose the multiplier suitable to the baseball, javelin, etc.

If the Throw roll fails, then the object lands at some random distance from the target. Compare the closeness of the die roll result to the highest number which would have indicated success, and choose a distance in yards between target and thrown object that feels comparable.

TRACK (10%)

With Track, an investigator can follow a person, vehicle, or animal over soft earth and leaves. Subtract 10% from the chance for success for each day that has passed since the tracks were made. Rain may make tracking impossible. A being cannot be tracked across water, over concrete, or at night except in unusual circumstances. ■

SANITY & INSANITY

In daring the perils of the Cthulhu mythos,
player-characters risk their very souls.
But even an insane investigator
can lead the way to light.

Some of the information and concepts in this chapter first appeared in the Chaosium publication *Taint of Madness*. That book contains in-depth information relating to this chapter, including broad historical background, considerations of law, discussion of asylums, problems of institutionalization, and historical asylums.

Most of those who suffer from serious mental illness have done so from an early age, and will be dealing with the illness for their entire lives. Call of Cthulhu player-characters typically start sane and mentally competent. In the course of play, however, they confront knowledge and entities of alien horror and terrifying implication. Such experiences shake and shatter belief in the normal world.

Sanity in the game is modeled after the behavior of protagonists in H.P. Lovecraft's fiction, who more than a few times faint or go mad. The characteristic SAN (Sanity) is the game's register of investigator flexibility and resilience to emotional trauma. Those characters who start with high SAN find it easier to rationalize traumatic events or to repress horrific memories. Those with lower SAN are mentally fragile and more susceptible to emotional upset. Though other gruesome, comparatively ordinary sights and events also cause emotional disturbance, center stage in the game belongs to the Cthulhu Mythos.

In an unnerving or horrifying play situation, the keeper will test the resiliency and emotional strength of the player-characters. He does this by calling for Sanity rolls. A success is a D100 roll equal to or less than the current Sanity points. An unsuccessful Sanity roll always costs the character Sanity points. A successful roll costs no points or relatively few. See the nearby box for examples of costs.

Insanity in a character is triggered when too many Sanity points are lost in too short a time, causing *temporary insanity* or *indefinite insanity*, defined later in this chapter.

To remain active in the game the character's insanity must be of a sort that can be effectively roleplayed. If time is of the essence, the keeper may roll on one of the temporary insanity tables, but as a matter of course the keeper should choose the insanity to match the situation which prompted it, and attempt to characterize the insanity in concert with the player and the investigator.

An insane character may return to sanity after a few game rounds, or may need months to recover. If Sanity points reach zero, the character needs lengthy hospitalization, and he or she probably will not return to play.

A character may regain Sanity points, and even increase his or her maximum Sanity points if POW increases. An increase in the Cthulhu Mythos skill always lowers the character's maximum Sanity points by the same amount.

How the Mythos Causes Insanity

War, abuse, or any other strong personal experience can scar feelings. To emphasize certain ideas he had concerning fear, the unknown, and humanity's lowly place in the scheme of things, Lovecraft posited new terrors for us. He suggested that what we believe to be the immutable laws of time and space are valid only locally, and only partly are true. Beyond our ken are infinities where greater realities hold sway. There are small and great alien powers and races who are sometimes actively hostile. Some encroach on our world. The real universe, Mythos authors suggest, is one of irrational event, unholy fury, endless struggle, and relentless anarchy. Human insanity opens a window onto this terrible realm. Through such an opening we can glimpse the dark and bloody truth at the heart of everything. Such sweeping cosmic visions are rare and climactic moments in the game.

Sanity is ordinarily lost in a few specific ways.

1) Knowledge is dangerous. The Cthulhu Mythos skill represents knowledge of the true universe. No amount of psychotherapy or rest can remove the danger of self-transformation in such knowledge. As Cthulhu Mythos increases, maximum Sanity lowers and limits current Sanity. In consequence, failed Sanity rolls become more frequent, and current Sanity drops.

2) Mythos magic is the physics of the true universe. In casting Mythos spells, characters perform visualizations of the

Examples of Sanity Point Costs

Sanity lost*	unnerving or horrifying situation
0/1D2	surprised to find mangled animal carcass
0/1D3	surprised to find corpse
0/1D3	surprised to find body part
0/1D4	see a stream flow with blood
1/1D4+1	find mangled human corpse
0/1D6	awake trapped in a coffin
0/1D6	witness a friend's violent death
0/1D6	see a ghoul
1/1D6+1	meet someone you know to be dead
0/1D10	undergo severe torture
1/1D10	see a corpse rise from its grave
2/2D10+1	see gigantic severed head fall from sky
1D10/1D100	see Great Cthulhu

successful roll cost / failed roll cost

unimaginable, and their minds must follow alien ways of thought. These wound the mind. Such traumas are ones for which the casters volunteered, it is true, but they are shocks all the same.

3) Mythos tomes add to the Cthulhu Mythos skill, and teach Mythos spells. When studying and comprehending Mythos books, all that we know as true becomes like shadow. The burning power of a greater and more horrible reality seizes the soul. Whether we try to retreat from the experience or hunger greedily for more of it, we thereby de-emphasize and lose confidence in what we once believed, and are more taken up by the encompassing truth of the Cthulhu Mythos.

4) Nearly all creatures and entities of the Mythos cost Sanity points to encounter. Aliens are intrinsically discomforting and repelling. We never lose awareness of their slimy, stinking otherness, which Lovecraft often characterizes as obscene or blasphemous. This instinctive reaction is part and parcel of every human being. Even losing Sanity does not erase this antipathy.

5) Non-Mythos shocks can also cost Sanity points. This includes witnessing untimely or violent death, experiencing personal mutilation, treachery, loss of social position, failure of love, and whatever else the keeper can devise as a challenge. In this category we also can lump our world's common supernatural events or agents, such as hauntings, zombies, vampires, werewolves, curses, etc.

Using SAN; Current Sanity Points

Use the investigator sheet to record SAN relationships. There are three kinds.

1) *Characteristic SAN.* It is equal to the character's POW x5. This number rarely changes.

2) *Maximum Sanity points.* This amount equals 99 minus present Cthulhu Mythos points. Maximum Sanity points may be more than, equal to, or less than characteristic SAN. Maximum Sanity is a cap amount, indicating the highest possible number of current Sanity points. This number occasionally changes.

3) *Current Sanity points.* This is the most important amount to keep track of. The following paragraphs discuss it. This number often changes.

When investigators encounter a sanity-threatening situation, the keeper may ask for a Sanity roll. The players roll D100 for each of their characters. A success is a roll equal to or less than the investigator's current Sanity points.

In published statistics and scenarios, Sanity loss rolls are shown as two numbers or rolls separated by a slash, as for instance *1/1D4+1*. The number to the left of the slash is the amount of Sanity points lost if the Sanity roll succeeds. The die roll to the right of the slash is the number of Sanity points lost if the Sanity roll fails.

Thus a successful roll means that the investigator loses no Sanity points or else a minimal amount. A failed Sanity roll always means that the investigator loses several or many Sanity points. The amount lost depends on the spell, book, entity, or situation actually encountered.

Losing more than a few Sanity points at one time may cause an investigator to go insane, as described further below. If an investigator's current Sanity points drop to zero, he or she is permanently insane, and normally can no longer be played.

GETTING USED TO AWFULNESS

At some point, constant exposure to the same Mythos tome or to the same Mythos creature has no added effect. For instance, having read and comprehended a particular Mythos tome and taken the Sanity loss and added the points necessary to Cthulhu Mythos, an investigator can consult the book over and over without further penalty.

Similarly, once an investigator has lost as many Sanity points for seeing a particular sort of monster as the maximum possible for the monster, he or she should not lose more Sanity points for a reasonable interval. "Reasonable interval" may be a game day, or a game week, or the duration of an adventure. The keeper decides. For instance, during a reasonable interval no investigator could lose more than 6 Sanity points for encountering deep ones (0/1D6 SAN), even though he or she saw a hundred of them. Still, we never truly get used to seeing alien obscenities. After a time, the horror of them will rise up freshly in any character.

Neither does learning and casting spells ever become a normal thing to do. Every spell is discrete, and most are cast with malevolent intent. Every spell achieves an effect impossible in the normal world. The necessary recreation of horrible effect and alien mind-set always costs Sanity, even if the same spell is cast twenty times a day. Spellcasting is a bargain with darkness, and must be paid for.

Insanity & the Cthulhu Mythos

Insanity stemming from non-Mythos causes yields no Cthulhu Mythos knowledge. But each time an investigator reels from Mythos-induced trauma, he or she learns more of the Mythos, and this is reflected in the arcane Cthulhu Mythos skill.

The first instance of Mythos-related insanity always adds 5 points to Cthulhu Mythos. Further episodes of Mythos-induced insanity each add 1 point to the skill.

Example: *Harvey Walters finds a manuscript in Crowninshield Manor. After comprehending it, he has 3% Cthulhu Mythos skill, but lost no Sanity points. When he steps outside, Harvey sees a nightgaunt fly overhead. He goes insane, his mind quailing before the unearthly manifestation. Since this is Harvey's first Mythos-related insanity, his player must add 5 percentiles to Harvey's Cthulhu Mythos skill, raising it to 8%. Harvey's maximum Sanity points drop to 91 (that is, 99 minus 8 Cthulhu Mythos).*

The emotional traumas of ordinary life, the fifth category, also can be gotten used to for a while. Later on, the "reasonable interval" passes for these events as well, and we experience the horror or terror anew.

Increasing Current Sanity Points

Some keepers feel that the notion of relentless self-improvement conflicts with Lovecraft's dark vision, and do not allow it. Others cheerfully promote it, since it makes players happy, and since their investigators will continue to go insane regardless how many Sanity points they have. (Current Sanity points can never increase above maximum Sanity points, but they can increase above original SAN.) Here are ways to raise current Sanity points.

BY KEEPER AWARD: at the end of a successful adventure, keepers routinely specify die rolls intended to increase investigator current Sanity. Keeper award rolls are the same for all participants, but are rolled individually by players for their investigators. Such rewards should be proportional to the danger the group faced. However, if the investigators were cowardly, brutal, or murderous, they deserve no reward. Keepers also may grant reward rolls for unusually good roleplaying. This should be done sparingly and perhaps in private if all are not to share.

BY INCREASING POW: procedures exist in the Magic chapter for increasing investigator POW. This is a rare accomplishment, but if POW rises, so does the SAN characteristic, which always equals POW x5. Remember to check increases against maximum Sanity points.

BY INCREASING A SKILL TO 90%: when an investigator attains 90% or more ability in a skill, he or she has mastered the skill. Add 2D6 points to current Sanity points to represent the discipline and self-esteem gained. Of all skills, only Cthulhu Mythos cannot be mastered.

BY DEFEATING UNNATURAL ENTITIES: natural animals and human enemies might terrify, but they usually do not horrify. Victory in wrestling a bear yields no Sanity point reward. Capturing a deep one might. When an investigator defeats, dispels, or slaughters something strange and alien, as a wraith or a byakhee, his or her confidence naturally increases. The game reflects that as an increase in Sanity points.

"Defeat" is necessarily vague. What were the goals of the monster? Did the investigators foil its intent? Did the investigators work purposefully toward the thing's defeat?

Such a reward should not exceed the Sanity loss roll for encountering the thing. If several or many such things were defeated, then award the maximum points for encountering the thing: for example, the 1D6 roll for one shantak would increase to six points flat for victory over a group of them.

BY PSYCHOTHERAPY: the therapist must have the skill Psychoanalysis. Intensive psychoanalysis can return Sanity points to the patient. Current sanity points can be restored up to the value of POW x5 or up to the maximum Sanity point cap posed by 99% minus Cthulhu Mythos, whichever is lower.

Once a game month, make a D100 roll against the analyst's Psychoanalysis skill, to learn the progress of the therapy. If the roll succeeds, the patient gains 1D3 current Sanity points. If the roll fails, add no points. If the roll is 96-00, then the patient loses 1D6 Sanity points and treatment by that analyst concludes: there has been some sort of serious incident, and the relationship has been broken.

In the game, Psychoanalysis does not speed recovery from insanity, but it can strengthen the investigator by increasing Sanity points, giving him or her a larger reserve for the active days to come. "Recovery" is independent of Sanity points. The use of Psychoanalysis is different in the game world than in the real world. In the real world, Psychoanalysis will not work against the symptoms of schizophrenia or psychotic disorders, or bipolar disorders (manic depression) or severe depression.

Psychoanalysis is the game's equivalent of mental First Aid. In real life progress with Psychoanalysis is slow and uncertain. In any case, permanent insanity is impervious to the "talking cure". The investigator's mind is in such disarray he or she cannot participate coherently.

BY PSYCHIATRIC MEDICATIONS: though drugs were administered to patients in the 1890s and 1920s, sometimes with promising results, only today are drugs broadly and consistently effective in treating the symptoms of emotional trauma. As long as the investigator can afford a psychiatric drug and is able to take it, his or her player can avoid roleplaying the *symptoms* provoked by mental distress. If the drug is unavailable, the player's roleplaying should begin to reflect the absence of the drug. Taking psychiatric medications does not make a character immune to further Sanity loss.

Drugs for several different sets of symptoms might be necessary: overlapping medications could provoke strong side effects of the keeper's choice. For each month of successful psychiatric drug therapy, add 1D3 current Sanity points. Keepers should not try to combine psychiatric medications with Psychotherapy in the 1890s or 1920s, since the drugs were full of side effects and some were addictive as well.

Once a character improves, he or she may feel a temptation to stop the regimen of medication and the sometimes palpable side effects resulting from it, feeling that he or she has been cured or perhaps even denying that an illness existed in the first place. If so, the madness returns.

Insane Insight: An Option

At the keeper's option, a character who has just gone insane may have an insight into the situation or entity which provoked the insanity. The player needs to roll D100 and receive a result greater than the character's INT x5. The keeper should offer the insight promptly.

Insanity

In the game, insanity is induced by traumatic experiences and ghastly comprehensions connected to the Cthulhu Mythos. The duration of the insane state depends upon the number or proportion of Sanity points lost. Three states—*temporary insanity*, *indefinite insanity*, and *permanent insanity*—can result.

Temporary Insanity

If an investigator loses 5 or more Sanity points as the consequence of one Sanity roll, then he or she has suffered enough emotional trauma that the keeper must test the character's Sanity. The keeper asks for an Idea roll. If the Idea roll fails, then the investigator has repressed the memory, a trick the mind uses to protect itself. Perversely, if the Idea roll succeeds, then the investigator recognizes the full significance of what has been seen or experienced, and goes temporarily insane. The effects of temporary insanity begin immediately. For the duration of temporary insanity, see the nearby tables.

In any occurrence of insanity, keeper and player together should choose an appropriate form, or else agree to a random roll on one of the tables. Most of the symptoms of temporary insanity are self-explanatory. The keeper might choose the duration more appropriate to the investigator's recent emotional strain.

When the temporary insanity is over, a mild phobia might remain as a reminder of the experience, but the most likely souvenir will be some degree of post-traumatic stress disorder, see under anxiety disorders, p. 115.

Indefinite Insanity

If an investigator loses a fifth (round up fractions) or more of current Sanity points in one game hour, he or she goes indefinitely insane. Indefinite insanity may remove a character from play for some time. The average duration for indefinite insanity is 1D6 game months.

When a character suffers from indefinite insanity, a random roll on a table of lunacies trivializes the massive shock to the afflicted person. If no obvious diagnosis for indefinite insanity is apparent, the keeper might mull over the choice until the end of the session, or until the beginning of the next session. Meanwhile play can continue. For the moment, the character is haunted by a powerful sense of foreboding. Since disorders provoking indefinite insanity do not simply suddenly appear, the player of the insane character may be able to contribute a good reason for choosing a particular insanity.

The symptoms of some indefinite insanities are continuous (amnesia, depression, and obsession, for example). Other indefinite insanities are transient and only manifest themselves at particular moments (multiple personality or

Results of Temporary Insanity

Short Temporary Insanity
(1D10+4 COMBAT ROUNDS)

Roll 1D10.

no.	result
1	fainting or screaming fit
2	flees in panic
3	physical hysterics or emotional outburst (laughing, crying, etc.)
4	babbling, incoherent, rapid speech, or logorrhea (a torrent of coherent speech)
5	intense phobia, perhaps rooting investigator to the spot
6	homicidal or suicidal mania
7	hallucinations or delusions
8	echopraxia or echolalia (investigator does/says what others around him do/say)
9	strange or deviant eating desire (dirt, slime, cannibalism, etc.)
10	stupor (assumes foetal position, oblivious to events) or catatonia (can stand but has no will or interest; may be led or forced to simple actions but takes no independent action)

Longer Temporary Insanity
(1D10 X10 GAME HOURS)

Roll 1D10.

no.	result
1	amnesia (memories of intimates usually lost first; languages and physical skills engaged, but intellectual skills absent) *or* stupor/catatonia (see short duration table)
2	severe phobia (can flee, but sees object of obsession everywhere)
3	hallucinations
4	strange sexual desires (exhibitionism, nymphomania or satyriasis, teratophilia, etc.)
5	fetish (investigator latches onto some object, type of object, or person as a safety blanket)
6	uncontrollable tics, tremors, or inability to communicate via speech or writing
7	psychosomatic blindness, deafness, or loss of the use of a limb or limbs
8	brief reactive psychosis (incoherence, delusions, aberrant behavior, and/or hallucinations)
9	temporary paranoia
10	compulsive rituals (washing hands constantly, praying, walking in a particular rhythm, never stepping on cracks, checking one's gun constantly, etc.)

dissociative identity disorder, conversion disorder, intermittent explosive personality, etc.). Both sorts of symptoms offer good opportunities for roleplaying.

For such situations and stresses that investigators come to know, some sort of anxiety disorder can often be the most appropriate.

For instance, after a life-threatening event, a person persistently re-experiences the trauma in some way, perhaps through images, dreams, flashbacks, or mental associations. There are marked symptoms of increased anxiety. Dissociative symptoms may also follow. These include (1) a subjective sense of numbing, detachment, or absence of emotional response; (2) decreased awareness, dazedness; (3) the world seeming like a stage or having a two-dimension feel to it; (4) the person perceiving that he or she is not real; and (5) amnesia.

Permanent Insanity

Investigators who reach zero Sanity points go permanently insane. "Permanently" may mean a game year or a lifetime. In real life, an asylum patient stays in an institution an average of four years and some months. In the game, the duration of permanent insanity is entirely at the keeper's discretion.

No difference between indefinite insanity and permanent insanity exists, except as a prognosis made by an attending psychiatrist and confirmed by a judge. In the real world, all insanity is indefinite insanity, since no one in real life can hope to predict the future as accurately as can a Call of Cthulhu keeper.

Many disorders, especially congenital conditions, offer little hope of recovery. Lovecraft concludes more than one story with the intimation that a lifetime of madness for the

A Hero Gone Mad: An Example

Armed with a shotgun, Harvey Walters enters Castle Kriegs. There he discovers the horribly mutilated corpse of Kurt, his manservant, hanging from a hook. Harvey reels back from the terrible scene. The keeper indicates that this may be a sanity-affecting event. Harvey's SAN characteristic is 45. He has 36 current Sanity points. Harvey's player rolls a 38 on D100, two points too high to succeed.

The keeper requests an Idea roll. Harvey's player rolls D100 and gets a 72, a success. Harvey's intelligence betrays him. He has completely understood that Kurt's mutilated body dangles in front of him.

Harvey's player lowers Harvey's Sanity points to 30. The keeper assures her that the insanity is Mythos-induced, saying that a cult rune has been drawn on the wall. That being so, she also increases Harvey's Cthulhu Mythos by 1 (to a total of 9) and lowers his maximum Sanity points to 90.

Harvey is temporarily insane. The keeper chooses not to roll on either temporary insanity table, instead ruling that Harvey faints for three rounds, then awakens with strong feelings of claustrophobia. Harvey's player says that after he wakes, Harvey goes outside for a while, to calm down. He emerges onto a battlement and breathes in the cool evening air.

Dismal shrieks are heard from above. He looks up and quails—a flock of terrifying winged things! (The keeper describes them as "gigantic, squawking, stinking winged things with glinting claws.") The keeper knows they are byakhee, but Harvey has never seen such things. Still feeling claustrophobic, he grits his teeth and shrinks back into the shallow mouth of the doorway, trying to hide. The door is firmly locked from within, so this is no opportunity for real escape.

The byakhee flap hideously not twenty feet overhead. Harvey's player must make another Sanity roll, since these things have a Sanity loss to encounter. This time the

result of his roll is 54, which is another miss. The Sanity loss is 1/1D6 for byakhee, the keeper knows, but because there are many byakhee, the keeper rules that Harvey must lose the full 6 Sanity points possible—6 points. Had there been only one byakhee, Harvey's player could have rolled 1D6 and the Sanity point loss might have been smaller.

When play began, Harvey had 36 Sanity points. He has now lost 12 Sanity points in rapid succession. Since that is more than a 20% loss in a reasonable interval of time, Harvey now goes indefinitely insane. The keeper may now choose an insanity. He elects for something relatively simple to play, a phobia, figuring that this will not be Harvey's last brush with emotional upset.

The keeper halts the action for a moment, to talk over the situation with Harvey's player. She suggests that the attack from above has reinforced Harvey's claustrophobia. The keeper (who had been thinking that zoophobia was not a good solution anyway) quickly agrees: severe claustrophobia is the choice. The player changes Harvey's current Sanity points to 24, adds another point to Cthulhu Mythos (now at 10), and lowers maximum Sanity points to 89. Play resumes.

Harvey's players states that her investigator views the swarm of winged things as a lowering dome of flesh that threatens to pin Harvey inside it forever. Harvey is frantic. The byakhee do not attack, but the frenzied investigator lets loose with both barrels of his shotgun. The keeper says that Harvey's panic prohibits proper aim, and rules that the pellets whiz harmlessly past the creatures and do no damage. The sudden roar from the gun startles them, though, and they flap up from the battlements far into the sky.

Harvey seizes the moment to bolt from the doorway, and after a panicky search finds steps winding down to the valley below. The next morning he is found beside a road, trembling with cold and fear.

narrator will follow. Every keeper must work out what end-point of madness satisfies his or her game.

Now and then a quiet release might be made from a local asylum. Some thin, unnaturally pallid person, almost unrecognizable after soul-wracking terrors, can walk shyly into downtown Arkham or elsewhere, cast keen eyes about, and attempt to plumb the surrounding darkness, but no player should count on such privilege as a right.

Playing Insanity

The threat of insanity in the Call of Cthulhu rules characterizes the Mythos in a way which allows no compromise. Exposed to it, few sane humans freely choose the Mythos, for the Mythos is intrinsically loathsome and foul. The connection of Sanity points and Cthulhu Mythos points emphasizes the power of the Mythos, which corrupts and ruins by proximity and association. The sanity rules prove to us our own fragility. All that which we thought strong becomes delusory and false, while madness sometimes becomes a necessary condition for truth. Humor and laughter around the game table become vital counterbalances. Good feelings promote harmony and cohesion during the darkest moments in the game.

Dealing with the Verge

If an investigator has even one point of Sanity remaining, the player has firm control. The aesthetics of how the player chooses to present a nearly-mad investigator represents the essence of roleplaying. As the investigator weakens, evidence of the weakening should become apparent. Thus near-insanity calls for stronger roleplaying, not for less player control.

Such an investigator should speak about his mental condition, so that the others understand the situation, and can act with due regard and sympathy. It is not good roleplaying to murmur "My guy's Sanity points are low." Such a statement is dull and makes nothing happen. But a player who can vividly describe his investigator's anxiety or terror, and relate how that affects the game, deserves applause.

If an investigator has ten or fewer Sanity points, he or she certainly knows the situation is serious. In such straits in real life, most people would pull back from the action and perhaps put themselves in sanitariums. So should investigators.

The Quality of Insanity

Investigator insanity characterizes the power of the Mythos by causing the investigator to adopt behavior which is limited in what it can achieve, yet expressive and interesting to roleplay. Even an indefinitely-insane investigator does not always have to be parked in a sanitarium, if a good alternative can be negotiated with the keeper. The choice can be serious, or conceivably eccentric and twisted, or even ridiculous, but it should not upset the tenor of the game.

Dangerousness Criteria

When a person seems to be at risk for self harm or for harm to others, and apparently cannot care for himself or herself, a medical doctor can certify that the individual should undergo psychiatric assessment and/or become an involuntary patient. With this affirmation, often of a comprehensive nature, the state can hold an individual for observation and potentially for treatment. The duration of institutionalization varies by state, but the term is rarely less than 60 game days if for a legal assessment, and frequently up to 180 days. This fate is most likely for an investigator who attempts bodily assault or murder without apparent motive, or who intelligently shams mental disturbance to avoid serious criminal charges. The doctor also can revoke the capacity to manage personal finances, the right to drive an automobile, the right to make treatment decisions, and so on.

DR. SHINY IS IN: AN EXAMPLE

Arrested after breaking into a construction site and attempting to steal dynamite, Harvey Walters keeps babbling about saving the world from the Cthulhu cult and the forces of the Mythos, especially the evil wizard Carl Stanford. The court decides to have Harvey assessed by a local psychiatrist. Dr. Shiny listens carefully during an interview, then decides to make Harvey an involuntary patient. (1) Harvey poses a risk to others, in the person of Carl Stanford; (2) Harvey poses a danger to himself, in stealing the dynamite and blasting caps; and (3) Harvey has a psychiatric disorder, in his delusions concerning cultists and the Cthulhu Mythos. During his history-taking, Dr. Shiny learns that recently Harvey has been in five car accidents involving chases, as well as one hit-and-run. Of the last, Harvey explains that he had to run over an evil cultist. Tsk-tsk! Dr. Shiny therefore also declares Harvey unfit to drive. But he finds that Harvey is financially competent, able to explain all his assets and how he earns money, and so Harvey retains the right to continue to manage his own financial affairs. Nonetheless, Harvey Walters is committed to the institute for assessment.

A few nights later, Harvey escapes from the institute and heads toward Arkham. Naturally Dr. Shiny wants to protect all involved, so he notifies the police. He also calls Carl Stanford regarding the escape. "Yes, Mr. Stanford, Harvey may be dangerous . . . ."

As a minor example, suppose that an investigator shows insanity by obsessively insisting on wearing two hats day and night. He argues that were he not to do so, his head would be unprotected if he tipped his hat to a lady while the sky was falling. Since the hats can be seen, keeper characters freely notice and comment or criticize the foible. In defense, perhaps all the investigators begin to wear two hats. No restaurant will seat them, since their behavior is so

Insanity & Treatment

Medications and Treatments in the 1920s and 1930s

Medications

Paraldehyde: a cyclic ether, introduced in 1882 as a hypnotic. It is an effective treatment for alcohol withdrawal symptoms, anxiety, and insomnia. It is metabolized in the lungs, and has an offensive taste and ubiquitous odor.

Barbiturates: introduced in 1903 as a sedative. Hypnotic drugs of first choice until the 1960s, when benzodiazipines were introduced. Barbiturates have a high potential for abuse. Used for anxiety, insomnia, and apprehension. Overdoses are frequently fatal. Intoxication symptoms include confusion, drowsiness, irritability, hyporeflexia, ataxia, and nystagmus.

Reserpine: historically, the first antipsychotic drug. It is a constituent of the shrub rauwolfia, which is native to India, Africa, and South America, and used in folk medicines for centuries. It was used in the 1920s, but the paper describing its effectiveness in treating mania and hypertension was written in 1931.

Treatments

Acupuncture: an ancient Chinese treatment, acupuncture is the stimulation of specific points of the body with a twisting needle. The stimulation is associated with specific points which relieve certain symptoms and are identified with certain organs. Chinese doctors have sworn this treatment is effective for a variety of disorders, and modern psychiatrists say it may have some effect in treating some depression and substance dependence (e.g., nicotine, caffeine, cocaine, heroin).

Insulin Coma Therapy: introduced in 1933. It was thought that some schizophrenics who went into a coma appeared to have decreased symptoms. Insulin was used to induce a coma lasting 15-60 minutes. The risk of death or cognitive impairment was high. The treatment was abandoned in the 1950s, with the introduction of antipsychotic medication.

Carbon Dioxide Therapy: introduced in 1929. Patients inhaled carbon dioxide, resulting in abreaction (verbal discharge of emotion) with severe motor excitement after removing the breathing mask. The treatment was used for neurotic patients. It was always considered a dubious treatment, and was soon abandoned.

Continuous Sleep Treatment: a symptomatic method of treatment in which the patient is sedated with a variety of drugs in order to induce twenty hours of sleep a day, sometimes for as long as three weeks in severely agitated patients. Klaesi introduced the name in 1922 and used barbiturates to obtain deep narcosis. The treatment is no longer used.

Hypnosis: originated by Mesmer (1734-1815). The term hypnosis originated with Baird, in the 1840s. In the late 19th century the French neurologist Jean-Martin Charcot studied it further. Sigmund Freud, who studied with Charcot, used hypnosis early in his career to help patients recover repressed memories. He noted that patients relive traumatic events while under hypnosis, a process known as abreaction. Freud later replaced hypnosis with the technique of free association.

Biological Therapies, 1845-1934

1845: Hashish intoxication proposed as a model of insanity.

1869: Chloral hydrate introduced as a treatment for melancholia and mania.

1875: Cocaine introduced as a treatment in psychiatry (Freud). Stopped once its addictive properties became evident.

1882: Paraldehyde introduced.

1892: Research with morphine, alcohol, ether, and paraldehyde in normal persons (Kraepelin).

1903: Barbiturates introduced.

1917: Psychosis of syphilis treated with malaria fever therapy (Wagner-Jauregg).

1922: Barbiturate-induced coma (Klaesi).

1927: Insulin shock for schizophrenia (Sakel).

1931: Reserpine introduced for treatment of schizophrenia (Sen and Bose).

1934: Pentylenetetrazol-induced convulsions (Meduna).

Present-Day Medications and Treatments

Medications

Antipsychotics: a variety of drugs used for the treatment of schizophrenia and other psychotic disorders. Drugs include chlorpromazine, thioridazine, haloperidal, and newer or specialized ones such as risperidone and clozapine. These drugs are also called neuroleptics, and they can have motor abnormality side effects such as restlessness and erratic body movements. They take a few weeks to begin to reverse the psychosis, but any sedational effects are dose-dependent from the beginning. Stopping the drug in a chronic psychotic condition results in the patient re-entering the psychotic state.

Antidepressants: used to treat depressive symptoms, usually in major depressive episodes. These include Elavil and other tricyclic drugs, Parnate and other monoamine oxidase inhibitors, and Prozac and other selective serotonin reuptake inhibitors. It often takes a month or six weeks to begin to treat a major depressive episode. If the drug is stopped before the episode is over (six months to a year), the patient re-experiences the symptoms.

Mood Stabilizers: used in bipolar disorders, especially in manic phases, these drugs acts as an umbrella to prevent the moods of a person with this illness from swinging too high or low. The classic drug is lithium, followed by various anticonvulsants such as carbamazapine, valproic acid, and gaba-pentin. Lithium can be very toxic, and if taken as an overdose (or if a person becomes dehydrated, etc.), the person can enter into seizures and coma.

Anxiolytics: sedatives used to treat anxiety symptoms. The first ones used were barbiturates such as secobarbital, but they were highly addictive. They were abandoned for benzodiazipes (Valium, etc.), which are addictive as well, but to a lesser degree, and without so many side effects. These drugs are often sold as street drugs, under many names ("Red Devils" is a street term for secobarbital).

Many Others: for movement disorders, beta-blockers, anticholinergics; for dementia, Aracept; for eating disorders, mood stabilizers and antidepressants; for opiod addiction, methadone weaning; and so forth.

Treatments

Electroconvulsive Therapy: seizure inducements have been used to treat psychosis since the 16th century. Electroconvulsive therapy (ECT) was introduced in 1934, first with injections of camphor to produce seizures, and then with electrically induced seizures in 1938. Alternating currents of electricity are passed through the patient's head between two electrodes that are placed over the temples. This causes unconsciousness and seizures. Though ECT produced good results, it also produced such violent seizures as to routinely fracture patients' bones! With the advent of anaesthesia and paralysis drugs in the modern era, patients avoid this problem. In the United States, ECT treats depressive disorders, manic episodes, and other serious disorders in 50,000 to 100,000 patients annually. The main side effect is that patients suffer from short-term memory loss, and often they entirely lose the memories of the hours or days connected with ECT.

Light Therapy (Phototherapy): used to treat mood symptoms coinciding with seasonal changes. A bright artificial light bathes the patient every day as long as the symptoms last. Response occurs in a few days, the only side effects being occasional headaches, eye strain, or nervousness.

Psychosurgery: surgical modification of the brain, including lobotomies and cingulotomies. This extreme procedure was widespread in the 1940s and 1950s, then nearly abandoned when antipsychotic drugs were introduced. It is resorted to now only when all else fails.

Biological Therapies, 1936-Present

1936: Frontal lobotomies (Moniz).

1938: Electroconvulsive therapy (ECT) begun (Cerletti and Bini).

1940: Phenytoin introduced as an anticonvulsant (Putnam).

1943: Lysergic acid diethylamide (LSD) synthesized (Hofmann).

1949: Lithium introduced as mood stabilizer.

1952: Chlorpromazine introduced as antipsychotic.

1955-1958: Tricyclics and monoamine oxidase inhibitors introduced as anti-depressants.

1960: Chlordiazepoxide introduced (minor tranquilizers, benzodiazipines).

1960-present: Introduction of newer and target anxiolytics, antipsychotics, antidepressants, light therapy, and a plethora of other therapies.

Today: New drugs constantly are being moved through the R&D, testing, and approval process. These new therapies are big business.

Present-Day Mental Disorders

For more information about the elements in this outline, see the referenced pages in the Mental Disorders chapter of the Keeper's Lore section. The Chaosium book *Taint of Madness* also contains a great deal of information concerning insanity and treatments, written on a historical basis. This outline is an incomplete summary, especially in that it ignores childhood disorders.

Many psychiatric terms used in the outline were coined recently, and lack the color and flavor of the language in earlier eras. In the 1930s and earlier, many disorders would have been described carefully on an individual basis but recorded merely as "anxiety" or "psychosis", and might not have been evaluated as separate disorders.

1) Schizophrenia & Other Psychotic Disorders (p. 114)
    Schizophrenia
    Brief Psychotic Disorder
    Shared Delusional Disorder (*Folie à deux*)

2) Mood Disorders (p. 114)
    Depression
    Mania
    Bipolar Disorders (Manic-Depression)

3) Substance-related Disorders (pp. 114-115)

4) Anxiety Disorders (pp. 115-116)
    Generalized Anxiety Disorder
    Agoraphobia
    Obsessive Compulsive Disorder
    Post-traumatic Stress Disorder
    Simple Phobia and Mania

5) Somatoform Disorders (p. 116)
    Somatization Disorder
    Conversion Disorder
    Hypochondriasis
    Body Dysmorphic Disorder

6) Dissociative Disorders (p. 116)
    Dissociative Amnesia
    Dissociative Fugue
    Dissociative Indentity Disorder (MPD)

7) Psychosexual Disorders (p. 117)

8) Eating Disorders (p. 117)

9) Sleep Disorders (p. 117)

10) Impulse Control Disorders (p. 117)
    Intermittent Explosive Disorder
    Kleptomania
    Pyromania
    Pathological Gambling

11) Personality Disorders (p. 117)

12) Other Disorders (p. 117)

uncouth. That two-hatted madman never left the game—the game widened to accommodate him.

A player may try to act out too many elements of his investigator's insanity. If that gets in the way of the game, the keeper must quash the interruption. Not to do so would be unfair to the other players.

This edition of the rules offers a more realistic version of the gamut of insanity. That is useful information from which to start, but information should not control the direction of the game. Waste no time trying to reproduce a particular disorder: let the way your investigator handles lengthy insanity evolve. It will, over time.

Treatment of Insanity

Temporary insanity ends quickly enough that schedules of treatment are entirely pointless. On the other hand, treatment of permanent insanity mostly has no meaning, since by definition the character will never recover, no matter how good the facility. Temporary insanity concludes soon enough that one merely need protect the sufferer from further upset or harm. Similarly, permanent insanity is essentially beyond treatment because its boundaries and duration are determined solely by the keeper. Only indefinite insanity offers real scope for intervention and treatment.

After 1D6 game months, therefore, safe from further trauma and with the agreement of the keeper, the indefinitely insane character finds enough mental balance to re-enter the world. Three sorts of care might have helped to get the character to this point. In choosing among them, keeper and player should consider the character's resources, his/her friends and relatives, and how wisely he or she has behaved in the past.

Private Care

The best care available is at home or in some friendly place where nursing can be tender, considerate, and undistracted by the needs of competing patients. If Psychoanalysis or psychiatric medications are available, roll D100 for each game month that one or the other is used. A result of 01-95 is a success; add 1D3 Sanity points for Psychoanalysis or psychiatric medications, whichever (but not both) is used. On a result of 96-00, the analyst fumbles or the character rebels against taking the drugs. The character loses 1D6 Sanity points, and no progress is made during the next game month.

Institutionalization

The next-best care is commitment to an insane asylum. Asylums may be said to have an advantage over home care in that they are relatively cheap or even a free service provided by the state. But in any of the game eras, these institutions are of uneven quality, and some may be potentially harmful. Some are creative places of experiment and advanced therapy, while others merely offer rude confinement. Presently, in the United States, most institutions are full or accessible only to the criminally insane. In any era, concentrated and nourishing treatment by strangers is rare.

Supervised activity, manual therapy, psychiatric medications, and hydrotherapy are frequent, as is electroconvulsive treatment today. Psychoanalysis is unavailable, and sometimes an institution can convey an uncaring sense that undermines the useful effects of psychiatric medications, leaving the character with a sense of anger and loss, and likely to be distrustful of outpatient support once he or she has left the institution. Roll D100. A result of 01-95 is a suc-cess; add 1D3 Sanity points for psychiatric medications. On a result of 96-00, the character rebels against taking the drugs. He or she loses 1D6 Sanity points, and no progress can be made during the next game month.

Wandering and Homeless

The investigator becomes a wandering derelict, struggling for survival. The wanderer gains no Sanity points unless able to join a group of the homeless, and finds at least one friend among them. To find a friend, roll equal to or less than current Sanity + POW on D100 each game month. If a friend appears, add 1 Sanity point per game month.

Each game month, roll D100 for survival. On a result of 01-95, the character survives. On a result of 96-00, the character dies of disease, exposure, or murder. ∎

A Psychiatric Glossary for the Present Day

Affect—the external expression of a patient's mood (sadness, anger, joy, fear). May be inconsistent with patient's mood, depending on the disorder.

Anorexia—loss or decrease of appetite.

Catatonia—various strong motor anomalies, for instance *catatonic stupor* (slowed activity to the point of immobilization); *cera flexibilitas* (the person can be molded into strange postures that are maintained), and *catatonic excitement* (agitated, purposeless movements).

Compulsion—the need to repeat an act repetitively, including various personal rituals, dipsomania, kleptomania, nymphomania, satyriasis, trichotillomania (pulling out hair), etc.

Delirium—a reversible syndrome of bewilderment, restlessness, confusion, and disorientation, associated with fear and hallucinations, all caused by some underlying medical condition.

Delusion—a firmly fixed false belief, one not based in reality. It can be bizarre, as in schizophrenia, or systematized as in delusional disorders.

Dementia—a loss of cognitive function, often first manifesting in memory loss.

Depersonalization—subjective feeling of being unreal, or unfamiliar to self.

Derealization—a subjective feeling that the environment is strange or unreal; for instance, feeling the world to be a stage or a two-dimensional painting.

Dissociation—confusion in the unitary sense of self and identity.

Formication—the feeling that insects are crawling all over one's body, a tactile hallucination caused by cocaine and delirium tremens.

Hallucination—a perception of a sensory stimulus in the absence of sensory stimulus.

Illusion—the misperception of a sensory stimulus; for instance, seeing the rustling branches of a tree as tentacles.

Logorrhea—copious, coherent, logical speech.

Mania—a mood characterized by elation and increased activity.

Mood—a pervasive feeling that is experienced internally.

Neurosis—this term refers to the theory of intrapsychic conflicts resulting in symptoms of depression, anxiety, etc. The neurotic patient is in relatively good mental health compared to a schizophrenic.

Noesis—a revelation in which immense illumination occurs in association with a sense that one has been chosen to lead and command.

Obsession—an idea or thought that constantly intrudes into consciousness.

Paranoia—persistent, consistent, plausible, and ingenious delusions of persecution or jealousy. New information always seems to support the increasing threat of some great conspiracy. Paranoia is more a symptom than a disorder, as it can appear in schizophrenia, mania, etc.

Psychosis—symptoms consisting of thoughts and perceptions that are out of touch with reality.

Somnambulism—sleepwalking.

Somnolence—abnormal drowsiness.

Synthesia—sensation caused by another sensation; for instance, seeing sound.

Tic—involuntary spasmodic motor movement.

Trailing Phenomenon—perceptual abnormality associated with hallucinogens in which moving objects are seen in a series of discrete discontinuous images.

Trance—focused attention and altered consciousness, usually seen in hypnosis, dissociative disorders, and ecstatic religious experiences.

EXAMPLE OF PLAY

Portraying a Call of Cthulhu game and including use of some of the game mechanics which have already been explained.

The era is the 1920s. The investigators are trying to find out why Boss Morgan, a notorious gangland figure, has vanished. Notice that though the players have different ways of referring to their characters, the keeper easily sorts out their statements, and feels no need for consistency.

KEEPER: Well, what's your plan?

PAULA: Let's sneak around Boss Morgan's house, looking for clues. *All the investigators agree to Paula's plan.*

JOE: Let's go! I'll drive us over in my Hupmobile. Is there anyone on the street? We're leaving at midnight.

KEEPER: Nobody is in sight.

CATHY: My private eye Jake can pick the lock on the back door. *The players agree to the plan.*

PAULA: I'll keep watch.

ARNOLD: I'll stay in the car for now—my investigator is still very nervous.

JOE: I'll go with Paula.

KEEPER: Paula, make a Listen roll.

PAULA: I succeeded.

KEEPER: You hear the house's front door quietly open. And you get a check for your Listen skill.

PAULA: Right. *She makes a check on her sheet.* I'm going to try to hide behind the garbage cans. *She rolls D100.* My Hide roll worked. What happens?

KEEPER: Since it's night, and there are no street lamps near, you can't see much. A hulking figure leaves the house and creeps towards the street. When it reaches the middle of the street, it pulls up a manhole cover and drops inside. You hear a splash. *The keeper makes a dubiously liquid sound.*

PAULA: Did he lock the door behind him?

KEEPER: Not only is it not locked, it's wide open.

PAULA: I'll sneak back and tell the others. Oh, and don't I get a check for my Hide?

KEEPER: No, it's too dark to matter. The rest of you, Paula told you that the front door is open.

JOE and **CATHY** together: Let's go inside.

KEEPER: What do you do, Arnold?

ARNOLD: Are you kidding? My professor go in there? No way.

CATHY: He can stand guard while the rest of us go inside.

ARNOLD: All alone? He's coming inside.

KEEPER: It's very dark inside.

PAULA: Joe, let me use your flashlight. I'll take the lead. Everyone else keep theirs doused—we don't want to be seen from the street.

KEEPER: You are in the bungalow's hallway. You can go left through an arch into the living room, or right through an open door into a study. In front of you is a stairway leading up. Beneath the stairs is a closed door. Ahead your beam picks up wet patches on the floor, possibly footprints. The water in the patches is dirty and stinking.

PAULA: Where do the footsteps come from?

KEEPER: You can't tell. Make Spot Hidden rolls. *All fail to notice droplets of water on the underside of the stairs banister.* What do you want to do?

PAULA: I'll search the study.

JOE: I'll search the living room.

ARNOLD: The professor checks out the hall closet.

CATHY: Jake looks upstairs.

KEEPER *(Since the group has split up, the keeper now deals individually with each.):* Paula, there are bookshelves here, but only a few books. There are two unlocked filing cabinets, a locked desk, a chair for the desk, and three big leather easy chairs.

PAULA: I'll open the desk first.

KEEPER: It's locked. Make your Locksmith roll or oppose Strength 9 on the Resistance Table.

PAULA: I succeed with my Locksmith.

KEEPER: Fine. Check your Locksmith skill. Now, inside the desk you find two things of interest, a sealed envelope marked "Last Will & Testament" and a small ledger which is titled "Innsmouth Shipping Co." Do you want to look at them now? *Paula wants to very much, and the keeper turns his attention to Cathy.* Cathy, as Jake gets to the top of the stairs, make a Luck roll.

CATHY: I succeeded.

KEEPER: You feel beads of water underneath the wooden banister, as though water accumulated here after something wet touched the railing.

CATHY: Uh-oh. Jake proceeds cautiously.

KEEPER: There are two bedrooms and a bath on this floor. The door to the right-hand bedroom is open.

CATHY: He peeps in through the open door.

KEEPER: Gore is everywhere. The fully clothed corpse of Boss Morgan is draped over the bed. The top of his head has been torn off and the insides crudely scooped out. You can see all this because a faint green phosphorescence has been tracked over most of the room. Please make a Sanity roll for him.

CATHY: Ooops, I failed.

KEEPER: Okay, Jake loses. Roll 1D6. *Cathy rolls: Jake loses 4 Sanity points.* He turns green and gets sick at the gruesome sight, but not before he shouts to alert the others. The rest of you hear Jake scream from upstairs.

ALL: We rush to aid him.

KEEPER: Good. Each of you make a Sanity roll to see the body. *They do, with various results.*

CATHY: After Jake has gotten control of himself, he finds a bathroom and wipes off his trench coat.

KEEPER: What are the rest of you going to do?

JOE: I want to inspect the body closely but without touching it. Also I'm warning the others not to step in the blood.

PAULA: I'm searching the other rooms up here.

ARNOLD: The professor comes with you.

KEEPER: Joe, you can see more of the filthy water splashed over the corpse. Some of it is even inside his brain pan. There are some abrasions on what is left of his face. Try an Idea roll.

JOE: I succeeded. Now what?

KEEPER: Seven feet up the wall is a bloody, watery hand print. Claw marks are visible, and the print is at least eight inches across the palm, though the fingers are quite stubby. It's not smeared at all, and you can make out the lines of the palm in the print.

JOE: Wow! I'm hissing for Paula, Jake, and the professor to get in here. Does he have his camera with him, Arnold?

ARNOLD: Dang it! I knew the professor forgot something! Uh, he presses a sheet of paper from a notebook against the print for a copy.

KEEPER: He gets the print. Arnold, your professor also notices strange symbols on the opposite wall. As he studies them, they seem to swirl hypnotically.

ARNOLD: Oho! He wants a closer look.

KEEPER: He doesn't have the time. Everyone try Listen rolls for your investigators. *Joe, Arnold, and Cathy fail. Paula succeeds.* Paula, you hear a clanging noise in the street. The rest of you hear nothing.

PAULA: I wonder what that could be? I hope it's not the manhole cover banging down!

KEEPER: The front door suddenly slams closed, and you can hear someone stomping up the stairs. *The keeper stomps on the floor and hunches his shoulders.*

ARNOLD: My professor is jumping out the window.

PAULA: I'm shining my light out the bedroom door, trying to see what is coming.

CATHY: Jake pulls out his .38 snub-nose and looks over Paula's shoulder.

JOE: I'm cowering behind Jake and Paula but I'm getting out my trench knife, just in case.

KEEPER: Arnold, your investigator's back is turned, so he can't see what the others do. Please step into the next room for a moment while I describe the scene. *Arnold obligingly goes to the kitchen for another can of soda.*

The KEEPER continues: Shuffling into the room is a ghastly parody of a man. It stands almost eight feet tall, with deformed, twisted extremities. Its face is a mass of wrinkles. No features are visible. Its sickly brown-green skin is loose and strips of decaying flesh flap from its limbs. It drips the filthy brown water seen earlier. You three try Sanity rolls for 1/1D10 points each.

JOE: I made my roll successfully.

CATHY: I blew it, but Jake lost only 3 Sanity points.

PAULA: Uh-oh! I'm really scared! I lost 9 points.

KEEPER: Let's see. *He examines her investigator's sheet.* Paula, your investigator isn't indefinitely insane, since you had 76 Sanity points, but unless you roll higher than his INT x5 on D100, he's going to faint dead away. *Paula rolls a 04 and her investigator faints.*

The KEEPER continues: Since Paula's investigator was holding the flashlight, it's now rolling on the floor, flashing wildly about the room. And Arnold's professor has turned around: he has seen, as he would had he checked earlier, that the windows are barred with iron gratings. The only way outside seems to be past the Thing.

ALL (*in confusion*): I'm trying to pound open the bars with a chair! Where's my flashlight? Does anyone know what this thing is? I'm shooting at its face. Help! Help!

Do the grills on the windows unlock and swing back? Do the symbols on the wall actually represent a Gate? Does the monster attack? Did Paula's investigator remember to bring along the ledger and legal documents he found? Does Jake's .38 revolver affect the monster? ■

MAGIC

Wherein are considered the magical forces of the Cthulhu Mythos, its books of ghastly lore, the casting of spells, and warnings and admonishments pertaining thereto.

Whether or not investigators gain much by knowing Mythos magic, they always find Mythos magic inconvenient to apply. When they do use Mythos spells, even for benevolent purposes, they lose Sanity points in consequence. Few Mythos spells can be quickly performed. Spells learned in the course of published scenarios may prove useful only in the course of a single adventure. Consequently, though all players are invited to study this chapter, only keepers are likely to get much advantage from it.

The magic of the Cthulhu Mythos is traditional in scope, centering on perilous summonings of horrible entities and the desperate manipulation of inimical forces. Spells are formally constructed. One wrong word or gesture can cancel an effect. Investigators learn spells by poring over cryptic manuscripts and ancient books of lore. Artifacts can be enchanted. Though this is rare for investigators, cultists and sorcerers also may be taught by their fellows and, through vision and visitation by the great and unseemly things that lurk beyond the normal senses, the dread Great Old Ones and the Outer Gods.

For human characters, Mythos magic is rare and difficult to use. Spells must be approached warily, since often what they do and what they cost is utterly unknown. For investigators, Mythos magic can be a dangerous trap, for in using it investigators lose Sanity points and add Cthulhu Mythos, more and more becoming like those whom they seek to defeat. Mythos magic bewilders, shocks, disorients, and debilitates its human practitioners. With enough exposure, the psychic contradictions involved in using this magic drives humans insane.

In the game, investigators mostly experience magic from the outside, as the targets of it, or by witnessing the effect of spells cast by someone else. An investigator rarely becomes a mage, since the requisite knowledge and experience usually leads to madness first.

In This Chapter

This chapter discusses spells, enchantments, and the books of the Cthulhu Mythos. It tells how to learn about such things, and what then to do with the knowledge. It discusses the occult versus the magical, and tells ways to increase characteristic POW.

This chapter does not contain spells. Hundreds of Mythos spells are in the Grimoire, found in the Reference section of this book, far more than any investigator could ever learn. (See the Grimoire chapter, starting on p. 191, for the complete spell listing.)

What Is Magic?

"Gilman had some terrible hints from the dreaded Necronomicon *of Abdul Al-hazred . . . and the suppressed* Unaussprechlichen Kulten *of von Junzt to correlate with his abstract formulae on the properties of space and the linkage of dimensions known and unknown."* —H.P. Lovecraft, "The Dreams in the Witch House".

After World War I, astronomers confirmed that the thirty or forty thousand light years of easily observed stars and dust nearest us comprised only a minor corner of the universe. There was not one Milky Way, as astronomers had once believed, but thousands and millions of galaxies, most so faint and so distant that the truth of the nebulae had long been argued, but never before solved. The notion of island universes—galaxies, as we now say—was a bombshell. In the 1920s, humanity's perception of the unbounded universe's true size increased by orders of magnitude.

Writing as such discoveries took place, Lovecraft gradually evolved a background myth incorporating them, and added some flavorings from Einstein and Planck. These new "universes", so he seems to have speculated, were truly islands. Their separation included their natural laws. Isolated by hundreds of thousands or millions of light years, the stuff of life could differ wildly. Very quickly, these islands also took on a Riemannian association of existing in or being connected to other dimensions.

The magic of the Cthulhu Mythos is the unifying logic of this universe of universes. The magic works everywhere. It models and defines the greater reality; it is the ultimate expression of natural law, the will of the Outer Gods made palpable, and the arbiter of time, space, and matter.

In comparison, earthly science and religion seem of little avail. It is apparent that we understand far less than we flatter ourselves as knowing. Is imperfection in what we believe or in how we have come to believe it? Perhaps there is a poverty in our souls or our equations that forestalls ultimate knowledge and revelation. The Mythos mocks human pretensions.

Mythos Tomes

In Lovecraft, one usually learns Mythos magic by finding and following written instructions. The volumes of arcane lore mentioned by the Lovecraft Circle writers represent the intellectual invasion of the Cthulhu Mythos.

In particular, these ancient manuscripts and suppressed publications included recipes for the admission or the return of the Great Old Ones and the Outer Gods, as in Lovecraft's classic, "The Dunwich Horror". At least by implication, such writings also indicated how to force away or dispel those entities. This breakthrough information is nowhere else available.

It takes time to learn, even from textbooks which have been carefully written and specially laid out just for that purpose. Studying the crabbed, idiosyncratic, and infinitely more difficult Mythos books takes much more time. Successfully learning to cast a specific spell from such a book demands more time yet.

Consider: these fat books are clumsily scribed by men whose sanity has been erased by the horror of their experiments and trials. The text is often handwritten in cramped archaic script. Many manuscripts are not even in a known alphabet—some are older than time, in languages long lost; others are written in occult ciphers to stymie witch-finders or the Inquisition, and now must be cracked before the would-be reader can ponder the black truths they conceal.

Even if a sorcerer wrote for others who were familiar with the arcane and occult, he wrote for adepts and cultists, not laymen. He would see no reason to explain, and would employ strange terms and ideas without explaining them. Valuable annotations might be made by a succession of owners, each perhaps in a different language or with a different aim, and some or all in error.

The present-day apparatus of scholarship does not exist in such books. There are no indices, no glossaries, no tables of contents, no careful definitions. There may not be numbered pages, chapters, paragraphs, punctuation, or even breaks between words.

Different books will have been written centuries apart from each other, by authors of different experience and different cultures. These writers, of widely varying philosophical persuasion, inevitably use different technical vocabularies. One must learn the jargon anew for each book. Who would comprehend such a book must read deeply, considering every syllable and comparing ideas and procedures with related books.

Example: Harvey Walters notices a reference to "Arthur's Grail" in an arcane book. His player fails the requested Occult roll to remember the reference. Harvey doesn't realize that the Holy Grail of Arthurian lore echoes the Black Cauldron of Celtic myth, and so he doesn't think of the Black Cauldron resuscitating dead men boiled in it, or that it came from Hell. Then his player misses an Idea roll, and Harvey does not realize for months that the phrase "he drank from Arthur's Grail" might refer to somebody raised by the Resurrection spell. And if Harvey knows nothing of the Resurrection spell, that phrase might remain meaningless to him forever.

A book may be physically difficult to read. Many are of enormous age and must be handled with care. Some are delicate: the reader must wear thin gloves and turn the pages with padded forceps. Only in the present do photocopy machines exist with which to make quick and accurate copies.

Some books are of great length. They are repetitive and boring, poorly written and obscure in style. Studying such stuff is tiring and may seem pointless. A dulled reader misses facts and allusions, so study must halt until the mind is refreshed. This also takes time.

A formula has been derived to determine an individual's reading times for a particular Mythos volume. Factors include the investigator's intelligence, education, language, Cthulhu Mythos or Occult skill percentage, and a rating for the library in which the tome is studied. See the Keeper's Lore chapter, "Research Modifiers", p. 125.

Describing Mythos Tomes

A spread of pages in this chapter summarizes information concerning the books of the Cthulhu Mythos most often mentioned in the fiction. These short, systematic entries give the impression of total understanding. Do not be deceived! Sorcerer madmen do not belong to the Book-of-the-Month Club. Their work is never proofed or marketed, and no editor ever has the chance to take aside the author of such a book and say, "Exactly what did you mean here?" Get the game information from those summaries, but the keeper and players also must wrestle with the reality of them as books.

Some Mythos volumes are recent enough in origin to have been printed with movable type. Those editions were short press runs, and upon publication copies often were sought out and destroyed, as was *The King in Yellow*. Surviving copies often have been ill-treated by the crazed or malicious, or rebound to disguise their blasphemous contents. Bound manuscripts were never regularized by typesetting and printing, of course, and their wavering, blotted handwriting may be wholly incomprehensible for pages at a time, a situation remedied only by great dedication and scholarship.

Tome Record Sheets

If precise records are of interest, consider a separate entry for each Mythos or occult tome which an investigator reads or has access to. Entries might include the following.

■ title / author / edition

■ language / era of publication or creation

■ Cthulhu Mythos +

■ Sanity points to skim / Sanity points to read

■ spells appearing in book

■ book's physical condition, size, binding, damage, completeness, etc.

■ which investigators have read the book

Examples of Occult Books

Owners of Mythos tomes are likely also to own occult volumes. An occult book always adds at least one point to the Occult skill after reading. There are thousands of occult volumes. This page is a small sampling.

Reading an occult book usually costs no Sanity, but not always—it might be lost because of dullness, complexity, length, or incomprehensibility. Otherwise the same sorts of rules apply to occult books as to Mythos books, if occult books come into play. No indication for time of reading has been given; the keeper should assign the relative interval he or she deems appropriate—2D6 weeks, 4D6 weeks, or 8D6 weeks. Keepers are free to add a Mythos spell in a margin or on a flyleaf if they think it appropriate, but (with the exception of the *Malleus Maleficarum*) the tone of these volumes is anything but evil or dangerous.

BEATUS METHODIVO—*in Latin, attributed to St. Methodius of Olympus, c. 300 AD.* Of Gnostic complexion, this work is written as a prophetic Apocalypse. It foresees the history of the world. It recounts how Seth sought a new country in the east and came to the country of the initiates, how the children of Cain instituted a system of black magic in India, more. Relatively short. *No Sanity loss; Occult +2 percentiles*. No spells.

THE EMERALD TABLET—*trans. into many languages, apparently from a Phoenician original, author or authors unknown, c. 200 AD.* The central alchemical text for medieval Europe, mercifully short but as cryptic and allusive as the *Tao Te Ching* of classical China. *No Sanity loss, though obsessive study of it could be a symptom of disorder; Occult +1 percentile*. No spells.

THE GOLDEN BOUGH—*in English, by Sir George Frazer, 1890, in two volumes.* An expanded thirteen-volume edition was published 1911-1915. A classic work of anthropology exploring the evolution of magical, religious, and scientific thought. An abridged version is available in most U.S. libraries. *Sanity loss 0/1D2; Occult +5 percentiles*. No spells.

I CHING—*in classical Mandarin and many trans., including the Wilhelm/Baynes into English, 1950, long a version preferred by English-speaking occultists.* One of the Five Classics of Confucian China. A subtle and poetical system of divination easily applied but capable of deep situational allusion. Contemplation of meaning is nearly irresistible, and therefore it is handy to turn to in a session, but the book is so good that the user risks overpowering the sense of the campaign. *No Sanity loss; Occult +8 percentiles*. No spells.

THE KEY OF SOLOMON—*trans. in various languages from Latin; written about the 14th century, but its claimed authorship is by King Solomon.* Composed of two books, the first indicating how to avoid drastic mistakes when dealing with spirits, and the second discussing the magical arts. The complexity of its magic rituals supply plenty of reasons why any spell cast might not succeed. *No Sanity loss; Occult +5 percentiles*. No spells.

MALLEUS MALEFICARUM—"Hammer of Witches". *In Latin, by Jakob Sprenger and Heinrich Kramer, 1486 AD, then many translations.* A guide for inquisitors in the Middle Ages on the identification and torturous persuasion of witches. This terrible book helped send an estimated nine million people to their deaths. The German translation of 1906 has the excellent title *Der Hexenhammer. No Sanity loss; Occult +3 percentiles*. No spells.

ORACLES OF NOSTRADAMUS—*the language varies by quatrain in the original, by Michel de Nostradame* [Nostradamus], *1555-1557*. Contains about a thousand four-line verses, purporting to be prophecies concerning human events up until the year 3797 AD. The prophecies are non-specific and imagistic, lending themselves to all sorts of applications. Numerous interpretations have been made for many of these prophecies. Possibly handy to keepers as an ongoing device in an extended campaign. *No Sanity loss; Occult +1 percentile*. No spells.

PERT EM HRU—"Coming Forth by Day". *Egyptian hieroglyphic version in some two hundred chapters; the "Scroll of Ani" contains most chapters; French and English translations have been published.* Concerns the beatification of the dead, who were imagined as reciting the chapters in order and thereby gaining privileges for their new lives after death. These instructions and magical procedures protect the dead against dangers they face in reaching the other world. Many spells to preserve the mummy against mold, assist in shape-shifting, and assist the dead to become as gods themselves. *No Sanity loss; +3 Occult percentiles*. Contains many related spells from dynastic Egypt.

PRINCIPLES OF NATURE, HER DIVINE REVELATIONS AND A VOICE TO MANKIND—*in English, by Andrew Jackson Davis, New York, 1847.* In which the "Poughkeepsie Seer" writes his "Harmonial Philosophy" as revealed to him by Galen and Swedenborg, prophesying a new dispensation to mankind, though one preceded by a social revolution. *No Sanity loss; Occult +1 percentile*. No spells.

THE WITCH-CULT IN WESTERN EUROPE—*in English, by Dr. Margaret Murray, 1921.* A modern English octavo with dust jacket; many editions and printings since. Connects the so-called covens of the Middle Ages with pre-Christian beliefs surviving as superstitions or in a more organized sense driven underground by the Church. This volume is often found in libraries and bookstores. *No Sanity loss; Occult +1 percentile*. No spells.

THE ZOHAR—*written in Aramaic, many editions and trans. to Latin, German, English, French, etc., by Moses de Leon, 1280 AD.* The fundamental work of medieval Jewish mystical thought, representing the effort to know or to reach God through contemplation and revelation. Long, dense, and difficult. *Sanity loss 1/1D3+1; Occult +7 percentiles*. No spells. ■

Even though each book's summary in the rulebook is uniform, assume that each copy of a Mythos book can be different from its fellows. Though the logic of that potential diminishes for recent books such as *Azathoth and Others*, even then bindings may be broken, pages torn out, and signatures missing or miscollated. Contents may be ink-stained or acid-scarred, pages half-burnt, and the words made illegible or utterly defaced by madmen or by sane men who sought to destroy the dangerous information. Unique information may be written as marginalia or jotted down on note paper and inserted here or there. Invaluable hand-colored plates may be tipped in, or may have been ripped and pinned on some long-burnt wall.

Sorcerers and cultists are not librarians. They are unreasonable and uncharitable. They are unconcerned with the needs of posterity. They intend themselves to live forever.

DISCOVERED EDITIONS

If an original language version is found of a work that until then was known only in translation, then the original version is more informative. Add three percentiles to the *Cthulhu Mythos* + amount. Treat the original edition as another edition. The keeper chooses the book's original language, and can make up its title in that language as well.

If the investigator has already read another edition of the same book, but the new version has a higher *Cthulhu Mythos* +, ignore any difference in Sanity point loss, but add the extra points of Cthulhu Mythos after reading the new version.

If a keeper creates a new Mythos tome for some purpose, he or she should have a name for it, know the language of its composition, know what it looks like, know how many Sanity points are lost in reading or skimming it, know how many Cthulhu Mythos points its comprehension adds, and be able to determine what spells if any can be found within it.

Despite the dangers, investigators will choose to study this or that terrifying book. The process of reading can be leisurely, and can be suspended at any point for as long as need be. "Study" and "reading" are synonymous in this context.

Reading Mythos Books

Any book listed as adding Cthulhu Mythos points therefore takes study to comprehend. In the summaries of Mythos books in this chapter, reading times for books are given in weeks. The keeper should never feel at the mercy of such numbers, and should shrink them or increase them as appropriate. An outstanding academic with pertinent language skills will read a book faster than an earnest but uneducated and disoriented journalist. Time of study need not be consecutive days, weeks, or months.

The keeper indicates when enough time has passed. If in other than the investigator's native language, the investigator needs a successful language roll on D100. With a success, the investigator gets an experience check for that language as well. A language failure means that the reader has been able to skim the book and loses some current Sanity points, but adds no Cthulhu Mythos points and learns no spells.

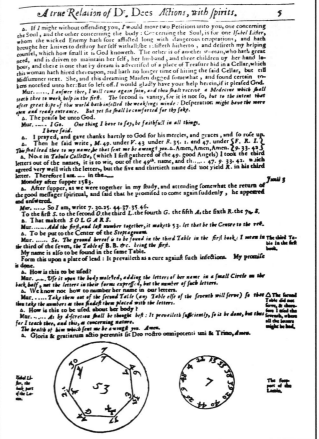

A TYPICAL PAGE FROM AN ELIZABETHAN OCCULT TOME

If a book is written in a language unknown by the investigator, then a translator is needed. What gets translated, how quickly, and how accurately is for the keeper to decide. If the language is unknown or long forgotten, the investigators must come up with a plan for a procedure that convinces the keeper, or the book baffles them.

With success, or if no skill roll is needed, the investigator now comprehends the book. The player adds the stated percentiles of Cthulhu Mythos, lowers maximum Sanity by the same number of points, and subtracts lost current Sanity points. Having read and comprehended the book, the investigator loses nothing more for further readings of it. (However, see "Discovered Editions", further above, for a possible complication.)

Current Sanity points are always lost for successfully reading or skimming a book. The book or manuscript must be in the reader's own language, or the reader must receive a successful language roll, or a third party must reliably translate the book. Unless one of those conditions can be satisfied, the book cannot be read. No Sanity points are lost for looking it. Sanity points are never lost for consulting or rereading a Mythos book which the investigator has already read.

SKIMMING A MYTHOS BOOK

An investigator can skim a book to learn what it is about and to guess at what spells it might contain. Skimming always succeeds if the language can be read.

Major Books of the Mythos 1

This section discusses important human writings that describe some portion of the Cthulhu Mythos. Some of this information is commonly known by bibliophiles, historians, and those in the book trade. Notes about even more additional editions of these writings exist in the *Keeper's Companion*, available from Chaosium. Many other versions of these volumes as well as lesser Mythos volumes exist, as do incidental notebooks, diaries, and letters.

Bulleted entries indicate different versions of the same original. Two dates are noted for three Mythos books: the latter date in each case is the date ascribed in the original story. If available at all, the number of copies listed reflects those known held in public and private collections. More existing copies are very likely.

Dimensions given are traditional, since actual sizes often vary between copies. Folios range from 12.5"x20" to 10" x15". Quartos vary between 10" x12.5" and 7.5" x10". Octavos range between 6.25" x10" and 5" x7.5".

Each entry consists of the title, following by the language of the edition, author or translator, and date of completion or publication. Some dates are conjectural. Descriptive notes then follow. Concluding each entry is the Sanity point loss for skimming and reading the book, and the points of the Cthulhu Mythos skill increase. Likely spells contained in each volume are then noted; keepers are free to add appropriate spells to these lists. The concept of the spell multiplier has been dropped.

These summaries also now include average weeks of study per book. When using such numbers, take into account the individual reader's skills and profession. Use the times given here as comparative indicators of difficulty. Each investigator will study and comprehend a book at a difference rate.

AL- AZIF—see *Necronomicon*

AZATHOTH AND OTHERS—*in English, written by Edward Derby, 1919.* A collection of the Arkham-born poet's early works. Published in Boston in a pocket-sized edition, 3.5" x5.5", and bound in black. About 1400 copies were printed and sold. *Sanity loss 1/1D4; Cthulhu Mythos +4 percentiles; average 1 week to study and comprehend.* Spells: none.

BOOK OF DZYAN—in English, author and trans. unknown, reputedly of ancient origin. Long referred to by theosophist Helena Blavatsky, a copy of this tome has never been verified. Said to be a translation of manuscripts original to Atlantis. Also called the *Stanzas of Dzyan*. Portions of this work was translated as *The Secret Doctrine*, but that includes no spells or other Mythos information. *Sanity loss 1D3/1D6; Cthulhu Mythos +9 percentiles; average 14 weeks to study and comprehend.* Spells: Call Forth Childe of the Woode (Summon/Bind Dark Young), Call Forth Wind Spirit (Summon/Bind Byakhee), Call Forth the Unseen

Walker (Summon/Bind Dimensional Shambler), Dream Vision (Contact Cthulhu).

Book of Eibon
(three versions follow)

- **LIBER IVONIS**—*in Latin, trans. Caius Phillipus Faber, 9th century AD.* Although the original is said to have been written by Eibon, wizard of Hyperborea, no earlier versions than the Latin have been verified. Never printed, six bound manuscript versions have been listed in library collections. *Sanity loss 1D4/2D4; Cthulhu Mythos +13 percentiles; average 36 weeks to study and comprehend.* Spells: Call/Dismiss Azathoth, Call/Dismiss Rlim Shaikorth, Contact Formless Spawn of Zhothaqquah (Tsathoggua), Contact Kthulhut (Cthulhu), Contact Yok Zothoth (Yog-Sothoth), Contact Zhothaqquah (Tsathoggua), Create Barrier of Naach-Tith, Create Gate, Create Mist of Releh, Deflect Harm, Eibon's Wheel of Mist, Enchant Brazier, Enchant Knife, Levitate, Voorish Sign, Wither Limb.

- **LIVRE D'IVON**—*in French, trans. Gaspard du Nord, c. 13th century AD.* Bound, handwritten manuscript of which thirteen specimens, partial or complete, are known to exist. *Sanity loss 1D4/2D4; Cthulhu Mythos +12 percentiles; average 36 weeks to study and comprehend.* Spells: as per *Liber Ivonis*.

- **BOOK OF EIBON**—*in English, trans. unknown, c. 15th century.* A flawed and incomplete translation. Eighteen copies by various hands are known to exist today. *Sanity loss 1D4/2D4; Cthulhu Mythos +11 percentiles; average 32 weeks to study and comprehend.* Spells: as per *Liber Ivonis*, except that Call/Dismiss Rlim Shaikorth, Create Barrier of Naach-Tith, Deflect Harm, and Voorish Sign are absent.

CELAENO FRAGMENTS—*a holographic manuscript in English, by Dr. Laban Shrewsbury, 1915 (1938).* A single copy is known to exist, deposited at Miskatonic U. Library shortly before the author mysteriously disappeared. *Sanity loss 1D4/1D8; Cthulhu Mythos +9 percentiles; average 15 weeks to study and comprehend.* Spells: Brew Space Mead, Call Cthugha, Elder Sign, Enchant Whistle, Summon/Bind Byakhee.

Cthaat Aquadingen
(two versions follow)

- **CTHAAT AQUADINGEN**—*in Latin, author unknown, c. 11-12th century.* A comprehensive study of the deep ones. Three copies of this Latin version exist, identically bound in human skin said to sweat when the humidity drops too low. One is at the British Museum, and the other two are owned by British collectors. *Sanity loss*

1D8/2D8; *Cthulhu Mythos +13 percentiles; average 46 weeks to study and comprehend.* Spells: Bring Forth the Great One (Call/Dismiss Bugg-Shash), Call The Black, Dreams from God (Contact Cthulhu), Dreams from Zattoqua [Tsathoggua], Dreams of the Drowner [Yibb-Tstll], Speak with Sea Children (Contact Deep Ones), Speak with Father Dagon, Speak with Mother Hydra, Speak with God-Child (Contact Star-Spawn of Cthulhu), Nyhargo Dirge (this last spell is a modification of the reversed Resurrection spell used to destroy revenants).

- **CTHAAT AQUADINGEN**—*in Middle English, author and translator unknown, c. 14th century.* A comprehensive study of the deep ones, but in an incomplete and deeply flawed translation. A single bound manuscript is held by the British Museum. *Sanity loss 1D4/2D4; Cthulhu Mythos +6 percentiles; average 29 weeks to study and comprehend.* Spells: Bring Forth the Great One (Call/Dismiss Bugg-Shash), Dreams from God (Contact Cthulhu), Dreams of the Drowner [Yibb-Tstll], Speak with Sea Children (Contact Deep Ones), Speak with Father Dagon, Speak with Mother Hydra, Speak with God-Child (Contact Star-Spawn of Cthulhu).

CTHULHU IN THE NECRONOMICON—*in English, written by Dr. Laban Shrewsbury, 1915 (1938).* Handwritten notes toward an intended book. Deposited at Miskatonic U. Library shortly before the author mysteriously disappeared. Tells of Cthulhu's power to affect men's dreams, warning of a worldwide cult dedicated to the creature's return. *Sanity loss 1D3/1D6; Cthulhu Mythos +6 percentiles; average 14 weeks to study and comprehend.* Spells: Contact Cthulhu, Contact Deep Ones, Elder Sign.

CULTES DES GOULES—*in French, by François-Honore Balfour, Comte d'Erlette, 1702?* Published in 1703 in France (Paris?), in a quarto edition. The Church immediately denounced it. Catalogues a large cult practicing necromancy, necrophagy, and necrophilia in France. Fourteen copies are known to exist, the most recent surfacing in 1906. *Sanity loss 1D4/1D10; Cthulhu Mythos +12 percentiles; average 22 weeks to study and comprehend.* Spells: Black Binding, Call/Dismiss Nyogtha, Call/Dismiss Shub-Niggurath, Contact Ghoul, Resurrection, Shrivelling, Summon/Bind Byakhee, Summon/Bind Dark Young, Voorish Sign.

DE VERMIIS MYSTERIIS—*in Latin, by Ludwig Prinn, 1542.* Black letter folio printed in Cologne, Germany, in the same year. Suppressed by the Church. Fifteen copies have survived. In part discusses the Arab world, and things supernatural there. *Sanity loss 1D6/2D6; Cthulhu Mythos +12 percentiles; average 48 weeks to study and comprehend.* Spells: Contact Byatis, Contact Yig, Create Liao Drug, Create Scrying Window, Create Zombie, Invoke Demon (Summon/Bind Byakhee), Invoke Child of the Goat (Summon/Bind Dark Young), Invoke Invisible Servant (Summon/Bind Star Vampire), Prinn's Crux Ansata, Spirit Transfer, Summon Ghost, Voorish Sign.

ELTDOWN SHARDS—*in English, by Rev. Arthur Brooke Winters-Hall, 1912.* Questionable translation of mysterious hieroglyphs found on clay fragments in southern England, in an edition of 350 pamphlets, 64 pages. Tells of beings who could exchange minds with others across space and time. *Sanity loss 1D4/1D8; Cthulhu Mythos +11 percentiles; average 6 weeks to study and comprehend.* Spell: Contact Yithian.

G'HARNE FRAGMENTS—*in English, by Sir Amery Wendy-Smith, 1919 (1931).* Scholarly study and translation of shards inscribed with curious dot patterns. Discusses the lost city of G'harne in great deal, including its location. The shards were discovered by Windrop in North Africa. The original edition was 958 copies printed at the author's expense as a humble sixteenmo (4.5" x5.75"). *Sanity loss 1D6/1D10; Cthulhu Mythos +10 percentiles; average 12 weeks to study and comprehend.* Spells: Contact Chthonian, Contact Elder Thing, Contact Shudde M'ell, Red Sign of Shudde M'ell.

THE KING IN YELLOW—*in English, trans. unknown, c. 1895.* The original is in French, apparently, but that edition was seized and destroyed by the Third Republic just after publication. The English edition is a thin black octavo volume across the front cover of which is embossed a large Yellow Sign. (The Sign costs 0/1D6 Sanity points to see for the first time only.) The text is an ambiguous, dream-like play which opens readers to madness. *Sanity loss 1D3/1D6+1 ; Cthulhu Mythos +5 percentiles; average 1 week to study and comprehend.* Spells: none.

LIBER IVONIS, LIVRE D'IVON—see *Book of Eibon*

MASSA DI REQUIEM PER SHUGGAY—*in Italian, by Benvenuto Chieti Brodighera, 1768.* An opera score and libretto never published and believe to have been performed only once. Deals with rape, incest, and other degradations. Knowledgeable musicians pronounce portions of it unplayable. Copies are held by the British Museum, the Bibliothéque Nationale in Paris, and probably the Vatican's Z-collection. *Sanity loss 1D3/1D6; Cthulhu Mythos +4 percentiles; average 2 weeks to study and comprehend.* Spells: performed with full chorus and orchestra, Call Azathoth is cast about midway through the third act.

MONSTRES AND THEIR KYNDE—*in English, author unknown, 16th century.* A single folio version of this handwritten book existed, and that was stolen from the British Museum in 1898. Rumors of other copies continue to persist to this day, though none has been verified. Contains a jumble of topics drawn from the *Necronomicon, Book of Eibon*, and a variety of other tomes. Many entities are discussed, including Cthulhu, Yog-Sothoth, and Lloigor, the twin of Zhar. *Sanity loss 1D4/1D8; Cthulhu Mythos +8 percentiles; average 36 weeks to study and comprehend.* Spells: Command Faceless One (Summon/Bind Nightgaunt), Command Ice Demon (Summon/Bind Byakhee), Command Invisible Servant (S/B Star Vampire), Command Night Beast (S/B Hunting Horror), Command Star Walker (S/B Dimensional Shambler), Enchant Altar, Enchant Blade, Enchant Pipes.

continued next page

Major Books of the Mythos II

Nameless Cults

(three versions follow)

- **UNAUSPRECHLICHEN KULTEN**—*in German, by Friedrich Wilhelm von Junzt, 1839.* A quarto, possibly printed in Hamburg. This volume, long referred to as the *Black Book*, tells of von Junzt's connections to various cults and secret societies. Other editions are rumored. Six copies are known to be in major libraries in Europe and America. The original edition boasts the horrific engravings of Gunther Hasse. *Sanity loss 1D8/2D8; Cthulhu Mythos +15 percentiles; average 52 weeks to study and comprehend.* Spells: Address Zhar (Contact Zhar), Approach Brother (Contact Ghoul), Barrier of Naach-Tith, Beckon Great One (Contact Dagon), Call Aether Devil (Contact Mi-Go), Call Forth the Sun (Call/Dismiss Azathoth), Call Forth Cyaegha (Call/Dismiss Cyaegha), Call Forth the Horned Man (Call/Dismiss Nyarlathotep), Call Forth That Which Should Not Be (Call/Dismiss Nyogtha), Call Forth the Woodland Goddess (Call/Dismiss Shub-Niggurath), Command Airy Travelers (Summon/Bind Byakhee), Command the Trees (Summon/Bind Dark Young), Command the Unknown (Call/Dismiss Ghatanothoa), Contact Children of the Deep (Contact Deep Ones), Revivify (Resurrection).

- **NAMELESS CULTS**—*in English, trans. unknown, published 1845.* An unauthorized translation published by Bridewell of England (probably London) in an octavo edition. At least twenty copies are held in various collections. Badly flawed text. *Sanity loss 1D8/2D8; Cthulhu Mythos +12 percentiles; average 48 weeks to study and comprehend.* Spells: as per *Unausprechlichen Kulten*, but most of these spell versions are incomplete or faulty. Roll POW x2 or less on D100 to find a working version of a particular spell.

- **NAMELESS CULTS**—*in English, trans. unknown, published 1909.* An expurgated version of the faulty Bridewell text, published by Golden Goblin Press, New York. Contains only descriptions of spells, not the complete rituals of the earlier editions. With some looking, this edition can be found in used bookstores. *Sanity loss 1D8/2D8; Cthulhu Mythos +9 percentiles; average 30 weeks to study and comprehend.* Spells: none.

The Necronomicon

(five versions)

- **AL-AZIF**—*in Arabic, by Abdul al-Hazrad (Abd al-Azrad), c. 730 AD.* Original form is unknown, but numerous manuscript versions were long circulated between medieval scholars. As early as the 12th century this version was referred to as lost. It is an immense compendium touching on nearly every aspect of the Mythos, and a capable reference on most subjects, including charts and star maps. *Sanity loss 1D10/2D10 Sanity points; Cthulhu Mythos +18 percentiles; 68 weeks to study and comprehend.* Spells: Call/Dismiss Azathoth, Call/Dismiss Cthugha, Call/Dismiss Hastur, Call/Dismiss Nyogtha, Call/Dismiss Shub-Niggurath, Call/Dismiss Yog-Sothoth, Contact Ghoul, Contact Nyarlathotep, Contact Sand Dweller, Dominate, Dread Curse of Azathoth, Dust of Suleiman, Elder Sign, Powder of Ibn-Ghazi, Resurrection, Shrivelling, Summon/Bind Byakhee, Summon/Bind Fire Vampire, Summon/Bind Servitor of the Outer Gods, Voorish Sign.

- **NECRONOMICON**—*in Greek, trans. by Theodoras Philetas, c. 950 AD.* Early manuscript versions are unknown. A small printing in (Florence?) Italy in a folio edition was suppressed by the Church; it lacked any drawings, maps, or charts. Last known copy burned in Salem, 1692. *Sanity loss 1D10/2D10; Cthulhu Mythos +17 percentiles; average 68 weeks to study and comprehend.* Spells: as per *Al Azif.*

- **NECRONOMICON**—*in Latin, trans. by Olaus Wormius, 1228 AD.* First circulated in manuscript form, then printed in Germany (late 15th century) as a black-letter folio. A second, nearly identical edition was published in Spain in the early 17th century. One copy of the former edition and four copies of the latter are known to exist. *Sanity loss 1D10/2D10; Cthulhu Mythos +16 percentiles; average 66 weeks to study and comprehend.* Spells: as per *Al-Azif.*

- **NECRONOMICON**—*in English, trans. by Dr. John Dee, 1586.* An accurate but expurgated version of the Greek translation. Never printed; exists in bound manuscript form only. Three nearly complete copies are known. *Sanity loss 1D10/2D10; Cthulhu Mythos +15 percentiles; average 50 weeks to study and comprehend.* Spells: Call Forth the Angel Yazrael (Call/Dismiss Yog-Sothoth), Call Forth the Lord of the Pit (Call/Dismiss Nyogtha), Command the Angel Dilyah (Summon/Bind Servitor of the Outer Gods), Consult Dark Servant (Contact Ghoul), Consult Ye Spirit of the Earth (Contact Nyarlathotep), Dominate, Dust of Suleiman, Elder Sign, Powder of Ibn-Ghazi, Voorish Sign.

- **SUSSEX MANUSCRIPT**—*in English, trans. by Baron Frederic, 1597.* A muddled, incomplete translation of the Latin *Necronomicon*, printed in Sussex, England, in an octavo edition. Properly known as the *Cultus Maleficarum*. *Sanity loss 1D3/1D6; Cthulhu Mythos +7 percentiles; average 36 weeks to study and comprehend.* Spells: as per *Al Azif*, but possibly dangerously flawed in form and intent.

PEOPLE OF THE MONOLITH—*in English, by Justin Geoffrey, 1926.* A volume of poems, 4" x6.75", bound in dark red buckram at Erebus Press, Monmouth, Illinois, in an edition of 1200 copies. The title poem is acknowledged as Geoffrey's masterwork. *Sanity loss 1/1D3; Cthulhu Mythos +3 percentiles; average 1 week to study and comprehend.* Spells: none.

PNAKOTIC MANUSCRIPTS—*in English, author and trans. unknown, 15th century.* Five bound manuscript versions of this book are catalogued in Europe and America. The apparent precursor volume, the *Pnakotica*, was written in classical Greek, and that book may trace its origins to the prehuman crinoids who seeded life on Earth. *Sanity loss 1D4/1D8; Cthulhu Mythos +10 percentiles; average 45 weeks to study and comprehend.* Spell: Contact Winged Thing (Contact Elder Thing).

PONAPE SCRIPTURE—*in English, by Captain Abner Ezekiel Hoag, 1734.* Published posthumously c. 1795, in Boston, as a sextodecimo, 4" x6.75", but inferior in accuracy and completeness to Hoag's manuscript, copies of which purportedly still exist. Details a South Sea islander cult of humans who worship and breed with the deep ones. *Sanity loss 1D3/1D6; Cthulhu Mythos +5 percentiles; average 10 weeks to study and comprehend.* Spells: the printed version has no spells. The manuscript original contains Contact Deep Ones, Contact Father Dagon, Contact Mother Hydra.

REVELATIONS OF GLAAKI—*in English, by various authors, 1842-1865.* Nine folio volumes were published by subscription, the last in 1865. Since then, three more volumes are said to have been composed and privately circulated. Copies of the original nine folio volumes are held by many major libraries. Each volume is by a different cultist, discussing a different aspect of Glaaki, associated entities, and their cults. This version of the text was apparently expurgated, but much information survives. The range of spells gives a good idea of the general contents. *Sanity loss 1D6/2D6; Cthulhu Mythos +15 percentiles; average 32 weeks to study and comprehend.* Spells: Call/Dismiss Azathoth, Call/Dismiss Daoloth, Call/Dismiss Shub-Niggurath, Contact Byatis, Contact the Crystallizers of Dreams, Contact Eihort, Contact Glaaki, Contact Ghroth, Contact M'nagalah, Nyhargo Dirge, Summon/Bind Being from Xiclotl.

R'LYEH TEXT—*in Chinese, author unknown, c. 300 BC.* Supposedly the clay tablet originals have been destroyed, but scroll copies and recent English and German translations are said to exist. The text apparently concerns Dagon, Hydra, star-spawn, Zoth-Ommog, Ghatanothoa, and Cthulhu, and tells of the sinking of Mu and R'lyeh. *Sanity loss 1D8/2D8; Cthulhu Mythos +15 percentiles; average 54 weeks to study and comprehend.* Spells: Call Cyaegha, Contact Cthulhu, Contact Deep Ones, Contact Father Dagon, Contact Mother Hydra, Curse of the Stone, Grasp of Cthulhu, Wave of Oblivion.

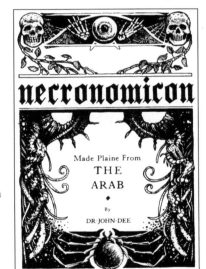

SEVEN CRYPTICAL BOOKS OF HSAN—*in Chinese, written by Hsan the Greater, c. 2nd century AD.* Seven scrolls, each on a different topic. An English translation, *Seven Cryptical Books of Earth*, is said to exist. The books discuss elements of the Mythos of particular importance or interest to those who live in the Middle Kingdom. *Sanity loss 1D4/1D8; Cthulhu Mythos +8 percentiles; average 40 weeks to study and comprehend.* Spells: Call Down Spirit (Summon/Bind Byakhee), Call Forth the Earth Spirit (Contact Chthonian), Contact Ghoul, Contact Hound of Tindalos, Contact Nyarlathotep, Door to Kadath (a gate to Kadath), Restore Life (Resurrection).

THAUMATURGICAL PRODIGIES IN THE NEW-ENGLAND CANAAN—*in English, by Rev. Ward Phillips, 1788?* Published in two editions, the second in Boston, 1801. Primitive American octavo in imitation black letter. The interiors of the editions are the same, except for changes in printer, place of printing, and edition date. Commonly found in major libraries and historical society libraries in New England. Describes the blasphemies of witches, warlocks, shamans, and other Colonial-era evildoers. Details of events in and around Billington's Woods. *Sanity loss 1D3/1D6; Cthulhu Mythos +4 percentiles; average 8 weeks to study and comprehend.* Spells: none, but annotations by Rev. Phillips in his personal copy reveal Call/Dismiss Ithaka (Ithaqua), Contact Narlato (Nyarlathotep), Contact Sadogowah (Tsathoggua), Contact Yogge Sothyothe (Yog-Sothoth), Elder Sign.

TRUE MAGIC—*in English, by Theophilus Wenn, 17th century.* A small and crumbling hand-bound manuscript, nonetheless describable as a veritable encyclopedia of Devil's lore. *Sanity loss 1D4/1D8; Cthulhu Mythos +6 percentiles; average 24 weeks to study and comprehend.* Spells: Call for Spirit of the Air (Summon/Bind Star Vampire), Call Forth the One (Summon/Bind Servitor of the Outer Gods), Call Forth the Winged One (Summon/Bind Byakhee), Speak with the Dark One (Contact Nyogtha).

ZANTHU TABLETS—*in English, by Prof. Harold Hadley Copeland, 1916.* A brochure subtitled "A Conjectural Translation" printed in 400 copies. Translates carvings found on black jade tablets drawn up from the Pacific Ocean by fishermen. The author claims the carvings are hieratic Naacal, the high language of ancient Mu. The brochure describes the worship of Ghatanothoa, Shub-Niggurath, and Cthulhu. *Sanity loss 1D3/1D6; Cthulhu Mythos +3 percentiles; average 8 weeks to study and comprehend.* Spells: the text is partially expurgated and contains no spells. The original Muvian tables contain Contact Cthulhu, Contact Ghatanothoa, Contact Lloigor, Contact Yuggya, Contact Zoth-Ommog. ■

Above: frontspiece of the Dee Necronomicon.

■ Skimming a printed or typescript book takes one hour per hundred pages. Skimming a handwritten manuscript takes one hour per ten pages.

■ Skimming a Mythos book costs half the current Sanity points needed to read the book, or as the keeper indicates.

■ Skimming never increases Cthulhu Mythos.

■ After skimming, reading the book costs the full Sanity-point roll, minus any Sanity points actually spent in skimming the book.

MYTHOS BOOKS AS REFERENCES

Once a tome has been read, the percentiles entered for its *Cthulhu Mythos* + also quantify its usefulness as a Mythos reference. As seems appropriate, such a book may be able to provide a specific fact about the Mythos (such as how long a chthonian takes to reach maturity, or where Y'golonac's body awaits its resurrection).

The investigator spends 1D4 game hours poring through the book. The player then multiplies the Cthulhu Mythos percentiles of the book by 5, and attempts a D100 roll equal to or less than that number. With a success, the investigator finds the fact or an allusion to the fact (the keeper can express the information as obscurely as desired). If the roll failed, the book does not hold the information. The user of the book will want to note what was or was not contained.

Occult Books

These ideas for handling the information in Mythos books can apply to non-Mythos books as well. An occult book by definition grants points of the Occult skill after being read. An occult book does not contain knowledge increasing the Cthulhu Mythos skill or it would be classified as a Mythos book. Some occult books may well include discussions of non-Mythos magic, including instructions for spells. An occult book may cost Sanity points if its writing is tangled and confusing.

Published Scenarios

Especially in published scenarios, the procedure for deciphering Mythos tomes often has been condensed, sometimes drastically, in order that the drama of the situation stay sharp and immediate. For instance, an adventure may suggest that the investigators can spend only 1D4 game days studying *Nameless Cults*, and that they then have a

More Mythos Tomes 1

title	language, date	author	wks.	sanity loss	C.M.	story/author
Black Book of the Skull	Greek	J'cak Igguratian	29	1D4/1D8	+6	"The Seven Cities of Gold", Burnham
Black God of Madness	English, 1930s	Amadeus Carson	7	1D3/1D6	+4	"The Salem Horror", Kuttner
Black Rites	Atlantean	Luveh-Keraphf	41	1D6/2D6	+11	"The Suicide in the Study", Bloch
Black Sutra	Burmese, c. 700	U Pao	18	1D4/1D8	+5	"Where Yidhra Walks", DeBill
Black Tome	Latin	Alsophocus	37	1D6/2D6	+10	"The Black Tome of Alsophocus", Lovecraft & Warnes
Book of Iod	ancient tongue	unknown	51	1D6/2D6	+12	"Bells of Horror", Kuttner
Book of Iod	English trans.	Johann Negus	10	1D3/1D6	+4	"Bells of Horror", Kuttner
Book of Skelos	Aklo	unknown	54	1D6/2D6	+10	Conan the Buccaneer, Carter & deCamp
Cabala of Saboth	Greek, 1686	unknown	16	1D3/1D6	+3	"The Mannikin", Bloch
Chronike von Nath	German	Rudolf Yergler	22	1D4/1D8	+6	"Music of the Stars", Rimel
Confessions of the Mad Monk Clithanus	Latin, c. 400	Clithanus	29	1D6/2D6	+9	"The Passing of Eric Holm", Derleth
Cthonic Revelations	Laotian	Thanang Phram	18	1D4/1D8	+7	"Where Yidhra Walks", DeBill
Daemonolatreia	English, 1595	Remigius	28	1D4/1D8	+8	"The Festival", Lovecraft [actual book]
Dhol Chants	Burmese	unknown	62	1D6/2D6	+10	"The Horror in the Museum", Lovecraft & Heald
Dhol Chants	German, 1890s	Heinrich Zimmerman	17	1D4/1D8	+7	"The Horror in the Museum", Lovecraft & Heald
Dwellers in the Depths	French	Gaston Le Fé	12	1D4/1D8	+8	"The Aquarium", Jacobi
Ethics of Ygor	Latin	unknown	13	1D3/1D6	+4	The Great White Space, Cooper
Fischbuch	German, 1598	Konrad von Gerner	8	1D2/1D4	+3	"Name and Number", Lumley
Fourth Book of D'harsis	English	D'harsis	42	1D6/2D6	+11	"Clock of Dreams", Lumley
Geph Transcriptions	English	unknown	20	1D4/1D8	+7	"Name and Number", Lumley
Ghorl Nigral	Muvian Naacal	Zakuba	46	1D8/2D8	+14	"Zoth-Ommog", Carter
Green Book	English	unknown	50	1D8/2D8	+13	"The White People", Machen
Hydrophinnae	Latin	Mr. Gantley	7	1/1D4	+3	"The Aquarium", Jacobi
Ilarnek Papyri	English	unknown	15	1D4/1D8	+6	"The Doom That Came to Sarnath", Lovecraft
In Pressured Places	English	Hartrack	3	1D3/1D6	+5	"De Marigny's Clock", Lumley
Invocations to Dagon	English	Asaph Waite	16	1D4/1D8	+9	The Trail of Cthulhu, Derleth
Johansen Narrative	English	Gustaf Johansen	6	1D3/1D6	+4	"The Call of Cthulhu", Lovecraft
Legends of Liqualia	English	Oswald	9	1D2/1D4	+4	"De Marigny's Clock", Lumley
Liber Damnatus Damnationum	English, 1647	Janus Aquaticus	34	1D4/1D8	+10	"House of the Toad", Tierney
Life of Eibon	French	Cyron	8	1D2/1D4	+3	"The Fishers from Outside", Carter
Magic and the Black Arts	English	Kane	12	1D3/1D6	+5	"The Scourge of B'moth", Russell
Marvels of Science	English	Morryster	11	1D2/1D4	+3	"The Festival", Lovecraft [actual book]
Mum-Rath Papyri	Latin	Ibn Shoddathua	10	1D3/1D6	+4	"The Fairground Horror", Brian Lumley
Naacal Key	English	Churchward	2	1/1D2	+1	"The Fishers from Outside", Carter

50% chance to learn some spell crucial to the adventure in the book.

If such inconsistency annoys you, change the name of the book or manuscript to one you have made up, or redesign the adventure so that the pressure of time has no consequence. At heart, the Call of Cthulhu rules assume months or years of play with the same keeper and players, assume that the mysteries involved are mostly created by the keeper and not hatched from a book, and assume that episodes merge like streams into a river. You, by choice or by circumstance, may not play that way.

Using Magic

Points increasing the Cthulhu Mythos skill widen the horizons of the student and chip away at his or her mental reserves. But the point of learning about the Mythos is that the knowledge lets the scholar change reality in specific ways. These packets of information are organized as spells. They require activation, measured in the game by magic points.

Magic Points

Magic points can be expended to cast spells, to energize artifacts and magical gates, to fight magical attacks or manipulation via Resistance Table rolls, and so on. An investigator cannot expend more magic points than he or she possesses. The number of magic points cannot regenerate above his or her points of POW.

Spending or sacrificing magic points or points of Power takes only the will of the owner. No special process is needed. Doing it may leave sensations of pleasure mingled with regret, or a numbness of the soul, or not be noticeable at all.

Some magical attacks leach magic points or POW from unwilling targets. In those cases, Resistance Table rolls may be characterized as being painful, or as leaving a headache or other minor symptom. Involuntary loss of POW would be a stronger sensation than that of losing the same amount of magic points.

■ If magic points reach zero, the investigator falls unconscious until at least one magic point regenerates.

■ Regeneration of magic points is a natural function, returning at one quarter of user POW per six hours (round down any fractions). After 24 hours, all magic

More Mythos Tomes II

title	language, date	author	wks.	sanity loss	C.M.	story/author
Necrolatry	German, 1702	Ivor Gorstadt	20	1D6/2D6	+12	"Dreams from R'lyeh", Carter
Night-Gaunt	English	Edgar Gordon	4	1/1D3	+1	"The Dark Demon", Bloch
The Occult Foundation	English, c. 1980	J. C. Wassermann	16	1D3/1D6	+5	"House of the Toad", Tierney
Of Evil Sorceries Done in New England	English, c.1600	unknown	9	1D3/1D6	+4	"The Lurker at the Threshold", Lovecraft & Derleth
Othuum Omnicia	Latin	unknown	12	1D2/1D4	+3	"The Last Rite", Lumley
Parchments of Pnom	Hyperborean	Pnom	31	1D6/2D6	+11	"The Coming of the White Worm", Smith
Polynesian Mythology, with a Note on the Cthulhu Legend-Cycle	English, 1906	Harold H. Copeland	8	1/1D3	+3	"Zoth-Ommog", Carter
Prehistoric Pacific in the Light of the Ponape Scripture	English, 1911	Harold H. Copeland	7	1D2/1D4	+4	"Zoth-Ommog", Carter
Prehistory in the Pacific: A Preliminary Investigation...	English, 1902	Harold H. Copeland	4	1/1D2	+1	"Zoth-Ommog", Carter
Reflections	English	Ibn Schacabao	27	1D4/1D8	+8	"The Festival", Lovecraft
Remnants of Lost Empires	German, 1809	Otto Dostmann	5	1/1D3	+2	"The Black Stone", Howard
Revelations of Hali	English, 1913	E. S. Bayrolles	5	1D2/1D4	+4	"The Inhabitant of Carcosa", Bierce
Saducismus Triumphatus	English, 1681	Joseph Glanvill	6	1D3/1D6	+4	"The Festival", H.P. Lovecraft [actual book]
Sapientia Maglorum	Latin	Ostanes	40	1D6/2D6	+10	"The Seed of the Star-God", Tierney
Saracenic Rituals	English, 19th C.	Clergyman X	6	1/1D3	+3	"Lord of the Worms", Lumley
Secret Mysteries of Asia, with a Commentary on the Ghorl Nigral	German, 1847	Gottfried Mulder	16	1D4/1D8	+7	"Zoth-Ommog", Carter
The Secret Watcher	English	Halpin Chalmers	10	1D2/1D4	+4	"The Hounds of Tindalos", Long
Song of Yste	Greek	Dirka Family	11	1D3/1D6	+5	"The Abyss", Lowndes
Soul of Chaos	English	Edgar Gordon	7	1D2/1D4	+4	"The Dark Demon", Robert Bloch
Testament of Carnamagos	Greek, 12th C.	Carnamagos	23	1D3/1D6	+6	"The Treader of the Dust", Smith
The Tunneler Below	English, 1936	Georg Reuter	2	1/1D3	+3	"The Terror From the Depths", Leiber
Tuscan Rituals	Italian	unknown	3	1/1D3	+2	"What Dark God?", Lumley
Unter Zee Kulten	German, 17th C.	Graf Gauberg	17	1D3/1D6	+6	"Return of the Deep Ones", Lumley
Uralteschrecken	German, 19th C.	Graf von Konnenberg	22	1D3/1D6	+6	"Where Yidhra Walks", DeBill
Visions from Yaddith	English, 1927	Ariel Prescott	1	1D2/1D4	+4	"Visions from Yaddith", Carter
Von denen Verdammten Oder	German	Karaj Heinz Vogel	24	1D6/2D6	+12	"Darkness, My Name Is", Bertin
Von denen Verdammten	German (repr.),1907	Edith Brendall	10	1D3/1D6	+5	"Darkness, My Name Is", Bertin
Watchers on the Other Side	English, 1940s	Nayland Colum	2	1D2/1D4	+3	"The Keeper of the Key", Derleth
We Pass from View	English, 1964	Roland Franklyn	1	1D3/1D6	+4	"The Franklyn Paragraphs", Campbell
Yhe Rituals	Egyptian	Niggoum-Zhog	14	1D4/1D8	+9	"The Thing in the Pit", Carter
Yuggya Chants	English	unknown	11	1D3/1D6	+4	"Out of the Ages", Carter

Harvey's First Spell: An Example

*A*fter spending a few game months totally crazed, Harvey Walters begins to recover from his indefinite insanity. Still in Germany, he rummages through the asylum's library and comes across a manuscript in medieval Latin. Its existence has long been ignored. The manuscript has no title, but Harvey comes to think of it as the Red Book, *after its crimson leather binding. His player declares that Harvey will skim the book to see if it is worth studying. The keeper, who has placed it there to give Harvey something to do while he recovers, agrees, and says that skimming the* Red Book *will cost Harvey 1D3 Sanity points. (That statement is an admission of the book's value as well as a show of concern for Harvey's fragile sanity—the keeper is not obliged to supply such information beforehand.) The player accepts the penalty, rolls a 1, and Harvey loses one current Sanity point from reading the book without other consequence.*

The keeper summarizes the Red Book *as a crumbling, worm-riddled record of alchemical researches made in the 13th century by one Gustaf the Dark. Though Harvey is expert in Latin, important parts of the text are in cipher and in cryptic abbreviations, which will take time to comprehend. Harvey spies one clear reference to "the appeal to flying servants of the great ones," the keeper adds. The player says that Harvey chooses to study the book.*

The keeper privately notes that deciphering the Red Book *will take Harvey three game months. The keeper could have rolled 2D6 for a random number of months, but he has already calculated that Harvey will recover in five game months total, and has plans for him then.*

Sessions of play continue. Every other session or so, the keeper calls for a Psychoanalysis roll for Harvey. After four months, Harvey's current Sanity points have increased to 33. The keeper declares that Harvey has read the Red Book, *that it has* Cthulhu Mythos +8 percentiles, *and that Harvey loses 1D6 current Sanity points in comprehending the tome.*

Harvey's player adds 8 points to Harvey's Cthulhu Mythos, raising it to 20. She lowers Harvey's maximum Sanity points to 79. She rolls 1D6 and gets a 3, but since Harvey had already lost 1 sanity point in skimming the Red Book *she subtracts just 2 current Sanity points to make his new total 31.*

Harvey suspects that the "appeal to flying servants" in the Red Book *is a Mythos spell. He needs time to learn if there is a complete spell in it—three game weeks, the keeper says. At the end of that time, the keeper calls for a D100 roll equal to or less than Harvey's INT (17) x3. Harvey's player must roll 51 or less. She fails, with a 77.*

The keeper sighs inwardly, but says smoothly that the asylum's librarian agrees to let Harvey borrow the book

indefinitely. Harvey can continue to study the spell while participating in other adventures: for how long until the next attempt, the keeper privately rolls 2D6, with the result of six weeks.

After an intervening adventure (at the end of which Harvey's current Sanity points rise to 38), he is ready to try the spell again. This time he succeeds.

The spell is Summon/Bind Byakhee (to which the keeper continues to refer to as Appeal to the Flying Servants). Though Harvey now knows the spell, it calls for an enchanted whistle, for which Harvey begins a search. After another adventure, he has gained such a whistle and, after being stranded on a large, barren rock in the middle of the North Atlantic, is ready to try the spell.

The spell commentary made it clear that the more magic points Harvey puts into the spell, the better his chances.

Harvey's low POW gives him no more than 9 magic points. His player sacrifices 8 magic points, leaving Harvey with one point so he can stay conscious. Casting the spell costs 1D3 Sanity points, lowering Harvey's current Sanity to 36.

Eleven minutes later, a dark and hideous winged figure flaps down from the sky and alights on the rock. It screeches loathsomely, and looks toward Harvey. This vision (a byakhee, the keeper knows) costs 1/1D6 Sanity points to encounter. The player fails a Sanity roll for Harvey, and rolls 1D6 to learn how many current Sanity points Harvey must lose. Harvey loses 4 more points.

Within a reasonable amount of time, Harvey has lost 6 from his starting total of 38 current Sanity points, more than 5 and so enough for temporary insanity, but in proportion less than 20% and so not enough for indefinite insanity.

The kindly keeper grants a Luck roll to the player, and it succeeds. In consequence, the keeper says, Harvey manages to point westward and shriek, "Take me to land!" and climbs on the thing's back before he begins to gibber and hallucinate.

The keeper rules that Harvey's temporary disorder lasts 20 game hours. The next morning, a disheveled Harvey wanders into a small Newfoundland town. Clutching the bat-like hide of the flying servant while it brought him to safety has left in him feelings of gratitude toward bats. From now on, he takes an approving interest in bats, and as he learns about them will more and more risk injury to defend these beneficent creatures.

Harvey has also learned that casting Mythos spells can be a very traumatic experience. He may be more careful when doing so in the future. ■

Above: silhouette of a byakhee (or a "Flying Servant" as Harvey knows them).

points should be regenerated unless the investigator has spent more in the meantime.

■ Were a character to obtain magic points of quantity greater than his or her POW, he or she could spend the excess but not regenerate it.

Learning a Spell

A wide selection of spells for the game are presented alphabetically in the Grimoire chapter, starting on p. 191.

■ In itself, learning a Mythos spell does not cost Sanity points. Casting a Mythos spell does.

■ Any individual can learn a spell. Studying the Mythos is the last thing a person should do, since increasing Mythos knowledge always brings the character closer and closer to the time when insanity or the Mythos stakes its claim. Sometimes circumstances demand such sacrifice.

■ Knowledge of a spell can be transferred in three ways. Learning from a book is by far the most common method.

LEARNING A SPELL FROM A MYTHOS BOOK

Sorcerers drive themselves insane by cruel experiment and heedless exposure to Cthulhu Mythos knowledge. Investigators seek out their records because their writings may offer quick solutions to problems of supernatual scope. Reading a sorcerer's notes and procedures can be horrifying and sanity-shaking, and should not be done heedlessly.

If a book contains spells, the keeper will indicate their presence and summarize each of them in a sentence or two. He or she probably will not use the rule book name for a spell, but might offer a description like "broughte forth a Great Winged Beast from ye void which did sore Crowde my place of Busyness" in place of the too accurate and too bland Summon/Bind Byakhee.

To learn a spell from a Mythos book requires that the book containing it has been read, and that 2D6 game weeks of study then takes place, or other game time as the keeper indicates. Just as with reading a Mythos book, learning a Mythos spell may be taken up, put aside, then taken up again, as convenient. The investigator chooses the spell to study. When the game time has elapsed, study is completed. The player then rolls D100 equal to or less than investigator INT x3 (or as the keeper sees fit). With a success, the spell is learned. Failing, the study time is lost, but the investigator may start over.

LEARNING A SPELL FROM ANOTHER PERSON

Having learned a spell, a character may teach it to others. Teaching person to person is quicker than one person learning from a book. To learn a spell from another person, roll D100 equal to or less than the student's INT x3 for each game week spent studying the spell. Succeeding, the student knows the spell and now may teach it to others.

LEARNING A SPELL FROM A MYTHOS ENTITY

At will, any intelligent entity might supply a book or a scroll detailing some spell. More characteristically the entity imparts such knowledge by means of dream or vision, each episode disturbing and alienating, and gnawing away at the character's sanity and will. This may happen quickly or slowly, as the story requires. An entity might imbue a complete spell in a character's mind via telepathy, though such a powerful experience also might send the character directly to the asylum.

Once the process is complete, the target needs a successful Idea roll to retain knowledge of the spell. Failing, the process must be started anew.

Imparting or imbuing a spell in this fashion is rare. Investigators rarely receive information in this manner. Cultists of the Cthulhu Mythos often do.

How Sorcerers Get That Way

Though investigators rarely have the chance, sorcerers and cultists sometimes swagger around with unseemly amounts of Power. Where did it come from? The following ideas are mostly intended to rationalize non-player characters.

Increasing Power increases the SAN characteristic, but does not increase current Sanity points.

■ When a character successfully casts a spell requiring magic points or POW to be matched on the Resistance Table, a chance exists for the caster's POW to increase through this "exercise". Subtract the caster's POW from 21 and multiply the difference by five: the product represents the percentage chance that the caster's POW increases by 1D3. Roll D100 equal to or less than that percentage chance to effect the increase.

■ As a reward for any Luck roll result of 01, POW can be said to be exercised. Subtract POW from 21 and multiply the difference by five: the product represents the percentage chance that the caster's POW increases by 1D3. Roll D100 equal to or less than that percentage chance to effect the increase.

■ Willful and ruthless individuals behave strangely. When created, an investigator may trade 10 current Sanity points for 1 POW. Lower maximum Sanity by ten. The process may repeat: if current Sanity points reach 9 or fewer, instincts of self-preservation take over. This procedure also might cost more current Sanity points, as the keeper sees fit to levy.

■ The character may be able to arrange a gift of or a trade for POW from some Great Old One or Outer God. This rationale is best left to the keeper. Such an event likely increases Cthulhu Mythos as well, and would cost additional current Sanity points besides those lost in communicating with the entity.

LEARNING NON-MYTHOS MAGIC

Not all magic originates from the Cthulhu Mythos, but Mythos magic is the most efficient agent of manipulation, and in the fiction it represents the best magical map or representation of the universe. Other earthly magic or religiosity can be significant and can have effect, though just how much is for the keeper to determine.

Mechanics and procedures for such magic should be the same as those for Mythos magic, though the means and aims of earthly magic will differ. Horrific deeds should always cost Sanity points.

Casting Spells

Manipulating the forces of the Cthulhu Mythos costs Sanity points, in amounts varying by spell. If some awful creature arrives in response to a spell, encountering it costs yet more Sanity points. Having no Sanity points does not prohibit spells from being cast—if it did, there would be no cultists.

Nearly all spells and many magical artifacts also require magic points (or Power, if that is the need) to be expended, or the spell does not activate. Nothing happens.

Physical components may be necessary. The component may be reusable, such as are the great menhirs necessary for summoning He Who Is Not to Be Named. Other components may be consumed in the course of the spell, such as the drinking of space-mead.

All spells need time to cast, from a few seconds or a game minute to as much time as a game week.

The caster must know the spell. He or she must reiterate a sometimes complex and lengthy chant in authoritative tones. Usually the caster must have complete freedom of movement, since gesture can be as important as chant.

SPELL RANGE

In the game, spell range is usually one of three: touch, 100 yards, or sight with the unaided eye. These general choices are easy to visualize and understand. Greater ranges get to be engineering problems, not examples of horror. Avoid telephone spells, internet spells, letter-bomb spells, cruise missile spells, spells sent by telescope, microbe spells, microwave transmission spells, and other contrivances. Like roleplaying, magic and horror are personal effects.

RESISTANCE TABLE MATCHES

Quite a few spells match caster and target magic points on the Resistance Table. Lacking other instructions, first subtract any caster magic points needed to cast the spell, then match the remaining magic points of the caster against those of the target's. To affect the target, first the spell must get there.

Evidence of Spells Being Cast

The damage done by a spell is probably obvious. A visible manifestation for a spell being cast may not be apparent. If it is, one might spot a peculiar hand gesture or body movement, or notice some unusual item or necessary ingredient. In themselves, such effects will begin to establish a tone for Mythos magic, so keepers are cautioned to keep such effects more low-key than not. But the effects could be wide-ranging, from hideous roars from beyond, gouts of fire, lines of electrical force, pale nimbuses, and auroras of various colors to the rushing of winds, raised hackles, ionized air, prickly sensations, the stench of sulfur, howling and hissing animals, murmuring voices, alarming moans, or whatever the keeper thinks fitting. ■

"One afternoon there was a discussion of possible freakish curvatures in space, and of theoretical points of approach or even contact between our part of the cosmos and . . . as fabulously remote as the tenatively conceivable cosmic units beyond the whole Einsteinian space-time continuum."

—Lovecraft, "Dreams in the Witch-House"

THE CTHULHU MYTHOS

*Themselves invulnerable and indifferent,
the entities of the Mythos may leave human
affairs to human worshipers and agents, who
may be foiled by clever investigators.*

LOVECRAFT once wrote, "All my tales are based upon the fundamental premise that common human laws and interests and emotions have no validity or significance in the vast cosmos-at-large." He further imagined that the fundamental truths of the universe were so alien and horrifying that mere exposure to them might result in madness or suicide. While humanity might crave both comfort and the truth, only one or the other was possible to it.

The human mind was an inflexible container. It could not maintain both more truth and complete sanity—more of one poured in must spill out more of the other. Humans desperate for the power cloaked within truth might choose to forgo all remnants of sanity in exchange for becoming adept at manipulating the secrets of time and space. Their devil's bargains made, these merciless sorcerers would whistle down devastation and doom to this world in new exchange for yet more knowledge and power.

Lovecraft's working-out of these ideas in his fiction became known as the Cthulhu Mythos. The term encompasses a complex and broad group of sometimes contradictory narratives, stories, essays, letters, and deductions, so extensive as to be impossible to summarize in detail—and not the least because new Mythos material continues to be written around the world. Adding to the confusion, one of his perceptions was that the truly alien is genuinely unknowable. The Mythos becomes not just mysterious, but protean and contradictory: not only do we not know it, we never can know it.

As it transpires, we have only our own names for most of these things. We do not even know their names for themselves, or if they have names.

A General Summary

Though their interrelations are dim, we know that some entities of the Cthulhu Mythos are clearly superior or inferior in their powers. Gods are the mightiest, followed (at some distance, apparently) by the Great Old Ones. Both may be attended by lesser servitor races, often of a characteristic species.

Outer Gods, Elder Gods, Other Gods

Depending on which author one reads, the universe is ruled by beings variously known as the *Elder Gods*, *Outer Gods*, or *Other Gods*. Only a few of these deities are known by name. The majority are both blind and idiotic. They are all extremely powerful alien beings, and some may be of extracosmic origin.

The Outer Gods rule the universe and have little to do with humanity, except for Nyarlathotep. Humans meddling with these entities suffer for it, usually ending mad or dead. Names for a few Outer Gods are known. They appear almost to be true gods, as opposed to the alien horror of the Great Old Ones, and some may personify some cosmic principle. Only a few of these deities seem to take interest in human affairs or to acknowledge the existence of the human race. When they do, they often are shown trying to break through cosmic walls or dimensions in order to wreak new destruction. All the races and lesser deities of the Mythos acknowledge the Outer Gods, and many worship them.

The Outer Gods are controlled to some extent by their messenger and soul, Nyarlathotep. When the Outer Gods are discomforted, Nyarlathotep investigates. Azathoth, the daemon sultan and ruler of the cosmos, writhes mindlessly to the piping of a demon flute at the center of the universe. Yog-Sothoth, either a second-in-command or co-ruler, is coterminous with all time and space, but locked somehow outside the mundane universe. Yog-Sothoth can be summoned to this side only through the use of mighty spells, whereas Azathoth theoretically might be met by traveling far enough through space. A group of Outer Gods and servitors dance slowly around Azathoth, but none are named.

The term *Elder Gods* sometimes refers to another race of gods, neutral to and possibly rivals of the Outer Gods. The Elder Gods, if they exist, do not seem to be as dangerous to humanity

as Azathoth and its ilk, but they have even less contact with humanity. Nodens is the best known Elder God.

Outer and Elder Gods sometimes have been lumped together and confusingly called the Other Gods, though primarily gods of the outer planets and not of our Earth. They would seem seldom called here, but when they do appear they are second to nothing in horror. (And, just to thoroughly confuse you, a set of minor Outer Gods are known collectively as the Lesser Other Gods!)

Species associated with these deities (shantaks, hunting horrors, servitors of the Outer Gods, dark young of Shub-Niggurath) are correspondingly rare on Earth.

The Great Old Ones

They are not as supernatural as the Outer Gods, but are nonetheless god-like and terrible to human eyes. Humans are much more likely to worship Great Old Ones, who are comparatively near at hand and who occasionally participate in human affairs or contact individual humans, than they are to worship Outer Gods. Entire clans or cults may secretly worship a Great Old One. Lone madmen, on the other hand, seem to prefer the Outer Gods. Beings serving the Great Old Ones frequently inhabit the remote fastness of the Earth. Investigators most often encounter their worshipers and alien servants.

The Great Old Ones themselves appear to be immensely powerful alien beings with supernatural-seeming abilities, but not to be true gods in the sense that the Outer Gods are reported. Each Great Old One is independent of the rest, and many seem to be temporarily imprisoned in some way.

It is said that "when the stars are right" the Great Old Ones can plunge from world to world. When the stars are not right, they cannot live. "Cannot live" need not mean death, as the famous couplet from the *Necronomicon* suggests.

> That is not dead which can eternal lie,
> And with strange aeons even death may die.

Cthulhu, the most famous creation of Lovecraft, is a Great Old One. With the rest of his race, he sleeps in a vast tomb at the bottom of the Pacific Ocean. Cthulhu seems to be the most important Great Old One on Earth. Others of differing forms exist, and they are recorded as being both less powerful and more free. Ithaqua the Windwalker roams at will across Earth's arctic latitudes. Hastur the Unspeakable dwells near Aldebaran, and Cthugha near Fomalhaut. Other Great Old Ones doubtless infest other worlds, and it may be common for a world to be ruled by dominant Great Old Ones. All those known on Earth are invoked or worshiped by humans but, by the evidence of the stories, Cthulhu is worshiped more than the rest put together. Minor Great Old Ones such as Quachil Uttaus usually have no worshipers, but wizards may know spells to summon them. Such entities fill the role of demons within the hierarchy of the Mythos.

But even Cthulhu is known of by few, and interventions by Great Old Ones in human affairs are isolated. Some commentators suspect that these greater beings rarely think about human beings or take them into account. Humanity is negligible and unimportant.

Servitor Races

Particular species are often associated with particular Great Old Ones or Outer Gods—byakhee with Hastur, for instance, or nightgaunts with Nodens. These are servitor species, and frequently a god or Great Old One manifests accompanied by several such servitors. Representatives may act as hitmen, messengers, spies, and delivery boys, frightening off investigators and bulking out confrontations. In comparison, Outer Gods and Great Old Ones should be met with exceedingly infrequently.

Independent Races

Other alien species are also important, and sometimes have been able to hold their own against Great Old Ones. The independent races vary in power, and some are extinct. They are intimately connected with our planet, as described in "At the Mountains of Madness" and "The Shadow Out of Time". In these stories Lovecraft gives the true history of the Earth. Some species, such as dholes or flying polyps, make no association with particular gods or else, as with elder things and the Great Race, take no special interest in magic. Whether one is *greater* or *lesser* seems to depend on the relative danger posed by the average individual.

At the dawn of the Cambrian age, beings known only as the elder things flew to the Earth. They inhabited much of the land, warred with other species, and finally were pushed back to Antarctica. The elder things, perhaps mistakenly, bred organisms eventually to become the

dinosaurs, mammals, and humanity. They also bred the horrible shoggoths, whose ultimate revolt led to the semi-extinction of the elder things.

Eons ago, indigenous cone-shaped beings had their minds taken over by the Great Race of Yith, mental beings from the stars. The Great Race survived in their adopted bodies until about 50 million years ago, when they were defeated by terrible flying polyps not native to this Earth, which the Great Race had imprisoned in vast caverns beneath the surface. However, the Great Race had already transmitted their minds forward in time to escape their doom.

The star-spawn of Cthulhu came down upon the Earth and conquered a vast reach of land in the primordial Pacific Ocean, but were trapped when it sank beneath the surface.

The beings referred to as the fungi from Yuggoth (or mi-go) established their first bases on the Earth in the Jurassic period, about a hundred million years ago. They gradually reduced their bases to the tops of certain mountains, where they maintain mining colonies and such.

Dozens of other races also participated in this antediluvian parade, such as the serpent people who built cities and a civilization in the Permian, before the dinosaurs had evolved, and a winged race which succeeded the Great Race of Yith. Even species from Earth's future are mentioned, such as the beetle-like organisms which succeed man, and the intelligent arachnids who are prophesied to be the last intelligent life on Earth, billions of years hence.

At present, humans share the planet with deep ones and ghouls (which seem related to humanity in some fashion), and with a handful of mi-go. Other species occasionally visit Earth, or are sleeping, or are dormant.

What Was Left Out

The designer has taken it upon himself to ignore a portion of the current Mythos which does not appeal to him, and which he feels was not in Lovecraft's original concept. He has left out the "war in heaven" in which the Great Old Ones battled and were defeated by the Elder Gods, supposed deities of good opposed to the cosmic evil of the Great Old Ones. This idea of a cosmic war is never found in Lovecraft's own works; more alarmingly, it vitiates some of the stark horror found in the original ideas. Carrying Elder Signs around like crucifixes and holy water and always having the white-hat Elder Gods in the background, ready to save one's bacon if things get too bad, greatly weakens the original horror of the bleak uncaring universe, to which mankind is left naked and defenseless.

He has also left out the concept of the various Great Old Ones being somehow connected to the Greek elements of Earth, Water, Fire, and Air (exemplified by Nyarlathotep, Cthulhu, Cthugha, and Hastur, respectively). This idea falls apart under close inspection (if Cthulhu is a water god, why is he currently dead due to being under the sea?), and weakens the premise of the Great Old Ones being monstrous alien beings.

Naturally, if these conceptions seem good and well done to the keeper, use them at will. Call of Cthulhu is your game.

The Mythos Prehistory of the Earth

4.5 Billion Years Before Present: in the earliest times, when the Earth is still cooling, Cthugha and its fire vampires servitors appear. They are the first life on the planet. Earth is covered by warm shallow seas from which continents periodically emerge.

1.8 Billion BP: earliest fossils of aquatic fungi and algae.

1 Billion BP: elder things arrive on Earth. Landing in what is now the Antarctic Ocean, they establish an undersea colony. Using organic material mined from the ocean floor, they invoke or generate the primal shoggoth mass called in the *Book of Eibon* Ubbo-Sathla, the father of all life. All terrene life more complex then bacteria and blue-green algae is born of this creature. Using the shoggoth-spawn of Ubbo-Sathla, the elder things construct their first great undersea city.

750 Million BP: the mysterious flying polyps arrive on Earth from outer space. Settling on land that far later becomes Australia, they erect great windowless cities of basalt and feed upon the cone-shaped beings they find living there.

450 Million BP: throughout the aeons the elder things have continued their creation and exploitation of primitive life forms. When some of their experiments escape the elder things deign to allow them to evolve on their own, resulting in the creations of the first vertebrates—fish—and other life forms.

By this time the planet's crust has formed major continents in the northern and in the southern hemispheres. The two continents slowly move toward each other.

400 Million BP: the minds of the Great Race of Yith travel across time and space to inhabit the bodies of the cone-shaped beings of Australia. The Yithians begin a war of subjugation against the polyps, which are surprised, quickly defeated, and sealed away in subterranean vaults. The Yithians build guard cities atop them.

350 Million BP: the two supercontinents collide, forming the supercontinent of Pangaea and giving rise to the mountains of Scotland and Scandinavia. This cataclysm also causes new land masses to form in the Pacific Ocean, among them K'naa Ponape, Yhe, and R'lyeh. These are the places that will one day be known as Mu.

In the wake of this upheaval Cthulhu and his spawn seep down from the distant star-system of Xoth, claiming Mu for their own. War begins with the elder things for dominance of the planet, but a truce is eventually declared between the two alien races.

300 Million BP: another great cataclysm shakes the Earth, plunging the lands of Mu beneath the waters of the Pacific Ocean. At this same time Cthugha and his fire vampires are banished from the Earth, and possibly other Great Old Ones are imprisoned.

275 Million BP: the beginning of serpent folk civilization, in Valusia, a land at the center of Pangaea. This is the famed First Empire of the serpent people. A parallel race of tailless reptile men co-exists to the east. These latter, who may or may not be related to the serpent people, built the Nameless City.

250 Million BP: the shoggoths revolt against their masters. In a war of survival the elder things finally win victory. The near-extinction of their slave-beasts signals the beginning of the long decline of the elder things.

225 Million BP: this begins the Age of Reptiles. The dinosaurs reign across Pangaea. The arrival of the dinosaurs causes the downfall of the First Empire of the serpent people. Many serpent people are killed, but others hibernate or go into hiding deep beneath the Earth, forming civilizations such as Yoth.

190 Million BP: a great east-west crack appears across Pangaea, separating Laurasia in the north from Gondwanaland in the south. The remnants of Valusia are plunged beneath the waves, into what will one day be the Mediterranean Sea. A separate Antarctic/Australian landmass has drifted free of Gondwana toward the South Pole. About this time India breaks loose from it and heads north toward Asia.

160 Million BP: the mi-go, the fungi from Yuggoth, arrive and establish their first colony in the Appalachian Mountains. These beings war with the elder things, who are forced to retreat southward. Soon the Earth is divided, with mi-go in the north, elder things in the south, and the Great Race in the lands surrounding Australia.

70 Million BP: a comet or asteroid strikes the Yucatan. Severe climatic consequences accelerate the doom of the dinosaurs. South America and Africa have separated, as have Antarctica and Australia. North America has broken free of Europe and is heading westward. Hyperborea is also freed and sliding north. Africa later crashes into the Near East, creating the Alps, Carpathians, and Pyrenees. In this time the new Atlantic Ocean and Mediterranean Sea are clearly noticeable while much of central Europe is submerged. Geologic forces thrust up the Andes and the Rockies.

65 Million BP: mammals become the dominant form of life.

50 Million BP: a cataclysm shakes the Earth, destroying the ancient prisons of the carnivorous flying polyps. The Yithian minds suddenly flee their cone-shaped bodies to inhabit another species existing far in the future of the planet. Deprived of Yithian intelligence the cone beings are soon overwhelmed and exterminated by the polyps. Afterward the polyps nearly disappear from the world. In the Antarctic the largest elder thing city is destroyed by the same earthquake that gives rise to the Mountains of Madness. After the cataclysm the elder things lay the foundation of a new city, the last surface structure they build.

40 Million BP: the Indian subcontinent crashes into the belly of Asia, raising the Himalayan Mountains.

26 Million BP: the continents approach their present positions.

3 Million BP: the civilization of the voormis of Hyperborea begins. They worship Tsathoggua and his spawn.

1.7 Million BP: the age of the oldest ice found in modern Greenland, which is a fragment of ancient Hyperborea. It marks the decline of the Voormis civilization.

1 Million BP: the ice age begins, marking the fall of the voormis of Hyperborea, as well as an advanced human civilization in Zobna. A civilization of humans rises in Hyperborea, and the survivors of Zobna found the new land of Lomar. In the Antarctic the climate chills and the elder things develop artificial heating.

750,000 BP: numerous glaciations have occurred in the north, but now the Riss episode destroys the human civilizations of Hyperborea and Lomar. The elder things of Antarctica retreat to an undersea Antarctic city.

500,000 BP: Lemuria rises in the Atlantic. A human civilization which rules for 100,000 years is founded there.

200,000 BP: a human civilization has arisen in the lands of Mu, where Cthulhu and his spawn once ruled. It will last until 163,844 BP, when it is destroyed by the curse of Ghatanothoa.

25,000 BP: the serpent men raise their Second Kingdom on the Thurian contient, which has arisen in the Atlantic from the ashes of Lemuria and Atlantis. They are eventually overthrown by humans.

20,000 BP: a great disaster sinks the Thurian continent.

12,000 BP: the Hyborian Age is the last time of great civilization before the modern age. Its countries cover Africa and western Europe.

11,550 BP: another great catalysm strikes the Earth, changing the topography of the Hyborian lands, destroying many ancient civilizations, and sinking the last remant of old Atlantis. From their ashes are formed countries such as Khem, in Northern Africa, and cities such as Sarnath, in the Middle East.

10,000 BP: the fall of Sarnath.

9,000 BP: rise of new hamlets in the Middle East.

7,000 BP: first great cities of Africa and Asia. Beginning of the fall of Khem.

5,000 BP: height of Sumerian civilization; first dynasty of Egypt; first date in Mayan chronology.

4,500 BP: legendary sage-kings of China; paper invented.

3,300 BP: escape of the Israelites from Egypt. Yog-Sothoth is freed from his Earthly prison.

2,500 BP: republic of Rome; Thucydides, the human Father of History, is born. ∎

THE NECRONOMICON

*Summarizing all that careful scholars of
this day might reckon upon without
themselves having to plumb the mind-wracking
pages of this ghastly tome.*

THOUGH more ancient works are known, in human languages it is the *Necronomicon* that best relates the reach and meaning of the Cthulhu Mythos. This dark tome contains a chant to Yog-Sothoth which can open the Way to this world, information on the powder of Ibn Ghazi, and a description of the Voorish Sign. Doubtless Lovecraft left other cantrips and formulae unmentioned. The tome also discusses many hundreds of places and things, a few of which poor Danforth babbles about at the end of H. P. Lovecraft's "At the Mountains of Madness".

The *Necronomicon* is encyclopedic, bafflingly. Allusions are definitions, inflections are explanations, wishes are proofs, and decoration and design are indistinguishable. The vocabulary is as interior as that of a dream.

Because references and clues within the *Necronomicon* have already led to investigations, cognoscenti cite this work as a Rosetta Stone for the black arts. It would be best, however, if investigators never get their own copies. Let the work continue to tantalize and beckon. The *Necronomicon* is not like a set of file cards, nor should it be used as a roundhouse through which to railroad investigators from one track to another. It is too powerful and too terrible for that. For its students, the *Necronomicon* is the gate to insanity, the way through which humans pass, metamorphose, and emerge unrecognizable, themselves newly made into mysteries.

History

The original version of the *Necronomicon*, known as the *Kitab Al-Azif*, was written around the year 730 A.D. in Damascus by the Arab, Abdul Al-Hazred (Abd al-Azrad). A student of magic as well as an astronomer, poet, philosopher, and scientist, al-Azrad was born around 700 A.D. in Sanaa, in Yemen. Before composing his great work he spent years visiting the ruins of Babylon, the pits of Memphis, and the great southern desert of Arabia. He died in Damascus in 738, according to his 12th-century biographer, Ebn Khallikan, devoured in broad daylight by an invisible demon.

Manuscripts of the *Al-Azif* circulated secretly among philosophers and scientists of the age, but it was not until the year 950 that the work was translated into Greek by the Byzantine Theodorus Philetas, who renamed it the *Necronomicon*. Numerous copies of Philetas' manuscript were made. The increased circulation of the blasphemous tome led to its eventual condemnation in 1050 by the Patriarch Michael of Constantinople. Many copies were confiscated and destroyed, their owners suffering harsh penalties.

In 1228 Olaus Wormius effected a Latin translation of the Greek version, all copies of the original Arabic having by this time been lost. Its rapid circulation among philosophical circles led to its banning in 1232, both the Latin and Greek versions placed on the *Index Expurgatorius* by Pope Gregory IX. Olaus did not retitle the Greek *Necronomicon*, and the work is thereafter commonly referred to by that name.

The year 1454 saw the first practical printing press using moveable type and before the end of the century a black-letter version of the Latin *Necronomicon* had been printed in Germany, probably in Mainz. The text does not identify the date or place of printing.

In the early 16th century, probably before 1510, a version of the Greek translation was printed in Italy. Although again lacking any identifying marks, this version is generally believed to have come from the press of Aldus Manutius, founder of the Aldine Press, famous for its printing of unedited Greek and Latin texts.

In 1586 an English translation of the *Necronomicon* was produced by Dr. John Dee, mathematician, astrologer, and physician to Queen Elizabeth of England. Never published, Dee's translation is believed to have been made from a Greek edition discovered by the doctor during his travels in eastern Europe. Although accurate, it is incomplete, partially expurgated by its translator.

A second printing of the Latin version was made in Spain in the early 17th century. As usual, the printer is unidentified but the poorer cut of the type distinguishes it from the finer German work. It is in all other ways faithful to the earlier edition.

Other Versions

Other versions and partial copies of the *Necronomicon* also exist. The *Sussex Manuscript*, also known as the *Cultus Maleficarum*, is an English translation made by a Baron Frederic from the Latin text, published in Sussex in 1597. The muddled and incomplete *Al-Azif—Ye Booke of ye Arab*, written in provincial English, was made in the late 16th century and circulated in hand-copied manuscript. The 116-page medieval *Voynich Manuscript*, presently in the collection of the University of Pennsylvania, is written in Greek and Latin using Arab script. Studies of the Latin versions have been made by such men as Feery and Shrewsbury, and fragmentary translations are found in books published by both these scholars.

Surviving Copies

Condemned and destroyed by the Church, only five copies of the *Necronomicon* are known to exist today, although an unknown number of copies may still be held in private collections. Copies that reach the open market are usually purchased by libraries or private collectors who appreciate the book only for its rarity, or possibly for its blasphemous nature and wicked reputation. The resultant increase in value has driven the price beyond the range of most serious students of the occult. Few can afford to obtain their own copies of this dark and powerful book, and, given the value and fragile conditions of the existing copies, few public institutions allow unrestricted access.

The documented extant copies are all Latin versions, four from the surreptitious 17th-century Spanish printing and the fifth a single surviving specimen of the fine 16th-century German edition. The four remnants of the edition printed in Spain are presently held in the collections of the Bibliothèque Nationale in Paris, the Miskatonic University Library in Arkham, the Widener Library at Harvard, and the library of the University of Buenos Aires. The precious single copy of the edition printed in Germany resides in the British Museum in London.

Although the last known copy in Greek is believed to have perished in flames during the chaos of the Salem witch trials in Massachusetts, rumors of other Greek copies occasionally surface. The most recent of these claimed that a copy was owned by the New York artist Richard Upton Pickman. If true, the book apparently disappeared along with the artist in 1926.

Handmade copies of the Dee version, most of them damaged and incomplete, are still occasionally unearthed. The most recent find was made by Miskatonic University, which now has a nearly complete Dee *Necronomicon* in its enviable collection. The decidedly less rare *Sussex Manuscript* also can be found in Miskatonic's collection and in many other large libraries as well. It is generally believed that no copies of the Arabic original have survived to the present day, although persistent rumors suggest that a copy surfaced in San Francisco shortly before the disastrous earthquake and fire of 1906. The claim that an Arabic copy is part of the collection in the British Museum has been recently disproved.

Physical Descriptions

All known printed editions of the *Necronomicon* are folio-sized. The Latin editions printed in Spain and Germany alike measure 18 by 11-1/2 inches and contain 802 pages, one leaf being bound in as a tabbed insert. Records suggest that the Greek version was several pages longer. The type style is black-letter gothic, and numerous woodcuts illustrate the text. Bindings, as with all books of this period, are individual, reflecting the tastes of the books' original owners. (Until the mid-19th century most books came from printers unbound, wrapped in paper.)

The *Necronomicon* found in the British Museum is in a 15th-century leather binding still in fair condition. Printed in Germany, the text is in good condition but lamentably lacks seven different leaves, each cut away and removed with great care. This volume was among the three libraries of books bequeathed to the people of England which led to the founding of the British Museum in 1753.

The copy found in the Bibliothèque Nationale is in poor condition, bound in the cheap, crumbling pasteboards common to the era. The text is in similarly bad condition, with many torn pages and several pages missing altogether. Other pages are indecipherable, badly stained by what some identify as blood. The acquisition of the book is shrouded in mystery, the volume deposited at the front desk in 1811 by a furtive man of foreign caste. The mysterious donor was found a day later in a rat-infested apartment, a victim of poison.

The University of Buenos Aires' copy is said to have come to South America in the late 17th century. Although the text is in only fair condition, it is unique for its odd marginal notes, written in unknown glyphs.

The Widener Library at Harvard contains a *Necronomicon* of poor condition. Its binding is original, but badly cracked and split. The text is complete but many pages have separated and others are crumbling. Restoration efforts are underway. The book was part of the library of Harry Elkins Widener, American millionaire, and it is said that he obtained the volume shortly before he boarded the *Titanic* in 1912.

The copy at Miskatonic University was obtained late in the last century by a young Dr. Armitage, then only recently hired by the school. Purchased from the private collection of Providence businessman Whipple Phillips, the Miskatonic's edition of the *Necronomicon* was rebound, probably in the early 18th century, in sumach-tanned goatskin. A false title, *Qanoon-e-Islam*, is embossed in gold on the front cover. The text is complete and in fair to good condition. ■

HOWARD PHILLIPS LOVECRAFT

Describing Lovecraft,
his original circle,
and mentioning a few of those writers
who have come later.

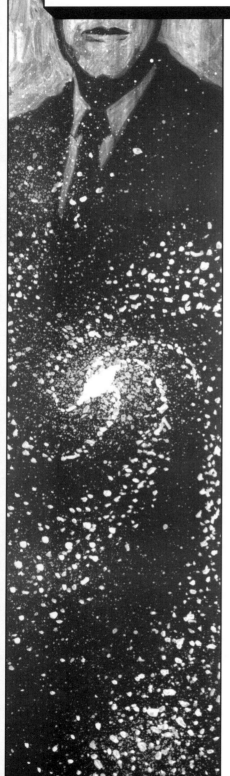

IN A 46-year lifetime H. P. Lovecraft wrote or collaborated on more than 65 stories, penned dozens of articles and essays, and hundreds of poems, and wrote perhaps as many as 100,000 letters. Occasionally referring to his Cthulhu and Yog-Sothoth cycles, to the best of anyone's knowledge Lovecraft never used the term Cthulhu Mythos.

Although nearly all his tales can be linked by common references to people, places, and things, for the most part they lack a true central structure or anything resembling a preconceived history and mythology. It was not until late in Lovecraft's career—and then probably only at the urging of some of his younger correspondents—that he began to integrate into his later stories some of the creations found in his earliest tales. In "The Shadow over Innsmouth" (1931) we find the deep one hybrids worshiping Dagon, a creature not mentioned since the story "Dagon" (1917), his second piece of adult fiction.

Similarly, the fictional city of Arkham and its Miskatonic University, first used as backdrops in "The Picture in the House" (1920) and "Herbert West—Reanimator" (1921-1922), are finally developed in his later stories beginning with "The Dunwich Horror" (1928) and continuing through "The Whisperer in Darkness" (1930), "The Dreams in the Witch House" (1932), and "The Thing on the Doorstep" (1933). "At the Mountains of Madness" (1931) and "The Shadow Out of Time" (1934-1935) contain detailed histories of prehuman Earth describing the different alien beings that had in the past visited and colonized the planets. Some of these races, such as the fungi from Yuggoth and the Cthulhu spawn, were from earlier stories and were carefully integrated into these late-devised histories.

The dreaded *Necronomicon*, one of the Lovecraft's most famous creations, undergoes a gradual evolution. First mentioned in "The Hound" (1922), it is here attributed to an Abdul Alhazred, an Arab poet mentioned in an earlier story, "The Nameless City" (1921). Alhazred was, in fact, the boyhood persona of a five-year-old HPL, his youthful imagination inflamed by his grandfather's copy of *A Thousand and One Arabian Nights*.

The term Cthulhu Mythos is generally attributed to August Derleth, a young writer and early fan of Lovecraft who later founded Arkham House publishers, dedicated to keeping in print the collected works of H. P. Lovecraft. Fans and scholars have since debated the definition of this term, argued the Cthulhu Mythos content of various of Lovecraft's tales, constructed experimental pantheons of gods and deities, postulated histories, and made vain attempts to explain all the facets of the literary Mythos.

In the meantime dozens, perhaps hundreds, of writers both professional and amateur have continued to write Mythos-inspired stories expanding upon Lovecraft's original concepts while simultaneously developing their own, sometimes inconsistent with HPL and rarely consistent with each other. For the purposes of Call of Cthulhu, Chaosium has incorporated most of Lovecraft's creations, as well as those of other authors, in a loosely cast Mythos that allows keepers to add or delete particular creatures and conceptions as they will.

Influences

Lovecraft enjoyed but little success during his lifetime. Although he early attracted a small core of avid fans—many of them writers themselves—he never achieved more than semiregular publication in the pulp magazines of the day. Never as popular as writers like Seabury Quinn, Lovecraft earned most of his always meager income revising and rewriting the works of others, even ghostwriting "Under the Pyramids" (1924) for escape artist Harry Houdini. It was through publication in amateur magazines and later in *Weird Tales* that Lovecraft was to come into contact with other authors of the macabre tale.

These contacts included already accomplished professionals like Clark Ashton Smith and Robert E. Howard, as well as talented young writers like Derleth, Frank Belknap Long, and a teenage Robert Bloch. As fate would have it, Lovecraft would make the personal acquaintance of only a few of these people, but long-standing friendships were maintained through voluminous correspondence—long, discursive letters filled with lengthy discussions of literature, philosophy, and science. Before his death this circle of correspondents would include such recognizable names as Henry Kuttner, C. L. Moore, J. Vernon Shea, E. Hoffman Price, and Fritz Lieber. Some of these letters are collected in the five Arkham House volumes and others are published by Necronomicon Press. Brown University, in Lovecraft's hometown of Providence, Rhode Island, maintains a catalogued Lovecraft collection with thousands more.

Lovecraft's fictional worlds and histories were often discussed, as were the worlds created by Smith and other writers. It was not long before Smith and Lovecraft carried over this sharing of ideas into their fiction, referring to each other's creations in their stories. It was Smith who gave birth to such deities as Tsathoggua, Atlach-Nacha, and Abhoth, and who created the magical tome, the *Book of Eibon*. It was Smith's magical, prehistoric Hyperborea that Lovecraft frequently referred to in his tales. This idea was soon picked up by other authors. Robert E. Howard—whose most famous creation is still Conan the barbarian—created the dreaded *Unausprechlichen Kulten* and the mad poet Justin Geoffrey, author of the terrible *People of the Monolith*. These were also incorporated into Lovecraft's stories, along with references to Howard's prehistoric Cimmeria.

The young Robert Bloch provided the blasphemous books *De Vermiis Mysteriis* and the *Cultes des Goules* as well as the interstellar and invisible star vampire that devoured a thinly disguised HPL in Bloch's "Shambler from the Stars" (1935). Bloch's creations were quickly absorbed by Lovecraft, who also revenged his "murder" by dispatching protagonist Robert Blake in the "The Haunter of the Dark" (1936). Long-time friend Frank Belknap Long brought to the collection both the hounds of Tindalos and the Space-Eaters, as well as Chaugnar Faugn, who appeared in "The Horror in the Hills", a story by Long based on one of Lovecraft's many vivid dreams.

August Derleth added the most to the now-growing collection of Great Old Ones and alien races. Continuing to write new Cthulhu Mythos stories long after Lovecraft's death in 1937, he created, among others, Cthugha, the Tcho-Tcho people, Ithaqua, and the sand-dwellers. Basing a number of his tales in Lovecraft's fictional towns of Arkham, Dunwich, Innsmouth, and Kingsport, he introduced such characters as Dr. Shrewsbury, who, with the use of magicks, voyaged through space to visit the vast alien library circling the star Celaeno. Although many disagree with Derleth's interpretations—his desire to create a pantheon of good gods based on Lovecraft's Nodens, and his attempts to define Cthulhu and Nyarlathotep as elementals—none will deny this man's tireless efforts in keeping the works of Lovecraft in print and available to the public in the decades following HPL's death.

One of Derleth's favorite additions to the Mythos was Hastur, a great being supposedly trapped beneath the Lake of Hali near the city Carcosa on a planet circling the star Aldebaran. Although briefly mentioned by Lovecraft in early tales, these were actually the creations of Ambrose Bierce (1842-1914?), American journalist and early exponent of the weird tale. Bierce was an early influence on HPL, as were a number of other writers. His favorite author was always Edgar Allan Poe (1809-1849), and Poe's influence can be clearly seen in some of Lovecraft's first adult fiction. "The Outsider" (1921) perhaps most closely emulates Poe's style and subject matter. Arthur Machen (1863-1947) was another early influence; his story "The Great God Pan" (1894) is very similar in theme to Lovecraft's "The Dunwich Horror." Robert W. Chambers (1865-1933) also left his mark on Lovecraft. A mysterious play, *The King in Yellow*, figures in some of Chambers' stories and probably inspired Lovecraft to create the *Necronomicon*, the *Pnakotic Manuscripts,* and the other tomes of eldritch lore for which his tales are famous. It was Chambers who first borrowed from Bierce the Lake of Hali and Carcosa, perhaps inspiring Lovecraft to attempt transpositions.

Lord Dunsany (1878-1957) was probably Lovecraft's strongest contemporary influence. It was Dunsany's *The Gods of Pegana* (1905) that encouraged Lovecraft to write several dream-based stories and first provided him with the idea of an artificial pantheon of gods. Algernon Blackwood, another contemporary admired by HPL, drew upon Native American legends for the version of the Wendigo later adapted into the Mythos by August Derleth, which is there called Ithaqua.

Lovecraft Himself

Although chronic nervous disorders prevented Lovecraft from regular attendance at school, he was a precocious child and an avid reader. His father institutionalized when Lovecraft was only three, he and his mother moved into the house owned by his maternal grandfather. It was in the library of Grandfather Whipple that Lovecraft first discovered the Arabian Nights, the myths of Greece and Rome, and Edgar Alan Poe. He wrote his first story, "The Little Glass Bottle", at the

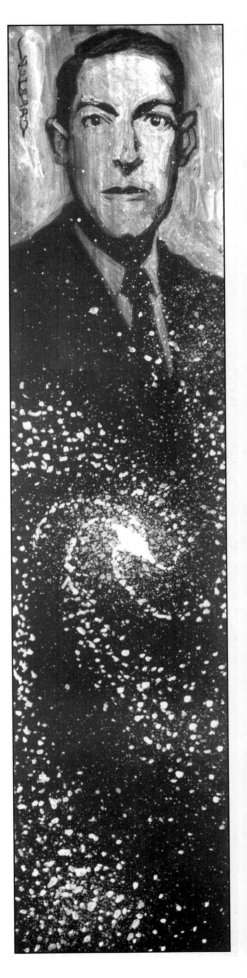

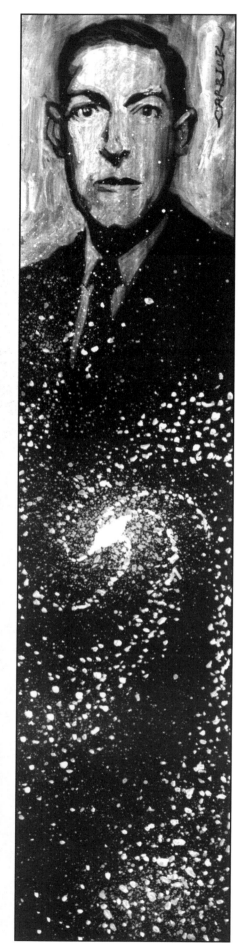

age of six, about the time he had his first dreams about the terrible, faceless nightgaunts (throughout his life he had vivid dreams). It was also through this library that Lovecraft developed a taste for Georgian thought and literature that would remain with him throughout his life.

But Lovecraft, who would later describe himself as a "mechanist materialist", was also attracted to the sciences. In 1899 he began publishing a small journal called the *Scientific Gazette*, followed

shortly thereafter by the *Rhode Island Journal of Astronomy*. These small, hectographed publications were sold door to door by a bicycle-mounted HPL. At age thirteen, Lovecraft's beloved grandfather died. His father had already passed away, succumbing to his illness in 1898, still confined to Butler Hospital. A series of business failures had depleted the Whipple family fortune, forcing Lovecraft's mother and aunts to sell the family home and move to smaller quarters. This was a great blow to Lovecraft. Another attack of nerves led to his withdrawal from high school in 1905 and again in 1908. Lovecraft, two and a half years short of graduation, never returned.

Lovecraft never held a job, supporting himself on the dwindling family fortune and by what little he could earn as a ghostwriter and revisionist. Always the aristocrat, he was throughout his life to remain torn between the professional writer's desire for success and money and the detached, amateur gentleman's desire to reach for aesthetic goals unfettered by commercial demands. Despite this, his first attempts to sell his fiction met with unqualified success, the editor of *Weird Tales*, Edwin Baird, accepting the first five stories sent to him by Lovecraft. His stories appeared in nine of eleven issues published between late 1923 and early 1925.

When the editorship of *Weird Tales* passed to the hands of Farnsworth Wright, Lovecraft's fortunes changed. Wright, an able editor, possessed a blind spot regarding Lovecraft's work and now HPL more often met with rejection than success. Stories now considered classics, such as "The Call of Cthulhu", were only published after meeting repeated rejections from *Weird Tales*. His half-hearted attempts to provide what Wright demanded of commercial fiction were only partially successful. Wright rejected both "At the Mountains of Madness" and "The Shadow Out of Time", now-famous stories that were eventually printed by *Astounding Stories*. The superb "The Case of Charles Dexter Ward" didn't see publication until years after Lovecraft's death. Lovecraft, crushed by the repeated rejections, began refusing to submit his stories, and "Dreams in the Witch House" only saw print because August Derleth secretly submitted it to Wright, urging him to accept it.

An Expanding Circle

Ironically, it was during this time that HPL was doing the bulk of his professionally published revision work, much of it no less than actual ghostwriting. Lovecraft might provide a nearly complete text of a story based on a few root ideas supplied by the "author". Stories such as Zealia Bishop's "The Curse of Yig" and "The Mound", and Hazel Heald's "The Horror in the Museum" and "Out of the Aeons" were in fact 90% or more the product of H.P. Lovecraft. While these stories were quickly accepted by Wright, Lovecraft's work under his own name continued to be rejected.

The practice of trading deities, books, and themes from one writer's stories to another was in full swing at this time, and Lovecraft seemed to join in the game with his revision tales. Bishop's two stories are set in the American southwest and here we find Lovecraft's Cthulhu and Smith's Tsathoggua, along with the introduction of Yig. All three are worshiped by a heretofore unguessed-at race of subterranean humans. "Out of the Aeons" introduces a new deity, Ghatanothoa, described through the vehicle of Robert E. Howard's *Nameless Cults* and linking both to Lovecraft's own fungi from Yuggoth. "The Horror in the Museum" introduces us to dimensional shamblers and a Great Old One known as Rhan-Tegoth.

The 1940s and '50s saw a quiet expansion of the Mythos. Robert Bloch and James Wade added a few stories to the canon, but it was August Derleth who contributed the most, producing a number of original tales as well as posthumous collaborations based on Lovecraft's story notes. It was not until 1964 that the appearance of a young Britisher named Ramsey Campbell heralded a renewed interest in the Cthulhu Mythos.

Encouraged by August Derleth, Campbell's first published collection, *The Inhabitant of the Lake and Other Less Welcome Tenants* (1964), was a series of Lovecraft-inspired pastiches set in England's Severn Valley. These stories described a number of different beings, races, and histories similar to, but distinct from Lovecraft's. His most famous Mythos creations include Y'golonac, Glaaki, the insects from Shagghai, and a host of other creatures and god-like beings. 1971 saw the emergence of another Britisher, Brian Lumley, who brought to the Mythos the underground chthonians, the mysterious *G'harne Fragments*, and the modern-day sorcerer Titus Crow.

Numerous other contemporary contributors directly influenced by Lovecraft include Gary Myers, Basil Copper, T.E.D. Klein, David Drake, and Thomas Ligotti. Many others, such as Stephen King, have made special contributions to anthologies of new Mythos tales. Few writers of modern horror fiction can claim there is no Lovecraft influence in their work.

Lovecraft died in near obscurity in March of 1937, at the age of 46 a victim of Bright's disease and virulent cancer. His mother had died in 1921 after two years' confinement in the same institution where his father had died. A brief, two-year marriage accompanied by residence in New York proved disastrous, though divorce was never made final, and in 1926 Lovecraft had fled home to Providence to live out his years a bachelor, sharing quarters with two aunts. These last years saw a reduced output of fiction but it was during this period that he produced some of his most memorable tales. He also found time to travel, visiting places that tickled his antiquarian heart: Maine, Philadelphia, Quebec, St. Augustine, Charlotte, New Orleans, Salem, and Nantucket. Traveling by bus, sleeping in YMCAs, and eating crackers, cheese, and canned beans, Lovecraft was able to indulge his personal tastes for the old, the antique, and the decaying.

Plenty of evidence exists to show that Lovecraft was, by any assessment, an odd individual. Predisposed to hypochondria and a premature pose of old age, for much of his life he was committed to social and artistic views more suitable to centuries past than the one he lived in. Allergic to cold and repulsed by seafood, he was also a scientist and a philosopher possessed of an inquiring mind and sharp wit. Most who came to know him during his lifetime were left profoundly changed by his friendship. Encouraged and enlightened by his erudition and no-nonsense philosophies, many went on to achieve fame far greater than their mentor ever enjoyed during his lifetime. He has the same effect today, generations after his death. His name is better known than ever and those who discover him, whether through his stories, through films, games, comics, or trading cards, find themselves as fascinated by his bizarre creations and nightmare worlds as were his contemporaries so many years ago. ■

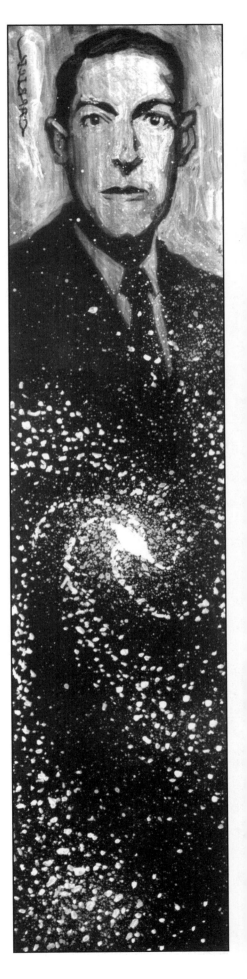

IN RERUM SUPERNATURA

"The Nature of Things Supernatural", exploring the influence of the Cthulhu Mythos as supplied by evidence in various languages

by Phileus P. Sadowsky

These notes discuss the *Necronomicon*, its author, mighty Cthulhu, evidences of Mythos knowledge in earlier times, and more. They are a summary of researches by Herr Doktor Phileus P. Sadowsky, late Professor of Arabic Literature and Philo-pseudology, University of Sofia [Bulgaria].

The Necronomicon

This key work of Mythos lore is a book familiar to students of arcana, although few alive have had opportunity to study it first-hand. Squeamish scholars have deemed the *Necronomicon* accursed and destroyed nearly every copy which can be found. Much of what is popularly known about the book is due to the writings of H. P. Lovecraft. According to his researches, *Necronomicon* is actually the title of a Greek translation made c.950 AD by Theodorus Philetas, from an original Arabic manuscript. A Latin version of the Greek translation was made in 1228 AD by Olaus Wormius, to whose name we may append "the Elder", so as not to confuse him with the 16th century scholar of the same name. His Latin version is the one known to have survived to the present. An analysis of Lovecraft's researches regarding the *Necronomicon* can be found in *Lovecraft: a Biography* by L. Sprague de Camp.

The meaning of the Greek title *Necronomicon*, which the Latin version retains, is something like "things pertaining to the customs, practices, or laws of the dead", *nekros* meaning "dead" and *nomos* meaning "custom" or "law". The original Arabic title of the work was *Kitab Al-Azif*, "book of the howlings of the desert demons or Jinn" or, more poetically, as "book of the Approacher".

The Author's Name

A major error in Lovecraft's description of the book is one not of his making. It seems to have been a scribe's error which found its way into the medieval manuscripts, and which is worth correcting at this point. The author of the *Necronomicon* is said to have been a mad Arab who died around 738 AD, named "Abdul Al-Hazrad". No Arab ever would have had such a name. Although in English popular fiction Abdul is perhaps the most popular surname given to an Arab character, it is not actually an Arab name. "Abd" in Arabic means either "slave" or "worshiper", as in *Abd al-Malik*, meaning "slave of the king", *Abd al-Rahman* (or *Abdurrahman*), meaning "worshiper of the generous one" (namely God), or *Abd Allah*, more commonly written in English as *Abdullah*, meaning "worshiper or slave of God". *Al* or *ul* in all these names means simply "the". Even Allah actually means "the (only) God". Abdul means merely "the worshiper/slave of —". Standing alone, it makes no sense in Arabic, needing a noun to complete the meaning.

The name *Abdul Al-Hazrad* is obviously a clerical error on the part of Theodorus Philetas or (more likely) by Olaus Wormius the Elder who, knowing no Arabic, translated Philetas' Greek version into Latin. Thus the correct rendering of the *Necronomicon's* author is *Abd al-Hazred*.

Hazred is not an Arabic word. It probably is a textual corruption from which one might reconstruct the original. Medieval authors often didn't fully understand foreign languages, and had no bilingual dictionaries available. They often made mistakes even in transliterating, according to how they heard proper names pronounced. For example, *hashisheen* in Arabic became *assassinus* in Latin and *assassin* in English. The Arabic name Ibn Rushd became Averroes in Latin. If Hazred is a similar case, I would speculate that the actual original was *Azrad*, the elative form of the Arabic verb *zarada* meaning "to strangle or devour". Thus the correct name for the Necronomicon's author is probably *Abd al-Azrad*, translatable as "the worshiper of the great strangler / great devourer".

A Famous Couplet

The most widely-known words from the *Necronomicon* are often quoted. The Arabic original of these lines contain an important piece of information, hitherto unknown, dealing with the cult of Cthulhu. The Arabic quoted is from Arabic Manuscript No. 2781, the *Necronomicon*, of the Magyar Tudomanyos Akademia Orientalisztikai Kozlemenyei. Lovecraft gives an English version as follows.

That is not dead which can eternal lie,
And with strange aeons even death may die.

The original Arabic verses have identical meter for each four-beat line, the stresses falling upon the slashes:

- / - - / - - / - - /

Transliterated, the Arabic sounds like this:

la mayyitan ma qadirun yatabaqa sarmadi
fa itha yaji ash-shuthath al-mautu qad yantahi.

لاَ مَيِّتًا طا قَادِرًا يَتَبَقَى سَرْمَدِى
فَإِنَّا يَجِىءُ ٱلشُّذَّاذُ ٱلْمَوْتُ قَدْ يَنْتَهِى

The Original Arabic

Literally (and unpoetically) translated, the Arabic original has the following meaning:

> *That thing is not dead which has the capacity to continue to exist eternally,*
> *And if the abnormal (bizarre, strange) ones (things, times?) come, then death may cease to be.*

One Arabic phrase, *yaji ash-shuthath*, perhaps gives a clue to a deeper mystery. It is plural, and it literally means "the abnormal", referring to people or to things, depending on the context. *Yaqi* means "comes" or "are coming". Colloquial Arabic often transforms the soft j-sound into a hard g-sound, and many times the vowel endings are left off and the words slurred together, as we often do in English. Therefore a possible rendering of this phrase in colloquial Arabic would be *yag-shuthath*, with a slight change in the quality of the vowels easily recognizable as Yog-Sothoth.

The couplet may have been part of an antedating ritual created by Arabian devil-worshipers who during ceremonies would chant *Yag-shuthath! Yag-shuthath!* meaning "The Abnormal One (or Times) are coming!" This is obvious reference to the return of the Great Old Ones or the Outer Gods, central goals for the worshipers of the Cthulhu cult, as reported by Legrasse, Armitage, and other students.

The Hungarian Necronomicon[1]

The manuscript is catalogued as the *Kitab al-Azif*, Arabic Manuscript 2781 of the Magyar Tudomanyos Akademia Orientalisztikai Kozlemenyei. The folded manuscript measures 21 by 16 centimeters on coarse parchment which is quite decayed and worm-eaten, and it is partially burnt on the lower right corner, as if it had been cast into a fire and then rescued before being consumed.

The text is written in a shaky hand, perhaps that of an old man, but certainly not that of a professional scribe. The type of parchment and the style of Arabic script allow the manuscript to be dated to the eighth century, probably from Syria or Iraq. Due to the decayed nature of the manuscript, only fragments of the text so far can be recovered with certainty, but there is enough to allow a reconstruction of the original Arabic names of many deities in the Cthulhu Mythos—with some philological comments on those names.

The original Arabic text of Abd al-Azrad passed through several recensions in Arabic and was translated into Greek, from Greek into Latin, and from Latin into English. Furthermore, such was the fame of this dread occultic work that there developed a large body of spurious *Necronomicon* manuscripts created by charlatans who had no connection to the authentic Mythos, but who wished to try to profit from it.

Recently, books bearing the name have been published in English, each claiming or imputing to incorporate the authentic tradition. At least one was printed as a mass-market paperback! None of these efforts has any establishable connection with the original manuscript, with the possible exception of H.R. Geiger's work, which is infused with the spirit of the original.

Post-Classical References to Mythos Entities, by Language

There were many difficulties in translating proper names from one language to another in medieval times. Arabic names often appeared in corrupt Latin forms—Al-Qahira became "Cairo", for instance—partly because the vowels of Arabic were seldom written, only consonants appearing in the usual script. The untrained foreign reader finds a large range of possible pronunciations of the same word. Different regional dialects pronounced the same syllables differently. One always finds transformations when names are transmitted from one language to another. This is certainly true of names connected with the Cthulhu Mythos, as they appear in various editions of the *Necronomicon*.

Azathoth

Azathoth, the Daemon Sultan, is the ruler of the Outer Gods according to the Cthulhu Mythos. His name is apparently a compound of two different particles, *aza* and *Thoth*. Thoth is clearly related to the name of the ancient Egyptian deity *Tahuti*, whose name is mispronounced in Greek as Thoth. *Aza* is a slight verbal corruption of the Arabic word *izzu*, meaning power, might, or

Azathoth

عِزّ طحوتي

in Arabic

ϽΛϽϗΘϴϴ

in Greek

Chthonians

الغاريون

in Arabic

ΧΘΟΥΙΟS

in Greek

Dark Young

المُظلِمون
الشباب

in Arabic

strength. The name written in Arabic would thus be *Izzu Tahuti*, or "Power of Thoth". Apparently Theodorus Philetas translated *Tahuti* into *Thoth*, to him the more familiar form. In Greek the full name became *Azathoth*, and so the deity would later become known in Latin and in English.

Latin: *Azathoth*

Greek: *azathoth*

Arabic: *Izzu Tahutiz*

Whether Thoth or Tahuti, both are code-names used by sorcerers in secret reference to Nyarlathotep, the Cthulhu Mythos deity most worshiped in ancient Egypt. Translated or interpreted, the name Azathoth means "Power of Nyarlathotep", since Nyarlathotep fulfills all the commands of Azathoth: he is Azathoth's power or agent, and thus Nyarlathotep is backed by Azathoth.

Chthonians

The word "chthonian" is a direct Latinization of the Greek word *xthonios*, meaning "dweller under the earth", which is exactly what the chthonians are in the Cthulhu Mythos. The original Arabic name for this race, according to the Arabic *Necronomicon*, is *al-ghariyun*, meaning literally "those of the cave", the singular being *ghari*, or "of a cave".

Latin: *chthonius*

Greek: *xthollios*

Arabic: *al-ghariyun*

The spot at which the chthonian race has most been claimed to emerge is at the city of G'harne, somewhere in north Africa. The similarities between the city name G'harne and the Arabic *al-ghariyun* are so vast as to need no comment.

Dark Young of Shub-Niggurath

This name has undergone a great deal of corruption in its transmission from Arabic into Greek, Latin, and English, and is in reality a composite of various epithets from those languages. Part of the problem comes from the fact that the name Shub-Niggurath, commonly taken to refer to the "Mother of the Dark Young", may be the title of the dark young themselves. Their Mother being known more accurately as "The Black Goat of the Woods With a Thousand Young".

Latin: *juvenis nigritiae*

Arabic: *ash-shubab al muthlimun*

The name is best understood by breaking it down into composite phrases. "Shub" is probably more correctly written in Arabic as *shabb*, meaning "youth" or "a young man". This word could clearly have reference to the "young" component of "dark young". "Niggurath" is apparently a corruption of the Latin *nigritiae*, meaning "blackness". Thus, Shub-Niggurath would seem to be a word combining Arabic and Latin, meaning "A Young One of Blackness"—one of the dark young. The Arabic term used by Abd al-Azrad for these entities is in the singular, *ash-shabb al muthlim*, or "the dark young ones"; made plural it is *ash-shabb al-muthlimun*. Unfortunately the portion of the Greek *Necronomicon* which discusses these matters is damaged by water, mold, and worms, and is illegible. Part of the difficulty could be resolved if we knew how Theodorus translated the Arabic phrase into Greek, but this is unknown.

How did this barbarous compound word of Latin and Arabic arise? When the Roman Empire fell, classical Latin accelerated corruption into the ancestral dialects of such modern languages as French, Italian, Spanish, Portuguese, Rumanian, and Romansch. Many Latin dialects developed in medieval Italy—modern Italian is a descendant only of the Florentine dialect. Many other dialects were and are spoken in Italy. The original Latin phrase for dark young, *juvenis nigritiae*, meaning literally "a young creature of blackness", also transformed.

It would seem that the dark young were worshiped by decadent fertility cults in medieval Italy and the dark young were referred to by these cultists as *juvenis nigritiae*. When the Muslims conquered Sicily in the ninth century their language and culture was spread throughout that island. Sicily was evidently a stronghold of worship of the Dark Young, and the Arab immigrants were caught up into this religion. The Arabs corrupted *juvenis nigritiae*, translating *juvenis* into Arabic as *shabb*, while corrupting the pronunciation of *nigritiae* into *niggurath*. When Olaus translated the *Necronomicon* into Latin in 1228, he was apparently familiar with the Sicilian cult, and translated the Greek phrase referring to them as Shub-Niggurath, a phrase by which the cult would possibly be known to a few Italian scholars and churchmen. This phrase transferred unaltered from Olaus' Latin version into English.

What would be the Arabic name of the creature (probably mistakenly) known in the Cthulhu Mythos as Shub-Niggurath? In the Arabic *Kitab al-Azif*, the phrase "Black Goat of the Woods with a Thousand Young" occurs alternatively as *Al-Ma'iza as-Sauda al-Ghabati* ("The Black Goat of the Woods"), *Umm al-Alf Al-Muthlimun* ("The Mother of the Thousand Dark Things"), or *Umm ash-Shabab al-Alf* ("The Mother of the Thousand Young Ones").

Ghouls

The ghouls mentioned in the Necronomicon are directly related to that mythical creature of Arabic legends, the *ghul*.

Arabic: *ghul*

According to Arabic sources, the *ghul* has a human form, but a canine or monstrous appearance. They haunt tombs and graveyards, feasting on the corpses therein, and attempting to lure away passers-by. This description clearly corresponds to the ghouls mentioned in various Mythos-related works.

Nyarlathotep

Nyarlathotep is presently the only name in the Mythos which can be traced to ancient Egyptian antecedents. The name is a contraction of *ny har rut hotep*, meaning "there is no peace (safety, rest) at the gate". The significance of this title is apparently that Nyarlathotep, in his role as messenger of the Outer Gods, is the "gateway" between the planes, and specifically between their dimensions and ours, or at least that is how the ancient Egyptian cultists viewed the matter.

These ancient Egyptian Cthulhu cultists used the name of the Egyptian god Tahuti (or Thoth) as an alternative name for Nyarlathotep, as both Thoth and Nyarlathotep served similar functions in their respective pantheons.

Latin: *Nyarlat Hotep*

Greek: *niarlat hotep*

Arabic: *niyharlat hotep*

Egyptian: *ny har rut hotep*

The key to the corruption of the word is that in New Egyptian the letter L, signified by a couching-lion glyph, also doubled for the Greek r-sound. Thus the "r" in Cleopatra is written by using the same glyph. Presumably, when Abd al-Azrad (or whomever transliterated the Egyptian into Arabic) read the word *ny har rut hotep*, he mistook the "r" in *rut* for an "l" and the phrase became, in Arabic, *niharlat hotep*.

In Greek, the letter "H" can only appear at the beginning of a word. Theodorus could not transliterate the "h" in *niyharlat*, instead choosing *niarlat* in Greek. Olaus Wormius continued the corruption by changing the letter "I" to the homophonous letter "Y", and English translators finished the process by combining the phrase into Nyarlathotep, the single word known today.

Shudde M'ell

Shudde M'ell, the ruler of the chthonians, is in the Arabic *Necronomicon* written as *al-Mu'ell* (or *al-Mu'ill*), meaning "The Causer of Destruction".

Arabic: *al-mu'ell*

The referred-to destruction is doubtless the chthonian power to provoke earthquakes. The word "Shudde" is almost certainly a corruption of the Arabic *shidda*, meaning "violence". Thus, Shudde M'ell (or perhaps more correctly *Shidda al-Mu'ell*) properly refers only to the earthquakes caused by this deity and its minion chthonians; that is, earthquakes are the violence, *shidda*, caused by *al-Mu'ell*, the deity.

World-Wide Forms of "Cthulhu"

The name Cthulhu represents an attempt to transliterate into Greek a difficult Arabic word which appears frequently in the Arabic *Necronomicon*. The Greek form is Cthulhu. Although this is a difficult phrase in English, Latin, or Greek, it makes perfect sense in the original Arabic. Cthulhu is sometimes called *Khadhulu* in the Arabic *Necronomicon*.

Latin: *Cthulhu*

Greek: *xthulu*

Arabic: *khadhulu*
    or *al-khadhulu*

Ghouls
in Arabic

Nyarlathotep
in Arabic
in Egyptian
in Greek

Shudde M'ell
in Arabic

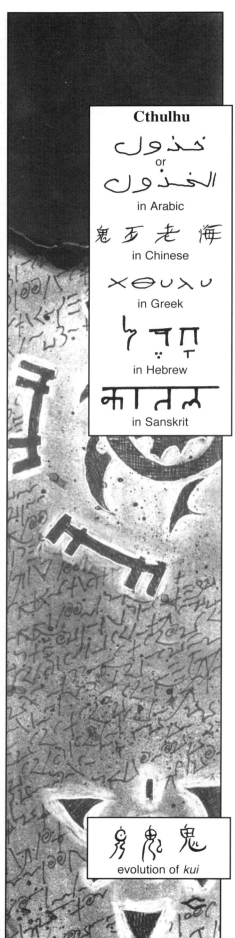

Cthulhu

نذلو
or
الخذون

in Arabic

鬼歹老海

in Chinese

XӨUХU

in Greek

כזִ ד ַ ל

in Hebrew

कातल

in Sanskrit

evolution of *kui*

In Arabic, *khadhulu* means "abandoner" or "forsaker". The term is used thus in the *Koran* 25:29 by Muhammed the Prophet, where it states, "For Mankind Satan [in Arabic, *Shaytan*] Is Khadulu". Muslim commentators have traditionally taken this to mean that Satan is a forsaker of mankind—on Judgment Day, Satan will forsake those who followed him in this life.

However, as *khadhulu* is used extensively in the Arabic *Necronomicon* to refer to a powerful deity, and is translated by Theodorus as *xthulu* and by Olaus in Latin as Cthulhu, it is possible to translate this verse as "for mankind Satan is Cthulhu", thus identifying the entity Cthulhu, worshiped by a cult of pagan Arabs before Muhammed, with the Satan of the Judeo-Christian tradition. Cthulhu worship in pre-Islamic Arabia may have centered on the famous Nameless City, also known as the City of Brass or Many-Columned Irem—in Arabic, *Iram dhat al-imad*.

On the other hand, there are reports of small tribes in the isolation of Greenland who refer to this pre-Christian deity as Cthulhu or a near-equivalent, despite the improbability of their having had contact with the *Koran* or with the Wormius version of the *Necronomicon*. Perhaps Cthulhu or some similar sound is the true name of this entity, and the similarity of the word *khadhulu* led Cthulhu's Arab worshipers to refer to their deity by a term understandable to them.

The Semitic cultures in particular, in all their various branches throughout the Middle East, retain vestiges of ancient Cthulhu worship. One of the oldest Semitic languages is Assyrian, which originated in the second millennium BC, and which shows clear references to Cthulhu worship. A common word for "demon" in Assyrian is *alu'u*[2]. When this word is combined with the Assyrian word *khatu*[3], meaning "ominous" or "evil", the result is *khatu alu'u*, and is clearly related philogically to Cthulhu. An ancient Babylonian scribe makes reference to *alu'u lemnu sha pa la ishu atta*, meaning "the *alu'u* (demon) who has no mouth"[4]. This could refer to Cthulhu himself, whose face is a mass of tentacles, and therefore appears as a demon who has no mouth. Even if not, the horror of the image points at Mythos origin.

Hebrew, another ancient Semitic language, also makes oblique reference to Cthulhu worship. This identification necessarily must remain tentative, since the oldest Hebrew texts we possess are of the Bible, the writers of which clearly and wisely would have been antagonistic toward any Cthulhu cultists. The prophet Isaiah, who lived in the 8th century BC, wrote "I shall look upon man no more among the inhabitants of *chadhel*" (Isaiah 38:11).

Hebrew: *chadel*

The last Hebrew word of this verse, *chadhel*, is directly related semantically to the Arabic *khadhul*. This word is generally thought to be a euphemism for Sheol or Hell[5]. However, if the word is taken as a proper name, the significance of the verse drastically changes. *Chadhel* is most likely an ancient Hebrew form of the word Cthulhu, as the Hebrew "dh" in this case is, in linguistic terms, an emphatic form equivalent to the English "th", an aspirant form of the same sound. "The inhabitants of Chadhel" comes to mean "those who dwell with Chadhel" or "the people of Chadhel" (*i.e.*, Cthulhu), and thus clearly refers to a cultist sect. The meaning of the verse should be "I shall look upon man no more among the people of Cthulhu", a form of ritual and well-deserved cursing of the evil cultists. The name Chadhel had such horrendous overtones to the Hebrews that in medieval interpretations it became synonymous with Hell, giving rise to the modern faulty interpretation of the verse.

Indo-European languages also mention dread Cthulhu. For instance, the Sanskrit word *katala*) refers to a large fish or sea-monster[6].

Sanskrit: *katala*

This word is simply a Sanskrit pronunciation of Cthulhu, who of course qualifies nicely as a sea monster.

The name Cthulhu transliterates from Chinese characters thusly:

Chinese: *kui tai lao hai*

The meaning is *kui* (demon), *tai* (evil), *lao* (ancient), and *hai* (ocean)[7]. In idiomatic English, the phrase signifies "ancient evil oceanic demon".

Important is the derivation of this name from the archaic form of kui. Mandarin characters evolved from pictographs, wherein the character drawn was an abstract picture symbolizing a word or idea. In later times these pictographs were further abstracted into the current Chinese characters. The character for *kui* went through an evolution, arranged chronologically from left to right in a nearby box[8].

Scholars will easily recognize the symbols as archaic drawings of Cthulhu, including the tentacles attached to the head. We can conclude that a generic Chinese character for "demon", *kui*, evolved from the very early need to refer to Cthulhu. Awareness of that entity must be ancient indeed in China for it to have affected the language so profoundly.

Conclusion

Traces of ancient Cthulhu worship exist in the records of all major Old World civilizations: in Mesopotamia to the Assyrians as *Khatu alu'u*, the "evil demon"; in Palestine to the Hebrews as *Chadhel*, a name equivalent to Hell; in Arabia as *Khadhulu*, "Satan the forsaker"; to the Hindus as *Katala*, the "sea monster"; and to the Chines as *Kui tai lao hai*, the "ancient evil ocean demon". All label Cthulhu as malignant. Only in Egypt has no reference to the worship of Cthulhu been found. Perhaps the worship of Nyarlathotep (in the guise of Thoth) drove out competing cults.

The widespread nature of the Cthulhu cult—the only god shown to have been worshiped simultaneously in all three major centers of ancient civilization—had hitherto gone unnoticed by scholars. One wonders: if such a powerful cult could have remained so well-hidden in antiquity, what obscene rituals in hidden places might yet be practiced to this alien horror?

End Notes

1   Alarmingly, neither the document nor that catalog number currently exist. Here we have only Herr Doktor Sadowsky's unimpeachable reputation for the truth as corroboration.

2   Ignace J. Gleb, *et. al. The Assyrian Dictionary* (Chicago University Press, 1964, in progress), vol 2, pp. 355Ff.

3   *Ibid.*, vol. 6, p. 158. Spoken swiftly and slurred (as is often done in human speech) it probably would sound like *khatulu'u*, easily recognizable as a variation of the word Cthulhu.

4   *Cuneiform Texts from Babylonian Tablets*, 1627:8.

5   *Gesenius' Hebrew-Chaldee Lexicon* (Eerdmans, 1982), p. 262.

6   Monier-Williams, *Sanskrit-English Dictionary* (rev. version of 1899 edition: New Delhi, Minshiram Manohalal, 1981), p. 270a.>

7   These Chinese characters can be examined in the following sources: Bernhard Karlgren, *Analytical Dictionary of Chinese and Sino-Japanese* (New York: Dover, 1974 reprint of the 1923 Paris edition) hereafter referred to as ADC, and L. Wieger, *Chinese Characters* (Dover 1965 reprint of the 1915 edition) hereafter referred to as CC. For the specific characters: *kui* (or *kuei*) = "demon, spirit" ADC 460, CC 548; *tai* = "bad, evil" ADC 959; *lao* = "old, ancient" ADC 515, CC 88; *shai* = "sea, ocean" CC 595.

8   *Ibid.* These drawings are analyzed in CC 112, 548. ■

MENTAL DISORDERS

*Being a listing of
many mental disorders, from
Schizophrenia to various
personality disorders*

Terminology changes rapidly. A psychiatrist of the 1920s would recognize some of these terms, but others would be baffling. Most strikingly, phrases of a hundred years ago like "lunatic" have become deliberately neutral in tone.

Schizophrenia and Other Psychotic Disorders

In general, psychiatric medications may be of high value in treating such disorders. Beyond the symptomatic behaviors, those who lack such medications also should suffer skill reductions while the effect is strong.

Schizophrenia (schizophreniform disorder, dementia praecox): Mental concentration greatly diminishes; halve all skills requiring concentration. Symptoms include bizarre delusions, paranoia, auditory hallucinations, incoherent speech, seeming emotional detachment, social withdrawal, bizarre behavior, and a lack of the sense of self.

Psychotic Disorders: interesting behavioral and culture-bound syndromes are known. There is a Capgras's Syndrome, for instance, in which everyone is perceived as having been replaced by impostor duplicates. In Cotard's Syndrome (*délire de négation*), one is convinced that not only his possessions and status have fallen away, but his body literally loses blood, and the heart, the intestines, etc., begin to rot. In autoscopic psychosis, a phantom is thought to follow and imitate the person's movements. Many more such behaviors exist, and appropriately metaphorical new ones can be imagined and made up.

Many culture-bound syndromes are of briefer duration:

Amok—Malaysia. "Running amok", an outburst of violence and aggressive or homicidal behavior directed at people and property. Amnesia, return to consciousness, and exhaustion occur following the episode. The killing spree will be done using whatever weapons are on hand. (*Ahade idzi be* is the Navajo equivalent.)

Boufeé Délirant—West Africa, Haiti. Sudden outburst of aggressive, agitated behavior, marked confusion, sometimes with visual and auditory hallucinations or paranoia.

Brain Fag—Nigeria. Impaired concentration and feeling fatigued; pains in the neck and head; the sense that worms are crawling inside the head. Usually attributed to witchcraft.

Ghost Sickness—Navajo. Weakness, loss of appetite, feeling suffocated, nightmares, and a pervasive feeling of terror. Attributed as a sending from witches or malign supernatural powers.

Piblokto—Inuit. "Arctic madness" wherein the afflicted rips off his clothes and runs howling like an animal through the snow. (*Myriachit*, Siberia.)

Susto—Spain. A variety of somatic and psychological symptoms attributed to a traumatic incident so frightening that it dislodged the victim's spirit from his body.

Taijin Kyofusho—Japan. "Face-to-Face", anthropophobia, an intense anxiety in the presence of other people; fearfulness that one's appearance, odor, or behavior is offensive.

Voodoo Death—Haiti, Caribbean. Belief that a hex or witchcraft can bring about misfortune, disability, and death through "spiritual" mechanism. Often the victim self-fulfills the hexer's prophecy by refusing to heat and drink, resulting in starvation and dehydration. (*Mal peusto*, Spain).

Wacinko—Sioux. Anger, withdrawal, mutism, and immobility, leading to illness and suicide.

Wendigo Syndrome—Cree, Ojibwa, Salteaux. The afflicted believes he is a personification of the Wendigo, a cannibalistic thing with an icy heart. Compare with *Ithaqua* in the "Creatures" chapter.

Shared Paranoid Disorder (shared delusional disorder, *Folie à deux*): the character takes on the delusional system of another paranoid as a result of being in close contact.

Mood Disorders

Depression: symptoms include change in appetite, weight gain, weight loss, too much or too little sleep, sluggishness, feelings of worthlessness or guilt, and suicidal thoughts, hallucinations, delusions, or stupor. Skills lowered by 10 to 30 percentiles. There is a predisposition to use alcohol or other substances in an attempt at self-medication.

Mania: character has a fairly constant euphoric or possibly irritable mood. Symptoms include a general increase in activity, garrulousness, increased self-esteem to the point of delusion, decreased need for sleep, easily distracted, willingness for dangerous or imprudent activities such as reckless driving, hallucinations, delusions, and bizarre behavior. Lower skills by 10 to 30 percentiles. A predisposition exists to use alcohol or other substances in an attempt at self-medication.

Bipolar Mood Disorder: character oscillates between mood states for weeks at a time, crashing into different mood states, or sometimes states with mixed features (such as being depressed but full of energy).

Substance Abuse Disorder

The character finds solace in using a drug, becomes physically addicted, and spends much time maintaining, concealing, and indulging the habit. Drugs include alcohol, amphetamines, cocaine, hallucinogens, marijuana, nicotine, opium (esp. morphine and heroin), sedatives, plutonian drug, space mead, etc.

A character under the sway of such a substance should feel the personal struggle daily. POW rolls might be used to resist or succumb symbolically to cravings. Modifications of -20 percentiles or more could occur to skills because of withdrawal symptoms. Sanity losses could occur from binges or bad trips. Particular characters might find that drugs promote communication with alien entities and gods, and that dreams about them become ever more vivid and horrifying. Conversely, such substances might function as self-medications, deadening a character's fears and offering temporary defenses against Sanity loss.

See p. 116 for a list of abused substances which often lead to substance-related disorders.

Anxiety Disorders

Generalized Anxiety Disorder: character suffers from a variety of physical and emotional symptoms groupable into certain categories.

Motor tension—jitteriness, aches, twitches, restlessness, easily startled, easily fatigued, etc. (halve physical skill percentiles).

Autonomic hyperactivity—sweating, racing heart, dizziness, clammy hands, flushed or pallid face, high resting pulse and respiration, etc.

Expectations of doom—anxieties, worries, fears, and especially anticipations of misfortune.

Vigilance—distractible, inability to focus, insomnia, irritability, impatience (reduce intellectual skills by one fourth).

Panic Disorder: a discrete period of fear in which symptoms develop rapidly. Within minutes palpitation, swearing, trembling, choking, etc. appear, strong enough that the person fears immediate death or insanity. Burdened with the recurrence of these episodes, he or she fears their return. This often leads to a developing agoraphobia.

Agoraphobia: the character needs a successful D100 roll against POW times a multiplier of 1-5 in order to leave home or engage socially. May be linked to panic disorder, as per just above.

Obsessive Compulsive Disorder: character involuntarily experiences persistent ideas, thoughts, impulses, etc. involving violence and self-doubt. These ideas are frequently repugnant to the character, but they are so strong that during times of stress the character may be unable to concentrate apart from them, even if necessary for survival.

Compulsions: ritual actions performed by the character intended to affect the future. Though the character may agree the actions are senseless, the need to perform them is overpowering and may last for D10 combat rounds. Even in times of great stress, the character may ignore his or her survival in order to perform the ritual. In a severe condition, for instance, a sufferer might need hours to clean up before he or she was able to leave one room for another.

Post-traumatic Stress Disorder (in WWI, "shell shock"): after a traumatic event, perhaps years later, the character begins to relive the trauma through persistent thoughts, dreams, and flashbacks. Correspondingly, the character loses interest in daily activities. He or she may return to normal once the memories are well explored and understood, but that process will perhaps take years. Today, quicker clinical treatments exist,

such as eye movement desensitization and refocusing, or EMDR.

Simple Phobia or Mania: the individual persistently fears a particular object or situation. He or she realizes that the fear is excessive and irrational, but the fear is disturbing enough that he or she avoids the stimulus. In severe cases, the object of the phobia is imagined to be omnipresent, perhaps hidden.

There are as many phobias as one cares to notice or name. Manias are rarer. In a mania, the character is inordinately fond of a particular stimulus, and takes great pains to be with it or near it. When the character's sexuality is involved, the mania is termed a fetish.

Phobic and manic reactions were stressed in earlier editions of Call of Cthulhu, partly from lack of imagination and partly because such reactions are easy to identify and apply, and sometimes amusing to communicate. In truth, the disturbed human mind is a complex maze of behaviors, symptoms, and concepts, one not nearly so easily described. See the nearby phobia listing.

Somatoform Disorders

Somatization Disorder: character suffers symptoms from dizziness and impotence to intense pain and blindness. Medicine cannot explain the symptoms, but the character does not believe they represent a specific disease.

Conversion Disorder: character reports physical disfunctions suggesting a physical disorder but, though involuntary, the symptoms provide a way to avoid something undesirable or to garner attention and caring. Symptoms range from painful headaches to paralysis or blindness.

Hypochondriasis: character believes he or she suffers from a serious disease. No physical cause for reported symptoms will be found, but the character continues to believe the disease or condition exists, often with serious consequences to the person's normal life.

Body Dysmorphic Disorder: character suffers from perceived flaws in appearance, usually of the face, often of the hips or legs. Behavior may alter in unexpected ways to cover up the flaws or to calm anxieties.

Dissociative Disorders

Dissociative Amnesia (Psychogenic Amnesia): inability to recall important personal information, brought on by a desire to avoid unpleasant memories. The character needs a POW x1 roll to recall such details or the cause of the amnesia. Since the horror of the Mythos is the probable cause of this amnesia, the keeper may choose to reset Cthulhu Mythos to 0 and maximum Sanity to 99 while this disorder holds sway: the horror returns when the character's memories do.

Dissociative Fugue: character flees from home and/or work, and cannot recall his or her past. Once the flight halts, the character may assume an entirely new identity.

Dissociative Identity Disorder (Multiple Personality Disorder, or MPD): character appears to harbor more than one personality, each of which is dominant at times and has its own distinct behavior and even different social relationships. Players may need several or many investigator sheets for their investigator's different personalities.

Addictions (Substance-Related Disorders)

Substance use and abuse occurs in all segments of all societies. By definition, abuse indicates decreased work or school performance, accidents, intoxication while working or driving, absenteeism, violent crime, and/or theft. Urine and blood tests can confirm suspected abuse. Substance use may worsen or mimic other psychiatric disorders relating to depression, anxiety, mania, or psychosis.

Many people successfully use substances recreationally, without substantial or even observable changes to their lives. A fraction are not so fortunate. Their lives change, as they increasingly cling to and come to depend on one or more such substances.

Alcohol, amphetamines, cocaine, and the opioids (opiates) are addictive substances most frequently resorted to in earlier game eras. They and more are used in the present day.

Abuse often leads to dependence, which is characterized by developing tolerance, withdrawal states, and a pattern of increasing procurement of the substance. Dependence may be emotional and social in context.

Therapy includes making sure someone hasn't overdosed, ruling out other substances possibly present in the blood, and medical support. Long-term treatment lasts six months to a year, with the goal of creating longer and longer periods of abstinence.

Alcohol: symptoms include poor judgment, talkativeness, mood changes, aggression, impaired attention, amnesia-like states. Use can also cause a flushed face, uncoordination, and slurred speech. Withdrawal can cause mild shakiness, hangovers, and other symptoms. Delirium tremens can include seizures and delirium requiring active medical intervention.

LSD, mushrooms, peyote: 8-12 hour duration of high with flashbacks after abstinence, visual hallucinations, paranoid thoughts, false sense of achievement and strength, suicidal or homicidal tendencies, depersonalization, derealization. Treatment requires talking down; for severe agitation, sedatives or antipsychotics plus restraints may be needed. Lysergic acid diethylamide was synthesized in 1943.

Amphetamines and cocaine: the user may be alert, talkative, euphoric, hyperactive, irritable, aggressive, agitated, sometimes paranoid. There may be visual and tactile hallucinations such as formication, the feeling that insects are crawling across one's skin. Cocaine use may be quickly followed by a crash phase. Craving for these drugs can last for years.

Opiods (opium, morphine, heroin): symptoms include euphoria, drowsiness, anorexia, lessened sex drive, hypoactivity, and passivity; physically, nausea and slow heart rate. In themselves, needle tracks in arms and legs can develop into a medical problem. Treatment is a weaning-off process using methadone(unknown until recently), itself highly addictive.

Phencycladine (PCP, Ketamine, "Special K"): 8-12 hours duration of high, hallucinations, paranoid thoughts, catatonic state, violent behavior, convulsions, anesthesia (for instance, can punch a hand through a windshield and shatter every bone in the arm, but not feel it until the drug wears off). If attempting to talk down such a user, the talker may get his face punched in, or more. Isolate until the behavior calms; use antipsychotics if the person is on a rampage. These and similar drugs are new, and exist only in the present era.

Psychosexual Disorders

This is an exceedingly diverse group. Homosexuality is no longer considered a mental disease, but it was believed such until the 1960s. Recognizable disorders include transsexualism, impaired sexual desire or function, nymphomania and satyriasis, and the paraphilias. Most of these disorders are so explicit as to be not playable in most roleplaying groups.

Eating Disorders

Since nearly all such cases are diagnosed in the United States and Canada, anorexia nervosa and bulimia nervosa might be classified as cultural syndromes, but they are conditions that may continue for many years, sometimes to the considerable danger of the patients.

Anorexia Nervosa: the character has an overpowering fear of becoming fat, and consequently loses weight (SIZ) and CON at a rate decided by the keeper. Even when skin and bones, the character is sure to feel too fat. Without intervention, death may follow.

Bulimia Nervosa: the character frequently eats high caloric food during secret binges. An eating episode may continue until abdominal cramping or self-induced vomiting occurs. Feelings of depression and guilt frequently follow such episodes.

Sleep Disorders

These include insomnia (character has difficulty falling asleep or staying asleep) and narcolepsy (character frequently falls asleep, almost anywhere). Characters performing demanding tasks such as driving a car or flying a plane may need CON rolls to stay awake.

Night Terrors: sleeping character awakes after several hours of sleep, usually screaming in terror. Pulse and breathing are rapid, pupils are dilated, and the hair stands on end. The character is confused and hard to calm down.

Somnambulism: sleepwalking. As with night terrors, this behavior occurs in the first few hours of sleep. An episode may last up to thirty game minutes. During the sleep-walk the face is blank and staring, and the walker can be roused only with difficulty. Waking, the walker recalls nothing of the activity.

Impulse Control Disorders

These include pathological gambling, pathological lying, kleptomania, and pyromania.

Intermittent Explosive Disorder: the character is recognizably impulsive and aggressive, and at times sustains uncontrollable rages which result in assault and/or destruction of property.

Personality Disorders

These long term disorders are often unpleasant to be around, even if only roleplayed. Some general types include antisocial, avoidant, borderline symptoms of many sorts, compulsive, dependent, histrionic, narcissistic, passive-aggressive, paranoid, schizoid, and schizotypal. Keepers who investigate these

Phobia Listing

Acrophobia: fear of heights
Ailurophobia: fear of cats
Androphobia: fear of males
Aquaphobia: fear of water
Astraphobia: fear of lightning
Astrophobia: fear of stars
Bacteriophobia: fear of bacteria
Ballistophobia: fear of bullets
Belonephobia: fear of pins and needles
Botanophobia: fear of plants
Blennophobia: fear of slime
Claustrophobia: fear of enclosed spaces.
Clinophobia: fear of beds
Demonophobia: fear of demons
Demophobia: fear of crowds
Dendrophobia: fear of trees
Doraphobia: fear of fur
Entomophobia: fear of insects
Ergophobia: fear of work
Gephyrdrophobia: fear of crossing bridges
Gynephobia: fear of females
Hematophobia or Henophobia: fear of blood
Iatrophobia: fear of doctors
Ichthyphobia: fear of fish
Monophobia: fear of being alone
Necrophobia: fear of dead things
Noctophobia: fear of night
Nyctophobia: fear of darkness
Ondontophobia: fear of teeth
Onomatophobia: fear of a certain name
Ophidiophobia: fear of snakes
Ornithophobia: fear of birds
Pediphobia: fear of children
Phagophobia: fear of eating
Pyrophobia: fear of fire
Scoleciphobia: fear of worms
Spectrophobia: fear of ghosts
Taphephobia: fear of being buried alive
Thalassophobia: fear of the sea
Tomophobia: fear of surgery
Vestiophobia: fear of clothing
Xenophobia: fear of foreigners
Zoophobia: fear of animals

disorders will find much to work with within the category, but their consistent expression in roleplaying may foster anger and unpleasantness within the group, and disappoint players with different expectations.

Other Disorders

These are mostly symptoms, or specific instances of disorders already mentioned above. They existed in the previous edition of the rules, and functioned as quickly understood characterizations for roleplaying. Among them were criminal psychosis, panzaism, quixotism, and megalomania. Any disorder mentioned in previous rules is still playable. ■

KEEPER'S LORE

Getting Ready to Play; Keeper Strategy;
Relying on Possessions; Descriptions;
A Toolkit; Surviving or Dying; Investigator
Life Spans;Civil Authority; Tournament Play.

Players need to read or to be familiar with Orientation, About Investigators, Game System and Skills, and Sanity and Insanity chapters. Keepers need to understand them, and in addition the Magic, Cthulhu Mythos, and Necronomicon chapters. They also should have browsed through the book just to know what's there.

The present chapter is background—play first, then thumb through here as convenient.

The hundreds of symptoms, notes, statistics, characters, and spells later in this section do not need to be studied, but remember their presence as a whole so that, in time, individual chapters or notions can be sought out and read.

Thumb through the last sections, Scenarios and Utilities. They include four scenarios, investigator sheets, a summary of tables, an index, some brief historical lists, ready-made investigators, record sheets of various sorts, and play aids.

Lovecraft Stories

To present a game of Call of Cthulhu, it's useful to be familiar with the works of H .P. Lovecraft. Read anything written by him. The following stories are among his best. They make a great introduction. Titles with asterisks are longish, up to a novelette in length.

"The Call of Cthulhu" (near the front of this book)
"The Case of Charles Dexter Ward" *
"The Dunwich Horror"
"The Haunter of the Dark"
"The Lurking Fear"
"The Shadow Out of Time" *
"The Shadow over Innsmouth" *
"The Shunned House"
"The Whisperer in Darkness" *

If you liked the ones above, why stop?

"At the Mountains of Madness" *
"The Colour Out of Space"
"The Dreams in the Witch-House"
"The Doom That Came to Sarnath"
"Herbert West—Reanimator"
"The Outsider"
"Pickman's Model"
"The Rats in the Walls"
"The Silver Key"
"The Thing on the Doorstep"

A keeper who knows five or six of these titles is more than equipped to run this game. Players should at least read "The Call of Cthulhu" to get context for their investigations.

New Keepers

Getting Ready to Play

Use common sense. You'll want a comfortable, reasonably quiet room, with enough chairs and a table large enough for everyone to sit at. Extra dice may be handy, as will be extra pencils and sheets of scratch paper. Farsighted keepers stock blank investigator sheets. Since Call of Cthulhu is a simple game to play, players may not need to bring their rulebooks. Photocopies of the Creating An Investigator spread, the weapon table, and the play aids can be convenient.

Try to keep your rulebook for yourself, because you are responsible for the rules: if you do not remember a rule, you should be able to look it up. If you are presenting a scenario from this book, you need this book.

Expect players to bring their own investigators, copies of the rules if they want them, their own dice, and any miniature figures they want to play with in the game. People who bring all of that usually bring their own writing materials as well. Pencil erasers sometimes wear to nubs in half an hour—a large, fresh gum eraser can be very helpful.

Most of the keeper's energy necessarily goes into preparing the adventure to be presented. Read published scenarios carefully beforehand, and give yourself enough time to ponder changes. Note inconsistencies: you will think of things that do not occur to authors and editors, or to anyone else. Review the printed statistics in light of player and investigator tendencies and motives, as well as by what you want to accomplish for the evening.

If you use miniatures, round up the sort you'll need. Marking pens and large sheets of paper are convenient for reproducing floor plans or sketching out terrain.

Call of Cthulhu is not suited well to solitaire play, though it is excellent with a keeper and one or two players. An average of three or four players is sufficient for adventures.

By custom, each player plays one investigator, but only good reason should stop someone from playing two if desired. More than two investigators per person threatens confusion and imbalance in the adventure.

Most keepers like to look over investigator sheets before play begins. The idea behind this inspection is not to allow the keeper to construct the hardest or easiest possible situations, but to see if any of the crucial situations in the play to come will be unduly hard or easy for the group to overcome. If no problem jumps out at the keeper, the player should be not much concerned. Having said this, though, it can be useful to photocopy the sheets so that a roll can be made in secret now and then, or so that the shreds of someone's sanity can be considered.

The investigators who were being played last time should continue to be played, unless it's a new story, or unless the keeper and players have negotiated the difference.

Players always control their investigators, with rare exceptions, amd make all the die rolls relevant to those investigators, rolling when the keeper directs. Keepers operate all the non-player-characters, making all rolls for them. Unless your style is very different, it's a good idea to let die roll results be visible to all. Occasionally, the keeper may rule that the investigators should not know if some action succeeded. Ideally then the keeper preserves the dice as they were rolled, perhaps shielding them beneath an inverted cup, to be shown with a flourish when the time is right.

Keeper's Choice

Keepers new to Call of Cthulhu find that the game demands full comprehension. There are few charts to consult, and even fewer to show to players in order to prove some point of controversy. Everywhere the rules appeal to judgment and reasonableness, and suggest that you make up your own mind. "Oh, no," you think, "I wanted rules!"

Statements indicating in effect "keeper's choice" mean that the decision has no ramifications, and that the keeper can determine the matter according to personal taste and local custom, without other ramification.

Accept this wise course. You can be expert in the Call of Cthulhu rules after six or seven sessions, and thereafter use them as a transparent vehicle for presenting a story.

Keeper Strategy

Call of Cthulhu is a game of mood. Keep your campaign full of bumps in the night, sinister strangers, and dark and stormy nights. Try to make your runs spooky enough to give your players the creeps. One good source of ideas for scenarios are television series and horror movies. Another good source is horror stories: M. R. James, Saki, A. E. Coppard, Ramsey Campbell, Arthur Machen, Roald Dahl, Shirley Jackson, Karl Edward Wagner, T. E. D. Klein, and Thomas Ligotti are among the finer writers. Many more authors offer ingenious and exciting tales. especially those writing in the Cthulhu Mythos. Lovecraft's essay, *Supernatural Horror in Literature*, gives dozens of sources for good ideas, many virtually unknown today.

Maxims

Stoke your love for the mysterious and the horrifying. That enthusiasm is more important than a complicated plot or mastering many different voices for your different characters. You need be articulate only enough to set a scene, to wrap it up conclusively, and to answer player questions directly.

Charts for random encounters, wandering monsters, and similar things are the bane of Call of Cthulhu. Craft events, so that the players get meaningful thrills and chills.

Always read published scenarios thoroughly before presenting them: you want to surprise the players, not yourself.

Many of the monsters in the Mythos are so potent that the best prepared party cannot defeat them. In such cases, the main goal of the expedition could be to avoid and escape the monster! Don't force a horror upon a party without giving them some warning. Not much warning is necessary: a blast of cold air, a howl in the night, or the cessation of the whippoorwills' chirping is enough, but be sure to have spooky things happen often enough that the investigators don't expect some horrendous monster to show up every time.

When an investigator reaches 0 Sanity points, he or she is retired unless the keeper and player can come up with a better idea. Rarely should he or she become a cultist, for that dishonors a life resisting the evil of cults and gods. If an investigator goes mad, the madness is his or her own.

Keep down the number of non-player characters which you must roleplay in a scenario. Too many individuals, especially if not organized by house or city or in some other way, are confusing to players and keeper alike.

Don't put Mythos deities into play unless the investigators are ready for them. Limit the involvement to fanatic cults and lesser Mythos races, then gradually lead matters to greater races, and only then let the players encounter a god.

As a foulness shall ye know them: the Mythos corrupts or injures. Investigators who pursue Mythos knowledge should do so through thickets of nightmare and moral dilemma. Acquiring Mythos knowledge should never be bland or routine.

Since guns kill in Call of Cthulhu, resist tendencies to turn the game into gunfights. Guns kill investigators, too. Encourage investigators to retreat unless there is good roleplaying to be done by staying. (Monsters often are little affected by impaling weapons, anyway.) Wean investigators away from their arsenals by limiting the applications for such equipment. Investigators who stick around to blaze away at major entities will soon pay the predictable price.

Shy away from mass combats. Portraying mass combat is a concept for miniatures play. In roleplaying, descriptions can be broad but action must be intimate.

Kill investigators dramatically. Death should mean something. If an investigator faints, let him lie there instead of having the monster eat him. When an investigator with a non-player character hireling sleeps in a haunted house, and the Inhabitant Therein looks for prey, have it make away with the hireling unless you wake the investigator somehow, and give him a fighting chance. Investigators should not lead charmed lives, but neither should they be snuffed out casually. If death is to have any meaning—that is, if it is to conclude the story of a life—death should come as the consequence of choices freely made.

Lovecraft didn't confine himself to Cthulhu Mythos stories, and neither should the keeper. Lovecraft also wrote psychological horror stories about ancestral memory, cannibalism, grave-robbing, and curses: let your imagination roam.

Attentive keepers have attentive players. As investigator plans change, remain flexible and adaptable. Accommodate events and change scenarios to suit them. In return for your efforts, Call of Cthulhu will provide vivid, memorable play.

An Example Of A Plot

A scenario in Call of Cthulhu can be organized like the layers of an onion. On the surface, suppose that the scenario looks like it's about a conventional haunted house. It might even look like a hoax. As the investigators penetrate the first layer, they should discover another beneath. These layers might go on and on, until the investigators themselves decide they are getting too deep and stop their investigations.

As the investigators delve more deeply into the mystery, hints and notes should situate the haunted house in some greater scheme. As the player characters investigate, these hints lead on to other adventures.

In Lovecraft's "The Case of Charles Dexter Ward," for example, young Ward begins by investigating the ancient writings of his wizard ancestor. As he investigates further (the first layer of the onion), he discovers a technique to raise the dead. He tries it, and is able to raise his ancestor, who proves to be a near twin of Ward in appearance. This ancestor then becomes Ward's mentor in the arcane arts (the second layer of the onion). However, young Ward proves too squeamish and his ancestor murders him and takes his place. That's the end of the scenario for Ward, and the end of the first onion for us.

Young Ward's doctor then starts *his* investigations, researching along the same lines Ward began. This is the initial layer of a new onion. Dr. Willett finds that the ancient house of the sinister ancestor still stands and visits it (the second layer of this onion). In the house's vast basements Willett encounters horrific sights and beings, and discovers how to lay to rest the evil ancestor whom he suspects has displaced his patient, young Ward (this is the third layer of the new onion). Now full of knowledge and determination, Willett visits the insane asylum where the evil ancestor masquerades as the young Ward. There Willett recites the Resurrection spell backward, destroying the ancestor and finishing the second onion and the story as well.

Although Lovecraft goes no further, other steps could be taken: a Being destroyed some of the ancestor's cronies, but were there others? Were there surviving notes and/or devices (and guardian monsters) at the homes of those cronies? At the ancestor's centuries-old house there were deeper crypts than the doctor wished to explore. What was in them? Was the malignancy of the Being that the doctor unleashed limited only to the ancestor and his brother wizards? Or does it now have diabolic plans of its own?

Each layer of a scenario should present the investigators with two or three choices as to where to proceed. Players should never be certain that they have delved to the bottom of a mystery, except for their own purposes, nor should they ever be certain of the keeper's intentions. Obviously, the keeper cannot make his scenarios infinitely deep and complex, so either he breaks off play when the investigators get too deep, or he improvises. If he breaks off play, it should only be till he manages to extend his scenario further and give more depth to the mysteries.

Building a Scenario

Plots, the scope allowed for free investigation, the extent of narrative, the compression and emphasis of detail, and the points at which a scenario begins and ends comprise the essential differences. The adventure's characters are the vehicles for this expression. How well a keeper or an author transcends, meshes, and refreshes these elements reveals his skill as a storyteller, or as a story killer.

The best structure cannot rescue stodgy, dull, or obvious ideas. But if your enthusiasm for the game and your enjoyment of your friends take center stage, you cannot go far wrong—clichés, errors, forgotten connections, and misplaced clues will be gratefully cherished if you can come up with an original twist now and then. Since most Cthulhu adventures are mysteries whose solutions lead to understanding, their structures are progressive and problem-solving, and in outline are much more alike than different. First come the facts of the situation for the keeper, set out as clearly and as succinctly as possible. Then information available to the investigators is parceled out by the keeper—this forms the bulk of the text. Investigator information includes the scene of the action, descriptions of scenario characters and clue, and problems of alternate choice. Following the onion-layer metaphor, each set of the following points could represent a layer in a campaign, or each point could be an entire layer in a single scenario.

1) *A mystery or crisis is posed.* This may be dramatized or offered low-key, such as in a letter, but there is always a cause, even if the investigators merely stumble across the situation by chance. Since there is a cause, a conclusion is also possible.

2) *The investigators become linked to the problem.* They need a stake in the outcome. It may be money, reputation, friendship, love, pity, charity, suspicion, or curiosity, but it must be agreeable to the players before they will enter into the spirit of play.

3) *The investigators attempt to define the mystery.* They look for clues and try to gather evidence about the mystery. In campaigns and longer scenarios this process can be extensive and complex, taking up many sessions, so that investigators deal with a variety of personalities and overlapping encounters. Attacks and other sorts of encounters also occur in this stage, for the most part related to the central mystery. Most of the keeper's descriptions and roleplaying occurs at this stage, which amounts to much of the total length of play.

4) *The investigators use the clues and evidence to confront the danger.* This may be a monster, a sorcerer, or something else entirely. The situation demands their intervention. In a short scenario, there may be only one dangerous encounter. In lengthy scenarios there may be many, but the climactic one usually will be clearly identified. This stage is simpler for the keeper in some ways, as the investigators are now focused and intent. The keeper still must make the roleplaying rewarding and justify previous effort, especially if investigators have already died.

5) *The mystery or problem is solved.* This may conclude the matter or lead to new problems. At this point well played investigators typically get Sanity point rewards and collect any fees. A gift or acquisitionsuch as some book or artifact can lead to new adventures.

Linked Scenarios: A Campaign

Two or more scenarios could lead to the same dark secret, simplifying the life of the keeper and presenting the atmosphere of a sinister network of secrets to the players. For example, the old Starry Wisdom cult chapel in Boston could lead the investigators to Innsmouth and the Esoteric Order of Dagon. Later, investigators of swamp cults in Louisiana could find that they have connections to a master cult in New England, centered in Innsmouth, called the Esoteric Order of Dagon.

The keeper need not have a different mystery for each scenario. That would make his life too complex, and perhaps his plots too repetitious.

First, make up several scenarios, each only two or three layers deep. The keeper will also need to think of a couple of deeper secrets and subsequent scenarios for the players to delve into if they succeed in solving a mystery.

The scenarios ought to be arranged like the branches of a tree. The players start out fooling around with the very tips and edges of the Mythos, where there are dozens of myths, legends, clues, and adventures. As they gain more knowledge and experience, the investigators will work their way inward, where there are fewer roots, to follow the metaphor, but ones of greater importance. At the center of the Mythos reside the hideous Outer Gods.

Sprinkled among the scenarios should be hoaxes and meaningless trails. These will keep your world from degenerating into a mass of monsters and their kin. Gamblers, spies, religious fanatics, drug smugglers, white slavers, grasping entrepreneurs, venal labor bosses, terrorists, movie stars, nefarious politicians, and piratical sea captains are also available.

An occasional scenario with dangers originating from this world might divert your players, but keep in mind that the main goal of the game is to meddle in the Cthulhu Mythos. A scenario, especially at the start of a campaign, with a werewolf, ghost, or vampire will be interesting and oddly comforting to experienced players, though new players will want to press on to the main event.

Relying On Possessions

Roleplayers rely on character, not on possessions or powers. Roleplayers experiment with and amuse each other with made-up personalities. The point of roleplaying is to involve the player characters in dangerous, patriotic, macabre, thrilling, exciting, suspenseful, embarrassing, horrifying, comfortable, curious, shocking, comical, creditable, lusty, insane, dismaying, rewarding, and stupefying experiences.

The quality of such experiences does not depend on numbers, physical simulation, or technical procedure. Roleplaying succeeds by evoking emotions. Their evocation and release is a major reward of the game. That being so, do not leave the emotions out of player responsibilities.

For instance, if a player wants to introduce some new weapon or spell into play, require that the player also supply a

Die Rolls Add Drama

Die rolls during a scenario cannot explain game action, but they are in themselves naturally dramatic and understandable.

Example: Harvey Walters, two other investigators, and six porters enter the wrong cave on a Polynesian isle and find themselves confronting the head of Cthulhu himself. Harvey gets favorable Sanity rolls, as do three bearers and one associate, and they lose only a couple of points each, but three other bearers and one investigator get failed Sanity rolls. They fall down in a faint on the cave floor. The keeper rules that Cthulhu's facial tentacles automatically snatch up these four, since they are unmoving. Since the actual Sanity point losses to Harvey and the others were minimal, all decide to turn and run—the proper response when meeting Cthulhu.

In the next round, mighty Cthulhu reaches out with the four tentacle attacks to snare more prey. The attacks are automatically successful, but Harvey and two of the islanders get successful Dodge rolls and survive. The fourth tentacle scoops up the other investigator. The keeper, feeling charitable, allows a Luck roll for the investigator to wriggle free. But the roll is a 94. The unlucky investigator, kicking and screaming, is crushed in Cthulhu's maw. Meanwhile, the islanders and Harvey turn a corner in the cave and streak wide-eyed for the safer and saner world above.

corresponding risk or a consequence for his investigator, one comparable to the value of the item or power.

Every introduction of a significant purchase or acquisition should have this sort of price. In roleplaying, money means little, but risk is important.

Negotiate the consequence, but let the investigator feel it at least as long as he has the acquisition. For instance, that glistening H&K assault rifle is a more dubious benefit if the previous owner used it to commit an unsolved murder. This sort of consequence easily leads to interesting new episodes of play.

A GREAT RELUCTANCE

Keepers are justifiably reluctant to allow exotic magic or heavy armament into their games. Contrary to what players might believe, this is not because the scenario might be completed too easily, though that might be a trivial result, nor is it because a Shrivelling spell or a stabilized turret gun might imbalance the game: with opponents like Cthulhu and Nyarlathotep, game balance is unlikely to shift very much.

Introducing higher and higher potency material reduces the chance for roleplaying. The effect of more powerful weapons or deadlier magic is progressively to isolate the owners from the events of adventures and the ordinary challenges of play, and paradoxically to limit the range of responses players and investigators feel safe in contemplating. Since the point of a roleplaying game is to roleplay, insulating investigators with technology or magic and then introducing greater countering power to re-establish the balance is a sad and pointless effort. The keeper is not quite like the military commander who had to destroy the hamlet in order to save it, but close enough.

Some players persist in dreaming that owning more possessions and new powers is the point of play. Requests for heavy weapons are among the most common, because the appeal of firepower is clear-cut. Again, if you allow introduction of some new element, the player should show first how the item or effect makes roleplaying better and more exciting. That effort of imagination is the true responsibility of the roleplayer.

Descriptions

Call of Cthulhu offers special problems of description to keepers. There are madmen who seem normal, monsters which are formless blobs of jelly, and angles and symbols which move and cannot quite be comprehended. There is an emphasis on darkness and mystery, and yet the investigators' choices must be clear enough to be just and appropriate. How should a keeper describe such matters?

Trust And Fairness

The crucial component of good description is psychological. If players and keeper feel comfortable together, and if all parties work together to create an enjoyable group fantasy, then a good outcome is predictable. Trust comes from evidence of fairness: everyone must be willing to suggest, to listen, and to agree. Normally, keeper and players combine to flesh out scenes by means of description, questions, replies, inferences, and negotiations.

Investigators will volunteer for risky missions when their players feel that the keeper always poses problems fairly, so that they can fairly evaluate the dangers. It is worth mentioning to players that keepers are willing to put in extra effort developing interesting, exciting adventures when the players appreciate and pay attention to such efforts.

Even when an investigator has gone mad with a criminal psychosis, only in the rarest circumstances should the keeper promote or allow an investigator to turn against his companions. If the players enjoy competitive back-stabbing, then indulge them to the hilt, but generally the Mythos causes more than enough trouble for a team. Internal bickering and betrayal lose sight of the point of investigation.

Reasonable Deduction

When the keeper sets a scene, his or her most important ally is invisible, one which no scenario-writer ever puts on paper. "Reasonable deduction" consists of all which is in the room, cavern, aircraft, or other physical setting which is not described as being there, but which logically can be inferred as being there.

For instance, the investigators are in the library of a mansion. Specifically mentioned are the many massive bookcases lining the walls, two leather armchairs, a desk and chair, and a billiards table. What else might there be?

Books, certainly, and lots of them. Cues, chalk, and billiard balls. Writing material. Paintings on the walls. Lamps and light switches. Windows, maybe lots of them. Rugs on the floor. A fireplace, and fireplace tools. Lots of odd things in the desk drawers, including scissors, a letter opener, glue, stamps, twine, tape (if it's the right era), and an address book. Perhaps correspondence files. Matches for the fireplace. Cigars in the humidor. Brandy on the side table.

Some of these things are useful weapons—thrown billiard balls are dangerous, for instance, and a swung cue is an excellent club, as is the poker beside the fireplace. The windows offer entry or escape. One might bind a captive with twine, or with sash cord from the drapes. (There are drapes, of course, on the windows—this is a mansion.) One might spirit out a captive by rolling him up inside a rug. One might torch the room, or build a torch from a rug fragment wrapped round a pool cue, held with twine and soaked with brandy. The key to the library door may not be in the door but, if not, it is very likely in a desk drawer. An electrical cord can be stripped to contacts and used (cautiously) as a weapon, as long as the electricity lasts.

Ingenious players or keepers can come up with much more. The point is that every setting offers things potentially of use in specific situations, things which may not be specifically mentioned in the text.

Describing Spells

The investigator enters the contest as Lovecraft's characters did, innocent, full of hope and trepidation, ignorant of the future and what the future brings. For the keeper to offer events as a mystery, now then he or shee needs verbal camouflage. As with creature names, spell names need disguising. The keeper's perhaps lurid descriptions can lend flavors to spells more gothic and evocative than the staccato Grimoire arrangment of Call Awarassa, Call Atlach-Nacha, Call Azathoth, and so forth.

Summon/Bind Star Vampire, for instance, is a name far too dull and lacking mystery. Far better to call it something appropriate to the manuscript or author where it is found— "Old Cobbit's Terror", say. Or it might be named more poetically after its effect: "Cloud of Blood", after the star vampires it aids in summoning, or "Recipe for the Veined Laugher" (perhaps too broad a clue), or "Ye Invisible Eater", a little misleading but helpfully dire. If you're stuck for something good, give the player a single word to cling to for the moment, then let the rest be understood when you (or the player) have come up with something appropriate.

A fresh name is introduced into play, the keeper can playfully explore possibilities, and mystery is preserved, perhaps enhanced. Be sure to note the spell's equivalent somewhere while it's still fresh in mind: keepers want to baffle players, not themselves.

Since the name need not be precise, neither need be what is called or created. The keeper may model a different version. Thus the spell Become Spectral Hunter need not be taken by the keeper as a demand for the exact creature—*that* creature exists in the 1983 campaign *Shadows of Yog-Sothoth*, along with the spell. The spell exists in this rulesbook to be a suggestive pattern. Rename the spell, remake the effect, make up a substitute creature, choose one from the Mythos chapter, or consult that campaign.

Details can be added to spells, to considerable effect, since the rulesbook little describes the spells and usually leaves the evidence of their casting up to the keeper.

However, since spells generally represent attacks, take care in staging them. Every spell should have a maximum range, for instance: the default ranges in the game are touch, sight with the unaided human eye, or 100 yards. Never present a spell unlimited in function or range; that would not be fair.

Understand whether several targets can be attacked at once, or must be attacked in succession. It will be useful to the players, of course, if the casting of a spell against them is betrayed by certain hand movements, or necessary items, or colored auras, or lightning-bolt-like discharges. Does it smell like ozone in here? —maybe that sorcerer is back!

Playing Alien Entities

Only the keeper knows how these things should behave. Anything they do may be important. They are capable of influencing observing investigators in all sorts of ways, because you've specifically mentioned it. Frequently, though, monsters just snarl or trumpet and then attack. This is a shame sometimes, because predictable behavior is not mysterious.

Intelligent creatures might build, experiment, worship, learn, perform magic, question, torture, or anything else humans might do. They might do much more as well. If the investigators are able to observe aliens for very long, the creatures also should do things which are odd, inexplicable, or incomprehensible. These motifs are difficult to create, but worth keeping in mind. The keeper will be served if behaviors are dark or mysterious in tone. Conversely, if aliens do ordinary things like brush their fangs before bed, play may be bet-

ter served if the investigators do not learn that they do, or if what seems obvious behavior actually has entirely different meanings or functions.

The same take on spell names holds with monsters. When a mysterious creature disappears into the coastal fog, make the player characters dare to get closer in order to see corroborative details, take special photos, try to use Spot Hidden and Track rolls, and so on. The identification of a monster takes away mystery and reveals details about the plot. Don't let investigators get information for free. If they get closer to the thing, it is still not a deep one—it is a dark, wet shape, half-submerged, draped with seaweed, stinking like a long-dead fish.

When monsters die, it is up to the keeper whether or not they exhibit symptoms of distress, simply collapse, vanish, or evaporate.

Mythos creatures who do die often dissolve and evaporate, the noxious cloud soon replaced by a damp spot and clean air, as happened to Wilbur Whateley in Miskatonic's library. This conveniently leaves the investigators short of evidence. Other things might happen, just as with spells—liquefying, splitting in two, igniting into flame, healing all damage, or winking in and out of existence.

Descriptions need not be entirely visual. Descriptions are more concrete if two or more senses can be involved. Did the thing leave some goo behind? Describe its texture. Does it expel disagreeable odors? Let wafts of fog drift about and fill the room with noxious perfume. Don't strain for effect, or break off the narrative to try to come up with the right word, but keep in mind texture, odor, taste, and quality of light as possible factors.

SCENE: WEREWOLF UNDER THE FULL MOON

A Keeper's Toolkit

Here are some ideas for keepers who like to tinker. Some may conflict with each other. All are optional. Use any that feel right. These are for browsing through and thinking about. Wholesale adoption is not recommended.

CHARACTERISTIC ROLLS

A characteristic roll is the value of a characteristic multiply by some number to create a threshold target for D100 resolution. Idea, Know, and Luck rolls are characteristic rolls which do not change. This kind of roll increases the ability of an investigator or group of investigators to solve problems or pass tests, since high percentiles in a specific skill are not needed to succeed. More fixed characteristic rolls might be adopted: CON x5 might be formalized as the endurance roll, for instance. APP x5 might be the charm roll. STR x5 might be the lift roll, and so forth.

COMBAT CRITICALS, FUMBLES

If the D100 result for a weapons skill is 01-05, the player has rolled a *critical success.*

With a critical, if the target is armored, ignore the armor and apply the rolled damage. If the target is unarmored, double the damage roll. If the target is extraterrene, the critical result does normal damage.

If the D100 is 96-00, the roll is a *fumble* — the combatant drops his weapon, fires some ridiculous ricochet, trips over his sword and breaks it, can't get his holster unsnapped, and so on. Something embarrassing, humiliating, or deadly happens. Even monsters can fumble but an attack of 100% is always perfect and cannot fumbled

If this rule somehow conflicted with the impale, the impale would give way: one could not have a critical impale, for instance. The advantage of this concept is that it could work with all skills, not just certain weapons.

COMBINATION ROLLS

Use two skills together to accomplish some related task, or to solve a problem not apt to a single skill. When apt, the keeper calls for a single D100 roll. For a success, the result must be equal to or lower than the skill with fewer percentiles. A success with one of the two skills might represent a partial success, or total failure. Linking two skills this way may not be believable if they are not relatively equal in percentiles.

Example: Harvey Walters wishes to read a passage from an unknown book in Count von Wertheim's Latin library. Harvey reads Latin. After long hours, the keeper declares the search over, and calls for a combination roll. Harvey has 65% Library Use and 50% Latin. His player rolls a 51, a success for Library Use but a close miss for Latin. A success would be 50 or less. Deciding to indicate a partial success, the keeper says that Harvey found the right book, but needs help understanding the many medieval references and obscure terms in it. (Harvey does get an experience check for Library Use.)

CONSECUTIVE ROLLS

The same skill or function roll may be called for several times in a row, each success presumably narrowing or redefining the focus of the effort, inquiry, etc. Such a set of rolls should not be resorted to often, for they fritter away play enthusiasm. Such rolls might help emphasize some essential mystery, but the keeper should have something good in mind, since few investigators will be able to get four or five successes in a row. Only the final success in such a series should grant an experience check.

CONTROL OF THE GAME

Sometimes an evening of play threatens to dissolve into chaos. There are so many reasons for this to happen, and so many ways to handle it if it does, that only a halo of advice is useful.

Roleplaying is not different from the rest of life. Make sure you deal with the players first as people, and only then go on to consider the rule interpretation or misunderstanding that seems to be in question.

Games sometimes dissolve when a keeper persists in trying to be too perfect—worrying too much about the map, the monsters, or the music, and too little about the players. Deal with the players as friends, not as people to impress. The players' fun comes from laughing together, feeling companionable, and facing challenges together. Everything else is secondary.

If the problem stems from clashing player personalities, and if disruptions persist despite your best efforts over several evenings, you will have to ask one player to leave the game, or else put up with the situation indefinitely.

If all else fails, close the game for the evening, making clear your reasons for doing so. If the game is to continue next week, try to get everyone to agree to start fresh. Remind them of your reason for doing this, and that you'll want things to go differently when you reconvene.

Don't be afraid to compromise. The keeper does control the game. The players are never obliged to play.

CREATING A SKILL

Keepers might create new skills for their games, or retain older skills now renamed or abolished. Talk to the players about the idea, and test its use. If everyone is pleased, write down a definition, to make clear to everyone what the skill means and what it is intended to achieve. Extra spaces for additional skills occur on the investigator sheets.

DODGE OPTION

If the keeper wishes, characters may attempt the Dodge skill for up to three attacks per combat round. These are rolled for at full Dodge percentage, 2/3 Dodge percentage, and 1/3 Dodge percentage, respectively, in the DEX rounds of the attacks. Round up fractions. Failing one Dodge roll in a round has no effect on the others.

EDU AND INT MULTIPLIERS

In creating characters, the EDU and INT multipliers for occupations and personal interests can be changed, since what is right to one keeper may be absurd to the next. It also has been suggested that one skill be chosen at 70%, two at 60%, three at 50%, four at 40%, and so on down through the 10% level. Another scheme is to allot 1000 points per investigator, with no restrictions. If adopting a scheme different from the "Creating an Investigator" spread, use it to create investigators who have human weaknesses and flavor.

HYPNOSIS, AN OPTIONAL SKILL

Keepers should decide if investigators may have this skill.

To hypnotize someone successfully, the target must be willing and the hypnotist must receive a successful Hypnosis skill roll.

Hypnosis influences a single individual at a time. The target must be physically close to the hypnotist. If a Hypnosis roll fails, the hypnotist is unable to hypnotize that particular subject. If the initial Hyponosis roll succeeds, the hypnotist can hypnotize the target whenever the target agrees.

Use Hypnosis in several ways:

1) As an aid to Psychoanalysis. If an investigator has 10 or more percentiles of Psychoanalysis and has hypnotized a subject, add 25 percentiles to his or her Psychoanalysis skill when treating that patient thereafter.

2) As a post-hypnotic suggestion. It causes the target to perform a single particular action without apparent thought. The target will not accept a suggestion contrary to his or her normal behavior and desires.

3) As an aid to memory. Fragmented or buried memories can sometimes be dredged up through hypnosis. Someone who went temporarily insane from the sight of something moving in the bottom of a dark well may remember the fear but not remember what was seen. Hypnosis can bring these memories to light, but also (in cases where Sanity was lost) cost Sanity points for reliving the incident.

4) As a way to alleviate pain. Hypnosis can ease or temporarily erase symptomatic pain in a patient, but the pain itself makes the target more difficult to hypnotize. For a success, match POW against POW on the Resistance Table in addition to a successful Hypnosis roll.

5) As disinformation. If a hypnotist begins to influence NPC memories of an incident, the keeper may begin to supply false information in return.

Characters who already might reasonably have Hypnosis (physicians, entertainers, etc.), start at 20% or at half Psychoanalysis or Medicine, whichever is higher

RESEARCH MODIFIERS FOR TOMES

Each tome has a research time, given in weeks. We assume these are 30-hour weeks—six hours a day, five days a week. Any more than that will require some rolls. Anyway, hours or weeks, the time required is modified by the following factors, which add up to make the Research Modifier (RM):

■ INT: Every point above 14 counts as 1.

■ EDU: Every point above 14 counts as 1.

■ Language Skill: Divide the appropriate language by 5. Round down. If you don't have the language at all, you'll need to use a translator's skill or work through dictionaries and incur a -100 penalty.

■ Cthulhu Mythos/Occult: Divide Cthulhu Mythos by 5. *Alternatively,* divide Occult by 20, and go with whichever is higher. Round down.

■ Library Rating: each library gets a rating of 1-20. Miskatonic, the Bibliothèque Nationale, and the British Museum are all in the 18-20 range. Dogpatch Public Library probably has about a 2.

Tally the numbers for the RM. Subtract the RM from 100. The result is the percentage of full-time effort it actually takes a particular researcher to finish the book.

Example: *Professor Henry Armitage (INT 18, EDU 24, Cthulhu Mythos 18%, Occult 25%, German 70%) is trying to read and absorb* Unaussprechlichen Kulten *at Miskatonic. He gets the following modifier: INT = +4, EDU = +10, German = +14, Cthulhu Mythos = +3 (it's higher), MU Library Rating = 20. Total RM = 51. 100-53=49. It takes 52 weeks to study the book, but Armitage will do it in 49% of the time, or 25.4 weeks.*

SKILL CLASSES

Sometimes investigators are drugged, hypnotized, made to drink too much, or otherwise fall prey to gases, chemicals, or magic which affect how they think, move, or speak.

One way to show this is by using the skills divisions noted in the Play Aids section: *communication, manipulation, perception, physical movement,* and *thought.*

A drug might affect only skills in one class, typically halving the effect percentages for a few minutes or hours. All of the classes might be affected by too much alcohol, for instance, while exposure to cold might affect only the skills for physical movement and manipulation. A glass of win might temporarily boost communication skills by ten percentiles, even while it lowered thinking skills.

SPECIALS

A special is a D100 skill result less than or equal to one fifth of the investigator's current skill percentage. Rolling this result always results in a skill check, and the keeper should look for ways to dramatize the excellence of this success. A special result in a combat attack represents an impale, and probably more.

SPELL MULTIPLIER, AN OPTIONAL RULE

This formerly determined the rate for learning spells.

Any book that contains a Mythos spell can be rated with a spell multiplier. Roll the reader's INT times the spell multiplier to yield the reader's chance to learn the spell. The higher the spell multiplier, the better the chance.

Other factors, such as the condition of the book or manuscript, its authenticity (earlier versions are always better), and the number of spells and their presentation could also cause the spell multiplier to change. Do not use the spell multiplier if learning a spell from another person. ■

Since Call of Cthulhu is an investigative game, the evidence that something leaves behind—pools, prints, fragments, flakes, etc.—or the damage it has done is a much more interesting way to lead to the deduction of its identity. Sets of clues that add up to a baffling monster can make fascinating play.

Atmosphere

The action and setting of the scenario should work together well enough that the tone of the adventure springs out. Music, special maps and plans, interesting new figures, or whatever else the keeper wants to bring to play can be of help.

But play aids will not convince players that an adventure is something special. If the adventure plays flat and dull, no quantity of props can save it. If it is exciting, then nothing else is much necessary. The keeper must thoroughly understand the story presented. No tabletop marvel can make up for bad timing, misunderstood events, or misapplied characterizations.

If you're relying on alien worlds or other dimensions to add atmosphere to your game, by the way, tell the investigators in some sense what to expect, so that their players' dread or anticipation can help out the narration. If there are twisting angles and things which can't quite be seen, give some thought to one or two interesting touches which characterize such effects. "The Unnamable" apart, you can't keep saying that something is indescribable and have it remain very interesting to the players.

An International Game

Nearly half of Cthulhu players are not U.S. citizens and may never visit or live in the United States. Keepers abroad who try accurately to present material set in the United States occasionally have special problems understanding references or special meanings. In the scenarios, we include a little historical material for context, and sometimes discuss particular historical points, but books of rules and scenarios cannot be history texts as well. Any good guidebook holds a wealth of information. Even if it is out of date, get one.

The same sort of problem holds true for U.S. keepers trying to set adventures in France, Malawi, or anywhere beyond U.S. borders. One always wants more background, more anecdote, and more filler with which to vamp across narrative gaps. A good encyclopedia is the best place to start. In it, careful cross-referencing of major topics can turn up a surprisingly large amount of material, and help define specific questions. Methodical web-browsing locates as much or more information, often with pictures sources as well, but finding it takes time. Historical maps can be jewels, though they tend to be large files. Small topics, like small towns, can left to the keeper's imagination, but general reference books have an extraordinary capacity for firing the imagination. Immersing oneself for an hour in information about a place can work wonders

If you and your players have friendly stereotypes of how people of other lands live, start with that common agreement.

History

Similarly, players and keepers usually are not intimately acquainted with the 1890s or the 1920s: how do I know how to act? What can I do? I don't want to say that there are flash-

bulbs when there are none, or talk about electricity when everyone really used kerosene lanterns.

Use the same sorts of solutions as for international play. Again, apply friendly stereotypes—broad strokes of how characters react to play. If it is important to you whether or not people in the 1890s used stick deodorants, or what they did with all the horse manure which fell on their streets and by-ways, then be prepared to do some scholarly digging. History vital to a published scenario is usually touched upon in that piece.

Surviving or Dying

Investigator deaths are sometimes unanticipated, but many deaths can be associated with the styles and the preconceptions of players and keepers. Incautious players lose investigators. Although some of the best horror stories, loved for generations, conclude with the agonizing deaths of protagonists, roleplaying campaigns which kill off favorite investigators every session will soon end.

The keeper understands the frustration of players who lavish exciting details upon new investigators, only to watch them be torn to bits, burnt to ashes, or swallowed whole and wriggling after an adventure or two. Carefully played investigators have survived full-length campaign adventures, gone on for more, and ended up writing their memoirs. When investigators die, it is not enough that they die bravely if they die too soon.

Keep the scale of violence low, the pace of play moderate, and provide time to recover. If the investigators insist on pressing forward into certain death, the keeper with integrity may not long resist, but the keeper who chides players into combats soon discourages the players.

Mythos monsters are terrible beings, capable of driving investigators mad or of shredding them. Human weapons have little effect against most of these alien horrors, and the scant magic available to investigators is itself dangerous.

Read published scenarios attentively beforehand to make certain that their challenges are apt to your players and their investigators. Tailor the missions to your style of play and sense of aesthetics. Adjust numbers, powers, and anything else if it will make a better adventure for your purposes. Only you know your preferences and needs. Published scenarios are always aimed at a typical group, but no typical group exists.

In playing members of minor Mythos races such as mi-go, serpent men, and deep ones, remember that they are often more intelligent than humans, lead much longer lives, and sometimes are vastly more knowledgeable. Who among these semi-immortals willingly risk death for some momentary victory over beings to them the equivalent of chimpanzees? If a greater power than them calls for their sacrifice, that command should be made clear to the player characters. Lacking reason to fight, intelligent creatures retreat before danger. Try not to have them negotiate, though, for that exposes motives and inevitably makes them human-seeming.

Shoggoths and other entities of lesser intelligence are more daring, unpredictable, and rancorous than mi-go or deep ones. Such creatures may well launch all-out attacks, and can be terrible in their wrath. Here the challenge is physical, and the keeper is obliged only to give reasonable warning of impending doom. Attacking the shoggoth who lives in the cave can be an episodic problem, one that can be returned to until the player characters destroy the thing.

Even if the entire party faints, the keeper is not obliged to kill everyone or anyone. Mysterious entities can do mysterious things without loss of credibility. A creature need not devour a soul, or it may be satisfied with one, or perhaps it merely wants to sample a limb or two. Perhaps it craves only the left forefingers of right-handed people, so that the day of the forefinger is ever after remembered by the players. Communicating some quality of decision from an alien, unintelligent thing is not too difficult, for brutish motivation is self-evident.

Investigator death is one possible outcome of a dangerous encounter, one not specially desirable until an investigator's death acquires a sense of justness. Stupid or careless activity is one way for that sense to arise, and pressing one's luck is another. Keepers can allow cads to wander into disaster but, as arbiters of justice, keepers should refrain from naked revenge. Crippling or disfiguring an investigator is a good way to underscore the consequences of haphazard play without eliminating the investigator from play.

Aside from crippling injuries that reduce DEX or CON, investigators can suffer grievous scars that lower APP (perhaps along with Credit Rating and skills like Persuade that may depend on facial expression). Debilitating diseases can lower investigator stats while still allowing a lengthy career. Judicious insanities can slow down an investigator, or leave him or her vulnerable to particular temptations. Brain damage, caused by injury or the attack of some creature, can lower INT without killing. Similarly, physical injuries can affect the circulation or internal organs, lowering an investigator's CON.

A slow-developing metamorphosis in an investigator (the Innsmouth taint) is another option. Although the character remains functional, his appearance over time may provoke Sanity point losses in viewers. Not all the tainted complete their physical change, so a sane hybrid is perfectly possible.

Although these alternatives to death or madness may sound like tortures, such experiences are often the things that investigators point to with pride: "Did I ever tell you exactly how I lost this eye?"

What the Players Can Do

Players fail their investigators by hurrying investigations, bullying bystanders, neglecting evidence, barging into cultist headquarters without plan or backup, alienating the police, and forcing weakened investigators into new shocks. But if players do not feel that their investigators are doomed from the outset, they try harder to keep their characters alive.

Investigators need to improve skills, learn how to conduct efficient investigations, and make allies and connections outside themselves. Incidental friends and acquaintances form the true boundaries of the game, analogues to friendships inspired between the players.

Preparing for the End

As an investigator gains Cthulhu Mythos, his or her reserve of sanity shrinks, but the pressure does not end. He or she will need to cast a spell to defeat some awful thing, or be trapped into witnessing awful rites to some foul god, and a little more

Cthulhu Mythos will come. As an investigator's sanity narrows, the player misses more and more Sanity rolls and feels anxiousness about new horrors, simulating quite well the effect of slowly losing one's mind. The investigator with low Sanity points feels the breath of doom.

The best-loved investigator is usually played to his or her doom, for the player never wishes to sever the connection to the investigator. The wise keeper will not interfere in this process, except occasionally to encourage players to let their investigators retire early.

Even the luckiest investigator must sooner or later collect so many Cthulhu Mythos points that his or her maximum Sanity is drastically low, and cannot be relied on in the field. Retired, the investigator can pass on the legacy of his career to a favored specialist or younger relative or friend. Handing over the course of your investigations to a close companion or relative increases the feeling of continuity within the campaign. Although the investigator may have changed, the understanding of the Cthulhu Mythos continues to grow. Those who retire can remain semi-active, researching questions, conducting interviews, and sharing in what the others learn in new adventures. Just as Sherlock Holmes emerged from retirement in a time of great need, so may an investigator be lured back — very occasionally — from safety and security to plumb just one more mystery.

As possible, players might alternate investigators, or play a pair rather than one. Singular identification is for many players the crucial enjoyment of roleplaying, however, and many resist diluting it.

Lacking player forbearance, the keeper cannot much defend the investigators without ruining the game and despoiling his own integrity and enjoyment. Life must go on. Allow a few moments of recognition for the fallen hero or the madman, then give a hearty welcome to the new investigator.

Civil Authority

Players know the general goals of their investigators, but keepers may be less certain of their own roles as policemen, prosecutors, judges, coroners, and doctors of psychiatry. Keepers will not be able to lavish attention on every character, yet agents of civilization inevitably clash with the investigators. What do these authorities wish to accomplish, and what problems does their existence pose to the keeper?

ATTITUDES

The keeper must define the function of the authority in the scenario. A sheriff or a judge, for instance, can be a great help or a great obstruction to an investigation: he may control evidence or the access to evidence, he may willfully pursue his own theories concerning a crime rather than cheerfully adopting the ideas of the investigators, and he may even blindly order the arrest of the investigators as suspects or hold them as material witnesses.

There is a rough justice in uniformly portraying authorities as sleazy opportunists, corrupt fools, and rigid bumpkins, but such clichés corrode the heart of the game. Call of Cthulhu assumes that humanity and human civilization are worth defending and worth saving. It's undramatic to say that humans are not as bad as the Mythos—for dramatic contrast, humans and human institutions must be better. Since investigators risk their lives to save such people, some authorities must be shown to be worth the struggle. The simple truth is that some are and some are not.

If the investigators encounter authorities with well rounded characters, freely capable of good and bad, they can make up their own minds about the value of society and the glory or depravity of human character. The keeper then becomes an artist, not an ideologue whose agenda does not vary.

If an authority has a major role in an adventure, be alert to ways to make him or her approachable. A casual meeting on the street or help with an automobile may be enough that the investigators can evaluate his character. If it's needed, evidence of hobbies or past experiences often appears on office walls—citations, mounted game fish, family photos, trophies, souvenirs, and so on. This is of wide enough variety that at least one investigator may have enough Natural History, say, or Swim that a conversation can open, and an acquaintance made. Friendships then kept or betrayed are that much more powerfully experienced.

BRIBES

Threatened with arrest for criminal behavior or with commitment for insane behavior, the investigator who does not resist may try to talk his way out. Some will try bribes. Whether this

Keeper's Tools: A Sanity Loss Guide

Sanity is lost by encountering a supernatural entity, by witnessing or experiencing some horrible natural event, by reading a book or manuscript pertaining to the Mythos, and by spell-casting. But how much Sanity should be lost?

1 or 1D2 SANITY: *Discomfort or slight confusion.* A low level of loss barely noticed by the investigator, and not enough to create excitement or apprehension in the players, though it should remind them of what lurks in the wings for their investigators. Rarely used, with the exception of the weakest spells.

1D3 SANITY: *Fright, confusion, or disgust.* Three or four such experiences in a short time might drive an unstable investigator insane. Most scenario events that are not particularly awful should cost this much Sanity.

1D4 SANITY: *Panic, disorientation, or loathing.* Few go insane from one instance of this level of Sanity loss. Use it to harass but not incapacitate the investigators. A natural event might provoke such loss. Only mechanical or ethereal monsters cost so little Sanity. Most new books of Mythos lore should be in this range, so as to control "magic inflation."

1D6 OR 1D6+1 SANITY: *Nausea or stupefaction.* This is the average level of Sanity loss experienced in an average published scenario, and is the lowest level from which an investigator is likely to go insane. Monsters in this category, if alien or bizarre, should be puny: for example, mi-go are shockingly alien, but not large, poisonous, or otherwise frightening in appearance. Dangerous terrestrial monsters might also get these values—the vicious, poisonous but not particularly alien serpent people and deep ones are examples. Spells in this category should be fairly powerful.

1D8, 1D6+2, 2D4 SANITY: *Shock.* Since the average loss is not far below 5 points, this level may drive investigators temporarily insane. Monsters provoking such Sanity losses are worthy of respect. They should not be physically puny unless they are truly horrible, sneaky, or pathetic in compensation for that weakness. Spells in this category should cause impressive results.

1D10 SANITY: *Major shock.* From here on, insanity is increasingly likely from one encounter. The average result here is 5-6. Monsters generating such results should have something very alien or deadly about them. Unimpressive but important deities such as Tsathoggua fit into this category. Weird events or rash actions should rarely cost so much. A spell at this level should be darned impressive.

2D6 OR 2D8 SANITY: *Mind-damaging horror.* Rarely used in the rules for monsters, but recommended to keepers to avoid "monster inflation." This is the highest level for spells, although one much higher spell has been published. Since the dread *Necronomicon* itself is only 2D10, Mythos tome charges should not exceed the 2D6/2D8 level. About half of normal investigators can be sent screaming into insanity with one application of this level, and about one fourth will be. This level of Sanity loss is potentially devastating to your story, particularly if in the early stages.

1D20, 2D10, 3D6 SANITY: *Extreme horror.* This is the highest level of Sanity loss which a majority of investigators in a party are likely to weather—most will risk going insane. Be chary of such potency. Monsters must be appalling, diabolical, lethal, or wildly alien. This level of loss includes minor deities such as Abhoth, and the average Great Old One. Few experiences other than Resurrection ever should so mangle the Sanity of any investigator.

3D10 SANITY: *Ye liveliest awfulness.* Few encounters in, on, or off this world are worthy of such Sanity loss. Single-handedly and willingly causing the destruction of the human race might qualify. Only one published spell has ever cost this much to cast.

D100 SANITY: *Ultimate cosmic evil.* Do not use for any new monsters or events, no matter how terrible. Reserve it for encounters with the incredibly powerful and alien deities of the Mythos—Cthulhu, Nyarlathotep in many of his ghastly forms, the sphery horror of Yog-Sothoth, and so on. This scale of loss has been published a few times for other causes, but that is no longer recommended. No deed, spell, or book is ever worth such cost.

works depends on the officer's character, which the keeper can create.

If he feels that the officer may take a bribe, the keeper can calculate the effective bribe according to (1) the officer's daily rate of pay, (2) the seriousness of the offense in the eyes of the officer, and (3) the likelihood that the officer will be found out. Accepting a bribe is a good deal only if the officer gains money without much risk; if there is risk, the cash needed goes up precipitously.

Nominal daily pay for a police officer in the 1890s is $2.00 to $2.50, in the 1920s is $2.50 to $4.00, and in the 1990s is $150 to $200.

To avoid a fine, a bribe would be half or less of the amount in question; for misdemeanors, up to a day's pay; for private civil matters such as animal disputes and for property crimes such as car theft or breaking and entering, up to a week's pay; for armed offenses, up to two weeks' pay; for capital offenses, a month's pay or more.

Serious or well publicized cases will involve several people, perhaps even a whole layer of civil servants.

If possible, keepers also might convey that people who take bribes are likely to continue to take bribes. Such characters will be as quick to betray the investigators as they were to betray the public trust.

ARRESTS

Apprehension and jailing for later review, trial, and punishment imply a hierarchy of authority and function. Reasons for arrests vary.

■ The investigators look suspicious—they should be arrested before they can do anything. (this is called *preventive arrest*, an idea in bad odor with honest courts; a 24-hour version of it, *detained for questioning,* is often found.)

■ The investigators committed a crime of property or violence, or they outraged local custom or public decency.

■ The investigators have valuable goods or information which the authority wishes to confiscate, to learn about, or to keep secret.

■ The investigators are sole witnesses to a serious crime or are endangered by threats from others.

■ The investigators are obviously insane and dangers to themselves, or are dangerous to others. Society must be protected.

Arresting authorities also weigh questions pertaining to themselves. Is arrest for a minor crime worth the anger of powerful people? Do those who might be arrested have important contacts who might make life difficult? What are the consequences of an arrest or a prosecution—how best will society be served?

An arresting officer must show that he has the authority to detain, question, and arrest. If an arrest, there must be a charge, but need or desire is enough for questioning within a limited time, perhaps 24 hours. Those in custody will be disarmed. If a detainee resists, appropriate force may be used.

At the police station, the officer registers the arrest and delivers his prisoners. Those arrested are questioned and asked to make legally significant statements of fact. They are isolated, and their stories checked against each other.

If charged, the investigators usually are told what the charges are, but not always. In some countries, the charge may be a general one ("enemy of the state" is a classic), and the actual charges may be instanced only at the time of the trial.

The arrested may or may not be allowed to communicate with the outside, and in some countries the fact of their arrest may be kept secret. Further questioning, grilling, and outright torture may be used to gather evidence or confessions. Torture and threats of violence are generally illegal, but their employment depends on the policy of the department and the moral sense of the questioners.

In some countries, the trial itself may be secret. The admissibility of evidence and witnesses varies greatly between judges, let alone countries.

The punishment may fit the crime, or it may reflect the danger the investigators pose to an individual, group, or the state. The length and severity of sentence often varies with the apparent cooperation of the sentenced person with the authorities, and with the putative intent of the crime.

COMMITMENT TO AN ASYLUM

Investigators may want to stay at an asylum or sanitarium, perhaps to gather information or to hide from someone. They should have little trouble entering it if they can pay for the care. A private institution with an available room will accept someone without symptoms who merely wishes a rest and counseling. All institutions ask for references, however.

A medical practitioner licensed within the state can arrange that an investigator be held for psychiatric observation, for up to 72 hours. If evidence of serious disorder is gathered, the patient may be placed in an asylum for 90-120 days, for purposes of observation and evaluation as spelled out by state law. Then the court will discharge or commit for treatment depending on the asylum's report.

Those committed for treatment are subject to yearly review, but they may be in an institution for many years. It requires another formal presentation to the court, in which an investigator would have to be found mentally incompetent to act on his own behalf, or else might voluntarily surrender specific legal rights in return for treatment. The soundness of these proceedings can vary widely; brusque *pro forma* evaluations are not unusual, and much depends upon the character and dedication of judge, counsel, and examining physician or physicians.

■ Someone (physician, family member, or the arresting officer) brings evidence of the investigator's incompetence to the notice of the court.

■ A hearing is held, and evidence bearing on the investigator's mental competence is admitted. No jury is involved. If the court, having duly weighed the medical evidence and opinion, decides the investigator is competent to act in his own behalf, he or she is released.

■ If the court decides for mental incompetence, then a responsible guardian is chosen, who thereafter in theory acts to benefit the individual. Normally the guardian is a relative or someone else whom the court has reason to assume to wish to act in the individual's best regard. Lacking other candidates, the court appoints itself.

- Unless the investigator is criminally insane (in which case the court must be the guardian), the guardian now decides what is best for the investigator. This may indeed be commitment, but it might also be home care, or a therapeutic sea voyage, etc. Lacking other indication, the court will accept any reasonable plan which seems to have the backing of medical opinion.

- If the guardian commits the investigator to an institution, the guardian continues to have general authority over the investigator, assigning day-to-day care and authority to the sanitarium staff.

- Thereafter the investigator has three ways to leave: he may convince the guardian to remove him from the institution; he may convince the institution's staff to bring notice of his restored mental balance before the awarding court and that court takes upon itself the guardianship and grants his freedom; or he can simply climb over the institution's wall and run for his life.

Playing for Keeps: Tournament Games

Tournament games, usually run at game conventions, offer players a gaming experience very different from standard campaign play. Tournament scenarios are self-contained, carefully plotted "one shots". They are designed to be finished in a limited time, usually two to four hours. Players are given pregenerated characters with defined skills and backgrounds, and are usually judged on their abilities to play their characters to the hilt. Tournament scenarios, with their rigid time limits and premade characters, might seem at first glance to be much more restrictive than a more standard campaign game. Keepers who design tournament Cthulhu games soon find, however, that the tournament environment gives them much more freedom, and offers the opportunity to create a truly unique brand of terror.

As with any Call of Cthulhu game, the keeper's primary goal is to scare the players. Keep the contestants guessing; throw them off balance whenever possible. The anxiety the players feel will push them to better roleplaying, which will in turn inspire the staff to scare them even more. To build a Call of Cthulhu tournament scenario, the keeper needs the same elements required of any story: plot, characters, and atmosphere. In a tournament setting, however, these elements take on a whole new blasphemous form.

Plot

In a tournament round, the keeper has absolutely free reign when designing the plot of the scenario. Obscure settings or historical eras are not a problem—there's no need to worry about how a group of 1920s investigators might logically end up in the outback, or on Mars. Want to go to Mars? Build a round around a group of astronauts. Always been fascinated by

a period of history? Keepers need not worry about sustaining a high level of historical detail for an entire campaign—a few hours of research will do nicely. Plots set in Ancient Rome, Colonial China, the Renaissance, and the Near Future are not only feasible, they're encouraged. Why stick to the three conventional eras when all history can be your canvas?

Tournament rounds free the keeper from consequences. Want to play a game that culminates in the destruction of the Earth? Go ahead! There won't be any session next week where the players will have nothing to do. Monsters or events which might derail or overbalance a campaign can have free reign. Also, not all of the characters need necessarily survive to play again next session. Tournament rounds can be very deadly as a result. Keepers should be careful not to carry this trend too far: while a no-holds-barred attitude toward death definitely makes life scarier for the players, they do pay money to play in tournaments, and will be upset if they get knocked out of the running too arbitrarily.

While a closed plot can be a devious keeper's best friend, he or she must always remember that the timed tournament format is his or her greatest enemy. However brilliant the plot, it needs to fit in the time provided. In tournaments with several levels of play, building a two-part scenario to resolve a particularly complex plot is possible (bringing with it a nice opportunity for a dramatic cliffhanger) but, for the most part, keepers should always be aware of time, and be looking for ways to cram the most thrills into the least time. Playtesting is absolutely critical, as is proper timekeeping during play. Finally, always remember to allow time for the players simply to roleplay, as they will most certainly take it!

In a tournament, keepers can wed the plot to the characters in ways that campaign games usually can't. Instead of coming to the aid of an old friend or relative in trouble, the horror can be personal. *You* are infected with the hideous disease. *You* wake up in a strange place with complete amnesia. *Your* house is haunted. There's a bug in *your* head. What do you do? As the narrator of any of Lovecraft's tales could tell you, the horror is much more acute when you are the victim rather than just a friend or associate.

Characters

As described above, the characters of a tournament round can (and should) be integral to the plot—their skills and abilities can be specifically tailored to the challenges at hand, and their backgrounds can already incorporate strong hooks into the plot. Keepers should always bear in mind, however, that the characters are not just means to an end—as the component of the round that they will experience the most, the pregenerated characters must be well realized and well fashioned. Players stymied by weak characters will never be able to enjoy the plot, however brilliant it may be.

What makes a good character? First and foremost, the character must be interesting—paint in broad strokes, and make free use of archetypes. Also, give each character definite goals or interests, with details thrown in to add color. Players must adopt their roles in five minutes (or less!). The more "handles" a character has, the easier a player can get into the game. Also, each character should have a role within the group, and ideally have a moment in the plot to shine, when his or her skills or knowledge are the key to success. Devious keepers are advised to sprinkle crucial information into the character backgrounds—the best players are the ones who were paying attention during the setup, and who will be ready with the critical clue or skill when the need arises.

Tournament characters should, first and foremost, be fun to play, but should also be challenging. The same wide palette the keeper uses for building the plot is also available here. Why not build a group of insane characters, each with his or her own derangements? How about pushing the players to play non-humans like ghouls or Yithians? A player expecting a tense bloodbath of a scenario will be hard pressed indeed when he's forced to play an 8-year-old boy. Even more devious tricks are possible—halfway into the scenario, begin a flashback sequence where the characters are taken away from the players and each is given a remote ancestors as new characters. Watch the players scramble to keep up! Over the course of the round, characters can learn that all of their memories are wrong, or that they're really androids. These sorts of challenges separate the strong players from the weak, and keep all of them coming back for more.

Atmosphere

Many tournament games are run in a specific enclosed environment—a hotel room, lecture hall, or classroom. If the tournament has the time and resources to invest, a tournament round can become a multimedia extravaganza: half game, half one-act play. It is recommended that tournament staff assign at least two keepers to every round. One will act as the primary narrator, and the other can run groups that split up (eliminating dead time when players are waiting for the keeper's attention) and take charge of any effects. Experiment with lighting, by the way—black lights, strobes, and even pitch darkness can be used to great effect. Lighting the room with a single, dim lamp or candle can create a tense, brooding atmosphere that will rub off on the players. Other effects are possible—a cooler full of dry ice can bathe the gaming table (or the entire room) in mist. Staffs are also encouraged to create lavish props. Realistic, intricate handouts heighten the players' enjoyment, as well as giving them concrete objects to perform with. The Chaosium book *Cthulhu Live* has some excellent tips on building props.

If the staff has portable tape or CD players that can be conscripted for the weekend, mood music and sound effects can easily be incorporated into a tournament round. Seek out the soundtracks of scary films: a gold mine of atmosphere awaits. With a little research before hand, the staff can assign specific tracks to specific encounters. Sound effects tapes and CD's are widely available, and can bring gunshots, explosions, or thunderstorms to life. Music is often the least expensive special effect a staff can add to an event, and is also one of the easiest to manage. The results are worth the effort.

Making it Happen

To run a successful tournament, a keeper needs more than the elements detailed above. First and foremost, he needs a staff, a dedicated group who will help run the events, manage the effects, and keep everything rolling. The more preparation the staff can sink into the tournament before it begins, the more enjoyable it will be for all involved. The hours spent making props or toiling over a scenario will all pay off when the players' eyes all widen in amazement or terror.

Second, the staff needs to be ready to handle the logistics of the event. How will it be scored? While most Cthulhu tournaments base advancement completely on roleplaying, the staff must decide whose choice is final. Will the players be given a vote, or are the keepers' decisions final? Both simple ranking systems (where each player is given a "place" and then total scores are tallied) or "speaker point" systems (where each player is given a score from 1 to 100) are common, and are often used in combination. The staff must be ready with ballots and record sheets to ensure that the tournament flows smoothly. For every round, make sure that every player's name, badge number, and character name are recorded. Finally, be sure that the staff can keep track of all of its gear. If other events will have access to the gaming space, security can become a problem.

The Pay-off

Well executed tournament rounds offer some of the best game experiences either keepers or players will ever have. At their best, these rounds become wonderful exercises in improvisational acting mixed with problem-solving and a strong dose of terror. The quality of the roleplaying can prove far superior to a standard home-grown campaign. The players will usually have paid money to participate, and are, after all, competing for a prize. The focus that a tournament environment brings to the players also pushes them to give more to the game than they would if at home with the same old group of players, after a hard day of work or school. By the end of the convention, both players and staff should be exhausted—if they are, then they've done something right.

Bringing It All Home

Of course, keepers who don't have the time to direct a Call of Cthulhu tournament, or who don't have access to a game convention, can take all of the above suggestions and apply them to their home games. Vary the pace of your campaign with a well constructed one-shot. Need a break from a long investigation? Spend a session on Yuggoth, or in the Middle Ages. In a well designed one-shot, both keeper and players can play like there's no tomorrow. ■

CREATURES OF THE MYTHOS

Being notes and statistics for scores of species and entities of the Cthulhu Mythos, the first of several chapters offering information on the divers entities of the world and universe.

Entries are made alphabetically, usually by key word or phrase: thus *Insects from Shaggai* is found here as *Shaggai, Insects from*. The coleopteran version of the Great Race appears in this book following the Yithians' conical form, as *Great Race, New*. The exact forms for entries occur in the Monsters by Type box, p. 134. There the entries are classified according to one version of a hierarchy for the Mythos. For deities, see that chapter beginning on p. 160.

The listing of a servitor species for a single god or Great Old One does not preclude independent use or the choice of another entity.

This section is not a complete selection of Mythos entities—every horror fan can think of some terror not present. These are the ones found in the most important stories, or that frequently appear in stories and scenarios, or that are commonly referred to. Many more than appear here can be found in the *Creature Companion*, forthcoming from Chaosium.

Entry Format

Each entry starts with a quote and description for the entity, and includes a story source. If discussing a god or Great Old One, notice of any human cult comes next. The rest of the notes consider any peculiarities of habit, habitat, or attack. A deity may be discussed as it is only after it has been summoned or otherwise encountered. Subheads may break up lengthy and complex material.

The relative length of entries has nothing to do with the importance of the entity or species within the Mythos, nor with the likelihood of encounter it. Ghouls, for instance, are among the most likely denizens of the Mythos to be encountered, yet their entry is much shorter than the one for the rare flying polyp—but, as described by Lovecraft, the flying polyp has remarkable properties demanding more space to summarize.

THE STATISTICS

Mythos statistics include STR, CON, SIZ, POW, and DEX, but not APP, EDU, or SAN, since those qualities in such alien creatures are not meaningful. Unintelligent beings also lack INT. Entities such as zombies that lack will of their own usually have only 1 POW.

Individual creatures are given exact statistics, but species statistics include a dice-roll range: when a specific monster is called for, the keeper can use those rolls as guides. Average scores for species are also given, and can be transcribed directly when speed is needed.

HIT POINTS: the number of points which a monster must lose before death follows. This is the average for the species, figured by averaging SIZ and CON. Bigger or healthier monsters have more hit points than smaller or sicklier representatives. Gods cannot be truly slain, though they have hit points. If an Outer

God, Elder God, or Great Old One is somehow reduced to 0 or negative hit points, the thing is dispelled or forced back whence it came. Mere damage will not destroy or even harm these powers. If they are forced or persuaded to leave, they can return.

MOVE: if two Move numbers are separated by a slash, the second number is the monster's maximum Move in another medium (water, air, etc.), as listed next to the statistic.

DAMAGE BONUS: those for individuals are the actual rolls to be added to damage results, and those for species are given as an average roll-for an individual of the species, calculate the damage bonus from its SIZ + STR. The notation +*db* indicates that the damage bonus should be included in the attack.

WEAPONS: among Mythos creatures, these are usually natural weapons, as opposed to artifacts. Here the entity's characteristic attacks and chances to hit are shown, plus damage done. Gods often get to attack at 100%—how could any deity miss a Bite attack? Again, those given for species represent averages, while those for individuals are the exact chances to hit. The entry +*db* stands for *plus damage bonus*. Bite attacks do not receive damage bonuses unless the bite is the primary means of attack.

DAMAGE: if an entity drains points of characteristics from a target, consider them gone permanently, unless the entry clearly states that the loss is temporary.

ARMOR: represents a number subtracted from the hit points of damage actually rolled for a successful attack. The creature may have a hard shell or thick hide, be able to regenerate flesh, or be immune to certain sorts of attacks, perhaps explained in an accompanying note. Many Great Old Ones or gods regenerate hit points. Most can be dispelled only if attacks lower their hit points to zero. This is very hard to do.

SPELLS: notes if an individual monster or a species can cast spells or particular spells. The choice of spells should include appropriate ones: a deep one is more likely to Contact Spawn of Cthulhu than to Summon Fire Vampire, for instance. The keeper can always add more spells. The use of magic is never required, for an entity may not notice humans any more than humans notice crouching mice. To speak of the Great Old Ones or the Outer Gods as knowing or not knowing specific spells is silly—aspects of their wills are expressible as spells, but these entities are mostly seamless and indefinable. They know what they want to know when they want to know it.

SKILLS: monsters may not have skills shown, though most or all might have the effect of skills such as Listen, Sneak, or Spot Hidden. Keepers should add skills or set skill roll thresholds as they need.

SANITY LOSS: how many Sanity points the investigator loses when encountering a member of the race. The actual amount lost might increase if more than one monster is seen, but the amount charged should never exceed the maximum possible loss that a single creature could cause. "To see" is appended as a way of saying "to witness", "to experience", or "to perceive." Player characters are affected whether or not they close their eyes.

BYAKHEE, Lesser Servitor Race. *There flapped rhythmically a horde of tame, trained, hybrid winged things ... not altogether crows, nor moles, nor buzzards, nor ants, nor decomposed human beings, but something I cannot and must not recall.*—H. P. Lovecraft, "The Festival."

This interstellar race often serves Hastur the Unnamable. Composed of conventional matter, they are vulnerable to ordinary weapons such as pistols. Byakhee can fly through space and carry a rider each, though such riders need protection from the vacuum and cold by suitable spells or potions. Byakhee do not have bases on Earth, but may be summoned to perform deeds or to serve as steeds.

In combat, a byakhee may either strike with both claws simultaneously (getting two attacks in the round), or attempt to bite the target. If the bite strikes home the byakhee remains attached to the victim and begins to drain his or her blood. Each round the byakhee remains attached, including the first, the blood drain subtracts 1D6 hit points of STR from the victim, until death. The byakhee characteristically remains attached with the Bite attack until it is slain or until the victim is drained of blood.

Escaping death, let the victim rest and regain blood by transfusion as well, at up to 1D3 STR per day.

BYAKHEE, the Star-Steeds

char.	rolls	averages
STR	5D6	17-18
CON	3D6	10-11
SIZ	5D6	17-18
INT	3D6	10-11
POW	3D6	10-11
DEX	3D6+3	13-14
Move 5/20 flying		HP 14-15

Av. Damage Bonus: +1D6.

Weapons: Claw 35%, damage 1D6+db
Bite 35%, damage 1D6+blood drain

Armor: 2 points of fur and tough hide.

Spells: byakhees of POW 14 or more know at least 1D4 spells, normally spells relating to Hastur and associated beings.

Skills: Listen 50%, Spot Hidden 50%.

Sanity Loss: 1/1D6 Sanity points to see a byakhee.

BYAKHE

Chaosium Pronunciations of Mythos Names

These are not official, but it's how we say them. All-capital syllables are stressed. Lovecraft developed unpronounceable names sometimes, to drive home their alien quality. Some of these entries are found in the Deities chapter.

Consonants are hard. All S's are sibilants. An apostrophe indicates a compacted short-I sound. A short-O is written O; a broad-O is written AU; a long-O is written OE. A short-A is written A; a broad-A is written AH; a long-A is written AE. A short-E is written E or EH; a long-E is written EE. A short-I is written I or IH; a long-I is written IGH. A short-U is written U or UH; a long-U is written OO. With one exception, the letter Y is pronounced as it is in "yore." OI is pronounced as in "noise."

entity	*pronunciation*
Abhoth	AB-hauth
Atlach-Nacha	AT-lach NACH-ah
Azathoth	AZ-uh-thoth
Bast	BAST
Bokrug	BOE-kruhg
Byakhee	b'YAHK-ee
Chaugnar Faugn	SHAHG-ner FAHN
Chthonian	kuh-THOEN-ee-un
Cthugha	kuh-THOOG-hah
Cthulhu	kuh-THOO-loo
Cyaegha	sigh-AE-guh
Dagon	DAE-gaun
Daoloth	DAE-oe-lauth
Dhole	DOEL
Eihort	IGH-hort
Ghast	GAST
Ghatanothoa	gah-tahn-oe-THOE-ah

entity	*pronunciation*
Glaaki	GLAH-kee
Gnoph-Keh	nauf-KAE
Gug	GUHG
Hastur	has-TOOR
Hydra	HIGH-drah
Hypnos	HIP-noes
Ithaqua	ITH-uh-kwah
Lloigor	LOI-goer
Mi-Go	MEE-goe
Nodens	NOE-denz
Nyarlathotep	NIGH-ar-LATH-oe-tep
Nyogtha	nee-AUG-thah
Quachil Uttaus	KWAH-chil oo-TAUS
Rhan-Tegoth	ran-TEE-gauth
Shaggai	shah-GIGH
Shantak	SHAN-tak
Shoggoth	SHOE-gauth
Shub-Niggurath	shub-NIG-er-ath
Shudde M'ell	shood-ih-MEL
Tcho-Tcho	Choe-choe
Tindalos	TIN-dah-loes
Tsathoggua	tsah-THAUG-wah
Tulzscha	TUHLZ-chuh
Ubbo Sathla	OO-boe SATH-lah
Xiclotl	ZIGH-klaut'l
Y'golonac	ee-GOE-laun-ahk
Yibb-Tstll	yib-TIS-tuhl
Yig	YIG
Yog-Sothoth	YAHG-sau-thauth
Yuggoth	YUG-gauth
Zhar	ZAR

CHTHONIANS, **Greater Independent Race.** *Flowing tentacles and pulpy gray-black, elongated sack of a body . . . no distinguishing features at all other than the reaching, groping tentacles. Or was there—yes—a lump in the upper body of the thing . . . a container of sorts for the brain, ganglia, or whichever diseased organ governed this horror's loathsome life!*—Brian Lumley, *The Burrowers Beneath.*

These creatures are like immense earth-bound squids, and their elongated worm-like bodies are coated with slime. A chanting sound accompanies them. These powerful burrowers live more than a thousand years, and are protective of their young. A jumble of remarkable properties, chthonians bear little resemblance to else on this planet. The most important individual chthonian is the gigantic Shudde M'ell.

All stages of chthonians communicate via telepathy and can thus reach another of their race anywhere in the world, and can sense other minds. Only adults can telepathically control members of other species with this power.

■ They can tunnel through rock as though it were butter, and have no need to breathe.

■ Adult chthonians can withstand enormous temperatures, up to 4000°C (7200°F). It may be that the majority of chthonians live toward the core of this planet, and that only outcasts, wanderers, and those accidentally caught up in pluming magma explore the cold outer crust where man thrives. Perhaps they migrate here to give birth, since the younger stages cannot withstand extreme heat. We do not know their motives.

■ Full adults can cause powerful earthquakes.

■ Chthonians are extremely susceptible to water. While their slime coating protects them from small amounts of water, general immersion destroys a chthonian. Burrowing, these monsters avoid significant water by distinguishing the relatively low echo profiles of water and watery sediment, avoiding such areas.

■ Chthonians are worldwide, even found in basalt under the oceans. In western Africa is a mystery city called G'harne, which they frequent. They may have been imprisoned there once, aeons ago.

The general discussion and initial statistics concern the full adult, the last and largest stage (instar) between molts. This is the sort which investigators are most likely to meet. A closing section compares all six stages, since a nest of younger chthonians may be encountered, or a band of chthonians with varying age groups could be met with.

CHTHONIAN TELEPATHIC CONTROL: chthonians can use telepathy to control humans, though they do not often do so unless the target has something they want, such as odd spherical mineral formations.

Match the POW of a single chthonian against the target's POW on the resistance table. Overcome, the victim is bound to the area where physically attacked. At first the target has mobility of a mile or so, but this progressively lessens as the chthonian draws nearer, until the victim may not be able to leave a particular room, or even a particular chair. The target immobilized, the chthonian erupts through the floor and collects its due. If the victim becomes aware of the mental influence of a chthonian, the hold may be broken by successfully matching POW against the chthonian's POW. Once a victim has experience of chthonians, a successful Idea roll constitutes awareness.

A chthonian can telepathically contact a known human anywhere on the Earth, but it may take time before it can find his mind.

It costs a chthonian one magic point to communicate with a human or to bind a human to a site for a day. Each ten miles of distance from a binding also costs another magic point. Several chthonians may contribute magic points to compensate for distance, but only one of their POWs may match at a time on the Resistance Table.

It costs no magic points to contact another chthonian, no matter at what distance.

Anecdotal evidence suggests that adults may be able to drain away a percentage of a human's magic points, but nothing definite is truly known.

EARTHQUAKE ATTACKS: all adult chthonians can create earthquakes. Figure an earthquake's force by totaling the POW of participating chthonians and dividing by 20. The result is the

ADULT
CHTHON-

PARENTE

Monsters, By Type

Independent Races	Great Race of Yith	Shaggai, Insects from	Glaaki, Servants of
Chthonians	Great Race, New	Shoggoths	Cthulhu, Star-Spawn of
Colours Out of Space	Gugs	Star Vampires	Formless Spawn
Dholes	Hounds of Tindalos	Xiclotl, Beings from	Hunting Horrors
Dimensional Shamblers	Leng Spiders		Nightgaunts
Elder Things	Lloigor	**Servitor Races**	Rat-Things
Flying Polyps	Mi-Go—The Fungi from	Byakhee	Sand-Dwellers
Ghasts	Yuggoth	Dark Young	Servitors of the Outer Gods
Ghouls	Moon-Beasts	Deep Ones	Shantaks
Gnoph-Keh	Serpent People	Fire Vampires	Tcho-Tchos

earthquake's magnitude on the Richter scale, but only in the first diameter of 100 yards. In the next 100 yards, the Richter force is lessened by one, and so on each additional 100 yards until the strength of the quake can be ignored. Alternatively, the chthonians might limit the force in the center diameter, and instead extend the quake's diameter-of-effect or maximum effect by multiples of 100 yards.

At least half of the participants must be directly under the center of the earthquake. Each chthonian must spend magic points equal to the highest Richter force number generated for the quake. Historically, the highest Richter numbers have been approximately 9s, but geological evidence exists of quakes that have been much stronger.

TENTACLE ATTACKS: each round, a chthonian can attack with 1D8 tentacles, each of which do damage equal to half the creature's damage bonus (round down). If a tentacle strikes home, it clings and worms its way into the victim's vitals, and begins to drain off blood and fluids, costing 1D6 CON each round. Reaching 0 CON, the victim dies. CON lost to a chthonian is gone for good. While a tentacle is draining a victim, only 1D8-1 other tentacles can attack each round, and so forth. Results of less than 1 indicate that no tentacles attack that round. However, tentacles draining their targets will continue to sap CON. Each tentacle could attack a different target, or they could all attack the same one.

CRUSH ATTACKS: a chthonian may use its immense bulk to crush a foe. If crushing, a chthonian cannot attack with tentacles, but it can continue to hold and drain victims that are already caught. The chthonian rears up and crashes down on a group: the crush area is circular, striking equally all within. The crush area equals a diameter in yards of the chthonian's SIZ divided by ten.

Within the crush area, an investigator must succeed with Dodge or Jump, or lose hit points equal to the creature's full damage bonus.

CHTHONIAN FULL ADULTS, Tentacled Burrowers

char.	rolls	averages
STR	3D6 x5	52-53
CON	3D6 + 30	40-41
SIZ	3D6 x5	52-53
INT	5D6	17-18
POW	5D6	17-18
DEX	2D6	7
Move 6/1 burrowing		HP 46-47

Av. Damage Bonus: +5D6 or 6D6.

Weapons: Tentacle 75%, damage 2D6 or 3D6 + blood drain
Crush 80%, damage 5D6 or 6D6 +db

Armor: 5-point hide and muscle; regenerates 5 hit points per round after wounded, but dies immediately upon reaching zero hit points.

Spells: a full adult possess spells if an INT x3 roll on D100 succeeds; it then has 1D6 spells connected with Shudde M'ell and Great Old Ones tied to this earth, such as Cthulhu, Y'Golonac, Yig, etc.

Sanity Loss: 1D3/1D20 Sanity points for a full adult; 1/1D10 Sanity points for the lesser instars; no Sanity points to see a hatchling.

Mythos Comparative Sizes

This table equates approximate weight with game SIZ. In Call of Cthulhu, SIZ pertains not only to weight but to volume and height as well. This table should not be relied on absolutely: it will not be useful for creatures lighter than air, gaseous, able to change mass, or made of plasma or ectoplasm. From SIZ 330 on, SIZ is exactly 1/10th the creature's weight in short tons. Thus, a dhole of SIZ 8000 weighs 80,000 short tons. See also the comparative size illustrations on pp. 146-147.

SIZ	English Weight	Metric Weight
1	1-12 pounds	.5-5.5 kg
4	38-51 pounds	17-23 kg
8	109-120 pounds	50-55 kg
12	156-168 pounds	71-76 kg
16	220-239 pounds	100-109 kg
20	310-338 pounds	141-154 kg
24	440-479 pounds	200-218 kg
32	880-959 pounds	400-436 kg
40	1760-1919 pounds	800-872 kg
48	3520-3829 pounds	1600-1741 kg
56	7040-7649 pounds	3200-3477 kg
64	7.1-7.7 tons	6455-7000 kg
72	14.1-15.4 tons	6.4-7 metric tons
80	28.2-30.7 tons	12.8-14 metric tons
88	56.5-61.5 tons	25.7-28 metric tons
96	96 tons	44 metric tons
104	104 tons	47 metric tons
112	120 tons	54.5 metric tons
120	144 tons	65.5 metric tons
128	176 tons	80 metric tons
136	216 tons	98 metric tons
140	240 tons	109 metric tons
144	264 tons	120 metric tons
152	320 tons	145.5 metric tons
160	384 tons	174.5 metric tons
168	456 tons	207 metric tons
176	536 tons	244 metric tons
184	624 tons	284 metric tons
192	720 tons	327 metric tons
200	824 tons	375 metric tons
208	936 tons	425 metric tons
216	1056 tons	480 metric tons
224	1184 tons	538 metric tons
232	1220 tons	555 metric tons
240	1364 tons	620 metric tons
256	1516 tons	689 metric tons
264	1676 tons	762 metric tons
272	1844 tons	838 metric tons
280	2020 tons	918 metric tons
288	2204 tons	1002 metric tons
294	2396 tons	1089 metric tons
304	2596 tons	1180 metric tons
312	2804 tons	1275 metric tons
320	3020 tons	1373 metric tons
330	3300 tons	1500 metric tons
340	3400 tons	1546 metric tons
350	3500 tons	1591 metric tons

CHTHONIAN LIFE CYCLE

The full adult is shown above; hatchlings are at the end of this write-up. INT and DEX do not change.

	1st instar	2nd instar	3rd instar	4th instar
STR	3D6	3D6 x2	3D6 x3	3D6 x4
CON	3D6+10	3D6+15	3D6+20	3D6+25
SIZ	3D6	3D6 x2	3D6 x3	3D6 x4
POW	1D6	2D6	3D6	4D6
Max Temp	100°C	250°C	600°C	1500°C
HP Regen.	1	2	3	4
Armor	1	2	3	4
Av HP	15-16	22-25	29-33	34-42
time	9-10 mon.	8-15 years	unknown	unknown

Max Temp—maximum temperature that the instar can withstand without pain and injury. A temperature double that listed quickly kills the creature.

HP Regen—hit points per round that the instar regenerates.

Av HP—the hit points for an average individual of that stage.

HATCHLINGS: Chthonian eggs resemble geodes or other spherical mineral formations. They are a foot or less in diameter, and have shells two or three inches thick.

Hatchlings are the initial stage of chthonian growth, before first instar, and exist only for a few months right after hatching. Out of their shells, each is the size of a large earthworm, has 1 hit point and 1D6 points of POW, and can withstand only 40 degrees C. A burning cigar could wither and kill one.

COLOURS OUT OF SPACE, Greater Independent Race. *The shaft of phosphorescence from the well [brought] a sense of doom and abnormality which far outraced any image their conscious minds could form. It was no longer shining out, it was pouring out; and as the shapeless stream of unplaceable colour left the well it seemed to flow directly into the sky.*—H. P. Lovecraft, "The Colour Out of Space."

A Colour is a sentient organism which manifests itself as pure colour—it is not gaseous, it is insubstantial. When it moves, it is visible as an amorphous, glistening patch of color, rolling and shining in shades of its pale colors that match nothing in the known spectrum. This patch pours over the ground or flies in a living fashion. When it feeds, its victim's skin and face glow with the Colour.

Though incorporeal, its passing nonetheless feels like the touch of a slimy, unhealthy vapor. Geiger counters register its presence as a distinctive burst of radiation. With 1990s light-intensification gear, it shows as a bright patch of luminosity. Infrared viewers are useless.

Colours come from the depths of space, where natural laws differ. Adult Colours create embryos, harmless three-inch spheres seemingly empty. Deposited on verdant soil or in shallow waters, the embryo begins to germinate. After a few days, the outer shell dissolves and the new creature, which we may term a larva, emerges.

The jelly-like larva can grow to great size. As it infiltrates the ecosystem, local vegetation exhibits a tremendous but unhealthy growth. Fruit tastes bitter. Insects and animals are born deformed. At night, all plant life glows with the Colour, and the vegetation begins to twist and writhe at night, as though in a strong wind. Even humans shine with the spectral light. After a few months, the larva transforms into a young Colour.

It now makes brief trips from its lair to feed, and begins to drain the life-force from the area previously affected by the larva. When it drains enough energy, it departs the planet for space and adulthood. In so maturing, the Colour may drain life-force from an area of five acres or so if rich in life, or perhaps 10-20 acres of moor or grassland. The area drained is ruined thereafter, and no plant can grow.

Bright light inhibits a Colour. It spends daylight hours in dark, cool hideaways, preferably underwater: cisterns, wells, lakes, reservoirs, and oceans are all suitable.

ATTACKS AND EFFECTS: since a Colour is so efficient an attacker, as a warning keepers sometimes may wish to allow INT x4 or x5 to detect its slight glow, or to notice a sudden presence of ozone.

If it is feeding, match the Colour's POW against the victim's current magic points. For every 10 full points by which the Colour exceeds its victim, it permanently drains 1 point each of STR, CON, POW, DEX, and APP from the victim, and costs him or her 1D6 hit points as well. Each POW so drained increases the Colour's POW. The victim is aware of a sucking, burning sensation, and progressively withers and grays. His face sinks, and his skin ages with hideous skin cracks and wrinkles. Once drained, the victim dies.

Colours of low POW feed on humans by using Mental Attack. A Colour can weaken the minds of nearby sentient beings. For each day of residence in the Colour's vicinity, each person must match his or her INT against the Colour's POW or lose 1D6 magic points and 1D6 Sanity points. Magic points so-destroyed cannot be regained without leaving the area. The influence also strongly binds the victim to his or her home, and the influence becomes increasingly irresistible as the victim's will weakens. To decide to leave the area, he or she must receive a success of current magic points x5 or less on D100, or stay.

A Colour can focus its energies to disintegrate a hole through almost any material. This ability is used primarily to excavate a lair underground. The same effort to melt a cubic foot of titanium removes several cubic yards of pine wood. The sides of the hole appear melted, but no heat is generated.

Finally, a Colour can concentrate and solidify a part of itself. That part becomes translucent. It can then use its STR to grapple humans, to grab weapons, or to manipulate other objects.

COLOUR OUT OF SPACE

COLOURS OUT OF SPACE, Life Force Feeders

char.	rolls	averages
STR	1D6 per 10 POW or fraction	7
SIZ	equal to POW	10-11
INT	4D6	14
POW	2D6*	10-11+
DEX	2D6+12	19
Move 12 pouring/20 flying		HP N/A

base amount, which then increases as a Colour feeds

Av. Damage Bonus: +0.

Weapons: Feed 85%, damage 1D6 + characteristics loss
Mental Attack 100%, damage 1D6 magic points + 1D6 SAN
Disintegrate 100%, damage physical disintegration
Grasp 85%, no damage

Armor: none. Invulnerable to physical attack except by strong magnetic fields, which can imprison it. Vulnerable to magic.

Spells, Skills: none.

Sanity Loss: 0/1D4 Sanity points to see a Colour; 1/1D8 Sanity points to see a victim of a Colour.

DAGON & HYDRA, Deep One Greater Servitors. *Vast, Polyphemous-like, and loathsome, it darted like a stupendous monster of nightmares to the monolith, about which it flung its gigantic scaly arms.*—H. P. Lovecraft, "Dagon."

Father Dagon and Mother Hydra are deep ones who have grown enormously in size and age, each over 20 feet tall and perhaps millions of years old. They rule the deep ones and lead them in their worship of Cthulhu. This pair is active and mobile, unlike Cthulhu and his minions, but are rarely met. Dagon's and Hydra's characteristics are identical. It is possible that more than two deep ones have grown to the enormous size and strength comparable to that described in Lovecraft's "Dagon."

DAGON or HYDRA, Rulers of the Deep Ones

STR 52	CON 50	SIZ 60	INT 20	POW 30
DEX 20	Move 10			HP 55

Damage Bonus: +6D6.

Weapon: Claw 80%, damage 1D6 +6D6

Armor: 6-point skin.

Spells: each knows all spells to summon/bind the lesser servitor races of the Mythos.

Sanity Loss: 1/1D10 Sanity points to see Dagon or Hydra.

DAGON

DARK YOUNG, Greater Servitor Race. *Something black in the road, something that wasn't a tree. Something big and black and ropy, just squatting there, waiting, with ropy arms squirming and reaching . . . . It came crawling up the hillside . . . and it was the black thing of my dreams—that black, ropy, slimy jelly tree-thing out of the woods. It crawled up and it flowed up on its hoofs and mouths and snaky arms.*— Robert Bloch, "Notebook Found in a Deserted House."

These beings are enormous writhing masses, formed out of ropy black tentacles. Here and there over the surfaces of the things are great puckered mouths which drip green goo. Beneath the creatures, tentacles end in black hooves, on which they stamp. The monsters roughly resemble trees in silhouette —the trunks being the short legs, and the tops of the trees represented by the ropy, branching bodies. The whole mass of these things smell like open graves. Dark young stand between 12 and 20 feet tall.

Such entities are the "young" referred to in Shub-Niggurath's epithet, "Black Goat of the Woods with a Thousand Young". They are closely connected to her, and are found only in areas where she is worshiped. Dark young act as proxies for Shub-Niggurath in accepting sacrifices, accepting worship from cultists, devouring non-cultists, and spreading their mother's faith across the world. Luckily, they are rarely met with.

ATTACKS & SPECIAL EFFECTS: in its masses of tentacles, a typical dark young has four thicker sinuous tentacles with which it attacks. Each of these thicker tentacles can strike out to injure or to grab and capture once per round, conceivably at four different targets. If a victim is grabbed, he or she is held to one of the horrible sucking mouths and drained of 1D3 STR per round. This STR loss cannot be restored. While being drained, a victim is capable only of ineffectual writhing and screaming. The dark young can also trample with its massive hooves, typically hooting and bellowing as it does.

DARK YOUNG of Shub-Niggurath

char.	rolls	averages
STR	4D6+30	44
CON	3D6+6	16-17
SIZ	4D6+30	44
INT	4D6	14
POW	5D6	17-18
DEX	3D6+6	16-17
Move 8		HP 30-31

Av. Damage Bonus: +4D6.

Weapons: Tentacle 80%, damage db + STR drain
Trample 40%, damage 2D6 + db

Armor: dark young are of non-terrene material and make-up, so that any successful firearm attack does only 1 point of damage. A firearms impale does 2 points of damage. Shotguns are exceptions, and do minimum possible damage, whatever that is. Hand-to-hand weapons do normal damage; attacks dependent on heat, blast, corrosion, electrical charge, or poisoning have no effect.

Spells: each dark young knows a number of appropriate spells equal to half its INT; round fractions up.

Skills: Sneak 60%, Hide in Woods 80%.

Sanity Loss: 1D3/1D10 Sanity points to see a dark young.

DARK YOUNG

DEEP ONES, Lesser Servitor Race. *I think their predominant color was a greyish-green, though they had white bellies. They were mostly shiny and slippery, but the ridges of their backs were scaly. Their forms vaguely suggested the anthropoid, while their heads were the heads of fish, with prodigious bulging eyes that never closed. At the sides of their necks were palpitating gills and their long paws were webbed. They hopped irregularly, sometimes on hind legs and sometimes on four . . . their croaking, baying voices . . . held all the dark shades of expression which their staring faces lacked.*—H. P. Lovecraft, "The Shadow over Innsmouth."

The deep ones are an amphibious race that serve primarily Cthulhu and two beings known as Father Dagon and Mother Hydra. Locked in the timeless depths of the sea, their alien, arrogant lives are coldly beautiful, unbelievably cruel, effectively immortal. They come together to mate or to worship Great Cthulhu, but do not crave touching or being touched as humans do. They are a marine race, unknown in freshwater environments, and globally have many cities, all submerged beneath the waves. One is off the coast of Massachusetts, near Innsmouth.

Some deep ones interact with humans. They appear to have a monstrous lust to produce human/deep one hybrids. The reason may lie in the breeding cycle of these beings, of which little is known. Deep ones may be worshiped by humans with whom they regularly interbreed, for deep ones are immortal, unless slain, and so are any hybrid offspring. Typically, hybrids inhabit remote coastal villages.

Such a hybrid begins life as a human-looking child who gradually becomes uglier and uglier. Suddenly, over a period of a few months, the human undergoes a monstrous transformation into a deep one. The changeover usually takes place at the age of 1D20+20 years, but some individuals change earlier or later, or only partially.

DEEP ONE

DEEP ONES, Gilled Humanoids

char.	rolls	averages
STR	4D6	14
CON	3D6	10-11
SIZ	3D6+6	16-17
INT	2D6+6	13
POW	3D6	10-11
DEX	3D6	10-11
Move 8/10 Swimming		HP 13-14

Av. Damage Bonus: +1D4.

Weapons: Claw 25%, damage 1D6 + db
Hunting Spear* 25%, damage 1D6 + db
*impaling weapon.

Armor: 1-point skin and scales.

Spells: at the discretion of the keeper, deep ones with POW 14 or more know at least 1D4 spells.

Sanity Loss: 0/1D6 Sanity points to see a deep one.

DHOLES, Greater Independent Race. *Below him the ground was festering with gigantic Dholes, and even as he looked, one reared up several hundred feet and leveled a bleached, viscous end at him.*—H. P. Lovecraft and E. Hoffman Price, "Through the Gate of the Silver Key."

Dholes are gigantic worm-like burrowing horrors. They are not native to the Earth, and none seem to have been brought here for more than brief periods, fortunately, for they seem to have riddled and left waste several other worlds. They dislike light, though it does not visibly harm them. They are only rarely seen in daylight, and then only on planets that they have thoroughly conquered. Some unknown relation between dholes and chthonians may exist. Similar creatures, *bholes,* exist in the Dreamlands.

ATTACKS & SPECIAL EFFECTS: *Goo Attack.* In lieu of swallowing or crushing a target, a dhole can spit a gob of slimy goo from its mouth up to a range of 2-3 miles. The globe covers a circular area with a diameter equal to 5% of the monster's SIZ in feet: thus a dhole of SIZ 400 spits a glob 20 feet across, big enough to bring down an airplane.

Any living thing struck by the glob is stunned and engulfed. Climbing out of a mass of goo requires a roll of STR or less on D100; make one attempt per round. While buried in the frightful slime, the investigator cannot breathe, and must make drowning checks as if asphyxiating each round. In addition, the caustic slime costs the investigator 1 hit point per round her or she is held. Once the victim escapes, the burning damage stops.

Engulf. If a dhole swallows (engulfs) someone, it scoops clean an area equal in size to the area of its goo attack. If a dhole crushes (crawls over) an investigator, death is automatic. With a successful Luck roll, his companions find enough to bury.

DHOLES, Burrowing Horrors

char.	rolls	averages
STR	1D100X10	505
CON	1D100+100	151-152
SIZ	STR+1D100	555-556
INT	2D6	7
POW	10D6	35
DEX	1D4	2-3
Move 18 Crawl/10 Burrow		HP 353-354

Damage Bonus: enough to flatten a battleship.

Weapons: Spit Goo 50%, damage special
Engulf 80%, damage swallowed
Crush 30%, damage death

Armor: points equaling the dhole's POW.

Spells: none

Sanity Loss: 1D4/1D20 Sanity points to see a dhole.

DIMENSIONAL SHAMBLERS, Lesser Independent Race. *Shuffling towards him in the darkness was the gigantic, blasphemous form of a thing not wholly ape and not wholly insect. Its hide hung loosely upon its frame, and its rugose, dead-eyed rudiment of a head swayed drunkenly from side to side. Its forepaws were extended, with talons spread wide, and its whole body was taut with murderous malignity despite its utter lack of facial description.* —H. P. Lovecraft and Hazel Heald, "The Horror in the Museum."

Little is known about these beings save their name and a description of a hide. It is assumed that they are entities capable of walking between the planes and worlds of the universe, spending little time at an one planet, but wandering about. They occasionally serve an Outer God or a Great Old One. They can leave a plane at will, signaling the change by beginning to shimmer and fade. This transition costs them 4 magic points and takes a round to complete. During this time they may be attacked, but they may not attack back.

A shambler can take objects or beings with it when it fades into another dimension. By clutching the desired object in its talons and expending an additional magic point per 10 SIZ points of the object or creature, that which is held makes the transit also. Objects and victims lost are never found again.

DIMENSIONAL SHAMBLERS,
the Murderously Malign

char.	rolls	averages
STR	2D6+12	19
CON	3D6+6	16-17
SIZ	2D6+12	19
INT	2D6	7
POW	3D6	10-11
DEX	3D6	10-11
Move 7		HP 18

Av. Damage Bonus: +1D6.

Weapons: Claw* 30%, 1D8 + db
*can attack with both foreclaws at once, at the same DEX rank.

Armor: 3-point thick hide.

Spells: a shambler knows one spell per point of INT over 9.

Sanity Loss: 0/1D10 Sanity points to see a dimensional shambler.

ELDER THINGS, Lesser Independent Race. *They represented some ridged barrel-shaped object with thin horizontal arms radiating spoke-like from a central ring and with vertical knobs or bulbs projecting from the head and base of the barrel. Each of these knobs was the hub of a system of five long, flat, triangularly tapering arms arranged around it like the arms of a starfish.* —H. P. Lovecraft, "Dreams in the Witch House."

A very complete description of one of these beings is in "At the Mountains of Madness", also by Lovecraft, but it is too long to include here. It notes that the entity stands about eight feet tall, with a six-foot torso, and that it has wings which neatly fold up into slots. In that story this race is referred to as the *Old Ones*. Elder things communicate by piping whistles and can sense without light.

Elder things came to Earth a billion years ago, and may have accidentally started terrestrial life. They created the blasphemous shoggoths to serve as slaves. Their race began to degenerate before man evolved, and they at least partially lost their former ability to fly through space on their membranous wings. After numerous wars with other races, the mi-go and the star-spawn prime among them, and the rebellion of their former slaves, the shoggoths, the amphibious elder things were eventually driven back to Antarctica in the last few million years, where their last city remains frozen under a glacier. Their civilization was eventually wiped out by the cold of the ice age. The elder things are extinct on land, but may still have colonies in the deepest waters. Elder things also may be met by time travelers and non-degenerate elder things still live among the stars.

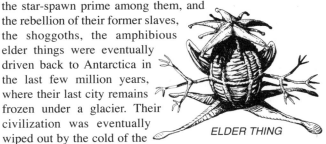
ELDER THING

In hand-to-hand combat, an elder thing may use all five tentacles at once, but no more than three may be used versus a single target. Once a tentacle grips, it clings to the victim, and each round thereafter the victim loses hit points equal to half the elder thing's damage bonus in constriction and crushing damage.

See also the "Alien Technology" chapter for a few more notes on elder things, p. 156.

ELDER THINGS, City-Builders Eons Old

char.	rolls	averages
STR	4D6+24	38
CON	3D6+12	22-23
SIZ	8D6	28
INT	1D6+12	15-16
POW	3D6	10-11
DEX	3D6+6	16-17
Move 8/10 flying		HP 25-26

Av. Damage Bonus: +3D6.

Weapons: Tentacle 40%, damage 1/2 db in constriction

Armor: 7-point skin.

Spells: each has INT x3 chance to know 1D4 appropriate spells.

Sanity Loss: 0/1D6 Sanity points to see an elder thing.

FIRE VAMPIRES, Lesser Servitor Race. *These appeared as thousands of tiny points of light . . . . The myriad points of light were living entities of flame! [Where] they touched, fire sprang up.* —August Derleth, "The Dweller in Darkness."

They are minions of Cthugha and, like him, dwell on or near the star Fomalhaut. They come to Earth when summoned, or when accompanying Cthugha. They appear to be a form of intelligent gas or plasma, a fairly frequent Mythos concept.

FIRE VAMPIRE

A DUAL ATTACK: fire vampires attack by touching their victims, and can set flammable objects alight by touch. They damage humans by heat-shock. To determine the heat-shock damage, roll 2D6 for the vampire's attack and match this against the investigator's CON on the resistance table. If the heat wins, the investigator loses hit points equal to the rolled damage. If the investigator wins, he loses hit points equal to half the rolled damage (round fractions up).

In the same attack, the vampire may try to steal magic points from its target: match its current magic points against the magic points of the target on the Resistance Table. If the vampire wins, it steals 1D10 magic points from the victim. If the fire vampire loses the resistance struggle, it loses one of its own magic points. Thus, in each attack by a fire vampire, roll twice—once to determine heat damage and once to determine magic point loss.

FIRE VAMPIRES, the Flame Feeders

char.	rolls	averages
STR	N/A	—
CON	2D6	7
SIZ	1	1
INT	3D6	10-11
POW	2D6+6	13
DEX	3D6+6	16-17
Move 11 flying		HP 4

Damage Bonus: N/A

Weapons: Touch 85%, damage 2D6 burn + magic point drain

Armor: most material weapons cannot harm them, including bullets, etc. Water costs a fire vampire one hit point per half-gallon poured over it, a typical hand-held fire extinguisher does 1D6 hit points of damage to it, and a bucket of sand costs it 1D3 hit points.

Spells: Fire vampires with a POW of 17 or more have at least 1D3 spells.

Sanity Loss: seeing a fire vampire costs no Sanity points.

FLYING POLYPS, Greater Independent Race. *A horrible elder race of half polypous, utterly alien entities . . . . They were only partly material and had the power of aerial motion, despite the absence of wings . . . . Suggestions of a monstrous plasticity and of temporary lapses of visibility . . . singular whistling noises and colossal footprints made up of five circular toe marks seemed also to be associated with them.*
—H. P. Lovecraft, "The Shadow Out of Time."

This unnamed species came to Earth out of space as conquerors about seven hundred and fifty million years ago. They built basalt cities with high windowless towers and inhabited three other planets in the solar system as well. On Earth, they were warred on and finally forced underground by the Great Race of Yith, but near the close of the Cretaceous era (about 50 million years ago) they rose up from their subterranean haunts and exterminated the Great Race.

The polyps still remain in their caverns and seem content to remain there, annihilating the few beings chancing across them. The entrances to their dwellings are mostly deep within ancient ruins where there are great wells sealed over with stone. Inside these wells dwell the polyps still, ferocious alien fighters with a bewildering variety of attacks.

They have the power to control great winds. Each of the polypoid wind abilities cost them a magic point per round to use.

WIND BLAST ATTACK: the wind blast has a base range of 20 yards and a 10-yard diameter cylinder of effect emanating from the polyp, doing damage equal to the polyp's damage bonus. The cylindrical blast can extend further than 20 yards, but loses 1D6 damage for each multiple of the base distance—thus a target at 39 yards would take 4D6, and a target at 41 yards would take 3D6 damage respectively. Victims of the wind blast literally have their flesh stripped from their bones and their skin dehydrated and wind-burned, and are blown backwards for a number of yards equal to the hit points they have lost.

FIXING ATTACK: this is for capturing prey, and is most mysterious. In this mode, the wind attack has a range of 1000 yards, and can blow without diminishment around corners or up through winding corridors. Although the wind emanates from the polyp, it has a peculiar sucking effect on the target, slowing down him or her, and forcing the player to make a Resistance Table roll each round of the target's STR against half of the polyp's POW. If the polyp wins, the victim cannot move away that round. If the target wins, he or she may move normally. At ranges of 200 yards or less, the target must resist against the polyp's full POW. The flying polyp can move at full speed while using this ability, so it may be both chasing interesting prey and slowing it.

This technique may be used on multiple targets within 30 yards of one another. Add 5 percentiles for each target to the chance of each who resists. The polyp may choose not to affect some targets in order to affect others more strongly.

FLYING POLYP

WINDSTORM ATTACK: a polyp can generate a wind in conjunction with its fellows. The windstorm has a speed of 1/2 mile per hour per point of POW of the participating polyp. This windstorm is local, losing 5 mph of force for every 200 yards it travels. A group of polyps can generate hurricane-force winds within an area of a few square miles. Base the damage done to targets by Luck rolls, starting at POW x5 and descending to x4, x3, etc., for every 15 mph of wind above 60 mph. The target takes 1D4 damage for each Luck roll missed.

TENTACLE ATTACK: polyps continually form and dissolve tentacles from their bodies. Each round, roll 2D6 to determine how many tentacles may attack in that particular round. Tentacle damage is always 1D10. Because of the partially non-material nature of these entities, the tentacle's damage is done directly to the target's hit points, ignoring any body armor. The wound takes the form of a wind burn or desiccation of tissue.

INVISIBILITY: by spending a magic point per round, a polyp can turn totally invisible, but it still can be roughly located by the constant nauseating piping sound that always accompanies it. Anyone trying to hit an invisible polyp must receive a successful Listen roll to tell where it is and subtract 50 percentiles from the chance to hit. Thus a marksman with 90% Rifle who fires at an invisible polyp has a 40% chance to hit.

Polyps always are phasing in and out of visibility, so a polyp's POW is subtracted from the attacker's chance to hit if the polyp is not entirely invisible. When a polyp is invisible, it does not attack with its tentacles, but may still use one of the wind attacks, or cast spells.

FLYING POLYPS, Terrors from the Blackness Below

char.	rolls	averages
STR	4D6+36	50
CON	2D6+18	25
SIZ	4D6+36	50
INT	4D6	14
POW	3D6+6	16-17
DEX	2D6+6	13
Move 8/12 flying		HP 38

Av. Damage Bonus: +5D6, but use only for wind blast.

Weapons: Tentacle 85%, damage 1D10
Windblast 70%, damage db lowered by 1D6 per 20 yards distance.

Armor: 4 points, plus invisibility. The extraterrene flying polyp takes only minimum damage from physical weapons—a gun doing 2D6+3 points of damage would automatically do only 5 points of damage to a polyp, with this reduced 4 points more by the monster's skin armor. An impale would do doubled minimum damage reduced by 4, or actual damage done of 6 points. Enchanted weapons do full normal damage, as do forces such as heat or electricity.

Spells: roll 1D20. If the roll is higher than the polyp's INT, it knows no spells. Otherwise, the polyp knows a number of spell equal to the die roll. The kindly keeper chooses those which seem appropriate.

Sanity Loss: 1D3/1D20 Sanity points to see a flying polyp.

FORMLESS SPAWN, Lesser Servitor Race. *When the men of K'n-Yan went down into N'Kai's black abyss with their great atom-power searchlights, they found living things—living things that oozed along stone channels and worshiped onyx and basalt images of Tsathoggua. But they were not toads like Tsathoggua himself. Far worse—they were amorphous lumps of viscous black slime that took temporary shapes for various purposes. The explorers of K'N-Yan did not pause for detailed observations, and those that escaped alive sealed the passage.* —H. P. Lovecraft and Zealia Bishop, "The Mound."

These black, protean beings change shapes in an instant, from toad-like lumps to elongate things with hundreds of rudimentary legs. They ooze through small cracks and enlarge their appendages at will. They are closely associated with Tsathoggua, often found in his temples or in sunless caverns.

Due to their extreme fluidity and the countless different forms available to them, each has at least four attack forms which they may vary at will from round to round, though not within a single round. Only one attack, Bite, is complex.

FORMLESS SPAWN

BITE ATTACK: the victim is instantly swallowed. Each round thereafter the victim takes 1 point of damage from constriction, the damage done per round progressively increasing by 1 point (e.g., on the second round he takes 2 points of damage, and so forth). While swallowed, the victim may take no action whatsoever, though friends may attempt to slay the monster to free him or her. A formless spawn can make one Bite attack per round and can continue to swallow prey until having swallowed its own SIZ in prey. While digesting a victim, a Spawn may continue to fight but may not shift location without disgorging what it has swallowed.

FORMLESS SPAWN OF Tsathoggua

char.	rolls	averages
STR	1D6+6 to 6D6+6	9-27
CON	3D6	10-11
SIZ	1D6+12 to 6D6+12	15-33
INT	2D6+6	13
POW	3D6	10-11
DEX	2D6+12	19
Move 12		HP 13-22

Av. Damage Bonus: +1D6.

Weapons: Whip* 90%, damage 1D6
Tentacle** 60%, damage db
Bludgeon*** 20%, damage db
Bite 30%, damage special
may seek to Grapple rather than do damage; range is always the monster's SIZ in yards.
**may strike at 1D3 opponents in a round, and may seek to Grapple rather than do damage; range equals the monster's SIZ in yards.*
***always a 20% chance, damage equal to 2D6 or actual damage bonus, whichever is higher.*

Armor: they are immune to all physical weapons, even enchanted ones, and wounds made by them simply snap closed after being opened. Spells may affect them, as may fire, chemicals, or other forces.

Spells: a formless spawn knows one spell if its INT+POW or less can be rolled on D100. A few spawn know many spells.

Sanity Loss: 1/1D10 Sanity points to see a formless spawn.

GHASTS, Lesser Independent Race. *Repulsive beings which die in the light . . . and leap on long hind legs . . . a pair of yellowish red eyes . . . . Ghasts have indeed an excellent sense of smell . . . something about the size of a small horse hopped out into the grey twilight, and Carter turned sick at the aspect of that scabrous and unwholesome beast, whose face is so curiously human despite the absence of a nose, a forehead, and other particulars . . . . They spoke in coughing gutturals.*—H. P. Lovecraft, "The Dream-Quest of Unknown Kadath."

GHAST

Ghasts are restricted to the underworld and vast caverns where sunlight never comes. Exposed to direct sunlight, they sicken and eventually die. Ghasts are cannibalistic and eat one another as well as other beings they catch.

The horrible semihuman bipeds which are ridden by the highly scientific but morally degenerate humans inhabiting the cavern of K'n-Yan may well be relatives of or even be examples of ghasts. If this is the case, then ghasts are likely a result of serpent people genetic experimentation. Ghasts are evidently tamable, though very primitive and savage.

GHASTS, Unwholesome Scabrous Beasts

char.	rolls	averages
STR	3D6+12	22-23
CON	4D6	14
SIZ	4D6+12	26
INT	1D6	3-4
POW	3D6	10-11
DEX	2D6+6	13
Move 10		HP 20

Av. Damage Bonus: +2D6.

Weapons: Bite 40%, damage 1D10
Kick 25%, 1D6 + db
A ghast is able to kick once and bite once in a combat round.

Spells: none.

Skills: Sneak 70%.

Sanity Loss: 0/1D8 Sanity points to see a ghast.

GHOULS, Lesser Independent Race. *These figures were seldom completely human, but often approached humanity in varying degree. Most of the bodies, while roughly bipedal, had a forward slumping, and a vaguely canine cast. The texture of the majority was a kind of unpleasant rubberiness.*—H. P. Lovecraft, "Pickman's Model."

Ghouls are rubbery, loathsome humanoids with hooflike feet, canine features, and claws. They speak in what are described as gibberings and meepings. They are often encrusted with grave mold collected as they feed.

Lovecraft's ghouls are horrible creatures dwelling in tunnel systems beneath many cities. They have ties to witches and occasionally attack humans. It may be possible for a human to transform into a ghoul over a prolonged period of time.

GHOUL ATTACKS: it may attack with both claws and its bite in a single combat round. If the ghoul's bite strikes home, then in hangs on instead of using claw attacks and worries the victim with its fangs, continuing to do 1D4 Bite damage automatically. A successful STR against STR Resistance Table roll dislodges the ghoul, breaking what amounts to a successful Grapple, and ending the Bite damage.

GHOULS, Mocking Charnel Feeders

char.	roll	averages
STR	3D6+6	16-7
CON	2D6+6	13
SIZ	2D6+6	13
INT	2D6+6	13
POW	2D6+6	13
DEX	2D6+6	13
Move 9		HP 13

Av. Damage Bonus: +1D4.

GHOUL

Weapons: Claws 30%, damage 1D6 + db
Bite 30%, 1D6 + automatic worry

Armor: firearms and projectiles do half of rolled damage; round up any fraction.

Spells: roll D100—if the roll is higher than the ghoul's INT, it knows no spells; if equal to or lower than INT, it knows that many spells, as chosen by the keeper.

Skills: Burrow 75%, Climb 85%, Hide 60%, Jump 75%, Listen 70%, Scent Decay 65%, Sneak 80%, Spot Hidden 50%.

Sanity Loss: 0/1D6 Sanity points to see a ghoul.

GLAAKI, SERVANTS OF, Lesser Servitor Race. *A hand came scrabbling up out to lever it up! . . . the hand of a corpse—bloodless and skeletal, and with impossibly long, cracked nails.*—R. Campbell, "The Inhabitant of the Lake."

Glaaki's slaves are undead things created by his spines. They share Glaaki's memories and become almost a part of the Great Old One, though they can still perform many individual actions. At first they look human enough, if stiff and corpse-like, but in time they wither and look like the undead monsters they are. After six decades of half-death, the servants of Glaaki become subject to the Green Decay if exposed to intense light, such as daylight. The Green Decay begins rot on the spot, destroying one so-exposed in a few hours.

SERVANTS OF GLAAKI, Decaying Slaves

char.	rolls	averages
STR	3D6	10-11
CON	3D6x2	20-22
SIZ	2D6+6	13
INT	2D6+6	13
POW	3D6	10-11
DEX	1D6	3-4
Move 5		HP 17-18

ZOMBIE SERVANT OF GLAAKI

Av. Damage Bonus: +0.

Weapons: Grapple 20%, damage special
Sickle 40%, damage 1D6 + 1 + db

Armor: none.

Spells: retains any known when alive, plus any new spells taught by Glaaki.

Sanity Loss: no Sanity point loss if human-seeming; 1/1D8 Sanity points lost if in living-corpse aspect; if dead from Green Decay, 1/1D10 Sanity points to see.

GNOPH-KEH, Greater Independent Race. *Gnoph-Keh, the hairy myth-thing of the Greenland ice, that walked sometimes on two legs, sometimes on four, and sometimes on six.*—H. P. Lovecraft and Hazel Heald, "The Horror in the Museum."

In earlier stories, Gnoph-Keh appears to be a single being, but later it seems to be a race of beings, possible even a degenerate tribe. Here we assume that it is a sparse race of rare beings, associated with Ithaqua. Usually only one gnoph-keh is encountered at a time, and the race is generally restricted to glaciers, ice caps, and extremely cold and icy areas. Especially harsh winters may bring them down into the lowlands. If a human tribe have indeed named themselves after the fabled gnoph-keh, perhaps they worship the gnoph-keh as a deity, or use it as a totem beast.

GNOPH-KEH

BLIZZARD & COLD ATTACKS: the gnoph-keh has the power to summon a small blizzard about itself, restricting visibility to 3 yards maximum. This costs the creature 1 magic point per hour, and yields a blizzard with a radius of 100 yards. That radius may be increased by 100 more yards for every extra magic point expended. On the rare occasions that two or more gnoph-kehs work together, they may combine their magic points to create gigantic blizzards. The blizzard will always be more or less centered on the gnoph-keh. Every 15 minutes that an investigator spends within such a blizzard, the player must roll CON x5 or less or have his or her investigator lose a hit point to freezing damage if not properly protected against the ice and wind.

The gnoph-keh can also create an intense cold around its body by expending magic points. For each magic point the gnoph-keh spends, the temperature goes down by 20°F for an hour in a 100-yard radius, as with the blizzard. If the creature desires, it can combine the cold and blizzard attacks to create a terrifying local storm.

OTHER ATTACKS: in any given melee round, the gnoph-keh may attack with its horn, and none, two, or four claws of its six. If it uses no claws, then add 2D6 to its damage bonus when jabbing with its horn, as it has a better grip in the snow. If it uses two claws, use its normal damage bonus. If it uses four claws, subtract 2D6 from its normal damage bonuses, including for the claws, as it must spend some energy staying upright instead of investing force in its blows.

GNOPH-KEH, Legends of the Ice

char.	rolls	averages
STR	2D6+24	31
CON	3D6+12	22-23
SIZ	2D6+24	31
INT	1D6+12	15-16
POW	6D6	21
DEX	4D6	14
Move 9		HP 27

Av. Damage Bonus: +3D6.

Weapons: Horn Gore 65%, damage 1D10 + db
Claw 45%, damage 1D6 +db

Armor: 9 points of gristle, fur, and hide.

Spells: roll 1D20—if the result is equal to or less than the creature's INT, it knows that many spells. Otherwise, it knows none.

Sanity Loss: 0/1D10 Sanity points for seeing a gnoph-keh.

GREAT RACE OF YITH, Greater Independent Race. *Enormous, iridescent cones, about ten feet high and ten feet wide at the base, and made up of some ridgy, scaly, semi-elastic matter. From their apexes projected four flexible, cylindrical members, each a foot thick, and of a ridgy substance like that of the cones themselves. These members were sometimes contracted almost to nothing, and sometimes extended to any distance up to about ten feet. Terminating two of them were enormous claws or nippers. At the end of a third were four red trumpetlike appendages. The fourth terminated in an irregular yellowish globe some two feet in diameter and having three great dark eyes ranged along its central circumference . . . . Surmounting this head were four slender grey stalks bearing flowerlike appendages, whilst from its nether side dangled eight greenish antennae or tentacles. The great base of the central cone was ringed with a rubbery grey substance which moved the whole entity through expansion and contraction.*—H. P. Lovecraft, "The Shadow Out of Time."

Their bodies are native to this Earth. They were a species of mental entities, fleeing their own world's destruction. They came to Earth and took over the minds of the cone-shaped beings dwelling here. The combination of the Earth-born bodies and the minds of the aliens made the Great Race. They taught their young their own technology and culture. Those young grew up as true inheritors of the mentalists, and the new bodies were natural to them. In the aeons that followed the Great Race divided up the Earth between themselves, the mi-go, and Cthulhu's kin. Cthulhu and his kind ruled from the Pacific, and the lost lands of R'lyeh and Mu. The mi-go controlled the north. In the south the Great Race were supreme. Their greatest city was Pnakotus, in modern-day Australia.

This race flourished from about four hundred million years ago until fifty million years ago, when they were exterminated by the flying polyps, an ancient race which they had imprisoned when they first came to Earth. However, the minds of the Great Race had already fled their doomed bodies into the future bodies of a beetle-like race to succeed mankind—the New Great Race.

The Great Race reproduce by means of spores, but do so infrequently because of long individual life spans (4,000 to 5,000 years). Members feed solely on liquids.

The Yithians are a race of socialist individuals. They value intelligence above all else, and use it as their criterion for

NEW GREAT RACE

immigration. Resources are shared among their kind out of a sense of intellectual logic and proportion. Strife is rare. The Great Race worship no gods.

TIME TRAVEL: the Great Race are so-named because they conquered time so thoroughly—the only race known to have done so. A member of the race can send its mind forward or backward through time and across space, pick out a suitable subject, and trade minds with it; whenever a member of the Great Race takes over the body of a being, that being's mind is put into the body of the Great Race individual, there to stay until the being now inhabiting its old body sees fit to return and trade places once more. With this technique the race has traveled *en masse* through time and space, and conquered other planets.

Keen students of history, an individual exchanges places with a select individual in the era it wishes to study. The minds are switched for about five years. On Earth, friends notice many differences about the substitute: an Idea roll would be appropriate to notice this.

The victim who has been forced into the alien Great Race body is caused to write down everything he knows about his own time. The Great Race are fairly kindly and permit their captives to travel about and see the country, as well as allowing them to meet other victims like themselves, generally from far distant planets or eras. When the time comes to restore a victim to his own body, the Great Race blank his memory of what has happened to him while he was trapped in their age. This erasure is imperfect: the victim may dream and have nightmares of being held by the Great Race.

OLD GREAT RACE

A cult on present-day Earth aids and abets Great Race visitors. In exchange, the visitors share technological or magical knowledge. Time-travel is the primary means by which a member of this race could be met in its original cone-body, though there have been scattered cases involving stasis cubes and sorcerous summonings across the aeons.

ATTACKS: in combat, a member of this race may use both pincers simultaneously. However, this civilized race avoids hand-to-hand combat, preferring camera-shaped weapons that fire great gouts of electricity, weapons that were originally created to destroy the flying polyps.

There are many varieties of lightning-guns. A common one contains a pack of 32 charges, and takes 1 round to reload. As many charges as desired may be fired as a single shot, but each charge past 4 fired at once gives a 5 percentile accumulating chance of burning out the gun. Thus, if 7 charges were fired at once, the gun would be ruined on a separate D100 result of 15 or less.

Each charge does 1D10 points of damage to the target, so that 3 charges would do 3D10 points of damage. The gun has a basic range of 100 yards. For each 100 yards fired past that base, subtract 3 points from the total damage done and subtract 20% from the chance to hit.

See also the "Alien Technology" chapter (p. 156) for a few more notes on the Great Race.

GREAT RACE OF YITH, Mental Time-Travelers

char.	rolls	averages
STR	12D6	42
CON	4D6+12	26
SIZ	8D6+36	64
INT	4D6+6	20
POW	2D6+6	13
DEX	2D6+3	10
Move 7		HP 45

Av. Damage Bonus: +6D6.

Weapons: Pincer 40%, damage 1D6 + db
Lightning Gun 30%, damage 1D10 per charge

Armor: 8-point skin

Spells: they rarely learn magic; a random member has a chance equal to its INT or less on D100 to know 1D3 spells.

Sanity Loss: 0/1D6 Sanity points to see one of the Great Race.

GREAT RACE (New), Lesser Independent Race. *The hardy coleopterous species immediately following mankind, to which the Great Race was some day to transfer its keenest minds en masse in the face of horrible peril . . . .*— H. P. Lovecraft, "The Shadow Out of Time."

Under assault from the subterranean flying polyps, the Great Race of Yith mentally transferred far into the future of Earth, well beyond the extinction of humanity, into swarms of intelligent beetle-like creatures.

Each individual is a hive-mind, composed of 2D4 x500 insects which can walk or fly. Though their bodies are dark or jet-black, their wings when spread reflect brilliant metallic hues of blue, gold, and green. Viewing a swarm at work, an observer always gains an impression of intelligence and decisive judgment. These superior beings need few tools of war, but might quickly produce any conceivable weapon.

In each swarm the hive-mind remains intact until at least 75% of the swarm has been destroyed. After that there is rapid loss of coordination, and the swarm becomes an undirected mass of individuals. Such a swarm can fly for up to 100 yards, or walk. Typically, half the swarm flies ahead and lands, then the rest fly to catch up or to leap-frog ahead.

Swarms are effectively immortal, since new insects are born as old ones die. In the stats, STR, CON, and SIZ are for individual bodies. POW, INT, and DEX are for the swarm.

NEW GREAT RACE, the Coleopterans

char.	rolls	averages
STR	1D2	1-2
CON	1D3	2
SIZ	1	1
POW	2D6+6	13
INT	5D6+6	23-24
DEX	2D6+6	13
Move 4/10 walk/fly		HP 1-2

Damage Bonus: N/A

Weapon: Bite 35%, damage 1D2

Spells: this species finds magic upsetting to its intellectual disciplines, but a swarm has an INT% chance of knowing 1D3 spells.

Sanity Loss: 0/1D4 Sanity points to see a New Great Race swarm.

GUGS, Lesser Independent Race. *It was a paw, fully two feet and a half across, and equipped with formidable talons. After it came another paw, and after that a great black-furred arm to which both of the paws were attached by short forearms. Then two pink eyes shone and the head of the awakened Gug sentry, large as a barrel, wabbled into view. The eyes jutted two inches from each side, shaded by bony protuberances overgrown by coarse hairs. But the head was chiefly terrible because of the mouth. That mouth had great yellow fangs and ran from the top to the bottom of the head, opening vertically instead of horizontally.*—H. P. Lovecraft, "The Dream-Quest of Unknown Kadath."

In worshiping various Great Old Ones, the gugs of the Dreamlands indulged in ceremonies so abhorrent that somehow they have been banished into the Dreamlands' Underworld. Gugs gleefully eat any surface dwellers they can lay their four paws upon. Gugs are huge—an average gug is at least 20 feet tall.

GUG

In combat, a gug may either bite, or hit with one arm. Each arm has two forearms, and thus two claws, so that the arm strikes twice when it hits. Both claws must strike at the same opponent.

GUGS, Unclean Giants

char.	rolls	averages
STR	6D6+24	45
CON	3D6+18	28-29
SIZ	6D6+36	57
INT	2D6+6	13
POW	3D6	10-11
DEX	3D6	10-11
Move 10		HP 43

Av. Damage Bonus: +5D6.

Weapons: Bite 60%, damage 1D10
Claw(s) 40%, damage 4D6 each (no db)
Stomp 25%, damage 1D6 + db

Armor: 8-point skin, hair, and cartilage.

Spells: Some gugs know a few spells. To simulate this, roll D100 for each random gug. Only if the die roll is equal to or lower than the gug's POW does it know magic, a number of magic spells equal to the die roll.

Sanity Loss: 0/1D8 Sanity points to see a gug.

HOUNDS OF TINDALOS, Greater Independent Race. *"They are lean and athirst!" he shrieked . . . . "All the evil in the universe was concentrated in their lean, hungry bodies. Or had they bodies? I saw them only for a moment, I cannot be certain."*—Frank Belknap Long, "The Hounds of Tindalos."

The hounds of Tindalos dwell in the distant past of the earth, when normal life has not yet advanced past one-celled animals. They inhabit the angles of time, while other beings (such as mankind and all common life) descend from curves. This concept is hard to imagine, and only seems to be used with respect to them. The hounds lust after something in mankind and other normal life, and follow victims through time and space to get it. They are immortal.

Just what these creatures look like is unknown, since those who meet them seem not to survive. A hound of Tindalos is hardly likely to look like a hound dog, but the name from the story is so evocative that is how they always are pictured.

Because of their relationship with the angles of time, they can materialize through any corner if it is sharp—120° or less. The rooms of most human houses have walls that meet at 90°. When a hound manifests, it first appears as smoke pouring from the corner, from which the head and then the thing's body emerges.

Once a human has become known to one of these creatures, it will follow through anything to get to him. To figure the time before the hound of Tindalos reaches its prey, determine the number of years between the prey's present time and the time when spotted by the creature. Then divide the number of years by 100,000,000 to get the number of days travel time for the hound. Driven off by a target, a hound of Tindalos usually gives up. Unfortunately, such a creature is difficult to drive off. Friends who come to a target's aid also will be attacked.

EXAMPLE: Harvey Walters has found a mysterious gem which, when meditated upon, allows him to see into the distant past. He looks 3,000,000,000 years back, sees a hound of Tindalos, and is seen as well! Though Harvey faints, breaking the connection, the hound of Tindalos is out for blood! The travel time for the creature is about 30 days. Harvey has a month to prepare for an unwelcome visitor.

ATTACKS: it may use its paw or its tongue to attack within a round, but not both. It usually attacks with its paw. For random determination, roll 1D6. On a result of 1-4, it uses its paw. A result of 5-6 indicates a tongue attack.

A hound of Tindalos is covered with a sort of bluish pus. When a victim is struck by a paw attack, a gout of this mucoid stuff is smeared over him. This pus-like stuff is alive and active, doing poison damage to the target as if he or she had ingested a poison of POT 2D6, and new damage is done in the same amount for each round that the ichor remains on the victim's body. The ichor can be wiped off with a rag or towel with a DEX x5 or less roll on D100. It could also be rinsed off with water or some other agent. Fire would kill the ichor, though 1D6 hit points would be lost to burns from the flame.

With a successful tongue attack, a deep penetrating (though bloodless and painless) hole is formed. The victim takes no physical damage, despite his peculiar wound, but loses 1D3 POW permanently.

HOUNDS OF TINDALOS, Scavengers of Time

char.	rolls	averages
STR	3D6+6	16-17
CON	3D6+20	30-31
SIZ	3D6+6	16-17
INT	5D6	17-18
POW	7D6	24-25
DEX	3D6	10-11
Move 6 / 40 flying		HP 23-24

Av. Damage Bonus: +1D6.

Weapons: Paw 90%, damage 1D6 + ichor + db
Tongue 90%, damage 1D3 POW drained per round

Armor: 2-point hide; regenerates 4 hit points per round, unless dead; mundane weapons have no effect on a hound, though enchanted weapons and spells do full damage.

Spells: each knows at least 1D8 spells, as the keeper finds appropriate.

Sanity Loss: 1D3/1D20 Sanity points to see a hound of Tindalos.

HUNTING HORRORS, Greater Servitor Race. *And in the air about him were great viperine creatures, which had curiously distorted heads, and grotesquely great clawed appendages, supporting themselves with ease by the aid of black rubbery wings of singularly monstrous dimensions.*—August Derleth, "The Lurker at the Threshold."

HOUND OF TINDALOS

They resemble enormous ropy black serpents or worms possessing bat-like or umbrella-like wings. Their forms continually shift and change, twitching and writhing, so it is hard to look at them. They may have only a single large wing rather than two. They speak in great harsh voices. A hunting horror's length averages forty feet.

These beings are dispelled by daylight. A strong enough burst of light (from a nuclear reaction, perhaps) could sear one to dust. Hunting horrors move swiftly and are harrier-creatures for some of the gods, particularly Nyarlathotep. They can be summoned in their own right, and sent to seek out blood and lives.

A hunting horror may attack with both bite and its tail tentacle attack in a single round. The tail grapples and wraps around the victim, keeping him from moving. The hunting horror may then fly off with him, or keep fighting. The victim can only break loose as the result of a successful STR-against-STR Resistance Table roll.

Comparative Size Illustrations

The three panels to the right illustrate various denizens of the Cthulhu Mythos, providing some idea of the relative sizes of these creatures. Note the various unfortunate investigators splattered about the monsters.

Some of these creatures, notably Cthulhu, are able to alter their mass and size at will; the illustration shows only one version of such images.

STAR VAM-

MOON-BEAST

HUNTING HORROR

DARK YOUNG

GUG

YITHIAN

SHUDDE M'ELL

When a victim is caught in the tail, the hunting horror may only make a bite attack, nibbling at the dangling victim at +20% chance to hit. The grappled one may not be able to fight back in any physical way, since his arms are usually pinioned, but some magic spells might be used.

HUNTING HORRORS, Great Viperine Flyers

char.	rolls	averages
STR	5D6+12	29-30
CON	3D6	10-11
SIZ	5D6+24	41-42
INT	1D6+12	15-16
POW	6D6	21
DEX	3D6+3	13-14
Move 7 / 11 flying		HP 26-27

Av. Damage Bonus: N/A.

Weapons: Bite 65%, damage 1D6
Tail 90%, damage Grapple

HUNTING HORROR

Armor: 9-point skin; cannot be impaled by bullets.

Spells: roll D100. If the result is equal to or less than the monster's INT, it knows a number of spells equal to the D100 roll.

Sanity Points: 0/1D10 Sanity points to see a hunting horror.

LENG SPIDERS, Lesser Independent Race. *There were scenes of old wars, wherein Leng's almost-humans fought with the bloated purple spiders of the neighbouring vales.*
—H. P. Lovecraft, "The Dream-Quest of Unknown Kadath."

They are huge, purplish spiders, with pustulently bloated bodies and long, bristly legs. Their color, a pale mottled violet on their abdomens, shades to indigo on their forebodies, with legs and chelae tipped in black. A Dreamlands entity, the spiders of Leng are intelligent, dangerous, and gigantic. New-hatched specimens are as

LENG SPIDER

NIGHT GAUNT

BYAKHEE

ABHOTH

MI-GO

GREAT CTHULHU

FATHER DAGON

DEEP ONE

SHOGGOTH

ELDER THING

big as Shetland ponies. Some valleys in the Plateau of Leng are almost completely webbed over. Many spiders worship Atlach-Nacha.

LENG SPIDER

Though intelligent, these spiders do not cooperate, and sometimes feed on their own kind. The bite of a Leng spider injects a deadly poison. Very large spiders are known.

LENG SPIDERS, Immense Web-Spinners

char.	rolls	averages
STR	8D6	28
CON	5D6	17-18
SIZ	10D6	35
INT	3D6	10-11
POW	4D6	14
DEX	3D6+6	16-17
Move 6		HP 26-27

Av. Damage Bonus: +3D6.

Weapons: Bite 40%, damage 1D3 + poison*
Web Toss 60%, damage entangle**
* poison POT equals spider's CON.
** entangle STR equals half of spider's SIZ; to free, roll target's STR against spider entangle STR on Resistance Table.

Armor: 6-point chitin.

Spells: roll 1D20; if the result is equal to or less than the spider's INT, it knows 1D3 spells of the keeper's choice.

Skills: Hide 50%, Sneak 80%.

Sanity Loss: 1/1D10 Sanity points to see a Leng spider; very large spiders might cost as much as 1/1D20 Sanity points.

LLOIGOR, Greater Independent Race. *"Invisible ones from the stars." These latter, he said were definitely aliens on our earth, and the chief among them was called Ghatanothoa, the dark one. They sometimes took forms, such as the monster on the tablet—who was a representation of Ghatanothoa—but existed as vortices of power in their natural state.* —Colin Wilson, "The Return of the Lloigor."

The twin of Zhar, Lloigor or Lloigornos, should not be confused with this race.

They are vortices of power in natural form, and completely invisible to human eyes. On rare occasions they can create tangible, visible bodies for themselves. These bodies are monstrous and bear some resemblance to enormous reptiles, though inspection reveals their utter dissimilarity to any reptiles that ever walked the face of the Earth.

The minds of lloigor are not divided into layers of consciousness. Lloigor do not forget, nor do they have imaginations or subconscious to mislead or distract them. Their outlook of absolute pessimism results in an atmosphere of gloom that makes lloigor minds and actions incomprehensible to humans. Mind-contact with lloigor always leads to suicidal depression for the human partners.

It is believed that the lloigor originally came to Earth from the Andromeda galaxy and that their first earthly colony was on a lost continent somewhere in the Indian Ocean, possibly the same sunken continent that now bears the city of R'lyeh

and its star-spawn with it. The lloigor used human slaves to perform their will, and used cruel disciplines to control recalcitrant slaves, such as amputating limbs or causing cancer-like tentacular growths to sprout on them. Earthly lloigor continued to decay and decline, and they retreated under the earth and seas, where they still husband their failing energies.

Wales, Rhode Island, and Iraq are places where lloigor are known to have acted in recent years. They are hinted at in the folklore of Haiti, Polynesia, and Massachusetts. Lloigor are sometimes linked with the Great Old One Ghatanothoa, now resting beneath the waves of the Pacific, and with Ithaqua.

THEIR USES FOR HUMANS: typically their human servants come from families with histories of mental instability, The lloigor need humans to survive: these immaterial entities must draw energy from intelligent beings to perform necessary tasks. By expending one of its own magic points a lloigor may drain 1D6 magic points from a sleeping human to use in performing some magical action. A lloigor can drain energy from several sleeping humans at once, from up to several miles away despite intervening obstacles. The next morning, the victims wake complaining of headaches and bad sleep.

MAGIC POINT ATTACK: lloigor may drain magic points from a particular sleeping target, keeping that character's magic points at zero, or close to it. Such an unnatural condition seriously weakens the victim physically and spiritually, leading to sickness and possibly death. After each full day spent unconscious with 0 magic points, the victim's player must attempt to roll CON x5 or less on a D100. If the roll succeeds, the investigator has fended off the attack, regains a magic point, and wakes. With a failure, the investigator loses a hit point and continues unconscious, and with a failing result of 96-00, the investigator loses a point of CON and continues to sleep.

TELEKINETIC EFFECTS: the lloigor can push people and manipulate objects such as a compass needle or a door latch via telekinesis. The (presumably immaterial) lloigor must be directly present, and within a few yards of the effect. It takes 10 magic points to create a telekinetic force of STR 1 above ground, 6 magic points to create telekinesis of STR 1 in a sub-surface but open area, such as a river bed or canyon, and 3 magic points to cause telekinesis of STR 1 in a tunnel or cave. A group of lloigor might combine telekinesis and perform potent deeds.

VORTEX ATTACK: The lloigor's most fearsome weapon is a type of implosion sounding like the roll of distant thunder. Things in the blast area are generally torn to pieces, and the ground is ruptured and discolored. At least 100 magic points are needed for an area ten meters in diameter. Each thing within the circle loses D100 hit points. An alert investigator notices the telltale effects of swirling lines appearing in the air and a half-unheard throbbing noise penetrating his body.

LLOIGOR AS REPTILE

REPTILIAN MANIFESTATIONS: to shape as a monstrous distorted reptile, a lloigor must expend magic points equal to the lloigor's reptile SIZ. Once the body is formed, it may be maintained indefinitely or dissolved at will. If the lloigor is slain in reptile form, it dies permanently. Several lloigor may combine their magic points to permit a single one to create his physical form quickly. A lloigor in reptile form has all the powers of one in the immaterial mode, except that it cannot pass through walls and is not invisible.

When in reptilian form, a lloigor has all the characteristics listed below. When immaterial and intangible, it lacks the parenthesized characteristics, skills, etc., possessing only INT, POW, and DEX.

LLOIGOR, Masters of the Tentacle

char.	rolls	averages
(STR)	3D6+30	40-41
(CON)	8D6	28
(SIZ)	2D4x10	50
INT	4D6+6	20
POW	4D6	14
DEX	3D6	10-11

Move 7 / 3 through stone as immaterial   (HP) 39

(Av. Damage Bonus:) 5D6.

(Weapons:) Claw 30%, damage 1D6 + db
Bite 50%, damage 2D6

(Armor:) 8-point reptilian hide. In the immaterial state it cannot be harmed by any physical weapons, magical or not.

Spells: lloigor know at least 1D4 spells.

Sanity Loss: 0/1D8 as reptile; invisible, no Sanity loss; mind contact costs 1/1D4 Sanity points.

MI-GO, the Fungi from Yuggoth, Lesser Independent Race. *They were pinkish things about five feet long; with crustaceous bodies bearing vast pairs of dorsal fins or membranous wings and several sets of articulate limbs, and with a sort of convoluted ellipsoid, covered with multitudes of very short antenna, where a head would ordinarily be. . . . Sometimes [they] walked on all their legs and sometimes on the hindmost pair only.* —H. P. Lovecraft, "The Whisperer in Darkness."

The fungi from Yuggoth are an interstellar race, with a main colony or base on Yuggoth (Pluto). There are mining colonies in the mountains of Earth, where the mi-go seek rare ores. The mi-go have definite connections with fungi, and are clearly not animal. They communicate with each other by changing the colors of their brain-like heads, but they can speak human tongues in buzzing, insect-like voices. They worship both Nyarlathotep and Shub-Niggurath, and possibly others. They hire human agents to simplify their operations, and are sometimes connected with cults. Lovecraft somewhere credits them with being the source of the Abominable Snowman stories long told in the Himalayas.

They are unable to eat terrene food, and must import theirs

from other worlds. They are able to fly through the interstellar aether on their great wings. but maneuver clumsily in an atmosphere. Ordinary photographic plates will not take an image of these beings, though a good chemist could devise an emulsion that would work. After death, a mi-go dissolves in a few hours.

They are capable of astounding surgical feats, including the placing of living human brains in life-sustaining metal tubes. They can then attach speaking, listening, and seeing devices to the tubes, so that the brains can interact with those about them. This way they can carry with them those who cannot withstand the vacuum and cold of space.

Fungi from Yuggoth may attack in hand-to-hand combat with two nippers at once. If the target is hit, the mi-go will try to grapple the victim (roll STR against STR on the Resistance Table to break free), and fly into the sky to drop the victim from a height or take the victim so high that his or her lungs burst.

See the chapter "Alien Technology" for a few further notes.

MI-GO, the Fungi From Yuggoth

char.	rolls	averages
STR	3D6	10-11
CON	3D6	10-11
SIZ	3D6	10-11
INT	2D6+6	13
POW	2D6+6	13
DEX	4D6	14

Move 7 / 9 flying   HP 10-11

Av. Damage Bonus: +0.

Weapons: Nippers 30%, 1D6 + grapple

Armor: none, but the extraterrene body causes all impaling weapons to do minimum possible damage.

Spells: each has an INT x2 chance to know 1D3 spells.

Sanity Loss: 0/1D6 Sanity points to see a mi-go, from Yuggoth or elsewhere.

MOON-BEASTS, Lesser Independent Race. *Great greyish-white slippery things which could expand and contract at will, and whose principle shape—though it often changed—was that of a sort of toad without any eyes, but with a curious vibrating mass of short pink tentacles on the end of its blunt, vague snout.*—H. P. Lovecraft, "The Dream-Quest of Unknown Kadath."

The moon-beasts are an alien race encountered primarily in the Dreamlands. They have a great colony on the moon of the Dreamlands, and some say that they may have a presence on the moon of the Waking World as well. They serve Nyarlathotep for his favor, and enslave other races. If sadism can be said to have any meaning for a race so alien, it can be said that these beings are monstrously cruel, frequently torturing members of other races that fall into their paws.

Although the only weapon listed here for the beings is the spear, they can be expected to have many more technological marvels. Many of their soldiers are members of various slave races, primary among them the men of Leng.

MI-GO

MOON-BEASTS, the Torture Lovers

MOON
BEAST

char.	rolls	averages
STR	3D6+6	16-17
CON	2D6+6	13
SIZ	3D6+10	20-21
INT	2D6+9	16
POW	3D6	10-11
DEX	2D6+3	10
Move 7		HP 17

Av. Damage Bonus: +1D6

Weapons: Spear 25%, damage 1D10 + 1 + db

Armor: none, but their peculiar body substance and arrangement causes them to lose minimum possible hit points from successful firearms attacks.

Spells: moon-beasts know at least 1D3 spells.

Sanity Loss: 0/1D8 Sanity points to see a moon-beast.

NIGHTGAUNTS, **Lesser Servitor Race.** *Shocking and uncouth black things with smooth, oily, whale-like surfaces, unpleasant horns that curved inward toward each other, bat wings whose beating made no sound, ugly prehensile paws, and barbed tails that lashed needlessly and disquietingly. And worst of all, they never spoke or laughed, and never smiled because they had no faces at all to smile with, but only a suggestive blankness where a face ought to be. All they ever did was clutch and fly and tickle; that was the way of nightgaunts.—H. P. Lovecraft, "The Dream-Quest of Unknown Kadath."*

Nightgaunts are Dreamlands creatures that serve Nodens by, among other things, grasping and carrying off intruders, who are unceremoniously dumped in the most dismal and horrible places imaginable and left to die. Nightgaunts are stationed at various spots in the lonely parts of the Dreamlands, and come out at night. In primeval times they dwelled in the Waking World as well, and may still. They are not very intelligent, but can understand some languages (such as the gibberings of ghouls), and are friendly to some occult races. Nightgaunts attempt to sneak up quietly on victims, grasp their weapons, and overpower them.

Two or more nightgaunts can combine their strengths to grapple with a strong victim.

Nightgaunts can only tickle foes who have already been grappled. A successful tickling attack is extremely unnerving, for the barb of the tail is razor-sharp and perilous even while its light application does no damage: the target becomes bewildered, humiliated, and disoriented, and focuses more and more upon the maniacal threat. Nightgaunt tails can snake up through holes and openings, slice through thick clothes, and find even the interstices of metal armor.

NIGHTGAUNTS, the Faceless

char.	rolls	averages
STR	3D6	10-11
CON	3D6	10-11
SIZ	4D6	14
INT	1D6	3-4
POW	3D6	10-11
DEX	2D6+6	13
Move 6 / 12 flying		HP 12-13

NIGHT
GAUNT

Av. Damage Bonus: +0.

Weapons: Grapple 30%, damage held for tickling
Tickle 30%, immobilized 1D6+1 rounds.

Armor: 2-point skin.

Spells: none.

Skills: Hide 90%, Sneak 90%.

Sanity Loss: 0/1D6 Sanity points to see a nightgaunt.

RAT-THINGS, **Lesser Servitor Race.** *The bones of the tiny paws, it is rumoured, imply prehensile characteristics more typical of a diminutive monkey than of a rat; while the small skull with its savage yellow fangs is of the utmost anomalousness, appearing from certain angles like a miniature, monstrously degraded parody of a human skull.*—H. P. Lovecraft, "The Dreams in the Witch House."

Resembling ordinary rats, and easily mistaken for them at a distance, rat-thing heads are nonetheless evil caricatures of human heads, and their paws are like tiny human hands. All have extremely strong, sharp teeth. These unnatural creatures are created by malign sorcery, which allowed deceased cultists to be transformed and thus continue to serve their masters. Though they do not die naturally, they are now very rare. Brown Jenkin, the familiar of Keziah Mason, the witch, may have been a rat-thing. Attacking rat-things climb the legs or clothes of human opponents, or drop down from ceilings. Once a Bite attack succeeds, the rat-thing clings and keeps on biting. Tearing away a rat-thing costs 1D3 hit points.

RAT
THING

RAT-THINGS, Malevolent Mockers and Scuttling Spies

char.	rolls	averages
STR	1D3	2
CON	2D6	7
SIZ	1	1
INT	3D6	10-11
POW	2D6	7
DEX	4D6+4	20
Move 9		HP 4

Av. Damage Bonus: -1D6.

Weapon: Bite 35%, damage 1D3

Armor: none, but subtract 40 percentiles from the chance to hit a running rat-thing, and subtract 20 percentiles from the chance to hit one attached to somebody.

Spells: those of INT 14 or more know 1D3 spells of the keeper's choice; those who knew spells in life retain that knowledge as rat-things.

Skills: Dodge 95%, Hide 80%, Sneak 65%.

Sanity Loss: 0/1D6 Sanity points to see a rat thing; if the rat-thing was known to the observer in life, however, it costs 1/1D8 Sanity points to see it.

SAND-DWELLERS, Lesser Serv-itor Race. *Then out of one of the caves came a Sand-Dweller—rough-skinned, large-eyed, large-eared, with a horrible, distorted resemblance to the koala bear facially, though his body had an appearance of emacia-tion. He shambled toward me, mani-festly eager.*—H. P. Lovecraft and August Derleth, "The Gable Window."

This obscure race appears in only a few sto-ries. Sand-dwellers look as though they are encrusted with sand. They dwell in caverns and come out at night. They are known to live in the American Southwest and may live in other deserts of the world as well. They usually serve the Great Old Ones, and often dwell near them.

In combat, a sand-dweller may use both claws at once.

SAND DWELLER

SAND-DWELLERS, Stalkers of the Wastes

char.	rolls	averages
STR	3D6	10-11
CON	2D6+6	13
SIZ	3D6+6	16-17
INT	3D6	10-11
POW	3D6	10-11
DEX	2D6+6	13
Move 8		HP 15

Av. Damage Bonus: +1D4.

Weapons: Claw 30%, 1D6 + db

Armor: 3-point rough hide.

Spells: those of POW 14 or more may know 1D8 spells the keeper thinks appropriate.

Skills: Hide 60%, Sneak 50%, Spot Hidden 50%.

Sanity Loss: 0/1D6 Sanity points to see a sand-dweller.

SERPENT PEOPLE, Lesser Independent Race. *They walked lithely and sinuously erect on pre-mammalian members, their pied and hairless bodies bending with great suppleness. There was a loud hissing of formulae as they went to and fro.*—Clark Ashton Smith, "The Seven Geases."

They resemble upright serpents, with ophidian heads and scales, but with two arms and legs. They possess tails and in their great days often dressed in robes. Yig is the greatest god of the serpent people, for he is the father of all snakes. Some blasphemers chose instead to pray to Tsathoggua in ancient times, but they were destroyed by a venge-ful god millions of years ago.

The serpent people's first kingdom—Valusia—flourished before even dinosaurs walked the Earth, some two hundred and seventy-five million years ago. They built black basalt cities and fought wars, all in the Permian era or before. They were then great sorcerers and scientists, and devoted much energy to calling forth dreadful demons and brewing

potent poisons. With the coming of the dinosaurs two hundred and twenty-five million years ago, the first kingdom fell, and serpent people retreat-ed in strongholds far underground, the greatest of which was Yoth. In these times the serpent people became great scientists as well, able to manipulate life itself.

In human prehistory the serpent people raiesd their second kingdom at the center of the Thurian continent. It fell even more rapidly then the first Valusia, overthrown this time by humans, who later claimed the land as their own. Again and again the serpent people retreated before the human hordes until their last citadel of Yanyoga was destroyed in 10,000 B.C.

A few lurking sorcerers survive, as do pockets of dwarfed degenerates. These diminutions are likely to include an occa-sional atavistic, fully capable serpent per-son who is still favored by Yig. Degenerate serpent people are likely to have characteris-tics lessened by as much as a third. In addition there are cer-tain hibernating serpent people—the sleepers—who have rest-ed for thousands of years or more. On occasion these serpent people waken, to humanity's regret. This third class of serpent people are typically more intelligent and powerful than their lurking brothers, and often know great sorcery.

Serpent people may use all weapons known to man, clutch-ing them effectively in taloned hands. Use the same base chances as for humans. In hand-to-hand combat the Bite attack can be made simultaneously with most weapon attacks.

A common spell among them is an illusion which trans-forms the caster's appearance into that of a normal human, allowing him to mingle in human society.

See also the "Alien Technology" chapter (p. 156) for a few further notes on serpent people.

SERPENT PEOPLE, Full Atavism

char.	rolls	averages
STR	3D6	10-11
CON	3D6	10-11
SIZ	3D6	10-11
INT	3D6+6	16-17
POW	2D6+6	13
DEX	2D6+6	13
Move 8		HP 10-11

Av. Damage Bonus: +0.

Weapon: Bite 35%, damage 1D8 + poison*
* POT equals the serpent person's CON.

Armor: 1-point scales.

Spells: full serpent folk know at least 2D6 appropriate spells; degenerate forms are not likely to know magic.

Sanity Loss: 0/1D6 Sanity points to see a serpent person.

SERVITORS of the Outer Gods, Greater Servitor Race. *Toad-like creatures which seemed constantly to be changing shape and appearance, and from whom emanated, by some means I could not distinguish, a ghastly ululation, a piping.*—August Derleth, "The Lurker at the Threshold."

These amorphous beings progress by rolling or slithering. They resemble frogs, as well as squids or octopi. Their ever-changing shapes are hard to describe specifically.

Servitors accompany their masters as required, though they are most commonly found in Azathoth's court. These are the demon flautists that play the flute-like music for their masters to dance by. They sometimes play for groups of cultists as well, as a sort of background dirge, or in order to summon various deities, etc.

The god or entity arrives 1D3+1 rounds after the servitor announces it, and departs when dismissed by the servitor, or 2D6 rounds after the servitor's death, or when the god pleases. Summoning costs the servitor a magic point, and another magic point each five rounds that the summoned being remains.

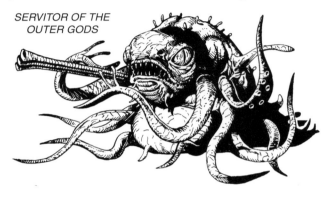

SERVITOR OF THE
OUTER GODS

SERVITORS of the Outer Gods

char.	rolls	averages
STR	4D6	14
CON	3D6+6	16-17
SIZ	4D6+6	20
INT	5D6	17-18
POW	2D6+12	19
DEX	3D6+6	16-17
Move 7		HP 18-19

Av. Damage Bonus: +2D6.

Weapons: Tentacle* 45%, damage db x2**
*2D6 of them make the attack; ** minimum of 1D6 always.*

Armor: none, but no physical weapon can harm one; spells and magical weapons do normal damage; regenerates 3 hit points per round until dead.

Spells: each knows at least 1D10 spells, always including 1D10 Summon/Bind and Call spells.

Sanity Loss: 1/1D10 Sanity points to see a servitor.

SHAGGAI, Insects From, Lesser Independent Race.

Even though they flew so fast I could, with the augmented perception of terror, make out many more details than I wished. Those huge lidless eyes which stared in hate at me, the jointed tendrils which seemed to twist from the head in cosmic rhythms, the ten legs, covered with black shining tentacles and folded into the pallid underbelly, and the semi-circular ridged wings covered with triangular scales—all this cannot convey the soul-ripping horror of the shape which darted at me. I saw the three mouths of the thing move moistly, and then it was upon me.—Ramsey Campbell, "The Insects from Shaggai."

These insect-beings never feed, as they live by photosynthesis, and they spend their time in decadence, in aesthetic enjoyment of abnormality, and in torture of their many slave races. Shans, as they also are known as, are extremely long-lived, taking centuries to reach adulthood, and are scientifically advanced. They have many weapons and devices which operate by focused mind-power (magic points). The shans worship Azathoth with many complex rites and systems of torment.

The shans are now a fugitive race. Shaggai itself was destroyed by a great catastrophe, but many shan escaped in temples made of an indestructible gray metal, teleporting them to other worlds. Earth's atmosphere contains some component which prevented the shan from teleporting away once they arrived here, and also keeps individual shan from flying any great distance.

The insect-beings now dwelling on Earth have brought with them certain beings from the planet Xiclotl as slaves and guards. At one time they ruled a human witch-cult dedicated to finding sacrifices for Azathoth. The largest colony of shan is near Goatswood, one of the villages of England's Severn Valley.

MENTAL ATTACK: Shans are parasitic and not wholly material. One of these pigeon-sized creatures can fly right through human tissue into a target's brain, wherein it crawls about and reads its host's memories, affects target thought processes, and injects specific memories and ideas of its own. During the day, the insect is not active within the brain, leaving the victim to do more or less as he or she pleases. But at night the shan wakes, and begins to implant memories. It can implant Sanity-destroying sights which the insect has witnessed, or riddle memory-fragments to entice the victim into performing certain actions. Eventually the host is so hypnotized that he or she gladly helps the shan. Often such progressively increasing control causes the victim to go raving mad, and thus become an unsuitable host.

SHAN

NERVE WHIP ATTACK: the nerve whip is a small technical device which projects a chattering line of pallid light. When the light strikes a target, match the shan's magic points against the target's magic points. If it wins, the target is overcome by agony, and can do nothing but writhe on the ground until the weapon is turned off. If the attack fails, the target is still in pain, and skill chances are effectively reduced by 20% for the next 24-CON hours. The attack may be renewed each round.

INSECTS FROM SHAGGAI, Mental Parasites

char.	rolls	averages
STR	1D3	2
CON	1D3	2
SIZ	1	1
INT	3D6+6	16-17
POW	5D6	17-18
DEX	2D6+24	31
Move 4/40 flying		HP 2

Av. Damage Bonus: N/A.

Weapons: Meld 60%, damage is progressive control after insect enters brain of target
Nerve Whip 50%, damage special

Armor: none.

Spells: roll 1D20—if the result is less than or equal to the shan's INT, that many spells are known by it, usually including Call Azathoth.

Sanity Loss: 0/1D6 Sanity points to see a shan.

SHANTAKS, Lesser Servitor Race. *Not any birds or bats known elsewhere on earth . . . for they were larger than elephants and had heads like a horse's . . . . The Shantak-bird has scales instead of feathers and those scales are very slippery.*—H. P. Lovecraft, "The Dream-Quest of Unknown Kadath."

Shantaks brood in cavernous holes and their wings are encrusted with rime and nitre. They are always described as noisome and loathly, and are used as steeds by various of the servants of the Outer Gods. They have an extreme fear of nightgaunts and always retreat from them. Shantaks can fly through space, and have been known to carry an unwary rider straight to the throne of Azathoth.

SHANTAKS, Elephantine Mounts

char.	rolls	averages
STR	4D6+20	34
CON	2D6+6	13
SIZ	4D6+36	50
INT	1D6	3-4
POW	3D6	10-11
DEX	2D6+3	10
Move 6/30 flying		HP 32

Av. Damage Bonus: +4D6.

Weapon: Bite 55%, 2D6 + 2

Armor: 9-point hide.

Spells: none.

Sanity Loss: 0/1D6 Sanity points to see a shantak.

SHOGGOTHS, Lesser Servitor Race. *The nightmare, plastic column of fetid, black iridescence oozed tightly onward . . . . A shapeless congerie of protoplasmic bubbles, faintly self-luminous, and with myriads of temporary eyes forming and unforming as pustules of greenish light all over the tunnel-filling front that bore down upon us, crushing the frantic penguins and slithering over the glistening floor that it and its kind had swept so evilly free of all litter. Still came that eldritch mocking cry—"Tekeli-li! Tekeli-li!"*—H. P. Lovecraft, "At the Mountains of Madness."

Shoggoths are among the most horrible of all the monsters of Lovecraft. Abdul Alhazred himself attempted desperately to claim that there were none on Earth itself, save in crazed dreams. Shoggoths are often found as servants of deep ones and other

SHANTAK

SHOGGOTH

races, and are amphibious. They are surly servants at best, ever becoming more and more intelligent, more and more rebellious, more and more imitative. They fought their former creators, the elder things, in a rebellion. They communicate in whatever manner their master race wishes, forming special organs for the purpose.

A typical shoggoth is roughly a 15-foot diameter sphere when floating free. In combat, it covers an area 5 yards square. All within the area are attacked separately, and each must receive a successful match of STR against the shoggoth's STR on the Resistance Table, or be sucked apart. If the shoggoth attacks more than one target, it must divide its STR among all targets. Those held within the shoggoth's black bulk can strike back only on rounds in which their players successfully roll STR or less on D100. Each round a victim is held within a shoggoth, he or she loses hit points equal to the shoggoth's damage bonus, the damage describable as rupturing, crushing, and being sucked into pieces.

SHOGGOTHS, Fetid Iridescences

char.	rolls	averages
STR	18D6	63
CON	12D6	42
SIZ	24D6	84
INT	2D6	7
POW	3D6	10-11
DEX	1D6	3-4
Move 10 rolling		HP 63

Av. Damage Bonus: +8D6.

Weapons: Crush 70%, damage is db

Armor: none, but (1) fire and electrical attacks do only half damage; (2) physical weapons such as firearms do only 1 point of damage, impaling or not; (3) a shoggoth regenerates 2 hit points per round.

Spells: none, normally.

Sanity Loss: 1D6/1D20 Sanity points to see a shoggoth.

STAR-SPAWN OF CTHULHU, Greater Servitor Race. *They all lay in stone houses in their great city of R'lyeh, preserved by the spells of mighty Cthulhu for a glorious resurrection when the stars and the earth might once more be ready . . . .* —H. P. Lovecraft, "The Call of Cthulhu."

These gigantic octopoid beings resemble Cthulhu himself, but are smaller. Not all the inhabitants of R'lyeh were trapped when it sank. Some still live on in the deep trenches beneath the ocean, where they are tended by deep ones. Related entities dwell in the stars, such as the beings said to infest the lake of Hali on a planet near the star Aldebaran, in the constellation Taurus.

A star-spawn may attack with tentacles or with claw. It may use 1D4 tentacles each round, or a single claw. Tentacle

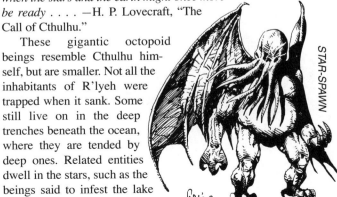

STAR-SPAWN

damage equals half the creature's damage bonus, while claw damage equals its full damage bonus.

STAR-SPAWN OF CTHULHU, Satraps of The Sleeper

Char.	Rolls	Averages
STR	2D6x10	70
CON	3D6x5	52-53
SIZ	3D6x10	105
INT	6D6	21
POW	6D6	21
DEX	3D6	10-11
Move 20 / 20 Swim		HP 79

Av. Damage Bonus: +11D6.

Weapons: Tentacles 80%, damage equals 1/2 db
Claw 80%, damage equals db

Armor: 10-point hide & blubber; regenerates 3 hit points per round.

Sanity Loss: 1D6/1D20 Sanity points to see a star-spawn.

SCENE: SUMMOR YE BLASPHEMOUS HORROR (A DARK YOUNG)

STAR VAMPIRES, Lesser Independent Race. *The dim outlines of a presence came into view; the blood-filled outlines of that unseen shambler from the stars. It was red and dripping; an immensity of pulsing, moving jelly; a scarlet blob with myriad tentacular trunks that waved and wavered. There were suckers on the tips of the appendages, and these were opening and closing with ghoulish lust.... The thing was bloated and obscene; a headless, faceless, eyeless bulk with the ravenous maw and titanic talons of a star-born monster. The human blood on which it had fed revealed the hitherto invisible outlines of the feaster.*—Robert Bloch, "The Shambler from the Stars."

These loathsome things are normally invisible, their presence signaled only by a sort of ghoulish tittering. After feeding, they become visible through the blood they drink. Summoned from the depths of space, some can be controlled to serve powerful wizards or other beings.

In an attack, 1D4 talons can grasp a given target at once. The victim will then be drained of blood, whether or not dead, and living victims lose 1D6 STR per round, as blood loss. If not killed, the victim replaces this loss quickly, in three days or less.

Against an invisible creature, halve the chance to hit, even if it is tittering. After feeding, the star vampire remains visible for six rounds, when the fresh blood metabolizes into a transparent equivalent. While it can be seen, attacks can be made at a normal chance to hit.

STAR VAMPIRE (caption, right margin)

STAR VAMPIRES, Invisible Raveners

char.	rolls	averages
STR	4D6+12	26
CON	2D6+6	13
SIZ	4D6+12	26
INT	3D6	10-11
POW	1D6+12	15-16
DEX	1D6+6	9-10
Move 6 / 9 flying		HP 20

Av. Damage Bonus: +2D6.

Weapons: Talons 40%, damage 1D6 + db
Bite 80%, damage 1D6 STR blood drain per round

Armor: 4-point hide. Bullets do only half damage to the extra-terrene integument of the star vampire.

Spells: though magical attack is unusual, a D100 roll of INT x3 or less gives 1D3 spells to a star vampire.

Sanity Loss: 1/1D10 Sanity points to see a star vampire or experience its attack.

TCHO-TCHOS, Lesser Servitor Race. *Our attackers ... were a horde of little men, the tallest of them no more than four feet, with singularly small eyes set deep in dome-like, hairless heads. These ... attackers fell upon the party and had* *killed men and animals with their bright swords almost before our men could extract their weapons.* —August Derleth and Mark Schorer, "The Lair of the Star-Spawn."

The blasted Plateau of Tsang in Tibet is one of the incursions of dread Leng into our space-time. On it and in a few other far-removed regions dwell the tribes of the Tcho-Tchos. In the beginnings of time, Chaugnar Faugn made a race of beings, the Miri Nigri, to serve him. The Miri were a race of dwarfs fashioned from the flesh of primitive amphibians. The Tcho-Tchos are said to come from humans who intermingled with the horrible Miri, forming a hybrid race of evil intent. Descendants are outwardly human-like, and actually of various sizes and costume, but the taint of the Miri curses all Tcho-Tchos with half-normal sanity at birth, rapidly eroded by horrid ceremonies and deeds.

The various Tcho-Tcho tribes worship a variety of Great Old Ones, not just Chaugnar Faugn. A Tcho-Tcho priest or acolyte knows at least three spells, usually including a Contact Deity spell and Voorish Sign.

Use human stats. Halve SAN for children, lessen Sanity points to 0 in adults.

TCHO-TCHO

XICLOTL, Beings from, Lesser Independent Race.

I had almost collided, I thought, with a metallically grey tree . . . about sixteen feet high with very thick cylindrical branches . . . cylinders further divided into six flat circular extensions. This might merely have been a natural distortion, and such an explanation might also have accounted for the strange arrangement of the branches in a regular circle at the apex of the trunk; but I could reach for no natural explanation when those branches nearest me suddenly extended clutchingly in my direction, and from the top of what I had taken for a trunk rose a featureless oval . . . an orifice gaping at the top. —Ramsey Campbell, "The Insects from Shaggai."

XICLOTLAN

These carnivorous aliens come from the planet of Xiclotl. The Xiclotlans are enslaved by the insects from Shaggai for their great strength and feeble intellect, and are used as brute laborers. On their home world, the Xiclotlans worship a legendary species of plant-creature, periodically voluntarily sacrificing themselves to these plants.

ATTACKS: Xiclotlans can simultaneously use all six of their tentacles in combat. Each tentacle does damage equal to half the creature's damage bonus.

Once seized, the victim's player must make a successful STR against STR roll on the Resistance Table or the victim is lifted to the being's mouth in the next round. The Xiclotlan can swallow one creature a round but cannot swallow anything larger than one-third its SIZ. Normally a Xiclotlan tears into pieces prey too large to swallow. Victims who are swallowed whole take damage each round equal to the devourer's damage bonus.

After the Xiclotlan has eaten prey of total SIZ equal to the Xiclotlan's own SIZ, it can no longer swallow prey, though it can continue to fight.

XICLOTL, Beings From

char.	rolls	averages
STR	6D6+30	51
CON	3D6+24	34-35
SIZ	4D6+30	44
INT	2D6	7
POW	3D6	10-11
DEX	4D6	14
Move 8		HP 39-40

Av. Damage Bonus: +5D6.

Weapons: Tentacle 50%, grasp + 1/2 db
swallows whole—does 5d6 damage per round thereafter

Armor: 8-point hide.

Skills: Hide 60%, Sense Hidden 50%, Sneak 60%.

Spells: usually none.

Sanity Loss: 0/1D6 Sanity points to see a Being from Xiclotl. ■

"It is absolutely necessary, for the peace and safety of mankind, that some of earth's dark, dead corners and unplumbed depths be let alone; lest sleeping abnormalities wake to resurgent life, and blasphemously surviving nightmares squirm and splash out of their black lairs to newer and wider conquests."

—*Lovecraft, At the Mountains of Madness*

ALIEN TECHNOLOGY

*Being an overview of the
technology of four alien races: Elder Things,
Mi-Go, Serpent People, and Yithians.
Also, notes on other races.*

Although most investigators tend to see creatures of the Mythos as little more than malignant monsters, in truth many of them have vibrant and technologically advanced societies. The technology of four advanced races—elder things, mi-go, serpent people, and Yithians—is highlighted below. Notes on a few other races follow.

Elder Things

A billion years ago elder things descended upon Earth from the stars, their technology hundreds of years advanced beyond what humans know in the late twentieth century. They were able to create life with their technology, according to some the source of all life on Earth.

CRYSTAL OF THE
ELDER THINGS

However, as the eons progressed, the elder things degenerated. They lost both their greatest technologies and their ability to fly through space unaided. Once they had colonized the entire planet, but through the ages they fell back until they controlled only one city. In the end they barely had the technology to create artificial heaters, and so preserve their existence a few centuries more.

Thus, while it is known that the elder things once had great technology, and while it is believed that there are still elder things among the stars and that they still remember their ancient secrets, the elder things of Earth left almost no traces of their technological mastery. The two items that follow scarcely hint at the esoteric technological secrets that the elder things of Earth's earliest ancestors knew.

CRYSTAL OF THE ELDER THINGS

Large crystalline storage containers constructed to harness the power needed to bind shoggoths to elder thing will. These crystals store magic points. The smallest shards might store 5 magic points and the largest 100. A caster can draw some or all of the magic points from a crystal while casting a spell. Most elder thing cities had 50-magic-point crystals at their hearts.

When empty these crystals are room temperature, but they become colder as more magic points are stored in them.

THE GREAT WHITE SPACE

A strange other dimension. It is unknown if the elder things actually created this dimension, but there is no doubt that they actively exploited it. It connects places light years apart and is or was used by the elder things to traverse the universe. The elder things created at least one portal to the Great White Space on Earth, deep in the mountains of China.

Mi-Go

Not only is mi-go technology advanced several hundred years beyond that of Earth, but they also are eager to use it; technology is very much part of their daily life. The mi-go originally came to Earth to steal certain minerals they could not find on their own worlds. Thus, most technology that the mi-go have brought to Earth relates to mining or to war.

The mi-go also touch upon the edges of the dark technology of the Outer Gods, perhaps more so than any other Mythos race. They created Ghadamon, a larval Great Old One, from a Seed of Azathoth; they formed the Shining Trapezohedron, which has a peculiar power over an aspect of Nyarlathotep; and they constructed a network of magical gates which tie together many of their outposts.

Mi-go advanced knowledge of medical and surgical techniques must be noted. They are able to remove a human brain from its body and preserve it for thousands of years, totally functional. In addition they can create very authentic-looking biological automatons, and engage in many surgical techniques that humans would consider miraculous.

BIO-ARMOR

In dangerous situations, mi-go typically don these webs of semi-luminous green slime. The harnesses provide 8 points of armor against blows, flame, electricity, etc., but do not protect against impaling attacks.

BIO-ARMOR

These bio-webs may be worn by humans, but they do a point of damage each time they are taken off as they rip away hair and flesh. A web will slowly degrade because humans do not exude the proper nutrient solutions to care for it. Each time it is worn by a human, a web of armor decreases in protection by one point.

BRAIN CYLINDER

These shiny cylinders are used to preserve extracted brains. Lovecraft described them as "a foot high and somewhat less in diameter, with three curious sockets set in an isosceles triangle over the front convex surface." Each cylinder is filled with a nutrient solution which sustains the brain within, and the inner surface of each cylinder is lined with a complex array of sensory filaments which detect electrical activity within the captive brain, interpret it, and channel neural impulses to a complex microcomputer behind the sockets. It in turn sends impulses through the sockets into connected machines, or funnels input from those machines back to the brain via a network of electrodes which directly stimulates the neurons in specific centers of the brain within.

Three accessory machines—a tall rig with twin lenses mounted on front, a box with vacuum tubes and a sounding board, and a small box with a metal disc on top—comprise the mi-go sensing apparatus. These machines, when connected to the proper sockets (an Idea or Spot Hidden roll allows an investigator to deduce which connector goes where), provide the brain with the faculties of sight, speech, and hearing. The mi-go, not possessed of human senses, have done their best but in approximation. All visual input is grainy, of low general resolution, and the audio is flat, like that of a monaural phonograph. Speech, with all its nuances of inflection and emotion, is utterly lost on the fungi. The speech machine talks with a mechanical, monotone voice, devoid of emotion. When the sensory machines are disconnected or deactivated, the encased brain falls into an semi-insane sleep state filled with strange dreams and hallucinations.

BRAIN CYLINDER

Every game month a human in a brain cylinder must match INT vs. POW. If INT wins, the character loses 1D3 SAN.

EARTHQUAKE MINING MACHINE

A massive cube, twenty feet on a side. The sides are covered with small convex windows of a cloudy, glass-like substance, spaced irregularly. When the device is activated it can be adjusted to pull a deeply buried stratum up through intervening layers of rock. The machine can reach down four to five miles, and can affect an area up to one cubic mile in area at a time. However, the machine has the unfortunate side effect of causing earthquakes when it is used. The size and depth of the area affected are directly correlated to the magnitude of the earthquake. For this reason mi-go tend to use such machines only in largely uninhabited areas, to avoid detection. A human unfamiliar with mi-go technology would be unlikely to be able to use the earthquake mining machine, except perhaps accidentally.

MINING MACHINE

ELECTRIC GUN

This weapon looks like a warty, doorknob-sized lump of black metal, covered in tiny wires. Mi-go fire this weapon by clutching it tightly and changing the electrical resistance of the lump. When activated, the weapon fires a bluish bolt of sparks doing 1D10 points of damage to the target. When it hits, the electric jolt acts like a taser, causing violent muscle spasms which immobilize the victim for a number of rounds equal to the damage inflicted. Finally, the target must successfully match his or her hit points against the damage done on the Resistance Table, or the target dies of heart failure. Mi-go take normal rolled

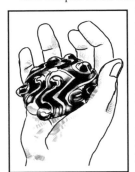
ELECTRIC GUN

damage (surface burns to the carapace) from these weapons, but do not have electrical nervous systems, and are hence immune to other damage from electrical charges.

To be able to fire this alien weapon, humans must realign the wires on the electric gun, a feat requiring two Electrical Repair rolls. So jury-rigged for human use, the weapon fires uncertainly. Roll 1D6 when attempting to fire: the weapon actually fires only on a result of 1-2.

MIST PROJECTOR

A cluster of twisted metal tubes projecting a cone of icy mist in a fat cloud about ten feet across. The mist looks like thick white fog, and is intensely cold. The mist does 1D10 points of damage per round of exposure, less one point if dressed in warm clothing or three points for thick, arctic clothing. Hiding inside a car affords four points of protection, but the mist freezes automobile engines, running or not, and they will not start or restart until they have warmed. The weapon's projection can be sustained—mi-go generally play mist over a target for several rounds, ensuring the death of unprotected humans.

MIST PROJECTOR

An investigator can figure out how to use this weapon with a successful Idea roll. The base chance of the weapon is 25%. Because the mist travels much more slowly than a bullet, investigators who have seen mist projectors in action and who have freedom of movement can dodge the slow-moving mist streams with a successful DEX x3 or INT x3 roll. The weapons carry enough charge for twenty shots, each potentially lasting an entire combat round.

Serpent People

Many serpent people kingdoms were based on sorcery and alchemy, but there is at least one—which originated deep below the Earth in Yoth and then migrated to Hyperborea—which raised science to new levels. It is believed that these serpent people were at least as advanced as the humans of the late twentieth century, but in the science of biology they excelled.

The serpent people of Yoth were able to manipulate lifeforms as they desired. It is believed that both ghasts and voormis are their creations, each bred to carry out certain tasks for their ophidian masters. Not only could the serpent people adjust the genetic structure of a creature in its prenatal state, so it changed as it grew, but they also developed serums which could evoke the most remarkable transformations in fully grown specimens. Cloning and accelerated growth were also well within the serpent people's ability.

Another particular area of serpent people interest was the creation of various poisons and toxins. Some killed, while others simply induced sleep. Some acted quickly, while others might take a century to take full effect. Some were blatantly obvious—so as to cause fear—while others were incredibly subtle. No other race has come close to approaching the level of knowledge of poisons enjoyed by the serpent people.

The later Hyperborean civilization of the serpent people, which preserved many of the secrets of Yoth, fell almost a million years ago, and since then the technology of the serpent people has almost utterly disappeared. Some modern serpent people strive to regain their lost technology, but they are few.

CAROTID TOXIN

A very rare POT 20 poison which causes a slow degeneration of the carotid arteries. If the imbiber fails his resistance roll

against the toxin, he is doomed. The toxin slowly eats away at the carotid arteries. In CON days the carotid arteries disintegrate, causing massive internal bleeding and almost instantaneous death. On a successful resistance roll the imbiber becomes extremely sick 1D6 days after the toxin is administered, as his body tries to fight it off. His STR and CON temporarily drop to 3 and he will be confined to bed, utterly exhausted and hallucinating. No doctor will find evidence of disease.

CAROTID TOXIN

CON days after the toxin was administered the victim will begin to recover, regaining most of his vigor in 1D6 days, but permanently losing 1 STR and 1 CON from the ordeal.

DOMINATION SERUM

A colorless serum with the faintest taste of raspberries. No more than ten drops are required for full effect. Unless he succeeds at a Luck roll the imbiber becomes very suggestible, but only to serpent people. Something in their peculiar smell or the specific intonation of their voices is the key to this suggestibility. The victim will do almost anything for serpent people, short of endangering his own

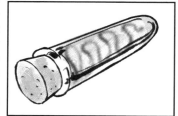

DOMINATION SERUM

life or the lives of those he loves dearly. The serum metabolizes slowly. It takes 1D10+10 days for a victim to be free of its effects, provided he does not imbibe more in the meantime.

Yithians

Of all the known alien races, the Yithians are the most technologically advanced. However—perhaps due to the Yithians'

philosophical view of life—they are oddly reluctant to use their technology. They tend to be reactive, quickly and adeptly formulating new technology as it is required, but in general their curiosity does not drive them toward invention.

Of particular note is the Yithians' conquest of time—the reason for their being called the Great Race. They are the only technical race able to move up and down the time stream at will. Somehow they even avoid the hounds

LIGHTNING GUN

of Tindalos, who pursue many others who traverse time and attract their attention. Although the Yithians' temporal abilities are largely mental, they have also invented devices which affect the fourth dimension.

LIGHTNING GUN

A rare Yithian weapon, this device was created by the race shortly after their arrival on prehistoric Earth. Built to combat the carnivorous flying polyps, it is a camera-shaped weapon that fires great gouts of electricity. Numerous varieties exist. A common one contains a pack of 32 charges, and takes 1 round to reload. Multiple charges can be fired at once, though each charge used above four at one time gives a 5% cumulative chance of burning out the gun. Each charge does 1D10 damage. Base range is 100 yards. Each additional 100 yards decreases the chance to hit by 20 percentiles and decreases the damage roll result by 3. An investigator can figure out how to use this weapon with a successful Idea roll. Base chance to fire a Lightning Gun is 30%.

Other variants of the lightning gun have fixed-size charges or affect only flesh.

STASIS CUBE

These devices appear in a number of different shapes and sizes, but they all have a single purpose: to slow the flow of time. Older cubes give ratios of 1 second internal time per thousand years external time, but in the future the Yithians will advance this to 1 second internal time per million years external time. The smallest stasis cubes were used to store

STASIS CUBES

books in Pnakotus. Larger stasis cubes have been used to fling Yithians into the future. Almost all stasis cubes are simple in design, made from metal or plastic with no sign of external circuitry. Most stasis cubes are deactivated by pushing a button or opening up the stasis cube, but some have complicated panels allowing the programming of set periods of stasis. These more complicated devices would likely be incomprehensible to someone who did not understand Yithian technology, but anyone could use the simpler ones, perhaps even by accident.

TABULA RASA DEVICE

This device was invented by the Yithians to erase the memories of those entities they displace through time. It is a small, slim, rectangular copper box covered with tiny indentations. From one side of the box five flexible metal tubes extend, ending in inch-long metal needles. The needles are inserted into the victim's head, which takes five rounds. Once the device is activated, the victim is paralyzed unless he or she makes a successful POW x1 roll each round that the device is connected.

Each round the machine erases up to a year's worth of memories or removes a point of INT, at the operator's discretion. These memories and thoughts are stored in the copper box. The erasure of memories is not always complete. Every year there is an INT x1 chance that some memory returns in

TABULA RASA

the form of dreams. The function of this device may also be reversed, feeding the stored memories to the original victim or

Adventure 2: Mystic Alliances Campaign
The Serpent Person

The Serpent Person is a one-night Mystic Alliances adventure about an inhabitant of the planet Yoth who hangs around various bookstores in the Seattle area. He is particularly interested in books on chemistry to do with preparing curotid toxin and domination serum. He is interested also in old science fiction novels by H. Rider Haggard to do with a talk he recently attended at a legal research CLE that focused around 'future internet technologies' where a spokesman from Eastside Health Alliance discussed SHE (shared holographic environment) and the implication of this virtual reality plan to those who engage in research and are interested in 'research tools'. The Serpent Person is interested in anything he can find on where this technology came from and believe it to be somewhat related to some research being done by university students on a massively multiplayer game of some sort that is based of novels by H. Rider Haggard.

The PCs will first run across indications that The Serpent Person is watching them when they attend the meeting of the Cryptonomicon society at Third Price Books, a gathering of teenagers and one older member called Thomas Henry. Thomas Henry is interested in a book that just came out called Lest We Forget which is a volume of poetry by authors who have written previously for the popular ezine strange Publications and also reprints Poe's famous poem The Raven with an all new analysis which links The Raven to other writer's writings.

The serpent person will watch the scene unfold carefully. He is dressed in a long brown trench coat and will attempt to slink into the shadows so his attempts to watch the group aren't fully noticed. A dead giveaway is his red eyes, so he will be wearing dark mirrored sunglasses. If spotted he will attempt to leave the bookstore via a side passage that leads into Sunset Boulevard Video where a clerk, Mandy Morgan will approach the group and say, "Are you interested in renting a scary movie for Halloween. We have some of the scariest around town. For example, there's a new film called Thrill Kill that's the coolest. Do you want to rent it?"

alternatively to another entity entirely. The tabula rasa device is very complex, and can only be used by those familiar with Yithian technology.

TEMPORAL COMMUNICATOR

These devices are sometimes supplied to humans who aid the Yithians in their travels through time. Made of bronze and

covered with intricate carvings, they stand nearly a foot tall when assembled and are surmounted by a red jewel. Each jewel is attuned to a specific Yithian. When power is switched on the jewel begins to glow red. After a few minutes contact is established with the faraway Yithian. A hologram is projected, and the Yithian can see into the time and space occupied by the machine and can communicate with those who have contacted it. A Yithian temporal communicator is easy to use,

COMMUNICATOR

provided that an investigator can determine which carving turns it on.

Other Races

Considerably less is known about the technology of other Mythos races. Earthlings have seen less evidence of it, thus in many cases it has been assumed that these races are not technologically advanced. What follows are scant notes on three other races with notable technologies.

DEEP ONES

Being derived underwater, without the benefit of fire, the technology of the deep ones is almost unrecognizable to humans. Beyond basic Stone Age constructs, most of the technology of the deep ones is organic. It is believed that they discovered the first hints of their organic technology when they first allied with the shoggoths and discovered how those creatures had been made by the elder things and how they could be controlled. In the modern world deep one cities are not as much constructed as grown. On occasion other useful tools are grown as well. Technology does not influence deep one society nearly as much as it does humanity's, but it is still an important force.

FLYING POLYPS

The malicious flying polyps colonized Earth aeons ago, apparently after flying to Earth on their own power. The flying polyps did build great basalt cities—the very ones they were later sealed in—but there is no other evidence of their technology. We must assume it is at least at the level of humanity's during the late Middle Ages.

SHAGGAI, INSECTS FROM

The technology of the shan seems most like that of the migo—it has been predominantly turned toward the dark science of the Outer Gods. They fly through space in great pyramidal space ships, and at the center of each of these craft is a nuclear reactor which is also Azathoth. Weaponry is a particular area of shan advancement. Their cruel nervewhip is just one of the many weapons they have designed. ■

> *"Scientists to the last—what had they done that we would not have done in their place? God, what intelligence and persistence! What a facing of the incredible, just as those carven kinsmen and forebears had faced things only a little less incredible! Radiates, vegetables, monstrosities, star-spawn—whatever they might have been, they were men!"*
>
> —Lovecraft, At the Mountains of Madness

DEITIES OF THE MYTHOS

*Being notes and statistics
on the fearsome gods of
the Cthulhu Mythos, before which
even the alien races quaver.*

Although many of the alien races of the Cthulhu Mythos are terrifying, they are nothing before the might of the Mythos gods—immense creatures barely within our scope of understanding, all the more horrifying for the fact that they do not care about the fate of humanity.

These descriptions are in the same format as the creatures of the Mythos (see pp. 132-155). Specific notes are also included on the cult of the god, where appropriate.

Classifications of Deities

The deities of the Mythos are divided into several classifications. These categories are not always consistant, but the following are the most frequently used.

It should also be noted that many deities have avatars. These are specific forms, sometimes with specific attributes, that the gods may appear in. Cults often worship avatars of gods rather than the gods themselves. Nyarlathotep is particularly well known for his thousand avatars (or masks). Though there are no avatars in this chapter, some appear in *The Creature Companion.*

ELDER GODS: the deities of the Mythos which seem uncaring of humanity, or even friendly toward it. They are often enemies of the Great Old Ones and Outer Gods, and may even be the inventors of the Elder Sign. Some elder gods are far-removed from Earth while others—such as Bast and Hypnos—have been worshiped as mostly benevolent human deities.

GREAT OLD ONES: the malevolent deities of the Mythos which are most frequently worshiped by humans. Many participate in the affairs of humanity, always to the detriment of the species. A number of Great Old Ones are imprisoned on Earth, often beneath Elder Signs.

OUTER GODS: the greatest deities of the Mythos. They may be true gods or simply cosmic principles. They are almost universally known—and feared. Nyarlathotep is the messenger and the soul of the Outer Gods, though what this entails is not entirely known.

ABHOTH

ABHOTH, Outer God. *He descried . . . in the pool a grayish, horrid mass that nearly choked it from rim to rim. Here, it seemed, was the ultimate source of all miscreation and abomination. For the gray mass quobbed and quivered, and swelled perpetually; and from it, in manifold fission, were spawned the anatomies that crept away on every side through the grotto.* —Clark Ashton Smith, "The Seven Geases."

Manifestly not native to this planet, Abhoth's protean form and cynical mind imply relation to Tsathoggua. The black caverns wherein it dwells and which it never leaves may well be part of N'Kai, an underground world beneath North America. Some reports place these caverns directly beneath the New England village of Dunwich.

CULT: Abhoth has no known human worshipers. Underground horrors or Abhoth's own spawn may worship it.

OTHER CHARACTERISTICS: obscene monsters constantly form in the gray mass and crawl away from their parent. Abhoth's tentacles and limbs grasp many offspring and devour them again, returning them to the primal mass, but more manage to escape. If someone nears Abhoth, the various monstrous spawn which continually detach from its body become more and more numerous, and these may harry or attack investigators. Spawn of Abhoth are manifold and varied in appearance; particulars are best left to the keeper. Its spawn are no larger than SIZ 1 to 3D6, at least at first—after a year or so of feeding and growing, a spawn may be any size.

If a party is unfortunate enough to come upon Abhoth itself, bubbling uncleanly in its pool of filth, Abhoth will put forth a probing hand or member which will feel over the intruders, and then drop off and crawl away. The visitor will then either be seized and devoured by other appendages of Abhoth's or ignored, at the keeper's option. Abhoth is known to speak telepathically with intruders, but few have returned from the meeting.

ABHOTH, Source of Uncleanness

STR 40	CON 100	SIZ 80	INT 13	POW 50
DEX 1	Move 0			HP 90

Damage Bonus: varies by pseudopod, usually not more than +1D6

Weapon: Appendage 60%, Grab and Absorb

Armor: No weapon using kinetic force can harm Abhoth permanently. Abhoth regenerates from all kinetic damage at the rate of 20 points per melee round. Fire or magic will cause normal damage. If Abhoth is reduced to 0 hit points, it withdraws and sinks far away down into the earth where it is inaccessible to further damage. It oozes toward the surface after healing from its injuries.

Spells: None, but it may give someone that it takes a fancy to a portion of its own body, which could be used to create a creature identical to the spawn of Abhoth.

Sanity Loss: seeing Abhoth costs 1D3/1D20 Sanity points.

ATLACH-NACHA, Great Old One.

A darksome form, big as a crouching man but with long spider-like members . . . . He saw that there was a kind of face on the squat ebon body, low down amid the several-jointed legs. The face peered up with a weird expression of doubt and inquiry; and terror crawled through the veins of the bold huntsman as he met the small, crafty eyes that were circled about with hair. —Clark Ashton Smith, "The Seven Geases."

Atlach-Nacha superficially resembles a huge and hideous black hairy spider with a strange, re-motely human face and little red eyes rimmed with hair. It lives underground, eternally spinning a fan-tastic web, bridging an unguessably deep chasm for unknown purposes. Old books cite the belief that when the web is completed, the end of the world will come. In the remote past Atlach-Nacha's dwelling was far beneath the continent of Hyperborea—modern Greenland. Now it may dwell beneath South America.

CULT: Atlach-Nacha is superstitiously believed to rule all spi-ders, perhaps because of its body form. It has no cult among humans, but gives some sorcerers spells and POW. Sorcerers sometimes summon Atlach-Nacha via various elder spells—a dangerous approach, however, for the spider-god hates leaving its eternal work of spinning. The children of Atlach-Nacha in the Dreamlands—called the Leng Spiders—are known to wor-ship Atlach-Nacha.

ATTACKS & SPECIAL EFFECTS: Who stumbles into Atlach-Nacha's web is trapped. To escape, the victim must match STR against the web's STR 30 on the Resistance Table. Friends may add their strengths to pull free the victim—roll against the total. In an hour or a day, Atlach-Nacha appears to dis-pose of the captive.

The spider god can first fling more strands over the victim and then bite, or it can bite at once.

When it bites, it injects a para-lyzing poison, leaving the victim incapable of action or defense. Atlach-Nacha then sucks the victim's body juices at the rate of 1D6 STR per combat round. If uncared-for, the husk soon dies. If rescued, the victim's STR returns at a rate of 1D4 points per game month of bed-rest. During this time the vic-tim's hit points can never exceed his or her STR.

ATLACH-NACHA, the Spider God

STR 30	CON 75	SIZ 25	INT 15	POW 30
DEX 25	Move 15			HP 50

Damage Bonus: +2D6

Weapons: Bite 60%, penetrates any armor and injects POT 35 paralyzing poison
Cast Web 80%, entanglement with STR 30 web

Armor: 12 points of chitin and fur. If hit points reach zero, it flees across its complex web to a secret lair where it heals.

Spells: all Contact spells.

Sanity Loss: 1/1D10 Sanity points to see Atlach-Nacha

AZATHOTH. Outer God.

That last amorphous blight of nethermost confusion which blasphemes and bubbles at the centre of all infinity—the boundless daemon sultan Azathoth, whose name no lips dare speak aloud, and who gnaws hungrily in inconceivable, unlighted chambers beyond time amidst the muffled, maddening beating of vile drums and the thin monot-onous whine of accursed flutes. —H. P. Lovecraft, "The Dream-Quest of Unknown Kadath."

Azathoth is the ruler of the Outer Gods, and has existed since the begin-ning of the universe. It dwells beyond normal space-time at the center of the universe, where its amorphous body writhes unceasingly to the monotonous piping of a flute. Lesser gods dance mindless-ly round Azathoth to the same music. Azathoth is described as

---

Deities, By Type

Elder Gods
Bast, Goddess of Cats
Hypnos, Lord of Sleep
Nodens, Lord of the Great Abyss

Outer Gods
Abhoth, Source of Uncleanness
Azathoth, the Daemon Sultan
Daoloth, the Render of the Veils
Lesser Other Gods
Nyarlathotep, the Crawling Chaos
Shub-Niggurath, the Goat with a
    Thousand Young

Tulzscha, the Green Flame
Ubbo Sathla, the Unbegotten Source
Yibb-Tstll, the Patient One
Yog-Sothoth, the All-In-One

Great Old Ones
Atlach-Nacha
Bokrug
Chaugnar Faugn
Cthugha
Cthulhu
Cyaegha
Eihort

Ghatanothoa
Glaaki
Hastur
Ithaqua
Nyogtha
Quachil Uttaus
Rhan-Tegoth
Shudde M'ell
Tsathoggua
Y'golonac
Yig
Zhar
Zoth-Ommog

both blind and idiotic, a "monstrous nuclear chaos." The urges of Azathoth are immediately fulfilled by Nyarlathotep.

CULT: Azathoth is little-worshiped, for the god offers not even gratitude in return. Usually humans call upon Azathoth by accident, and thereby unwittingly bring disaster and horror. Only the criminally insane would knowingly worship such a being. Nonetheless, such worshipers may have special insights into the nature of the universe, its origin, powers, and meaning, insights perhaps understandable only by other madmen.

OTHER CHARACTERISTICS: Azathoth always manifests with a servitor flautist to play its music, and 1D10-1 Lesser Other Gods. Summoners risk Azathoth striking out in irritation, the percentile chance equal to 100% minus ten percentiles for each Other God who arrived, and minus another five percentiles for each magic point which the sorcerer expends to placate the god. The magic points sacrificed must be renewed each round. If Azathoth angers, it grows: on the first round that it attacks, it also burgeons out from its summoned confines, and its pseudopods have a reach of 50 yards. On the second combat round it has a reach of 100 yards, the third round giving it 200 yards, and so on, doubling each round indefinitely.

There is also a chance that Azathoth voluntarily departs if it becomes angered, equal to ten percentiles per round minus one percentile per lesser other god that arrived with it.

An area equal to its pseudopod radius is blasted by Azathoth and totally ruined, with cracked boulders, pools of alkaline water, and dead splintered trees, but damage to investigators is done by specific pseudopod.

AZATHOTH, Seething Nuclear Chaos

| STR N/A | CON 300 | SIZ varies | INT 0 | POW 100 |
| DEX N/A | Move 0 | | | HP 300 |

Weapons: Pseudopod* 100% or less, damage D100 hit points + corroding the surface

As the last action in a combat round, roll 1D6 to learn the number of pseudopods with which Azathoth lashes out that round and the chances that anyone is hit:

| 1 = 100% | 3 = 33% | 5 = 20% |
| 2 = 50% | 4 = 25% | 6 = 16% |

Investigators cannot Dodge these massive blows. Allot attack at multiple targets if desired.

Armor: none, but at 0 hit points Azathoth is dispelled and not slain, and can return at full strength in 1D6 hours. It takes 3D6 damage from an Elder Sign, but destroys the Sign.

Spells: commands all the lesser Other Gods and much of the universe; fortunately it has 0 INT.

Sanity Loss: 1D10/1D100 Sanity points to see Azathoth.

BAST, Elder God. *Beauty—coolness—aloofness—philosophic repose—self—sufficiency—untamed mastery—where else can we find these things with even half the perfection and completeness that mark their incarnation in the peerless and softly gliding cat?—H. P. Lovecraft, "Cats and Dogs."*

Lovecraft loved cats. It is proper that the Cat Goddess have a position of importance. She is represented as a cat or as a woman with a cat's head. In ancient Egypt she was often shown with a sistrum in her

right hand, an aegis surmounted with a lion's head in her left hand, and a small bag slung over her left arm. She is also called Bastet or Ubasti. Bast may have dominion only over Earth and its dreamlands, for the cats of Saturn in the Dreamlands are inimical to Earth's cats.

CULT: the goddess of ancient Bubastis, in Egypt, Bast's cult eventually came to major Roman cities, including Pompeii. When she was actively worshiped, she was both a deity of the home and a lioness war goddess. Her worshipers always regarded her affectionately. Her cult seems not to have survived among humans, except in the Dreamlands, but she may not care. All cats worship her in their savage hearts.

BAST

OTHER CHARACTERISTICS: like the other Elder Gods, Bast rarely takes action. If a person is remarkably cruel to cats, she may act through her feline minions. If they cannot solve the difficulty she may come personally. She always appears with an entourage of large, sleek felines—mostly house cats, but including at least one lioness, tigress, or other big cat.

ATTACKS & SPECIAL EFFECTS: If Bast must participate in a fight, she can transform one or both of her delicate arms and hands into the tawny forelimbs of a lioness and swipe with them. Bast can both Claw and Bite in a round. Her attack penetrates armor without diminishment of damage, and the dripping wounds do not heal until treated by magic or by a successful Medicine roll.

BAST, Goddess of Cats

| STR 48 | CON 25 | SIZ 12 | INT 35 | POW 30 |
| DEX 45 | APP 21 | Move 40 | | HP 19 |

Damage Bonus: +3D6

Weapons: Claw 100%, damage 1D8 + 3D6
Bite 100%, damage 1D10

Armor: none, but note spells entry below.

Skills: Dodge 100%, Hide 100%, Sneak 100%, Track 100%.

Spells: her general powers include the following:

(1) Commands all felines, anywhere in the world. She can summon any number of cats, but they must travel normally to reach her.

(2) Heals damage to herself or to a cat by expending one magic point per point of damage.

(3) Evades up to three attacks per round and still can Claw and Bite once each per round.

Sanity Loss: no Sanity point cost to see Bast.

BOKRUG, Great Old One. *They worshiped a sea-green stone idol chiselled in the likeness of Bokrug, the great water-lizard; before which they danced horribly when the moon was gibbous.—H. P. Lovecraft, "The Doom That Came to Sarnath."*

Bokrug is a greenish-blue, iguana-like creature about twelve feet long. Its scales are metallic in texture, and its eyes glow bright yellow-green. Feelers on its lower jaw replace the dewlap of a true iguana, and the spines along its back are razor-sharp. It has webbed feet and

BOKRUG

a tail flattened for swimming. Bokrug dwells near the ruins of Sarnath in the Dreamlands' Mnar, though legends claim it originally landed in the Middle East of the Waking World.

CULT: one of the few Great Old Ones dwelling in the Dreamlands, its only worshipers were the flabby beings from Ib, who were destroyed by the men of Sarnath. Bokrug now accepts propitiatory worship by the folk of Ilarnek, who correctly credit him with the destruction of Sarnath. Bokrug's wrath may not descend for centuries, but his utterly destructive anger expunged mighty Sarnath in a single night.

OTHER CHARACTERISTICS: if ever encountered, D100 ghosts of Ib accompany Bokrug.

ATTACKS & SPECIAL EFFECTS: Bokrug attacks each round with one or both weapons.

BOKRUG, Great Old One

STR 30	CON 65	SIZ 25	INT 10	POW 24
DEX 20	Move 18			HP 45

Damage Bonus: +2D6

Weapons: Bite* 80%, damage 3D6 + 2D6
Tail Lash** 80%, damage 2D6 + db + grapple
succeeding, he can keep a grip and swallow another 3D6 hit points each turn until the target is swallowed.
**succeeding, the target is bound and can escape only with a Resistance Table success of STR against STR. After grappling, Bokrug can hurl his victim away, bite him, or simply hold him.*

Armor: 9 points of tough beaded hide.

Spells: all Contact spells plus Raise Ghost of Ib (1D10 ghosts per magic point), plus mainly minor spells at the keeper's option.

Sanity Loss: 0/1D8 Sanity points to see Bokrug.

CHAUGNAR FAUGN, Great Old One. *The ears were webbed and tentacled, the trunk terminated in a huge flaring disk at least a foot in diameter . . . . Its forelimbs were bent stiffly at the elbow, and its hands—it had human hands—rested palms upward on its lap. Its shoulders were broad and square and its breasts and enormous stomach sloped outward, cushioning the trunk.*—Frank Belknap Long, "The Horror from the Hills."

Chaugnar Faugn squats in a cave in mountainous Asia, guarded day and night by subhuman thralls only vaguely manlike, who hold rites so foul that none dare describe them. Usually Chaugnar Faugn remains immobile on his pedestal, a grotesque statue. Legends say that one day the "White Acolyte" will come to bear Chaugnar to a new land.

CULT: Chaugnar Faugn is primarily worshiped by the subhuman Tcho-Tcho people of the Tsang Plateau. In addition he has scattered cults among the humans of central Asia. Some of these have begun to spread, such as The Blood, which migrated to Montreal, Canada in the 18th century.

OTHER CHARACTERISTICS: at night, Chaugnar Faugn may stir and hungrily feed on a sacrifice, or upon anyone at hand. Day or night, he may lurch from his pedestal to annihilate unbelievers who enter his precincts. The disk-like snout at the end of his trunk is an organ which drains blood from a victim. Laid on an open wound, that wound never heals.

A 5% chance exists that Chaugnar Faugn sets free an exceptionally brave victim whose player's roleplaying has won the keeper's admiration. If not hungry, the Great Old One may merely maul a victim for 1D6 hit points.

The Great Old One may choose a human as a companion, and thereafter that mesmerized person loses 1D10 Sanity points daily until mad. At night Chaugnar Faugn lays his snout-disk on his companion, incidentally inducing the captive's nose and ears gradually to grow into caricatures of Chaugnar Faugn's. Psychically linked to the companion, Chaugnar Faugn controls his or her will. If no other victim is handy, the elephantine god suckles from the companion, who loses 1 CON each time.

ATTACKS & SPECIAL EFFECTS: if Chaugnar Faugn loses more than 90 hit points, he becomes inert and lifeless. Depending on the alignment of the stars, he requires months, decades, or centuries of rituals and sacrifices to be restored to life.

CHAUGNAR FAUGN, Horror from the Hills

STR 65	CON 140	SIZ 40	IN 25	POW 35
DEX 30	Move 70			HP 90

Damage Bonus: +6D6.

Weapons: Grapple 80%, grapples first to hold immobile for Bite
Bite and Drain 100%, lose 1D6 hit points each round.
Psychic Sending 100%, the target dreams of Chaugnar Faugn and his greatness. If of a sensitive nature, the target may become obsessed by these dreams.
Heart Attack* 100%, damage as keeper chooses.
Mesmerize Sacrifice** 100%, causes target to go to Chaugnar Faugn to await destruction.
to ward off this attack, target must receive a result of CON x5 or less on D100; succeeding, the roll must succeed a second time or target loses 1D6 hit points and fall unconscious.
**but target may break the trance if receiving a result of his or her POW x1 or less on D100.*

Armor: no ordinary weapon or mechanical device does damage; defends against enchanted impaling weapons with 10 points of super-dense hide; resists even the most powerful forces for 15 minutes before disincarnation.

Spells: Contact Chaugnar Faugn, Curse of Chaugnar Faugn, Summon/Bind Brother of Chaugnar Faugn, others as the keeper desires.

Sanity Loss: inert, he costs 0/1D6 Sanity points to see; animated and active, he costs 1D4/2D6+1 Sanity points; seeing Chaugnar Faugn's mutated companion costs 1/1D6 Sanity points.

CTHUGHA, Great Old One. *But even though we had shielded out eyes, it was impossible not to see the great amorphous shapes streaming skyward from this accursed place, nor the equally great being hovering like a cloud of living fire above the trees.*—August Derleth, "The Dweller in Darkness."

Cthugha resembles an enormous burning mass continually varying in shape. It dwells at or near the star Fomalhaut, whence it may be called. It is one of the most obscure and remote of all the Great Old Ones.

CULT: no cult appears to be connected with Cthugha, though scattered fire cults to it have existed in the past, such as the church of Melkarth in ancient Rome. It is served by entities known as fire vampires. In some books, the fire vampires are stated to be ruled by a being known as Fthagghua; perhaps this is just another way to spell Cthugha.

OTHER CHARACTERISTICS: Cthugha has the telepathic abilities common to the Great Old Ones, but does not seem to communicate with humans in any fashion, and must be summoned to be dealt with.

ATTACKS & SPECIAL EFFECTS: *Automatic Scorch Attack.* summoned, Cthugha brings D100 x10 flame vampires with it, which immediately begin to set the area alight. Cthugha itself floats above, scorching and burning the entire site. Humans in the area lose hit points to the heat, starting in the round after Cthugha comes. Each round the players must attempt to roll CON x5 or less on D100. Upon failure, the investigator loses 1 hit point per round until death. The only way to survive is to flee the area, a roughly circular area with a diameter of 2D10 x20 yards. Cthugha does not depart until that area has been thoroughly blasted and burned, unless first dismissed by means of a spell.

Pseudopod Attack. Each round, Cthugha can form 1D4 pseudopods from its formless mass with which to flail or squeeze individual targets. Each attack can be upon a different target.

Flame Burst Attack. It may belch forth fire instead of using pseudopods. A flame bust has a range of 150 yards and blankets the target site with fire, incinerating an area 20 yards across. Players of all within the area must roll their investigators' CON against Cthugha's POW on the Resistance Table: a failing roll indicates damage equal to Cthugha's POW. A success indicates hit point loss equal to half Cthugha's POW, a dubious benefit. Body armor is of no help against this attack, but an intervening wall or embankment would be.

CTHUGHA, The Living Flame

STR 80	CON 120	SIZ 140	INT 28	POW 42
DEX 21	Move 0 (aerial drift)			HP 130

Damage Bonus: 13D6.

Weapons: Pseudopod 40%, damage 1D6 + 13D6
Flame Burst 60%, special

Armor: (1) Any attacking hand-to-hand weapon magically takes 14 points of damage in the round in which it strikes Cthugha. The hit points are lost before Cthugha is struck and, if the weapon is destroyed, Cthugha takes no damage. (2) Bullets and other projectiles do normal damage to Cthugha, but only after 14 has been subtracted from the amount of damage actually done. A result of 0 or less does 0 damage to Cthugha.

Spells: all spells concerning entities of flame and itself.

Sanity Loss: 1D3/1D20 Sanity points to see Cthugha.

CTHULHU, Great Old One. *A monster of vaguely anthropoid outline, but with an octopus-like head whose face was a mass of feelers, a scaly, rubbery-looking body, prodigious claws on hind and fore feet, and long, narrow wings behind. This thing . . . was of a somewhat bloated corpulence. . . . It lumbered slobberingly into sight and gropingly squeezed its gelatinous green immensity through the black doorway . . . . A mountain walked or stumbled.*—H. P. Lovecraft, "The Call of Cthulhu."

Great Cthulhu's body form is not fixed. He can warp and modify it at will, extending new limbs, retracting old ones,

CTHUGHA

greatly increasing his wings' area and reducing his body's size to enable flight, or elongating a single limb or tentacle to enable it to writhe through yards of corridor. However, his overall shape is tied to the form described. Thus he might expand or contract his wings, but would never completely absorb them. All of his forms are recognizable as caricatures of Cthulhu.

Cthulhu dwells in the corpse city of black R'lyeh, sunken deep beneath the surface of the Pacific. He is in a living death while there, but someday the city will rise and he will wake, freed to raven and slay across the world. In the city are also entombed other members of Cthulhu's race. Cthulhu is evidently the high priest and ruler of them all, and is by far the most potent.

CULT: Cthulhu's cult is the most widespread and popular cult of the earthly Great Old Ones. This cult believes that Cthulhu plunged from the stars with his kin and built a great prehistoric city at R'lyeh, ruling the world. When the stars changed, their continent sank beneath the sea, and the city and its inhabitants fell into a death-sleep where they await their reawakening by members of Cthulhu's cult. When R'lyeh rises above the waves, members of the cult will be required to come to it and open the vast black door behind which Cthulhu dreams, whereupon he will awaken and rise to revel across the world in wild abandon with the faithful.

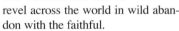

CTHULHU

Entire tribes are recorded as worshiping Cthulhu. Remote Inuits are mentioned. So are degenerate Louisiana swamp-folk. He seems to be most worshiped among sea-folk, or beings that live near the sea. He is served by the beings known as the deep ones as well as by the octopoid things known as the star-spawn of Cthulhu. Cthulhu's cult is prehistoric and of many variants, and Cthulhu himself has many names, most of which can be traced back to their original form. Thus two of his names are Tulu and Thu Thu.

OTHER CHARACTERISTICS: though in millennial sleep, Cthulhu is known to send horrifying dreams to mortal men, which may have tipped some people into madness.

ATTACKS & SPECIAL EFFECTS: each round 1D3 investigators are scooped up in Cthulhu's flabby claws to die hideously. If Cthulhu were just emerging from a vast hole, or if he were to stoop over, the investigators might also be attacked by Cthulhu's facial tentacles, which can grab four people per round and which can penetrate small openings.

At 0 hit points, Cthulhu bursts and dissolves into a disgusting, cloying greenish cloud, then immediately begins to reform. He needs 1D10+10 minutes to regain full solidity and, when he does, he then has a full 160 hit points once again.

Cthulhu could try to grab a plane or similar object with his claws to keep it from hitting him. If he so tries, he is automatically successful.

GREAT CTHULHU, Master of R'lyeh

STR 140   CON 110   SIZ 210   INT 42   POW 42

DEX 21   Move 24 Stride/20 Swim/16 Fly   HP 160

Damage Bonus: +21D6.

Weapon: Claw 100%, damage 1D6 + 21D6

Tentacle 100%, damage 11D6

Armor: 21 points of transdimensional muck and muscle; additionally, he regenerates 6 hit points per round.

Spells: knows hundreds of spells but not Summon/Bind Nightgaunt and Contact Nodens; he might impart Contact Deep Ones or Contact Cthulhu via terrifying dreams.

Sanity Loss: 1D10/1D100 Sanity points to see Cthulhu.

CYAEGHA, Great Old One. *They saw that it was a gigantic eye staring down at them. Around the eye, the sky split; deep clefts opened through which darkness began to ooze, a darkness blacker than the night, which crawled down as a set of slimy tentacles, taking on more form, more definite shape . . . something was standing, outlined against the black sky, something which had tentacles of darkness and a green-glowing eye.*—Eddy C. Bertin, "Darkness, My Name Is."

CYAEGHA

Cyaegha is an enormous black mass with one huge spherical green eye. It is possible that Cyaegha's form is simply that of the huge eye surrounded by long tentacles.

CULT: Cyaegha is worshiped by the residents of a small village over its resting place in a remote part of western Germany. The cult holds human sacrifice, but Cyaegha cares little for worship, only for the day of its release.

ATTACK & SPECIAL EFFECTS: if freed, Cyaegha drifts over an area, surveying all below, randomly picking human targets to crush and squeeze with its tentacles.

Attacking, Cyaegha deploys 1D10 tentacles per round.

CYAEGHA, Great Old One

STR 80   CON 120   SIZ 200   INT 20   POW 35

DEX 14   Move 25 flying   HP 160

Damage Bonus: +0.

Weapon: Tentacle 100%, damage 8D6.

Armor: none, but takes minimum damage from impaling weapons. Reaching 0 hit points, Cyaegha retreats underground.

Spells: whatever Call/Dismiss or Contact spells the keeper wishes.

Sanity Loss: 1D10/1D100 Sanity points to see Cyaegha.

DAOLOTH, Outer God. *Not shapeless, but so complex that the eye could recognize no describable shape. There were hemispheres and shining metal, coupled by long plastic rods. The rods were of a flat gray color, so that he could not make out which were nearer; they merged into a flat mass from which protruded individual cylinders. As he looked at it, he had a curious feeling that eyes gleamed from between these rods; but wherever he glanced at the construction, he saw only the spaces between them.*—Ramsey Campbell, "The Render of the Veils."

A strange, geometric being, Daoloth does not appear to be particularly malign. It lives somewhere beyond our universe, but may be summoned into it.

DAOLOTH

CULT: Daoloth is currently worshiped on Yuggoth and other alien worlds, but seems to have little earthly cult. His astrologer-priests can see the past and future, and perceive how objects extend into the last dimension. They gain the power to travel into other dimensions and to see other types of reality. Seeing Daoloth is disastrous, for the human eye attempts to follow the god's outline, and that speedily causes madness. Daoloth's few human cultists summon the god only in absolute blackness.

CHARACTERISTICS: the god's presence causes disaster among humankind. If he is not carefully held inside some magical barrier, his form expands and engulfs anyone nearby. Those engulfed by Daoloth are immediately send to distant and dismal worlds or alternate dimensions, from which they rarely return.

Daoloth moves unconventionally, either by expanding his shape or by slipping through dimensions. He expands at 8 meters radius per round, and can continue expanding to any size.

DAOLOTH, The Render of the Veils

STR N/A   CON 100   SIZ varies   INT 50   POW 70

DEX 30   Move 8   HP 100

Damage Bonus: N/A.

Weapon: Engulf, automatic success, sends victim to other plane.

Armor: anything striking or penetrating Daoloth is transported to another dimension, but any spell which the keeper thinks appropriate might do harm to hit points.

Spells: it might know any spell dealing with seeing or traveling to other worlds, planes, and dimensions, and whatever other spells the keeper thinks appropriate.

Sanity Loss: 1D10/1D100 Sanity points in the first round the god is visible; in succeeding rounds automatically lose 1D10 Sanity points while nearby.

EIHORT, Great Old One. *Then came pale movement in the well, and something clambered up from the dark, a bloated blanched oval supported on myriad fleshless legs. Eyes formed in the gelatinous oval and stared at him.*—Ramsey Campbell, "Before the Storm."

Eihort is a monstrous being which lives in a labyrinthine network of tunnels, deep beneath England's Severn Valley.

CULT: Eihort's only known cults are in the Severn Valley, particularly in the cities of Brichester and Camside. Typically a group of demented humans is led by a group of Eihort's Brood, which have formed themselves into the simulacrum of a human.

ATTACKS & SPECIAL EFFECTS: Eihort's Bargain. Cornering a human victim, Eihort questions the captive, and if the captive refuses Eihort, he smashes him or her dead.

Whoever would survive must accept Eihort's Bargain, and accept implantation of immature Brood into his or her body. Progressively horrible and Sanity-wracking dreams begin, costing 1D4 Sanity points and adding 1D3 Cthulhu Mythos, affecting the victim in the coming months. The maturing Brood fight the Bargainer for control of his or her body. After D100 months, the struggle climaxes as terrifying visions wrack the Bargainer's brain, and at last the mature Brood split open the Bargainer's body and emerge from within and scuttle off. The Bargainer always dies.

Eihort's Brood. They are small, globular, white grub-like or spider-like creatures, easily slain. Their systematic destruction risks Eihort's wrath. After their grisly birth, the Brood hide until the Great Old Ones walk the Earth again. Then they will metamorphose into smaller versions of Eihort, and thereafter attend him. Brood are not intelligent or aggressive, but they can gnaw motionless targets to the bone. In 1D10 minutes a group can do 1 hit point damage to a defenseless target.

EIHORT

BROOD

EIHORT, God of the Labyrinth

STR 44	CON 80	SIZ 50	INT 25	POW 30
DEX 12	Move 8/1 surface/burrowing			HP 65

Damage Bonus: +5D6.

Weapons: Bite 70%, damage 5D3 + paralytic poison POT 15
Crush 85%, damage 5D6 to all in 10-foot radius

Armor: none. All physical attacks do minimum damage. Additionally, Eihort regenerates 3 hit points per combat round. Brought to 0 hit points, his remains ooze into the ground and he regenerates somewhere far within the earth.

Spells: Cloud Memory, all Contact Deity spells, Create Gate, Summon/Bind Chthonian, Summon/Bind Ghoul.

Sanity Loss: 1D6/1D20 Sanity points to see Eihort.

GHATANOTHOA, Great Old One. *Nothing I could say could even adumbrate the loathsome, unholy, non-human, extra-galactic horror and hatefulness and unutterable evil of that forbidden spawn of black chaos and illimitable night.*—H. P. Lovecraft and Hazel Heald, "Out of the Eons."

Ghatanothoa is known to be exceedingly horrible, with myriad tentacles, maws, and sensory organs, with a definite dreadful outline. In ancient Mu Ghatanothoa dwelt in a burrow beneath a city originally built by fungi from Yuggoth, though generally inhabited by primeval humans. The burrow was surmounted by a truncated volcanic cone. When Mu sank, the god's home was overlaid by the waves and he was no longer free.

Sometimes tectonic upheavals force Ghatanothoa's dwelling place to the surface, as if in horrific preparation for that awful day when it will rise, along with R'lyeh, to sink no more. Investigators might beware any island between New Zealand and Chile that matches the description of Ghatanothoa's abode.

CULT: Ghatanothoa is sometimes tied to Iloigor. At present, no human cultists are known for him. In ancient times, the priests of Mu unwillingly offered periodic human sacrifices to Ghatanothoa, lest he rise from his extinct volcano and work greater carnage. Certain fungi from Yuggoth also served Ghatanothoa in these ancient times.

ATTACKS & SPECIAL EFFECTS: Curse of Ghatanothoa. Anyone in visual proximity to a perfect image of Ghatanothoa receives this curse. Each round that the image of Ghatanothoa is present, the human witnesses must attempt CON x5 rolls on D100. Upon failure, the investigator loses 1D6 DEX, muscles stiffen, and creeping paralysis begins. If an investigator's DEX is brought to zero, complete immobilization occurs, a petrifaction process normally irreversible.

In a few minutes, the victim's flesh and sinews rapidly harden to the consistency of leather and bone. The brain and other internal organs remain fresh and alive in this hard, immobile case, aware yet unbearably imprisoned. Only the destruction of the brain can end the victim's suffering. The blind, numb victim loses 1D6 Sanity points per day until reaching permanent madness or the forgiving release of death.

When he is at less than 0 hit points, the Great Old One's curse is inoperative. Once regenerating to at least +1 hit point, petrifaction proceeds normally.

GHATANOTHOA, Lord of the Volcano

STR 90	CON 80	SIZ 140	INT 20	POW 35
DEX 8	Move 9			HP 110

Damage Bonus: N/A.

Weapon: Tentacle 80%, damage 7D6

Armor: 10-point hide; regenerates an additional 10 hit points per round.

Spell: knows all Summon/Bind spells, as well as Contact spells for Great Old Ones, Chthonians, Deep Ones, Flying Polyps, Ghouls, Star-Spawn of Cthulhu, and Sand Dwellers.

Sanity Loss: 1D10/1D100 Sanity points to see Ghatanothoa, but that's the least of the investigator's troubles.

GLAAKI, Great Old One. *From an oval body protruded countless thin, pointed spines of multi-colored metal; at the more rounded end of the oval a circular, thick-lipped mouth formed the center of a spongy face, from which rose three yellow eyes on thin stalks. Around the underside of the body were many white pyramids, presumably used for locomotion. The diameter of the body must have been ten feet at its least wide . . . long stalks [were] twisting above it . . . [the] shape towered, pulsing and shaking with deafening vibration . . . a spine stiffened toward a victim].*—Ramsey Campbell, "The Inhabitant of the Lake."

GHATANOTHOA

Glaaki currently dwells at the bottom of a lake in the Severn River

Valley (in England) from whence it summons new cultists by a "dream-pull"—the sending of hypnotic dreams to potential initiates. Glaaki is weak now, and without the strength drawn from the initiation process, it cannot send the dream-pull any distance. But whenever someone comes to live nearby it can send the dreams, or it can dispatch servants of Glaaki to capture or guide new initiates.

GLAAKI

CULT: Glaaki heads a particularly loathsome cult in which most members are undead. On occasion living humans have worshiped Glaaki but currently the area around his lake is deserted.

ATTACKS & SPECIAL EFFECTS: *The Dream-Pull.* Glaaki mainly uses the dream-pull to draw victims to the lake for initiation. The target's chance to be overwhelmed by the dream is equal to Glaaki's magic points minus the victim's magic points on D100. For each half-mile of distance between the victim and Glaaki's lair, add 1 magic point to the victim's total for the effect of this calculation. Glaaki can try once per night, for as many nights as desired.

For initiation, the novice stands on the lake shore while Glaaki rises from the deep. Glaaki drives one of its spines into the victim's chest and then, on the next round, injects a fluid into the victim. Normally the spine kills the human victim. The spine detaches from Glaaki, and from it grow protrusions through the victim's body. When growth is complete, in a night or two, the spine drops off, leaving a livid spot which does not bleed and from which emanates a network of red lines. The victim is then an undead slave, a servant of Glaaki.

Conditions: if the damage from the spine fails to kill the target before the fluid is injected, the victim becomes an undead horror, but is not subject to the will of Glaaki. If possible Glaaki has its servants capture such an individual and hold him or her while it drives in another spine to force proper servitude. If the victim manages to break off the spine during the round in which he or she is stabbed and before the fluid is injected, he or she dies anyway but does not become an undead slave of Glaaki. In the rare instance that the Spine does not cause enough damage to kill the victim, and is broken off before the fluid is injected, the victim can remain a normal human being. Glaaki's undead slaves may hold novices tightly to prevent them from breaking off spines prematurely.

GLAAKI, the Inhabitant of the Lake

STR 40	CON 60	SIZ 90	INT 30	POW 28
DEX 10	Move 6			HP 75

Damage Bonus: N/A.

Weapon: Spine 100%, damage 7D3

Armor: 40-point integument; each spine has 4 points of armor and 6 hit points.

Spells: Glaaki knows most spells, and teaches many to his worshiper-slaves.

Sanity Loss: 1D3/1D20 Sanity points to see Glaaki.

HASTUR The Unspeakable, Great Old One. *Utterly alien landscape . . . . Foreground a deep lake. Hali? In five minutes the water began to ripple where something rose. Facing inward. A titanic aquatic being, tentacled. Octopoid, but far, far larger—ten-twenty times larger than the giant Octopus apallyon of the west coast. What was its neck alone easily fifteen rods in diameter. Could not risk chance of seeing its face.*—August Derleth, "The Gable Window."

Hastur the Unspeakable dwells near the star Aldebaran in the constellation Taurus. He is connected with the mystic Lake of Hali, the Yellow Sign, and Carcosa, as well as the things that dwell therein. He may be connected in some way with the power of flight through space. His appearance is disputed. In a reported instance of possession by Hastur, a corpse took on a bloated scaly look, and the limbs became boneless and fluid. The things in the Lake of Hali look octopoid from a rear view and are related to Hastur. They also have unbearably horrible faces. Still, Hastur's appearance is largely up to the individual keeper. Hastur is served well by the byakhee, an interstellar flying race.

CULT: the cult of Hastur is moderately common on Earth, and the abominable Tcho-Tcho peoples are reputedly among his worshipers, as are the Brothers of the Yellow Sign.

HASTUR

Hastur's cult is particularly loathsome, and is more widely known of than it is belonged to. Worshipers refer to Hastur as He Who Is Not to Be Named. This may be a misapprehension, stemming from his title, "The Unspeakable."

OTHER CHARACTERISTICS: Hastur is summonable only at night. When Hastur is present each round three individuals within 20 yards of the horror must successfully Dodge or be grasped by Hastur and destroyed on the following round. Hastur does not normally attack friends or worshipers. He must always leave that portion of the Earth where Aldebaran is below the horizon.

HASTUR, He Who Is Not to Be Named

STR 120	CON 200	SIZ 100	INT 15	POW 35
DEX 30	Move 20/50 flying			HP 150

Damage Bonus: +13D6.

Weapons: Tentacle/Claw 100%, damage death

Armor: 30-point thick, scaly, rubbery, and baggy hide.

Spell: Brew Space Mead, all Call and Contact spells, Summon/Bind Byakhee, and others the keeper finds appropriate.

Sanity Loss: 1D10/1D100 Sanity points to see Hastur.

HYPNOS, Elder God. *Young with the youth that is outside time, and with a beauteous bearded face, curved, smiling lips, Olympian brow, and dense locks waving and poppy-crowned.*—H. P. Lovecraft, "Hypnos."

We also learn that his true form is as distorted and fear-some as the worst of nightmares. As the god of sleep, his nature is tied to the sleep-boundary between the waking world and the Dreamlands, and dreaming sleepers travel through his dominion.

CULT: though Hypnos has on occasion visited the Waking World, he has not had a known cult there since the time of the Greeks. In the Dreamlands Hypnos is worshiped by certain nonhuman entities.

OTHER CHARACTERISTICS: should a dreamer overreach himself or attract Hypnos' attention, the god may transform the sleeper into a form more suitable to him. A transformed sleeper is altered as Hypnos desires, though no characteristic can increase above 50. The victim's skills do not change, except as a new shape prevents or promotes their use. New abilities may be granted, or old abilities taken away. Generally the victim must dwell with Hypnos forever, and never returns to Earth.

HYPNOS

HYPNOS, Elder God, Lord of Sleep

STR 20	CON 100	SIZ 12	INT 80	POW 85
DEX 30	APP 30	Move 8		HP 56

Damage Bonus: +1D4.

Weapon: Transform 100%, damage is the transformation

Armor: immune to everything which does not simultaneously exist in the Dreamlands and the Waking World; thus is endangered only by dreamers in their dreams, and by deities.

Spells: transformation ability.

Sanity Loss: seeing Hypnos' true form costs 1D6/1D20 Sanity points.

ITHAQUA, Great Old One. *The stars had been blotted out . . . the great cloud which had obscured the sky looked curiously like the outline of a great man. And . . . where the top of the "cloud" must have been, where the head of the thing should have been, there were two gleaming stars, visible de-spite the shadow, two gleaming stars, burning bright—like eyes!* — August Derleth, "The Thing That Walked on the Wind."

Ithaqua is reported from the Arctic and sub-Arctic, where Native Americans encountered him. He is known to stalk the wastes, tracking down hapless travelers and carrying them off. Such unfortunates are sometimes found alive, and they linger living for a while, unable to explain what has happened to them. Most are found dead weeks or months later, buried partway as if dropped from a height, frozen solid in positions of great agony, and missing random body parts.

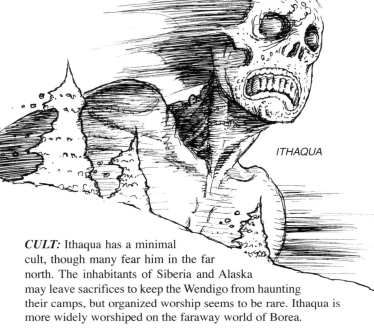

ITHAQUA

CULT: Ithaqua has a minimal cult, though many fear him in the far north. The inhabitants of Siberia and Alaska may leave sacrifices to keep the Wendigo from haunting their camps, but organized worship seems to be rare. Ithaqua is more widely worshiped on the faraway world of Borea.

ATTACKS & SPECIAL EFFECTS: if Ithaqua is within a few dozen yards, he can use mighty winds to attempt to whisk victims into the air. Players of those attacked this way must roll on the Resistance Table, matching the investigator's STR against Ithaqua's STR on the Resistance Table. If Ithaqua is attacking several investigators, divide his STR among them.

If within reach, Ithaqua may grab with one mighty claw per round. Anyone grabbed is automatically held as well, if Ithaqua desires.

ITHAQUA, the Wind-Walker, the Wendigo

STR 50	CON 150	SIZ 100	INT 10	POW 35
DEX 30	Move 10 / 100 flying			HP 125

Damage Bonus: +8D6.

Weapons: Wind Gust 100%, damage lift and drop*
Claw 80%, damage 6D6 (damage ignores any armor)
*1D10 x10 feet. Each 10 feet dropped equals 1D6 damage.

Armor: 10 points of skin and thick rime.

Spells: All Call and Contact spells.

Sanity Loss: 1D10/1D100 Sanity points to see Ithaqua; 1/1D6 Sanity points to hear the howl of the Wendigo on the North Wind.

LESSER OTHER GODS, Outer Gods. *To which detestable pounding and piping dance slowly, awkwardly, and absurdly the gigantic Ultimate gods, the blind, voiceless, tenebrous, mindless Other Gods whose soul and messenger is the Crawling Chaos Nyarlathotep.*—H. P. Lovecraft, "The Dream-Quest of Unknown Kadath."

In addition to named gods who may attend Azathoth, there is a company of entities seemingly minor or less important, the Lesser Other Gods. They number among the beings known to dance for Azathoth, as well as several others worshiped in various places. These spawn monstrous larvae which may grow into new gods.

CULT: the lesser Other Gods possess only small cults, and the keeper should determine any names needed. Most are as mindless as their master, Azathoth, but they possess less power and are safer to approach. A lesser god may grant protection to worshipers, or they may be able to exploit the god by getting it to unwittingly complete tasks for them.

OTHER CHARACTERISTICS: since these gods are at least a little different from one another, vary their powers and attacks. In conjunction with their masters they might manifest much greater power. Types other than the one described here exist, some with INT, greater SIZ, and so forth.

LESSER OTHER GODS, Minor Deities

char.	rolls	averages
STR	4D20	42
CON	1D100+20	70-71
SIZ	1D100+50	100-101
INT	0	0
POW	1D100	50-51
DEX	1D10	5-6
Av. Move 1D8-1		HP 85-86

Av. Damage Bonus: 8D6.

Weapons: Smash 60%, damage equals db

Armor: usually none, but 0 hit points merely dispels them.

Spells: they are able to will servants and slaves to aid them, and each has at least one servitor to fetch for it; they may be without formal spells, being gods, since this might merely mean that they could use magic, but not teach it.

Sanity Loss: 1/1D20 Sanity points to see a lesser other god.

N**ODENS, Elder God.** *And upon dolphins' backs was balanced a vast crenelate shell wherein rode the grey and awful form of primal Nodens, Lord of the Great Abyss . . . . Then hoary Nodens reached forth a wizened hand and helped Olney and his host into the vast shell.* — H. P. Lovecraft, "The Strange High House in the Mist."

He usually takes the form of a normal human, gray-bearded and hoary. Nodens often rides in a chariot formed from a huge sea shell drawn by unearthly monsters or fantastic beings from earthly legend.

LESSER OTHER GOD

NODENS

CULT: at times, Nodens is almost friendly to humankind. He has visited Earth on occasion, and is known to have aided some who were pursued or harassed by the Great Old Ones or Nyarlathotep. Nodens has no cult on Earth. He is served by nightgaunts.

ATTACKS & SPECIAL EFFECTS: Nodens never physically attacks a foe. Faced by a weak opponent, he summons nightgaunts in sufficient quantity to carry off the target. Facing a powerful foe, Nodens attempts to dismiss the enemy: in dismissing a foe, roll the foe's POW or less on D100. With a success, the foe remains and Nodens voluntarily departs in order to avoid a struggle. If Nodens is forced to leave because of some such being's resisting his dismissal, he has been known to take a favored human with him partway, left in some random location. He is recorded as having taken a human on trips to the outer reaches of the galaxy (and back again).

NODENS, Lord of the Great Abyss

STR 42	CON 45	SIZ 15	INT 70	POW 100
DEX 21	APP 21	Move 12		HP 30

Damage Bonus: +3D6

Weapons: Staff* 100%, damage 4D6 + 3D6
staff damage ignores protective armor.

Armor: none to start, but may choose to add armor by spending 1 magic point per point of armor desired—this armor lasts until either moonset or sunrise.

Spells: can call nightgaunts to his aid at the rate of 1D10 nightgaunts per magic point expended; Nodens may summon other servants at a rate of one per magic point expended; he heals himself by expending a magic point per point of damage; keepers should add other spells as thought characteristic of this god.

Sanity Loss: no Sanity points loss for seeing Nodens.

N**YARLATHOTEP, Outer God.** *A tall, slim figure with the young face of an antique pharaoh, gay with prismatic robes and crowned with a pshent that glowed with inherent light . . . the fascination of a dark god or fallen archangel, and around whose eyes there lurked the languid sparkle of capricious humor.*—H. P. Lovecraft, "The Dream-Quest of Uknown Kadath."

Nyarlathotep is the messenger, heart, and soul of the Outer Gods. He is the only one to have a true personality, and he claims to have a thousand different forms. To him, causing madness and insanity is more important and enjoyable than mere death or destruction.

Only a few of Nyarlathotep's forms have been described. The Black Pharaoh is an Egyptian-looking human. The Bloody Tongue is an enormous monster with clawed appendages and a single long blood-red tentacle in place of a face. This tentacle stretches forward when the Thing howls at the moon. The Haunter of the Dark is black and winged, with a trilobed red eye, and cannot withstand light. The Bloated Woman is a mammoth woman whose body convulses with numerous tentacles. The Beast takes the form of Egypt's Sphinx, but its face is filled with stars. There is some evidence that the Black Man of witch ceremonies is also a form of Nyarlathotep.

CULT: Nyarlathotep is typically worshiped though one of his forms, or Masks. There are numerous such cults, spread across the entire globe. The Brotherhood of the Black Pharaoh is centered in Cairo and has a powerful branch in London. The Cult of the Bloody Tongue is known in Kenya and New York. The Starry Wisdom Cult of Providence worships the Haunter of the Dark, as does the Cult of the Sand Bat in Australia. Other known cults include Shanghai's Order of the Bloated Woman and the global Brotherhood of the Beast.

In addition those worshiping the Outer Gods often do so in hope of gathering Nyarlathotep's favor. Rewards to loyal slaves usually come through the Crawling Chaos, as the other Outer Gods are too mindless to care. Nyarlathotep may grant worshipers knowledge of a spell, impart some destructive fact or divisive religious belief, or grant a servitor monster as an assistant. Nyarlathotep's gifts always seem to provoke turmoil among humanity, and are particularly likely to bring suffering and terror to a gift's recipient.

Besides servitors of the Outer Gods, Nyarlathotep has special servants, including the shantaks and hunting horrors. He may gift any type of creature to a worshiper if he deems it good. Such a bequest involves at least the permanent donation of POW or other characteristic to Nyarlathotep and the other Outer Gods.

OTHER CHARACTERISTICS: Nyarlathotep enacts the will of the Outer Gods, and is accurately referred to as their soul. He always attempts to bring madness to humanity, and several prophecies, including the stories "The Crawling Chaos", "Nyarlathotep", and the poem "The Fungi from Yuggoth" seem to state that someday Nyarlathotep himself will destroy humanity and possibly the entire planet. Nyarlathotep is always a mocking figure, evidently contemptuous of his masters.

All invocations to the Outer Gods include Nyarlathotep's name, possibly recognizing him as their messenger. He is known and feared by all Mythos species, and he occasionally requires things of them.

ATTACKS & SPECIAL EFFECTS: in human form Nyarlathotep may try to corrupt or trick his foes by appearing as a friend, and is generally reluctant to reveal his supernatural powers unless pressed. Nyarlathotep usually reacts to challenges by summoning beings to carry off or otherwise dispose of foes.

Nyarlathotep can summon a member of any servitor or independent race in this book (plus more that are not), at the cost of 1 magic point per POW

point the creature possesses. When in monster form, he tends to grasp his victims and then carry them off with him.

When in human form, Nyarlathotep can be slain by normal physical means. If so slain, after collapsing the body begins to quake and swell, bursting to release a huge clawed monster (or some other monstrous form described previously). This unwelcome colossus then rises from the split corpse and disappears into the sky without further molesting the killer. When in monster form, Nyarlathotep is difficult to slay, but slaying does dispel him.

Nyarlathotep's clawed demon form changes continually, but each round he will have at least two claws capable of attacking.

NYARLATHOTEP, the Crawling Chaos

char.	human	monstrous
STR	12	80
CON	19	50
SIZ	11	90
INT	86	86
POW	100	100
DEX	19	19
APP	18	—
HP	15	70
Move	12	16
db	+0	+10D6

Human Fighter: Any Weapon 100%, damage as per weapon

Monstrous Fighter: Claw 85%, 10D6 +10D6

Armor: none, but brought to 0 hit points, he collapses on the ground, changes form (always to a more monstrous one, which causes his viewers to lose Sanity points), and then flies into interstellar space.

Spells: Nyarlathotep knows all Mythos spells; he can summon monsters at the rate of 1 magic point per POW point the monster has; he may summon a shantak, hunting horror, or servitor of the Outer Gods at the cost of a single magic point.

Sanity Loss: no loss to see his human form; in many of his other 999 forms, 1D10/1D100 to see Nyarlathotep.

NYOGTHA, Great Old One. *An insidious odor began to penetrate the room. It was vaguely reptilian, musky, and nauseating. The disk lifted inexorably, and a little finger of blackness crept out from beneath its edge* [came] *a great wave of iridescent blackness, neither liquid nor solid, a frightful gelatinous mass.*—Henry Kuttner, "The Salem Horror."

Nyogtha is a minor deity reported to inhabit underground caverns on Earth. It may be related to Cthulhu. Nyogtha resembles a blob of living darkness which may throw out black tentacles or pseudopods at will.

CULT: Nyogtha has a few worshipers, mostly witches and their ilk. It teaches them spells on occasion in return for sacrifices and POW. In the Dreamlands Nyogtha is worshiped by a band of ghouls. Some ghouls in the Waking World may practice this worship as well.

ATTACKS & SPECIAL EFFECTS: unless driven off by appropriate spells, Nyogtha grabs and drags its victim off to underground pits. If Nyogtha strikes for damage, each target within 10 yards takes 1D10 points of damage from numerous small wounds.

NYOGTHA, The Thing That Should Not Be

STR 85	CON 40	SIZ 80	INT 20	POW 28
DEX 20	Move 10			HP 60

Damage Bonus: N/A.

Weapons: Tentacle 100%, damage 1D10 or entrap and grapple

Armor: Nyogtha ignores the first 10 points of damage received each round from all sources; at 0 hit points, Nyogtha is dispelled and will leave.

Spells: all Call and Contact spells; Create Gate.

Sanity Loss: 1D6/1D20 Sanity points to see Nyogtha.

QUACHIL UTTAUS, Great Old One. *It was a figure no larger than a young child, but sere and shriveled as some millennial mummy. Its hairless head, its unfeatured face, borne on a neck of skeleton thinness, were lined with a thousand reticulated wrinkles. The body was like that of some monstrous, withered abortion that had never drawn breath. The pipy arms, ending in bony claws, were outthrust as if ankylosed in the posture of an eternal dreadful groping.* —Clark Ashton Smith, "Treader of the Dust."

Quachil Uttaus' two legs are drawn tightly together and are as immobile as his arms. He is said to dwell in a dark limbo beyond time and space. Mentioned only in the exceedingly rare *Testament of Carnamagos*, Quachil Uttaus is interested in, attuned to, and possibly influences time, death, and decay.

CULT: Quachil Uttaus has no known cult, though occasionally wizards have called upon him to beg immortality.

ATTACKS & SPECIAL EFFECTS: when Quachil Uttaus is called, a shaft of gray light appears from above, focused on Quachil Uttaus' intended target: the victim cannot escape from this light. The god then swiftly, silently descends on the shaft of light, reaching toward the target. Unless summoned to grant immortality, Quachil Uttaus' touch causes near-instant aging and death, leaving a pile of dust for a corpse. He then departs the way he came, his small footprints in the remains the only trace of his visit.

QUACHIL UTTAUS (image label)

QUACHIL UTTAUS, Treader of the Dust

STR 12	CON 20	SIZ 6	INT 19	POW 35
DEX 3	Move special			HP 13

Damage Bonus: N/A.

Weapon: Touch 100%, damage is instantaneous death.

Armor: immune to all physical and magical attacks; upon attack, weapons instantly age to dust and dissolution.

Spells: as the keeper wishes, including any which have to do with life, death, time, and aging.

Sanity Loss: 1D6/1D20 Sanity points to see Quachil Uttaus.

RHAN-TEGOTH, Great Old One. *An almost globular torso, with six long, sinuous limbs terminating in crab-like claws. From the upper end a subsidiary globe bulged forward bubble-like; its triangle of three staring, fishy eyes, its foot-long and evidently flexible proboscis, and a distended lateral system analogous to gills suggested that it was a head.* —H. P. Lovecraft, "The Horror in the Museum".

This minor god ruled what is Alaska today, feeding on stringy hominids who ran squealing before his might. Perhaps as late as the last glacial cycle, Rhan-Tegoth entered into a deep hibernation from which he would not or could not wake. Rediscovered by modern men, most mistake the unmoving god for a ghastly statue.

CULTS: in ancient times Rhan-Tegoth was worshiped by a primitive human people, perhaps of the Inuit. Since he has gone into hibernation, his cult has faded. The bestial gnoph-keh of the northern wastes may also have some relation with Rhan-Tegoth.

ATTACKS & SPECIAL EFFECTS: a fetid amphibian-like being, he requires blood sacrifices of at least SIZ 15 daily. To feed, he grasps a screaming victim and draws him or her into the mass of tentacles. There the tentacles begin to drain the prey of blood, organic fluids, and STR, 1 point per round. For every 2 such points, increase Rhan-Tegoth's CON by 1, to a maximum of 160 CON. Excess points are lost. A victim who survives such an attack thereafter has hit points equal to half his or her CON. Unfed, Rhan-Tegoth loses 2D6 CON each day until reaching 60, and then re-enters semipermanent hibernation.

A sacrifice fully drained by Rhan-Tegoth is left flattened and riddled with hundreds of tiny puncture wounds. The blood and body fluids sucked out, only the crushed shell of the corpse remains. Seeing such a corpse costs 1/1D6 Sanity points.

RHAN TEGOTH (image label)

RHAN-TEGOTH, Terror of the Hominids

STR 40	CON 60*	SIZ 30	INT 15	POW 35
DEX 15	Move 10/14 swim			HP 45*

*base amount; increases as he feeds.

Damage Bonus: +3D6.

Weapons: Claw 80%, damage 1D6 + 3D6
Innumerable Tentacles 100%, damage drain 1 STR per round, plus 1D3 acid damage per round

Armor: 10 points from thick, slime-covered skin and tentacles. Also regenerates 1 hit points per round.

Spells: all, except those for the Outer Gods and their minions.

Sanity Loss: 1D8/1D20 Sanity points to see Rhan-Tegoth.

SHUB-NIGGURATH, Outer God. *"Iä! Iä! Shub-Niggurath! The Black Goat of the Woods with a Thousand Young!"* —H. P. Lovecraft, "The Whisperer in Darkness."

Shub-Niggurath is never met personally in Lovecraft's stories, but is often referred to in rituals and spells. It has been guessed that she is a perverse fertility deity.

In one of her few descriptions, Shub-Niggurath is said to be an enormous cloudy mass. This mass doubtless boils and festers. It is likely that parts of the mist coalesce at times, forming horrendous body parts, ropy black tentacles, slime-dripping mouths, or short

SHUB-NIGGURATH

writing legs, ending in black hooves which may account for the titular reference to "goat." When she arrives, she may bud off dark young.

Recent information suggests that her milk may have remarkable properties, but keepers must establish this.

CULT: worshiped extensively, she may have connections with druids and similar groups. Worshipers of Shub-Niggurath generally form into gangs or congregations, as do Cthulhu's cultists. Her emissaries and stand-ins, the dark young, may represent the aid she grants worshipers.

Summoned, Shub-Niggurath attacks nonworshipers present. She is often summoned specifically to accept sacrifices. Shub-Niggurath can be dismissed by those who know her summoning spell, and it is possible to hurt her enough to make her leave.

ATTACKS & SPECIAL EFFECTS: Shub-Niggurath has dozens of tentacles, but only one can attack a given victim in a round. With a successful catch, the investigator is whipped to the goddess' body to be drained of body fluids by one of her many mouths, the bite permanently draining 1D6 STR from the victim per round.

While being drained, the victim is held absolutely helplessly, and may not cast spells, expend magic points, or perform any act whatsoever except to writhe in pain and scream.

In battle against more powerful beings, Shub-Niggurath still attacks with one tentacle per opponent, but after a tentacle strikes it holds on, and a second tentacle attacks, and so on. Each additional successful attack permits a new mouth to begin to drain her gigantic victim.

Shub-Niggurath may trample beings of SIZ 60 or less. The trample attack is effective against all such beings in her path, which averages 10-20 yards across.

SHUB-NIGGURATH, The Black Goat of the Woods

STR 72	CON 170	SIZ 120	INT 21	POW 70
DEX 28	Move 15			HP 145

Damage Bonus: +11D6.

Weapons: Tentacle 100%, damage automatic catch
Trample 75%, damage 11D6
Bite 100%, damage is 1D6 STR drained per round

Armor: Shub-Niggurath has no armor, but her slimy mist body is immune to physical weapons. Magical weapons, or fire, electricity, or similar energies damage her normally. Her ropy tentacles and gooey vapors can rejoin, effectively allowing her to regenerate points of damage. Each magic point she expends enables her to heal 2 points of damage.

Spells: Shub-Niggurath knows at minimum all spells pertaining to the Outer Gods; she is known to have imparted Create Gate, Curse of Azathoth, and Voorish Sign to favorites.

Sanity Loss: 1D10/1D100 Sanity points to see Shub-Niggurath.

SHUDDE M'ELL, Great Old One. *A great gray thing a mile long chanting and exuding strange acids . . . charging through the depths of the earth at a fantastic speed, in a dreadful fury . . . melting basaltic rocks like butter under a blowtorch.* —Brian Lumley, *The Burrowers Beneath.*

He is pre-eminent among the chthonians and apparently is the largest and most evil of his kind. According to legends he once was imprisoned beneath G'harne, but is now free to wander the Earth with his kin.

CULT: chthonians, Shudde M'ell among them, are not much worshiped by humans now, though druids are rumored to have done so in the past and remnant Stone Age tribes may continue the practice. Perhaps the races that built G'harne did so to honor Shudde M'ell.

ATTACKS & SPECIAL EFFECTS: by himself, Shudde M'ell can cause a local earthquake of shocking intensity. In conjunction with other chthonians, he can create very strong earthquakes of regional size, strong enough to topple buildings or destroy bridges.

If Shudde M'ell attacks directly, a vast hole opens up, accompanied by a terrible chanting noise and slobbering, sucking sounds. Everything over the hole, which is at least 1D10+10 yards across, is sucked in and destroyed. Chthonians then pour out of the hole and attack survivors.

SHUDDE M'ELL

SHUDDE M'ELL, the Burrower Beneath

STR 90	CON 80	SIZ 120	INT 20	POW 35
DEX 15	Move 8/8 burrowing			HP 100

Damage Bonus: +12D6.

Weapons: Tentacle 100%, damage 6D6 + 1D6 CON drain
Crush 90%, damage 12D6 to all within 12 yards radius

Armor: 8-point skin; regenerates 5 hit points per round.

Spells: knows all spells the keeper finds appropriate; has taught many concerning the Great Old Ones and servitor races.

Sanity Loss: 1D3/1D20 Sanity points to see Shudde M'ell.

TSATHOGGUA, Great Old One. *He discerned in a dark recess the formless bulking of a couchant mass. And the mass stirred a little at his approach, and put forth with infinite slothfulness a huge and toad-shaped head. And the head opened its eyes very slowly, as if half awakened from slumber, so that they were visible as two slits of oozing phosphor in the black browless face.* —Clark Ashton Smith, "The Seven Geases."

He dwells in the black gulf of N'Kai, where he first arrived on Earth from Saturn. He is one of the less malevolent beings of the Cthulhu Mythos, though still terrible. Tsathoggua is usually represented as having a fat furry body and a toad-like head with bat-like ears and fur. His mouth is wide and his eyes always are half-closed, as if sleepy. It is also said that he can freely change his shape.

CULT: Tsathoggua was worshiped by serpent people and the furry subhuman voormis in ancient times, and by sorcerers and wizards in later times. He has given magic gates and spells to the faithful in the past. He is served by a race of entities known, for lack of a better name, as the formless spawn. They dwell in N'Kai and in his temples.

OTHER CHARACTERISTICS: if Tsathoggua is encountered, he has a 50% chance of being hungry, or the keeper may prefer to ask for a Luck roll from the investigator who enters first. If Tsathoggua is not hungry, he ignores the investigators and pretends to be asleep.

ATTACKS & SPECIAL EFFECTS: if hungry, Tsathoggua grabs an investigator and pulls the victim to him: in each following round the character loses one point from each characteristic until they are gone or until Tsathoggua is driven off. The victim will be in great agony, with acid burns, vitriol running through his veins, body punctures everywhere, etc. In this case, a full month of hospital care restores one point to each characteristic.

TSATHOGGUA, the Sleeper of N'kai

STR 50	CON 120	SIZ 30	INT 30	POW 35
DEX 27	Move 24			HP 75

Damage Bonus: +4D6.

Weapons: Tentacle 100%, damage Grapple
Characteristics Drain 100%, damage 1 point per characteristic per round

Armor: regenerates 30 hit points per round from wounds and punctures, but fire, electricity, and other such forces have normal effects on the monstrous god.

Spells: broad magical powers, as befits a Great Old One; he is recorded as having taught Create Gate and various Summon/Bind spells to humans.

Sanity Loss: 0/1D10 Sanity points to see Tsathoggua.

TULZSCHA, Outer God. *A belching column of sick greenish flame . . . spouting volcanically from depths profound and inconceivable, casting no shadows as healthy flame should, and coating the nitrous stone with a nasty, venomous verdigris. For in all that seething combustion no warmth lay, but only the clamminess of death and corruption.*—H. P. Lovecraft, "The Festival."

At the court of Azathoth it is a blazing green ball of flame, dancing with brethren Outer Gods before the Daemon Sultan. Called to our world, it assumes a gaseous form, penetrates the planet to the core, then erupts from below as a pillar of flame. It cannot move from where it emerges.

CULT: A few pockets of cultists worship this obscure entity, generally in subterranean temples, and especially during equinoxes, solstices, and important conjunctions. Tulzscha thrives on death, corruption, and decay.

TULZSCHA

TSATHOGGUA

TULZSCHA, Outer God, The Green Flame

STR 60	CON 36	SIZ 78	INT 15	POW 15
DEX 12	Move 0 on surface			HP 57

Damage Bonus: as energy, not applicable.

Weapon: Flame Gout 80%, damage special*
* *Effective at 50 feet or less; 1 attack per round. The gout of green fireballs may be dodged. With a successful attack, the target ages 2D10 years. The target needs CON x5 and POW x5 rolls on D100, with the losses expressed as 1/1D6 CON and 1/1D6 POW, respectively. A second POW x5 roll is necessary, as well; failing it, roll 1D6: 1-2 = lose 1 STR; 3-4 = lose 1 DEX; 5-6 = lose 1 APP.*

Armor: none, but immune to impaling weapons and to heat, cold, acid, and electricity. Explosives and all other physical attacks do minimum damage. Magic affects it normally, but Tulzscha can only be driven away by reaching 0 hit points.

Spells: all in the Greater Grimoire, and as the keeper wishes.

Sanity Loss: 1D3/1D20 Sanity points to see Tulzscha.

UBBO-SATHLA, Outer God. *There, in the gray beginning of Earth, the formless mass that was Ubbo-Sathla reposed amid the slime and the vapors. Headless, without organs or members, it sloughed off from its oozy sides, in a slow, ceaseless wave, the amoebic forms that were the archetypes of earthly life.* [About it] *there lay the mighty tablets of star-quarried stone that were writ with the inconceivable wisdom of the premundane gods.*—Clark Ashton Smith, "Ubbo-Sathla."

This god dwells in a cold, dank cavern, and never leaves its lair unless called or disturbed. The grotto can be entered through deep fissures in the Antarctic ice or through secret entrances from the Cold Waste of the Dreamlands. Other routes may exist.

CULT: Ubbo-Sathla has no human cult, although the mi-go and other alien races may worship it. The *Book of Eibon* and the *Necronomicon* mention this god.

OTHER CHARACTERISTICS: The Unbegotten Source may have spawned the prototypes of all earthly life, an idea also whispered of about the elder things. It was from Ubbo-Sathla's tissues that the elder things created their dread shoggoths. Within the grotto of Ubbo-Sathla, several tablets of star-wrought stone rest, said to contain great knowledge and secrets of the Elder Gods. These tablets, the Elder

UBBO-SATHLA

Keys, remain an enigma. Seeking these tablets, even the most powerful sorcerers have failed to return.

ATTACKS & SPECIAL EFFECTS:

an observer sees hundreds of pseudopods forming, flailing about, grasping prey, and being absorbed back into the body mass at all times. Remaining more than a few minutes in the god's presence insures that one or more investigators will be attacked. Each pseudopod has a reach of 100 yards. Any spot touched by Ubbo-Sathla is left devoid of life.

Spawn of Ubbo-Sathla. It continually produces 1D10 offspring per round, some of which it eats and others which escape. Those surviving fulfill every whim and urge of their primal, mindless sire. Generally encountered only in Ubbo-Sathla's primal grotto, no two spawn are exactly alike. All prefer surprise attacks from ambush: some attack with sticky filaments, some with pseudopods, some with gelatinous tentacles, and so on. Whatever the attack, a success draws the target into the spawn's body, where it is digested at the rate of 1D6 hit points per round. Once swallowed, no action is possible, though friends may attempt to free the victim.

UBBO-SATHLA, The Unbegotten Source

STR N/A	CON 200	SIZ 200	INT 0	POW 75
DEX N/A	Move 0			HP 200

Damage Bonus: N/A.

Weapon: Pseudopod 90%, damage grasp and absorb.

Armor: regenerates 25 hit points per round. Immune to impact, projectile, and cutting weapons; fire, spells, and enchanted weapons do normal damage. Loses 3D6 HP to an Elder Sign, but destroys it. Reaching 0 hit points, the god seeps back into its cavern or a fissure, and regenerates fully.

Skills: Generate Spawn 100%.

Spells: none, but Ubbo-Sathla controls its spawn at any reasonable distance.

Sanity Loss: 1D8/5D10 Sanity points to see Ubbo-Sathla.

SPAWN of Ubbo-Sathla, Greater Servitor Race

char.	roll	averages
STR	1D6 to 6D10+6	3-4 to 39
CON	3D6+6	16-17
SIZ	1D6 to 6D10+10	3-4 to 41
INT	zero	0
POW	3D6	10-11
DEX	4D6	14
Move	1D10+3	HP 19-20

Av. Damage Bonus: +1D4 to +4D6.

Weapon: Swallow Attack (various) 75%, 1D6 per round when swallowed

Armor: immune to blows and cuts; fire, magic, and enchanted weapons harm them normally.

Spells: none.

Skills: Sneak 90%.

Sanity Loss: 1/1D8 Sanity points to see a spawn of Ubbo-Sathla.

Y'GOLONAC, Great Old One.

He saw why the shadow on the frosted pane yesterday had been headless, and he screamed. As the desk was thrust aside by the towering naked figure, on whose surface still hung rags of the tweed suit, Strutt's last thought was an unbelieving conviction that this was happening because he had read the Revelations *. . . but before he could scream out his protest his breath was cut off, as the hands descended on his face and the wet red mouths opened in their palms.—Ramsey Campbell, "Cold Print."*

Y'golonac is delineated in the *Revelations of Glaaki*, an arcane book. It is a bloated, glowing figure who dwells underground in a vast ruin behind a wall of bricks. This prison may be near the Severn Valley city of Brichester, for it is known to frequent that place. Y'golonac is known to come when its name is read or spoken while evil is present. It is a minor god, but malignant.

Y'GOLONAC

CULT: Y'golonac has little cult, but strives mightily after more worship, entrapping those who are subtly evil to be his priests. Y'Golonac's notion of evil seems to be a shallow one, however.

OTHER CHARACTERISTICS:

Y'golonac may appear to be a normal, somewhat neurotic and flabby human. When he manages to contact a person that is debased in evil, the victim is possessed and absorbed by the deity, and thereafter his shape can change at will from the form of the possessed individual to Y'golonac's true form—glowing, headless, naked and huge, with wet mouths opening in the palms of the hands.

ATTACKS & SPECIAL EFFECTS:

to fight off a psychic attack, the target's player must roll his investigator's POW x5 or less on D100 each round to avoid being overcome. Once overcome, the investigator loses 1 INT and 1 POW each round until Y'golonac is forced away or until his soul and mind are destroyed, and replaced with Y'golonac's—and Y'golonac departs only if he loses all his hit points. Y'golonac normally attacks people who have become aware of him, usually through reading at least a page of the *Revelations of Glaaki*. Y'golonac is clever at getting persons to read passages from that horrid book without knowing they have done so.

In combat against more than one enemy, Y'golonac uses his mouths to devour and destroy foes. Damage done by the mouths does not heal naturally, and INT and POW loss is permanent, since the suppurating wounds never close.

Y'GOLONAC, Great Old One

STR 25	CON 125	SIZ 25	INT 30	POW 28
DEX 14	Move 10			HP 75

Damage Bonus: N/A.

Weapons: Touch 100%, lose 1 INT & 1 POW each round
Devour 100%, damage 1D4 non-healing damage

Armor: none.

Spells: Summon/Bind and Contact spells, and whatever else
the keeper thinks appropriate.

Sanity Loss: 1/1D20 Sanity points to witness human to
Y'golonac transformation; 1/1D10+1 to see Y'golonac.

YIBB-TSTLL, Outer God. *There, about the pulsating
black body of the Ancient One, hugely winged reptilian creatures without faces cluttered and clutched at
a multitude of blackly writhing, pendulous breasts!
[The eyes]* moved quickly, independently—sliding
with vile viscosity over the whole rotten surface
of Yibb-Tstll's pulpy, glistening head!*—Brian
Lumley, "The Horror at Oakdeene."

This horrible deity sees all time and
space as it slowly rotates in the center of its
clearing in the Jungle of Kled, in Earth's
Dreamlands. Beneath its billowing cloak
are a multitude of nightgaunts, suckling
and clutching at Yibb-Tstll's breasts.

YIBB-TSTLL

CULT: in ancient times Yibb-Tstll was worshiped as the god
Yibb, but now he has no known cult. Yibb-Tstll is often
approached by individuals—most often sorcerers—who either
crave the use of Yibb-Tstll's servitors, the nightgaunts, or ask
for his beneficent touch.

OTHER CHARACTERISTICS: Yibb-Tstll's blood, known
as The Black by sorcerers, can be summoned and
can take independent action, appearing as soft
dark flakes that adhere to the body of a target,
accumulate in great mass, and soon suffocate
him or her; use the rulesbook drowning rules.
Then The Black dissipates, taking the victim's soul back to Yibb-Tstll. Large quantities
of running water dispel The Black.

ATTACKS & SPECIAL EFFECTS: Yibb-Tstll's
touch commonly causes a drastic loss, one of the
keeper's choice—perhaps the immediate loss of all
Sanity points or a quick death from fearful convulsions, or perhaps running forward to suckle from
the thing before being ripped to shreds. Changes
might be physical. Sometimes are they beneficial.

YIBB-TSTLL, the Patient One

STR 40	CON 48	SIZ 52	INT 60	POW 65
DEX 16	Move 0			HP 50

Damage Bonus: +5D6.

Weapon: Touch 100%, damage is a drastic loss chosen by keeper
Blood 100%, damage is suffocation

Armor: 12-point cloak, and regenerates 5 hit points per round.
Loss of all hit points dispels Yibb-Tstll, but he can soon reform
or reappear somewhere else.

Spells: all Contact spells, Call Yibb-Tstll, Contact Yibb-Tstll,
Summon The Black, Summon/Bind Nightgaunt, others desired.

Sanity Loss: 1D6/1D20 Sanity points to see Yibb-Tstll.

YIG, Great Old One. *The half-human father of serpents
. . . the snake-god of the central plains tribes—presumably the primal source of the more southerly Quetzalcoatl or
Kukulcan—was an odd, half-anthropomorphic devil.*—H. P.
Lovecraft and Zealia Bishop, "The Curse of Yig."

Yig is never clearly described, but may look like a scaly
strong man with a serpent-like head or a normal head. He may
be accompanied by mobs of snakes. He seems to be mainly
a North American deity. The notorious "curse of Yig"
consists of madness and malformed children.

CULT: Yig is recorded as being worshiped by Plains
tribes and voodoo doctors, and may be somehow
connected to Quetzalcoatl. He is also worshiped by the serpent people and their kin.
Worshipers gain some immunity from poisonous snakes, the ability to talk to
snakes, and some arcane rituals and
spells. If someone exposes cult secrets or
does harm to the cult, Yig sends a sacred
snake to kill the offender.

ATTACKS & SPECIAL EFFECTS: a
manifestation of Yig would be signaled largely or entirely by a carpet of serpents—rattlers
in North America, puff adders or cobras elsewhere.

In hand-to-hand combat, the hand of Yig grasps, not
punches, doing crushing damage to an arm or leg. In the next
combat round, Yig draws the victim to him on a successful
STR against STR Resistance Table roll and bites him.

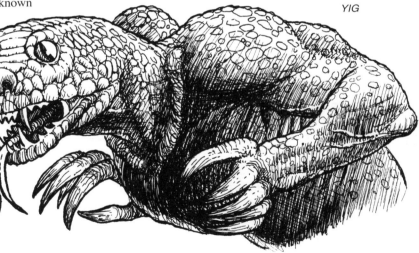

YIG

A sacred snake of Yig is always a very large individual of
a species native to the area where manifested, with a white
crescent on the top of its head. In North America, usually such
a snake would be an enormous tom rattler, at least 5-6 feet
long. The snake appears so swiftly that the victim is always
startled and automatically hit unless he or she can react swiftly (the player must roll DEX or INT x5 or less). On subsequent
rounds, the investigator must successfully Dodge to avoid
being bitten by the snake, which will pursue and continue to
attack unless it is killed. No anti-venin can save someone bitten by a sacred snake of Yig—bitten, he or she always dies
after a few minutes of agony.

YIG, Father of Serpents

STR 30   CON 120   SIZ 20   INT 20   POW 28

DEX 18   Move 10   HP 70

Damage Bonus: +2D6.

Weapons: Hand Grasp 90%, damage 2D6 no damage bonus
Bite 95%, damage 1D8 + instant death on penetration

Armor: 6-point scales. Impaling weapons do damage only on an
impaling roll, then doing normal damage and ignoring armor;
any other hit by an impaling weapon bounces off. Hand-to-hand
attacks do normal damage, and Yig's armor protects normally,
but any object penetrating Yig's scaly armor takes 3D6 points of
damage from the disintegrating effects of Yig's venomous blood.

Spells: has all the usual Summon/Bind and Contact spells, and is
more willing than most deities to impart
them; he is particularly expert
with chthonians; keepers
should add other spells as
desired.

Sanity Loss: 0/1D8 Sanity
points to see Yig.

YOG-SOTHOTH

YOG-SOTHOTH, Outer God. *Great
globes of light massing towards the opening . . . the breaking apart of the nearest
globes, and the protoplasmic flesh that
flowed blackly outward to join together
and form that eldritch, hideous horror
from outer space . . . whose mask was a
congeries of iridescent globes . . . who
froths as primal slime in nuclear chaos
forever beyond the nethermost outposts
of space and time!* — August Derleth,
"The Lurker at the Threshold."

Yog-Sothoth dwells in the inter-
stices between the planes which compose the universe. There it
manifests as a conglomeration of iridescent globes which are
always shifting, flowing into one another and breaking. This
conglomeration is large in size, but variable, so that at one time
it may appear to be 100 yards across and at another time half a
mile or more. Connections between Yog-Sothoth's appearance
and sightings of so-called flying saucers are obvious.

CULT: Yog-Sothoth is preeminently the deity of sorcerers and
wizards. He grants them the power to travel between the
planes, or the power to see into other planes via a piece of
magic glass or the like. Yog-Sothoth may also give its slaves
the ability to command various monsters from distant worlds.

In return for these gifts, worshipers open the way for Yog-
Sothoth to travel from his usual domains to Earth, to ravage
and plunder.

As Tawil at'Umr, all those wishing to travel to distant times
and places may safely deal with him. This form seems to be the
least malignant way in which to meet him but even then there
is always a danger that Tawil at'Umr will remove its veil and
cause utter madness and destruction to those dealing with it.

OTHER CHARACTERISTICS: Yog-Sothoth holds the
power to travel within the planes to reach any other time or
space. Yog-Sothoth itself is coterminous with all time and
space. Because of this, Yog-Sothoth has been called the Key
and the Gate. In Yog-Sothoth's aspect as Opener of the Way, it
is recorded as Umr at'Tawil [the correct Arabic form would be

Tawil at'Umr, which means the Prolonged of Life]. Yog-
Sothoth wishes to enter this plane to feast on the life it contains, but only can do so at certain times.

Yog-Sothoth can fly through our atmosphere at speeds of
hundreds or thousands of miles per hour.

Yog-Sothoth can transport one character per round anywhere in the universe or anywhere in time by touching him. If
the investigator is not willing to be thus transported, his player may successfully resist by rolling investigator POW x3 or
less on D100.

ATTACKS & SPECIAL EFFECTS: each
combat round, Yog-Sothoth may
touch one character with its slimy
spheres, and that character immediately loses 1D6 CON. This damage is
permanent and will not heal normally.
It takes the form of corrosion, with-
ering, or corruption of the body
part touched, and may also
involve an APP loss for the victim. Alternatively, Yog-Sothoth
may unleash bolts of silvery fluid
or fire (at a cost of 1D6 magic
points) which can reach over half
a mile, and destroy any normal
objects struck—knocking down aircraft, and
slaying or stunning any or all humans failing to
Dodge or jump out of the way. A gout of energy
covers an area about 5 yards across with its
effect.

YOG-SOTHOTH, the All-In-One

STR N/A   CON 400   SIZ varies   INT 40   POW 100

DEX 1   Move 100   HP 400

Damage Bonus: N/A.

Weapons: Sphere Touch 100%, damage 1D6 permanent CON
Silver Bolt 80%, damage death in 5-yard diameter

Armor: none, but only magical weapons can damage Yog-
Sothoth.

Spells: as many as he wants.

Sanity Loss: 1D10/1D100 Sanity points to see it in sphere
mode. No cost to see Tawil at'Umr form.

ZHAR, Great Old One. *The thing that crouched in the weird
green dusk was a living mass of shuddering horror, a ghastly mountain of sensate, quivering flesh, whose tentacles, far-
flung in the dim reaches of the subterranean cavern, emitted a
strange humming sound, while
from the depths of the creature's body came a weird
and horrific ululation.*
—August Derleth, "The
Lair of the Star-Spawn."

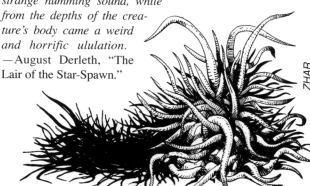

Zhar dwells in a dead city, buried under the Plateau of Sung or Tsang in China. There are two equally titanic monsters here. Possibly Zhar possesses two bodies, connected by long expanses of tentacles. The name lloigor is persistently associated with that of Zhar, and this second mammoth may be named Lloigor (do not confuse with the astral race of the same name), or the lloigor may simply be tied to Zhar as worshipers or exploiters.

CULT: the Tcho-Tcho people inhabit the Plateau of Sung (among other places), and are known to worship Zhar.

ATTACKS & SPECIAL EFFECTS: approached or disturbed, Zhar attacks by grasping with a tentacle. Anyone grasped completely disintegrates on the next round, leaving behind only unliving, inorganic objects. The tentacles reach at least 30 yards. Each round, Zhar may attack with one tentacle for each target.

ZHAR, the Twin Obscenity

STR 100　　CON 100　SIZ 100　　INT 30　　POW 28
DEX 30　　Move 20 / 50 flying　　　　　　　HP 100

Damage Bonus: +11D6.

Weapons: Tentacle 100%, damage is death in second round

Armor: 22-point blubbery flesh.

Spells: as the keeper wishes, including Summon/Bind Byakhee and Call Hastur.

Sanity Loss: 1D6/1D20 Sanity points to see Zhar.

ZOTH-OMMOG, Great One. *A body shaped like a broad-based, truncated cone. A flat, blunt, wedge-shaped, vaguely reptilian head surmounts this conical torso, and the head is almost entirely hidden behind swirling tresses. This hair, or beard and mane, consists of thickly carved and coiling ropes, like serpents or worms . . . . Through this repulsive*

ZOTH-OMMOG

Medusa-mane of ropy tendrils, two fierce, serpent-like eyes glare in a horrible intermingling of cold, inhuman mockery and what I can only describe as gloating menace. —Lin Carter, "Zoth-Ommog."

It has a cone-shaped body with a lizard-like head. From the head grows a mass of thick serpent-like tentacles. From the base of the neck project four thick pseudopods resembling starfish arms, one on each side of the body. Zoth-Ommog is evidently buried underneath the Pacific in the corpse-city of R'lyeh.

CULT: Zoth-Ommog has no active cult among humans. Some deep ones may worship this malign entity. Zoth-Ommog can manifest itself through one of the many statues of itself scattered apparently randomly around the world.

ATTACKS & SPECIAL EFFECTS: generally it assaults any human on sight, attacking either with one of its gigantic pseudopods or a bite.

ZOTH-OMMOG, Great Old One

STR 40　　CON 120　SIZ 60　　INT 20　　POW 35
DEX 12　　Move 50　　　　　　　　　　　HP 90

Damage Bonus: +5D6.

Weapons: Tentacle 90%, damage Grapple—on next round squeeze for 5D6 damage
Bite 90% damage 1D6 + 3

Armor: 10-point thick, blubbery hide; regenerates 3 hit points per combat round.

Spells: all Call and Contact spells, plus any that the keeper finds appropriate.

Sanity Loss: 1D6/1D20 Sanity points to see Zoth-Ommog. ∎

"The Old Ones were, the Old Ones are, and the Old Ones shall be. Not in the spaces we know, but between them, They walk serene and primal, undimensioned and to us unseen.

—Lovecraft, "The Dunwich Horror"

BEASTS & MONSTERS

*Being a selection of
natural and supernatural entities
useful to keepers in contrasting and
complementing the Cthulhu Mythos.*

Not all encounters, even deadly ones, need be with the Mythos. Here are included mammals, birds, insects, swimming things, and legendary supernatural entities of this planet.

BAT

More such beings certainly can be devised, and those presented here can easily be modified to represent another species. For instance, a keeper may want a Kodiak bear or a polar bear instead of the common black bear presented here. In that case add 1D6-3D6 to the STR, CON, and SIZ of the animal. Also increase the damage bonus, to reflect the damage that a bigger, stronger, tougher paw swipe from a bear would do.

Only supernatural creatures cost Sanity points to see. In the following stats, the absence of the *Sanity Loss* entry means that no Sanity point loss occurs in normal connection with the animal. Sanity point losses for ghosts and wraiths vary with their loathsomeness and how well they inspire terror.

BATS, LARGE, *Pteropus gouldii, et al.* Even the giant fruit bat of Central America congregates in dozens or hundreds. The smaller bats common to the United States gather in enormous cavern-based flocks of up to 50,000 individuals. Bats worldwide are under severe environmental attack from humans.

BATS, LARGE

char.	rolls	averages
STR	2D4	5
CON	2D6	7
SIZ	2D4	5
POW	2D6	7
DEX	1D6+18	21-22
Move 1 / 12 flying		HP 6

Av. Damage Bonus: N/A.

Weapon: Bite 40%, damage 1D2

Skills: Echo-Locate Prey 75%, Spot Hidden 75%.

Habitat: warm and temperate climates worldwide.

BOBCATS, *Felix rufus.* The bobcat is the most common large cat of North America, and is notoriously bad-tempered. It is found in mountains and woods everywhere on the continent, especially along watercourses. A bobcat attacks with both claws and its bite each combat round. If

BOBCAT

both claws hit, the animal hangs on, continuing to bite, and may rip with its hind claws.

BOBCATS

char.	rolls	averages
STR	2D6	7
CON	3D6	10-11
SIZ	1D4	2-3
POW	2D6	7
DEX	2D6+12	19
Move 12		HP 6-7

Av. Damage Bonus: -1D6.

Weapons: Bite 20%, damage 1D4
Claw 40%, damage 1D3 + db
Rip 80%, damage 2D3 + db

Skills: Climb 80%, Hide 80%, Sneak 90%.

Habitat: North America.

BLACK BEARS, *Ursus americanus.* By far the most common type of bear in North America. It is the only bear likely to be met in the eastern United States. It can attack twice in a round, using either two separate claw attacks or a bite plus one claw attack.

BLACK BEARS

BLACK BEAR

char.	rolls	averages
STR	3D6+10	20-21
CON	2D6+6	13
SIZ	3D6+10	20-21
POW	3D6	10-11
DEX	3D6	10-11
Move 16		HP 17

Av. Damage Bonus: +2D6.

Weapons: Bite 25%, damage 1D10
Claw 40%, damage 1D6 +db
Slap 25%, damage equals db

Armor: 3-point fur and gristle.

Skills: Climb 30%, Listen 75%, Scent Prey 70%.

Habitat: southern Canada to southern Mexico.

BUNYIPS, Greater Independent Race. *The eye is the size of a man's head, and is as inhuman as that of a squid, great and sad and timeless.*—Love, "Old Fellow That Bunyip."

A creature from the myths of native Australians. It's something like a crocodile, and something like an enormous seal. The eyes are glowing coals, and the hide is an unwholesome and unnatural combination of fur, scale, and feather. Swimming, its powerful flippers come into play. Walking, the hind legs allow it to stand erect, towering twelve feet or more. The hunting cry is the only sound made, as dire and desolate as death, or a savage, roaring paean of hate, rage, and hunger. The bunyip has long claws, and hugs its prey to death. It prefers eating women to men. It is found in ponds and spring-fed pools.

BUNYIP

BUNYIPS

char.	rolls	averages
STR	10D6+10	45
CON	4D6+12	26
SIZ	10D6+10	45
INT	2D6+12	19
POW	10D6	35
DEX	3D6+6	16-17
Move 10/16 walk/swim		HP 36

Av. Damage Bonus: +5D6.

Weapons: Bite 65%, damage 1D10
Claw 65%, damage is Grapple in first round and then 5D6 + db in second round.
Can Bite and Claw once each per round. The only escape is to overcome a bunyip's STR with STR on the Resistance Table.

Armor: 10-point hide.

Spell: a bunyip can at will raise and lower the water level of its pool or billabong.

Skills: Sense Life 95%, Swim Quietly 95%.

Sanity Loss: 1/1D10 Sanity points to see a bunyip; 1/1D3 Sanity points to hear its call.

BUSH PIGS, *Potamochoerus porcus.* These common African animals live in dense forests and travel in small herds of about twenty individuals. They are not domesticated. Their numbers have increased lately because the number of leopards has decreased.

BUSH PIGS

char.	rolls	averages
STR	2D6+4	11
CON	2D6+6	13
SIZ	2D6+4	11
POW	2D6	7
DEX	2D6	7
Move 10		HP 12

BUSH PIG

Av. Damage Bonus: none.

Weapon: Gore 30%, damage 1D8 + db

Armor: 3-point hair, hide, and muscle.

Skills: Scent Enemy 50%.

Habitat: Africa, south of the Sahara.

CAPE BUFFALOES, *Syncerus caffer.* They travel in large herds, sometimes of several hundred individuals, but also are met in smaller groups. The cape buffalo is the largest representative of this geographically diverse species. It is notoriously irritable and aggressive, and often is held to be the most dangerous large animal in Africa.

CAPE BUFFALOES

char.	rolls	averages
STR	4D6+20	34
CON	3D6+10	20-21
SIZ	4D6+20	34
POW	2D6	7
DEX	2D6	7
Move 12		HP 27-28

Av. Damage Bonus: +3D6.

Weapon: Charge 30%, damage 2D6 + db

Armor: 5-point hide and muscle.

Skills: Scent Enemy 65%.

Habitat: Africa, plains and open forest south of the Sahara.

CAPE BUFFALO

CONDORS, *Vultur gryphus.* The statistics do as well for a giant eagle or any other large bird. The condor's wingspread averages about nine feet. Only the largest birds will attack humans, though vultures will attack helpless prey of any sort. All birds have the special ability to cut an attacker's chance to hit in half while they are flying.

Larger birds live in the higher hills and mountains, which offer safe nesting sites and reliable updrafts for soaring. They perch among pinnacles or on rocky ledges, or even in trees that have grown close enough to support the considerable weight of up to a half-dozen large birds and their nest. The range of such birds is effectively the western hemisphere, but no reason exists that a keeper cannot say "A giant bird is diving at you" anywhere this side of Antarctica, where the giant birds only walk.

EAGLE

ANDEAN CONDORS, or any giant bird

char.	rolls	averages
STR	3D6+12	22-23
CON	3D6	10-11
SIZ	3D6+6	16-17
POW	2D6+6	13
DEX	2D6+12	19
Move 5/12 flying		HP 13-14

Av. Damage Bonus: +1D6.

Weapon: Bite 45%, damage 1D8
Claw 45%, damage 1D6 + db

Armor: 2-point feathers.

Skills: Spot Hidden 90%.

Habitat: North and South America.

CROCODILES, *Crocodylus niloticus.* This is the Nile crocodile, now rare in the lower Nile but still found in central Africa, Madagascar, tropical Asia, and northern and western Australia. Where there is water there may be crocodiles. Crocs eat anything they can catch, and come in great numbers to a kill to feed communally. Usually they will not attack a boat. Similar stats may be used for any *Crocodilia,* including alligators, caimans, and gavials—all long-snouted, lizard-like, and carnivorous.

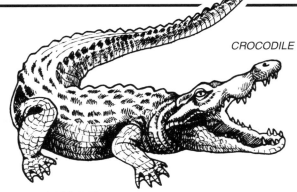

CROCODILE

NILE CROCODILES

char.	rolls	averages
STR	4D6+12	26
CON	3D6+8	18-19
SIZ	4D6+12	26
POW	3D6	10-11
DEX	2D6	23
Move 6/8 swimming		HP 22-23

Av. Damage Bonus: +2D6.

Weapon: Bite 50%, damage 1D10 + db

Armor: 5-point hide.

Skills: Glide Stealthily Through Water 75%, Hide 60%, Sneak 50%.

Habitat: tropics, esp. jungle marshes worldwide.

DOGS, ORDINARY, *Canis familiaris.* Our domestic friends are notable among animals for devotion and affection to their human masters. As hunters, they prefer to gather in packs of 1D8+3 animals minimum.

DOG

DOG, ORDINARY

char.	rolls	averages
STR	2D6	7
CON	3D6	10-11
SIZ	1D6+1	4-5
POW	2D6	7
DEX	2D6+6	13
Move 12		HP 7-8

Av. Damage Bonus: -1D4.

Weapon: Bite 30%, damage 1D6

Skills: Listen 75%, Scent Something Interesting 90%.

Habitat: wherever humans live.

ELEPHANTS, AFRICAN, *Loxodonta africana.* Everyone knows about elephants. Investigators should be safe enough unless they too closely approach a herd, are surprised by a rogue, or run afoul of a protective parent. This species is larger (averaging six tons in weight) and more feisty than its Asian cousin. An elephant can attack once per melee round. If the trunk grapples a target, the victim escapes by successfully matching his or her STR against half the elephant's STR on the Resistance Table. The trunk does negligible damage, but

ELEPHANT

each round following a successful grapple the victim can be hit by any of the elephant's other attacks with a 99% chance for success.

AFRICAN ELEPHANTS

char.	rolls	averages
STR	6D6+34	55
CON	3D6+16	26-27
SIZ	6D6+42	63
POW	2D6+6	13
DEX	3D6	10-11
Move 10		HP 45

Av. Damage Bonus: +6D6.

Weapon: Trunk 50%, damage Grapple
Rear & Plunge 25%, damage 8D6 + db
Trample 50%, damage 4D6 + db
Tusk Gore 25%, damage 6D6 + db

Armor: 8-point skin.

Skills: Listen 80%, Scent Something Interesting 95%.

Habitat: Central Africa; a smaller cousin species lives in tropical Asia.

GHOSTS. Each ghost should be crafted by the keeper to fit the circumstances of the adventure. Ghosts generally possess only INT and POW, appearing as dim, misty forms. They haunt specific locations, or sometimes specific objects such as a ship or automobile.

Ghosts may or may not be vulnerable to magic. Some ghosts may may not be exorcisable. Ghosts especially seem to haunt locations in order to communicate the awfulness which prompted their formation. Sometimes a ghost gives clues or instructions which, if carried out, let the anxious shade dissolve and find peace. Though all ghosts are terrifying, some are more loathsome than others: a 1D8 Sanity point loss is the maximum loss.

For a ghost's attack, match its POW against target POW on the Resistance Table. As this happens, the ghost may be glimpsed as clawing at, enveloping, or otherwise physically attacking the target.

If the ghost overcomes the target's POW, the character loses 1D3 POW. If the character can overcome the ghost, he or she causes it to lose 1D3 POW. The characteristic lost is forfeit. Ghosts of great strength may drain 1D6 POW or more from a victim in a single combat round, but such potent entities still lose only 1D3 POW if overcome by the victim in a particular round. Compare with the Wraith, below.

Individually crafted ghosts are good sources of spooky scenarios. Entire campaigns can be devoted to the study of and exorcism of ghosts. Books to read as sources for ideas about ghosts include *The Haunting of Hill House* (both the novel and the film, in fact) by Shirley Jackson, *The Shining* by Stephen King, any of William Hope Hodg-

GHOST

son's ghost stories (particularly the Carnacki—Ghost Finder tales), and the ghost stories of M. R. James. Henry James contributes a whole volume of ghost stories in his *Collected Works,* and Rudyard Kipling set some excellent tales of ghosts in England and in India. Like the ghosts they portray, some of these books may prove difficult to get hold of, but larger public libraries should have them.

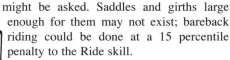

GORILLA

GORILLAS, *Gorilla gorilla.* These creatures do have the strength to rip apart human beings, but we have come to understand that they are shy and gentle, and nearly extinct.

If prodded into violence, a gorilla can bite and attack with both hands in one round. If the gorilla successfully attacks with both hands, it grapples its foe, doing the gorilla's damage bonus in damage to the victim in each successive round until the victim breaks the gorilla's grasp via a successful STR against STR match on the Resistance Table. With a second successful Grapple, any victim's hand-to-hand weapon is immobilized.

GORILLAS

char.	rolls	averages
STR	4D6+12	26
CON	3D6	10-11
SIZ	2D6+12	19
INT	1D6+1	4-5
POW	3D6	10-11
DEX	3D6	10-11
Move 8		HP 15

Av. Damage Bonus: +2D6.

Weapons: Bite 45%, damage 1D6 + db
Hand 45%, damage 1D6 + db

Armor: 2-point skin.

Skills: Browse For Food 50%, Hide 75%.

Habitat: mountains of Central Africa.

HORSES, *Equus caballus.* Horses offer many advantages to those who know their ways. For role-playing, divide them into riding horses, draught horses, and donkeys and mules.

Use of the riding horse is covered by the Ride skill. Single riders and small groups can easily cover forty miles in a day, given plenty of water and fodder such as oats and other grains.

Riding horses may spar with other horses, but they do not fight unless cornered. Even cavalry-trained horses are trained merely to stay their ground and control their nervousness. Nearly all horses will panic at the presence of some supernatural thing.

Draught horses are the largest of horses, usually broken to ride but not much actually ridden. To hitch them to wagons, a Drive Horses or similar roll

HORSE

might be asked. Saddles and girths large enough for them may not exist; bareback riding could be done at a 15 percentile penalty to the Ride skill.

Donkeys and mules mostly carry burdens, not riders, or draw wagons or carts. Stereotypically, they ignore commands when it pleases them, even brutal ones.

Among all horses, the tendency concerning bloody events, gunfire, monsters, angry crowds, and so on will be a sensible one, to flee.

RIDING HORSES

char.	rolls	averages
STR	3D6+18	28-29
CON	2D6+6	13
SIZ	4D6+12	26
POW	3D6	10-11
DEX	3D6	10-11
Move 12		HP 20

Av. Damage Bonus: +2D6.

Weapons: Bite 05%, damage 1D10
Kick 05%, damage 1D8 + db
Rear/Plunge 05%, damage 2D8 + db
Trample* 25%, damage 2D6 + db
horse must be trained for this attack.

Armor: 1 point of muscle.

Skills: Dodge 45%, Hide 25%.

Habitat: grasslands and high deserts, or where humans are.

INDIAN WILD DOGS (dholes), *Cuon dukhenensis.* This is no supernatural monster. The wild dog of India lives mainly in dense forests and is sometimes quite vicious. They travel in packs of up to a dozen individuals, all good enough hunters that they sometimes bring down water buffaloes.

DHOLE

WILD DOGS

char.	rolls	averages
STR	1D6+1	4-5
CON	3D6	10-11
SIZ	1D6	3-4
POW	1D6+6	9-10
DEX	2D6+6	13
Move 15		HP 7-8

Av. Damage Bonus: -1D6.

Weapon: Bite 05%, damage 1D6

Skills: Listen 40%, Track 80%.

Habitat: wooded areas of Central and South Asia.

LIONS, *Panthera leo.* The most famous of all the wild cats, lions travel in prides of a dozen or so animals, and hunt cooperatively. The male lions of southern Africa have denser and blacker manes than those further north.

A lion can make one claw attack and one bite attack each combat round. If both attacks hit, the lion hangs on, continues to bite the neck in order to close off the air supply, and may rake with its hind claws.

LIONS

char.	rolls	averages
STR	2D6+12	19
CON	3D6	10-11
SIZ	3D6+6	16-17
POW	2D6+6	13
DEX	2D6+12	19
Move 10		HP 13-14

LION

Av. Damage Bonus: +2D6.

Weapons: Bite 40%, damage 1D10
Claw 60%, damage 1D6 + db
Ripping 80%, damage 2D6 + db

Armor: 2-point skin.

Skills: Organized Hunt 25%, Track 25%.

Habitat: Africa and Near East.

MOUNTAIN LIONS, *Panthera concolor.* A wide-ranging predator averaging six feet in length. It is smaller, short-legged, and less social compared to its African cousin. The mountain lion rarely attacks adult humans, but children would be fair game. In the 1980s and 1990s it became a protected species in the United States, where its numbers have greatly increased.

In attacking, it attaches with both claws and bites each round. If both claws hit, the animal hangs on, biting or choking the target, and may rake with its hind claws.

MOUNTAIN LIONS, Pumas, Cougars

char.	rolls	averages
STR	3D6+6	16-17
CON	3D6	10-11
SIZ	2D6+8	15
POW	3D6	10-11
DEX	2D6+12	19
Move 12		HP 13

MOUNTAIN LION

Av. Damage Bonus: +1D4.

Weapons: Bite 30%, damage 1D10
Claw 50%, damage 1D6 +db
Rake 80%, damage 2D6 +db

Armor: 1-point fur.

Skills: Climb 80%, Hide 80%, Jump 40%, Sneak 90%.

Habitat: found throughout North and South America.

MUMMIES. These undead beings are similar to intelligent zombies. Some cults keep mummies in their temples as guardians. Like zombies, mummies must be hacked apart before they cease action. Contrary to popular belief, many mummies lack bandage wrappings and can move relatively swiftly. Mummies cannot naturally regenerate magic points.

A mummy has double its human STR, 1.5 times its original CON, and two-thirds of original DEX.

Because of the bitumen and bandages frequently used to preserve them, fire is particularly effective against Egyptian mummies: damage is normal, but the flames are more difficult to extinguish because of the bitumen in the wrappings.

MUMMIES, Average

char.	rolls	averages
STR	3D6 x2	20-22
CON	3D6 x1.5	15-17
SIZ	2D6+6	13
INT	3D6	10-11
POW	1D6+12	15-16
DEX	2D6	7
Move 6		HP 14-15

Av. Damage Bonus: +1D4.

Weapon: Fist 70%, damage 1D6 + db
Grapple 25%, damage special

Armor: 2-point skin; impaling weapons are useless unless severing a limb, head, etc.

Skills: Move Quietly 50%, Stalk 40%.

Sanity Loss: 1/1D8 Sanity points to see a mummy.

PYTHONS, *Python reticulatus.* In folk tales, pythons have the ability to charm prey, causing a target to stand unresisting until attacked, but investigators should mainly worry about being crushed and swallowed. A successful D100 roll of DEX x3 or less frees one investigator arm. From the victim's point of view, treat the Crush attack as a Grapple which does damage each round it succeeds. As the keeper sees fit, the victim's player also might need to roll CON x5 or less on D100, or the investigator falls unconscious.

PYTHON

Once stilled, the victim, of SIZ up to that of the snake, is swallowed dead or unconscious. If not dead when swallowed, death follows quickly from suffocation.

PYTHONS, or other Giant Snake

char.	rolls	averages
STR	3D6+12	22-23
CON	2D6+6	13
SIZ	5D6	17-18
POW	3D6	10-11
DEX	2D6+6	13
Move 6		HP 15-16

Av. Damage Bonus: +1D6.

Weapons: Swallow automatic, damage suffocation and digestion
Crush 40%, damage 1D6 + db

Armor: 2-point glistening skin.

Skills: Move Quietly 90%, Hide in Cover 75%.

Habitat: tropical forests.

RAT PACKS, *Rattus norvegicus.* Individual rats are not worthy opponents, but an infestation of rats can be daunting. Assume ten rats per pack, and per round damage of 1D3 hit

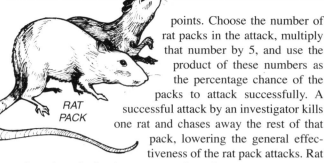

points. Choose the number of rat packs in the attack, multiply that number by 5, and use the product of these numbers as the percentage chance of the packs to attack successfully. A successful attack by an investigator kills one rat and chases away the rest of that pack, lowering the general effectiveness of the rat pack attacks. Rat packs exist only for the purposes of gaming.

RHINOS, *Diceros bicornis*. The two-horned animal described here is the irascible black rhino of Africa. This animal is aggressive, and may charge for no apparent reason. The larger white rhino is more placid and much less likely to charge. A typical black rhino is about twelve feet long and five feet high at the shoulder.

In order to use the Charge attack, a rhino must be able to charge for at least ten yards. A rhino attacks once per round, and does not hesitate to smite the car or truck as well as the passenger.

RHINO

BLACK RHINOS

char.	rolls	averages
STR	6D6+20	41
CON	4D6+6	20
SIZ	6D6+20	41
POW	3D6	10-11
DEX	2D6	7
Move 15		HP 31

Av. Damage Bonus: +4D6.

Weapons: Bite 25%, damage 1D10
Charge 50%, damage 1D10 + db
Trample 75%, damage 3D10 + db against downed foe

Armor: 10-point hide.

Skills: Be Annoyed 70%, Scent Danger 60%.

Habitat: sub-Saharan Africa, along with the white rhino; cousin species live in India and Indonesia.

SKELETONS, HUMAN. Animated skeletons are encountered in a few medieval legends, and rather more frequently in modern stories and especially in modern films.

Dried bones are fairly brittle, and snap and splinter easily from a heavy blow, but no area of a skeleton is more vulnerable than any other. To simulate this, ignore impales, critical hits, and so on. Any blow striking a skeleton has a chance of destroying it equal to or less than the damage done x4, as rolled on D100. For example, if an axe hit a skeleton and did 8 points damage, there would be a 32% chance of destroying the skeleton by shattering it. Unless the skeleton shatters, it remains totally undamaged.

SKELE-

Secondly, halve the chance to hit with an impaling weapon, since much of the target is simply air.

Animated skeletons traditionally use weapons rather than striking blows directly, perhaps because they shatter so easily. Equip as desired, typically small club or sword at a skill percentage of DEX x3.

No good explanation explanation exists for the continued mobility of the bones once muscles, tendons, and ligaments have rotted away.

HUMAN SKELETONS

char.	rolls	averages
STR	3D6	10-11
CON	N/A	—
SIZ	2D6+6	13
INT	3D6	10-11
POW	1	1
DEX	3D6	10-11
Move 7		HP N/A

Av. Damage Bonus: none.

Weapon: any hand-to-hand weapon DEX x3% chance, damage normal + db

Skills: Clatter Ominously 45%, Rise Unexpectedly 60%.

Habitat: ruins, tombs, treasure chests, dungeons, sorcerers' keeps.

Sanity Loss: 0/1D6 Sanity points to see an animated skeleton.

SQUIDS, GIANT, *Teuthoidea architeuthis*. The average size of the species is a body about twelve feet long, with tentacles up to an additional sixty feet in length. The statistics reflect a squid of this size. To make a whale-battler, add 1D6 of SIZ and STR for every two feet of increased span from tentacle tip to tip.

The beak and eight tentacles can attack simultaneously at up to eight different targets. The first tentacle striking a foe hangs on; when a second connects, the two constrict the target, and each does its damage each round.

GIANT SQUIDS

char.	rolls	averages
STR	6D6	21
CON	2D6+6	13
SIZ	6D6	21
POW	3D6	10-11
DEX	2D6+12	19
Move 4/10 swimming		HP 17

Av. Damage Bonus: +2D6.

Weapons: Beak 45%, damage 1D10 + CON = POT poison
Tentacle 45%, damage 1D6 + db of constriction

Armor: 2-point hide.

Skills: Hide in Cover 70%.

Habitat: deep oceans, preferably cool polar waters.

SQUID

TIGERS, *Panthera tigris*. The largest of all felines, tigers are notorious man-killers in India, where villages unwisely intrude into diminishing ranges. Tigers are solitary hunters. A tiger can attack with both claws and one bite each combat round. If both attacks hit. the tiger hangs on, continues to bite or choke, and may rake with its hind legs.

BENGAL TIGERS

char.	rolls	averages
STR	3D6+12	22-23
CON	3D6	10-11
SIZ	3D6+6	16-17
POW	3D6	10-11
DEX	2D6+12	19
Move 10		HP 13-14

Av. Damage Bonus: +1D6.

Weapons: Bite 45%, damage 1D10
Claw 70%, damage 1D8 + db
Ripping 80%, damage 2D8 + db

Armor: 2-point skin.

Skills: Hide in Cover 80%,
Move Quietly 75%, Track
50%.

Habitat: India to Java; a
Siberian cousin also exists.

TIGER

VAMPIRES. Every player will be interested in matching
wits with these blood-suckers, but stories about vampires
and their powers so conflict and contradict that the individual
keeper must determine which vampire facts are true in play,
and which are merely legendary. Here are some options.

■ A vampire casts no reflection.

■ A vampire may have to return to soil in which it originally
was buried in order to pass the daylight hours.

■ The third bite from a vampire causes a character to die, and
then to become one of the undead.

■ A vampire has no special powers in daylight, and may be
unable to move abroad, or be unable to move from its coffin.

■ In Catholic cultures, the cross gives protection from a vampire, at least for a while, and holy water touching the thing
sears and scalds its flesh.

■ A vampires never drinks . . . wine.

A vampire can change into smoke, mist, a wolf, or a bat at will.
If smoke or mist, it drifts at the rate of one yard / combat round.

   Once physical attacks have exceeded its hit points, the
vampire turns into smoke or mist at the end of the combat
round, thereafter regenerating hit points at the rate of 1 point
per round. However, if the vampire's hit points have been
reduced exactly to zero, its head has been hit: the vampire falls
and cannot transform into smoke. Then a stake driven through
its heart kills it forever.

VAMPIRE

VAMPIRES

char.	rolls	averages
STR	3D6 x2	20-22
CON	2D6+6	13
SIZ	3D6	10-11
INT	2D6+6	13
POW	2D6+6	13
DEX	3D6	10-11
Move species rate +2		HP 12

Av. Damage Bonus: +1D6.

Weapons: Bite* 50%, damage 1D4 first round + blood drain
   thereafter
Claw** 50%, damage 1D4 + db
Gaze***, match POWs on Resistance Table

*If a vampire's Bite attack does damage, maintaining the Bite
stifles any resistance from the target, and drains 1D6 STR
(blood) from the victim each round thereafter.*

**With a successful magic point against magic point roll on the
Resistance Table, the touch of a vampire drains 1D3 magic
points from the victim, transferring them to the vampire. This
happens each combat round. Each successful roll drains another
1D3 magic points. Magic points so acquired vanish after the
vampire's POW in hours. The victim can regenerate the magic
points normally.*

***If the Resistance Table roll succeeds (match POW against
POW), the target is always hypnotized, and can be made to follow simple instructions. If these instructions are self-destructive,
at the start of a round the target's player may roll INT x5 or less
to snap out of it.*

Armor: can reform after hit points are exceeded.

Skills: Human Psychology 60%, Scent Blood 75%.

Habitat: wherever innocence is undefended.

Sanity Loss: 0/1D4 Sanity points to be attacked; 1/1D3 to witness a transformation. Vampires of human appearance cost no
Sanity points to see.

WASP Swarms, or Bee Swarms. Such a cloud of stinger-
equipped flying insects attacks for 2D6 combat
rounds before halting pursuit. Unless the victims are completely covered (as with netting or by being enclosed in an
auto or by diving underwater) there is no protection against them. An investigator
who is stung extensively and
whose player fails a CON x5 roll
on D100 may experience profound immune system shock, fall
seriously ill, and (rarely) die.

   The Africanized bees coloniz-
ing the Americas in the 1990s are
more intent in their pursuit than
are honey bees or wasps, attacking
for up to 3D6 minutes. Being seriously stung by these so-called
killer bees occasionally results in death, since the attacks are
comparatively unrelenting and often more numerous. Each
minute of such attack might cost as much as 1D6 hit points.

WASP

BEE

WEREWOLVES, Humanoid or Full Wolf. As the first
sort, a normal human is cursed and occasionally thereafter turns into a monster, half human and half beast, classically
at the full moon. This unfortunate may be unaware of his curse

or may detest his fate. The second sort may fully transform into a wolf, glories in his transformations, and has more control over the metamorphoses than the first. Ravenous and savage attacks, much like the classical mad dog or the rabid human, are typical of both. The mass of the individual does not change, even though the shape does.

Both types apparently propagate by transmitting a transformational agent through the saliva while biting; thus even an unsuccessful attack is perilous.

WEREWOLF

In bestial form the werewolf is notoriously resistant to injury, regenerating 1 hit point every combat round. Scars and welts of such damage may remain after the ravener reassumes human form. Such healing is weakening, often forcing the shape-changer to spend days in bed. Werewolves are immune to most weapons, but they can be damaged or killed by fire or by silver weapons that impale. (Its fur set afire, the werewolf loses hit points faster than it can regenerate.)

Silver, the lunar metal, is poisonous to the werewolf. To determine damage, match the damage done by the silver weapon against the werewolf's CON on the Resistance Table. If overcome, the werewolf dies. If not overcome, the werewolf takes half the rolled damage and may not regenerate hit points so lost.

As humans, werewolves are outwardly normal, and have normal human characteristics. The Man-beast and Giant Wolf forms below share common attacks, armor, etc. The keeper may or may not charge a Sanity loss for the wolf form: if there is a Sanity loss, give the creature glowing eyes and other supernatural attributes to account for the perception in the mind of the character.

WEREWOLVES, Man-beast Humanoid Form

char.	rolls	averages
STR	6D6	21
CON	2D6+6	13
SIZ	3D6	10-11
INT	1D4+2	4-5
POW	2D6+6	13
DEX	2D6+6	13
Move 12		HP 12

Av. Damage Bonus: +1D4 or +1D6.

WEREWOLVES, Giant Wolf Form

char.	rolls	averages
STR	6D6	21
CON	2D6+6	13
SIZ	3D6+1D3	12-13
INT	1D4+2	4-5
POW	2D6+6	13
DEX	2D6+6	13
Move 13		HP 12-13

Av. Damage Bonus: +1D6.

Weapons: Werewolf Bite 30%, damage 1D8 + db
Infect 99%, if target's skin broken by Bite, the victim transforms into a werewolf at the next full moon

Armor: while in wolf or man-beast form, 1-point hide plus regeneration of 1 hit point per round.

Skills: Hide 60%, Track by Smell 90%.

Sanity Loss: 0/1D8 Sanity points to see a werewolf. 0/1D3 to see one change shape.

Habitat: wherever the full moon shines brightly.

WOLVES. They may hunt in packs when dogging herds of elk or caribou; they as often hunt singly or in family pairings. Wolves are normally shy, and verified attacks on healthy humans are said to be rare or nonexistent.

WOLVES

char.	rolls	averages
STR	2D6+6	13
CON	3D6	10-11
SIZ	2D6+1	8
POW	3D6	10-11
DEX	2D6+6	13
Move 12		HP 9-10

WOLF

Av. Damage Bonus: none.

Weapon: Bite 30%, damage 1D8.

Armor: 1-point fur.

Skills: Spot Hidden 60%, Track by Smell 80%.

Habitat: approximately the same ranges as larger cold and temperate climate ruminants and herbivores.

WRAITHS. This kind of wrathful, potent ghost seems to be created by overwhelming feelings of frustration and hate at the time of death.

Like ghosts, wraiths may haunt or guard specific locations, and like them have only INT and POW as characteristics. Each one should be carefully hand-crafted, always have some point of unique interest, and rarely should have POW of less than 13. Their INT may vary widely. Sanity loss to see a wraith is at least 1/1D8 Sanity points.

WRAITH

Wraiths live on the ethereal plane, and this gives them special powers and vulnerabilities. They are vulnerable to magic. Their POW acts like CON in dealing with magical attack. Some wraiths therefore have magic points, and if one loses all its magic points, it dissolves and cannot reform for at least a week. Others will not be able to reform at all, or be able to only at the cost of considerable Power. Others have no magic points, only POW, and in losing all POW are dispelled forever. No wraith negotiates, nor does one ever reveal its secrets. Leave that for ghosts.

No matter how the wraith is configured, the attack procedure is the same. First, match the wraith's POW against the target's CON on the Resistance Table. If the target loses, he or she loses 1D6-1 (0-5) points from STR, INT, or CON (from which depends upon the motive of the wraith). A victim reduced to zero in one of these characteristics either dies, is bed-ridden, or is a vegetable until the characteristic can be raised. These attacks may continue at the same level of damage until the target has lost all points in the characteristic, or until he or she manages to flee the room or other specific location.

If the target successfully resists, the wraith loses that amount of POW or magic points. If all magic points are lost, the thing is dispelled, perhaps permanently at the will of the keeper. A wraith never recovers lost characteristic points.

ZOMBIES. Though everyone knows what film zombies are like, not many stories have been written about these things. Zombies are almost immune to weapons which impale (including firearms), although such weapons will further damage the zombie's appearance. Any hit by an impaling weapon does 1 point damage to the creature's hit points. All other weapons do only half the damage rolled. A zombie literally must be hacked apart before it ceases to act. Setting one aflame also seems to be effective.

The spell creating the zombie supplies the point of POW motivating it. Each spell-caster directs what he or she creates: zombies have no wills of their own.

As the keeper wishes, a few spells and substances may deactivate these things. According to voodoo tradition, zombies could be destroyed by feeding them salt; their makers would first sew shut their mouths to guard against this. In addition to the voodoo tradition, we note also the notion in the Cthulhu Mythos of Resurrecting the dead (which, though, seem mostly in control of their faculties), and the new rationales that weird science or vile pollution might also create zombie-like things.

Since *Night of the Living Dead*, zombies are more eager to eat than to threaten; by the 1980s zombies were synonymous with the idea of cannibalism. The 1943 film *I Walked with a Zombie* remains the most evocative and interesting depiction of this terror.

ZOMBIES

characteristics	rolls	averages
STR	3D6 x1.5	15-17
CON	3D6 x1.5	15-17
SIZ	2D6+6	13
POW	1	1
DEX	2D6	7
Move 6		HP 14-15

Av. Damage Bonus: +1D4.

Weapon: Bite 30%, damage 1D3
Large Club 25%, damage 1D8 + 1 + db

Armor: none, but impaling weapons do 1 point of damage, and all others do half rolled damage.

Skills: Obey Command 99% or Pursue Human Flesh 99%.

Habitat: wherever created.

Sanity Loss: 1/1D8 Sanity points to see a zombie. ∎

"One might easily imagine an alien nucleus of substance or energy, formless or otherwise, kept alive by imperceptible or immaterial subtractions from the life-force or bodily tissues and fluids of other more palpably living things into which it penetrates and with whose fabric it sometimes completely merges."

—Lovecraft, "The Shunned House"

PERSONALITIES

Roleplaying versions of selected representative characters from Lovecraft's tales as models for new keepers and as resources and curiosities for all.

NOMINAL ages for these characters are those given or implied in the stories in which they appear. Some of the skills are intended as roleplaying notes for whomever uses them as non-player characters, and do not exist anywhere else.

Individuals who have other than zero damage bonuses are indicated by +*db*, not amount, to make clear the difference between weapon damage and damage bonus.

ARMITAGE, Dr. Henry. *In the end the three men from Arkham—old, white-bearded Dr. Armitage, stocky, iron-grey Professor Rice, and lean, youngish Dr. Morgan—ascended the mountain alone.*—H .P. Lovecraft, "The Dunwich Horror."

ARMITAGE, HENRY

After the library watchdog killed Wilbur Whateley while Whateley was attempting to steal the *Necronomicon*, Armitage learned some of the book's secrets. Accompanied by Rice and Morgan, Armitage traveled to Dunwich and there met and (with the aid of strange magicks) defeated Wilbur Whateley's terrible twin, the Son of Yog-Sothoth.

Dr. HENRY ARMITAGE, Age 73, Man of Letters and Librarian

STR 11	CON 8	SIZ 12	INT 18	POW 16
DEX 10	APP 13	EDU 24	SAN 55	HP 10

Damage Bonus: none.

Weapons: none.

Skills: Cryptography 75%, Cthulhu Mythos 18%, French 80%, German 70%, Greek 68%, History 65%, Latin 75%, Library Use 95%, Literature 75%, Occult 25%, Persuade 75%, Psychology 48%.

CARTER, Randolph. *He knew only that he wished to cross the barrier to the untrammelled land of his dreams and the gulfs where all dimensions dissolve in the absolute.*—H. P. Lovecraft, "Through the Gates of the Silver Key."

CARTER, OLD

He is the central character in several Lovecraft tales. Of independent means, Carter studied and wrote, and served with the French Foreign Legion during the Great War, but found no lasting satisfaction in the illusions of the waking world. Like Odysseus, he was a man never at a loss, and thereupon journeyed elsewhere. He disappeared from Arkham, returned and reported an astounding journey to a few friends, then disappeared again, perhaps forever.

RANDOLPH CARTER, Age 55 When Last Disappeared

STR 15	CON 17	SIZ 15	INT 18	POW 19
DEX 14	APP 15	EDU 21	SAN 50	HP 16

Damage Bonus: +1D4.

Weapons: .45 Revolver 60%, damage 1D10 + 2
Scimitar 75%, damage 1D8+1 + db

Skills: Appreciate Eccentric Artists 47%, Archaeology 14%, Chinese 25%, Colonial Architecture 59%, Credit Rating 60%, Cthulhu Mythos 10%, Deal With Publishers 15%, Dream Lore 70%, Dreaming 62%, English 90%, French 57%, History 48%, Library Use 55%, Love Old Books 79%, Military Tactics 35%, Navigate 65%, Persuade 55%, Philosophy 88%, Psychology 70%, Ride Unusual Mount 45%, Speak Cat 35%, Speak Zoog 20%, Yaddithian Lore 77%.

Magic Items: large silver key, Hyperborean scroll.

CURWEN, Joseph. *The subject* [of the painting] *was a spare, well-shaped man . . . with a thin, calm, undistinguished face which seemed somehow familiar to both Ward and the artist.*—H. P. Lovecraft, "The Case of Charles Dexter Ward."

CURWEN, JOSEPH

Dead at the hands of his 18th-century neighbors, the sorcerer Curwen left clues and magical suggestions which led great-great-great-grandson Charles Dexter Ward to resurrect his ancestor. Returned to life, Curwen soon found Ward "too squeamish", and slew him. Curwen in turn was returned to blue dust in 1928, when Dr. Marinus Bicknell Willet, realizing that Curwen had taken Ward's place, reversed Curwen's Resurrection spell.

JOSEPH CURWEN, Appears as Age 26, Cruel Sorcerer

STR 12	CON 14	SIZ 10	INT 19	POW 20
DEX 14	APP 11	EDU 21	SAN 0	HP 12

Damage Bonus: none.

Weapons: Dagger 35%, damage 1D4
Flintlock Pistol 70%, damage 1D6 + 1

Spells: Enchant Painting, Journey to the Other Side, Resurrection, Steal Life, Voice of Ra, Voorish Sign.

Skills: Accounting 15%, Alchemy 40%, Anthropology 30%, Astrology 55%, Bargain 80%, Blackmail 80%, Chemistry 10%, Conceal 60%, Credit Rating (as Ward) 70%, Cthulhu Mythos 29%, Fast Talk 65%, Greek 45%, Hebrew 48%, Hide 45%, History 67%, Interrogate 75%, Lack Mercy 90%, Latin 58%, Library Use 55%, Occult 50%, Persuade 45%, Pharmacy 20%, Psychology 70%, Sneak 35%, Torture 75%.

DE LA POER, The Last. *The rats continued their riot, stampeding with such force and distinctness that I could finally assign to their motions a definite direction. These crea-*

tures . . . were engaged in one stupendous migration from inconceivable heights to some depth conceivably, or inconceivably, below.—H. P. Lovecraft, "The Rats in the Walls."

Returning to his ancient family seat, the narrator unwittingly awakens the horrible taint in his blood. The last de la Poer, never given a first name but reassuming the ancient form of his family name, devolves from retired business-man to blood-hungry madman. The rats in the walls of Exham Priory, migrating hungrily to the horrible caverns below and with which he maintains a horrify-ing rapport, lead de la Poer to murder and insanity.

DE LA POER, LAST

DE LA POER, About Age 65, Last of the Line

STR 12	CON 11	SIZ 11	INT 15	POW 14
DEX 12	APP 10	EDU 16	SAN 0	HP 11

Damage Bonus: none.

Weapon: Hysterically Claw & Chew 35%, damage 1D4

Skills: Accounting 45%, Bargain 70%, Credit Rating 75%, Hear Rats 85%, History 40%, Listen 40%, Local Tales 55%, Love Cats 90%, Make Profits 85%, Psychology 40%, Spot Hidden 55%.

DERBY, Edward Pickman. *Blond and blue-eyed, he had the fresh complexion of a child; and his attempts to raise a moustache were discernible only with difficulty. His voice was soft and light, and his pampered, unexercised life gave him a juvenile chubbiness rather than the paunchiness of pre-mature middle age. He was of good height, and his handsome face would have made him a notable gallant had not his shy-ness held to seclusion and bookish-ness.—H. P. Lovecraft, "The Thing on the Doorstep."*

Weak-willed and dreamy, Derby was an easy target for Asenath Waite, who married him planning to exchange minds with him. Inside the shell of Asenath lurked the mind of sorcerer Ephraim Waite, her father. But Derby took revenge from within this perverse menage when he rose from the dead, quickening for a while after being in-stalled in Asenath's putrescent remains by the sorcerer.

DERBY, EDWARD

EDWARD PICKMAN DERBY, Age 38, Poet and Dilettante

STR 11	CON 10	SIZ 12	INT 16	POW 8
DEX 11	APP 13	EDU 16	SAN 15	HP 11

Damage Bonus: +0.

Weapons: none

Skills: Avoid Responsibility 35%, Craft Poem 85%, Credit Rating 75%, Cthulhu Mythos 33%, Debate Literature 60%, Drive Automobile 0%, History 45%, Imagine 90%, Know Arkham 95%, Library Use 65%, Occult 65%, Oratory 75%, Speculate 90%, Turn Away From Reality 40%.

LEGRASSE, Inspector. *It must not be fancied that Inspector Legrasse had the least interest in archaeology. On the con-*

trary, his wish for enlightenment was prompted by purely professional consid-erations. The statuette . . . had been cap-tured some months before in the wooded swamps . . . so singular and hideous were the rites connected that the police could not but realise that they had stumbled on a dark cult.—H. P. Lovecraft, "The Call of Cthulhu."

Legrasse's men broke up a large cultist gathering south of New Orleans. His subsequent interrogations best sum-marize the goals of those who worship the Great Old Ones.

LEGRASSE, JOHN

JOHN RAYMOND LEGRASSE, Age 40, Police Inspector

STR 12	CON 14	SIZ 11	INT 14	POW 15
DEX 13	APP 11	EDU 17	SAN 70	HP 13

Damage Bonus: none.

Weapons: .38 Revolver 45%, damage 1D10

Skills: Climb 35%, Credit Rating 30%, Cthulhu Mythos 2%, Dodge 34%, English 72%, French 44%, Grill Suspect 85%, History 27%, Law 35%, Library Use 31%, Listen 80%, Oratory 15%, Persist 70%, Photography 22%, Psychology 70%, Ride 45%, Sneak 39%, Spanish 18%, Spot Hidden 59%, Track 40%.

MALONE, Thomas F. *In youth he had felt the hidden beauty and ecstasy of things, and he had been a poet; but poverty and sorrow and exile had turned his gaze in darker directions, and he had thrilled at the imputations of evil in the world around.—H. P. Lovecraft, "The Horror at Red Hook."*

Malone is described as "large, robust, normal-featured, and capable-looking." A graduate of Dublin Univer-sity, he was as well equipped for the supernatural as any detective has a right to be, and yet he was overwhelmed immediately.

MALONE, THOMAS

THOMAS F. MALONE, Age 42, Police Detective

STR 14	CON 15	SIZ 15	INT 15	POW 14
DEX 11	APP 11	EDU 16	SAN 58	HP 15

Damage Bonus: +1D4.

Weapons: Fist/Punch 65%, damage 1D3 + db
Nightstick 38%, damage 1D6 + db
.38 Revolver 70%, damage 1D10

Skills: Bargain 65%, Climb 55%, Credit Rating 35%, Dodge 36%, Drive Automobile 35%, Fast Talk 70%, Greek 20%, Hebrew 8%, History 30%, Jump 50%, Know New York Streets 85%, Latin 38%, Law 40%, Library Use 55%, Listen 55%, Occult 16%, Persuade 20%, Psychology 60%, Sneak 25%, Throw 45%.

MASON, Keziah. *Old Keziah, he reflected, might have had excellent reasons for living in a room with peculiar angles; for was it not through certain angles that she claimed to have gone outside the boundaries of the world of space we know?—H. P. Lovecraft, "The Dreams in the Witch House."*

A woman of admitted evil in the era of the witch trials, Keziah Mason escaped retribution by fleeing to another dimension. Her anchor in this space-time appears to have been her Arkham home, known in later centuries as the Witch House. There Walter Gilman studied her reappearances and influences, and there Brown Jenkin gnawed out Gilman's heart.

KEZIAH MASON, Immortal Witch

STR 14	CON 15	SIZ 10	INT 21	POW 23
DEX 14	APP 8	EDU 25	SAN 0	HP 13

Damage Bonus: +1D4.

Weapons: Butcher Knife 65%, damage 1D6 + db

Spells: Contact Nyarlathotep*, Create Gate**, Dread Curse of Azathoth, Enchant Pipes, Shrivelling, Summon/Bind Hunting Horror, Summon/Bind Servitor of the Outer Gods, Voorish Sign.

MASON, KEZIAH

*This special relation is seemingly at will and without cost of magic points; the form contacted is that of the Black Man.

**The witch has a special grasp of Create Gate, and seems to be able to drag victims into other space-times against their will.

Skills: Astronomy 35%, Cthulhu Mythos 81%, Estimate Gate 80%, Fast Talk 70%, Hide 65%, History 40%, Kidnap 65%, Occult 65%, Organize Cult 80%, Persuade 85%, Pharmacy 70%, Poisons 70%, Psychology 50%, Sneak 30%.

Sanity Loss: 0/1D4 Sanity points to see Keziah Mason.

BROWN JENKIN, Keziah's Immortal Rat-Thing Familiar

STR 3	CON 5	SIZ 3	INT 14	POW 12
DEX 18*	EDU 3	SAN 0	Move 9	HP 4

*has four tiny human hands in place of paws.

Damage Bonus: -1D6.

Weapon: Bite 80%, damage 1D2

Skills: Gnaw 65%, Hide 85%, Listen 70%, Scuttle 75%.

Sanity Loss: 0/1D4 Sanity points to see Brown Jenkin.

PICKMAN, Richard Upton. [He] *was shewing what happens to those stolen babes—how they grow up—and then I began to see a hideous relationship in the faces of the human and nonhuman figures. He was, in all his gradations of morbidity between the frankly non-human and the degradedly human, estab-lishing a sardonic linkage and evolution. The dog-things were developed from mor-tals!*—H. P. Lovecraft, "Pickman's Model."

PICKMAN, RICHARD

The force of Pickman's canvases apparently depended as much upon the depiction of human hypocrisy as upon revealing the physical evolution of human into ghoul.

RICHARD U. PICKMAN, Age 43, Artist of the Macabre

STR 13	CON 17	SIZ 12	INT 18	POW 18
DEX 18	APP 11	EDU 16	SAN 15	HP 15

Damage Bonus: +1D4.

Weapon: .45 Revolver 55%, damage 1D10 + 2

Skills: Art (Oil Painting) 90%, Brush Technique 96%, Colonial Architecture 30%, Cthulhu Mythos 12%, Fast Talk 55%, Jump 50%, Latin 25%, Morbid Renderings 99%, Photography 25%, Psychology 90%.

SON OF YOG-SOTHOTH. *It was mostly a kind of force that doesn't belong in our part of space; a kind of force that acts and grows and shapes itself by other laws than those of our sort of Nature.*—H. P. Lovecraft, "The Dunwich Horror."

THE SON

This is Wilbur Whateley's fraternal twin, "who looked more like his father" than Wilbur did: "red eyes an' crinkly albino hair, and no chin, like the Whateleys . . . . It was a octopus, a spi-der kind o' thing, but they was a haff-shaped man's face on top of it, an' it looked like wizard Whateley's, only it was yards an' yards acrost." It was invisible and could be seen only with the aid of the Powder of Ibn-Ghazi.

SON OF YOG-SOTHOTH, Age 15

STR 35	CON 30	SIZ 50	INT 21	POW 24
DEX 21	Move 9			HP 40

Damage Bonus: +2D6.

Weapon: Grasp and Suck 100%, damage 1D6 hit points lost to crushing every round, plus loss of 1D10 hit points of blood drain every round after the first.

Armor: none, but cannot be harmed by physical weapons. Enchanted weapons do minimum damage. The creature is sus-ceptible to magic. It is invisible except when feeding.

Spells: Call Yog-Sothoth, Death Spell, Implant Fear, Stop Heart, Voorish Sign.

Sanity Loss: when invisible, 1/1D8 Sanity points; when visible, 1D8/3D10 Sanity points; conceivably players may need to roll twice.

WAITE, Asenath. *She was dark, smallish, and very good-looking except for overprotuberant eyes; but something in her expression alienated extremely sensitive people . . . . One of the Innsmouth Waites, and dark legends have clustered for generations about crumbling, half-deserted Innsmouth and its people.*—H. P. Lovecraft, "The Thing on the Doorstep."

WAITE, ASENATH

To preserve himself, sorcerer Ephraim Waite transferred his mind into that of his daughter, Asenath, but that effected he still desired the male brain's "unique and far-reaching cosmic pow-ers." Fearing for his life, Edward Derby murdered Asenath, but Ephraim ensor-celed Derby from beyond the grave.

ASENATH WAITE, Age About 23 [soul/mind of Ephraim Waite]

STR 12	CON 14	SIZ 10	INT 18	POW 18
DEX 13	APP 13	EDU 23	SAN 0	HP 12

Damage Bonus: none.

Weapons: Fist/Punch 60%, damage 1D3
Head Butt 50%, damage 1D4
Grapple 35%, damage special
Dagger 45%, damage 1D4 + 2

Spells: Alter Weather, Curse of Azathoth, Mind Exchange, Mists of R'lyeh, Wither Limb, and any six Call and Contact spells.

Skills: Arabic 60%, Cthulhu Mythos 72%, Drive Automobile 70%, Library Use 70%, Occult 55%, Swim 85%.

WEST, Dr. Herbert. *West was then a small, slender, spectacled youth with delicate features, yellow hair, pale blue eyes, and a soft voice . . . only an occasional flash of a cold blue eye. . . [told] of the hardening and growing fanaticism of his character under the pressure of his terrible investigations.—*H. P. Lovecraft, "Herbert West—Reanimator."

West obsessively reanimated dead tissue for some twenty years, but with no thorough-going success. Some of his partial successes at last hunted him down and slew him.

Dr. HERBERT WEST, M.D., At Age 30, Experimenter

STR 11	CON 13	SIZ 9	INT 18	POW 18
DEX 15	APP 12	EDU 23	SAN 10	HP 11

Damage Bonus: none.

Weapons: Scalpel 90%, damage 1D4
Hypodermic Syringe 80%, damage negligible*
*impale result enters vital organ or releases POT 16 poison.

Skills: Anatomy 80%, Bargain 75%, Chemistry 65%, Credit Rating 40%, Dodge 55%, Electrical Repair 55%, Fast Talk 50%, First Aid 65%, Hide 40%, Library Use 60%, Listen 5%, Make Plausible Excuse 60%, Mechanical Repair 45%, Medicine 79%, Pharmacy 60%, Photography 20%, Select Best Nervous System 55%, Sneak 39%, Spot Hidden 70%, Track 18%.

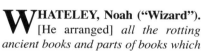

WEST, HERBERT

WHATELEY, Noah ("Wizard"). [He arranged] *all the rotting ancient books and parts of books which* 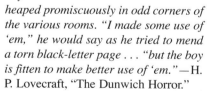 *during his own day had been heaped promiscuously in odd corners of the various rooms. "I made some use of 'em," he would say as he tried to mend a torn black-letter page . . . "but the boy is fitten to make better use of 'em."—*H. P. Lovecraft, "The Dunwich Horror."

Keenly intelligent, the self-taught sorcerer promoted the impregnation of his wife by Yog-Sothoth. She subsequently bore fraternal twins, Wilbur and the Son of Yog-Sothoth, who carried on Noah's work.

WHATELEY, NOAH

WIZARD (Noah) WHATELEY, Age 72, Sorcerer

STR 10	CON 11	SIZ 12	INT 18	POW 13
DEX 9	APP 8	EDU 7	SAN 0	HP 12

Damage Bonus: none.

Weapon: Staff 80%, damage 1D8 + 1

Spells: Alter Weather, Augur, Blight/Bless Crop, Call Horned Man*, Call Yog-Sothoth, Cause/Cure Blindness, Contact

Nyarlathotep, Death Spell, Dread Curse of Azathoth, Evil Eye, Implant Fear, Lame/Heal Animal, Shrivelling, Stop Heart, Summon/Bind Byakhee, Summon/Bind Star Vampire, Voorish Sign, Warding.

*A summary of this spell exists in *Return to Dunwich.*

Skills: Cthulhu Mythos 22%, Drive Sleigh 65%, First Aid 25%, History 15%, Library Use 10%, Occult 25%, Persuade 25%.

WHATELEY, Wilbur. *Though he shared his mother's, and grandfather's chinlessness, his firm and precociously shaped nose united with the expression of his large, dark, almost Latin eyes to give him an air of quasi-adulthood and well-nigh preternatural intelligence.—*H. P. Lovecraft, "The Dunwich Horror."

WHATELEY, WILBUR

Whateley and his ghastly twin intended to open the way for Yog-Sothoth and other gods, but Wilbur, the human-looking twin, was mauled to death in the Miskatonic University library by a watchdog. Wilbur had broken in at night to steal the *Necronomicon.* This episode alerted Dr. Armitage to the danger facing mankind.

WILBUR WHATELEY, age 15, Eager Pupil

STR 17	CON 18	SIZ 21	INT 21	POW 20
DEX 14	APP 7	EDU 15	SAN 0	HP 20

Damage Bonus: +1D6.

Weapons: Fist/Punch 65%, damage 1D3 + db
Kick 45%, damage 1D4 + db
Head Butt 55%, damage 1D4 + db
.45 Revolver 30%, damage 1D10 + 2

Spells: Augur, Blight/Bless Crop, Call Yog-Sothoth, Cause/Cure Blindness, Contact Nyarlathotep, Create Gate, Death Spell, Evil Eye, Implant Fear, Lame/Heal Animal, Powder of Ibn-Ghazi, Stop Heart, Summon/Bind Byakhee, Summon/Bind Star Vampire, Voorish Sign, Warding, Wither Limb.

Skills: Aklo 65%, Arabic 25%, Astronomy 25%, Climb 65%, Cthulhu Mythos 38%, Dodge 55%, Drive Wagon 55%, English 75%, Greek 45%, Hide 55%, History 35%, Jump 65%, Latin 65%, Library Use 25%, Listen 90%, Occult 45%, Psychology 45%, Sneak 45%, Spot Hidden 75%.

Sanity Loss: meeting the clothed Wilbur costs 0/1 Sanity points; meeting Wilbur naked costs 1/1D8 Sanity points since his body is hideous and alien.

ZANN, Erich. *He was a small, lean, bent person, with shabby clothes, blue eyes, grotesque, satyr-like face, and nearly bald head.—*H. P. Lovecraft, "The Music of Erich Zann."

An unnamed but inhumanly-great musician, perhaps an Outer God, pursued the man. Poor Zann died of fear and kept on playing.

ZANN, ERICH, About Age 60, Violist

STR 14	CON 10	SIZ 9	INT 14	POW 13
DEX 18	APP 9	EDU 10	SAN 15	HP 10

Damage Bonus: none.

Weapon: none.

Skills: Know Music 93%, Listen 90%, Play Viol 99%, Spot Hidden 0%, Write French 11%, Write German 63%, Write Music 99%. ∎

A MYTHOS GRIMOIRE

Spells alphabetized for keeper delectation and player dismay, scour'd from Divers Books of dire adventures in print still or now Rare and Collectable.

Precursor Mythos tales by Chambers, Machen, and Blackwood are some five generations since publication. Lovecraft fell silent more than sixty years ago. Since then have come new wizards of words, among them the writers and keepers of *Call of Cthulhu* adventures. These latter have created much, including here more than two hundred spells for use in the game. Spells make interesting browsing and can become useful models for keeper projects. These have been evaluated in play many times.

As always, keepers are not obliged to recognize any ensorcelment or incantation which has not become manifest in the course of play. Spells are a province of the keeper, not the players. Most spells are intended to be cast by evildoers, cultists, and madmen.

A handful of spells are the product of independent magical tradition—human tribal knowledge, the arcana of the Serpent People, the fathomless rationality of the Great Race, individual research, etc. A few spells have no Sanity point cost.

Spells are arranged in a single alphabetical list. Cross-references indicate a couple of spell name changes.

Five types of spells—Call/Dismiss Deity, Contact, Contact Deity, Enchantment, and Summon/Bind Servitor—form subclasses which include several or many spells. The rationales for some of these spells have been regularized for this edition. Enchantments include what were known as "artifacts"—permanent enchantments for which no spell of creation is known. The four that exist in this grimoire (Glass from Leng, Lamp of Alhazred, Plutonian Drug, Shining Trapezohedron) are mentioned under Enchantments, but are alphabetized individually in the general spell list.

The Spells

ALTER WEATHER: moderates or exacerbates any weather condition. Large groups may cast the spell to achieve great meteorological effects. The keeper establishes the base conditions. Every ten magic points sacrificed effects one level of change (see further below). The caster may expend as many magic points as he or she is able, as can any participant who knows the spell. Those ignorant of the spell can contribute 1 magic point only.

Casting the spell costs every participant 1 current Sanity point, and requires a song-like chant to be uttered for three minutes per level of weather change. The effective radius of the base spell is two miles; this area can be widened for a cost of ten magic points for each additional mile. The change in the weather lasts thirty minutes for every ten magic points of the total contributed, but violent weather such as a tornado lasts a much shorter time.

Five weather components can be changed, in varying levels of effect. One level costs 10 magic points to change: thus to change the two levels from *partly cloudy* to *heavy clouds* takes 20 magic points to change. For snow to fall, the temperature must be 30°F or lower, otherwise the precipitation is rain, not snow.

Cloud Cover Levels: (1) clear, (2) foggy, (3) partly cloudy, (4) cloudy, (5) heavy clouds.

Wind Direction Levels, the eight compass points: (1) north, (2) northeast, (3) east, (4) southeast, (5) south, (6) southwest, (7) west, (8) northwest.

Wind Speed Levels: (1) calm, (2) breezy, (3) gusty, (4) strong steady wind, (5) gale, (6) local hurricane, (7) tornado.

Temperature Levels: one level raises or lowers the temperature in the area of effect by five degrees Fahrenheit.

Precipitation Levels: (1) dry, (2) drizzle or mist, (3) rain [snow], (4) hail [snow], (5) heavy rain [heavy snow], (6) thunderstorm [blizzard].

APPORTION KA: the caster can place a portion of his life essence, or ka, into one or more of his vital organs. This done, the wizard can then remove the enchanted organ from his or her body. The organ continues to live and sustain the caster's identity. Having one's own insides removed costs 2D10 SAN and the permanent loss of 1 POW per organ removed.

This spell was first used by followers of the Dark Pharaoh, Nephren-Ka, who would remove vital organs and lock them away in safe places. This would make the caster virtually impossible to kill, if not for the spell's one weakness. The brain is the seat of the spell's power and, as such, could not be removed. If the brain was destroyed the other organs would lose their magical properties and the caster would die. (Other spells no doubt supplied the priests with means for seeing, touching, and so on.)

The priests of Nephren-Ka could not transplant themselves into other people. With transplant technology, today's sorcerer can. Even while disembodied, the caster is able to sense where the other parts are, and subtly guide the bodies toward each other. When two bodies are as close as a block or two, the caster regains full consciousness, with access to all memories, knowledge, and spells. The caster also takes command of these proximal bodies, and they all become of one mind. POW is his or her own, but the magic points are the sum of those he or she controls as well as owns. His or her own magic points regenerate, but the rest are one-time use only, and only as long as the caster maintains sway.

ATTRACT FISH: a fisherman's aid, to be cast over salt or fresh water. The cost is 2 magic points and no Sanity. Bait must be placed in the water and a simple sing-song chant uttered for two minutes. In 1D6 minutes, D100 local fish congregate in the area.

AUGUR: grants portents of the future if the caster is clever enough to understand them. Augur costs 4 magic points and 1D2 SAN to cast. Media varies, from animal entrails to tea leaves to the casting of stalks. The chance of understanding an augury is equal to or less than the augurer's POW x5. A portent may be vague, subtle, dream-like, or in a cryptic verse; if the future were easy to know, everyone would know it.

AWAKE ABHOTH: this spell wakens the sleeping god Abhoth to begin the great feast for which it waits and hungers. The spell costs 12 magic points, 1D10+2 Sanity points, and long rituals that prove the caster's faithfulness to the god.

BAIT HUMANS: causes the image of a fabulously large and beautifully cut diamond to float in the air before the target. The spell costs the caster 1 magic point per casting, lasts for five minutes, and can be repeated indefinitely. Approximate range of the spell is one mile. As a target approaches the illusion, the diamond recedes at approximately the same speed, in the direction the caster wills, presumably to where the hungry chthonian waits. As in sport fishing, the target decides whether or not to take the bait. Only chthonians have this spell. A variation, Bait Sand Dwellers, exchanges the image of a floating diamond for that of a tender human haunch, dripping flesh blood.

BALK BROOD: calls forth the Brood of Eihort from a victim. The spell requires three rounds to intone and costs 1D3 Sanity points per participant. The caster and other people who know the spell can expend as many magic points as desired. Those who touch the caster while the spell is intoned can add 1 magic point per person, though the Sanity cost remains at 1D3 points each. Learning the spell requires a roll of INT x2 or less on D100 and 15-INT days of study.

Using the Resistance Table, match the total of the magic points expended against the number of days elapsed since the injection of the Brood. If the spell succeeds, the Brood infesting the victim promptly cascade out of the victim's orifices, costing him or her 1D3 Sanity points for pain and embarrassment.

Spells Likely to Be Imparted

Particular sorts of alien entities are more likely to teach particular spells to worshipers.

From an Outer God—Call/Dismiss Azathoth, Call/Dismiss Shub-Niggurath, Call/Dismiss Yog-Sothoth, Contact Nyarlathotep, Create Gate, Dread Curse of Azathoth, Powder of Ibn-Ghazi, Shrivelling, Summon/Bind Dark Young, Summon/Bind Hunting Horror, Summon/Bind Servitor of the Outer Gods, Voorish Sign.

From an Elder God—Brew Space-Mead, Contact Nodens, Elder Sign, Summon/Bind Nightgaunt.

From a Great Old One or via a Servitor Race—Brew Space-Mead, Call/Dismiss Cthugha, Call/Dismiss Hastur, Call/Dismiss Ithaqua, Call/Dismiss Nyogtha, Contact Deep One, Contact Deity / Cthulhu, Contact Deity / Tsathoggua, Contact Deity / Yig, Contact Ghoul, Contact Mi-Go, Contact Star-Spawn of Cthulhu, Create Gate, Summon/Bind Byakhee, Summon/Bind Fire Vampire.

From an Independent Race—Contact Chthonian, Contact Deep Ones, Contact Ghoul, Contact Mi-Go, Contact Sand-Dweller, Contact Star-Spawn of Cthulhu.

The victim also loses 1 hit point for each day of infestation. The infestation may already have caused the victim great harm, which their presence keeps from being obvious. Removing the Brood actually may kill the victim, but he or she is doomed in any case.

At each casting of this spell, the participants risk the appearance of Eihort: the chance accumulates at 10 percentiles per cast. Eihort will attack the caster first.

BANEFUL DUST OF HERMES TRISMEGISTUS: similar to the Dust of Suleiman, it only affects creatures of nonterrestrial origin (that excludes humans, deep ones, ghouls, servants of Glaaki, sand dwellers, serpent people, and chthonians, but not flying polyps, elder things, mi-go, star-spawn of Cthulhu, or shoggoths). It costs 4 magic points and no Sanity to cast the creation spell; thereafter anyone may use the gold-colored dust created. Only the most fearsome entities continue to fight after an application of this powerful dust.

To apply the dust requires that the target be within reasonable Throw range. With a successful Throw roll, the dust burns the extraterrestrial creature for 2D6 points of damage. Armor does not protect against the dust. Each successful Throw of the dust does the same damage. If Thrown and missed, the nimbus of the dust still does 1 hit point of damage. The creature escapes damage only if the Throw roll is fumbled.

The dust's effects are horrible, and cost sensitive observers 0/1D3 Sanity points to see. The creature flinches and flails, and sometimes screams. Its body smokes and burns as if eaten by powerful acid.

The formula for the dust requires common chemicals and ingredients in a proportion of combined weight about equal to two pounds. Two ounces of this concoction is enough for one dose. Sixteen doses would be made each time the formula is followed. A successful Chemistry or Pharmacy roll is required for a batch to work; the keeper should make this roll, for the caster should have no idea if a batch will be effective.

BANISHMENT OF YDE ETAD: It sends home most transdimensional human or human-like intelligences that are under their own volition. It is not effective against servitors, hirelings, thralls, or any creature commanded by another intelligence. Correctly performed, the banishment is permanent and irrevocable. Each banishment is of an individual, not of a class.

At least three people must participate in the spell. All participants must know the spell. More participants add to the effectiveness. The total number of participants must be divisible by three. Each participant donates 1D4+3 magic points and loses 1D4 Sanity points. Learning this spell requires twelve hours of time, a roll of INT x4 or less, and 1D3 Sanity points.

This banishment works by destroying with ritual flames a sigil representing the target. The target's personal sigil is best, but a substitute can be prepared according to a formula described with the spell.

The spell must be performed in the open air in the middle of the night, ideally in a place of power associated with the subject. The target's known haunts, its last known location, or its point of entry into this dimension are all suitable sites. The spell casters must divide their numbers: one third remain outside a protective circle and the rest stand within.

Using a mixture of ground silicon dioxide, lime, or magnesium silicate, combined with dried and ground henbane or garlic, the larger group of spell casters inscribes a circle on the ground around them, one large enough to accommodate the group as well as leaving room for a fire in the center. As the circle is made, the casters must recite a complicated verse. Then more of the compound is used to trace a series of complicated symbols, accompanied at all times by the chanting of verses read aloud or declaimed from memory.

The spell casters outside the circle then trace a second larger circle of the compound, surrounding all. The casters in the central circle place their personal sigils (a sigil can be a handwritten signature, or something equally characteristic) at evenly spaced intervals around the inside perimeter of the inner circle. As the sigil is placed, that participant must speak his or her name aloud to the heavens. These personal sigils must remain in place until the ritual is completed. The protective circles complete, the casters in the inner circle build a ritual fire upon a grate suspended two to six inches above the ground. The fire must be of moderate size, with plainly visible flame. As the ritual fire is lit, all casters repeat yet another complicated verse. The fire must burn steadily from this time until the sigil is utterly consumed. If the fire flags or dies, the banishment fails, so the inner circle also must contain plenty of fuel.

Once the fire is burning steadily, the casters within the inner circle throw locks of their own hair and nail clippings into the flames, accompanied by more chanting. As the smoke rises from the clippings, the casters within the inner circle place the sigil of the intended target on the fire so that it is clearly visible to all the spell casters, and it must remain visible until utterly consumed. At that point the image of the thing to be banished appears, howls in fiery agony, and gradually returns to its own plane of existence. As it burns, the casters within the circle repeat a final verse, then remain silent until the fire dies, an additional 3D10 game minutes. The casters then may destroy the circles and freely move about.

BAT FORM: lets the caster assume the form and capabilities of a flying fox, while retaining his or her intelligence and intentions. The spell costs 12 magic points to cast; assuming the form of a bat costs 1D8 Sanity points. The spell must be cast while the sun is down, and its effects last only until the sun rises. Capabilities of a bat include those of flight and of acute hearing.

BECOME SPECTRAL HUNTER: turns the target into a monster which can attack while invisible. The spell requires 2 POW from the caster (who also may be the recipient), a small specially made figurine, the blood of several animals, and the loss of all Sanity points by the target of the spell. The target must be a knowledgeable volunteer. If the caster is not also the recipient, he or she loses 3D6 Sanity points in performing the ritual. The target transforms into a spectral hunter, a hideous humanoid described in the 1982 supplement *Shadows of Yog-Sothoth*. The new spectral hunter is psychically linked to the figurine which holds its soul. If this figurine is destroyed, the spectral hunter is injured or killed.

BIND ENEMY: either by physical attack or magical attack, the spell renders the target unable to harm the caster for the next seven days. A variable number of magic points are sacrificed into a small effigy of the target, and then matched against the target's POW on the Resistance Table. If the target wins, the spell fails. No Sanity points are expended. It takes about a day to gather the materials, construct the effigy, and chant the ritual that seals the magic points into the effigy.

The effigy must contain a few hairs or nail clippings from the target, or something else of a personal nature. The spell is broken if the caster attacks the target or if the effigy is destroyed.

BIND LOUP-GAROU (Cage of Kind): removes a werecreature's desire to control his or her shape-changing, quickly condemning him or her to the life of whatever animal the character's animal alternate is. Bind Loup-Garou needs 14 magic points per targeted loup-garou. It consumes 2D4 Sanity points per ceremony, no matter how many loups-garous are involved. A loup-garou so bound sheds its human side in a number of game days equal to its POW.

Once the spell is cast, the target loup-garou steadily loses his or her ability to choose when to shape-change. More and more he or she becomes the animal alternate when primal emotions such as rage, fear, lust, or hunger become strong. The shape-change is more and more triggered, and not a choice. The effect strengthens over time. After 1/2 POW days, the target spends half its time in its animal form. After POW days, the human side is utterly unattractive and tedious. The loup-garou then lives out the remainder of its life as an animal in the wild.

To perform this spell, the caster needs a bowl of solid silver or gold. The bowl must be inscribed with the incantations of the spell on its inner surface. The caster must also carve a circular talisman into the surface of the area where the spell is to be cast. Six candles are placed and lit clockwise around this talisman. Once the candles are lit, the caster may not leave the circle, or he or she must repeat the ceremony from the beginning.

At least six drops of uncoagulated human blood must be added to the bowl. To target an individual, place some of his or her body hair, fingernail clippings, personal possessions, etc., in the bowl. More than one person may be targeted at a time. Incantations must be chanted without interruption for an hour. If all goes well, the bowl briefly glows and the spell begins its work.

After the spell is cast, the targeted loup-garou experiences growing fears and desires based on the need of its animal side. For instance, if the loup-garou is half mountain lion, then while on the human side the loup-garou becomes increasingly aloof, predatory, and territorial with rivals. The affected loup-garou loses no Sanity unless it understands what has happened to it; then the Sanity loss is 1D3+1 SAN per day, until POW days have passed. Then it loses all remaining SAN and as a human is permanently insane.

BIND SOUL: allows the caster to imprison a human soul and thereby control or murder the body from which the soul came. Cost to cast the spell is 10 magic points and 3 Sanity points. The caster must be able to find the soul before it can be imprisoned; see Snare Dreamer for one way to achieve that. See Compel Flesh for a way to control the body.

The caster must defeat the target soul by matching POW vs. POW on the Resistance Table. If the soul is trapped, the victim's body begins to die, at the rate of 2 CON per day. When CON reaches zero, the body dies and the soul is released. If the soul is not trapped, the magic points and Sanity points are lost without effect.

A special vessel for the soul must have been prepared. That ritual takes three days. Anything that can be closed (a jar, a box, a bottle, etc.) will do as a vessel. The soul can be released by opening or breaking the vessel, if the vessel can be found. The powder of Ibn-Ghazi and similar magic can trace the link between body and soul: the location of the vessel can be calculated by triangulation or by expending considerable powder and simply following the spider-web-like link left tangible by the powder.

BLACK BINDING: offers a way to create an ordinary zombie, at a cost of 16 magic points and 1D6 Sanity points. A ritual liquid must be poured over a corpse, or into the grave in which a corpse lies. The keeper determines the ingredients of the liquid: at least one part should be difficult to obtain legally. The corpse is left to mature. At the end of a week, the caster comes to the grave and intones the Black Binding. At the end of the half-hour ritual, the corpse claws its way from the grave, and thereafter does the caster's will. A zombie made this way continues to rot after it has risen. A replacement must be created periodically.

BLESS BLADE: creates a blade capable of damaging or killing entities which cannot be harmed by ordinary weapons. Requires the blood sacrifice of an animal of at least SIZ 10, a point of POW, and 1D4 Sanity points from the creator. The blade of the knife must be of an elemental metal such as iron or silver. The blade may be of any size, but larger blades do greater damage; see the weapons table (p. 58) for sample damages. If the blade is broken, melted, or otherwise damaged, it permanently loses this ability, but it will not be harmed in attacks against supernatural entities.

BLIGHT / BLESS CROP: as the caster chooses, the spell causes one acre of vegetation to wither and die slowly, as if parched, or to blossom and grow with vigor. The spell in either version costs 6 magic points and as Blight Crop an additional 1D6 SAN to cast. "Blooding" the caster (striking the face hard enough to draw blood) breaks the spell.

BODY WARPING OF GORGOROTH: allows the caster to change his or her physical form. The caster must invoke Nyarlathotep and repeat the phrases of the spell for 1D6+4 minutes while expending 6 magic points and an additional magic point for each point of SIZ to be gained or lost in the body warping. This spell also costs 2D6 Sanity points and 1 point of POW each time cast. Only one alteration per casting is possible, and the effect is permanent until the spell is recast to change back again. This spell cannot be cast on another being.

The sorcerer can change to any shape and appearance, though retaining personal abilities. The form must be fleshly, thought it can appear to be of stone, wood, a rug, etc. Once changed into a new shape, the caster has the mobility of that shape. The caster's STR, CON, INT, POW, and DEX never change. If emulating a person, the sorcerer's APP becomes that of the individual emulated. The caster can take on only the form of what he knows.

BREATH OF THE DEEP: his or her lungs fill with sea water, drowning the target. The caster must be able to see the target. After mentally intoning the spell for a round, the caster sacrifices 8 magic points and 1D6 Sanity. Match POWs on the Resistance Table. If the caster wins, consult the drowning rules in the Game System chapter. D100 rolls begin at CON x5, then CON x4, etc., and the target must make them for 1D6 rounds. Each missed CON roll costs the target 1D8 hit points.

BREW DREAM DRUG: creates a drug which facilitates group entry into a world of dream. Casting the spell and making the drug takes about five hours and costs 4 magic points and 2 Sanity points to cast. After the first, each additional draught made at the same time costs one additional magic point—to make five draughts, for instance, would cost a total of 8 magic points and 2 Sanity points.

The drinker of a draught falls asleep very quickly, for about four hours. The subjective length of the dream may be long or short, and memories of the dream may be distorted. All who drink of the same drug together are together in the dream. By the origin and proportion of the ingredients (and by arrangement with the keeper), the caster may guide dream entry into a specific area correlative to the Waking World, such as a specific city or to some special place or other dimension.

A large number of herbs are required, some commonplace, others mystical and difficult to find. The result is a thin brown liquid. A mild narcotic effect relaxes the drinker and inclines him or her toward dreams.

BREW SPACE-MEAD: *a wonderfully golden liquid, which he kept in a carafe in his desk and served in tiny Belgian liqueur glasses in such small amounts that it seemed futile even to raise it to one's lips—and yet its bouquet and its taste . . . outdid even the oldest Chianti and the best Chateau Yquem to such an extent that to mention them in the same breath was to do injustice to the professor's brew. Fiery though it was, it had the additional effect of making me drowsy . . . —August* Derleth, "The House on Curwen Street."

This spell creates a magical drink that allows a human to withstand journeys through the vacuum and vicissitudes of space. For all such journeys, the effectiveness of space-mead also requires the expenditure of an equal number of magic points and current Sanity points, each equal to the log to base 10 of the journey's distance in light years (see the Space-Mead Effectiveness Table nearby).

Brewing the drink and taking the journey represent separate stages for the caster/user. Different types of space-mead exist, each with the same effects but all of them requiring different ingredients.

Space-Mead Effectiveness Table

Magic points and SAN each to be expended . . .	Distance in light years not to exceed . . .
1	100
2	1,000
3	10,000
4	100,000
5	1,000,000
6	10,000,000
7	100,000,000
8	1,000,000,000
9	10,000,000,000

. . . and so on: add another pair of points, add another zero; 10 magic points and 10 Sanity points might be enough to reach any point in the universe, at least as we understand the universe.

Brewing space-mead requires five special ingredients to be chosen by the keeper, and requires at least a week of brewing time. Once the mead is foaming and bubbling, the caster must sacrifice 20 magic points per dose into the brew. These magic points may be sacrificed over several or many days; the more points, the more doses. Each dose allows a person to withstand one journey through space of varying distance and time.

Once the space-mead has been enchanted, the traveler must find a mount: among others, the spell Summon/Bind Byakhee can provide an interstellar steed. The traveler then drinks a dose (presumably bringing a return dose along), climbs on and commands the mount, and the journey begins.

While in space, the traveler is in mental and physical stasis, nearly insensible to surroundings. Upon arrival at the destination, the effects of the brew conclude.

BRING HABOOB (Sandstorm): the caster focuses strong swirling winds. In a desert or among coastal dunes, this produces a sandstorm. The cost of the spell is 20 magic points, it takes an hour to cast, and also requires 1D4 Sanity points.

This very cost-effective spell produces a whirling storm roughly 20 miles across with winds averaging 30 mph and gusts of roughly twice that. See Alter Weather for a more systematic spell of greater extremes.

BRING PESTILENCE: *Dreamlands.* This foul spell infests its victims with dreadful diseases. Casting the spell costs 10 magic points and 1D10 Sanity points. The target must be touched by the caster and the target can resist the spell by matching POW against the caster's POW. A bit of decayed human flesh is required as a material component.

The first symptoms of the disease show up in 1D10 rounds. Symptoms of the illness vary, but its game effect is always the daily loss of 1D3 CON until the victim is cured or dead. Victims also suffer a daily cumulative 5-point loss from each skill. The victim may be cured with a successful Medicine roll, and cured dreamers regenerate all lost CON points in 2D6 hours.

Should an infected dreamer wake before perishing, he or she is saved. On the next visit to the Dreamlands no sign of the sickness exists. *This spell may be cast only in the Dreamlands.*

CALL / DISMISS ARWASSA: can bring Arwassa on the first night of the new moon. Costs the caster and other participants a varying amount of magic points to Call, and the caster loses 1D10 Sanity points. The arrival of the deity will cost more Sanity points.

Appearing, the fearsome Arwassa must be fed 100 SIZ or more of living creatures, including at least one human being. Since Arwassa's worshipers always provide sufficient fodder, what would happen if they fail is unknown. Arwassa is one of many little-known Great Old Ones. Stats for Arwassa appear in the *Creature Companion*, to appear soon.

CALL / DISMISS AZATHOTH: Calling this god is extremely dangerous. The spell costs the caster and other participants a varying amount of magic points, and the caster loses 1D10 Sanity points. The arrival of the deity will cost more Sanity points, and has the potential to fry the planet. The spell can be cast only at night, outdoors, but no other special preparations are needed.

CALL / DISMISS THE BEAST: this Call Deity spell summons a gigantic monster (Abu Hol is one name for it). Casting the spell costs the caster and other participants a varying

amount of magic points, and the caster also loses 1D10 Sanity points. The arrival of the deity will cost more Sanity points. The spell may be cast only at one special site on Earth. This spot is not given here, for the protection of those who have not yet played through the *Day of the Beast* campaign.

CALL / DISMISS CTHUGHA: brings Cthugha to the flame held by the caster. The spell costs the caster and other partici-

Call/Dismiss Deity Spells

Call/Dismiss spells bring the avatar, Outer God, or Great Old One before the caster. Casting this spell is perilous, even for cultists. Only cult priests or desperate people should choose to summon a Mythos deity. A handful are cited here, but Call/Dismiss spells likely exist for every Great Old One and for every form of Outer God.

A group or crowd can help power Call/Dismiss spells. The caster acts as the focus for the group. Everyone present expends 1 magic point. Those who know the spell can sacrifice as many magic points as they have. Total the magic points spent. That total is the percentage chance that the spell works. For each magic point cast, the group must chant for a game minute, but never for more than 100 minutes.

The caster also loses 1D10 Sanity points in casting the spell. Everyone present loses Sanity points if the deity appears.

The keeper plays the thing and must create some motivation for the thing's behavior. Mostly, when a Mythos deity arrives on Earth, it wants to stay.

Dismissing a Deity

A deity who does not want to leave Earth can be dismissed. Every Dismiss spell differs; the caster must know Call / Dismiss for the particular deity. First, allot 1 magic point per 5 POW (round up) possessed by the deity. This grants a 5% chance to dismiss the god, and it opens the way for the deity's dismissal. Example: Cthugha has 42 POW, and so 9 magic points are needed to open the way.

Once the way is prepared, the sacrifice of more magic points can tempt the deity into departure. In this, the second stage, each new magic point sacrificed increases the chance that the deity leaves by 5 percentiles. Sacrificing 10 more magic points adds 50 percentiles to the chance. Example: 9 magic points opens the way for Cthugha, representing a 5% chance for dismissal. Sacrificing 10 more magic points increases the chance to 55%. To have a 100% chance of dismissing Cthugha, those assembled must sacrifice 9+19 magic points in the two stages, a total of 28 magic points.

Roll D100 against the total chance for the dismissal.

As with Call Deity, the caster is the focus of the spell; other members of the group still can contribute magic points. Call Deity spells require special conditions and rituals, but the Dismiss portion of the spell can be cast any time, anywhere. Dismiss Deity costs no Sanity points.

OPTION: keepers may declare that a 00 result invalidates the spell. In that case, all the magic points sacrificed in the spell are lost.

pants a varying amount of magic points, and the caster loses 1D10 Sanity points. The arrival of the deity will cost more Sanity points. As the caster intones the spell, he or she moves the flame, usually a torch. The spell can be successfully cast only on clear nights when Fomalhaut clears the horizon. September to November are the best nights for Fomalhaut in North America.

CALL / DISMISS HASTUR: calls the deity to nine large blocks of stone in a V-pattern, always a sign of cult activity. The spell costs the caster and other participants a varying amount of magic points, and the caster loses 1D10 Sanity points. The arrival of the deity will cost more Sanity points. Each of the stone blocks needs a volume of nine or more cubic yards.

The spell can be cast only on clear nights when Aldebaran is above the horizon (roughly October to March). Each byakhee present during Call/Dismiss Hastur adds 10 percentiles to the chance for success.

If a point of POW has been sacrificed into each block, so that all are enchanted, the stone V adds 30 percentiles to the chance to Summon/Bind Byakhee.

CALL / DISMISS ITHAQUA: focuses the attention of Ithaqua, but the presence of the Great Old One may be noticed only as a whirlwind or icy wind. The spell costs the caster and other participants a varying amount of magic points, and the caster loses 1D10 Sanity points. The arrival of the deity will cost more Sanity points. The spell must be cast on an enormous mound of snow. Ordinarily, the spell can only be performed in the far north of the world, when temperatures are below freezing. It is possible that Ithaqua might be invoked from any high, snowy mountain.

CALL / DISMISS NYOGTHA: invokes the favor of Nyogtha, who then appears. The spell costs the caster and other participants a varying amount of magic points, and the caster loses 1D10 Sanity points. The arrival of the deity will cost more Sanity points. The caster must perform the spell ritual at the entrance to any cavern eventually connecting to the cave wherein Nyogtha dwells.

CALL / DISMISS SKINLESS ONE: *Brothers of the Skin.* Calls the Skinless One to its assembled cult. The spell costs the caster, priests, and other participants a varying amount of magic points, and the caster loses 1D10 Sanity points. The arrival of the deity costs more Sanity points. Calling the Skinless One is a dangerous task, even for a cultist.

At least one freshly flayed corpse must be offered, and each such cadaver increases the chance the Skinless One appears by one percentile. If the D100 roll fails, perhaps because of a 00 result, the Skinless One may still materialize to collect the sacrifices, but take that number again from among the worshipers present. The Skinless One is an avatar of Nyarlathotep; stats for it are in the *Creature Companion.*

CALL / DISMISS SHUB-NIGGURATH: calls Shub-Niggurath to a consecrated stone altar. The spell costs the caster and other participants a varying amount of magic points, and the caster loses 1D10 Sanity points. The arrival of the deity costs more Sanity points. This cult altar must be set in dank wilderness, and the spell must be cast from the altar. Call/Dismiss Shub-Niggurath may be cast only at the dark of the moon.

The altar is consecrated by bathing the stone in blood, to the amount of 200 SIZ or more. Each Call of the dark goddess requires fresh blood across the altar. A blooded altar in the amount of 40 SIZ or more adds 20 percentiles to the chance to Call Shub-Niggurath, and each dark young present adds another 10 percentiles.

CALL / DISMISS YOG-SOTHOTH: calls Yog-Sothoth to a specially constructed stone tower. The tower must be in an open area, and the sky must be cloudless. The spell costs the caster and other participants a varying amount of magic points, and the caster loses 1D10 Sanity points. The arrival of the deity will cost more Sanity points. The stone tower must be at least ten yards high. Each time the spell is cast, the cultists must designate a human sacrifice for the god's taking. This need be no more than an invitation—gesturing toward a nearby village, for instance, from which Yog-Sothoth then selects a victim.

At the cult's option, the stone tower may be enchanted, lowering the magic points needed for a successful cast of the spell. Each point of POW in the tower permanently improves the total chance of casting either Call or Dismiss from it by 5 percentiles.

CALL FISH: see ATTRACT FISH

CALL POWER OF NYAMBE: see POWER OF NYAMBE

CANDLE COMMUNICATION: allows two sentient beings to communicate magically by voice at a distance, without other apparatus. This requires two casters, and costs each 5 magic points and 1 Sanity point. At a pre-arranged time, each participant lights a candle and speaks the words of the spell over and over until the other's voice can be heard. This spell works clearly at up to ten miles; for each additional hundred miles or fraction thereof, the spell costs an additional magic point and is 10% less likely to be understood. Maximum range is one thousand miles. A blown-out candle flame breaks communication. The spell can be recast by both parties.

CAST OUT DEVIL: frees the target of possession by alien entities. This elaborate spell takes a full day to cast, requiring many components of African tribal magic. It costs no Sanity points. After a contribution of 10 magic points to energize the spell, match the POW of the exorcist against the POW of the foe possessing the victim. Willing assistants who also know the spell may add half of their POW (round fractions down) to the effort, and this spell is seldom attempted without such help. It might be used against many foes—to help a person possessed by Y'golonac, perhaps, or by a mind from the Great Race of Yith.

CAST OUT SHAN: expels a shan (insect from Shaggai) from any living host standing within a five-foot-wide pentagram drawn with the herb amica. The caster performs a ritual which takes one hour and costs 10 magic points, as well as 1 POW from the caster and each victim. (The caster could perform it on himself or herself for 2 POW.) After the ceremony, the pentagram is proof against a new shan intrusion for the next twelve hours. The spell does not destroy the shan, but has that effect if performed in direct sunlight.

CAUSE / CURE BLINDNESS: the target suffers complete and permanent blindness, as if by a stroke. The same spell can reverse blindness if the eyes and optic nerves are essentially intact. The spell costs 8 magic points for either version, and an additional 2D6 Sanity points for Cause Blindness. A day of ritual and a successful POW vs. POW match on the Resistance Table are also needed.

CAUSE DISEASE: afflicts the target victim with a feverish illness resembling cholera, malaria, pneumonia, etc. The caster may invest as many magic points as he or she can; match them against the target's POW on the Resistance Table. Casting time is five game rounds. If the target wins, there is no effect.

If the caster wins, symptoms such as high fever, nausea, vomiting, dehydration, and loss of concentration follow. The victim loses 2D6 STR, CON, and DEX (roll separately for each), at the rate of one point daily for each. If the victim survives, he or she regains these points. If any of the characteristics reach zero, the victim dies.

To cast the spell, the attacker obtains some personal item of the target, especially something that has touched the mouth. The object is buried in a deep hole with shreds of poisonous plants or bamboo. The hole is filled and a specially carved stone place on top. A short chant follows, and the spell is cast.

Bed rest is the only treatment that seems to maintain clarity of mind. Only curative magic truly helps. Retrieving the buried object breaks the spell, otherwise the spell runs its course.

CHANT OF THOTH: may increase the caster's chance to solve a particular intellectual problem. To cast it requires 30 minutes of time and 1D4 Sanity points. For every magic point spent in the chant, the caster adds 2 percentiles to his or her chance to gain knowledge, learn a spell, translate a passage, deduce the meaning of a symbol, etc. If the user's chance is less than 10%, the Chant of Thoth cannot help: thus for it to aid in translating a passage in Latin, the caster must know at least Latin 10%.

CHARM ANIMAL: causes the target animal to treat the caster as a friend. The spell costs 1 magic point for every SIZ point of the animal, and lasts for 24 hours. When it expires, the animal remembers nothing of its previous friendliness. No communication occurs. The animal friend cannot be used to run errands or engage in combat, but all will share their warmth during sleep, and a predator will share some of the game that it has killed.

CHIME OF TEZCHAPTL: with it, the caster can enchant a small bell or chime made of a pure metal such as gold or iron. Silver gives the best tone. The ritual takes six hours, and costs 1D6 Sanity points and the sacrifice of 2 POW. For each 100 feet above sea level, the effectiveness of the created chime increases by one percentile: made at 5500 feet, a chime works 55% of the time it is rung. Additionally, the caster must enact the Unspeakable Promise (in this chapter), imperiling his or her sanity and life.

The resulting chime defends against many spells which require song or music instruments in their casting—Free Hastur, Song of Hastur, Dampen Light, and Soul Singing are four examples. Rung softly, the chime absorbs the spell or spells if a D100 roll equals or is less than the chime's percentile rating. As the chime absorbs magic, its metal takes on a peculiar sheen and the chime's tone alters in timbre. Once it has absorbed a spell, the chime retains the spell's essence for 2D6 minutes.

During that interval, if the holder of the chime rings it loudly, the spell energy in it is released violently back at the caster who sang the spell, costing the target 1D6 hit points for each 2 magic points or point of POW the chime absorbed. A target's blood vessels erupt, and he or she bleeds from every pore. With the loss of more than half his or her total hit points, the eyeballs burst, inflicting total blindness. Using the chime in this fashion costs no magic points and no Sanity points. Witnessing the reflection of spell energy may cost Sanity.

CIRCLE OF NAUSEA: creates a powerful protective circle around the caster that will cause nausea and pain in anyone approaching it. Creating the circle costs 4 magic points, 2 points of Sanity, and 5 game minutes. The caster must inscribe a circle on the ground, then fortify the circle with four enchanted stones—  one at each of the four cardinal points of the compass. Enchanting the stones in this case requires the previous sacrifice of 4 magic points into each.

Breaching the circle requires a successful resistance struggle matching the character's POW against the magical STR of the circle (equal to the POW of the caster). Anyone who touches the circle but fails the POW struggle vomits for the next five minutes, or until he or she retreats at least 100 yards away. If anyone successfully breaches the circle, the spell collapses.

CLOAK OF FIRE: at the cost of great pain to the caster, this spell increases the caster's movement and augments his or her combat defense. Cloak of Fire costs 12 magic points and 1D10 Sanity to cast. Only the caster can benefit from the spell. It takes one round to cast, and its effect lasts 4D4 rounds. Viewing the Cloak in action costs 1/1D3 Sanity points.

The spell wreathes the caster in weaving, glittering points of light, each spark dragging a luminous trail and flickering white-hot. Sealed within the Cloak, the caster rises several inches off the floor so that his feet no longer touch. Nonetheless, body movements are precise. The nimbus of the Cloak is agonizing, costing 1D6 Sanity points to feel during the first cast. No hit points are lost because of the pain, however, and if the caster has not touched anyone, the pain stops when the spell does.

While the spell is in effect, double the caster's MOV and DEX. Decrease all chances for attack against the caster by 20 percentiles. All weapon attacks do minimum damage. Anyone attacking with Fist/Punch, Kick, etc., suffers exactly the damage done to the caster.

If the caster touches someone, treat it as a Fist/Punch attack doing 1D8 hit points of damage; each time this happens, the caster also suffers half of that rolled damage (round down) as his or her skin and flesh flash away to feed the Cloak's magical surface. Thus it is possible that this spell could lower the caster's hit points to zero, and cause death.

CLOUD MEMORY: blocks the target's ability to remember consciously a particular event. The spell costs 1D6 magic points and 1D2 Sanity points. The spell takes effect immediately. The caster must be able to see the target, and the target must be able to receive the caster's instructions. If the caster's magic points overcome the target's on the Resistance Table, the target's mind is mentally blocked with respect to one specified incident. If the incident was terrifying, the victim may thereafter still have nightmares vaguely relating to it. If the spell fails, the event in question becomes vivid in the target's mind.

The caster must know the specific event to be blocked. The caster cannot command something vague like "Forget what you did yesterday." Instead, he or she must cite a certain event, such as "Forget you were assaulted by a monster." This spell cannot block knowledge of spells or of the Cthulhu Mythos unless the knowledge is firmly tied to a specific event, nor can it undo a Sanity loss, or undo insanity.

CLUTCH OF NYOGTHA: a hideous attack spell costing 1D20 Sanity points. The caster must spend 1 magic point to start the spell, and the target must be within a conversational distance. If the caster overcomes the target's magic points with his or her own on the Resistance Table, the target feels as though a large hand is crushing his or her heart, and loses 1D3 hit points for each combat round that the spell is in effect. While under such attack, the target is temporarily paralyzed, as though having a heart attack. In the round that the target's hit points fall to zero or less, the target's chest ruptures and bursts, and the target's smoking heart appears in the hand of the caster.

Each round the spell lasts, the caster must spend magic points equal to twice the number of hit points in damage actually done. The caster must concentrate on the spell each round that it is to remain in effect, and the caster must overcome the target's magic points each round that he or she concentrates. If the caster is distracted or if the target successfully resists, the spell ends. Any damage already done remains.

COMMAND ANIMAL SPELLS: causes a specific animal or insect to swarm to obey a specific command. Published spells include ones for Driver Ant Column, Green Mamba, Leopard, and Spider Monkey. Though each such spell must be learned separately, all require 1 magic point each and no Sanity points. The command is answered naturally (the animal or insects moving by natural means to the caster). One does not want to call on some sort of creature which must take months to reach the caster. Command spells for any natural animal may exist, known by witch doctors or shamans somewhere.

Reaching the caster, the creature is able to comprehend and perform a command appropriate to it. To instruct a snake to "fly to Mexico" has no meaning to it, and the order to "bite Jonathan Kingsley" baffles a tarantula, since it has no way to identify the target. On the other hand, the command to "bite all humans in front of you" could be attempted by a creature of minimal intelligence.

COMMAND DHOLE: the spell must be chanted together by a large group of people, each of whom must know the spell, though not necessarily the intent. Each contributes 1 magic point to the summoning. The chant leader loses 1D6 magic points and 1D3 Sanity points. The chant lasts hours, until the dhole appears.

The chant leader can attempt to overcome the magic points of the summoned dhole with his own and, if successful, he commands the dhole when it appears. It remains controlled until the caster frees it, either voluntarily or by losing his concentration, falling asleep, etc., and at that point it disappears. If the command roll fails, the dhole attempts to eat everyone, then disappears. At present this spell does not exist in any earthly writing.

COMMAND GHOST: compels a ghost to come forth to answer specific questions. Casting the spell costs 10 magic points and 1D3 Sanity points. The casting must be performed at night. A mammal's blood is poured upon the grave or ashes of the dead person whom the caster wishes to contact. The spirit will refuse to re-enter this world, so the caster must overcome its magic points with his or her own on the Resistance Table, forcing it to appear. Sanity loss for viewing the ghost varies with the ghost, which appears in its form at death.

The ghost summoned by this spell responds to questions about events occurring while the spirit lived. Each question costs the caster one magic point and another Resistance Table struggle. When the spirit is victorious, or when a game hour elapses, it departs.

COMMAND SHARK / PORPOISE: for committing a human sacrifice to the gods of the sea. The spells originated in the South Pacific. Each casting costs 1 magic point; for each additional point, the chance of successfully bringing the creature rises by ten percentiles. The spell must be cast over salt water. To bring a shark, splash blood into the sea; for a porpoise, drop in small live fish. The creature follows the shouted commands of the caster. With a successful Luck roll, a second shark or porpoise accompanies the one called for, but the second one is not subject to magical control.

COMPEL FLESH: a person becomes a living zombie, capable only of following simple, understandable, spoken instructions. Compel Flesh costs 3 Sanity points and 5 magic points to cast plus an additional magic point for every ten game rounds that the spell is to remain in effect.

First the soul of the target must be bound; see Bind Soul above. Then the caster can use this spell to force the body of the target to perform actions. The body will follow instructions until a task is completed, or the body is killed, or the spell ends.

CONJURE GLASS OF MORTLAN: creates a way to view scenes from the past. Costs the caster 1D8 Sanity points and each viewer 1D6 Sanity points, plus any Sanity loss for what is viewed. A crystal ball and an enchanted brazier are required as well. Let the light from a candle shine through the crystal ball onto smoke from the brazier: a vision forms. The caster expends 6 magic points per spell attempt, with a chance for success equal to his or her Cthulhu Mythos skill. The Voorish Sign can help.

The vision is of the past. Unless the vision comes under the sway of a Great Old One (20% chance), the scene viewed is of the caster's choice. A Great Old One might cause visions to appear that were pertinent to itself or some artifact, instead of what was desired by the caster.

CONSUME LIKENESS: the caster can assume the living likeness of a person freshly dead, as seen by eye, video camera, X-ray, etc. The victim may be no more than 3 SIZ points different from the caster. For the next few days the caster consumes the victim and works the spell, expending 10 magic points every six hours, and permanently sacrificing 1 POW point. The caster could consume several likenesses, and thereby take on several guises. When a victim is consumed, the caster loses 1D20 Sanity points. This spell is known by many serpent people.

Once the spell is complete, the caster takes on the appearance of the victim at will, for as long as desired. The shadow of the caster remains as original. Similarly, the caster's skills and memories remain intact–the victim's are foregone.

Upon losing one or more hit points, the caster must revert to original form and rest 1D3 hours. To go from an assumed form to the original form takes 20 seconds. The original form must be reverted to before another form can be assumed. To go from the original to an assumed form takes 1D3 minutes.

CONTACT CHTHONIAN: the spell costs 5 magic points to cast, and 1D3 Sanity points. Unless there are no chthonians nearby, it succeeds automatically. The spell must be cast at a location which has known recent earthquakes, such as at G'harne in West Africa, or where hot spots and volcanoes offer relatively quick transport from the deep interior of the planet to the outer edge of the geologic crust.

CONTACT DEEP ONE: the spell costs 3 magic points to cast, and 1D3 Sanity points. Unless there are no deep ones nearby, the chanting succeeds automatically. This spell should be cast at the edge of a salt-water ocean or sea. To work best, it should be cast near a deep one city, such as the waters off Innsmouth, Massachusetts. Part of the ritual consists of throwing specially inscribed stones into the water.

CONTACT ELDER THING: the spell costs 3 magic points to cast, and 1D3 Sanity points. Unless there are no elder things nearby, the chanting succeeds automatically. The most likely locations are along the southern part of the Mid-Atlantic Ridge, or over the geological trenches nearest Antarctica.

CONTACT FLYING POLYP: the spell costs 9 magic points to cast, and 1D3 Sanity points. Unless there are no flying polyps nearby, it succeeds automatically. Flying polyps occur only in their rare underground cities, the largest of which is beneath the City in the Sands, in the western Australian desert. There the caster should first open a communication shaft for their egress.

CONTACT FORMLESS SPAWN: the spell costs 3 magic points to cast, and 1D3 Sanity points. Unless there are no formless spawn nearby, it succeeds automatically. The best place to cast this spell is at a temple of Tsathoggua whose altar statue of Tsathoggua is still present, or at a spot near an opening into the black abyss of N'Kai, somewhere near Binger, Oklahoma. Possibly other places in western or midwestern North America offer entry and exit points. One such cavern complete reputedly exists near Dunwich, Massachusetts.

CONTACT GHOUL: the spell costs 8 magic points to cast, and 1D3 Sanity points. Unless there are no ghouls nearby, it succeeds automatically. Ghouls are found wherever large concentrations of humans are, especially near graveyards and crypts. Places of burial more than a century old are propitious locations for this spell. Moonlit nights are best.

CONTACT GNOPH-KEH: this spell takes 6 magic points and 1D3 Sanity points. Unless there are no gnoph-keh nearby, it succeeds automatically. Gnoph-keh are usually found in Greenland or other frozen wastes near the North Pole. There it works automatically. The spell must be augmented with a successful Sing roll, and before doing so the caster must build a small effigy of the beast from ice and snow.

CONTACT HOUND OF TINDALOS: The spell costs 7 magic points to cast, and 1D3 Sanity points. If a hound of Tindalos is summoned, it will come automatically. There is no known way to bargain with a hound of Tindalos, whose motive for moving through the time stream is simple hunger.

CONTACT HUMAN: *Mi-Go.* With this spell, mi-go mentally command and inform their human servants. The spell costs 3 magic points to cast, and no Sanity points. It effects a telepathic link to a human who has in the past fallen under mi-go hypnosis. The contactee can respond, ask questions, etc. Each 5 rounds of contact after the first round costs the human 1 Sanity point.

CONTACT MI-GO: The spell costs 8 magic points to cast, and 1D3 Sanity points. Unless there are no mi-go nearby, it succeeds automatically. The spell must be cast at the base or the top of a high mountain in a range known to be mined or visited by the mi-go. Among such ranges are the Appalachians, Andes, and Himalayas, and some peaks in Central Africa.

CONTACT RAT-THING: The spell costs 2 magic points and 1D3 Sanity points. To bring forth a foul rat-thing, it must be cast at or near a site infested by rat-things. A population of these evil creatures reportedly exists in Yorkshire, England. Another report of similar creatures comes from Massachusetts.

CONTACT SAND-DWELLER: The spell costs 3 magic points to cast, and 1D3 Sanity points. Unless there are no sand-dwellers nearby, it succeeds automatically. The spell must be

Contact Spells

Contact spells are not Contact Deity spells. Those spells are found under the appropriate heading.

Using Contact spells, a cultist could get in touch with intelligent servitors and intelligent independent races, perhaps to learn more about history, magic, gods, or alien species. The caster should have a definite goal in mind. Procedures are much the same for each Contact spell, though particular conditions or requirements may be unique. Knowing one Contact spell is of no help in casting another. Many more Contact spells exist.

To cast, a Contact spell costs magic points equal to the minimum POW possible to the species: for instance, for hounds of Tindalos it is 7, the minimum possible from a 7D6 roll. Each Contact spell also costs 1D3 Sanity points. Cast properly, this spell always works, unless there are no such things living within a convenient distance (flying polyps might journey from the City in the Sands to some part of Australia, but might ignore the chance to fly to North America).

A Contact spell takes five to ten rounds to cast. The thing reached by the spell may appear in a game hour or take a game day or more to show up. For a random appearance in hours, roll D100. Entities living nearby will walk, swim, dig, or fly to the spell point. If the trip is too long, the thing called by the spell never shows up. Things from other dimensions appear in any characteristic or evocative manner.

The spell brings a random member of the species, presumably with its own motives. The caster should try to be alone, or to be with no more than a small group, in order not to seem threatening. Once the contacted thing appears, it is free to depart, so if the caster has something to offer it, the chances for an extended meeting greatly improve.

If a contacted species is large, such as are flying polyps, only one will likely appear. If it is human-sized or smaller, the keeper may cause several representatives to come as a group.

There is no guarantee that a contacted entity would rather bargain than devour the caster. It should have an alien motivation in any case, but if further contact seems of advantage to both sides, then some interesting role-playing may emerge.

cast in a suitable desert, such as in the Sahara, the southwestern United States, Saudi Arabia, or central Australia.

CONTACT SPIRITS OF THE DEAD: *Voodoo.* Many versions of this spell exist. The spell costs 3 magic points to the caster and 1D3 Sanity points to each attendee. A tent of white sheets is erected near a river and jugs full of the stream's water are placed inside. Songs are sung, and dances danced. An entreaty is made for the dead to appear. Add up all the magic points, multiply the sum by five, and let the caster's player try to roll D100 under that result. With a success, the voices of the dead emerge from the water jugs. One may hear them and discuss or question them by putting one's head in the tent. As with loas, politeness and communication skills are helpful. Remember that the dead mostly know only what they knew in life, and that some have not realized that they are dead.

CONTACT STAR-SPAWN OF CTHULHU: The spell costs 6 magic points to cast, and 1D3 Sanity points. Unless there are no representatives nearby, it succeeds automatically. It should be cast at the ocean shore, perhaps near a deep one outpost, or else near a spot where star-spawn may sleep. The spell works well in Polynesia, along the Massachusetts coast, and above R'lyeh.

CONTACT DEITY / CHAUGNAR FAUGN: opens communication with Chaugnar Faugn. For each attempt, the caster must sacrifice 1 POW and 1D6 Sanity points. The chance of success equals half of POW x5 (round up). On second and later tries, sacrifice the same amount and continue to decrease the Luck roll threshold to reflect the changes in POW, but halve the Luck roll only on the first cast. With a success, the deity sends the caster visions or nightmares which inform the dreamer of the god's desires, or lets him or her know if a petition to the god is to be favorably answered or rejected.

CONTACT DEITY / CTHULHU: opens communication with Cthulhu. For each attempt, the caster must sacrifice 1 POW and 1D6 Sanity points. The chance of success equals half of POW x5 (round up). On second and later tries, sacrifice the same amount and continue to decrease the Luck roll threshold to reflect the changes in POW, but halve the Luck roll only on the first cast. Cthulhu typically responds at night, during the caster's dreams. By dreams and nightmares he informs his followers of his desires.

CONTACT DEITY / EIHORT: little resembles other Contact Deity spells. Eihort's Bargainers sacrifice 1 magic point instead of 1 POW in casting it. The god automatically appears in dream form if the Bargainer is distant, and in person if within a few hundred yards. In imparting this spell into the Bargainer's brain, Eihort extracts 1 POW in compensation.

CONTACT DEITY / LOA: *Voodoo.* Opens communication with a specified loa. This spell may be cast by one person or a group, as the mambo prefers. For each attempt, there is a sacrifice of 1 POW, the first time by the caster, and of 1D6 Sanity points from the participants. The chance of success equals half the caster's POW x5 (round up). On second and later tries, sacrifice the same amount and continue to decrease the Luck roll threshold to reflect the changes in POW, but halve the Luck roll only on the first cast.

A particular loa must be chosen. Typically the ceremony involves a small congregation of worshipers dancing to drum. The particular loa's symbol (*vè-vè*) must be inscribed in the floor of the *humfor* [place of worship]. Offers are made, and a summons sung by those present. On second and later tries, a random person among the congregation is chosen by the loa to lose 1 POW. A random 1D6 participants each lose a Sanity point. Again the chance of success equals the caster's present POW x5 or less on D100.

If the result is a success, the sought-for loa possesses someone other than the caster. The host's INT and POW are replaced by those of the loa, and the loa's voice emerges from the host's mouth. The loa may be questioned politely or asked for advice, or may even agree to increase a supplicant's chance to complete a particular task. Communication skill rolls may be called for. The ceremony over, the possession ends. Payment is not normally accepted for casting Contact Loa—one must be invited to have it cast for him or her.

CONTACT DEITY / NODENS: opens communication with Nodens. For each attempt, the caster must sacrifice 1 POW and 1D6 Sanity points. The chance of success equals half of POW x5 (round up). On second and later tries, sacrifice the same amount and continue to decrease the Luck roll threshold to reflect the changes in POW, but halve the Luck roll only on the first cast. The Contact spell for Nodens can be cast only from a remote, unpeopled place such as the edge of a seacliff. If, later, Nodens contacts the caster, it will be when he or she is alone, and in a similar inaccessible place.

CONTACT DEITY / NYARLATHOTEP: opens communication with Nyarlathotep. For each attempt, the caster must sacrifice 1 POW and 1D6 Sanity points. The chance of success equals half of POW x5 (round up). On second and later tries, sacrifice the same amount and continue to decrease the luck roll threshold to reflect the changes in POW, but halve the Luck roll only on the first cast. This spell can be cast from anywhere, as befits this omnipresent god, but Nyarlathotep appears only at meetings of worshipers, or when new priests of the Outer Gods are anointed.

CONTACT DEITY / SKINLESS ONE: *Brothers of the Skin.* To contact the Skinless One, an avatar of Nyarlathotep, 1 POW and 1D10 Sanity points must be sacrificed, The chance of success equals half of POW x5 (round up). On second and later tries, sacrifice the same amount and continue to decrease the Luck roll threshold to reflect the changes in POW, but halve the Luck roll only on the first cast.

A freshly skinned corpse must be available. The Skinless One manifests in this corpse and, before the corpse liquefies and evaporates, answers up to three questions. Sanity loss for viewing this is 1/1D10 SAN. Seeing the Skinless One costs 1D10/1D100 SAN.

CONTACT DEITY / TSATHOGGUA: opens communication with Tsathoggua. For each attempt, the caster must sacrifice 1 POW and 1D6 Sanity points. The chance of success equals half of POW x5 (round up). On second and later tries, sacrifice the same amount and continue to decrease the Luck roll threshold to reflect the changes in POW, but halve the Luck roll only on the first cast. Tsathoggua may appear in spirit form, as a hazy and translucent projection of his real self, to which normal Sanity losses apply. He usually visits only if the caster is alone. He speaks audibly to the caster.

CONTACT DEITY / Y'GOLONAC: opens communication with Y'golonac. For each attempt, the caster must sacrifice 1 POW and 1D6 Sanity points. The chance of success equals half of POW x5 (round up). On second and later tries, sacrifice the same amount and continue to decrease the Luck roll threshold to reflect the changes in POW, but halve the Luck roll only on the first cast. This god responds by attempting to convert the caster to its worship. If the deity feels that the caster would be an unsuitable priest, it will psychically attack him or her, and try to eat the soul and mind. If the caster might be suitable, Y'golonac tries to possess a friend, who (controlled) approaches the caster to tempt him or her into service.

CONTROL SKIN: *Brothers of the Skin.* For purposes of disguise, the caster may meld, bend, and alter the skin of one general body area per casting. The spell costs 5 magic points and 1D6 Sanity to cast, and then the caster must overcome the target's magic points on the Resistance Table unless the target is willing. A spell for a single body area would take about thirty minutes to prepare and enact. The effect lasts 15 minutes to an hour. For permanent change, 1 POW per general body area is also needed. A second casting of Control Skin can undo the change, of course.

General body areas are head, torso, right arm, left arm, right leg and left leg. For 30 magic points, the entire body can be changed, with a corresponding cost of 6D6 Sanity.

CREATE BAD-CORPSE DUST: creates a barrier which zombies cannot cross, at a cost of 2 magic points and no Sanity points. This powder requires the intestines of a zombie, an ounce of flesh from the dust-maker (which he must bite out of himself), and the dried and powdered flowers of a rare jungle liana. The whole is carefully dried, pounded together, and chanted over for several hours, then poured in the desired trail or line, chanted over, and the magic points sacrificed. The dust becomes a magical invisible wall which zombies cannot cross. This barrier remains until the dust is washed or blown away. One such creation of the dust results in enough to form a barrier about 30 yards long.

CREATE BARRIER OF NAACH-TITH: this barrier provides both physical and magical defense. Each participant in this spell loses 1D10 Sanity points and a variable number of magic points. Each magic point expended in the creation gives the barrier 1D6 points of STR. The spell takes 1 game minute to cast (during which time all magic points to be used must be expended) and the resulting barrier lasts 1D4+4 hours. Anyone who knows the spell may participate in the casting and contribute magic points to the barrier.

The barrier is spherical in shape, and about 100 yards in diameter. It can be cast around the user, to protect him or her from harm, or it can be cast so as to englobe a monster or enemy. Any creature bisected by the barrier's boundary upon its creation is unharmed and thrust outside the barrier. Anything trapped within the barrier can get out only by beating down the barrier with a successful STR against STR roll on the Resistance Table (multiple entrapped victims cannot combine STR to escape). A bullet or missile can cross the barrier if the rolled damage to the barrier overcomes the barrier's STR on the Resistance Table. If penetrating the barrier, the object does the damage rolled, as if the barrier did not exist, and the barrier is destroyed.

A written copy of the spell is known to be in a great haunted library on a planet orbiting the star Celaeno, one of the Pleiades.

CREATE CURSE WHISTLE: makes magical musical pipes from owl bones. The creator must expend 256 magic points over the course of the night of the first full moon following the summer solstice. Creation costs no Sanity points.

The creator must be an Algonquian Indian shaman. He may be assisted in the magic-point expenditure by other shamans who know this spell. The finished whistle can be used to cast the spells of Soul Singing and Pipes of Madness.

CREATE FETCH STICK: makes a spear-like weapon which can damage or kill extraplanar monsters. To make a fetch stick, the sorcerer first obtains a bamboo staff and attaches a sharpened iron point to one end. Over the course of the next year, the sorcerer then sacrifices two humans and 2 POW to the fetch stick and attaches the second skull to the stick. This process should cost at least 20 Sanity points, and the keeper should describe it as gruesomely as possible. The result is used as a magic spear, but creatures resistant to impaling resist it normally. An impaling blow from a fetch stick instantly destroys a zombie or other animated corpse.

CREATE GATE: *The idea of a panel that would open on some remote world impressed Eibon as being rather fantastic, not to say farfetched.* —Clark Ashton Smith, "The Door to Saturn."

This important spell allows the user to step between other lands, dimensions, or worlds. A Gate connects to a single other location. Creation of a Gate requires the permanent expenditure of POW, in a sacrifice equal to the log to base 10 of the distance the Gate connects in miles. A Gate may take many forms, common ones being indicated by a pattern of painted lines on a floor or a peculiar arrangement of stones in a field.

Contact Deity Spells

Contact Deity spells and Contact spells are different. See Contact spells under their own heading.

Contact Deity spells are unused except by the insane priests of these deities, or by great independent sorcerers who hope to strike deals and win over some small fraction of the deity's powers. The deity sought for Contact can be an Elder God, a Great Old One, or an Outer God.

For each such spell, the cast must sacrifice 1 POW (slightly reducing the character's Luck roll) and 1D6 Sanity points. The chance of successfully contacting the deity equals half of the character's new Luck roll. On second and later tries, sacrifice the same amount and continue to decrease the Luck rolls to reflect the falling POW, but halve the Luck roll only on the first cast.

Once the Luck roll succeeds, the deity or some aspect of it will contact the caster in a semi-friendly manner after a few game hours or days. The deity is unlikely to give non-worshipers anything of value. If the caster bores the deity, or oversteps his bounds, the god will likely squash him or her, or drive him or her insane, and so get some pleasure from the situation.

Gate Creation & Travel Costs Table

POW (gate creation) or magic points (gate travel)	Distance in miles / light years up to . . .
1	100 miles
2	1,000 miles
3	10,000 miles
4	100,000 miles
5	1,000,000 miles
6	10,000,000 miles
7	100,000,000 miles
8	1,000,000,000 miles
9	10,000,000,000 miles
10	100,000,000,000 miles
11	1,000,000,000.000 miles
12	~ 1/2 light year
13	~ 5 light years
14	~ 50 light years
15	~ 500 light years
16	~ 5,000 light years
17	~ 50,000 light years
18	~ 500,000 light years
19	~ 5,000,000 light years
20	~ 50,000,000 light years

Sample Locations and Distances

distance from Boston	approx. furthest in miles / light years	POW / MP needed
Providence	40 miles	1
Peoria	1000 miles	2
Portland (Australia)	10,000 miles	3
empty space	100,000 miles	4
Moon	230,000 miles	5
Mercury	140,000,000	8
Venus	160,000,000	8
Mars	250,000,000	8
Jupiter	600,000,000 miles	8
Saturn	1,000,000,000	8
Uranus	1,900,000,000	9
Neptune	2,800,000,000	9
Yuggoth (Pluto)	4,600,000,000	9
Oort Cloud	9,000,000,000 miles	9
Proxima Centauri	4.3 light years	13
Sirius	8.3 light years	14
Fomalhaut	~ 22 light years	14
Vega	~ 26 light years	14
Aldebaran	~ 50 light years	14
Celaeno	~ 400 light years	15
far side of Milky Way	~ 70,000 light years	18
Galaxy M31	~ 2,800,000 light years	19
Azathoth	~ 10 billion light years	23
distant quasar	~ 15 billion light years	23
1 astronomical unit	~ 93,000,000 miles	7
1 light year	~ 5,900,000,000,000 miles	12
1 parsec	3.26 light years	13

Using the Gate costs a number of magic points equal to the POW originally used to make the Gate. Each trip through a Gate costs 1 Sanity point.

Lacking enough magic points for a trip, the keeper might rule that a traveler stays on this side, but unconscious and drained of magic points, or that the investigator might complete the trip but arrive unconscious, drained of magic points, and having sacrificed 1 POW for the fare. Return trips through a Gate always cost the same as the initial journey.

The far end of the Gate resembles the initial end. Ordinarily, anyone or anything can move through a Gate, though some have been built so that a certain word or gesture is needed to activate the portal. Gate are also known that change those who pass through, to aid survival on an alien world. There may also be Gates capable of more than one destination.

CREATE MIST OF RELEH: causes a dense mist to appear in an egg-shaped volume 10 x10 x15 feet, directly in front of the caster. The spell requires 2 magic points and no Sanity points. The long axis of the cloud is always at right angles to the direction in which the caster faces. The spell obscures vision for 1D6+4 game rounds, then evaporates without trace.

CREATE SCRYING WINDOW: makes a magic window which looks into the past. Using it costs the viewer 1D3 Sanity points per session, as well as incidental Sanity losses for viewing particular monsters.

To make a scrying window, enchant a central clear viewing glass with 10 points of POW. When the glass is enchanted, it must be keyed to a specific time in the past, an assessment relative to the date the glass is made. As a key, one could say, "800 years past", but not "1125 B.C." After the central glass is enchanted and keyed, 98 pieces of expensive colored glass must be enchanted, requiring 1 magic point each, and fitted carefully into a geometric mosaic with the clear viewing glass at the center. When finished, the central glass shows the site at which it is placed (though at the appropriate time in the past). The viewing site may be changed by expending 1 magic point and five game minutes of concentration per 100 miles or fraction thereof moved.

The glass has an obvious limitation: a given scene can be viewed once, for time passes on both sides of the glass, and the glass must be tuned to a spot where things actually happen.

The scrying window has an inherent danger. Any being viewed has a chance equal to its POW minus 20 or less on D100 to realize that it is being observed. It could then cast a spell through the window, including a Summon or Call spell which could manifest a monster on the observer's side of the window.

CREATE SELF-WARD: slows the advance of age as well as protecting its user from physical damage, at a variable cost of POW, magic points, and Sanity points. This is a rare and powerful enchantment. The caster must gather together personal effects, hair, nail clippings, etc., and place them within a small leather or cloth bag. The caster then spends one or several days in close contact with the bag, each day uttering ritual chants while expending a chosen number of magic points.

The subsequent rate of aging depends on the days spent in creating the Self-ward. If 3 days, 3 magic points per day are spent, and the caster thereafter ages one year for every three. If 6 days, 6 magic points per day are spent, and the caster thereafter ages one year for every six, and so on. On the final day of the ritual, the user must endow the bag with POW points equal to the number of days spent creating the Self-Ward, and 1D6 Sanity points for every point of POW.

Besides the benefit of longer life, the ward-bag if held or worn deflects damage equal to the number of POW points sacrificed in creating it. If the bag is not in the possession of the caster but has not been destroyed, he or she receives half of such protection (round up fractions).

If the bag is destroyed or emptied, or the caster is killed, this spell is broken. If the spell is broken, the caster rapidly ages until physical age agrees with chronological age. He or she also loses a number of CON points equal to the POW placed in the Self-ward.

CREATE TIME GATE: opens a time gate to the future or to the past. The spell resembles the Create Gate spell, but costs POW for the number of years traveled, rather than the number of miles. Use the nearby Gate Creation / Travel Costs Table, and substitute *distance in years* for *distance in miles*. The spell only yields a time approximate to that desired, though once such a Gate is created the exact interval between "now" and "then" remains the same. No written version of this spell exists.

CREATE WINDOW: a version of a Gate which is kept open entirely by the will (minimum POW 25) of a god or great sorcerer, and operated by him, her, or it. In this version, the energizing magic points come from the deity or sorcerer, not from those who actually use the window—the personal POW of the traveler does not limit the distance traveled by the user. As the creator wishes, no sign or symbol necessarily marks the exit or entrance, which may open and close at the creator's will. A Window may be one-way or two-way, as the caster wishes.

CREATE ZOMBI: *Voodoo.* The target is brought to near death by a paralyzing powder made partly of blowfish innards and alkaloids. (Costs for this are found in the last paragraph.) This POT 25 poison must be inhaled. The target then falls into a deep trance indistinguishable from death. Horribly, the target is still conscious, but incapable of movement.

The victim is put in a coffin and buried alive in the cemetery. So that he or she may breathe, a small tube connects the coffin to the surface. During this time, the target's player must succeed with a Sanity roll every three game hours, or lose 1D6 SAN. If the target goes insane during this period, he or she embraces the will of the *bokor*, or sorcerer, grateful that the terror of the grave has been dispelled.

Three nights later, the bokor comes to the grave site to cast Create Zombi. The spell costs 10 magic points and 4 Sanity points. If the bokor perceives mental resistance from the target, the caster may then match POW vs. POW on the Resistance Table to overcome the will of the target. Whether the target is insane or still sane, success with the spell drains away all but 1 POW. If the spell fails, the bokor may simply cover up the breathing hole and leave the victim to suffocate.

CREATE ZOMBIE: another way to create zombies. The spell requires a human corpse which retains sufficient flesh to allow mobility after activation. The caster puts an ounce of his or her own blood in the mouth of the corpse, then kisses the lips of the corpse and "breathes part of the self" into the body. One point of POW is lost, a gift to the corpse, and the caster loses 1D10 Sanity points. If the spell succeeds, the caster may give the zombie simple commands which it will carry out. Should the caster die, the zombie becomes inactive and rots away. Other than the caster's POW, the number of zombies that can be created is unlimited.

Part of the invocation refers collectively to the Outer Gods—every caster knows such entities exist, though no names are used. These zombies are those from the Beasts and Monsters chapter (p. 186), useful indefinitely.

CURSE OF CHAUGNAR FAUGN: eventually causes the target to be devoured by Chaugnar Faugn. Casting the spell requires a tiny fragment of flesh from the target as a focus and twelve hours of chanting per week. The caster must be a sworn worshiper of this Great Old One. The spell costs the caster 1 magic point per game hour of chanting. Each twelve hours of chanting cost 1D3 Sanity points. The target is affected by the spell regardless of distance, and success is automatic.

That night and for the nights thereafter, the victim's dreams fill with horrible visions sent by Chaugnar Faugn. Soon he or she suffers from trance states in which physical attempts are made to reach the god and be accepted as a living sacrifice. These trances become longer and more frequent until the victim succeeds. That interval might be the victim's POW in days, but strong-willed individuals may fight off the effects for POW x2 or even POW x3 days, as the keeper chooses. Eventually the victim is devoured. Then the flesh fragment possessed by the caster instantly rots, demonstrating that the spell need continue no longer.

CURSE OF DARKNESS: forces a being from another plane or dimension to return whence it came. The spell costs 1D6 Sanity points to cast, and a variable amount of POW. A group surrounds the person who casts the spell. All must know the spell, and all chant it for at least two or three minutes. Each participant must sacrifice 1 POW, except that the caster may contribute none or as many as wished. For each POW point sacrificed, the chance of success rises by 10 percentiles. The entity has no chance to resist or evade the spell once it is begun. To be effective, the being's name must be known, or it must have been seen by one of the circle or the caster. The alien must be nearby, within a couple of miles.

CURSE OF THE RAT-THING: a particularly horrible spell that, when cast upon a corpse dead within 24 hours, causes the target's spiritual essence to settle into the newly created body of a rat-thing. This spell costs 1D10 Sanity points and 20 magic points, plus 1 POW, and to cast it is dire and ungodly—not the sort of thing to do to a friend.

The disintegrating corpse forms the substance of the rat-thing. The rat-thing's face closely resembles a malevolent version of the victim's own face. As the keeper wishes, being reborn as a rat-thing may cost one's total Sanity, and perhaps force full-fledged membership in the evil species.

CURSE OF THE PUTRID HUSK: *Brothers of the Skin.* A sanity-attacking illusion. Cost to cast the spell is 5 magic points and 10 Sanity points; the victim's Sanity loss is 1D10 points.

The victim perceives that his or her skin is visibly rotting and corrupting. The outward appearance seems to deteriorate swiftly, so that great rents and tears occur through which internal organs begin to tumble out. Thereupon the victim faints and awakens in a few minutes whole and normal. The spell takes effect or is blocked by matching INT vs. INT on the Resistance Table; subtract 4 INT from the target at night, when he or she is sleeping. The entire cycle of effect takes about twenty minutes, including the faint.

This curse spell takes an hour to prepare and cast. The target must be known to the caster, and the caster must have as a focus some personal object belonging to the target. The experience of the spell is devastating, but each successful session of Psychoanalysis (the analyst gets a D100 roll equal to or less than his or her own Psychoanalysis skill) can help the victim come to terms with these inexplicable dreams and hallucinations, and restore half of each such Sanity loss. Psychiatric drugs do little to compensate for such an attack.

CURSE OF THE STONE: causes horrible hallucinations in the mind of the target. The spell requires two rounds to cast and costs 1D10 Sanity points and 9 magic points. The caster must overcome the target's magic points with his or her own on the Resistance Table or the spell fails. An ensorcelled stone tablet is also needed; one could be enchanted for the purposes of this spell by chiseling a sigil into a small stone slab and sacrificing 4 magic points.

Either the caster or the target of the spell must hold the tablet. The target must be visible. The spell being cast, the target is instantly overwhelmed with dreadful hallucinations, loses 1D4 Sanity points, and continues to be blinded and misled by these phantoms each round until his or her player can roll the character's POW or less on D100. Recovering, the target continues to be plagued by nightmares costing one Sanity point each night. To lift the curse the victim needs ingenuity: killing the caster would be heinous and maybe ineffective.

DAMPEN LIGHT: music from enchanted pipes or a flute creates a zone of darkness. The caster must be able to play the pan pipes or flute, and the instrument itself must be already enchanted. Casting the spell requires music from the pipes or flute, sacrifice of 1 or more magic points, and 1D3 Sanity points. Each magic point expended gives the zone of darkness 1 yard more of radius, centered on the musician and moving with him or her. The music must be played continuously for the spell's duration. The effect takes place three rounds after the music begins. All the light around the caster is drained away, blinding everyone nearby including the caster.

DEATH SPELL: causes the bewildered victim to burst into flame. It costs 24 magic points and 3D10 Sanity points. The target must be within ten yards of the caster, who must overcome the target's magic points with his or her own during each round of concentration. After 1D3 rounds of concentration, the victim's skin forms large blisters and he or she loses 1D3 hit points. In the next round, the victim loses 1D6 more hit points. On the third round, the victim bursts into flames, losing 1D10 hit points then and each round thereafter. The stench of burning hair and flesh is overwhelming. It is impossible to render aid, since the horrified victim burns from the inside out.

DEFLECT HARM: allows the caster to negate various physical attacks. The spell costs 1 magic point and 1 Sanity point. The caster invokes the names of the Outer Gods, then stretches out a hand toward an attacker. Until dropping the hand, the caster may deflect successive attacks by expending magic points equal to the rolled damage for each attack. If an attack would have missed, no magic points are expended. Upon dropping of the hand, the spell ends.

The spell may be recast. The caster may deflect any number of attacks until out of magic points. He or she may choose which attacks to deflect and from which attacks to take damage, but must choose before knowing what the damage will be. Lacking the magic points to stop a particular attack, the spell

ends, and the blow or missile hits or misses as it would in ordinary circumstances.

DETECT ENCHANTMENT: allows the caster to detect the baleful glow of curses, Evil Eyes, and other harmful enchantments that have been cast on humans, animals, or crops. It costs 6 magic points but no Sanity points.

DETRANSFERENCE: Brothers of the Skin. This spell reverses Transfer Body Part (see later in this list). It costs 10 magic points and 2 POW to cast. It takes five rounds to complete. Match the caster's magic points against those of the target on the Resistance Table. If the caster succeeds, then the borrowed organs and members appear in the caster's hands, sodden and rotting. Bereft of something vital, the target dies quickly.

The spell costs no Sanity unless it succeeds, in which case the rotting parts appear in the caster's hands. That costs 1D10 Sanity points unless the caster has had medical experience, or experience as a butcher.

DOMINATE: bends the will of the target to the caster's will. Dominate costs 1 magic point and 1 Sanity point. Match caster and target POW on the Resistance Table: with a success, the target obeys the commands of the caster until the next combat round concludes.

The spell affects one individual at a time, and has a maximum range of 10 yards. Obviously the command or commands must be intelligible to the target, and the spell may be broken if a command contradicts the target's basic nature. Dominate can be cast and recast as many times as the caster finds possible, allowing a target to be controlled without interruption for several minutes. Each cast of the spell has the same costs and limits. Recasting is almost instantaneous: Dominate can be cast once per round.

DREAD CURSE OF AZATHOTH: can drain POW from victim. It costs 4 magic points and 1D6 Sanity points to cast. By repeating the secret Name of Azathoth, one can generate respect and fear in any being conversant with the Mythos, for to know the Name implies that one knows the secret Last Syllable. Said alone, the Last Syllable may be directed against a foe. Match magic points on the Resistance Table. With a success, the target loses 1D3 POW.

DREAM VISION: causes the caster or a chosen target to experience a dream portending something about the future. The spell costs 3 magic points to cast. It may cost Sanity as well, depending on the content of the dream.

DUST OF SULEIMAN: this gray-green powder has the ability to harm unnatural beings from other planes. The powder requires the dust from an Egyptian mummy at least 2,000 years old, and each such mummy suffices for three doses of the magic dust. Also required are frankincense, sulfur, and saltpeter. An incantation must be said over the dust while it is being sprinkled. No Sanity points are needed to make or use this dust.

Sprinkled over an other-plane being, the entity loses 1D20 hit points per dose. It takes one round to apply a dose. The powder works only on beings for which a Summon/Bind or Call spell exists in this grimoire. Thus the powder would harm a nightgaunt, a byakhee, or Azathoth, but is useless against a shoggoth, Cthulhu, or a sand-dweller.

EIBON'S WHEEL OF MIST: evokes a whirling cylinder within which one or more persons can hide from select Mythos creatures. Each foot of height for the cylinder costs 1 magic point. The spell costs only 1 Sanity point.

A small bronze disk etched with a strange symbol resembling a three-legged swastika is needed. The caster lays the disk on the floor, stands atop it, intones the words of the spell, and expends the magic points and Sanity point. This generates a 5-foot-diameter wheel of spinning blue mist around the caster. Everything within the wheeling cylinder of mist is totally obscured. The desired wheel takes 1D3 minutes to form completely, and lasts for 1D20+10 minutes, then dissolves.

The mist hides people from creatures summoned by Nyarlathotep or in the name of Nyarlathotep. Such a creature acts as if the mist and those obscured by it are not present. The creature will not move through the wheel's position, even by accident. If the wheel blocks a path, the creature stops where it is or goes backward without knowing why. The wheel only affects his summoned minions, never Nyarlathotep.

As many people as can crowd into the mist can be obscured by the wheel, but if one's feet, head, etc., stick out then the illusion is ruined. To hide a group of normal-height investigators, 7 magic points are needed, unless players specifically indicate that they are crouching, bending, etc.

Creatures present before the wheel of mist is cast, or creatures called up by power other than that of Nyarlathotep, can see the wheel and move into it. The wheel can be stepped out of, but this ruins the illusion if the stepper is spotted, as does passing anything through the mist, such as a bullet or a sword. Anything passing from the outside of the wheel to the inside immediately gives away the illusion. Once the creature's attention is caught, and it realizes that an illusion might be in progress, the protection of the spell is lost.

ELDER SIGN: *Its decoration. . . was, rather, in the rough shape of a star, in the center of which there appeared to be a caricature of a single giant eye; but it was not an eye, rather a broken lozenge in shape with certain lines suggestive of flames or perhaps a solitary pillar of flame.*—August Derleth and H. P. Lovecraft, "The Lurker at the Threshold".

The spell activates a previously drawn Elder Sign. Each active Elder Sign takes a sacrifice of 2 POW to create, but costs no Sanity points. An Elder Sign may be formed into a leaden seal, carved in rock, forged in steel, etc. When made active beside an opening or Gate, it makes that path unusable to minions of the Great Old Ones and Outer Gods, as well as to those greater beings themselves. Without the spell, the symbol itself means nothing and has no effect.

The writings of certain scribes apart, the Elder Sign is worthless in personal defense if the monster or minion can evade the Sign—worn around the neck, for instance, an Elder Sign might protect a few square inches of flesh but the rest of the wearer's body would be completely vulnerable.

ENCHANT BOOK: aids in summoning star vampires by enchanting any book in which is inscribed the words of the spell Summon/Bind Star Vampire. The book's ink must contain the ichor of a star vampire. The caster sacrifices a varying amount of POW and loses 1D4 Sanity points, and meditates for three days. For each point of POW given to the book, add 10 percentiles to the caster's chance of success with Summon/Bind Star Vampire.

ENCHANT BRAZIER: allows the casting of Conjure Glass Of Mortlan, this step costing 1 point of POW and 1D4 Sanity points.

On the night of a full moon between the fall equinox and the winter solstice, the caster must sacrifice a small animal while intoning a formula and performing certain gestures. The chosen brazier is soaked in the animal's blood, and sprinkled with a handful of gold dust, platinum powder, or fixed mercury granules. The enchanter must then burn a piece of wood at least 500 years old, holding the brazier in its smoke. Upon completion, the brazier is enchanted and ready to use.

ENCHANT CANE: creates an artifact which drains POW points from victims and stores them as magic points usable by the owner. Casting the spell and creating the cane requires a week's work, a human sacrifice, 6 points of POW, and 1D6 Sanity points. Each use of the cane costs 1D3 Sanity points. Any inflexible object might be used, but a cane is typical.

When anyone but the cane's creator touches the enchanted object for more than 30 seconds, he or she loses a point of POW, and the object accumulates a magic point. The person losing the POW immediately feels suspicious and profoundly uneasy. The object usually is held against a victim who is held by force until POW is drained away completely, and the soul sucked into the enchanted object. When a magic point from the object is used in casting a spell, it is gone permanently and a point of POW may be drained from a victim to replace it.

ENCHANT CANDLE: *Voodoo.* Requires a day-long ritual, grants a variety of permanent effects, and costs the caster 4 magic points but no Sanity. The supplicant must sacrifice 1 POW and 1D4 Sanity points by reciting certain words, and may or may not be told what those words cause to happen.

The supplicant's fingernail clippings or hair scraps must be mixed into the wax when the candle is made, as must droplets of his or her blood, and the event the supplicant wishes to influence must be written on the side. As the candle burns, the

Enchantment Spells

A number of Enchant spells exist, each used to imbue magic into a different device or artifact. Each such spell involves a blood sacrifice, the sacrifice of at least 1 POW, the loss of 1D4 or more Sanity points, and at least a game day of time.

There are four enchanted items of permanent duration for which no spell of creation is known: the Glass from Leng, the Lamp of Alhazred, the Plutonian Drug, and the Shining Trapezohedron are included in this grimoire under their alphabetical entries, not in the list of enchantments.

To craft an enchantment or an artifact, consider keeper and player styles. It might have unpredictable advantages and disadvantages. It might be useful for probing more deeply into the Mythos, it might expose investigators to monstrous encounters, or it might offer a way to another dimension. Since the spell or the artifact is unlikely to vanish from play once introduced, consider it carefully before introducing it, and make sure what it does and what it costs is clearly stated and easy to understand.

supplicant must perform a pertinent activity—the skill to be improved, picturing in mind the person from whom he or she seeks undying love, and so forth.

ENCHANT DOLL: *Voodoo.* Requires a two-day ritual, causes pain and harm to the target, and costs 1 POW and 1D4 Sanity points each from caster and supplicant. The supplicant need only be present for the last hour of the ritual. The doll is soaked in an elixir which includes human blood, and then a lock of the target's pubic hair is affixed to the doll. When the doll is stabbed, the target receives a corresponding excruciating pain, or vertigo, nausea, impotence, etc. Roll D100 against CON to avoid halving physical skills during these attacks.

ENCHANT GATE BOXES: allows creation of twin magical boxes which, open, thereby form the two ends of a magical Gate. Going through a gate box costs exactly the same magic points and Sanity points as going through a normal Gate, and the transit procedure is the same.

First, two identical wooden boxes must be made to any desired SIZ. The boxes should be open only at one end. Then the necessary ritual, consisting of placing one's hands on the boxes and conceiving certain hyperdimensional lines and angles in one's mind for about five hours, must be performed. 1 POW is sacrificed at this time. Then the boxes automatically drain magic points equal to half of the maker's POW each day, until they have absorbed magic points equal to their total SIZ x100. (If the maker has odd-numbered POW, the boxes take an extra magic point daily.) 1 SAN is lost for every full week of magic point drain. Once the necessary magic points have been taken, the boxes become operative.

ENCHANT GRIS-GRIS: *Voodoo.* Requires a long ritual, grants a variety of permanent enhancements. It costs the caster 3 magic points, and from the new owner of the bag 1 POW, 1D4 Sanity points, and a variable number of magic points. A small animal must be sacrificed. A magical aura produced by items in the small drawstring bag improves one aspect of the wearer's life, specified before the creation of the bag— increasing by five percentiles a particular skill, for example, for each magic point the owner invests in the bag.

ENCHANT FLESH: *Brothers of the Skin.* A spell known only to one man. It allows the caster to preserve and ensorcel 1 SIZ point of the skin and flesh of a victim. After a day of preparation, the spell takes five minutes to cast and costs the user 1 POW and 3D4 Sanity points. The flesh must be cut away with an enchanted knife while the blood flows, and immediately thereafter the spell must be cast upon the flesh.

The SIZ point of flesh is now immune to damage from fire, electricity, strangulation, blunt weapons, impaling weapons (except for guns, which do minimum damage), and so forth. Enchanted weapons and magic do normal damage. Further, the flesh will age instead of the caster, adding a year to the caster's life. By adding new flesh yearly, the caster gains an indefinite extension of life.

If Graft Flesh is used, the flesh lasts forever. Otherwise the enchanted flesh lasts only for a number of weeks equal to the caster's POW x2. After that it loses its magical properties and goes the way of all flesh.

That number of flesh blocks equal to a person's SIZ can completely armor him or her. The resulting lumps and scars are impressive. See also Graft Flesh.

ENCHANT JU-JU: *Voodoo.* Requires day-long preparation and ritual to consecrate a ward defending against black magic. A sacrifice of 1 POW and 1D4 Sanity points is needed, as well as the sacrifice of a chicken with black feathers, to give notice to the spirits. When created, a ju-ju will be shunned by evil denizens of the voodoo world, sorcerers included. This ward can be anything the supplicant wants. The ju-ju may be worn to protect a person, or placed over a doorway or window to protect a home.

ENCHANT KNIFE: the enchanted knife increases the success chance for other spells. The caster sacrifices a point of POW and 1D4 Sanity points. The spell enchants a knife or dagger made of a pure metal such as gold or iron. With the knife blade a diagram is drawn on a flat surface; then the blade is used to kill an animal of at least SIZ 4. The creature's blood is then traced out to follow the lines of the drawn diagram, and the enchantment is complete.

Such a knife is suitable for use in casting Summon Dimensional Shambler. Each extra point of POW placed into it adds 10 percentiles to the chance for success in casting that spell. If this knife is used to slay the small animal for Enchant Brazier, the brazier so made adds 10 percentiles to the chance for successfully casting Conjure Glass of Mortlan.

ENCHANT LANCE: does 1D10 damage to any creature, and can impale any creature, including ones normally resistant to impaling weapons. The spell requires 1 POW, a week's work, 1D4 Sanity points, and a bellows-driven fire hot enough to melt steel. The lance must be made out of pure metal of some kind, and at least once the metal must be quenched in blood. The user needs good STR and DEX to wield the lance. To make a lance properly requires an appropriate Craft roll.

ENCHANT PIPES: augments the chance for success in casting particular spells. The spell enchants a set of pan pipes or a flute. The instrument must be at least 90% metal. An hour-long ritual of concentration and incantation must be performed over the musical instrument, during which 1D6 Sanity points are sacrificed by the caster, who must also sacrifice POW into the instrument. For each point of POW sacrificed, the musical instrument must steep in fresh warm blood for two hours. A new animal, of at least cat or rabbit size, must be slaughtered for each point of POW. For each point of POW it contains, the finished instrument adds 10 percentiles to the success chance of Summon/Bind Servitor of the Outer Gods, and other spells requiring the use of pipes or flutes to cast.

ENCHANT SACRIFICIAL DAGGER: to activate, perform this spell over a flame-shaped dagger. The dagger must then be used to kill a living being of at least 20 POW. Simultaneously, the enchanter sacrifices 6 points of his or her own Power. From then on, when the dagger is used properly to sacrifice chosen victims in the presence of Nyarlathotep, the POW of the victim flows into the dagger, and from the dagger the POW can be sent to any convenient storage site—the caster, perhaps, or an inanimate object.

ENCHANT SPEAR: creates a spear which always hits the target if the target is within range. The weapon must be a wooden spear with a point made from bird bone. The caster loses 4 POW, and 1D4 Sanity points. The spear must be decorated with feathers from at least 30 different species of birds, each plucked from a living bird. If a feather is lost in use, a new one must be obtained. To make the spear, the caster must perform a ritual with the chosen spear on the spring equinox for two consecutive years. At the end of the second ritual, the spear must be used to kill something. It is then enchanted. It always hits when thrown, but is otherwise an ordinary weapon. It does 1D10 damage, impales, and acts as a magical weapon against a Mythos creature unless the creature is resistant to impaling weapons.

ENCHANT STONE TABLET: this tablet must be made from black stone taken from the sunken city of R'lyeh. It must be carefully etched over a period of several weeks, and the caster must put 2 POW into it. Both a deep one and a human must be sacrificed to the tablet without shedding blood (usually by strangling or smothering). The caster loses 1D8 Sanity points and daily must place 1 magic point into the stone. When finished, the stone is enchanted.

Anyone owning this stone has nightmares of alien vistas and dimly-perceived oozing masses, all against a background of shifting colors and forms. Far-off slithering and gurgling is heard. If the stone's possessor destroys it, the effects of the dreams intensify, with the same result as if the spell Curse of the Stone had been cast upon the owner (except that he does not fall prey to instant hallucinations). The tablet also can be used in the spell Curse of the Stone.

If the tablet is tossed into the sea, it contacts (but does not bind) 1D8 deep ones. They return the tablet to the person who threw it away, perhaps sending the target over the edge of insanity. The time it takes them to bring back the tablet depends on the distance from the thrown tablet to the nearest deep one city. The dreams stop while the deep ones possess the tablet. If the thrower is very far inland, local cultists may do the job.

ENCHANT WANGA: *Voodoo.* Requires a three-hour ritual daily for eight days. It causes harm or bad luck to the wearer, and costs 3 magic points and 1D3 Sanity points from the caster and 1 POW and 1D4 Sanity points from the supplicant. A *wanga* is an object "mounted" by evil spirits, causing illness or bad luck while touched by the target. Often a personal object belonging to the target will be spirited away to be turned into a *wanga*—frequently a rosary or a crucifix. The victim's illness or bad luck (-20 percentiles for all skill rolls and Luck rolls) lasts until the *wanga* is identified and destroyed.

ENCHANT WHISTLE: augments the caster's chance to Summon/Bind Byakhee. The spell enchants a whistle, which must be an alloy of silver and iron meteorite. POW is sacrificed to the whistle in a day-long ceremony, and a rooster also must be sacrificed. The ritual costs the caster 1D4 Sanity points. For each point of POW sacrificed to the whistle, add 10 percentiles to the chance of successfully casting Summon/Bind Byakhee.

ENTHRALL VICTIM: entrances the target. The spell costs the caster 1D6 Sanity points and 2 magic points. The caster must be able to speak calmly with the target before the spell can take effect. After a round or so of talking, the caster matches his magic points against the target's on the Resistance Table. If overcome, the victim stands struck, numb and dumb, until relieved from the trance by physical assault or some similarly shocking event. If the caster fails to overcome the target, he or she may try the spell the following round.

EVIL EYE: causes a victim to suffer from bad luck. The spell costs 10 magic points and 1D4 Sanity points to cast. The target must be within sight of the caster. The victim will not necessarily sense the Evil Eye, but feels an odd chill or unease when the Evil Eye is cast.

The victim's chance for a Luck roll is halved. His or her chance for a DEX roll is halved. His or her guns jam on every roll of 75% or higher. The chances for Summon / Bind spells are halved. The effects continue until sunrise, until the caster removes the spell, until the caster is found and blooded (hit hard enough to bleed), or until the victim dies.

EXILE EIHORT: forces Eihort, a Great Old One, to remain in his English labyrinth for a year and a day. Learning the spell requires a roll of INT x2 or less on D100 and 25-INT days of study. The spell requires 3 rounds to intone and costs 1D4 Sanity points per participant. The caster and other people who know the spell can expend as many magic points as desired. Additional participants who touch the caster can add 1 magic point per person, though the Sanity cost per participant remains 1D4. Using the Resistance Table, match the total against Eihort's POW 30. They'll need at least POW 21 to have a 5% chance.

EXTEND: grants immortality to the caster. It costs 3 POW, 3D6 Sanity points, and 100 magic points. During the spell the caster builds a great fire and summons an ancient nameless being which costs 1D6/1D20 SAN to see. The ritual then creates a pact between the caster and the being, in which the being ages instead of the caster. If the caster dies somehow, the being replaces the caster on Earth, while the caster's corpse is magically sent to the dimension from which the being came.

EYE OF LIGHT AND DARKNESS: weakens many Mythos agents and servants. This powerful spell requires very large sacrifices of POW, but of varying amount for each time the spell is cast.

A great sigil of the Eye is worked into a hard natural substance such as granite, and then placed on a high place in the area to be warded. The Eye must be created in the afternoon before the full moon rises. At moonrise, the blood of an innocent (that is, someone without Cthulhu Mythos knowledge) must be used to fill the pupil of the Eye once per hour until the moon sets. Thus only a few ounces of blood are needed.

A number of participants must chant together as the first blood is given, repeating aloud *sa-ma, sa-ma, te-yo, sa-ma* and so on till the moon sets. When the moon next rises, the pupil of the Eye is activated and begins to glow. Once activated, the symbol disappears within the substance into which it has been chiseled or inscribed, and cannot then be removed by physical or ordinary magical agent or spell. When nearby, those who created it (and only they) always can see the dim nimbus emanate from the Eye.

The ward requires 100 POW from the people chanting for the spell, not necessarily given with their knowledge. Each hour of the chant, the Eye randomly leeches 1D4 POW from each chanter until exactly 100 POW or slightly more have been absorbed. A character losing all Power drops dead. If 100 POW or more is not accumulated before moonset, the activation of the ward fails, all leeched Power is lost, and the procedure must be started again from scratch if the ward is to be created.

An Eye of Light And Darkness is powerful. It weakens agents, monsters, and minions of the Outer Gods and Great Old Ones who enter the area it protects, damaging them at the rate of 1 magic point per hour. If such a servant remains within the Eye's effect until its magic points reach 0, it disintegrates. Contact, Call, and Summon/Bind spells may not be cast within the reach of the Eye.

The effect of the Eye extends in a 10-mile radius from it, but it does not penetrate more than 20 feet of rock or metal. If placed on a mountainside, for instance, the Eye would protect only that side of the mountain.

To destroy an Eye requires a spell unique to that Eye, the characteristics of which may take years to deduce.

EYES OF THE ZOMBIE: allows the caster to take direct control of a specially prepared zombie, and thereafter to perceive events from the zombie's viewpoint until the spell expires. Each cast costs 3 magic points and 15 Sanity points, and is effective for 1D3 months.

The eyes of the zombie are removed and placed in a special chemical bath. The caster's eyes are similarly removed as part of the ritual, and stored away for safety. Then the zombie's eyes are inserted into the caster's empty sockets, and a short phrase murmured. Then the caster can move, perceive, and react as though actually in the zombie body.

Replacing the eyeballs requires a similar spell cast.

FIND GATE: makes apparent to the caster any Gate to or from another world or plane, if it is within the caster's vision. The spell costs 1 magic point and 1D3 Sanity points. This spell locates: it does not empower anyone to open, close, create, or pass through any Gate.

FIST OF YOG-SOTHOTH: hits the target with an invisible blow of varying intensity. This spell costs a varying amount of magic points as well as 1D6 Sanity points. The caster must be able to see the target. The spell takes effect instantaneously. It affects a single target.

Each magic point included in the spell yields 1D6 STR of force. For every 30 feet of distance that the caster stands from the target, the STR of the blow decreases by 1D6.

When the target is struck, match the rolled STR of the blow against the target's CON+STR on the Resistance Table. If the blow overcomes the target, then the target is knocked unconscious. Whether or not the target is left unconscious, the target always is pushed away from the caster for a distance in feet equal to the rolled STR of the blow minus the target's SIZ.

The spell can be used against the STR of inanimate objects such as doors or walls. Results may be obvious, but sometimes keepers will have to determine these cases, perhaps by the result actually rolled.

FLESH WARD: grants protection against physical attack. The spell costs 1D4 Sanity points and a varying amount of magic points. Each magic point spent gives the caster (or the chosen target) 1D6 points of armor against nonmagical attacks. This protection wears off as it blocks damage. If a character had 12 points of Flesh Ward as armor, and was hit for 8 points of damage, his Flesh Ward would be reduced to 4 points, but he or she would take no damage. The spell takes five rounds to cast, and lasts 24 hours or until the protection is used up. Once cast, the spell may not be reinforced with further magic points, nor recast until the old spell's protection has been used up.

FOOD OF LIFE: cruelly and unnaturally extends the life span of an individual cultist. The spell costs 10 magic points and 1D8+1 Sanity points to cast. An unholy feast of several days' duration is key to the ritual. The cultist cannibal adds one month of life for every SIZ point of human flesh therein consumed.

FREE HASTUR: in conjunction with the nine stone monoliths required for the Call Hastur spell, this chant permits Hastur to enter and to remain freely within the area bounded by the monoliths. Only the leader of the chant needs to know the chant. Everyone else involved in the chant loses 1 POW. For every 10 such points sacrificed, 1-POW-worth of Hastur or his creatures gain access to Earth. Thus 350 chanters would be needed to bring Hastur, and 210 chanters needed to bring the average star-spawn of Cthulhu.

Once Hastur can freely remain, he need not return to the sky at sunrise and can remain active all year round. Hastur-connected spells are usable day or night within the bounded region. That region may be millions of square miles.

GLASS FROM LENG: *a great round window of a most curious clouded glass, of which* [Wilbur] *said only that it was a work of great antiquity, which he had discovered and acquired in the course of his travels in Asia. He referred to it at one time as "the glass from Leng" and at another as "possibly Hyadean in origin", neither of which enlightened me in the slightest.* — August Derleth and H. P. Lovecraft, "The Gable Window."

An enchantment. This magical glass allows the possessor to see in it random visions of other places. The previous owner would inscribe a pentagram in red chalk (presumably for protection), recite a brief verse, and then the glass would show a scene of beings from the Cthulhu Mythos. Unfortunately, such beings could also see through the glass to the user's side.

GRAFT FLESH: *Brothers of the Skin.* Allows the caster to graft enchanted flesh to his or her body, and have the flesh and its armoring effects last forever. The spell costs 10 magic points and 2D6 Sanity points to cast. The lengthy ritual involves hours of chanting and prayer to Nyarlathotep or another significant Mythos deity. The caster must also remove from his or her own body a corresponding area of flesh (costing 1D4 hit points and 2D6 Sanity points) before the enchanted flesh can be Grafted. After the spell has been completed, the properties of enchanted flesh are immediately available. See the spell the Enchanted Flesh.

GRASP OF CTHULHU: immobilizes one or more targets with crushing pressure, temporarily robbing STR as well. The charm costs 2D6 magic points per game minute, and 1D6 Sanity points for the cast. It can be extended for as many minutes as the caster's magic points can buy without additional Sanity point cost, but the caster must concentrate on the spell during that time. The spell's range is ten yards. Cast, the spell's effect begins immediately, and can affect more than one person at a time, but each additional target costs an additional 2D6 magic points per game minute.

Resolve this spell on the Resistance Table, separately matching the POW of the caster against the POW of each target. If the caster wins, the victim feels great pressure and is unable to move, as though wrapped by the mighty tentacles of Great Cthulhu. If there are multiple targets, one target may be attacked successfully while another target fends off the attack. For each minute the spell lasts, the target temporarily loses 1D10 STR points. If the target's STR drops to zero or less, he or she falls unconscious.

GRAY BINDING: a way to form an uncontrolled zombie. A ritual liquid must be poured over a corpse. The keeper determines the ingredients of the liquid. At least one part is costly or illegal.

Immediately after, the caster intones the spell, spending 8 magic points and 1D6 Sanity points. The ritual takes five minutes, after which the corpse rouses. It is nearly mindless, and is not under the control of its creator. The thing continues to rot after its creation, and so eventually decays into incapacity. The risen corpse is otherwise identical to the zombie on p. 186.

HANDS OF COLUBRA: turns the hands of the caster into the foreparts of venomous snakes. The spell costs 12 magic points and 1D10 Sanity points. It can be used only on the caster, and takes a full round to cast. The effect lasts 1D3+3 combat rounds. The transformed snakes can bite targets up to 8 feet distant. Each snake has the caster's DEX x5 chance to hit, each bite does 1D3 damage by itself, and each hit injects a venom of potency equal to the current magic point total of the caster. Match the potency of the venom against the target's CON on the Resistance Table. If the venom attack succeeds, the victim loses 1D10 hit points per round until the hit points lost equal the venom's potency. At that point the poison is neutralized and does no further damage, but a second bite starts a second, new attack. Sanity loss is 0/1D6 for witnessing the use of Hands of Colubra.

HEAL: maximizes the healing rate possible: with it the natural rate is 3 hit points per week, with First Aid it can be 6 hit points the first week, and with Medicine it can be 9 hit points the first week. The spell costs 3 magic points and no Sanity points. It takes 25 game rounds to cast. The recipient must be touched by the caster or the spell cannot take effect, and the spell must be reapplied each week to have effect for that week.

HEALING: after 2D6 game rounds, it can immediately heal 2D6 hit points lost to injury, disease, or poison. Ignore hit points restored in excess of normal. The spell cannot bring back the dead to life. Each cast costs 12 magic points and 1 Sanity point.

HEART'S COURAGE: a protective spell against those who know spells of any sort. It costs 1 POW and 4 Sanity points to cast. Those knowing no spells are unaffected. The caster must be a worshiper of Chaugnar Faugn, though the god may have other names than that. The caster carves certain runes into the wall or floor of the area to be protected, then prays to Chaugnar Faugn and sacrifices POW. From time to time, such a ward may need a new sacrifice of POW, but there is no automatic expiration.

When a target nears the runes, he or she must intone the god's name to be let past. Failing that, the target's player may attempt POW x3 or less on D100. With a success, the investigator keeps on walking and the spell has no effect.

With a failure, the target finds himself or herself paralyzed and frozen in place. The body otherwise functions normally. The target can speak and see. With a result of 96-00, the target falls before going rigid.

If left at the warding runes or carried past them, paralysis continues indefinitely, and the target may die in two or three days. If carried back away from the runes, the paralysis ends after the target's POW in game rounds. A character who was frozen by the ward can attempt to pass it again after his or her POW in game rounds has passed.

IDENTIFY SPIRIT: this spell creates a magical powder which temporarily exposes any alien entity inhabiting the target's mind or body. Making it costs 12 magic points and 2 Sanity points. Anyone can use this powder. When sprinkled over a human and a word of power is spoken, the powder then reveals the possessing entity for a game round.

The powder requires glass ground from a mirror at least 100 years old, a handful of gold dust, and two special ingredients of the keeper's choice. The caster then meditates for a day and a night in a silent cave or other lightless place. Once his or her mind is clear, the caster combines the ingredients, adds the blood of a mammal, sacrifices 12 magic points and 2 Sanity points, and utters a short incantation. If the vessel's contents burst into flame, the spell has succeeded. If not, the magic points are lost, and the ritual may be begun anew. The chance for success is the caster's POW x5 or less, rolled on D100. The result is a fine gray-blue powder as soft as fresh wood ash. It keeps indefinitely.

A pinch or two is enough. Sprinkled, blown, or thrown over a possible victim, the form of any existing foreign entity becomes visible as a life-size shadow superimposed over the host; the shadow vanishes at the end of the game round. Sanity losses are half normal, since only a shadow is revealed.

Y'golonac, a Great Race member, or an insect from Shaggai would be revealed. Serpent people using Cast Illusion would not be revealed by this spell, nor would people of ghoulish tendency, nor vampires or shape-changers. A wraith would be revealed.

IMPECCABLE THROW: reciting a short verse allows the caster to throw objects and have them land exactly where he or she desires, for a period of the caster's POW in game rounds. The spell costs 3 magic points and 1 hit point (for the effort), but no Sanity is lost. The spell guides a thrown object to a trajectory that will hit the target. The spell will adjust aim, but there must be sufficient force in the throw.

IMPLANT FEAR: grips the target with soul-chilling dread. It costs the caster 12 magic points and 1D6 Sanity points. The sudden unnerving costs the target 0/1D6 Sanity points and causes him or her to stop work or end concentration.

IMPLANT SUGGESTION: *Dreamlands.* This rare spell of compulsion is effective only against creatures with some human blood in them—Lengites, deep one hybrids, ghoul changelings, Little People, etc. Magic point and Sanity point costs for the spell vary. The range is 10 yards or less, and the target must be able to hear and understand the caster. The caster needs two rounds to intone the spell and to relate the suggestion to the target. When the spell is cast, the caster must overcome the target's POW with his or her own on the Resistance Table; extreme suggestions involving death or great harm require a second successful Resistance Table roll just before the suggestion is implemented.

The cost for the spell varies with the suggestion. For ordinary unthreatening suggestions (drop your sword, hand over your money and leave, etc.), the cost is 5 magic points and 1D3 Sanity points. Riskier suggestions, but not ones antithetical to the target (go to Inquanok, set fire to a building, etc.), cost 10 magic points and 2D3 Sanity. Dangerous or suicidal suggestions (kill a companion, kidnap King Kuranes, etc.) cost 15 magic points and 3D3+1 Sanity.

IMPRISON MIND: destroys the ability of an entity to move magically or naturally from mind to mind, possess other beings, or leave in any other way the body in which it is currently. The cost per participant is 10 magic points and 1D6 Sanity points.

The spell may be cast by an individual or a group. Once cast, match the casters' POW against the target's on the Resistance table. (The target is always the possessing mind.) If the target is overcome, it is forever trapped in its current body. If used against a Great Old One, Outer God, Elder God, or avatar, the spell traps the being for only 100-POW minutes. Y'golonac, for example, would be trapped for 72 minutes.

JOURNEY TO THE OTHER SIDE: self-entranced, the caster sends his or her spirit to another plane as desired, conceivably even to the location of a Cthulhu Mythos deity. This spell costs 15 magic points to cast, and a day-long ritual to achieve. The trance lasts 1D6+3 game hours. Unknown but possibly large Sanity losses result from the particular experiences.

KEENNESS OF TWO ALIKE: to a level which seems appropriate to the keeper, this spell heightens mental clarity, concentration, and retention for a period of 1D4+4 hours. It requires two casters of blood relation. Costs to each caster are 4 magic points and 0/1 Sanity point. Conclusions understood or perceived during the spell's effect are remembered when the spell ends, though the derivations of such conclusions may become mysterious.

Each casting takes one hour. The spell may be recast when a casting concludes. Two casters must participate following an elaborate ritual, one necessarily blood-incestuous. One caster receives the temporary intellectual enhancement, nominally equivalent to an extra 6 INT. Ritual and spell are from left-hand or black Tantra, and are not Mythos-connected.

LAME / HEAL ANIMAL: causes one animal, usually a farm animal like a horse or cow, to suffer painful inflammation of its tendons and ligaments or to become extraordinarily healthy and vigorous, as the caster chooses. The spell costs 4 magic points for either version, and 1D4 Sanity points to cast Lame Animal.

LAMP OF ALHAZRED: *The lamp of Alhazred was unusual in its appearance. It was meant for burning oil, and seemed to be of gold. It had the shape of a small oblong pot, with a handle curved up from one side, and a spout for wick and flame on the other. Many curious drawings decorated it, together with letters and pictures arranged into words in a language unfamiliar.*—August Derleth and H. P. Lovecraft, "The Lamp of Alhazred."

An enchantment. When lit, this lamp gives forth vapors that sends the minds of those who inhale the vapors into ecstasies of vision. These revelations are of the strange and weird landscapes of Mythos places and dimensions, and the ways of the entities there. If this lamp was actually used by al-Hazred, the author of the *Al Azif*, some of the breadth of his knowledge would be explained.

LEVITATE: causes the caster or a chosen target to float slowly through the air. Levitate requires 1 magic point per SIZ of the thing levitated, and 1D6 Sanity points. The caster must be able to see the levitation. The effect lasts several minutes. The spell levitates the target 3-5 feet off the ground or floor. If falling from a height, the target falls in slow motion and halts several feet off the ground. Each extra magic point expended after the spell is cast allows the user to move the target one yard horizontally or vertically. (If the target is a living being who is unwilling to be levitated, the caster must first overcome the target's magic points with his or her own.)

The target floats as the caster wills, helpless to stop moving except by grabbing a tree limb or similar brace. In that case match target STR against the caster's magic points (both in the spell and those still unexpended). If the target wins, the spell is broken. The target falls, of course.

LOOK TO THE FUTURE: hurls a willing target a varying number of years into the future. After a group chant for a game hour, all participants in the ceremony lose 1 POW each, except the caster of the spell, who loses 2D6 Sanity points instead.

Upon completion of the chant, the chosen volunteer (who need not himself chant) is then physically hurled into the future. One year passes for each point of POW expended during the ceremony. The spell is imprecise: subtract 1D10 years from the desired target date. If the result is a trip into the past instead, the target disappears from existence (one preferably wants at least eleven contributors of POW therefore). After a number of game hours elapse equal to the volunteer's POW, he or she snaps back to the present. To witnesses, the volunteer disappears, then reappears a round or two later.

Depending on what it achieves, this spell can provoke important historical paradoxes. In keeping with the tradition of the Cthulhu Mythos, a major paradox should lead swiftly, grimly, and immediately to the madness and death of the person initiating it. This powerful spell is known by Nyarlathotep, who may or may not teach it to a worshiper.

MELT FLESH: *Brothers of the Skin.* It heats dead flesh to its melting point in one round, requiring 1 magic point to melt 3 SIZ of flesh. This takes 5 rounds and costs 1D4 Sanity points to cast. If used on animate flesh, the cost changes, to 1 POW per 3 SIZ, and the attacker and target magic points first must be matched on the Resistance Table. Seeing human flesh melt off human bones costs 1/1D6 Sanity.

MENTAL SUGGESTION: causes the target to be controlled by the caster for one round, and to do exactly what is commanded. The spell costs 8 magic points and 1D8 Sanity points, and takes 3 rounds to cast. The sorcerer can cast it on any target visible to the unaided eye. Match the caster's magic points against the target's on the Resistance Table. Success is total, and can include the command to attempt suicide or make a murderous assault on a friend. The spell can be recast, as the sorcerer is able.

MESMERIZE: the user can command any being with human blood in its veins. The caster loses 1D6 Sanity points, but no magic points, and must have at least 50% Occult and 50% Cthulhu Mythos. The spell takes a DEX rank to cast.

Match caster and target POW on the Resistance Table. If successful, the target stops and accepts commands spoken by the caster. The target must be close enough to see the caster's eyes, which seem to glow while the spell operates. Mesmerization lasts for 5 rounds for each point of INT the caster possesses. If the INT of the target is higher than that of the caster, a successful POW vs. POW Resistance Table roll must be made every 10 rounds, or the spell is broken.

A single target is affected. The victim's physical action skills are halved. The victim carries out all that is commanded by the caster, even to self-destruction. The spell also works against modern serpent folk and deep ones who have interbred with humans, but doesn't work on nonhuman entities such as shantaks or dimensional shamblers.

MI-GO HYPNOSIS: *Mi-Go.* By introducing ultrahigh and ultralow frequency tones into its buzzing, the mi-go can put one or many humans listening to it into a trance state. An investigator within forty feet of a buzzing mi-go must receive a successful Resistance Table roll of POW vs. POW or become incapable of action. Thoughts and commands can then be given to a specific human via the Contact Human spell.

MINDBLAST: the victim of this spell loses 5 Sanity points and goes temporarily insane for at least one hour. The spell costs the caster 1D3 Sanity points and 10 magic points. To succeed, the caster must successfully match magic points with the target on the Resistance Table. The target is affected for 1D10 x10 game hours, after which he or she recovers. The concept of the insane insight would not apply to this induced temporary insanity.

MIND EXCHANGE: allows the caster to trade minds with another individual. The caster loses 1D3 Sanity points and must expend magic points equal to the target's POW the first time the spell is cast. Thereafter, the cost goes down 1 magic point per casting until it reaches 1, where it remains. The Sanity point cost does not increase.

The target must know the spell-caster and love or strongly favor him or her. If that affection is somehow lost before the spell's cost is reduced to 1, the exchange can no longer occur. Fresh affection renews the chance. The target loses Sanity points upon finding arriving in another's body, 1/1D3 Sanity points at minimum. Temporary insanity is a possible reaction.

This spell can be cast at any range. The caster must overcome the target's magic points with his or her own each time the spell is cast, until the cost for casting the spell has been reduced to 1, when he or she no longer needs to do so and can transfer at will, using only a strong mental effort. The spell caster cannot initially stay more than a few minutes inside the target's body, but progressively is able to longer and longer. Once the cost for transfer is 1 magic point, he or she can stay there indefinitely.

MIND TRANSFER: allows the caster permanently to trade minds with the target, perhaps to attain longer life at the target's expense. The spell requires 10 magic points to cast, and also takes a successful magic-points match on the Resistance Table. With success, the caster loses 1D10 Sanity points, and the victim loses 1D20 Sanity points.

If the exchange fails, the caster must immediately cast the spell again (lose 10 more magic points) or his or her soul dissipates into eternity. Running out of magic points has the same result. Once the transfer is begun, it cannot be broken off.

MIRROR OF TARKHUN ATEP: as harassment or warning, the caster is able to project his image onto the surface of a mirror or mirroring surface that is being gazed into by the caster's intended victim. This spell costs 5 magic points and 1 Sanity point. The victim can be anywhere on Earth.

The caster needs a mirror large enough to see his or her head and neck. Gazing within it and keeping an image of the target in mind, he or she utters the short incantation, makes the sacrifice of Sanity and magic points, and waits. When the target looks into a darkened window, a mirror, or any other mirroring surface, an image of the caster begins to form. If the caster tires before the target looks into a mirror, that loss of attention breaks the spell.

Sometimes the mirror image of the caster is looking directly into the eyes of the victim. At other times the caster is seen standing directly behind the victim in the reflection. If the victim wears glasses, images reflected from the lenses may even be resolved. Words and short phrases which the target can hear can be uttered by the caster. The caster can see through his or her mirror as well, and see the target and the target's surroundings.

NIGHTMARE: causes the target to experience a horrible nightmare, awake screaming, and lose 1D3 Sanity points. The spell costs 8 magic points and 1 Sanity point to cast. It affects a single sleeping individual, whose name must be known to the caster. The spell can take effect at any range. The shaken victim awakes in a cold sweat, but cannot remember the contents of the dream unless benefiting from a successful Psychoanalysis roll. The dream's content is chosen by the keeper, not the caster, and must be closely related to the life and habits of the caster.

PARTING SANDS: ancient Egyptian sorcery used to part nonliving obstacles (walls, doors, rivers, and so forth). The spell costs 2 magic points and 0/1D4 SAN to cast. Ordinary desert sand is enchanted. For each point of SIZ above the first two points, the spell costs an additional magic point. One could use this spell to part the Red Sea, but that would take a lot of magic points. To apply, spread a line of sand in the direction desired, and sacrifice the necessary points. The way that opens is wide enough and tall enough for men and horses. The spell takes about ten rounds to complete.

PERFECTION: given the permission of a god, the caster may convert points of Power into points of other characteristics with this spell, either for the caster or for his or her designated target. The god designates any costs involved—usually one for one in characteristic points. There is no Sanity charge per se, but contact with an Outer God or Great Old One is necessary, so the Sanity loss involved may be substantial.

PIPES OF MADNESS: drives hearers insane. This spell must be cast with the enchanted owl-bone pipes made by the ritual in the spell Create Curse Whistle. The caster plays a specific weird melody on the pipes and expends 5 magic points every 5 rounds of playing. It costs 1D6 Sanity points to cast the spell.

Call for Sanity rolls for all within earshot. Whoever receives a failure loses 5 Sanity points and immediately goes temporarily insane; roll on the longer duration table. With a successful Sanity roll, the listener loses 1D3 Sanity points and ordinarily does not go insane. Repeat the Sanity rolls every 5 rounds that the pipes are played and heard.

PLUTONIAN DRUG: *"I have here five pellets of the drug Liao. It was used by the Chinese philosopher Lao Tze, and while under its influence he visioned Tao. Tao is the most mysterious force in the world; it surrounds and pervades all things"*—Frank Belknap Long, "The Hounds of Tindalos."

An enchantment. This drug has the ability to send the user's mind back in time. In the story, it sometimes sent back users so far that they encountered the hounds of Tindalos, entities capable of traveling up and down time via its "corners." The hounds are attracted by such intrusion and soon appear to devour the interloper. The drug can appear in liquid or tablet form.

POSE MUNDANE (MASK): the spell makes a creature or object totally unremarkable in the minds of viewers. The caster must sacrifice magic points equal to the SIZ of the creature or object, plus one magic point per round to maintain the effect. An inanimate object can be masked indefinitely by the sacrifice instead of 1 POW during the casting.

People fail to notice the strange appearance, though frequent contact with the masked item allows a person to perceive that something about the object or creature is very unusual.

POWDER OF IBN-GHAZI: *Those without the telescope saw only an instant's flash of grey cloud—a cloud about the size of a moderately large building—near the top of the mountain. Curtis, who held the instrument, dropped it with a piercing shriek into the ankle-deep mud of the road. He reeled, and would have crumpled to the ground had not two or three others seized and steadied him. All he could do was moan half-inaudibly.*—H. P. Lovecraft, "The Dunwich Horror."

The spell makes visible magically invisible things by blowing the powder against the invisible thing. The powder must be compounded carefully, according to exacting instructions, and involves three special ingredients and the sacrifice of 1 magic point per dose. A dose is one application of the powder. The keeper determines the special ingredients. The powder is either blown from a tube or thrown over the target. The thing which is dusted stays visible for no more than ten heartbeats.

That which could be made visible includes the magical lines extending from a place enchanted for the Calling of a Mythos deity, the aura around a Gate, and a normally invisible creature such as a star vampire. Using the powder costs no Sanity points, but seeing what it exposes may.

POWER DRAIN: drains magic points from the target. The spell costs 1D8 Sanity points. Match the caster's magic points against the target's. If the caster wins, then the target loses 1D6 magic points, and the caster gains them. If the caster fails to overcome the target, the caster loses 6 magic points to the target.

POWER OF NYAMBE: grants the caster additional magic points perhaps useful in an emergency. The caster performs a ritual which requires many components of African tribal magic, and sacrifices 1 point of POW but no Sanity points. In return, the caster receives 2D6 extra magic points usable for any purpose. These points do not regenerate, and the POW does not return.

PRINN'S CRUX ANSATA: the spell creates an ankh which can temporarily or permanently banish individual Mythos creatures. The cost of enchantment is 5 POW and 1D6 Sanity. The object must be an ankh (looped cross) made of an unalloyed metal—pure copper, iron, silver, gold, or lead would be the easiest metals to find and to form. For 20-INT days the caster performs episodic rites and sacrifices, and then sacrifices 5 POW and 1D6 Sanity to enchant the ankh. It is ready to use.

To combat the Mythos, the caster intones a chant for three rounds, and expends any number of magic points to be matched against those of the target on the Resistance Table. Companions to the caster may contribute 1 magic point each; in token of the 5 POW, the caster adds 5 free magic points as well.

Any person who knows the chant may wield the ankh and attempt to banish a creature, but does not get the 5-magic-point bonus granted to the original caster. If the ankh-wielder and companions overcome the creature, it is dispelled to its home plane. If they fail to dispel the thing, it attacks the ankh-wielder first before turning its attention to others present.

RAISE NIGHT FOG: draws up a dense ground fog from a body of water. Casting it costs 3 magic points and 1D2 Sanity points. The ritual takes about twenty game rounds to complete and involves a bowl or cup for water, filled from the body of water where the fog is to form, then blowing softly across the surface of the container. The fog forms suddenly; if there is wind, it drifts with the wind. The spell can be cast only at night. The fog dissipates with the rising sun.

REACH: allows the caster to reach through intervening surfaces and volumes, to the physical extent of his or her arms or tentacles, and adjust things, implant new elements, or withdraw existing ones. Cost of the spell varies: match the number of magic points sacrificed against the STR of the surface or surfaces to be passed through. The spell also costs 5 points of Sanity.

RED SIGN OF SHUDDE M'ELL: causes one or several victims to die horribly. This spell takes 1 combat round, 3 magic points, and 1D8 Sanity points to cast. When formed correctly, a dull red symbol glows in the air as the caster's finger describes it. The sign's malevolent effects manifest the round after its creation. Once formed, the sign must be maintained by concentration, and the expenditure of 3 more magic points each additional round.

All those within 10 yards of the sign lose 1D3 hit points per round as their bodies quake and spasm, and their internal organs and blood vessels convulse. Those further than 10 yards but nearer than 30 yards lose one hit point each round. Those further than 30 yards take no damage. It is possible to escape the sign's effect by crawling behind a wall or other opaque barrier. The caster must stand next to the sign and concentrate. The caster loses 1 hit point each round because of proximity.

REMORTIFICATION: forces the appearance of the ghost of one whom the caster has personally killed. The spell takes 1 round to cast, and costs 1D6+1 Sanity points. The spirit re-enacts movements made just before its death. The spirit is immaterial. Objects pass right through it. It cannot physically harm anyone or anything, but may cost Sanity to see.

RESURRECTION: *He turned from the inscriptions to face the room with its bizarre contents, and saw that the kylix on the floor, in which the ominous efflorescent powder had lain, was giving forth a cloud of thick, greenish-black vapour of surprising volume and opacity.*—H. P. Lovecraft, "The Case of Charles Dexter Ward."

The spell reduces a corpse to its essential salts and compounds, a bluish-gray powder, or reverses the process to yield ultimately the form and soul of the deceased. A complete corpse is necessary. Either version of this rare, misleadingly named spell costs the caster 3 magic points and 1D10 Sanity points, for casting it is an unholy thing to do. Being Resurrected in this manner costs the victim 1D20 Sanity points.

If only part of the ashy powder is available for the spell, the sorcerer gets "onlie the liveliest awfullness" from what's then made flesh. But the successfully resurrected need not be all in one piece—as long as the coffin is intact and sufficient care is taken to scrape together all the fragments and dust within, the spell succeeds.

Reciting the spell backward returns the resurrected entity to dust. It can be retained or thrown away. In this process, the caster matches magic points against the resurrected's on the Resistance Table. If the caster wins, the victim returns to dust. If the victim wins, it may try to prevent the caster from reciting the spell again. Reciting the spell backward takes two rounds. In "The Case of Charles Dexter Ward", many of those resurrected were interrogated and tortured to reveal secrets of the past.

RIVER GOD'S CURSE: *Dreamlands.* This spell can be cast only by the River God Oukranos, after the target has earned his enmity. A devastating thirst plagues the target. In the Dreamlands, this curse takes effect every 1D3 days and lasts for 1D3 hours. In the Waking World, the afflicted cannot drink enough water ever to slake thirst. The target loses 1 CON daily, until death occurs or until he or she returns to the Dreamlands and fulfills some obligation. Once the River God is satisfied, the cursed recover 1 point of lost CON per week.

SEAL OF ISIS: protects inanimate objects against magical attack within a 50-foot cube. This warding spell requires 1 hour, 1 Sanity point, and as many magic points as the caster thinks useful. Spells cast at items in the warded area are resisted by the magic points sacrificed to the warding. Match the points on the Resistance Table. Seal of Isis does not defend people, and is not a physical barrier against intruders.

SEEK HEART: quickens and implants the will within a corpse to pursue and acquire a fresh heart to replace the one that has been taken from it. A cast of the spell costs six Sanity points and 8 magic points. The caster must be within a hundred yards of the corpse, and must be able to see the corpse to activate it.

When the spell is cast, the corpse searches for the first human target it can find. It attacks, striving to rip open the victim's belly and reach up and scoop out the victim's living heart. Insertion of the living heart within the attacker fulfills the seeking corpse, which enjoys a few fleeting game rounds of ecstasy. Shortly thereafter, the seeker collapses and begins to decay. It has been drawing upon latent energies in existing cells and muscles; once those energies have been drained, dissolution of the corpse is speedy.

The effect of the spell lasts for the corpse's former STR plus CON plus POW, in minutes. If by that amount of time the corpse has not taken a new heart, it emits profound lamentations, falls to earth, and putrefies. Seek Heart can be cast only upon a corpse, and then only once.

Each cast of the spell requires a relatively fresh corpse, one without significant putrefaction. The blood of the corpse must be drained, and the corpse's heart somehow removed. Preparation of the corpse and the casting of the spell take 1D3 hours.

SEKHMENKENHEP'S WORDS: the caster creates an intense bond with a large group of listeners. The spell costs 3 magic points and 1D6 Sanity points to cast, and an additional 3 magic points sacrificed at the end of each ten game minutes that the spell lasts. The caster then must speak extemporaneously and seemingly from the heart, and maintain the audience's attention. Each ten minutes therefore the caster also needs a successful communication roll as the keeper thinks appropriate (Bargain, Credit Rating, Fast Talk, or Persuade), or the speech ends indecisively and in confusion. At the end of a successful speech, the audience believes what has been said for 1D3 days.

SEND DREAMING: can be cast only during the dark of the moon, and only by one who possesses Alcheringa Dream Lore.

The caster sacrifices 1 POW into a fire. The fire burns yellow, then white, then blue as the night wears on. The caster then entrances himself and sends Dreamtime visions to the sleeping target, plunging that person's imagination into the Dreamtime without preparation or knowledge.

If the dream is horrifying, the target can wake with a successful INT x1 roll as it begins, or by a successful POW x1 roll at the end of each hour. A dream costs caster and target alike 1D6 Sanity points, and lasts for six hours. Once such a dream is underway, the target cannot be awakened by someone else. The same dream might be sent to two targets in one night for twice the cost of one.

SEND DREAMS: subjects the target to dreams specified by the caster. The spell costs a varying number of magic points, and 1D3 Sanity points. The caster must use a special bowl made of "the copper from above", an alien metal. Such a bowl is etched with certain runes, and filled with specified herbs and a dram of blood from the caster. The herbs are set afire. As weird greenish smoke rises, the caster concentrates and casts magic points into the spell. The magic points energizing the spell are matched against the magic points of the target, and a Resistance Table roll determines the winner. The spell lasts two minutes for every magic point put into it.

The target must be asleep and within 20 miles of the caster. The dreams may be anything the caster desires, but one usual use of the spell is to send visions of Mythos entities to lower the Sanity of the target. Sanity losses from such visions are one-tenth normal (round up fractions). A dream-vision of Azathoth, for instance, costs 1 Sanity point if the Sanity roll succeeded, and 1D10 Sanity points if it failed. The caster cannot send a vision of any entity whom he or she has not seen. The spell cannot transmit orders or wishes, nor hypnotize the dreamer, who knows only that he or she is having strange dreams.

SENDING OF THE DEAD: *Voodoo.* Causes significant harm or death to the target. It costs 10 magic points and 1D6 Sanity points from the caster and supplicant. The caster uses Contact Loa for Baron Samedi, who demands that the supplicant bring specific symbols to his *vè-vè* at midnight, as well as several handsful of earth. There the caster performs the spell. The supplicant must now lay the earth where the target will walk on it. When the victim does, the dead enter his or her body. Match the caster's POW against the victim's POW. If the caster wins, roll 1D8:

    1-4 Victim immediately loses 1D10 SAN.
    5-7 Illness costs victim 1D6 STR and 1D6 HP.
    8   Victim falls into a coma and dies in 1D6 days
          unless the dead are expelled.

SENSE LIFE: allows the caster to detect the general nature of life in a particular area. Casting this spell costs 1 magic point and 1 Sanity point. The target is an area equivalent to an average house. It must be within sight of the caster. The spell allows the caster to distinguish species (such as a dog or a person), but not to recognize specific individuals.

SHINING TRAPEZOHEDRON: [it was] *a nearly black, red-striated polyhedron with many irregular flat surfaces; either a very remarkable crystal of some sort, or an artificial object of carved and highly polished mineral matter. It did not touch the bottom of the box, but was held suspended by means of a metal band around its center, with seven queerly-designed supports extending horizontally to angles of the box's inner wall near the top . . . . exposed,* [Blake] *could scarcely tear his eyes from it, and as he looked at its glistening surfaces he almost fancied it was transparent, with half-formed worlds of wonder within.*—H. P. Lovecraft, "The Haunter of the Dark."

An enchantment. In the story, Robert Blake finds a peculiar metal box in which is mounted a stone about four inches thick. It rewards or damns those who look into it with visions of other worlds and dimensions—thus the stone shines with the interior light of things not of our world. The notes of a previous investigator refer to it as the Shining Trapezohedron, the correct description of the crystalline form. When the box is closed, a hideous avatar of Nyarlathotep comes, but one which either will not or dares not enter even the pale circles of light cast by street lamps.

The stone exercises great command over human psyches. Getting rid of it proves too much for poor Blake, who perishes when the electric lights of Providence fail during a thunderstorm and the avatar emerges.

SHRIVELLING: a powerful spell of attack. Casting it costs a variable number of magic points and half that many Sanity points (round up any fraction). It takes two rounds to intone. To succeed, the caster must then use the Resistance Table to overcome the target's magic points with the remainder of his or her own. If successful, the spell blasts and blackens the target—subtract 1 hit point from the target for each magic point invested in the spell.

SIREN'S SONG: the caster sings the spell, which if successful causes the target to believe that the caster is all that his or her heart desires. The spell takes two rounds to cast. Casting the spell costs 1 magic point and 5 Sanity points. The spell lasts for 4D10 hours. The target may resist POW vs. POW on the Resistance Table and, if the target succeeds, the spell has no effect. Siren's Song affects as many people as can hear it.

SKIN OF THE SEDEFKAR: *Brothers of the Skin.* Magically defends the caster. Casting the spell costs 10 magic points and 1D3 Sanity points. For twenty-four hours, the caster is protected against all kinetic attacks by ten points of invisible magical armor. However, each attack reduces the stopping power of that armor by 1 hit point; e.g., after two bullets hit, the spell stops only the first 8 hit points of damage from the third, and only the first 7 from the fourth. Casting the spell takes approximately one uninterrupted hour of time.

SNARE DREAMER: allows the caster to attract a particular soul if it is currently out of body. The spell takes twenty minutes to cast, and costs 8 magic points and 1 Sanity point. The caster and target must be within five miles of each other, and the target's player may attempt a POW vs. POW match on the Resistance Table to escape. With a failure, the soul is drawn into the presence of the caster and is subject to such spells as Bind Soul. If the soul evades capture, it wanders off to participate in more dreams. The dreamer sees the caster and location, though he or she may not recognize the location, and remembers this as a particularly vivid dream.

SONG OF HASTUR: a magical attack, the song is a wailing ululation costing the caster 1D4 Sanity points and 1D4 magic points each round it is performed. Roll D100 equal to or less than POW + DEX x2 in order to sing properly the alien melody.

The target must be visible to the caster. Though everyone can hear the song, the spell affects only the person chosen as target. This spell will not work except at night, and only if the star Aldebaran is visible.

Successfully cast, this spell causes the skin and flesh of the chosen victim to bubble and fester into pestilent blobs, costing the target 1D6 hit points per round. After every two rounds, scarring reduces the victim's APP by 1D6. After every four rounds, internal ruptures lower the victim's CON by 1D6. When the victim's hit points or CON reach 0, the body swells up, then bursts with a sickening pop as steamy gore spills onto the floor.

The song can be used defensively, to guard against another caster of this spell. Successful opposing castings neutralize each other.

SOUL EXTRACTION: *Voodoo.* Allows a person's soul to be hidden, for purposes of protecting it, often within a clay pot. The elaborate ceremony costs 8 magic points to the caster. The target then lives a relatively normal life, and benefits from a Luck roll's chance of defeating any voodoo spell cast against him or her. If an enemy gains control of the soul's container, spells may be cast directly at it, with the effect that each spell does maximum damage.

SOUL SINGING: causes the target to see and hear only what the caster desires. The spell costs the caster 8 magic points and 1D4 Sanity points. The caster also must play the enchanted bone pipes (see Create Curse Whistle). The spell takes effect when the caster's magic points overcome the target's on the Resistance Table.

Soul Singing is aimed at a single victim who, seeing what the piper wishes him to, is led entranced to some doom or destruction. The spell affects one target. Others present cannot hear the tune unless their players succeed in D100 rolls of POW x3 or less. Then they hear a faint, nondirectional piping of strange melodies.

SOUL-TRAP: allows the caster to trap the soul of a victim within a specially prepared talisman. Creating the talisman costs the caster 1 POW and 1D4 SAN points. The victim must be wearing it at his or her time of death, or the spell fails. If wearing the talisman, capture of the soul is automatic. Thereafter the victim's soul can be called forth by the caster with a few simple words.

The summoned soul takes the physical form it possessed in life, including clothes and accessories like rings or watches. The spirit can be questioned or called upon to perform tasks, but if it refuses or is hostile, the caster needs a successful POW vs. POW roll on the Resistance Table to compel it. A failing roll frees the soul, which quickly disappears.

Summoned, the soul remains apparent for the caster's POW in rounds, and may be summoned again following the same interval.

SPECTRAL RAZOR: creates the effect of an invisible blade which can be used to cut and slash victims. This immaterial weapon can be used at a range in yards equal to the caster's POW x3. Damage is 1D6 per round. The spell takes 2 rounds to cast and costs 2 Sanity points and 2 magic points. For each additional round of effect, the caster must pay another 2 magic points.

A Spectral Razor target must be visible. If concealed or half hidden behind obstacles or obstructions, the damage is done to intervening objects until the keeper believes enough damage has been done that the target is visible and vulnerable.

STEAL LIFE: drains life from a victim to make the caster younger. This cruel spell costs 8 magic points and 1D20 Sanity points. To cast the spell, the target must be within sight and hearing of the sorcerer, who must overcome the target's magic points in a match with his or her own on the Resistance Table. With a success, the target begins to age and decay while yet alive, the innate life and vitality draining into the sorcerer. Each combat round after the spell is cast, the target loses 1 point each of STR, CON, DEX, POW, and APP. For each point of characteristic drained from the target, the caster becomes a week younger. For example, if the spell were cast upon a random derelict who had 8 points in each characteristic, the caster would become 40 (8 times 5) weeks younger. Meanwhile, the target withers, turns gray, and flakes away. At the end of the spell, the target has become a horrid dry husk which costs 0/1D6 Sanity points just to see.

If this spell is not cast on the night of the full moon, the caster does not gain the benefits of restored youth, but the victim still dies. If the caster of the spell is slain before the victim dies, the spell cancels and the victim's lost characteristics return to him or her.

STOP HEART: causes the target to lose 4D6 hit points to a sudden massive heart attack. The spell costs 14 magic points and 2D6 Sanity to cast. An involved ritual occupies the caster for the day before the spell is cast. Once the ritual is ready, the casting takes only a round, though the target must be within sight of the caster. A POW vs. POW match on the Resistance Table must be won, or the heart attack does not occur.

SUMMON / BIND BAKA: *Voodoo.* The *baka* or evil spirit may grant a certain wish if the price is right. As with other Summon / Bind Servitor spells, the caster must contribute 1 magic point for each ten percentiles toward the chance for a successful spell, and both caster and client must sacrifice 1D3 Sanity points. Negotiations with a *baka* are usually tricky; only a successful Bargain roll creates payment terms that both parties understand and actually agree to. With a successful casting, however, the *baka* fulfills the wish within 1D6 days and then returns to the supplicant to exact payment.

SUMMON / BIND BROTHER OF CHAUGNAR FAUGN: diminutive versions of Chaugnar Faugn slumber in vaults of the Pyrenees, to awake when Chaugnar Faugn once more strides the Earth. Each magic point allotted to the spell increases the chance of success by 10%; a result of 96-00 is always a failure. Casting the spell costs 10 magic points, plus anything lost for the creature or creatures summoned. They are linked telepathically with their lord, who may choose to summon them when he wishes, or who can impart this right to favored humans. Brothers have statistics roughly half those of Chaugnar Faugn, and the Move entry is also less, 8/12 walk/fly. For greater Brothers, the Sanity loss is 1D3/1D8. For lesser Brothers, the Sanity loss is 1/1D4.

SUMMON / BIND BYAKHEE: a whistle must be blown during the chant. Magic point cost varies; for each magic point sacrificed, increase the chance for a successful cast by 10 percentiles; a result of 96-00 is always a failure. The spell also costs 1D3 Sanity points to cast. This spell is active only on nights when Aldebaran is above the horizon (October through March are the best months). The summoned byakhee will flap down out of the sky, still icy from space.

Summon/Bind Spells

Such spells deal with alien races and attendants, mostly those classified as *greater* or *lesser servitors*. Dimensional shamblers and star vampires are independent races: perhaps these spells suggest that they once were servitors and have somehow been freed.

The general procedures for these spells are the same, but conditions vary from spell to spell. Knowing one such spell is of no use whatsoever in attempting to cast another. Unless the keeper wishes otherwise, the summon and the bind portions of each spell are learned together.

With the exception of Summon/Bind Servitor of the Outer Gods, these spells require the sacrifice of 1 magic point per 10 percentiles chance for success. For example, 3 magic points gives a 30% chance for the spell to succeed. In general, for each magic point spent, the caster must chant another five game minutes chanting—the greater the chance for success, the longer the spell takes to cast. A result of 96-00 is always a failure.

The caster also loses 1D3 Sanity points per spell cast, whether or not the spell succeeds.

If a success, one being appears per spell, 2D10 game minutes after the chant concludes. The thing appearing may also require a Sanity loss to see it.

As the keeper wishes, the thing arrives bound or the keeper may ask that the remaining magic points of the caster and those of the thing then be matched on the Resistance Table. With a success, the thing is bound; with a failure, it attacks the caster, then returns from whence it came. Bound, the thing must obey one order by the caster, even to attacking its own kind, after which it is freed and returns from whence it came.

Form of the Command

The caster's command to the thing must be specific and limited in duration: "protect me from harm forever" would not be a valid command, but "slay that man in the corner" would be. The thing is bound to the caster until it fulfills a command (a bound thing without a command soon finds a way to leave). Orders might include carrying someone somewhere, presiding at some ceremony, being specially docile while being examined by a group of professors, appearing somewhere as a warning to those assembled—whatever can be imagined.

Keep commands simple. The best rule of thumb is that a command has no more words than the thing has INT. Simple gestures such as pointing will be understood. Assume that the thing is always able to understand a straightforward command, whether spoken in English or Urdu. *See also Separate Binding, next page.*

If the whistle is enchanted, each point of POW in its enchantment adds 10 percentiles to the chance for success. Such a whistle may be used again and again.

SUMMON / BIND CHILD OF ATLACH-NACHA: revivifies a fossil spider form. Useful only on certain rocks in the Andaman Islands, this spell calls up and brings to life one of many fossil spiders in the rocks, which will then carry out one attack as commanded. Magic point cost varies; for each magic point sacrificed, increase the chance for a successful cast by 10 percentiles; a result of 96-00 is always a failure. Each cast costs 1D3 Sanity points, and also requires expenditure of 1 magic point for every SIZ point of the chosen fossil. All children of Atlach-Nacha have statistics half those of Atlach-Nacha, plus or minus 1D6, including movement rate and Sanity loss.

SUMMON / BIND CHILD OF YIG: brings forth one of Yig's special snakes. Magic point cost varies; for each magic point sacrificed, increase the chance for a successful cast by 10 percentiles; a result of 96-00 is always a failure. Each cast of this spell also costs 1D3 Sanity points. Summon/Bind Child of Yig can be cast only in an area where Yig's worship is strong, or where it has been strong within the last few hundred years. Yig's special snake appears coiled around the caster's leg. The first time this happens costs an additional 1/1D4 Sanity points for surprise and dismay.

SUMMON / BIND DARK YOUNG: brings present a single dark young. The magic point cost varies; for each magic point sacrificed, increase the chance for a successful cast by 10 percentiles; a result of 96-00 is always a failure. Each cast of this spell also costs 1D3 Sanity points. A beast of at least SIZ 8 must be sacrificed. The summoner needs a knife to make certain ritual cuts in dispatching the victim. Cast this spell outdoors, in a wood, during the dark of the moon. A dark young will stalk out of the shadows after the summoning.

SUMMON / BIND DIMENSIONAL SHAMBLER: a single dimensional shambler gradually assembles itself out of thin air. The magic point cost varies; for each magic point sacrificed, increase the chance for a successful cast by 10 percentiles; a result of 96-00 is always a failure. Each cast of this spell also costs 1D3 Sanity points. The spell requires a dagger made from any pure metal such as copper or iron. Alloys such as brass will

Separate Binding

If a monster arrives unbound or is come upon unexpectedly, it may be bound on the spot. The caster must know the Summon/Bind spell for that type of thing, and must spend a game round chanting before the thing can be bound. The caster then matches magic points against the thing's magic points on the Resistance Table. Failing, chant the Bind portion of the spell again. Each cast of the binding costs 1 Sanity point but no magic points. A binding cast works on only one creature at a time.

An attacking creature cannot be bound by the person fighting, but it could be bound by a person able to hold back from the fray. A creature presently bound cannot be rebound until its present command is completed. A creature to be bound must be visible to the caster and within 100 yards.

not work. If the dagger is enchanted, the chance for success also rises by 10 percentiles per point of POW in the dagger. This spell may be cast day or night. One authority has written that shamblers are more easily confused in bright sunlight.

SUMMON / BIND FIRE VAMPIRE: causes one fire vampire to swoop down from the sky like a skittering star. The magic point cost varies; for each magic point sacrificed, increase the chance for a successful cast by 10 percentiles; a result of 96-00 is always a failure. Each cast of this spell also costs 1D3 Sanity points. A bonfire or other source of flame is required. The spell may be cast only at night when the star Fomalhaut is above the horizon (September through November are the best times in moderately northern latitudes).

SUMMON / BIND HUNTING HORROR: a single horror appears head-first, as though entering through a hole in the air. The magic point cost varies; for each magic point sacrificed, increase the chance for a successful cast by 10 percentiles; a result of 96-00 is always a failure. Each cast of this spell also costs 1D3 Sanity points. This spell may be cast only at night in the open air. The blood sacrifice of a sentient being is needed. The caster does not perform the sacrifice himself—the hunting horror seizes the sacrifice when it arrives. If no alternate sacrifice has been prepared, it takes the caster and vanishes.

SUMMON / BIND NIGHTGAUNT: a nearly silent swoosh of air comes, then the single ghastly form of the blank-faced flying servant of Nodens appears. The magic point cost varies; for each magic point sacrificed, increase the chance for a successful cast by 10 percentiles; a result of 96-00 is always a failure. Each cast of this spell also costs 1D3 Sanity points. To summon, a stone emblazoned with the cryptic Elder Sign must be present, but the stone itself need not be star-shaped. The spell can be cast only at night when there is no moon.

SUMMON / BIND SERVITOR of the OUTER GODS: a single servitor arrives amid haunting echoes of insane piping. The magic point cost varies; for each three magic points sacrificed, increase the chance for a successful cast by 10 percentiles; a result of 96-00 is always a failure. Spell costs are tripled because of the great power of these beings. Each cast of this spell also costs 3D3 Sanity points. A flute is also needed to cast this spell; if the flute is enchanted, it increases the chance for the spell's success by 10 percentiles per point of POW within the flute. Cultists cast this spell anywhere and at any time that is especially unhallowed—typical nights would be Midsummer's Eve, Mayday, Halloween, and Walpurgis Night.

SUMMON / BIND STAR VAMPIRE: curious rustling sounds are heard once this invisible thing lurks near. The magic point cost varies; for each magic point sacrificed, increase the chance for a successful cast by 10 percentiles; a result of 96-00 is always a failure. Each cast of this spell also costs 1D3 Sanity points. The caster also needs a book in which are written or inscribed the words of the spell. If the book is enchanted, the chance for success is increased by 10 percentiles per point of POW within the book. This spell can be cast only at night under a cloudless sky. The creature is invisible save when its veins fill with blood from some visible creature.

SUMMON EFFIGY OF HATE: the ritual for this spell takes eight hours to perform and can only be cast at night. It requires 12 magic points and 3 points of POW, the latter usually donated by an unwilling slave or captive. The caster must supply the magic points but the spell allows for the POW to be drawn from a designated victim. Successfully summoned, the Effigy inhabits a tall war totem specially constructed for this purpose.

Over the following two nights the Effigy emerges into our world, each night drawing three points of POW from the designated victim. Once the Effigy has fully coalesced, it begins to go about fulfilling the caster's deepest desire.

SUMMON PLAGUE: *Dreamlands*. Causes disease-infested rats and insects to swarm over an area, biting and stinging livestock and humans, spreading a terrible plague. If bitten or stung, a victim automatically contracts the plague, its first symptoms appearing in 1D3 days. The first day of illness sees the loss of 1D5 CON, followed by further losses of 1D4 CON every day until the victim dies or is cured. All skills drop by ten percentiles daily.

An infected dreamer may be cured with a successful Medicine roll, regenerating all lost CON overnight. Although surviving the plague makes one immune to further infections of the same disease, the spell produces a different disease with every use, rendering immunity to this magic unlikely.

The first disease-carrying rats and insects appear in 2D10 minutes, followed by additional hordes over the next 2D10 hours. The first day the affected area has a diameter of one mile, this area increasing by an additional mile until the plague is somehow banished. Summoned plagues are not contagious; the disease can only be transmitted by the bite of an insect or other animal. If an infected dreamer wakes before dying he is cured and shows no symptoms of the disease on his next visit to the Dreamlands.

This summoned plague may be banished by successfully casting the spell in reverse. However, anyone already infected must still be cured with Medicine or face a lingering death. Casting the spell costs 20 magic points and 2D10 Sanity points. Bits of rotting mammal flesh and human feces are required for successful casting.

SUMMON THRALL OF CHAUGNAR FAUGN: thralls are creatures of their creator, and only Chaugnar Faugn can bind or command them, but anyone can summon them. For each cast, 1D6+1 thralls appear, each costing the caster 1D2 magic points and 0/1D2 Sanity points.

Thralls can be summoned only in an underground room or chamber without windows or other close connection to the surface. The summoner squats naked upon the dirt or floor, concentrates on an image of Chaugnar Faugn, and chants and drums until self-entranced. In the caster's mind, Chaugnar Faugn may deign to appear. If it does, the vision of it speaks and roars, "To my greater glory!"

TRANSFER BODY PART: *Brothers of the Skin*. Allows the willful substitution of another hand, arm, etc. Casting the spell costs 1 POW, 1D10 magic points, and 1D10 Sanity points. If the donor is already dead, the transfer costs 2 POW. More complicated transfers cost more: the most expensive is 100 magic points for Transfer Head.

Preparation for the spell takes about an hour, including the creation of the magical thread that provides the initial connection of body to part, plus the transfer taking game minutes equal to the magic points required. Since the procedure is often clumsy, the caster usually Transfers the part to a second Brother. The Brothers look for particularly prize pieces of anatomy—an athlete's legs, a boxer's fists, and so on.

To return to an original body part, see the similar spell Detransference.

TRANSFER ORGAN: *Brothers of the Skin*. Replaces a human internal organ with its match from another human. Hearts cannot be moved or traded. The spell costs 63 magic points and 1 POW. Donor and receiver each lose 1D8 Sanity points. One of the participants can be the caster.

The donor must be alive. The donor's agreement is not needed for the effect of the spell.

A paste is made of blood from both participants, mixed with chameleon saliva. Donor, receiver, and caster are surrounded by a group who link hands and sing an ancient poem; the 63 magic points are drawn from them in equal or nearly equal amounts. This keeps both parties alive during the transfer.

Using the paste, the caster draws the symbol of the organ to be transferred on the respective areas of the participants. After an hour of meditation and visualization, the caster delves his hands into the donor body where the symbol is. Pinching off major connections, the organ is lifted out and placed on a circular stone table. The process is repeated for the recipient, and then the parts are installed in their new bodies and sewn into place.

UNMASK DEMON: it destroys any magical disguise used by a target, and costs a variable number of magic points and no Sanity points. The spell requires the participation of a group of at least three people who chant clearly and rhythmically while their leader breaks a raw unfertilized egg on which has been drawn an image of the target. To succeed, the casters must overcome the target's POW with their own combined magic points. Each participant may contribute as many as half his magic points to the spell. Sanity may be lost when the target's true form is revealed.

UNSPEAKABLE PROMISE: establishes a binding oath made to He Who Is Not To Be Named, and costs the caster 2D8 Sanity points. In return, Hastur grants the caster some benefit—a plausible gift would be an important ancient tome such as the *R'lyeh Text* or the yearly award of 3 POW for the rest of the recipient's life. Additionally, however, there is a non-cumulative chance of 2% per year that the caster transforms into a gruesome humanoid monster totally under Hastur's sway, one which the keeper may create afresh or draw statistics from the Unspeakable Possessor, in the *Creature Companion*.

VANISH: causes the caster to disappear in a puff of smoke, to reappear instantly in a location beside a previously prepared box. The box takes 2 POW to prepare. Each casting of the spell takes about two seconds, and costs 5 magic points and 1 Sanity point.

The location is defined by creating a charm made of a box containing components of the caster's body such as hair, teeth, or nails. The box is magically prepared, taking about a day, and the POW must be sacrificed. Then the Vanish spell may be cast any number of times. If the box is destroyed, or opened and its contents scattered, the POW points are lost. The box must be remade before the spell can work again.

The location of the box might be as far as several hundred miles distant. More than one box might be prepared at the same time.

VIEW GATE: cast at a suspected Gate, this spell allows the caster and companions to see what, if anything, is on the other side of the Gate without going through it. The cost varies with the number of magic points needed to activate the Gate. It always costs 1 magic point and 1 Sanity point to cast the spell. Viewing is a variable cost, one tenth of the Gate cost (round up fractions). Thus a Gate costing 7 magic points to pass through requires 2 magic points and 2 Sanity points to view through. The view lasts 1D6+1 rounds. The spell may be cast as often as the caster's magic points and Sanity points allow.

If there is something horrific to see, additional Sanity charges are in line for each viewer. If important to play, viewers may attempt appropriate skill rolls to learn where or when or what they are viewing.

VOICE OF RA: temporarily increases caster APP and certain related skills. The spell requires 5 magic points and 1 Sanity point. The ritual takes two hours to complete, and a variety of herbal components are burned during the casting. For 24 hours, the spell adds 1D10 APP to the caster, and increases by 20 percentiles each the caster's Bargain, Credit Rating, Fast Talk, Persuade, and Psychology skills.

VOID LIGHT: *Mi-go.* This spell subtly warps space, creating a sink from which photons will not emerge. The mi-go must spend one magic point for every cubic yard of blackness desired. No light can escape the affected area, making useful visual protection for these sometimes fragile aliens. Depending on how the spell is prepared, the darkness may be like a sheet or a spherical volume.

VOORISH SIGN: *They from outside will help, but they cannot take body without human blood. That upstairs looks it will have the right cast. I can see it a little when I make the Voorish sign*—H. P. Lovecraft, "The Dunwich Horror."

These magical hand gestures aid in Mythos magic. Making the Voorish Sign costs the user 1 magic point and 1 Sanity point. The passes and hand movements take only a few seconds, but they increase the chance to cast successfully a Mythos spell by 5 percentiles, and in some cases seem to make visible the invisible. In the canon, this sign is never described.

WANDERING SOUL: while he sleeps, this spell can send the caster's soul to some location, and thus scry out his enemies. The caster then wakes twelve hours later, having spent all but one magic point and sacrificed 1D4 SAN, and with a sense of exhaustion. The dream-like vision reveals information readily observable, but lamps cannot be lit, nor boxes and drawers opened, nor papers rifled.

While it is so wandering, those of POW 20 or more can see and identify the scrying soul. Those of POW 15 or more have the feeling of being watched. Those asleep see the face of the scrying soul and can identify it, for the soul has always the appearance of the caster, and cannot be disguised.

WARDING: makes a warding arrangement. Costs 1 magic point per stone used in the ward, and costs no Sanity points. A number of ordinary white stones are required. They are placed on the ground as the caster pleases, except that each must be within a yard of each of the others. The spell takes about fifteen seconds to cast, during which a shimmering heat haze can be seen over the stones. Thereafter if any stone is moved, the caster will be aware of the fact, even if asleep until then. Once this has occurred, the spell is broken.

WARDING THE EYE: this spell protects completely against the Evil Eye spell. It costs 2 magic points and no Sanity points, and involves a number of complicated hand gestures which may be made prior to or at the same time as the Evil Eye. Like the Evil Eye, this spell expires at midnight.

WAVE OF OBLIVION: causes a powerful ocean wave to smash down at the caster's direction. The caster must be in or on the water himself. The spell costs 30 magic points and 1D8 Sanity points to cast. Sufficient quantities of salt water must be present to create the wave, and the caster must be able to see the target. The wave volume is 3,000 cubic feet, enough to swamp or capsize a small sloop. Were several or many spells cast at once, a large ship could be swamped. Needless to say, people swallowed up by such waves vanish forever below the surface.

In another version, one sorcerer must know the spell and expend all but one of his or her magic points, but others can also contribute magic points to allow the creation of vast waves capable of sinking ocean liners, battleships, or Manhattan island. Those knowing the spell can contribute as many magic points as desired, and must expend 1D8 Sanity points. Those who do not know the spell can contribute 1 magic point each. The variant requires a minimum of 30 magic points, creating a wave ten feet long, ten feet wide, and thirty feet high. Each additional magic point adds a foot to the length and width of the wave.

WITHER LIMB: causes permanent damage to the target. The spell costs the caster 8 magic points and 1D6 Sanity points. It takes 1 round to cast and the target must be within 10 yards. Overcoming the target's magic points with his or her own on the Resistance Table, the caster causes the nominated arm or leg to wither and shrivel, leaving to the victim 1D8 hit points of damage and a permanent loss of 3 CON. The victim and any witnesses lose 0/1D3 Sanity points each.

WRACK: temporarily incapacitates a single target. It costs 3 magic points and one Sanity point to cast. The caster must be 10 yards or less distant. Match caster and target magic points with those of the target on the Resistance Table. Succeeding, the spell takes effect after one round of confusing hand gestures. Intense, wracking pains seize the target, the face and hands blister and drip fluid, and the eyes cloud with blood and become temporarily sightless. The effect lasts 1D6 rounds, after which sight returns. In 3D10 minutes, the target fully recovers and resumes normal activity. Traces of physical corruption fade quickly, and in 24 hours only faint blemishes can be seen on the skin. Each such experience costs the target 1/1D6+1 Sanity points. ∎

THE HAUNTING

More people have played this Call of Cthulhu scenario than any other. Under the title "The Haunted House" it has been included with the game since the beginning. For many it was their first Cthulhu adventure. Most people familiar with the game remember being baffled by it. Its title has changed to avoid confusion with another scenario in another book, and to encourage long-time keepers to give it a fresh look.

"The Haunting" is recommended for beginning investigators. Keepers can darken or lighten its tone by adjusting damages and Corbitt's motive: it offers genuine challenge, and one or more investigators easily can die at Corbitt's hand.

The *Liber Ivonis* is not central to play, and can be excluded if the keeper is unready to introduce the Mythos or a Mythos book.

The nominal year is 1920. It could be any era. The nominal location is Boston, Massachusetts, but wherever the keeper desires will do.

Call of Cthulhu maps are usually sketched free-hand, rather than drawn out precisely. The relationships shown are important, but exact distances and angles are not. Partly this is in expectation that the keeper or a player will sketch out larger freehand versions of the plans on the spot, and partly because traps in Call of Cthulhu are intellectual or emotional ones which the keeper can describe, rather than physical traps which are camouflaged and waiting to be sprung by some unlucky movement.

To lengthen play, increase the front part of this scenario, characterize the landlord, the negotiations with the investigators, and the process of uncovering the clues. To shorten the length of play, bring the investigators directly to the Corbitt house. Nearly all Cthulhu scenarios begin with the accumulation of evidence. The keeper may want to caution novice investigators about this if they do not get a chance to collect clues and conduct interviews. This adventure should take an evening to complete.

Study Corbitt's powers, and play them keenly. Most of the keeper's fun in this scenario comes from the baffling events in upstairs room #3.

Keeper Information

The body of Walter Corbitt is buried in the basement of a house. The mind of Walter Corbitt still lives, is still aware of events within the house, and still has influence in particular parts of the house. Corbitt knows Mythos magic that preserves his identity and enables him to animate his body after death. He sometimes vampirizes or otherwise preys upon the current residents of the house, and drives away or slays those who learn his secret. To solve the mystery posed to them, the investigators must learn about Corbitt. Corbitt will be aware of the investigators and will try to mislead them concerning the house. Failing that, he tries to murder them.

THE PROBLEM

A landlord asks the investigators to examine the old Corbitt house in central Boston. The former tenants were involved in a tragedy, and the owner wishes to understand the mysterious happenings at the house and set matters straight. He offers to reimburse the player-characters for their time and trouble.

How the landlord learns about the investigators, what he will pay, and even what he says he wants done can be negotiated by keeper and players.

Failing other ideas, try the following. (1) The landlord's cousin was friendly with one of the investigators at the university—whichever investigator had some interest in the mysterious and the occult. The cousin made the recommendation. (2) The landlord offers the investigators $20 per day total, with a bonus of $100 dollars when they can give his property a clean bill of health. (3) He wants their assurance that he can rent out the property again without provoking some new tragedy.

The landlord gives the investigators the keys, the address, and $50 cash in advance. The rest is up to them.

WHAT HAPPENED

The Macario family moved into the house in 1918. A year after moving in, the father had a serious accident and shortly thereafter went violently insane. He was committed. Within the last month, the mother also went insane. Both babbled of a haunting form with burning eyes. They told of inexplicable events in the house. Neither would enter one upstairs bedroom. The landlord knew the house was rumored to be haunted before he bought the place, but the property was too good a bargain to resist. The landlord wants the investigators to put the rumors and his mind at rest or else to exorcise the haunts.

Player Information

Now the players can do what they want. Acting as the landlord, the keeper should answer enough questions to give them lines for inquiry, but the landlord has never seen a haunting or strange event at the house, nor does he know what the Macarios saw. If the players cannot agree about what to do, they can roll dice to resolve the conflict. The evidence in the rest of this subsection is arranged in the most likely order of investigator encounter.

If the players immediately send the investigators to the Corbitt house, caution them but let them have their way.

THE MACARIO FAMILY

Husband and wife were committed to Roxbury Sanitarium, a few miles from Boston. Vittorio is still quite mad, and an interview with the mumbling, huddled man uncovers nothing. Gabriela is conscious and approachable, though the keeper should end the interview quickly since the questions greatly upset her.

Mrs. Macario has little to say. An evil presence lives in the house, one she hates to think of. At night she would sometimes wake to find it leaning over her. When it was angry, the thing might cause dishes or other objects to fly around the room. Mostly it hated her husband, Vittorio, and concentrated on him. The keeper can answer more questions, but she is unable to give specific information. After the investigators have visited the house, the keeper might let her be more precise and forthcoming.

The two young Macario boys are being cared for by relatives in Baltimore. The investigators can visit them, but they know nothing except that they miss their parents and that in their former home they often dreamed of a strange man with burning eyes.

NEWSPAPER ACCOUNTS

With a successful Idea roll, one of the investigators suggests using the morgue (the clippings files) at the *Boston Globe*, a daily newspaper of good repute. Coming as a group, the inves-

tigators need a successful Fast Talk or Persuade roll to get in, a letter of reference from the Mayor's office, or an authorizing telephone call from any editor on the paper.

The pertinent clippings are filed by street address. The stories concerning the Macarios are brief and uninformative: the *Globe* reported the facts as the investigators already know them.

Also present is a 1918 feature story which was never published. It states that in 1880 a family of French immigrants moved into the house but fled after a series of violent accidents left the parents dead and three children crippled. The house long stood vacant.

Sometimes facsimiles of newspaper accounts are supplied in adventures.

In 1909 another family moved in, and immediately fell prey to illnesses. In 1914, the oldest brother went mad and killed himself with a kitchen knife, and the heartbroken family moved out. In 1917, a third family rented the house, but they left almost immediately, after they all became ill at the same time.

About Call of Cthulhu Adventures

These adventures are ready to play. Most can be finished in an evening's play. Without considerable keeper embroidery, none need take more than two sessions of play. Having played these adventures, new keepers can plan their own creations, or draw from other published material.

Whether a scenario is home-grown or purchased, always study and think about it before you play it. Imagine how players will react to it, and consider solutions to problems the piece raises in your mind. Above all, understand the adventure well enough to be able to summarize the action in a few sentences, and be prepared to answer general questions about the plot.

SCENARIO FORM

Printed Call of Cthulhu scenarios have evolved over time. Newer scenario books are presented in a style very similar to the one for this book, down to skills and terminology. Keepers who own older materials will notice differences, sometimes considerable. The current form for character statistics has been used since 1989.

Statistics for individuals differ from those for groups of individuals, since by definition groups appear more or less at the same time, do not have individual functions in play, and do not need to be completely developed. The keeper can fill them out if he or she wishes. Statistics for Mythos entities may have various arrangements.

POSITION: in published scenarios which contain lots of character statistics, or in short ones where the same characters may appear at a variety of points, statistics are collected at the end of the adventure. The theory is that one place is better than every place. (the scenario "The Madman" is the exception in this book.)

VISUAL MATERIALS: some adventures include newspaper articles, letters, or maps as evidence. Photocopy these before play begins. When the time is right, pass them out rather than reading aloud from the book, so that the players can study them and reach their own conclusions.

SPELL REPEATS: in books of scenarios, spells from the Grimoire and other sources are usually reproduced near the caster's statistics, so that the keeper does not need to sort through a stack of books in order to play a single sorcerer. For spells instanced in the present scenarios, see the Grimoire chapter.

DAMAGE BONUSES: these appear independently and are added as applicable to listed weapons damages. Printed damage rolls may include +db notations, which refers to the damage bonus amount, found on a separate line.

STATISTIC ORDER: statistical information about individual characters usually occurs in the same order of presentation: name (and age if human), characteristics and hit points, damage bonus, weapons, spells (if any), armor (if any), skills, Sanity loss (if any).

ORDER OF CHARACTERISTICS: it's mostly a matter of tradition, but the fact that one line in the individual statistics ends in *POW* and that the other ends in *SAN* and *hit points* is not—those positions have blank space nearby where the keeper can pencil in changes to those values.

WEAPON ENTRY: in order, a weapon statistic is summarized by *type of weapon*, followed by *skill %* with that weapon, then by the *damage* done with the weapon by that particular character. The word damage is inserted to make plain that the entry does not represent the hit points of the weapon itself.

OPTIONS: boxed options may occur in a scenario, such as the effects of cold in "The Madman." Using or not using an option makes no difference to the play of the scenario. There is no right choice to make. Please yourself. In different books you may meet differing opinions about the same sort of subject—options are not consistent, just handy. An option is usually presented as a play balance mechanism (suppose the investigators bring along a company of state police in "The Madman"), or is an idea which seems to add realism or interesting detail but which may also slow play or make for clumsy play.

If an investigator successfully flirts with the librarian (APP x3 or Credit Rating roll), he or she happens to remark that the *Globe* files go back no further than a fire in 1878. The Corbitt House may be mentioned earlier than that.

THE MAIN LIBRARY

This worthy institution has several interesting items tucked away, but the investigators need a separate Library Use roll to find each of the following items.

- In 1835, a prosperous merchant builds the house, but immediately falls ill and sells it to a Mr. Walter Corbitt, esquire.

- In 1852, Walter Corbitt is sued by neighbors, who petition to force him to leave the area "in consequence of his surious [sic] habits and inauspicious demeanor".

- Evidently Corbitt wins the lawsuit. His obituary in 1866 states that he still lived in the same place. It also states that a second lawsuit was being waged to prevent Corbitt from being buried in his basement, as provided by his will.

- No outcome to the second lawsuit is recorded.

Each item is in a different newspaper and takes four hours to find.

HALL OF RECORDS

With a successful Library Use roll, civil court records show that the executor of Walter Corbitt's will was Reverend Michael Thomas, pastor of the Chapel of Contemplation & Church of Our Lord Granter of Secrets. The register of churches (also available in the Hall of Records) notes the closure of the Chapel of Contemplation in 1912.

If the investigators think to look up the Chapel of Contemplation in criminal court records, they find references to actions taken in 1912, but the actual records are not present. If the investigators have been courteous to the clerk, he points out that serious crimes would be handled in the county, state, or federal courts. A successful Law roll can indicate the same thing. The records of city officers participating in arrests or seizures are filed at Central Police Station.

HIGHER COURTS; CENTRAL POLICE STATION

Use a Law, Credit Rating, or Fast Talk roll to get access to the records. They concern a secret raid on the Chapel of Contemplation. The police raid was occasioned by affidavits swearing that members of the church were responsible for the disappearances of neighborhood children. During the raid three policemen and seventeen cult members were killed by gunplay or fire. Autopsy reports are singularly undetailed and uninformative, as though the coroner had not actually performed examinations.

Though 54 members of the church were arrested, all but eight were released. The records hint of illegal intervention in the proceedings by important local officials, offering an explanation of why stories of the battle—the biggest criminal action in the city's history—never appeared in print.

Pastor Michael Thomas was arrested and sentenced to 40 years in prison on five counts of second-degree murder. He escaped from prison in 1917 and fled the state.

THE NEIGHBORHOOD

Most of the people who lived in the area before WWI have moved away or died. New offices and businesses have replaced the nineteenth-century homes, and the Corbitt place with its overgrown front yard is now the only private residence on the block. The investigators do find a Mr. Dooley, a vendor of cigars and newspapers, who remembers the area vaguely. He is able to point out where the Chapel of Contemplation stood, a few blocks distant.

THE CHAPEL OF CONTEMPLATION

What is left of it stands at the end of a crooked, dingy street. The ruins of it are so weathered and so overgrown with greenery that the gray stone rubble seems more like natural stone than former walls and foundation. The investigators pass a slumping wall bearing white-painted symbols, apparently freshly swabbed—three Y's, arranged in a triangle so that the top elements of each Y touch the other two Y's. In the center so-created is painted a staring eye. When the investigators near the signs, they begin to feel irritating tingles in their foreheads, like headaches but not quite. While they remain near the chapel they continue to feel this, and finally cannot wait to get away from the area. When they leave, the irritations stop.

See the nearby player aid for an image of this symbol. Show it to the players.

Prowling the chapel, they find mostly blocks of granite, half-burnt rotted timbers, and ancient rubbish. At some point they become aware that the earth they stand on is covering weakened floorboards: call for DEX x4 or less on D100. Those who get failing rolls are unable to grab something secure when they feel the floor give way. They fall ten feet into the basement. Each falling investigator loses 1D6 hit points.

This part of the basement was sealed off from the rest, reached by a separate stairs buried under tons of rubble. Within it are two skeletons dressed in fragments of silk robes, apparently cultists who hid and perished in the fire.

Also in the room are cabinets of moldering church records. At one point (successful Library Use roll to find this) a journal of cult activities states that Walter Corbitt was buried in the basement of Corbitt's house "in accordance with his wishes and with the wishes of that One Who Waits in the Dark."

Chained to a rotting desk is an enormous volume bound in human skin—a successful Medicine or EDU x3 roll establishes this. It is a copy of the *Liber Ivonis*, hand-written in Latin, but rotten and worn-eaten so that whole sections no longer can be understood. Its stats are modified to 1D2/1D4 Sanity points, Cthulhu Mythos +5, no complete spells.

The Old Corbitt Place

HOUSE AND GROUNDS: the brick bungalow is overshadowed by taller, newer office buildings on either side. The house fronts the street. In the rear are overgrown plantings and a half-collapsed arbor. Access to the rear exists on either side of the residence.

Player Aid: Symbol in the Chapel

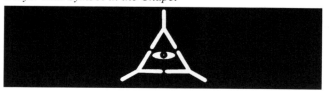

Studying the house, the observer is impressed by the way the house seems to withdraw into the shadows cast by flanking buildings, and how the blank curtained windows hide all understanding of what lies within. Investigators who have already undergone mysterious or occult events in their lives sense something ominous within, but can point to no evidence to support these feelings.

The front door is secured with a single lock. Four additional bolts lock the door from the inside. All of the bolts seem to have been added within the last year or two. If the investigators think to test the ground floor windows, they find that all of them have been nailed shut from the inside.

GROUND FLOOR INTERIOR

Study the plan provided.

ROOM 1: a storage room, filled with boxes and such junk as rusted water tanks and old bicycles. At the right end of the room is a cupboard, boarded shut. If it is wrenched open, three bound books are found within, the diaries of a certain W. Corbitt, a former inhabitant of the house, as the address on the flyleaf of volume one testifies.

The Corbitt Diaries are in plain English, though sometimes strangely-put. The three volumes take a total of two days to read, add +4 to Cthulhu Mythos, and cost 1D4 Sanity points. They describe Corbitt's various occult experiments, including a summoning and other magic, and clearly describes the technique for Summon/Bind Dimensional Shambler (*see the Grimoire for this spell*). No other spells exist in the diaries. This spell takes 2D6 weeks to learn after the diaries are read, likely too long to be useful in this adventure.

ROOM 2: a second storage room, this one mostly devoted to broken furniture and other items which might be broken up to burn in a wood stove.

ROOM 3: the mud room, where hang overcoats, galoshes, hats, and umbrellas. Several bags of coal for the living room's free-standing stove are here. A successful Idea roll notices that the side door is secured with three bolts and two locks.

ROOM 4: the living room. It contains conventional furnishings such as a radio, couch, stuffed chairs, and shelves laden with gewgaws. A successful Idea roll notices the unusual quantities of crosses, images of the Virgin, and other Catholic religious artifacts.

ROOM 5: the dining room, complete with a long mahogany table, a built-in sideboard, and seven chairs. Three places are set, and unused. Rice soup rots in a tureen.

ROOM 6: a conventional kitchen, with icebox, wood-fed stove and oven, and a meager larder. Some of the foodstuffs are edible yet—there is canned soup and meat, rice, several pastas, a few bottles of homemade wine. The produce which did not spoil has been eaten by rats, judging by the spoor left behind.

UPPER FLOOR

ROOM 1: an ordinary bedroom, with a double bed, bookshelf, and window view, apparently the room of Vittorio and Gabriela. More crosses are here, and a rosary and breviary rest on a table beside the bed.

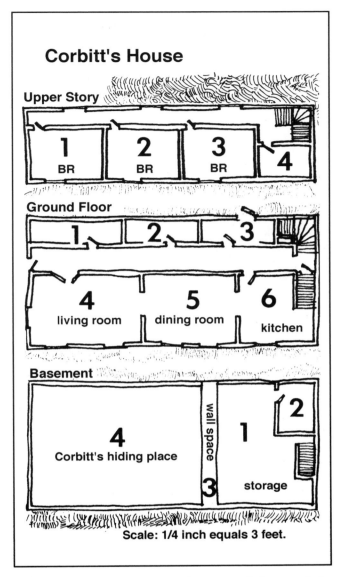

ROOM 2: two small beds, toys, dressers, and pictures of aircraft and cowboys mark this as the children's bedroom.

ROOM 3: it contains a bed frame, bare bed springs, and an empty dresser. Though unused, this room looks like the other two bedrooms. It was once the room of old Corbitt himself. He stayed here so long that his psychic influence lingers on, and he is able to will certain deeds to happen in this room. Whenever he does, a horrible smell manifests—a sure sign of the Mythos.

■ He can cause loud thumping noises to emanate from this room. These noises can be heard from anywhere in the house.

■ He can form a pool of blood (taken from rats he slaughters) on the floor, or to drip down from the ceiling or walls.

■ He can make a rattling, scratching sound on the windowpane or door.

■ He can impel the bed at good speed, fast enough to strike a strong blow against anything in the room.

Though Corbitt lays low at first, if the investigators seem determined to learn the secrets of the house then Corbitt tries to convince them that this room is the center of the psychic disturbance. To this end, he uses the pools of blood and the thumping.

If an investigator is unconvinced, Corbitt tries to lure him into this room and kill him, first attracting the investigator to the window by making it rattle, then causing the bed to move rapidly, hitting the investigator and throwing him through the window. The broken glass and fall costs the victim 2D6 hit points.

ROOM 4: sink, bathtub, and a water closet with an overhead tank. Towels and other possessions are still here, typical to a family of four. A brackish pool of water has collected in the bathtub, fed by a dripping faucet which cannot quite be closed.

THE BASEMENT

ROOM 1: the door to the basement has a lock and three bolts, able to open from the upstairs side only. Below is the main basement storage room. The stairs are in poor repair, and Corbitt has turned off the electricity to the basement at the fuse box upstairs in the kitchen. Each investigator must receive a DEX x7 or less roll, or lose 1D6 hit points from falling down the rickety stairs.

In the smallish room are scattered tools, pipe, lumber, nails, screws, and so forth. The side walls are of brick. The facing wall (#3) is of wood, as are the walls of the room under the stairs (#2).

THE FLOATING KNIFE: in Room 1, if an investigator searches through the mess and receives a successful Spot Hidden roll, he or she finds a old knife with an ornate hilt whose blade is coated with oddly-thick rust. This is Corbitt's magic dagger, and the rust is actually the dried blood of victims. Corbitt can make this knife float in the air and try to stab someone. Each such attempt costs Corbitt 1 magic point; he can make one attack per round, and his chance to hit the target equals Corbitt's current magic points x5 or less on D100. Because the knife moves magically, and does not partake of Corbitt's STR, do not add his damage bonus to a successful attack.

An investigator can try to parry the knife with a garbage can lid (base chance 30%)—nothing else suitable is in the room. Seeing the knife attack in this manner costs each investigator 1/1D4 Sanity points.

The investigator can try to grab the knife out of the air (he or she must receive a D100 roll of DEX or less). If the investigator gets hold, match his or her STR against Corbitt's current magic points. If Corbitt wins, the knife is wrested free and the investigator loses 1 hit point for sliced hands. Attempting to wrench the knife away costs Corbitt another magic point.

ROOM 2: an empty storage bin, once intended for coal. The door to the outside coal chute has been nailed shut firmly.

ROOM 3: the wall opposite the stairs is made of closely fitted boards. If they are broken through or removed, a crawl space is visible between two wooden walls. Foul odors emanate from the rat who nest here. If the investigators do not give the rats room to escape, they attack whoever tries to explore this space. There are six packs. The "Beasts And Monsters" chapter of this book contains notes and stats for them.

Carved into the inner wall are the words "Chapel Of Contemplation," but the irregular, scratchy carving takes a successful Spot Hidden roll to notice. If the investigators break through this wall, they find themselves in Room 4.

ROOM 4: this is Corbitt's hiding place. He lies motionless and seemingly dead on a pallet in the center of the room. He is described in the "Corbitt" subsection below. The floor is earthen, and there is a table in the southwest corner with some curled papers on it. They crumble to dust if touched. What the investigators can see looks like a horoscope. If they retrieve or photograph this material, the keeper should disclose its true nature in some later adventure.

Corbitt needs 2 magic points to move his body for five combat rounds, so he is reluctant to move at all unless threatened. Then he rises from his pallet, costing all viewers 1/1D8 Sanity points, and attacks.

While still on the pallet, he may decide to cast spells, if he has not already done so.

Conclusion

If the investigators have solved the mystery and overthrown Corbitt, the landlord pays off promptly and happily. If they report to him that nothing was wrong, he spends a night in the house to make sure, and is stabbed to death in the basement by Corbitt's magic dagger. The investigators then must prove the house is haunted to escape murder charges by the police.

REWARDS

If Corbitt is conquered and destroyed, each participating investigator gains 1D6 Sanity points.

Around Corbitt's neck is a black gem fastened on a chain. If the stone is fished out of his dust by an investigator, the stone dissolves in the investigator's hand and adds 1 POW to his characteristic. This magical stone helped fuel Corbitt's undead might.

The investigators can claim for their own the damaged *Liber Ivonis* from the Chapel. Use the statistics given there.

Finally, the Landlord gladly pays their fee and bonus.

EXTENSION

Keepers will have noticed the freshly-painted sign on the rubble at the Chapel, as well as the evidence of the cover-up following the raid in 1912. Connections to what may be a great conspiracy are available and might be returned to at some later time.

About W. Corbitt, Esq.

He is a drawn, wooden-looking, wizened figure of some six feet, skinny and naked, with ghastly wide-flaring, saucer-like eyes and a nose like a knife blade. He has lost all hair, and his shrunken gums make his teeth look very long. From him comes a sharp, sweet, churning scent, like rotten corn. He might be silent at first, but at some point it will be more convincing to have him growl, screech, cackle, or mock. He does not breathe at all.

Corbitt is not truly a vampire, nor any recognizable monster—he is a sorcerer in the process of transforming himself into something entirely inhuman.

Sunlight causes him pain and is too bright for him to see in comfortably. It might kill him, but whether it does is for the keeper to determine. And though he drinks blood for food, he could also eat carrots—drinking blood is just more fun.

His Flesh Ward spell operates as per that spell in the Grimoire chapter, but characterize its effect like this: bullets and blows only chip off pieces of his body, making him look even more horrific than he already does. Other Flesh Ward spells might work in ways which appear to be different.

His dried, iron-hard flesh is invulnerable so long as the spell holds. If damage exceeds the armor, his hit points reduce normally. He never heals. Reaching zero hit points, Corbitt crumbles into dust and never returns.

With his version of the Dominate spell, Corbitt can mentally cloud the mind of one investigator at a time, as long as the target is physically in the house. This costs Corbitt 1 magic point, and he must overcome the victim's POW with his own on the Resistance Table. If Corbitt succeeds, the target is in a daze for 2D3 combat rounds (keepers, note that this amount differs from the Dominate spell in the Grimoire). While in this dazed state, the victim is subject to telepathic commands from Corbitt. He or she will not commit suicidal acts, though homicidal ones or idiotic, reckless ones (such as trying to swallow a butcher's knife), might be attempted. Waking, the victim cannot recall what happened.

WALTER CORBITT, Undead Fiend

| STR 18 | CON 22 | SIZ 11 | INT 16 | POW 18 |
| DEX 7 | APP 1 | EDU 16 | SAN 0 | HP 17 |

Damage Bonus: +1D4.

Weapon: Floating Magical Dagger, magic points x5%, damage 1D4+2 (no db)

Claws* 50%, damage 2D3 +db

* Being wounded by these talons risks serious disease. A day later, the victim becomes delirious and remains so for 30-CON days, recovering at the end of that time with a D100 roll of CON x5 or less. Failing, he or she loses 1D3 CON, and continues in delirium for another 30-CON days, and the procedure repeats until the investigator recovers or dies. CON lost does not regenerate.

Spells: Dominate, Flesh Ward, Summon/Bind Dimensional Shambler.

Magical Artifact: floating dagger.

Skills: Conceal 30%, Cthulhu Mythos 31%, Lie 72%, Listen 60%, Mislead 64%, Sneak 80%.

Sanity Loss: 1/1D8 Sanity points to see him move. ∎

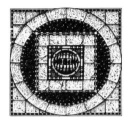 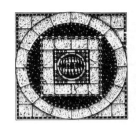

EDGE OF DARKNESS

At least four investigators are needed for this adventure. New investigators may not yet know one another; this adventure provides the opportunity to make one another's acquaintance and become friends and allies in an ongoing struggle against dark forces. The adventure begins in Arkham, Massachusetts, in the year 1928. The keeper should feel free to alter locations, dates, names, or anything else that pleases him. Little in the scenario makes it difficult to transfer the adventure to the 1890s or the present. It is assumed that the player-characters live close to Arkham.

They are called to the hospital bedside of a dying man, Rupert Merriweather, an elderly gentlemen fast succumbing to cancer. The investigators are all friends, relatives, past students, and former colleagues of the man. The exact relationship of each investigator must be decided ahead of time by the keeper andcan involve some close personal bond and a reason for trust. Each investigator receives word of the man's plight either by telephone, telegraph, or personal courier. They learn he is confined to St. Mary's hospital in Arkham and that he wishes them to visit tomorrow afternoon—a Thursday—at one o'clock.

Rupert Merriweather

St. Mary's hospital is located in central Arkham adjacent to Miskatonic University. The information desk in the main lobby provides directions to Merriweather's private, third-floor room. The investigators find the door to his room open

and the bed-ridden man engaged with two other visitors—his grieving 62-year-old wife, Agnes, and his sneering, weasel-like son, 33-year-old Bertrand.

In a rasping whisper Rupert introduces the investigators to his wife and son, and to one another. After pleasantries are exchanged Rupert asks his weeping wife and suspicious son to leave him alone for a moment with his friends. After making sure the door is shut, Rupert reveals why he has called them here.

A DARK SECRET

In the days of his youth, the old man says, he and some fellow students became involved in what they believed to be an innocent exploration of the occult. Led by a slightly older man named Marion Allen, the six men purchased an old farmhouse a few miles west of Arkham near the village of Ross's Corners. There they could conduct their seances and other psychic research in privacy. The unexpected result of their last experiment was the summoning of some evil force into this world. Instead of attempting to expel the thing, the young men abandoned the old house, confident that the magic which brought the evil to this world would keep it confined to the vacant house. However, the spell that binds the being to the house lasts only as long as the casters live. Rupert Merriweather is the last of the group and he fears that upon his death the thing will go free and wreak havoc on the countryside.

Rupert gestures weakly to an innocuous metal box on the night stand beside the bed. "Take the box," he croaks. "All the aid I can offer you lies within. You must find a way to send

Player Aid #1: Journal Entry, March 1882

We begin the ceremony as Marion instructed, according to that described in his book, *De Vermiis Mysteriis*. A fire is set in the fireplace and a pentagram chalked on the floor, marked with appropriate symbols and illuminated by two black tapers placed near the center flanking the piece of amber with its entrapped spirit. The others sit in a circle while I, the designated "watcher" who guards for malevolent spirits, sit in the far corner of the room.

Marion throws a handful of powder in the fire, producing an evil-smelling smoke and dampening the flames which now burn a sputtering green and brown. Those seated begin the Latin chant Marion Allen has transcribed from his book.

After nearly two hours I see a trail of smoke circling up from the piece of amber. Its surface seems to be bubbling, melting. Could this be it? Have we finally achieved success? I can see a form —

It is the following day. We have finished with our plans and have sworn a pact to never speak of what happened last night. We have satisfactorily explained the death of Robert, and in some manner the madness of Harold. The sheriff accepts the explanation of a carriage accident—we planned it well. Robert's neck was broken in the fall, we told him. Harold struck his head on a rock when the horse's leg broke and the carriage rolled. Would it be that it was only that. For the rest of us, we will be forever changed by what we experienced last night.

The thing formed in the center of the pentagram, shapeless, nearly invisible. Its terrible voice should have given us a clue but we were foolish. It spoke, then Marion cast that damned powder on the spirit, the Dust of Ibn-Ghazi he calls it, and that's when we could see it.

Words cannot describe the faceless thing with a thousand maws. It roiled and bubbled, never fully revealing itself. So terrifying was its aspect that I sat as though frozen to the floor, the pen falling from my nerveless fingers. Cecil and Marion seemed as lifeless as I, while a short, sharp cry issued from Crawford's mouth. Robert, however, rose to his feet and before anyone could stop him, stepped forward as though to embrace our horrible guest. With its arms, or those appendages that seemed most like arms, it took hold of poor Robert and twisted his head around as though it was a doll's head. The lifeless corpse was then thrown back in Harold's lap and that when he began that damnable shrieking—the shrieking that hadn't stopped even after we handed him over to the Sheriff's men.

We still had a chance, apparently. Marion now believes that if we had kept our wits, we could have reversed the chant and eventually forced back the creature to wherever it came from. But Crawford panicked and, mistakenly believing that it would dispel the creature, reached forward and destroyed part of the pentagram, breaking its effectiveness. Released from that binding symbol, the thing—with a screech that could only have been unholy satisfaction—fled the house, disappearing out the window as a roaring, screaming wind of boiling colors.

Marion believes that the thing could still be destroyed, or at least dispelled, but none of us who remain have the stomach for such an undertaking. It is believed that the spell we cast inextricably binds the thing to the house and it is true that when we went back a few days later to retrieve our things, we heard it bumping about in the attic over our heads. The warding signs so cheerfully carved by Marion Allen during better times—times that seem so long ago—apparently are effective and bar the thing entry except into the attic of the house.

that thing back to where it came from. You must see that this is done. Do this for me."

As soon as an investigator takes possession of the box but before he can open it, the ailing Rupert is choked by a sudden spasm. He doubles up, groans, then coughs forth a huge gout of blood and tissue—spattering any investigator standing near the night stand—then falls into a coma. All investigators present must roll against their current Sanity, losing 0/1 points depending on success or failure. Someone should call for a doctor.

The room quickly fills with interns, nurses, and Rupert's concerned wife and son. In the way, the investigators are asked to leave. Despite the hospital's best efforts, Rupert dies within the hour.

THE CONTENTS OF THE BOX

The investigators probably examine the contents of the box. Inside they find a yellowed envelope containing the deed to a house and the key to its lock, a small, sarcophagus-shaped gold box of ancient design, and a slim journal bound in leather. Deed and key are to the farm near Ross's Corners.

The ornate box opens easily but is empty. A successful History or Archaeology roll identifies the hieroglyphs decorating the box as Egyptian, of the Middle Kingdom, although those carved on the *inside* of the lid are distinctly different and not Egyptian at all.

If an investigator receives a successful Egyptian language roll, he or she receives Player Aid #4, a translation of the carvings found on the outside of the box. In a week or so, translation can also be made using dictionaries and grammars found in the Miskatonic University library, or the investigators might find that a scholar at the university can help them, perhaps for free or for a small fee.

A successful Occult skill roll result notices that the odd carvings on the inside of the box lid resemble writings attributed by certain occultists to the lost Pacific continent of Mu, but these inscriptions cannot be translated and remain a mystery in this adventure. Perhaps their meaning is learned in some later scenario.

The slim journal is a record of the Dark Brotherhood's activities at an old farmhouse on Boone Road. More about this is learned in a few paragraphs.

What Next?

By late afternoon Rupert Merriweather is dead. Investigators may do as they wish but certainly one of them will want to read Rupert's journal. Others may take it upon themselves to conduct research. Miskatonic's library is open evenings during the week: for what can be done there, see the sub-section "Research," further below.

If investigators speak with Merriweather's widow or son at the hospital, they quickly discern that neither knows anything about Merriweather's long-ago experiments, nor even of the existence of the farm property.

Investigation into Merriweather's illness reveals that he suffered from cancer. Though deadly, nothing about the illness was unusual, as a successful Medicine roll can confirm.

Neither son nor widow serve further purpose in this scenario. However, they are available should the keeper need to introduce new evidence or motivation into the plot. Agnes Merriweather, while going through her deceased husband's papers, may come across a piece of evidence or vital clue that can put stymied investigators on track. Mrs. Merriweather may personally deliver it to the farmhouse. Keep in mind that she has a weak heart and exposure to a sudden shock or horror might cost her life.

Bertrand, Merriweather's grasping son and only child, may decide to demand the contents of the box given to the investigators by his father—or go even further and show up later at the farm property, lawyer in tow, demanding they vacate the premises. The investigators have no legal right to be on the property nor will they find it easy to prove that Rupert Merriweather gave them special instructions and possession of the box before he died. It is likely, however, that the climax of the adventure takes place before the younger Merriweather can enlist the aid of an armed sheriff to evict the squatters from his property. Charges of trespassing are not serious, but there could be repercussions if the investigators refuse to vacate or attack or threaten the rightful heir.

As suits the keeper's mood, a nurse or orderly also could pop up to help the investigators. This person witnessed a strange, recurring nightmare that plagued the dying Rupert. The actual dream may be obscure, but some element within it can provide a clue needed by the investigators.

Reading the Journal

Bound in plain black leather, the journal entries date from June 1881 to March of 1882. Although the ink is faded, no English roll is necessary to understand it, and reading it requires only four hours' time. Reading the volume costs the reader 1D2 Sanity points and adds 1 percentile to his or her Cthulhu Mythos skill.

- A group of friends, playfully calling themselves the Dark Brotherhood, held their first meeting in the early spring of 1881. Rupert Merriweather became the recording secretary. The members numbered six including Marion Allen, the founder and their nominal leader.

- In June of 1881 they purchased an old farmhouse outside Ross's Corners, a place where they could conduct their experiments in privacy. Representing themselves as a student literary fraternity, they cleaned and furnished the place while Marion Allen carved special warding (protective) signs over the wooden doors and windows. At the time, the others were amused at such precautions.

- A series of experiments, innocent and apparently ineffective attempts to contact the spirit world, are then detailed.

- An entry dated February of 1882 notes Marion Allen's acquisition of an artifact, purportedly Egyptian, described as a small sarcophagus of gold with a hinged lid. Inside was a large piece of amber entrapping a specimen of some unknown species of arthropod. Allen is excited. The box corresponds to a description he found in an ordinary reference volume in the Miskatonic University library

- Allen says that in another book, a thick Latin tome titled *De Vermiis Mysteriis*, is an explanation of some purported powers of the box. The small animal trapped in the amber is said to contain a friendly spirit and guide to the spirit world.

- A date is set to conduct a ceremony intended to summon this spirit creature—a Saturday night in the middle of March.

- The next entry is reproduced as Player Aid #1. Hand a photocopy to the player of the investigator reading the book.

- The next entries are the names of those belonging to the Dark Brotherhood, followed by the dates of their deaths, all by the same hand, but in various inks.

Robert Menkin, March 1882
Harold Copley, August 1882
Marion Allen, August 1883
Crawford Harris, January 1915
Cecil Jones, March 1924
Rupert Merriweather —

- A small newspaper clipping, dated in August of 1883, is pasted next to the entry marking Marion Allen's death. Hand the player a copy of Player Aid #2.

- The last entry is reproduced as Player Aid #3. It is written in a noticeably weaker hand, and the ink is quite fresh.

Research Topics

Although Arkham supports a small public library, the famed library at Miskatonic University is by far the better source. Only students and faculty are allowed to borrow books but the library is otherwise open and available to the public. Hours are: 8 am to 9 pm Monday through Friday, and 10 am to 6 pm Saturday. The reference room is open Sundays 1 pm to 6 pm, but the stacks are closed and books cannot be withdrawn on that day. The M.U. library is large, containing over 400,000 volumes, and investigators must be able to state the topics they wish to research.

HISTORY OR EGYPTOLOGY

A four-hour search in these large section coupled with a successful Library Use roll turns up a copy of the book mentioned by Marion Allen in Merriweather's journal. It contains a draw-

Player Aid #2: Newspaper Article, August 1883

A MURDER AT THE DOCKS

NEW ORLEANS—The body of Mr. Marion Allen, late of Arkham, Massachusetts, was discovered early this morning near the Gulf & Panama docks. A victim of foul play, the man was identified by local witnesses who said that Mr. Allen had been seen in the locale the evening before. Although robbery was the apparent motive, police report that the victim's tongue had been cut out. Marion Allen had reportedly gone to police earlier this week claiming that he was being followed and that he feared for his life. He said his shadowy pursuers were after an Egyptian artifact which he no longer possessed.

---

ing and short description of the small box now in the investigators' possession. It notes that little is known about the box but that scholars believe it to have been the possession of the little-known Nophru-Ka, a would-be usurper of the Egyptian throne who lived sometime during the XIVth Dynasty.

The sarcophagus was supposed to have been given to Nophru-Ka by the gods and was said to contain spirits that Nophru-Ka could call upon to serve him. The sarcophagus actually contains a piece of unpolished amber encasing a trapped insect.

For years the golden box was owned by a noble family in Britain. It was stolen in a burglary in 1876, and not seen since. The article offers a translation of the inscription carved on the box (see Player Aid #4). The summary briefly mentions the odd glyphs carved on the inside lid but makes no attempt to explain or decipher them.

OCCULT

Four hours' research in this section along with a successful Library Use roll turns up a book about the fabled civilization of Mu. A reproduction of sea-eroded carvings purported to be Muvian in origin closely resembles those found inside the lid of the sarcophagus. The book offers nothing in the way of translation. The glyphs remain indecipherable.

DE VERMIIS MYSTERIIS

The catalog shows that the library owns a copy of this book and that it is locked away in a rare book collection upstairs. The librarian says that the old volume is on a special restricted list compiled by the head of the library, the aging Dr. Henry Armitage. Armitage's personal permission is needed to gain access to this volume.

Further questioning can establish that Armitage is in his office on weekday mornings, and that Armitage is presently preoccupied with special studies of those restricted books.

Recently alerted to the threat of the Cthulhu Mythos, and having no clear understanding of it, Armitage actively discourages visitors from reading these books. Without solid credentials or proper letters of reference, investigators find Armitage impervious to bribes and skill rolls such as Fast Talk. Only at the keeper's discretion can the investigators gain access to the library's Mythos holdings. As events prove, however, all that the investigators need to know is in the farm house.

NEWSPAPERS

Investigators might wish to check the library's bound collection of newspaper back issues, kept in the basement. It takes one hour's time to skim through a year's editions of the *Arkham Gazette*, *Arkham Advertiser*, or any other paper collected by the library. A successful Library Search roll uncov-

Player Aid #3: Final Journal Entry

I gravely fear that which I and my colleagues have loosed upon this countryside. Nothing of consequence has yet taken place but with my death the bonds will be broken and the thing then freed to come and go as it pleases. Lives and souls not yet taken already lie heavy on my conscience. The method of delivering the thing out of this world is still in that accursed house, the translation made by Marion Allen from the horrid De Vermiis Mysteriis. I am not strong enough to take on the task, but I know of those who perhaps are. Should they fail me, may God have mercy on my soul.

---

ers stories in both the *Gazette* and *Advertiser* dated March, 1882, describing the carriage accident that took the life of one student and grievously injured another. Rupert Merriweather and the others are mentioned by name.

Ross's Corners

Their research concluded, investigators probably visit the farmhouse. To get there, they must pass through Ross's Corners, a hamlet located a few miles west of Arkham. They can drive, or take the bus that passes through the village on a run from Arkham to Worcester and back each day. The fare is 80 cents each way. The bus stops at Ross's Corner shortly after 10 am on the way out and shortly before 2 pm on the way back.

Ross's Corners consists of a few tired buildings and homes. The prosperity of long farms has long been in decline. No more than forty people live here. A church and a combination general store, post office, gas station, and milk depot are the community's centers.

If the party stops to purchase supplies or gasoline, or to ask directions, they may try to open conversations with some of the locals. Residents are exceptionally dour, unsmiling, and suspicious. A successful Psychology roll tells an investigator that he is experiencing something besides proverbial Yankee reticence.

If the investigators are dressed well and act respectably, the people may warm up. Ask the players to choose one or more investigators as spokesmen. If they can tell good jokes, conduct their purchases in seemly manners, flatter the villagers with pious Fast Talk, or receive successful Credit Rating rolls, they can learn more.

If they ask about the old farmhouse, the investigators learn that the children say it is haunted. Ma Peters, who runs the general store, sniffs at those stories and states that the taxes are always paid on the place. A Mr. Merriweather in Arkham has owned it for years and done nothing with it, as nearly everybody knows. Country people make it their business to know who is responsible for local property.

If the keeper judges that any of the investigators have made a good impression on Ma Peters, she may confide that last night a local woman disappeared, a middle-aged farmer's wife who went out after dark to check on the barn and who hasn't been seen since.

"Any suspicious looks you mighta got today are on account of that. Folks are a little shy about strangers right now. Don't think nothin' of it."

Boone Road runs north out of town and is easy to find. The old farm lies to the north. If the investigators arrived by bus they can try to hire a local to give them a lift in a truck or wagon, who will be astonished to receive payment for saving someone a stroll of a mile and a half. Otherwise the investigators walk, carrying any equipment and supplies.

The Farm House

The ancient house sits atop a hill, visible from the road and about a hundred yards east of it. It is of early 18th century saltbox design with a high peaked roof and windows sealed by sagging shutters. Its single story has two rooms, with a windowless attic overhead and a root cellar below. A huge brick fireplace stands at the end of the second room. The roof is bowed, but all the shingles are intact.

> "Seeker of Wisdom, Servant [son] of Yugr [Yoag] Setheth, Deliverer of the people [slaves] of the water, Bearer of the spirits of Nar-Loth-hotep,
> child of Thoth, Seeker of Wisdom.

Player Aid #4: Translation of the Hieroglyphic

On lintels over all the doors and windows are carved symbols of a strange nature, identified with a successful Occult roll as symbols of power used to ward against otherworldly spirits, a good defense if left in place. Cut away from the house, they are useless. Knowing how to ward was lost when Marion Allen died.

The locked front door opens easily with the key which accompanied the deed. The back door, if checked, is found unlatched, standing a half-inch open.

Inspecting the grass and bushes around the house, a successful Spot Hidden roll finds a recently-dead raccoon laying in the knee-high grass. If the thirty-pound carcass is turned over, the cause of death is easily determined. The animal's breast is stained with clotted blood, and a large hole has been chewed into its chest. A little poking around and a Medicine or Natural History roll reveals that its ribs were gnawed apart and then its heart was neatly eaten out. A fox could have done it, but the investigator has an uneasy feeling after noticing the smooth edges of the wound.

THE FRONT ROOM

Within, the front room of the house is dirty and long untouched. Dust lies thickly on the mantel and empty shelves, while dead leaves and detritus cover the floor. The wooden floor is badly warped and stained, the result of water leaking through the roof and ceiling. Rot has eaten away at an old couch and matching wing chairs. Perhaps they are the source of the faint foul odor in the room.

At this point the keeper might secretly make Listen rolls for each investigator. A successful roll indicates an investigator hears a scuffling, scurrying, or bumping noise under the floor. Communicate that perception to the player.

THE BACK ROOM

Near the entrance to this room is a narrow opening in the floor revealing a steep flight of steps leading down to the cellar. A trap door set in the ceiling overhead leads to the attic, the wooden frame surrounding it decorated with the same occult carvings seen over the doors and windows of the house. The back door, slightly ajar, and the large fireplace are also important elements in the room.

Evidence points to recent occupation. The dust has been kicked up, and fresh footprints can be seen. The large fireplace contains the embers of a fire not long dead. Beside the fireplace a thick new wool blanket has been tossed, and nearby is an empty can of Campbell's pork-and-beans. Trace of the sauce are still liquid.

Nearby is a penny box of wooden matches, half empty, a can opener whose cutting edge approximates the sharp edges left on the pork-and-beans can, a dull jack knife, a dirty spoon, the stub of a candle, and wrinkled pictures of various attractive young ladies in advertisements. Depending upon the investigators' backgrounds, the keeper may or may not require an Idea roll to conclude that at least one hobo recently stayed here.

On a high shelf are materials mentioned in Merriweather's journal of the Dark Brotherhood: an old wooden cigar box and a thin sheaf of yellowed papers.

THE CIGAR BOX

The sheets of paper glued on it are peeling and yellowed, and an investigator must either smoke cigars or receive a successful History roll to date the brand in the 1880s.

Inside is a small metal canister containing a coarse, brownish powder, and a small wooden box with a sliding lid holding a small amount of a silvery, talc-like substance. A successful Chemistry roll identifies sulfur and an oxide of copper as important constituents of the brown powder.

The silvery talc defies identification, even subject to lab analysis. Like graphite, it adheres to the skin, coating it and imparting a greasy feel. The talc washes off easily. A successful Cthulhu Mythos roll identifies it as Powder of Ibn-Ghazi. If shown the talc, Dr. Armitage (from the university) also could make that identification.

THE SHEAF OF YELLOWED PAPERS

The papers are hand-written notes dated March, 1882. All the sheets are in a large, flourished hand (that of Marion Allen, though the investigators may never prove this), a hand unlike the neat, crabbed script of Rupert Merriweather. No sheet mentions the silvery Powder of Ibn-Ghazi.

There are six copies of the same Latin chant—separate copies for each of the members.

Three other sheets identify the chant as having been copied from a book called *De Vermiis Mysteriis* written c. 1542 by one Ludwig Prinn. They contain notes about the book and its history, and comment in passing that the chant "could be used to release the spirit trapped inside the ancient amber."

The tenth sheet includes a description of the pentagram, the symbols to be drawn, and the combination of chemicals to be burned in the fire.

The last three sheets discuss the ritual. They indicate that to dispel the spirit, the chant should be reversed, but that everything should be done the same, whether invoking or dispelling. A two-hour ceremony, begun at midnight, will drive off the unwanted spirit.

Although the ceremony can be performed by one person, Prinn suggests the use of several chanters, allowing individuals to occasionally interrupt their chanting without disturbing the potency of the casting. If the chant is continuous for two hours, at least one person at all times maintaining the rhythm, the spirit must succumb. But even the slightest disruption of the chant results in failure; another ritual must commence on a following night.

Prinn suggests that during this time—as during any summoning—that a "watcher be posted, lest the sorcerers be disturbed by the nuisances and distractions of malevolent spirits."

THE CELLAR

During this time the keeper may again secretly attempt Listen rolls for the investigators. The source of the noise from beneath the floor is a man called Red Jake, a hobo by trade.

Red Jake, generally an amiable fellow, made the mistake of trying to bed down here last night, only to be driven off by the unseemly noises and smells coming from the attic above. Fleeing the house in a panic, leaving his meager belongings

behind, he was set upon and almost killed by the monster spirit that inhabits the house.

His escape was narrow. Soon after, the ravening monster found, killed, and carried off the unfortunate farmer's wife. Her torn, heartless corpse now lies in the woods. Jake spent the night shivering in the woods.

The hobo sneaked back to retrieve his belongings, only to be surprised by the arrival of the investigators. He now hides in the dark cellar, paranoid and fearful, temporarily insane from last night's encounter with the horror. If left undisturbed Red Jake waits until the time is right and then bolts upstairs and out the back door, heading for the woods. Unless the investigators can run him down, he will not return.

If instead someone goes downstairs, perhaps investigating the strange noises, Jake jumps out of the shadows and makes a surprise attack with an old table leg. A successful Spot Hidden by the investigator spies the hiding hobo and nullifies any chance of being surprised. If Jake hits the investigator, the victim takes the rolled damage for Light Club and is stunned long enough for Jake to mount the stairs. He only wants to escape. He attacks those who stand in his way.

RED JAKE, Horrified Hobo

STR 15	CON 14	SIZ 15	INT 11	POW 10
DEX 12	APP 8	EDU 6	SAN 42	HP 15

Damage Bonus: +1D4

Weapons: Fist/Punch 65%, 1D3 +db
Table Leg 55%, 1D8 +db.

Skills: Climb 75%, Craft (Carpentry) 40%, Cthulhu Mythos 5%, Dodge 55%, Hide 75%, Jump 65%, Listen 55%, Sneak 55%.

If the investigators subdue the hobo, they find him rambling, almost incoherent. A successful Psychoanalysis roll might calm the man long enough to get a few scraps of information from him but these clues will be sketchy. What he says must be determined by the keeper.

If the investigators take their captive back to Ross's Corners and turn him over to Pa Peters, the Justice of the Peace, he is arrested by the state police and jailed in Salem, the county seat, as the prime suspect in the disappearance of the farmer's wife. Although he may be cleared of the charges, in the meantime the investigators will enjoy increased respect from the citizens of Ross's Corners.

If Red Jake escapes the investigators, he dies that night, the second victim of the terrible spirit creature in the attic. He may return after death to pay the investigators a surprise visit.

THE LURKER IN THE ATTIC

The thing in the attic waits soundlessly, listening to the intruders below, judging their intent and gauging their strength. Dwelling in this house for over forty years it has learned to eat well and is content, and it will use its intelligence and cunning to stay here.

Although the thing is careful to make no sound, some investigator may wish to explore the trap door in the ceiling. A ladder or shoulder-boost will be necessary. The door itself is stuck with a force of STR 12. Opening it requires a successful roll on the Resistance Table.

The Lurker waits until the intruder pokes his head up through the opening, then with a growling rush makes a grab for the target. It is so nearly invisible to the sight of this world that even a flashlight beam cannot much reveal it, but the investigator can hear the thing pummeling the floorboards toward him and, with a successful Dodge, is able to fall back and down to the floor below—losing 1D3 hit points upon landing but avoiding the talons of the fiend.

The attack evaded or completed, the trap door then slams shut and a growling, panting sound is heard coming from the attic above. Witnesses to these events, including the target, lose 1/1D2 Sanity points.

The Dodge roll failing, the investigator takes the rolled damage from the monster's attack, then falls and suffers the 1D3 additional points of damage. All present lose 1/1D3 points of Sanity to witness this successful attack. The victim, if surviving, suffers injuries to the head and face that leave permanent scars. The investigator's APP drops by 1D4 points.

If the blow kills the investigator, indicate that the talons have caught in the target's skull. The Lurker can haul up the dangling corpse, chew out its heart, then throw the carcass back down through the opening. Witnesses to this lose another 1/1D6 Sanity points. The rapidity of these psychic blows makes it likely that some investigators go indefinitely insane. Keep careful track of individual Sanity point losses.

About The Lurker

This creature is a nearly invisible and barely material manifestation from another dimension. Although not bound to the house, it regards the attic as its home and refuge. It is not physically harmed by light, but light causes the creature pain. It prefers darkened shelter.

The Lurker cannot be harmed by physical weapons. Spells that drain POW do affect it. It suffers no damage from fire, electricity, or acid. It becomes visible and takes on a semi-solid form if dusted with the Powder of Ibn-Ghazi or when feeding. It finds sustenance and pleasure in devouring the hearts of warm-blooded animals. If the investigators ever enter the attic they find it littered with the rotting corpses and skeletons of raccoons, possums, birds, and other small animals that have mistakenly explored here.

THE LURKER IN THE ATTIC, Nearly Invisible

STR 20	CON 18	SIZ 17	INT 12	POW 20
DEX 18	Move 12			HP 18

Damage Bonus: +1D6

Weapons: Claws* (2) 70%, 1D8 +db

launches one Claw attack per round.

Special Abilities: can animate and control a corpse; is able to pass through unwarded material obstructions without effort; generates stinking acid.

DISPELLING THE LURKER

The creature is impervious to most physical attacks. Unless the investigators have magic not in this scenario, dispelling the monster according to Marion Allen's notes is the only solution. Firing the house does not harm the creature, but encourages it to take residence nearer to Ross's Corners.

Dispelling the monster takes two hours of continual chanting, begun at midnight and coupled with a properly-drawn pentagram and a fire burning some of the brown chemical compound found with Allen's notes. These notes suggest that at least one person stand back from the ceremony in order to watch for malevolent spirits that may be drawn to the rites, but the investigators may do as they wish.

To dispel the Lurker, the words must be chanted in reverse. Individual chanters may stop now and then to catch their breaths, but at least one person must be chanting at any given moment. Each investigator participating in the chant donates 2 magic points every half hour; a chanter reaching zero magic points falls unconscious.

At sunset, long before the investigators can begin the ceremony, the creature leaves the house, whistling out of the attic and across the fields toward the nearby woods. No Listen rolls are necessary to hear it exit. Any investigators standing outside may see the thing leaving the house, each suffering a loss of 0/1D3 Sanity points at the sight of a faint, tangling vortex rolling through the air. An attack on watching investigators would probably succeed, but the Lurker intends to track down and kill the hobo who escaped its clutches the night before.

In this endeavor it is successful, if Red Jake has already escaped the house. The hobo dies a horrible death at around ten o'clock that night. Investigators receiving successful Listen rolls hear distant screams, ending too soon for them to take action.

The Ceremony

The ceremony begun, the Lurker quickly returns to the house, aware of the intent of the investigators. Unable to enter the warded rooms, it plunges into the attic above and begins a campaign of terror calculated to disrupt the proceedings. During this time call for more Sanity rolls. The danger of temporary insanity exists, as well as the possibility of indefinite insanity due to quickly accumulating losses. Insane investigators are unable to chant properly. Any investigator, sane or not, who flees the safety of the house is probably set upon by the Lurker and slain.

The first twenty minutes of the ceremony go smoothly. Then the monster returns, drawn home by the chant, landing in the attic with a loud thump. Investigators hear it snuffling heavily above them. All lose 0/1 Sanity points.

Within moments the creature sets up an awful howling, interspersed by grunts and foul curses spoken in a harsh guttural voice. The old house sways and creaks, the sudden jolts shaking it to its foundations. Objects on shelves and the mantel fall and roll across the floor. All lose 1/1D3 Sanity points.

This violence and noise continues for a half hour, then a horrible smell begins to creep down from the attic above, followed by a thick stinking goo that oozes through the ceiling and drips down the walls. Call for Luck rolls. Those receiving failures at some point are spattered by this alien acid and suffer 1D2 points of first- and second-degree-burn damage. This may leave scars, as the players wish.

Near the beginning of the second hour of chanting, the monster quiets and the investigators chant without distraction. A half-hour later, anyone who makes a Listen roll hears, from outside, a faint call for help—a woman's voice. An investigator looking outside sees something fifty yards away, crawling slowly through the high grass towards the house. A Spot Hidden roll, or artificial light, reveals the object to be a woman, middle-aged, obviously hurt. She lifts her head and calls toward the house. Her face is streaked with blood.

This is the swollen corpse of the missing farm wife, Maggie McPhirter. She has been dead for 24 hours, her heart chewed out by the thing that dwells in the attic. The monster has spent 5 magic points to animate the corpse and thereby disrupt the ceremony. Anyone going outside is attacked, either by Maggie's animated corpse or, if the keeper chooses cruelty, by the monster itself.

It may be that the monster has or will likewise animate the corpse of Red Jake, and use it to attack an investigator attempting to help the woman. If the animated dead fail to lure the investigators out, the monster has them assault the house, pushing in the doors or windows, screaming, shouting, hollering, and biting. They are fearsome, but not very difficult to destroy, and they cannot enter the house because of the wards. In most ways they can be treated like rulesbook zombies. The sanity losses they provoke may be their most dangerous aspect. Destroying an attacking undead results in Sanity awards of 1D6+1 for every investigator involved.

M. McPHIRTER, Corpse, animated by the Lurker

| STR 11 | CON 04 | SIZ 10 | INT 0 | POW 01 |
| DEX 03 | Move 5 | | | HP 07 |

Damage Bonus: none.

Weapons: Maul 65%, damage 1D6

Sanity Loss: 1/1D6

RED JAKE, Corpse, animated by the Lurker

| STR 11 | CON 04 | SIZ 15 | INT 0 | POW 01 |
| DEX 05 | Move 5 | | | HP 10 |

Damage Bonus: +1D4

Weapons: Maul 65%, damage 1D6 +db

Sanity Loss: 1/1D6

The Thing Appears

Nearing the last five minutes of the ceremony a wisp of smoke curls down from the ceiling, twisting toward the center of the pentagram on the floor. The creature from the attic manifests itself before the investigators' eyes. Four more minutes of chanting is all that is required to drive it back to its place of origin. As it begins to condense in the pentagram, it becomes partially visible—a horrible twisting mass of talons and maws and long appendages. Sanity loss to see this is 1/1D8 Sanity points, but subtract any points already lost in observing the thing leave the house at sunset.

Any investigator going insane sees not a horrible monster, but a compelling and attractive human figure. The insane investigator steps forward to embrace the creature. Unless stopped, he or she probably dies. The monster is confined to the pentagram but can attack anyone who crosses the symbol's perimeter.

If the investigators can finish the last few minutes of the chant, the creature is driven wailing from this world, banished to wherever from which it first came, leaving only the lingering unearthly foulness behind.

Conclusion

If the creature is banished, participating investigators each receive a Sanity award of 1D10+1 Sanity points. If they fail to banish the creature each suffers an additional loss of 1/1D4 Sanity points during the next week, as the monster takes three more victims before leaving the area forever.

Loose Ends?

The investigators' connection with this adventure may not be finished. What about Bertrand Merriweather and any legal troubles the investigators may have incurred at the start of the adventure? Are the investigators able to satisfactorily explain to the sheriff concerning corpses, heartless or otherwise, littering the property after the adventure?

Do the investigators benefit from Rupert's will? He considered them fine and trustworthy people, perhaps he rewarded them with a small, or even large gift from his estate.

What about the mysterious glyphs on the inside of the gold sarcophagus? It is possible that the *Zanthu Tablet*s, purportedly a history of Mu, contains enough notes to effect a partial translation of this obviously important inscription.

Who murdered Marion Allen years ago in New Orleans? Were they cultists desperately searching for the sarcophagus of Nophru-Ka? Could they possibly learn that it is now in the investigators' possession and come looking for it? Looking into the background of Marion Allen, the investigators may find that before turning up in New Orleans, Allen was briefly affiliated with the Chapel of Contemplation in Boston.

And what about the investigators' jobs? They may have now missed several days of work and need a story for their bosses. Certainly they can't tell the truth. ∎

"I say to you againe, do not call up Any that you can not put downe; by the Which I meane, Any that can in Turne call up something against you, whereby your Powerfullest Devices may not be of use. Ask of the Lesser, lest the Greater shall not wish to Answer."

—Lovecraft, "The Case of Charles Dexter Ward"

 # THE MADMAN

S et in New England in the 1920s, little in this short adventure needs to be changed or added to in order to relocate it or place it in another era. In the 1990s, keep the fire area inaccessible by cloaking the mountain in high winds and fog, and suggest that the strangely foul weather seems in some sense to be artificial.

Importantly, the alien enemies in this adventure are methodical and more technically advanced than the investigators. Our heroes need luck or outside help as well as skill to emerge victorious.

Interested keepers should photocopy the four newspaper stories on p. 234 and give the duplicates to the players, so that they can make their deductions.

No maps are provided, since distances and relationships are unimportant in the scenario. Strafton Mountain, Windham County, and Brattleboro are real places in southern Vermont. The west fork of the Windham River—if it exists—has been moved to suit the scenario.

Since the investigators must drive, the keeper needs to know what they decide to bring with them. Presumably they go in one or two cars—as a rule of thumb, allow each a suitcase for personal effects, and another 20-30 pounds each for guns, bulky high-quality cameras, and other special equipment. Only when a mystery is clearly defined, or if they must be absent for many weeks should a keeper allow much more. If the player-characters decide to buy more gear, they must go to a town or city where it reasonably would be sold. Little is for sale in Jenning except foodstuffs and stamps.

Keeper Information

Old Harny Rooger has gotten very eccentric. He attacked a postman for no reason. There are also tales that Harny's insanity has taken the form of mysterious rituals on hilltops, complete with bonfires and sacrifices of goats.

Rooger, never a stable man, has been contacted by a group of mi-go, the fungi from Yuggoth. These aliens wish to drive away or destroy the residents of Jenning so that they may mine the surrounding hills without interference. They are trying to clear out the humans by summoning Ithaqua the Windwalker to blast the town, killing all the people as if by a severe snowstorm. The mi-go will mop up survivors with their mist projectors. Over the course of a few months, the mi-go have managed to create a magical pathway to the top of Strafton Mountain, allowing Ithaqua to manifest itself this far south. They are attempting to summon that Great Old One with midnight chants and spells, but so far they have failed, since they have only a 20% chance for success in casting the spell Call Ithaqua.

Player Information

Recent stories appearing in the *Brattleboro Tattler* have been picked up by the Boston dailies. They concern strange noises and lights seen around Jenning, Vermont. The latest story tells of the disappearance of Bartley Hodges, the *Tattler*'s correspondent in Jenning. Suspecting Mythos activity, the investigators decide to drive to Vermont and inspect the situation, and incidentally earn the reward.

BRATTLEBORO TATTLER

The editor of the *Tattler* is happy to talk about the stories and about Bartley Hodges' disappearance. He has little information to add to the stories, except to say that Hodges, an ex-newspaperman who had retired to Jenning, was a reliable fellow. "Old Hodges liked to walk along Jenning's Notch. Mebbe he slipped into the river—mebbe not. If he went anywhere, he didn't tell no one." The editor shows the investigators four pertinent stories in the *Tattler*, all written by Hodges. They differ little from the versions printed in the Boston papers.

WINDHAM COUNTY CONSTABULARY

Also in Brattleboro are the offices of the county's sheriff. The deputies are guarded in their comments, except that the disappearance of Bartley Hodges is being treated as a bona fide missing person's case. They are uninterested in the fires, except as related to Hodges' disappearance.

Jenning, Vermont

Jenning is a small town of a few hundred people, tucked in the hills not far from Jenning's Notch, where the west fork of the Windham River rushes through to join the Connecticut. Its buildings are prim and well-repaired, but they are small and old—Jenning is not prosperous, and has not had a burst of prosperity since the Civil War.

INFORMATION IN TOWN

The grade school, general store, feed store, and church are the only public places to meet people. The use of Fast Talk or Persuade to get information is regarded as down-right pushy and rude. No one responds to such overtures. Some will deign to refer questions to the constable who drives in once a week and stops at the general store, to catch up on the local gossip. There is also a monthly town meeting, if the investigators would like to wait.

Approaching a citizen and using a successful Credit Rating roll gets better results, since people are impressed by well-dressed, responsible-seeming people, even if such people are strangers. He or she has seen or has heard that others have seen "unnatural things" in those hills. Nobody goes there at night now, "sure not now that they're settin' them fires."

Having gotten this far, a successful Fast Talk or Persuade can pry out more. The things are "sumthin' like big crawdads, big as a man, but with a little scrunch'd up face an' red all o'er, like they bin roasted."

What about Bartley Hodges? "Everybody knows they're makin' those fires. Bartley knew it too. Reckon he got too close. I'll lay a dime that poor old Bartley's got roasted too."

BARTLEY HODGES' HOME

If the investigators ask, any successful Credit Rating roll gets them directions to Bartley Hodges' home, a simple four-room clapboard house not far from the river. Crossing the broad front porch, they find the door unlocked, as is every door hereabouts.

Hodges lived alone. On the walls are memorabilia of the big stories he broke, and pictures of his now-departed wife. No matter how thoroughly they look, the investigators find nothing detailing secrets about Hodges or about the fires. Hodges was in all respects exactly who he seemed to be. The only sug-

gestive item in the house is in the wastebasket, on the back of a short note from the editor of the *Tattler*. It's penciled lightly on the paper, and takes a successful Spot Hidden to notice. This is all it says:

Harny Rooger

If the investigators miss this clue, have someone else in town mention that Harny Rooger lives closer to the fires than anyone else. Maybe he knows something.

HARNY ROOGER

If the investigators pursue this lead, townspeople explain that Harny is an old handyman who lives in an unpainted cottage four miles north of Jenning, at the end of a lane the width of a wheel barrow. The person giving directions can also say that the constable has already been up and talked to Harny, and that Harny had nothing to say—this is a small town, remember, and everybody knows everything. Almost.

Two miles northwest of the wooden shack rises the crest of Strafton Mountain, nearly 4000 feet high, where on the east

---

EXCERPTS FROM

The Brattleboro Tattler

FIRE ON STRAFTON MOUNTAIN

JENNING—Residents in the Jenning area report a large fire Tuesday night on the east side of Strafton Mountain. The local constabulary has been unable to locate the remains of the blaze, which apparently extinguished itself by Wednesday morning. No reports of damage have been received here from neighboring farmers or foresters.

STRANGE SOUNDS ON THE MOUNTAIN

JENNING—Another great blaze was seen Sunday evening on Strafton Mountain. Observers declare that this time the flames seemed to be accompanied by dull drummings or explosions of a rhythmical nature.

To their evident annoyance, again authorities proved unable to locate the source of these mystery blazes.

This scribe among them, certain residents hereabouts plan to deploy opportunely these next few evenings. We shall try to solve this mystery.

A SECOND NIGHT'S BLAZE

JENNING—Jenning-area neighbors spied another large fire on the east side of Strafton Mountain on Friday night. As the moon was up, watchers were able to get a better idea of its location on the mountain.

Reward Offered

MISSING TATTLER CORRESPONDENT

JENNING—Windham County authorities report that Bartley Hodges, retired newsman and Jenning correspondent for this newspaper, has not been seen since Tuesday night, and is declared missing.

Mr. Hodges is described as 67 years old and with silvery hair, about six feet tall, thin, spry, and a man of ready speech and wit.

Bartley Hodges is well known in this area as a convivial companion and an upstanding citizen. The Tattler will pay $500 reward to learn his present circumstances.

side the strange fires have been occurring. Alongside the house is an acre of gardens and vines, and a small orchard.

Rooger is a gangly, balding man who seems never to have entirely grown up. He is sinewy and rangy, and skillful with an ax — when the investigators come up, they see him split wood, round after round with never a miss and never a partial split.

Rooger is friendly enough during the day, but becomes increasingly uneasy as night approaches. He does not know what his "new friends" are planning to do to Jenning, and if he found out, he would turn against them. He drinks heavily of a clear liquid from an unlabeled bottle. He grows drunker as the day passes. If the investigators make a chemical analysis of this liquid, they find that it is 140-proof moonshine.

He answers such questions as he can but denies any knowledge of Hodges.

As time passes, he continues to drink, and begins to insinuate statements such as "My new friends knaow more th'n them perfessers from the U." "They kin mek it snow or rain." "My crops hev'n't failed oncst since m' new friends come along." "Daon' hev m' dawg no more — m' friends needed it to he'p call *their* friend. Iffka, I thin' his name be. Er, is it Ifkwa . . . Ittaw . . . Iffdkwa?"

Asked about Bartley Hodges, Rooger shakes his head sorrowfully, but finally grudgingly adds, "I did warn 'im, afore goodness I did."

If the investigators bribe and cajole Harny enough, they learn that the mi-go are certain that the "big-un" will soon come, but even the aliens do not know when. Harny does not know what will happen when he does: "Mebbe shan't be so blamed cold up thar then, ayup, an' then mebbe worser."

If an investigator insists on staying till nightfall, Harny threatens him with his shotgun and orders him to "Git! I be workin' naow!" Rooger intends to keep his appointment with the aliens, for their power impresses him.

If the investigators stay (perhaps they disarm Harny or hide in the nearby woods outside), they have time to prepare as they wish. When the sun goes down they see a mi-go fly out of the sky to the cabin (lose 0/1D6 Sanity points) and go inside to speak in a buzzing voice with Harny, ordering him to appear tonight. This is mi-go #2 in the statistics.

If the mi-go finds investigators inside, it attacks if there are one or two investigators, and it tries to flee if there are more than two. If it flees successfully, it fetches armed mi-go and they fly back, intending to hunt down and kill the meddling humans.

HARNY ROOGER, Age 58, Batty Handyman

STR 8	CON 13	SIZ 15	INT 8	POW 10
DEX 9	APP 6	EDU 4	SAN 18	HP 14

Damage Bonus: none.

Weapons: 20-gauge Shotgun 70%, damage 2D6/1D6/1D3 Wood Ax 85%, damage 1D8+2.

Skills: Craft (Gardening) 60%, Drive Automobile 40%, Electrical Repair 35%, Hide 45%, Mechanical Repair 45%, Natural History 33%, Track 65%.

The Mountain

Presumably the investigators survive the mi-go and stay on the case. Whether or not he is a captive, Harny will want to carry out his contract with the aliens. Jacketed, with fur cap and gloves, he sets out just after sunset, up Strafton Mountain. He is easy to trail.

Keeper Option: Cold

The effect of this option will be to postpone the action on Strafton Mountain until the investigators are better prepared, or else to whittle down the size of the investigator party which manages to stay at the top of the mountain.

As one climbs the slopes, the air quickly gets unnaturally cold. At the top, the temperature is well below zero. If the investigators are not wearing warm clothing, each player must roll CON x5 or less on D100 when called for, or lose a hit point to the cold provoked by the ceremonies to Ithaqua. When an investigator loses more than half of his or her hit points, unconsciousness from exposure sets in. The group should retreat from the mountain if this happens.

If an investigator has dressed warmly, only a few CON rolls will be appropriate.

Toward the top, each trailing investigator must receive a successful Sneak roll or be spotted by a patrolling mi-go, who then attacks.

If the investigators climb the mountain during the day and wait concealed until night, each needs a successful Conceal or Hide roll to keep from being seen by the mi-go when they arrive. In these cases, the keeper should make the die rolls. The investigators should not know if they are hidden well enough or not.

If a loud noise is made after sunset, such as a gunshot, then in 1D10 combat rounds several fungi from Yuggoth arrive to investigate. Three fungi patrol the mountain after dark on ceremony nights.

THE CEREMONY

Near the top of the mountain, on a barren spur which has a clear view to the north as well as the east, is a ring of irregular stones, each stone roughly three feet in diameter, each coated with thick layers of fresh frost and rime.

As the investigators wait in the dark, seven fungi from Yuggoth float out of the sky (check for Sanity loss) and begin to move about the hilltop. Harny joins them, and then three leave to renew their area patrol.

Then the chant begins, led by the awful buzzing voice of the leader, who is assisted by mi-go #5, while Harny and the two remaining mi-go chant responses. The leader and mi-go #5 each expend all their magic points but one, while Harny and the other two each expend one, giving them a 28% chance to succeed. As the beings hum and sway, a blue-white flame flickers in the circle of stones. A blast of icy air emanates from it — the flame is one of cold, as can be determined by the sudden growth of frost on the stones around it.

If the spell succeeds, a grotesque howling horror plunges out of the northern sky into the middle of the flame, extinguishing it, and then proceeds to ravage down the valley, bringing an unnatural arctic blizzard to the horrified Vermont hamlet. All investigators seeing Ithaqua lose 1D10/D100 Sanity points. Harny probably goes mad.

If the spell fails, then the flame flickers on for a while, then subsides, and the disappointed fungi call back their guards and flap off the mountain, leaving Harry to make his way back to his shack.

If Ithaqua is successfully called, the valley and its village will be destroyed by three days of 75 degrees-below zero weather. Huge snowdrifts block all roads.

The Mi-Go

Review the mi-go entries in the Creatures and Alien Technology chapters. All the aliens in this adventure carry pieces of twisted metal that look like metallic driftwood but actually are weapons. Mi-go #1, #5, and #7 also wear slimy webs which act as 8 points of armor against all weapons.

SEVEN MERCILESS MI-GO

	STR	CON	SIZ	DEX	POW	HP
#1*	10	14	14	22	13	14
#2	11	14	07	17	08	11
#3	11	10	13	14	08	12
#4	10	09	06	13	15	08
#5*	09	09	08	14	14	09
#6	08	15	11	15	12	13
#7*	14	14	10	18	10	12

* +8 armor for the web armor.

Damage Bonus: none.

Weapons: Nippers 30%, damage 1D6 + grapple
Mist Projector 80%, damage 1D10 cold

Armor: none, but impaling weapons do minimum rolled damage.

WEB ARMOR: the webs are half-alive artifacts of mi-go organic technology. If an investigator manages to steal an armor-web, he or she may wear it, but its clinging slime costs a hit point every time it is taken off, as it rips away skin, flesh, and hair. It will work as armor for a human, but since the human does not have the proper nutrient solution to soak it in after use, each new time it is used, it declines in effectiveness by 1 point of armor. Thus the second time it is worn, it is worth only 7 points of armor, then 6 points the next wearing, and so

on. This greenish armor-web looks quite grisly, drips goo behind the wearer, and cannot be worn on the street without attracting screams and shocked comments. When a projectile or weapon strikes the user, the web instantaneously hunches up and clumps around the target spot, softening the impact.

MIST PROJECTORS: each twisted metal thing projects an icy mist which looks like a thick fog. The fog expands at Move 16 speed to a fat cylinder about 10 yards across. The fog always engulfs the target unless the intended victim is able to move out of the area of effect.

When the fog engulfs the target, he or she loses 1D10 hit points of freezing damage. Roll the result, then subtract 1 point for thick clothing and 2 points for arctic-type clothing. If the victim is in a closed car, then subtract 4 from the hit points lost, but the car's engine freezes up and stalls unless the investigator can receive a successful Drive Automobile roll.

The weapon is normally played on a target for several successive rounds. Its advantage to the mi-go is that it leaves no marks on the victim, who appears to have frozen to death. If an investigator can get one of these weapons, he can master its use given a successful Idea roll.

An investigator who has seen such a weapon in action and who can move freely in any direction can evade a blast from a mist projector with either a successful roll of DEX x3 or of INT x3 on D100.

Conclusion

If the investigators have managed to foil the mi-go, the alien operations around Jenning are suspended indefinitely. Searching about the mountain they also find Bartley Hodges' frozen corpse, and duly collect the *Tattler*'s $500 reward.

For foiling the mi-go, each investigator also gains 1D10 Sanity points. Merely killing a mi-go nets no Sanity points, but killing all seven nets each investigator a full 6 Sanity points for which no die roll is necessary. ∎

DEAD MAN STOMP

This adventure suits beginning players and investigators, or experienced players who want to relax. Much of it depends on scene-setting. It may take a long evening of play to complete.

The events are set in a large American city of the 1920s, such as New York or Chicago. This adventure will not transfer well to the present without reconstruction.

Jazz music is theme and soundtrack to this scenario, and keepers might search out 1920s recordings as background— King Oliver's Jazz Band and Jelly-Roll Morton's Red Hot Peppers are good sources. Such music establishes an upbeat mood. Be sure to turn it down when things get dark.

This adventure is more complicated in its aim of depicting social background. It should be studied carefully by the keeper with an eye to maintaining the investigators fully in play, not relegated to the status of sideline observers.

SPECIAL COMMENTS

Race is important in this adventure. Identify the race of each investigator before play begins. Choice of race brings no penalty, but a questioner's race can determine the accessibility of information. Read this adventure before presenting it: if all the investigators are African-American, for instance, rather than a racial cross-section, or are all white, or are all Asian-

Americans, the keeper must devise some patches. The scenario presumes that the investigators are white.

"Black" can be an insult in this era; "Negro" is polite, if high-falutin'; "colored" is recognized everywhere in the U.S., and is relatively polite, but also exists in the sign-board phrase "no coloreds allowed". In the West and Southwest "colored" extends to Asians and Native Americans; "African-American" is known but is obscure to most, and will not be in vogue until the 1980s. "Ethiopian" is a derisive white term. "Nigger" is almost universally used by whites without apology; this term is always insulting, except in its ironical sense between blacks.

KEEPER INFORMATION

Leroy Turner is a jazz man. He has a broken heart, a drinking problem, and a curse. The last is in the form of an unusual trumpet, which he believes was given to him by Mr. Louis Armstrong In fact, the instrument was handed to him by Nyarlathotep. When played by a gifted musician, this four-valve trumpet raises the dead within hearing and drives the resurrected to vengeance. When the scenario begins, Turner does not know of this capability. When he discovers it, he goes mad.

A gangland kingpin, Archie the Boss Bonato, and his gang learn of Turner's astonishing ability. They treat it as a joke, but their treachery provokes tragedy and disaster.

The story begins at night, in the Blue Heaven Ballroom. Why the investigators are present is left to the keeper. They may be out on the town, or they may be meeting someone or searching for some clue as part of another adventure.

The Blue Heaven Ballroom

The Blue Heaven Ballroom is a nightclub that illegally serves liquor. Patrons break the law. Men should wear tuxedos, and women evening dresses, or expect to be hidden behind the palm trees next to the kitchen. Visitors without ties won't be admitted. No one would think of going out at night without a necktie. At least twenty dollars each is needed for an evening at the club, including drinks (booze or water costs the same), a light meal perhaps, and tips. Drinks cost two dollars each. The high-class joint is protected. Police and criminals alike come down on disturbances in the Blue Heaven.

The music is hot, the company is fine, and the hooch is genuine and imported at the Blue Heaven Ballroom, the swankiest speakeasy in town. Plenty of bribes go to keep the Blue Heaven open, so food and drink are expensive. The first show starts about 8 o'clock. The place is open every night till dawn.

Inside the unmarked blue door, two very large white men in tuxedos eye the passing customers; poor people, the casually-dressed, or non-whites who somehow slipped past the doorman get caught and ejected here. If some or all of the investigators are not white, they are refused entrance. If they do not enter the Blue Heaven, presumably they find a way backstage, from where they witness the succeeding events.

Beyond the guards, blue-carpeted stairs lead up to the ballroom. That floor is laid out much like a contemporary movie theater. The check room faces the stairs. To the left is the gentlemen's lounge and stairs leading up another floor to a posh casino (not pertinent to this adventure), to the right is the ladies' lounge and the entrance to the ballroom proper. Both lounges have blue and white marble tiles. Mirrors abound, as do gleaming chrome faucets and fittings.

The manager smiles as the investigators pass the swinging doors and into the main room. He signals that they should accompany him. Waiters hover. Jazz and the buzz of conversation fill the room.

The showroom is large. An opulent bar stretches out to the left, the faces of the bartenders shadowed by lines of bottles. A large stage opposite the bar holds the band. Between bar and stage are small round tables surrounded by plush armless chairs, and the dance floor. Each table holds a small lamp, for intimate lighting. Above, electric chandeliers cast subdued hues of blue and gold onto the faces of neat, pale-faced, portly men and the bleached hair of be-jewelled ambitious young women.

The Blue Heaven is a famous hangout. New York money-men and stage stars, Hollywood movie stars, honest politicians and those on the take, Chicago businessmen and mobsters, Detroit auto moguls, shipping magnates and railroad scions from San Francisco, oil men from Texas and Oklahoma, the rich and the cunning, the butter-and-egg men from around the world stop here when in town.

The 5-Star Band provides the music. Bartenders, waiters, busboys, chorus girls and boys, entertainers, and kitchen help at Blue Heaven are black; clientele, management, enforcement, and ownership is white.

Jazz bands in the 1920s, especially bands playing big clubs, were larger than is usual today. Instruments might include trumpets, trombones, saxes, clarinets, cornets, drums, bass or tuba, banjo or rhythm guitar, and a piano—every configuration was tried. Without amplification, at least eight or ten instruments were needed to fill a hall with sound. Smaller bands played for smaller rooms.

STARTING THE ACTION

When the investigators enter, the club is packed. The 5-Stars are in full swing, belting out a rousing version of "Doctor Jazz." Apologizing for the crowd, the manager finds seats for the investigators at a table in a corner near the bar. A stranger is already sitting alone at the large table. He nods agreeably, but puts one hand out to reserve the chair next to him—he is waiting for someone. Though the investigators don't know it, the man is Pete Manusco, a local accountant. He waits for Joey Larson, a minor mobster.

Manusco does not talk, nor is he listening to the music, as the nervous drumming of his fingertips on the table indicates. He is of average build, with eyebrows so bushy that they appear to be a single black furry line spanning his frowning forehead. Compared to the raucous crowd, his demeanor is prim and tense. A successful Psychology roll confirms that the stranger is nervous, and a successful Spot Hidden detects a sheen of sweat on his face. Though he directs his eyes at the band, avoiding the investigators, he doesn't seem to listen to the music.

The band finishes "Doctor Jazz" and launches into "Clarinet Marmalade."

An Incidental Incivility

A door behind the table opens, and a tall, thin black man in a suit, carrying a shiny trumpet, slowly emerges. He looks around and blinks. His intention clearly is to get to the stage, but seated as they are around the table, Manusco and the investigators completely block his path.

The horn man hesitates, the effect of several drinks apparent. He studies the faces before him, then chooses Manusco. "Sir, I got lost backstage. Uh, would you be so kind as to let me by? I really apologize for asking."

Mancuso would have to stand up to let a black man pass. Jittery nerves do not improve his manners. "Find some other way, boy, or I'll have you thrown out!" Mancuso snaps.

Investigators familiar with the town's night life may recognize the black man as Leroy Turner, an excellent young trumpeter who has fallen on hard times. Though Turner has had some drinks, he is not feeling suicidal enough to press the issue among a crowd of thugs, racists, and politicians. He backs away awkwardly, half-bowing. "Sorry, sir. Sorry, sorry."

The investigators can intervene, if they wish, rising to let Turner pass, or they can pretend to ignore the matter and by default force Turner back through the door. If they do, he almost immediately reappears out of another door and makes his way to the stage.

If the investigators let Turner pass, he thanks them sincerely, surprised to be treated decently. As he does, call for a Spot Hidden. A success notices that Turner's trumpet has four valves, not the usual three—musicians may find more unusual the crackled silver finish of the trumpet.

Across the room, the band leader makes an announcement. Their attention pulled to the stage, few notice a small, rat-like man in a snappy brown suit enter. He looks over the crowd, then eases along the bar toward Manusco.

"Ladies and gentlemen, his honor the Mayor is with us tonight—congratulations on re-election, Mr. Mayor! That reformer thought he had you beat, but you can't keep a good man down. This song's for you!"

Now on-stage, Leroy Turner's rumpled brown coat and pants contrast with the white jackets of the band, but so does the extraordinary strength and rippling precision of his tones as he joins them in a heated version of a new number, "Dead Man Stomp." The rhythms are irresistible, the musicianship top-notch, and soon most of the crowd is dancing enthusiastically—the new piece is a hit.

The Guest Arrives

Midway through the band leader's tribute to the mayor, the rat-like little man standing behind Pete Manusco moves forward. He is Joey Larson, a gunsel for Archie Bonato. Joey is the man for whom Manusco waits. As the music heats up, Joey pulls out a .45 almost as big as he is, and at point-blank range shoots Manusco once squarely in the back of the head.

Though the band is loud and the crowd is louder, at three feet nothing is louder than a .45's report. The investigator opposite Manusco is showered with brain and bone blasted through the gaping hole in Manusco's forehead. He or she loses 1/1D6 Sanity points, and other witnesses lose 1/1D3 Sanity points.

As the body hits the table, the investigators turn and—perhaps with Luck rolls—get clear looks at the gunman's face. Joey sees their faces. He doesn't stay to chat, but slides the revolver beneath his coat and coolly exits via the service door though which Leroy Turner entered. Then he takes a side door to the blue-carpeted steps and the outside.

Investigators may or may not be carrying guns. By the time pursuing investigators reach the bottom of the stairs and race pass the startled guards and doorman, Joey's on the street and

in a gray Packard, rolling away midway down the block. A successful Spot Hidden notices that the Packard's license plate has been removed.

Inside the Packard, Little Jimmy Foster hits the gas. If anyone gives serious pursuit, a mobster with a tommy gun in the back seat leans out and squeezes off 15 or 20 aimless rounds, to discourage such behavior. The doorman flings himself to the ground, and so should investigators who want to avoid being hit. Those who stand or pursue have a 25% chance of being wounded for 1D10+2 damage; a D100 result of 01-05 is an impale, doing 2D10+4 damage.

The Packard and Joey Larson always get away. Encourage pursuing investigators to return to the Blue Heaven and see what's happened.

A Dead Man Stomps

Back in the Blue Heaven, few people yet know about the shooting, but the news spreads quickly when "Dead Man Stomp" concludes. How could the news not spread? Manusco slumps across the table, face sideways in a sea of blood, brains, bone, and whiskey, giving everyone a look at the neat black hole in the back of his head and the red funnel through his forehead. He's dead.

But, as the band keeps swinging, the dead man's hands start to splat out time on the gore-covered table. Manusco pulls himself up to a sitting position. His eyes are rolled up. Blood courses from the huge exit wound in his forehead, but still he stands. A moan seeps from his lips. Any bystander with a successful Listen roll understands the word "Joey" was spoken. Then Manusco turns and staggers toward the main doors, now watched by most of the appalled crowd. The band falls silent. The manager gasps and collapses. Pete Manusco staggers out the swinging doors. From beyond them, muffled screams mark his progress down the stairs and into the night.

Sanity loss to witness this terrible resurrection is 0/1D6 Sanity points. Investigators with successes believe that, although serious, Manusco's hit looks worse than it is. Investigators with failing rolls know better.

News of the shooting brings shouts and screams as people rush out to avoid scandal. Nearly everyone, from Mayor to busboy, flees.

Some keep their wits and leave through the back alley, but most take the stairs, trying to push past the slow-moving Manusco. They bowl him over. He tumbles to the bottom of the stairs, and the terrified patrons trample him as they panic. Moaning, he tries to get to his feet, but they keep knocking him down, reducing him to a bloodier and bloodier ruin. Seeing the man die for a second time, the normally unflappable door guards leave and do not return.

When the wave of customers has gone, the remains of Pete Manusco stir. It gets to its feet and staggers into the street, searching for its murderer. "Joey!" it moans, "Joey!" The call has about it a dark, terrible patience.

The driver of the first squad car on the scene sees the bloody pulp that Pete Manusco has become, and loses control. The vehicle skids, and pins Manusco against a lamp pole, cutting him in half. Killed thrice now, Pete Manusco stirs no more.

SOME MINOR HELP

The band's leader, Mitch Wester, notices the investigator who is covered with Manusco's brains. "You're hit! My god, my god, you're hit! Are you all right?" Once it is apparent that the investigator was missed, not hit, Wester grabs his cornet and departs like everyone else.

Suddenly alone on the stage, Leroy Turner sits against a wall, wide-eyed, draining a half-pint bottle. When he hears sirens, he gets up and heads for a bathroom, to climb out a window. If the investigators are there, and if earlier they let him pass, he is not too drunk to speak to them.

"Y'all be in trouble soon, lest you be movin'. Come on, now—I know a way." He is as good as his word. Once they're outside, it's every man for himself.

AN IMPORTANT CLUE

In escaping out doors or windows, either Wester or Turner drops a business card from a funeral parlor.

Morgan & Dupuy
CHRISTIAN FUNERAL HOME
Serving Families of African Descent Since 1851
172nd and West Charles Streets
Elkhorn 6617

Handwritten in ink on the card are tomorrow's date and the words *11 A.M. sharp—bring your horn. New Orleans style.*

THE GOVERNMENT MAN

Roger Daniels is a Treasury agent in the Prohibition unit. He is in the Blue Heaven that night, and can witness the crime if the keeper wishes.

Daniels is part of a team documenting participation of elected officials in bootlegging. He is an honest man in his early thirties, tall with ginger hair. He carries a gun, but avoids gunplay. He dreams of commendations and fame, and intends someday to run for political office.

Daniels is available to thicken the plot. This "dry agent" may decide that the investigators are involved with bootlegging, perhaps with a rival gang. He may follow them, and provide opportune rescue. He might be an ally, an obstruction, or just comic relief. He is a keeper resource. He never, never takes a drink.

Investigations That Night

The investigators may remain at the Blue Heaven, to help the police. As long as they tell the truth, their statements are taken and then they're allowed to go home.

Investigators who left the Blue Heaven and missed Manusco's walk can be told about it by any drunk in the neighborhood. If the investigators have an automobile, perhaps some respectable couple hails them when taxis became scarce, and relate the story that way.

If the investigators try to find members of the band, few blacks admit to knowing anything to men of another race, even if fellow musicians. If the investigators press very hard, someone might suggest that Mitch Wester will be at Freddie Fayette's funeral tomorrow. Ukrezia Borden, a black woman old enough to be beyond fear, tells them to "leave that band alone. They ain't done nothin'. Buster Bedson the drummer, he keeps a chicken foot inside his drum. Yessir! You know what that means." This is not true, and is a red herring for voodoo-wary investigators.

SUMMARIZING THE EVENING

Allow the players the rolls needed to suggest that Manusco was somehow resurrected—Occult or Cthulhu Mythos, perhaps. An Idea roll can point out that the resurrection occurred while a new tune was played, "Dead-Man Stomp." If the connection to Leroy Turner is not made now, it must be forced at Fayette's funeral.

Depending on investigator responses, several courses are available to them. Importantly, they should lead to the Fayette funeral.

The Morning Papers

The morning dailies carry Manusco's shooting, and tell how the poor man, mortally wounded yet somehow indomitably willing himself to stay alive, tried to reach help only to be cut down, ironically by the very aid he sought. Ruminations on life's meaning see print in the next few days.

Peter Manusco is identified as a self-employed accountant, a man with a spotless record who in a moment of weakness entered the Blue Heaven Ballroom. Police think he was mistaken for some criminal foe.

The Mayor's office announces the padlocking of the Blue Heaven Ballroom, offering thanks that such a cesspool of vice and crime has been located. The manager of the club, Mr. Roland Marlow, is arraigned on various petty charges and quietly released on bail.

Government agent Roger Daniels testifies that the Blue Heaven was selling alcohol. Daniels manages to get his picture in most of the dailies. His career has begun.

THE EMANICIPATOR & UNION LEADER

There is also a black daily at the newsstand. Compared to the other papers, the difference in tone and coverage is astonishing. None of its front-page stories overlap with the white newspapers, except mention of disturbances in what is known then as the Anglo-Egyptian Soudan.

A long story discusses a Mr. Marcus Garvey, a black nationalist, photographed in flamboyant military costume. Another, by-lined by a Mr. Du Bois of the NAACP, discusses the sharecropping system in the South, and its implications for African-American health, education, and general livelihood. Other stories discuss black interests and personalities, and a successful Idea roll deduces that the other dailies are as specifically white in *their* coverage. Almost nothing overlaps between the black and wide dailies, not even the baseball stories. Manusco is not mentioned.

With a successful Luck roll, the investigators notice an advertisement for the Morgan and Dupuy Funeral Home.

Looking in the funeral announcements column, they see that a funeral and procession are scheduled for 11 a.m. today at Morgan and Dupuy, for Frederick Lincoln Fayette, brother-in-law of band-leader Mr. Mitchell Wester.

Research either at the *Emancipator's* office or at the library branch which is nearest the newspaper's offices (or in conversation perhaps with Mr. Wester, whose name appears in the telephone directory) establishes that Mr. Fayette died by accidental gunshot wound two days before. Elizabeth Wester Fayette survives him. Mr. Fayette owned his own truck, and worked as a drayer.

PETE MANUSCO

Manusco's office and home have listed telephones. Investigators who act quickly can beat the police to both locations. At the office, they find a broken lock and that all the "B"files have been removed. A successful Spot Hidden finds a scrawled note in the wastebasket.

> *Mister M. you shld meet me tonite at Blue Heavin for a meaningful discusn on youre helth and safety. J.*

A search of Manusco's apartment turns up a scrapbook of clippings about Archie the Boss Bonato. The clippings date back about a year and a half. Inspection of Manusco's savings passbook shows that monthly cash deposits of $1000 were made to his account over the same period.

A RUMOR FROM THE POLICE

Visiting central station or talking to investigating officers reveals that the coroner will testify that Manusco's head wound was immediately fatal. More than half the volume of the victim's brain was shredded or blown away. Manusco could not have done what the investigators witnessed.

The Fayette Funeral

At a black family funeral, those of other races can find whatever welcome they deserve: curiosity-seekers will be snubbed, rowdy gate-crashers will be threatened and expelled, those extending genuine sympathies will be appreciated, and the bereaved will be consoled. Let the investigators find their own depth.

At some point someone may casually ask the player-characters' relation to the deceased. It is a natural question. Whatever information the investigators give passes quickly through the crowd.

After the funeral is over, six pallbearers emerge from the hall, carrying a long pine coffin. Two black policemen on motorcycles lead the way and control traffic at intersections. Members of the 5-Star band strike up "I'll See You on Judgment Day", and the mourners fall in behind.

More people join in as the procession moves through the streets toward the cemetery. The 5-Stars play slow and soulful renditions, hymn after hymn. The musicians walk in a line behind the coffin, with Wester in front and the drummer in the rear, his bass drum strapped to his chest. All maintain a serious and noble bearing.

Passing some storefronts, the investigators have a special feeling of being watched. A successful Spot Hidden roll distinguishes Leroy Turner in a doorway across the street, smoking and watching the parade pass by, but identifying Turner does not extinguish the sense that someone else watches with ominous interest.

Turner extinguishes the cigarette and steps out, lifting his trumpet as the band strikes up "Closer Walk With Thee." He comes up alongside Wester, puts the horn to his lips, and starts to blow melancholy notes in fine counterpoint to Wester's cornet. A rolling murmur through the crowd testifies to the music's beauty.

But not twenty seconds after Turner's trumpet sounds, a successful Listen roll detects moaning from inside the coffin. Hearing this costs 0/1D2 Sanity points.

Another Dead Man Stomps

The pall bearers lurch as the weight in the coffin shifts. Startled, they look at each other in confusion and alarm. The crowd gasps, and the music dies. Then the coffin lid smashes open. As the bearers drop their burden and pull back, the late Frederick Fayette emerges—gray, puffy, bewildered. Shrieks, screams, and astonishment are general. Sanity cost to witness this is 0/1D6 Sanity points.

Various hands reach out to try to help Fayette, who continues to move and look about wildly. Whoever would keep him calm needs successful D100 rolls of STR x5 or less.

Lizzie Fayette steps in front of her dead husband, and lifts her mourning veil. Her cheeks are wet with tears, and she whispers "Freddie, is that you?" Fayette stops, lurches forward, looks at her in shock and begins to realize his situation. He throws back his head, and gives a terrible scream. He collapses at the knees of his wife, trembling arms folded round them, and he does not move. He is dead again, and does not revive.

Clamor sweeps the crowd, and anger begins to spark against the mortician, Mr. Dupuy, and two assistants who have accompanied the procession. The words most often heard are "Buried alive!" With the aid of police, these three escape injury.

The investigators may be able to intervene, using their Fast Talks or Credit Ratings. Any good-faith effort gains them favor among those present. Mitch Wester may recognize them from the night before.

THE WATCHER

During the disturbance, ask for another Spot Hidden. A success notices a short white man in a brown suit. He backs away and walks briskly to a waiting gray Packard. Investigators who were in the Blue Heaven last night recognize the man as Pete Manusco's murderer. The gray Packard is gone before any investigator can fight through the crowd to reach it. Joey Larson has been tailing the investigators. They got a good look at his face last night. Now he's nervous and beginning to think maybe he ought to take care of them. Having witnessed Fayette's resurrection in the same fashion as that of Manusco, he scurries to tell Boss Bonato what he saw.

Leroy Turner

If no one stops him, Turner slips away during the tumult. Turner's trumpet-playing has twice seemed to awake the dead—an unusual talent. If an investigator asks for a chat, Turner agrees, at the price of a drink. He leads the investigators to a neighborhood speakeasy.

He is bewildered by the events of the last day. "I played trumpet for ten year. Ain't nothin' happened like *this*." Any sympathetic or perceptive remark gets him started talking.

His new trumpet was given to him by no less than Mr. Louis Armstrong. A few days before, Turner was playing with a scratch band and, when he went outside for a reefer, Armstrong approached him in the alley. "You're such a good player, Leroy, that I want you to have one of my horns." Armstrong gave him the trumpet on the spot.

A successful Psychology roll agrees that the event took place as Turner relates it, but that he noticed something more. If asked, Turner adds: "Mr. Armstrong's eyes, man, they looked like they was pools of blackness. Real strange!" Turner does not repeat what else he suddenly remembers Armstrong/Nyarlathotep as saying—"You blow this horn, baby, you'll wake the dead!"

Instead of three valves, the trumpet has four. Its silver finish is crackled, like snake or alligator hide. And inside the bell of the trumpet can be seen an encircling ring of strange symbols—neither Occult nor Cthulhu Mythos rolls decipher them.

Turner will not sell or lend the horn. "This horn is my living. It sews my body and soul together. I ain't found no trumpet good as this."

INVESTIGATING LEROY TURNER

With Bargain, Fast Talk, Persuade, or Credit Rating rolls, and sometimes a little money, the investigators can learn something about Leroy Turner over the next day or so, especially if they are polite and friendly. Mentioning the Fayette funeral and the reawakening gives them information to exchange. Rumor about that affair is rampant. Alternatively, if an acquaintance with Mitch Wester has been established, all the information could come from him. Leroy Turner is not popular in the community, even among the musicians—he's too irresponsible. When he gets a gig, a week later he goes on a bender and loses it. What he says he'll do, he don't.

But people have some sympathy. Turner's heart is broken—after they'd come up together from New Orleans two years ago, his lover Marnie Smeaton was run over and killed. The gray car didn't stop. Folks think it was college boys.

Turner lives in a tiny room on 174th Street. He owns one trumpet, two suits, three shirts, four boxes of sheet music, and a framed photograph of a smiling young woman.

MR. LOUIS ARMSTRONG

With the intercession of a black theatrical agency, the investigators can get through to Mr. Armstrong. To complete the connection, they need a pocketful of quarters and two successful rolls among Fast Talk, Credit Rating, or Luck. Armstrong lived in Chicago 1922-24, played with King Oliver 1924-25, was in New York with Fletcher Henderson, and returned to Chicago in 1925.

Louis Armstrong is good-natured but baffled by the questions. He's heard of Leroy Turner, but never heard him play. He didn't give anyone a trumpet.

See the box "A Kidnaping," p. 242.

A Surprise For Joey

Bonato's thugs use a garage to unload shipments of liquor from out of town. Two heavy trucks wait inside to be unloaded, and they offer cover to following investigators. The wide room at the rear of the garage has been converted into an office and hangout. The shop backs up on an alley; the blinds are drawn, but their paper is old and ragged. Investigators in the alley can see and hear what goes on inside. Or they can enter and overhear via the unguarded front door.

Give them plenty of chances to interrupt what follows.

Turner is brought in through the garage, into the office, and tied to a chair. His hands and arms are left free. They hand him his trumpet. To one side stands Joey Larson. Two other gangsters stand about, deferring to the fifth and last man in the building, Archie Bonato, a big man in shirtsleeves, puffing a gigantic Havana cigar.

LEROY TURNER

A Kidnaping

Sometime after the funeral, Joey Larson kidnaps Leroy Turner. This action signals the scenario's end, so the keeper should stage it only when ready. The kidnaping might happen after the talk with the investigators, at night from Turner's room, or from wherever Turner wanders drunken and grieving. The investigators must witness the kidnaping—perhaps they've just finished investigating Turner's background—or the keeper must supply another connection to the Bonato gang.

Half a block away, Leroy Turner is about to cross the street when a gray Packard rolls around a corner. It pulls up alongside, then two white men get out and together force Turner into the back, and get in themselves. The car drives away. The snatch is over in seconds.

If the investigators have a car, they can follow. If on foot, a taxi is idling at the corner. In either case, they need a successful Drive Automobile roll to tail the Packard without being spotted; exstablish which investigator drives (Benny the cabbie has 60% Drive Auto).

If the roll fails, Little Jimmy (Drive Automobile 70%) tries to get away. Interested keepers may wish to be prepared for an auto chase. Or match Drive Automobiles on D100. The first to receive two successive failures loses, and the other driver has his way, either losing the pursuers or re-establishing the tail without being spotted again.

If the Packard gets away, successive Luck and Spot Hidden rolls are needed before it is found parked beside a large garage. It is a lonely spot, among weed-filled lots and tumbled-down buildings. The door to the garage is unlocked.

If tailed successfully, the Packard pulls into the alley and four people get out and enter the garage.

The intent of the scene is to confront Turner with the power of his horn, which will drive him insane.

Boss Bonato asks Joey if this is the boy, and Joey says yes. Bonato asks Joey to repeat what he saw. Joey describes the funeral and how dead Freddie Fayette got up and walked. Joey adds that Laurette, Joey's black girlfriend, says that this is from voodoo, and that the gang can use it. Bonato hums and puffs for a while, then asks if Joey's sure. Joey says he is.

"No screw-ups, Joey, like you did with Manusco."

Joey says, "No way, boss."

"That was a dumb piece of work, Joey. Keeping Blue Heaven closed is costing me dough—all you had to do was to warn the guy, Joey. Now I gotta get a new accountant."

Boss Bonato hums a bit more, and a flicker of expression passes between him and the gunmen to either side of Joey Larson. "Okay, Joey, I'll bite on what you say." He looks at Joey's hands. "I want you to shoot yourself." The room is silent. Joey Larson twitches, but doesn't move.

"Look, Joey, this here black boy can bring you back to life, like you say. What's the problem? Shoot yourself."

When Larson still doesn't act, Boss Bonato tells Little Jimmy to do it. In dire peril, Larson tries to pull his long-barreled .45, but the Boss easily shoots first, then puts a second shot through Joey's heart to be sure. Little Jimmy bends over the dripping corpse. "He's dead, Boss."

Archie the Boss shakes his head. "Joey, I always told you that gun was too big for a fast draw." He turns to Leroy Turner. "Okay, jazz man, blow."

Turner swallows hard, then starts up "High Society." Seconds pass. Joey twitches. Then he slowly rises. Everybody swears, including Leroy Turner, but Archie the Boss tells him to keep playing. Larson lurches toward Bonato, spitting blood. Little Jimmy opens up with his tommy gun, and empties twenty rounds into Joey Larson's corpse. Turner giggles and plays "Tiger Rag", while the walking corpse dances and jerks. The heavy slugs cut up the former Joey and rip him apart. Bullets whine around the room, the smell of blood and cordite is thick. The tommy gun is empty. Larson is all over the floor and the walls. Silently the boys cross themselves and pour drinks, while Archie the Boss swears in disbelief. Sanity loss for this scene is 1/1D6 points.

WHAT THEN?

Did the investigators do anything to distract the thugs? If not, perhaps the mobsters are so shaken that they cut Turner's ropes and push the sweating, shaking man out the door, and try to forget about this.

Or maybe Bonato thinks Turner might be useful. He gives the giggling, unresisting jazz man to Little Jimmy, and tells him to lock Leroy in the cellar of Mama Changelle's, a brothel that Bonato owns. On the way, though, Turner jumps out of the car and disappears into the crowd, stopping now and then to play a few bars.

Or maybe the investigators find some honest police who come on the scene before the mess is cleaned up. In that case, the gangsters are arrested. Among the evidence at the scene are the incriminating "B" files from Manusco's office.

In any case, whether he escapes from Bonato, from the investigators, or from the police, the deranged Leroy Turner makes his way to Marnie Smeaton's tombstone.

Leroy's Blues

Turner runs from the building. He disappears into the city. If the investigators don't guess, an Idea roll suggests that Turner, now insane, has gone to the cemetery to raise his love. Marnie Smeaton may be dead and in her grave, but her true love has the means to bring her back. Even after a couple of years there'll be something to animate. No matter how quickly the investigators figure this out, Leroy Turner always beats them to the cemetery.

There, the caretaker can find her plot, or perhaps they spot Turner's long, eager strides from hundreds of yards distant. Descriptions and Luck or Spot Hidden rolls might draw out the suspense. When they get there, Turner is poised near Marnie Smeaton's grave, trumpet tipped, cheeks flexed, foot ready to mark time. "Folks, this next number is for Marnie," he mumbles, and starts to play.

He plays for the waste of his life, for his love of booze, for the music he'll never make, for the loss of Marnie, for everything he's left undone or been cheated of. The trumpet notes have a sad sweetness, as light and as deft as life itself. The call is irresistible.

The ground stirs; the wing of a marble angel cracks and falls away; a slate tombstone tilts and crumbles. Wherever Turner's trumpet reaches, the dead groan and remember. Marnie

Smeaton hears her lover play, and struggles upward, a wrinkled, dessicated shape not living and not dead. In every direction come sounds of creaking and stirring, waking and shifting. The dead are rising. Loss to be here is 0/1D3 Sanity points.

Turner comes to his senses, and sees what is happening. If he can get away, he does, bounding over heaving graves and shuddering slabs, and past tombs grinding open. When he has space to play again, he does.

If Turner is fatally shot or stabbed, he staggers back, puts the horn to his bloody lips, shuts his eyes, and blows. A harsh note peals forth, his life's breath. He dies, but the echo resurrects him—he keeps blowing. Dead now, he need spare no air for breathing, so that the terrible notes continue, growling, resonant, and infinite. The trumpet call grows stronger, until its force pulverizes headstones and shatters mausoleum doors. Witnessing Turner's undeath costs 1/1D6 Sanity points.

Dead or alive, Turner plays on, until the whole cemetery struggles free and rises, each stumbling corpse remembering him or her who failed them, each dancing and staggering toward a separate cloudy vengeance, in each the notion of vengeance widening and expanding to encompass more and more of the living. Investigators now lose 1D6/1D20 Sanity points, and risk being attacked by random risen dead.

Looking on from the void, Nyarlathotep howls with laughter. Right to the center of the cosmos, to the court of Azathoth, Turner's trumpet reaches, blending indissolubly with the blind and idiot chorus of squealing charnel flutes.

Conclusion

If the corpses in the cemetery rise, the keeper determines their disposition, and how the living perceive them. Tales of this awakening are counted the ravings of lunatics. Authorities ascribe the disturbed graves to vandals.

If the investigators stop Turner, but kill him in the process, charge them 1D3 Sanity points. If Turner is stopped and still lives, grant 2D6 Sanity points. Destroying the trumpet gains 1 Sanity point.

Turning in Boss Bonato at the murder scene gains 1D3 Sanity points and a $1,000 reward from police to share, but in the end only Little Jimmy is convicted of manslaughter and possession of a concealed weapon. He gets out eleven months later. The Blue Heaven re-opens in ten days, newly painted and carpeted, ready for business.

If he survives, Leroy Turner spends a lifetime in an asylum, completely and irrevocably mad, silently playing for Azathoth's court, waiting each night for his loving Marnie to come to call.

If their relations have been good, a few weeks later Wester sends the investigators a copy of the first record by the 5-Star band, made days before Manusco's murder. One side, "Dead Man Stomp," features a solo by Leroy Turner on trumpet.

Statistics

The statistics occur in their scenario order. Those raised from the dead are zombies. Each loses only one hit point from a bullet or impaling weapon attack. All other attacks inflict half rolled damage. Each continues to attack until hacked apart at zero hit points. A zombie nominally costs 0/1D8 Sanity points to see. Consider the actual condition of the corpse in charging Sanity. Seeing many zombies, the maximum Sanity point cost is 8 points.

LEROY TURNER, Age 28, Alcoholic Sideman

| STR 12 | CON 14 | SIZ 16 | INT 11 | POW 09 |
| DEX 18 | APP 10 | EDU 09 | SAN 39 | HP 15 |

Damage Bonus: +1D4.

Weapons: Fist/Punch 50%, damage 1D3 + db
Unholy Trumpet 92%, 25 hp, music raises the dead

Skills: Hold Liquor 65%, Improvise Music 72%, Play Trumpet 92%.

JOEY LARSON, Age 24, Gunsel

| STR 12 | CON 11 | SIZ 08 | INT 10 | POW 07 |
| DEX 16 | APP 07 | EDU 11 | SAN 23 | HP 10 |

Damage Bonus: none.

Weapons: .45 Long-Barreled Revolver 60%, damage 1D10 + 2
Thompson Submachine Gun 45%, damage 1D10 + 2
Switchblade Knife 64%, damage 1D4

PETE MANUSCO, Age 40, Zombie Accountant

| STR 17 | CON 15 | SIZ 11 | INT 0 | POW 01 |
| DEX 06 | APP 06 | EDU 0 | SAN 0 | HP 13 |

Damage Bonus: +1D4.

Weapons: Fist/Punch 30%, damage 1D3 + db
Grapple 25%, damage special

MITCH WESTER, Age 39, Band Leader

| STR 14 | CON 14 | SIZ 15 | INT 15 | POW 17 |
| DEX 13 | APP 13 | EDU 10 | SAN 85 | HP 15 |

Damage Bonus: +1D4.

Weapons: none.

Skills: Compose 48%, Fast Talk 43%, First Aid 41%, Persuade 67%, Play Cornet 77%, Psychology 36%, Sing 54%, Spot Hidden 52%.

ROGER DANIELS, Age 31, G-Man

| STR 13 | CON 12 | SIZ 15 | INT 16 | POW 13 |
| DEX 12 | APP 11 | EDU 15 | SAN 65 | HP 14 |

Damage Bonus: +1D4.

Weapons: .38 Revolver 50%, damage 1D10
Grapple 50%, damage special
Fist/Punch 60%, damage 1D3 + db

Skills: Accounting 45%, Drive Automobile 60%, Law 55%, Listen 67%, Persuade 47%, Pharmacy 15%, Spot Hidden 62%, Track 13%.

FREDDIE FAYETTE, Age 27, Zombie Moving Man

| STR 24 | CON 27 | SIZ 17 | INT 0 | POW 01 |
| DEX 07 | APP 06 | EDU 0 | SAN 0 | HP 22 |

Damage Bonus: +2D6

Weapons: Throttle 35%, damage 1D8
Grapple 35%, damage special
Fist/Punch 20%, damage 1D3 + db

ARCHIE The Boss BONATO, Age 46

| STR 13 | CON 16 | SIZ 15 | INT 13 | POW 13 |
| DEX 14 | APP 09 | EDU 12 | SAN 47 | HP 16 |

Damage Bonus: +1D4.

Weapons: .45 Snub-Nose Revolver 60%, damage 1D10 + 2
Fist/Punch 64%, damage 1D3 + db

Skills: Fast Talk 71%, Find Bottom Line 59%, Law 13%, Listen 48%, Sneer 78%, Spot Hidden 51%.

LITTLE JIMMY FOSTER, Age 34, Get-Away Man

STR 17	CON 17	SIZ 18	INT 10	POW 14
DEX 12	APP 08	EDU 10	SAN 61	HP 18

Damage Bonus: +1D6.

Weapons: Thompson Submachine Gun 73%, damage 1D10 + 2
Brass Knuckles 58%, damage 1D3+2 + db
Baseball Bat 52%, damage 1D8 + db

JOEY LARSON, Age 24, Zombie Creep

STR 18	CON 17	SIZ 08	INT 0	POW 01
DEX 08	APP 03	EDU 0	SAN 0	HP 13

Damage Bonus: +1D4.

Weapon: Grapple 25%, damage special

LEROY TURNER, Age 28, Zombie Trumpeter

STR 18	CON 21	SIZ 16	INT 0	POW 01
DEX 09	APP 05	EDU 0	SAN 0	HP 19

Damage Bonus: +1D6.

Weapons: Grapple 25%, damage special
Unholy Trumpet 100%, 25 hit points, music raises the dead

SIX POLICEMEN

	STR	CON	SIZ	DEX	POW	HP
ART	13	16	14	16	13	15
BOB	17	14	13	12	11	14
FERGUS	13	12	12	11	09	12
NATE	12	11	15	11	10	13
ROY	15	13	13	10	11	13
STAN	16	10	12	08	15	11

Damage Bonus: +1D4

Weapons: .38 Revolver 40%, damage 1D10
Billy Club 40%, damage 1D6 + db
Grapple 40%, damage special

SIX MOBSTERS or FUNERAL-GOERS

	STR	CON	SIZ	DEX	POW	HP
ONE	13	15	15	16	12	15
TWO	12	14	14	10	11	14
THREE	12	17	17	12	09	17
FOUR	13	12	12	11	10	12
FIVE	12	11	15	11	11	13
SIX	14	12	12	08	15	12

Damage Bonus +1D4

Weapons: .38 Revolver 35%, damage 1D10 (mobsters only)
Club 40%, damage 1D6 + db
Fist/Punch 40%, damage 1D3 +db (all)

SIX RISEN DEAD

	STR	CON	SIZ	DEX	POW	HP
ONE	24	27	14	09	01	21
TWO	19	15	14	07	01	15
THREE	21	21	18	06	01	20
FOUR	21	18	14	06	01	16
FIVE	23	24	16	05	01	20
SIX	27	17	10	04	01	14

Damage Bonus: +1D6

Weapons: Grapple 25%, damage special
Bite 20%, damage 1D2 ∎

"To me there was nothing grotesque in the bones and skeletons that strowed some of the stone crypts deep down among the foundations. I fantastically associated these things with every-day events, and thought them more natural than the coloured pictures of living beings which I found in many of the mouldy books."

—Lovecraft, "The Outsider"

Lovecraft Country: Guide to Arkham

This spread and the next provide an overview of Arkham, its environs, and several events of note. Arkham would be a good place to base a Call of Cthulhu campaign. The *Compact Arkham Unveiled* and *Miskatonic University,* detail Arkham. Books such as *Dead Reckonings, Escape from Innsmouth,* and *Adventures in Arkham Country* contain more information.

Arkham, Massachusetts, is five miles north of Salem, and twenty miles north of Boston. Its population is 22,562. Arkham was settled in 1692, and incorporated in 1699. Textiles form the bulk of its present industry, but more and more it is becoming a genteel residential suburb of Boston. Arkham is the home of Miskatonic University and the point of departure for classic Lovecraft stories such as "The Mountains of Madness", "The Dunwich Horror", and "The Shadow Out of Time".

Sites in Arkham

1: ARMITAGE HOUSE—417 W. Miskatonic Avenue., SE corner of West St. Henry Armitage is the University librarian who recognizes the threat posed by the Whateleys of Dunwich and, accompanied by Profs. Rice and Morgan, goes there to stop the invocation of Yog-Sothoth. See the story "The Dunwich Horror."

2: ARKHAM ADVERTISER—389 W. Armitage Street (at West). One of two competing daily newspapers in town.

3: ARKHAM BUS STATION—411 N. West Street (at W. High Lane). Connects to Boston, Salem, Newburyport, Dean's Corners, and Kingsport, among others. This bus line does not go to Innsmouth; for that, see Innsmouth Bus Stop, below.

4: ARKHAM GAZETTE—350 W. Hyde Street (between Jenkin and Brown). One of two competing daily newspapers in town.

5: ARKHAM PUBLIC LIBRARY—630 Marsh Street (NE corner of Marsh at Hyde).

6: ARKHAM SANITARIUM—255 E. Derby Street (at Peabody).

7: BOSTON & MAINE RR DEPOT—298 W. High Lane. Direct connection to Boston, and points north and south.

8: COURT HOUSE AND JAIL—666 N. Peabody Avenue (NW corner of Hyde and Peabody).

9: FIRE DEPARTMENT—418 E. Armitage Street (at SE corner of Peabody).

10: HOTEL MISKATONIC—200 block, W. College Street. Offers the best lodging in Arkham. At five stories, Arkham's tallest building.

11: INNSMOUTH BUS STOP—705 Dyer Street (W. corner at Curwen). Joe Sargent picks up here twice daily, 40 cents one way.

12: LABAN SHREWSBURY HOUSE—498 W. Curwen Street (at West St.). He disappeared in 1915. Among his publications are the *Celaeno Fragments* and *Cthulhu in the Necronomicon*. See *The Trail of Cthulhu,* by August Derleth.

13: NATIONAL GUARD ARMORY—560 Marsh Street (SE corner at Hyde).

14: PEASLEE HOUSE—588 Crane Street (midway between Boundary and West, north side of Crane). Home of Nathaniel and Wingate Peaslee, who both go to Australia in 1935 to investigate photos of strange stone blocks. See the story "The Shadow Out of Time."

15: POST OFFICE—487 N. Peabody Avenue (at SW corner of Armitage).

16: OLD ARKHAM GRAVEYARD: between Lich, Parsonage, Church, and Peabody.

17: UNNAMABLE HOUSE—at 188 N. Boundary Street (between River and Main). Visited by Randolph Carter and Joel Manton in the story "The Unnamable."

18: WILMARTH HOUSE—118 W. Saltonstall Street. In a recent trip to Vermont, Dr. Wilmarth confronted aliens from beyond in "The Whisperer in Darkness."

19: WITCH HOUSE—197 E. Pickman Street (at NW corner of Parsonage St.) Here a brilliant young mathematician, Walter Gilman, learns part of the secrets of Keziah Mason, a witch. See "The Dreams in the Witch-House."

MISKATONIC UNIVERSITY

A: SCIENCE ANNEX

B: SCIENCE HALL

C: LIBERAL ARTS

D: DORMITORY

E: DORMITORY

F: MISKATONIC UNIVERSITY LIBRARY—a guard dog here kills Wilbur Whateley when he breaks in to steal the *Necronomicon.*. See "The Dunwich Horror."

G: PRESIDENT'S HOME

H: FACULTY/GRADUATE RESIDENCES

I: DORMITORY

J: LOCKSLEY HALL

K: ST. MARY'S TEACHING HOSPITAL

L: MISKATONIC UNIVERSITY EXHIBIT MUSEUM— 687 W. College Street, SE corner of West.

M: AXTON FIELD HOUSE & STADIUM—entire block between Boundary and West, and Crane and College.

N: DEAN HALSEY STATUE—(top center of campus) Hero of the terrible typhoid epidemic of 1905 . See "Herbert West—Reanimator." ∎

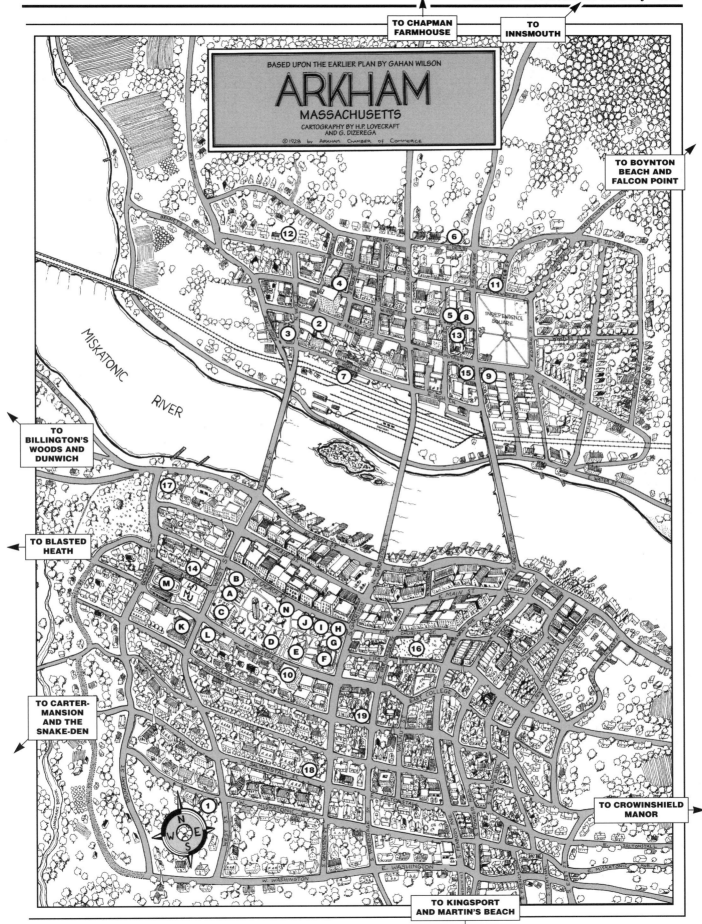

BASED UPON THE EARLIER PLAN BY GAHAN WILSON

ARKHAM
MASSACHUSETTS
CARTOGRAPHY BY H.P. LOVECRAFT
AND G. DIZEREGA
©1928 by Arkham Chamber of Commerce

TO CHAPMAN
FARMHOUSE

TO
INNSMOUTH

TO BOYNTON
BEACH AND
FALCON POINT

MISKATONIC RIVER

TO
BILLINGTON'S
WOODS AND
DUNWICH

TO BLASTED
HEATH

INDEPENDENCE
SQUARE

TO CARTER-
MANSION
AND THE
SNAKE-DEN

TO CROWINSHIELD
MANOR

TO KINGSPORT
AND MARTIN'S BEACH

Lovecraft Country: Locales & Events

To Dunwich—*about 70 miles northwest of Arkham.* Near the Vermont border. Population 376, settled in 1692. A small farming community. Formerly the site of several large lumber mills. Rumors persist concerning bizarre deaths here in the summer of 1928: see the story "The Dunwich Horror."

To Innsmouth—*6.5 miles northeast of Arkham.* Population 367, founded in 1643. Originally active in the China trade, this port town launched many privateers during the Revolutionary War and the War of 1812. Fishing is the main industry today. A small gold refinery operates. This is a curiously private town, and many of the buildings in it are now abandoned. See HPL's story "The Shadow over Innsmouth."

To Chapman Farm—*a couple of miles north of Arkham.* Dr. Herbert West accidentally burned down the farmhouse on this property. See "Herbert West—Reanimator."

To Boynton Beach—*a mile southeast of Innsmouth.* A few fisher families live here on a beach near the inlet's mouth. This settlement is close to Devil Reef, a danger to shipping oddly uncelebrated in these parts. Curious Fish Head Rock is at the north end of the beach, a massive rock greatly eroded now, carved by local shamans and their helpers long before the *Mayflower* landed. This broad outcrop reputedly represents the fish people said to haunt these waters.

To Billington's Woods—*a couple of miles northwest of Arkham.* The old Billington estate is on the south side of the Miskatonic River. Here are set mysteries concerning a stone tower, a colored glass window, and a mysterious entity. See *The Lurker at the Threshold*, by August Derleth and H. P. Lovecraft.

To Falcon Point—*a small fishing village just south of Boynton Beach.* Population 56, settled in 1696. It is named for the numerous raptors who line the high rocks anticipating the large schools of fish that regularly stir these waters into a frenzy.

To Blasted Heath—*a mile or so west of town.* A meteorite lands on the Nahum Gardner farm. It contains a strange entity which gradually drains life force from everything living in the vicinity. The only witness to it in the 1920s is a rustic farmer, Ammi Pierce, who lived nearby. See "The Colour Out of Space."

To Crowninshield Manor—*half-mile east of town* (end of E. High St.). Home to Edward Pickman Derby and his wife, Asenath. Derby was a poet and author of *Azathoth and Other Horrors*. Lovecraft chronicles the couple's ultimately deadly marriage in "The Thing on the Doorstep."

To Carter Mansion—*about three miles southwest of Arkham.* Just west of the road to Salem and Boston, on the slopes of Elm Hill. The family manse of the Carters is in ruins since Randolph Carter, a war hero and promising author, disappeared. See "The Silver Key", "Through the Gates of the Silver Key", and "The Dream-Quest of Unknown Kadath."

To Snake's Den Cave—The mouth opens in the dark woods near the Carter Mansion. Randolph Carter played here as a child. See the Lovecraft story "The Silver Key."

To Kingsport—*two miles south of Arkham.* Population 7834, founded in 1639, incorporated in 1651. Home port of numerous privateers during the Revolutionary War. A summer resort and artist colony, the town retains much of its original architecture. Fishing is the main industry. See the stories "The Festival" and "The Strange High House in the Mist."

To Martin's Beach—*two miles southeast of Arkham.* Population 867, first settled in 1644. Fishing village, now popular with tourists and summer people. Near the mouth of the Miskatonic River, it commands a fine view of stony Kingsport Head. Many landscapes of that landmark have been painted from Martin's Beach as the last light of day glimmers on the quaint building near its summit. This headland is the highest point on the Massachusetts coast.

ARKHAM
MASSACHUSETTS

A Chronology of Events

The followings dates are from Lovecraft's stories. Many, but not all, are located in Lovecraft Country.

1877—Disappearance of the Starry Wisdom cult in Providence, Rhode Island: "The Haunter of the Dark."

May 11, 1878—A mysterious mummy found on a new island in the South Pacific by Captain Charles Weatherby of the freighter bound from Wellington, New Zealand, to Valparaiso, Chile. Delivered to the Cabot Museum in Boston: "Out of the Aeons."

October 31, 1889—murder of Walker Davis by his crazed wife Audrey near Binger, Oklahoma: "The Curse of Yig."

June, 1892—mysterious meteorite falls in the yard of Nahum Gardner near Arkham: "The Colour Out of Space."

1893—disappearance of Edwin Lillbridge, reporter for the Providence *Telegram*, during investigation of the Starry Wisdom cult: "The Haunter of the Dark."

November 1, 1907—swamp cult near New Orleans broken up by police raid and 47 prisoners taken: "The Call of Cthulhu."

April 17, 1908—last sighting of Alonzo Typer before his disappearance in the Van der Heyl mansion, Attica, New York: "The Diary of Alonzo Typer."

1908—mysterious stone figurine displayed at annual meeting of the American Archaeological Society in St. Louis by Police Inspector John Raymond Legrasse: "The Call of Cthulhu."

February 2, 1913—Wilbur Whateley born in Dunwich (on Roodmas): "The Dunwich Horror."

May 17, 1922—Captain James P. Orne of the fishing smack *Alma* captures a one-eyed marine creature of colossal size, which is then preserved, placed on display in Boston, and an admission charged: "The Invisible Monster."

August 8, 1922—death of James P. Orne and over a dozen others to drowning under mysterious circumstances: "The Horror at Martin's Beach."

Mid-October 1923—death of Doctor Munoz, New York City: "Cool Air."

August 1, 1924—death of old Wizard Whateley, on Lammas. He is survived by his daughter Lavinia and his grandson Wilbur: "The Dunwich Horror."

August 8, 1924—death of Captain Edward Norrys, in conjunction with the sudden madness of a Mr. Thornton, a psychic investigator, and of Mr. Delapore, owner of Exham Priory, while in an underground grotto beneath the priory. Months later, Exham Priory is demolished: "The Rats in the Walls."

March 23 through April 2, 1925—madness and delirium of the young sculptor Henry Anthony Wilcox after strange dreams. He recovers, with loss of memory, on April 2: "The Call of Cthulhu."

April 2, 1925—crew of the *Emma* traveling from Auckland, New Zealand, to Valparaiso, Chile, encounter a strange volcanic island. While on the island, six crewmen die, and another goes mad. Captain Gustaf Johansen is the only survivor—a madman, he dies later aboard ship: "The Call of Cthulhu."

1926—the promising poet Justin Geoffrey dies in a madhouse: "The Thing on the Doorstep."

October 31, 1926—Lavinia Whateley dies. She is survived by her illegitimate son Wilbur: "The Dunwich Horror."

Winter 1926-1927—death of George Gammell Angell, Professor-Emeritus of Semitic languages at Brown University, after jostling by a sailor: "The Call of Cthulhu."

November 3, 1927—unprecedented Vermont floods carry strange bodies past observers: "The Whisperer in Darkness."

Winter 1927-1928—government investigation of Innsmouth, and detonation of waterfront warehouses; a submarine discharges torpedoes off Devil's Reef: "The Shadow over Innsmouth."

Early August 1928—after being killed by a guard dog in the MU library, Wilbur Whateley's inhuman corpse dissolves: "The Dunwich Horror."

August 1928—the ghost-mound near Binger, Oklahoma, is partially excavated by an ethnologist specializing in American Indian lore, but the ethnologist inexplicably refuses to do more than dig some preliminary scratches: "The Mound."

September 9 to 15, 1928—Professors Armitage, Rice, and Morgan from Miskatonic University dispel the Dunwich Horror on Saturday, the 15th of September: "The Dunwich Horror."

September 12, 1928—Albert Wilmarth from Miskatonic University visits Henry Akeley. Akeley disappears and Wilmarth flees: "The Whisperer in Darkness."

September 20, 1930—the Miskatonic University Expedition to Antarctica sets sail from Boston aboard the brig *Arkham*: "At the Mountains of Madness."

9 November, 1930—the M.U. Antarctic expedition puts ashore in McMurdo Sound: "At the Mountains of Madness."

January 22, 1931—Prof. Lake and companions fly far inland, there discovering unknown life forms, but radio communication ceases: "At the Mountains of Madness."

September 2, 1931—death of noted entomologist Henry Sargent Moore, Professor at Columbia University, NY, from sleeping sickness of an especially virulent nature: "Winged Death."

January 23, 1932—death of noted doctor and entomologist Thomas Slauenwite, in Bloemfontain, South Africa, from heart failure: "Winged Death."

December 1, 1932—two apparent thieves found mysteriously dead in Cabot Museum, Boston, evidently dying while trying to steal the *Eridanus* mummy delivered to the museum in 1878: "Out of the Aeons."

December 8, 1932—autopsy performed on mysterious *Eridanus* mummy, found in 1878. Results hushed up and never released: "Out of the Aeons."

July 17, 1935—archaeological expedition to Australia ends. It was headed by Nathaniel Wingate Peaslee, who was an amnesiac from 1908-1913. Miskatonic U. funded the expedition: "The Shadow Out of Time." ∎

Optional Rules: Vehicle Chases

These rules offer resolutions for simple chases and other situations involving wheeled vehicles. They are best played with two vehicles. The keeper should change or augment these ideas as desired.

Sequence Per Game Round: (1) speed change of vehicles, if any; (2) vehicles maneuver and check for crashes; (3) individual characters move or act on DEX rank.

CONCEPTS

Rated Speed: the maximum sustainable Speed of the vehicle. A vehicle may travel at top Speed or at any lesser Speed. All vehicles start at Speed 0, and accelerate up to travel speed.

Range: the relative interval between moving vehicles. There are five Ranges, as shown on the Vehicle Range Track. For every Speed faster than an opponent, a vehicle can move one Range closer to or further from the other vehicle per round of play—if ahead, the leading vehicle moves further from the pursuer; if behind, the pursuer moves one Range closer.

Accelerate, Decelerate: a vehicle can accelerate/decelerate #X Speeds per round—the Mercedes-Benz SSK, for instance, with 4X can increase or decrease by 4 Speeds in a single round.

Handling: ease and responsiveness of maneuver. Add or subtract rated handling for the vehicle from the character's Drive skill. See the Vehicles Table for this modifier.

Maneuvers: failing a maneuver, roll on the Trouble Table.

Turn: a turn may require a vehicle to decelerate by 1 Speed or more. A U-turn always requires a vehicle to slow to Speed 1. Success is automatic, part of normal driving.

High-Speed Turn: lower the Drive skill by 10 percentiles, then attempt a Drive roll. Success allows the turn without decelerating.

Bootlegger Reverse: lower the Drive skill by 25 percentiles, then attempt a Drive roll. Success sets the vehicle in a skid which concludes with the vehicle facing in the opposite direction. The vehicle is then moving forward at Speed 2 in the next round. Cannot be performed with horse-drawn vehicles.

Ram, Collide: the vehicle is caused to smash into or side-swipe a moving or stationary target. A ram does 1D6 hit points of damage to the vehicle or vehicles for the relative Speeds of the impact; affected characters in the vehicles lose 1D3 hit points per Speed.

Swerve, Evade: with a successful Drive roll, the driver can evade any single Ram, Throw, Climb, Jump, firearms attack, etc., but not more than one in a round.

VEHICLE DAMAGE

The Vehicle Table shows the hit points for a variety of models. When a vehicle collides or is rammed, subtract the rolled damage from its hit points. When damage is more than half its hit points, halve its top speed. When it has 5 hit points or fewer, it ceases to function. Successful Mechanical Repair can restore 1D6+4 hit points to a damaged vehicle, in the same number of hours. If a vehicle takes damage, the keeper may at his or her option call for a roll on the Trouble Table.

INDIVIDUAL ACTIONS

Side by side, characters can clamber around on vehicles and attempt to move one to another. Halve any Climb, Jump, Grapple, etc., skill rolls in such situations; allow a DEX x3 roll or a Luck roll to grab something in case of a missed movement. For firearms attacks, see Vehicle Range Track.

A NOTE ABOUT ROADS

In the 1890s, the principle streets of sizable towns and cities were paved, but even nearby residential areas might be linked by dirt streets. Country roads were uniformly dirt. Bridges were scarce: stream crossings would be by ford, and major rivers would be by ferry. Long distance travel was accomplished by railroad or ship.

In the 1920s, city and town streets are still two lanes, one in each direction. Major intersections are controlled by traffic officers. Back streets are still unpaved, single-car-width tracks. Main country roads are very narrow, frequently curving. Shoulders are uncleared and unmarked. Turnouts are rare. Direction signs and crossroads are unmarked. Farm animals and farm machinery will be encountered. ■

Vehicle Range Track

Side by Side	2 Car-lengths	Close	In Sight	Out of Sight
Range 1	Range 2	Range 3	Range 4	Range 5
firearms at normal skill	*halve firearms skill*	*one-quarter firearms skill*	*allow 01% chance to hit*	*no chance to hit*

show position with coins or other markers

Trouble Table

Use when a maneuver is failed or a vehicle is damaged. If a result greater than 10 is called for, roll an additional time and use both results.

D10   result

1   ***Flat Tire or Cracked Wheel:*** slows vehicle to Speed 1 until changed or repaired.

2   ***Engine Damage or Broken Harness:*** slows vehicle by 2 additional Speeds each round until stopped. Then cannot start without a successful Mechanical Repair roll.

3   ***Gas Tank Punctured or Dead Horse:*** no effect until second hit. Replace gas tank and fuel, or replace horse.

4-6 ***Skid:*** lower Drive skill by 20 percentiles in next round only.

7   ***Fishtail:*** lower Drive skill by 10 percentiles in next round only.

8   ***Fishtail:*** lower Drive skill by 15 percentiles in next round only, roll on table again, and add 2 to the result.

9   ***Bad Fishtail:*** lower Drive skill by 30 percentiles in next round only, roll on table again and add 4 to result.

10   ***Roll:*** vehicle careens off road, rolling once per Speed traveled. Each roll does 2D3 damage to vehicle, and 1D3 to each passenger (1D6 to horse-drawn passengers who are hurled free of the vehicle on its first roll). For automobiles, allow a ten percent chance of a gasoline explosion.

Drive Roll Modifiers

All modifiers are cumulative.

Hazard, etc.	percentile change
bootlegger reverse	-25
dirt road	-20
heavy rain	-20
limbs, rocks	-20
oily, icy	-20
snow	-20
long downhill grade	-10
flat tire	-10
fog	-10
gravel road	-10
high-speed turn	-10
night	-10
rain	-10
wind	-10
at max Speed	-10
handling	per vehicle
at Speed 1 or 2	+10

Monster Speeds

Average ratings for Mythos creature Speeds. Individuals will vary.

SPEED 0: Abhoth, Azathoth, Cthugha.

SPEED 1: byakhee (ground), chthonian, Daoloth, dark young, deep one, Father Dagon & Mother Hydra, dhole (burrowing), dimensional shambler, fire vampire, Elder Thing (ground and flying), flying polyp (ground and air), formless spawn, ghast, Ghatanothoa, ghoul, Glaaki, servants of Glaaki, gnoph-keh, Great Race of Yith, gug, hound of Tindalos (ground), hunting horror (ground and flying), Ithaqua (ground), Lesser Other God, lloigor, mi-go (ground and flying), moon beast, nightgaunt (ground and flying), Nodens, Nyarlathotep (human), Nyogtha, sand-dweller, serpent person, servitor of the Outer Gods, insect from Shaggai (ground), shantak (ground), shoggoth, Shudde M'ell, star vampire, being from Xiclotl, Y'golonac, Yig.

SPEED 2: Atlach-Nacha, byakhee (flying), Cthulhu (swimming and flying), dhole (ground), Hastur (ground), Nyarlathotep (monstrous), Shub-Niggurath, star spawn of Cthulhu, Tsathoggua, Zhar (ground).

SPEED 3: Cthulhu (striding), Cyaegha (flying), shantak (flying).

SPEED 4: Bast, hound of Tindalos (flying), insect from Shaggai (flying).

SPEED 5: Hastur (flying), Zhar (flying), Zoth-Ommog.

SPEED 10: Ithaqua (flying), Yog-Sothoth.

Sample Vehicle Record

vehicle _____

driver _____

Drive skill% _____   max Speed _____

accel/decel. _____   vehicle hit points _____

handling modifier _____   current speed _____

Vehicle Table

type of vehicle	max Speed	hit pts	hand-ling	driver & passengers	accel/decel
saddle horse	2	20	20	1	2X
one-horse shay	2	20	15	1+1+RBs	1X
4-horse carriage	2	30	-1	2+4	1X
4-horse wagon	1	35	-1	1+some	NA
Hispano-Suiza H6	8	30	7	4+RBs	3X
Mercedes-Benz SSK	10	20	12	2+RBs	4X
Model A Ford	5	25	4	5+RBs	2X
Model T Ford	3	25	2	5+RBs	1X
Packard Str. Six	7	40	0	5+RBs	2X
6-ton Truck	4	70	-6	3 (cab)	1X
Harley D Motorcycle	12	18	16	1(+1)	8(6)X
Corvette SR	15	25	14	1+1	8X
Taurus	11	30	12	5	7X
Pickup (6 cyl.)	12	45	11	3 (cab)	7X
18-Wheeler	9	90	4	3 (cab)	4X

Speeds & Distances

Throughout the 19th century and into the 20th century, the steam engine and then the steam turbine steadily compressed travel times. Up to and through World War I, the keys to travel were the steamship, the steam locomotive, and the horse-drawn or electric trolley.

World War I greatly improved the automobile and the airplane, but they were not the long-distance modes of choice until after World War II, when enormous sums were spent on new airports and interstate highways. At the same time rail transport, despite its efficiencies for commuters and freight alike, was dismantled almost everywhere in the United States. This revolution halted only recently, after most of an enormous rail net had been scrapped.

Prices for transportation can be found next, in the era Sample Gear and Price spreads, beginning on p. 254.

All the following speeds and ranges are nominal ones, for civilian transport.

Average Aircraft Speeds and Ranges, ca. 1928

• Single-engined fixed-wing aircraft, 120 mph (190 kph), 300-500 miles (480-800 km).

• Twin-engined fixed-wing aircraft, 90 mph (144 kph), 500-800 miles (800-1280 km).

• Zeppelin, 70 mph (112 kph), 1000 miles (1600 km).

Special preparations greatly extended ranges: Lindberg flew from Long Island to Paris in a single-engine aircraft; during WWI, a zeppelin made a 10,000 mile (16,000 km) voyage from Germany to Africa and back.

Average Aircraft Speeds and Ranges, Present

Single-engined fixed-wing aircraft, 200 mph (320 kph), 750-1,000 miles (1,200-1,600 km).

• Twin-engined fixed-wing aircraft, 275 mph (440 kph), 2,000 miles (3,200km).

• Lear jet, 500 mph (800 kph), 3,000 miles (4,800 km).

• Boeing 747, 550 mph (880), 7,000 miles (11,200 km).

• Two-seater civilian helicopter, 140 mph (224 kph), 400 miles (640 km), ceiling 9,500 feet (2,930 m).

Average Ship Speeds, 1890: Steam Launch, 12-15 knots (22-28 kph); Freighter, 10 knots (18.5 kph); Atlantic Liner, 15 knots (28 kph).

Average Ship Speeds, 1920: Motorboat, 20-25 knots; Freighter, 14 knots; Atlantic Liner, 25 knots.

Average Ship Speeds, Present: Motorboat, 35-45 knots (65-83 kph); Containership, 30 knots (55 kph); Tanker, 35 knots (65 kph); Factory Ship, 25 knots (46 kph); Cruise Ship, 30 knots (55 kph); Ferry Hovercraft, 50 knots (93 kph).

Average Speed on Horseback: 10-12 mph (16-18 kph).

Average Carriage Speed: 10 mph (16 kph).

Average Auto Speed, 1920s: 25 mph (40 kph); back roads 15 mph (24 kph).

Average Auto Speed, Present: 70-75 mph (110-120 kph) on U.S. interstate.

Average Long-Distance Rail Speed: 35 mph (55 kph). In the United States. This rate has not much changed in a century. High-speed trains of France and Japan, in contrast, routinely triple that speed, or more.

Charts

Nearby charts list air and sea distances for a variety of international cities, U.S. cities, and the Panama Canal. The Blue Ribband highlights the contest for naval speed, in a era when sea travel was prestigious and economically vital. ∎

Air Distances, International

Values are in miles; for kilometers, multiply by 1.609.

	Buenos Aires	Cairo	Calcutta	Cape Town	Hong Kong	Honolulu	London	Los Angeles	Manila	Mexico City	Montreal	Moscow	New York	Sydney	Tokyo
B. Aires	—	7,345	10,265	4,269	11,472	7,651	6,916	6,170	11,051	4,592	5,615	8,376	5,297	7,330	11,408
Cairo	7,345	—	3,539	4,500	5,061	8,838	2,181	7,520	5,704	7,688	5,414	1,803	5,602	8,952	5,935
Calcutta	10,265	3,539	—	6,024	1,648	7,047	4,947	8,090	2,203	9,492	7,607	3,321	7,918	5,685	3,194
Cape Town	4,269	4,500	6,024	—	7,375	11,534	6,012	9,992	7,486	8,517	7,931	6,300	7,764	6,843	9,156
Hong Kong	11,472	5,061	1648	7,375	—	5,549	5,982	7,195	693	8,782	7,739	4,439	8,054	4,584	1,794
Honolulu	7,561	8,838	7,047	11,534	5,549	—	7,228	2,574	5,299	3,779	4,910	7,037	4,964	4,943	3,854
London	6,916	2,181	4,947	6,012	5,982	7,288	—	5,482	6,672	5,550	3,282	1,555	3,458	10,564	5,940
Los Ang.	6,170	7,520	8,090	9,992	7,195	2,574	5,382	—	7,261	1,589	2,427	6,003	2,451	7,530	5,433
Manila	11,051	5,704	2,203	7,486	693	5,299	6,672	7,261	—	8,835	8,136	5,131	8,498	3,944	1,866
Mexico C.	4,592	7,688	9,492	8,517	8,782	3,779	5,550	1,589	8,835	—	2,318	6,663	2,094	8,052	7,021
Montreal	5,615	5,414	7,607	7,931	7,729	4,910	3,282	2,427	8,186	2,318	—	4,386	320	9,954	6,383
Moscow	8,376	1,803	3,321	6,300	4,439	7,037	1,555	6,003	5,131	6,663	4,386	—	4,665	9,012	4,647
New York	5,297	5,602	7,918	7,764	8,054	4,964	3,458	2,451	8,498	2,094	320	4,665	—	9,933	6,740
Sydney	7,330	8,952	5,685	6,843	4,584	4,934	10,564	7,530	3,944	8,052	9,954	9,012	9,933	—	4,866
Tokyo	11,408	5,935	3,194	9,156	1,794	3,853	5,940	5,433	1,868	7,021	6,383	4,647	6,740	4,866	—

Distances from Panama Canal

port	nautical miles	kilometers
Baltimore	1,901	3,521
Boston	2,157	3,995
Buenos Aires	5,450	10,094
New York	1,974	3,656
Callao (Panama)	1,346	2,493
Cape Town	6,574	12,175
Gibraltar	4,343	8,043
Hamburg	5,070	9,390
Havana	1,003	1,858
Hong Kong	9,195	17,029
Istanbul	6,166	11,419
Jacksonville	1,535	2,843
Le Havre	4,610	8,538
London	4,763	8,821
Manila	9,347	17,311
Naples	5,325	9,862
New Orleans	1,403	2,598
Portland	3,869	7,165
Port Said	6,268	13,270
Rio de Janeiro	5,345	9,899
San Diego	2,843	5,265
San Francisco	3,245	6,010
St. Petersburg	6,282	11,634
Shanghai	8,556	15,846
Singapore	10,506	19,457
Sydney	7,674	14,212
Tahiti	4,486	8,308
Tokohama	7,682	14,227
Valparaiso	2,616	4,845
Vancouver	4,032	7,467
Vera Cruz	1,420	2,630
Wellington	6,505	12,047

The Blue Ribband

When the passenger liner was a source of national prestige and seemed to indicate the vigor of a nation's navy, this trophy for speed across the Atlantic was greatly sought. Competition from jetliners ended interest in the prize, and the run. For kilometers, multiply knots by 1.852

year	passenger liner	tons	av. knots	direction
1891	Teutonic	9700	20.5	e-w
1892	City of Paris II	10,700	19.5	e-w
1892	City of New York	10,500	20.1	w-e
1893	Campania	13,000	21.3	w-e
1894	Lucania	13,000	21.8/22	e-w/w-e
1897	Kaiser Wilhelm D.	14,400	22.4	w-e
1898	Kaiser Wilhelm D.	14,400	22.7	e-w
1900	Deutschland	16,500	23.2/23.4	e-w/w-e
1906	Kaiser Wilhelm II	19,400	23.6	w-e
1907	Mauretania	32,000	23.7	w-e
1907	Lusitania	31,600	24.5	e-w
1908	Mauretania	32,000	24.5	w-e
1909	Lusitania	31,600	25.9	e-w
1909	Mauretania	32,000	26	e-w
1910	Lusitania	31,600	25.8	w-e
1911	Mauretania	32,000	25.9	w-e
1924	Mauretania	32,000	26.3	w-e
1929	Bremen	51,700	27.8/27.9	e-w/w-e
1930	Europa	49,800	27.9	e-w
1933	Bremen	51,700	28.5	e-w
1933	Rex	51,100	28.9	e-w
1935	Normandie	79,300	30/30.4	e-w/w-e
1936	Queen Mary	81,200	30.1/30.8	e-w/w-e
1937	Normandie	83,400	30.6/31.2	e-w/w-e
1938	Queen Mary	81,200	31/31.7	e-w/w-e
1952	United States	53,300	36/35.6	e-w/w-e

Air Distances, U.S.

Values are in miles; for kilometers, multiply by 1.609.

	Chicago	Denver	El Paso	Los Ang.	Miami
Chicago	—	920	1252	1745	1188
Denver	920	—	557	831	1726
El Paso	1252	557	—	701	1643
Los Ang.	1745	831	701	—	2339
Miami	1188	1726	1643	2339	—
Minneapolis	335	700	1157	1524	1511
N. Orleans	833	1082	983	1673	669
New York	713	1613	1905	2451	1092
San Fran.	1858	949	995	347	2594
Seattle	1737	1021	1376	959	2734

	Minneap.	N. Orlns	New York	San Fran.	Seattle
Chicago	335	833	713	1858	1737
Denver	700	1082	1613	949	1021
El Paso	1157	983	1905	995	1376
Los Ang.	1524	1673	2451	347	959
Miami	1511	669	1092	2594	2734
Minneapolis	—	1051	1018	1584	1395
N. Orlns.	669	—	1171	1926	2101
New York	1018	1171	—	2571	2408
San Fran.	1584	1926	2571	—	678
Seattle	1395	2101	2408	678	—

Water Distances from U.S.

Values are in nautical miles; multiply by 1.852 for kilometers.

port	New York	N. Orleans	S. Francisco
Aden	8,532	7,870	11,500
Bombay	1,820	9,536	9,780
Buenos Aires	5,868	6,318	7,511
Calcutta	9,830	11,239	8,920
Cape Town	6,815	7,374	9,898
Congo River	5,862	6,580	8,853
Hamburg	3,637	5,249	8,315
Le Havre	3,169	4,760	7,855
Hong Kong	11,431	10,830	6,086
Honolulu	6,686	6,085	2,097
London	2,233	4,507	8,038
Manila	11,546	10,993	6,289
Melbourne	10,628	9,437	7,040
Nome	8,010	7,410	2,705
Port Said	5,122	6,509	9,562
Rio de Janeiro	4,778	5,218	7,678
St. Petersburg	4,632	6,223	7,823
Shanghai	10,855	10,254	5,550
Singapore	10,170	11,500	7,502
Valparaiso	4,637	4,035	5,140
Vladivostok	10,001	9,410	4,706
Wellington, N.Z.	8,540	7,762	5,909
Yokohama	8,986	7,762	4,536

1890s Costs, Equipment & Services

Clothing

Men's Clothing
Tailored Prince Albert Suit ......$25.00+
Clerical or Professional Suit $18.00
Clay Worsted Dress Suit $12.50
Vicuna Cheviot Dress Suit $6.50
Oxford Bicycle Suit $3.25
Mackintosh Rain Coat..................$6.98
All-wool Spring Overcoat...........$9.45
Satin Smoking Jacket $5.95
Needle-toe Dress Shoes $2.95
Fancy Silk Vest...........................$2.50
French Percale Shirt ....95¢
Lace-front Wool Sweater $1.50
Felt Top Hat.................................95¢
Straw "Boater" Hat ....75¢
Deerstalker Hat (fore-and-aft)........45¢
Silk Windsor Tie............................55¢
Gentleman's Cane ....75¢
Flannel Night Shirt........................98¢
Embroidered Suspenders................55¢

Women's Clothing
Tailored Bolero Suit................$25.00+
French Silk Wrapper..................$11.00
Chelsea Cloth Wrapper $1.75
Silk Shirt Waist...........................$2.25
Silk Taffetta Moire Skirt $9.50
Full Sweep Satin Cape $8.00
Kid Button Boots $5.00

Cloth-top Lace-up Shoes..............$2.70
Bon Ton Rose Foliage Hat...........$3.50
Untrimmed Neopolitan Hat.............75¢
French Narrow-waist Corset $1.89
Muslin Camisole ....78¢
China Silk Parasol.......................$2.35
Reticule (Lady's Handbag) ....98¢
Four-button Kid Gloves $1.29
Reversible Beaver Shawl $3.95
Chantilly Lace Collar..................$2.25

Communication

Telegram
for 12 words ....12¢
per additional word ....1¢
international, per word $1.00

Postage
to 1 ounce ....2¢
to 2 ounces ....+1¢
each additional 2 ounces................+1¢

Messenger
per mile..4¢
per hour ....8¢

Telegraph Outfit $3.00
Long Distance Telephone.............$7.00

Newspaper.......................................2¢

Entertainment

Theater Tickets
Standing...75¢
Seated $3.00
Box $7.50

Music Hall Tickets $1.50
Vaudeville Tickets ....50¢

Spirits
Cocktail ....20¢
Fine Wine (bottle) $1.75
Ale ....5¢
Whiskey (glass)...............................6¢
Whiskey (bottle).........................$1.00

Upright Cabinet Piano..............$189.00
Concert Violin with Case $36.55
Graphophone Outfit $35.00
Graphophone Records....................50¢
Magic Lantern $9.50

Hand Camera $14.40
Film (48 exposures) $2.85
View Camera with Tripod..........$29.75
12 Dry Photographic Plates ....50¢
Complete Darkroom Outfit $98.00

Lodging & Dining

Hotels
Good Hotel (per night)...............$5.00+
Average Hotel
    per night $2.00
    per week (with service $10.00

Common Lodging (per night)
Double Bed.....................................20¢
Single Bed ....10¢
Rope Lean-to....................................5¢

House (rent per year)................$600.00
Apartment (rent per week)...........$3.50

Meals
Breakfast...25¢
Lunch..50¢
Dinner...$1.00

Medical Equipment

Medical Valise $1.10
Forceps ....75¢

Hypodermic Syringes...................$2.75
Electro Medical Battery $5.75
Surgeon's Instrument Set $20.00
Elastic Bandage (3x15 inches).....$1.15
Hickory Crutches $4.00
Nerve and Brain Pills....................88¢
Laudanum, 4 oz. (tinct. opium).......28¢
Paregoric 4 oz. ....18¢
Liquor Habit Cure, 24 doses...........50¢
Peruvian Wine of Coca, 16 oz. ....95¢

Outdoor & Travel Gear

Camping Equipment
Camp Cooking Kit $6.50
Mexican Woven Hammock..........$1.59
Folding Canvas Boat, 10 ft. $24.00
Wool Blanket..................................89¢
U.S. Folding Cot $5.95
Reflecting Lamp...........................$2.59
Arctic Sleeping Bag $13.00
Kerosene Tent Heater..................$6.50
Camp Stool....................................55¢
Spy Glass....................................$15.00
Deer-foot Hunting Knife $1.50
Two-bladed Pocket Knife...............65¢
Fishing Tackle and Lures $8.98
Steel Jaw Animal Trap $1.20
Dark Lantern $1.15
Match Safes, per doz......................40¢
Jute Rope, per lb. ....18¢

Luggage
Kit Bag (20"x 27")......................$1.20
Leather Gladstone Bag (8 lbs) $2.50
Packing Trunk (40 lbs.)................$3.95
Full Size Trunk (85 lbs.) $5.95

Tents
7 x 7 foot A-frame Tent................$3.65
12 x 12 foot Miners' Tent.............$5.80
16 x 24 foot Wall Tent................$22.70
24 x 30 foot Tarpaulin............... $20.25

Tin Canteen ....24¢
5 Gallon Steel Tank.....................$2.89
Wooden Barrel, 50 Gallons..........$3.25

Tools

Hand Saw ....50¢
Bit Brace (plus bits) $1.10
Pliers...45¢
Carving Tools ....82¢
Gasoline Blowtorch......................$3.00
Claw Hammer ....75¢
Hatchet ....45¢
Combination Vise.........................$7.50
Sharpening Stone ....30¢
Oak Frame Grindstone $2.25

Transport

Horses and Horse-drawn Vehicles
Riding Horse ....$50.00+
Draft Horse...............................$20.00+
Saddle $10.25
Bridle $2.40
Top Buggy (2 seats) $65.00
Canopy Surrey (4 seats).............$80.00
Canopy Carriage (4 seats)........$175.00
Farm Wagon (2 seats)................$45.00
Stable Fee ....25¢/day
Single Harness...........................$16.50
Double Harness..........................$22.40
Draft Harness $18.00

Train Fares
50 Miles...85¢
100 Miles....................................$1.50
500 Miles....................................$5.00

Sea Voyage (U.S. / England)
First Class (one way) $75.00
First Class (round trip) $110.00
Steerage $20.00

River Steamer Fare, local trip.........10¢
Bicycle.......................................$43.00

Ammunition & Weapons

Firearm Ammunition
For firearm prices, see the Weapons Table, pp. 58-59.
.22 Long Rifle (box of 100)............30¢
.25 Winchester (box of 100)...........70¢
.25-20 Marlin (box of 100) $1.10
.30 Short Round (box of 100)........44¢
.30-30 U.S. Army (box of 100)....$4.25

.32 Short (box of 100)....................80¢
.32 Long Colt (box of 100)............88¢
.38 Short Round (box of 100)........98¢
.38 Extra Long (box of 100) $1.67
.41 Short Round (box of 100)........72¢
.44 Smokeless (box of 100) $2.35
.45 Colt Army (box of 100) $2.98
12-gauge Shell (box of 25) $1.18
20-gauge Shell (box of 25) $1.15

Cavalry Saber $2.50
Blackjack.......................................40¢
Sword Cane $12.00
Shoulder Holster..........................$2.25
Cartridge Belt................................50¢
Meat Cleaver ....35¢
Scythe..50¢
Handcuffs $3.75

Miscellaneous

College Tuition (semester).....$190.00+
Professional Microscope $39.00
Pocket Compass $3.00
Aneroid Barometer......................$5.50
Dog Power Sawing Machine $15.00
Fountain Pen.................................12¢
Ink (2 oz.)......................................42¢
Writing Tablet..................................4¢
Sewing Machine.........................$13.50
Full Toupee.................................$15.00
False Beard (ventilated) $1.75
Fencing Foil (per pair) $1.35
Cheroot Cigars (250 cigars).........$3.65
World Atlas..................................$5.00
30 volume Encyclopedia............$25.00
Sewing Kit...................................$1.18
Stereoscope with Views $2.25
Tooth Brush.....................................5¢
Shaving Razor $1.25

1920s Costs, Equipment & Services

Clothing

Men's Clothing
Tailored Silk Dress Suit ....$75.00+
Worsted Wool Dress Suit $29.50
Cashmere Dress Suit $18.50
Corduroy Norfolk Suit $9.95
Dog Fur Overcoat.....................$37.50
Chesterfield Overcoat...............$19.95
Oxford Dress Shoes $6.95
Leather Work Shoes $4.95
Lace-bottom Breeches.................$4.95
Broadcloth Dress Shirt $1.95
Shaker Sweater...........................$7.69
Felt Fedora $8.95
Wool Golf Cap $1.95
Sealskin Fur Cap $16.95
Silk Four-in-hand Tie $3.69
Bat-wing Bow Tie ....55¢
Sock Garters ....39¢
Cotton Union Suit $1.50
Cuff Links ....40¢

Women's Clothing
Chic Designer Dress ....$90.00+
Silk Crepe Frock $16.50
Satin Charmeuse.........................$10.95
French Repp Dress $10.95
Worsted Wool Sweater $9.48
Cotton Crepe Negligee................$6.98
Spike-heeled Parisian Shoes $4.45
Leather One-strap Slippers...........$3.69
Snug Velour Hat $4.44
Satin Turban-style Hat $3.69
Rayon Elastic Corset....................$4.95
Embroidered Costume Slip $1.98
Silk Hose (3 pairs) $2.25

Velour Coat with Fur Trim........$39.75
Brown Fox Fur Coat $198.00
Silk Handbag $4.98
Dress Hair Comb...........................77¢

Communication

Telegram
for 12 words ....25¢
per additional word ....2¢
international, per word $1.25

Postage
to 1 ounce ....3¢
to 2 ounces ....5¢
each additional 2 ounces ....2¢

Console Radio Reciever.............$49.95
Desk Phone (bridging type) $15.75
Telegraph Outfit $4.25
Newspaper..5¢

Entertainment

Movie Tickets
Seated ....15¢
Nickelodeon ....5¢

Professional Baseball Ticket $1.00

Concert Hall or Ballet Tickets
Public Seating...............................$4.00
Box $10.00

Speakeasy Prices
Rotgut Gin (shot) ....10¢
Cocktail ....25¢

Wine (glass)......................................75¢
Beer (glass)......................................20¢
Whiskey (glass)................................25¢

4-string Jazz Banjo......................$8.00
Brass Saxophone $63.45
Cabinet Phonograph $45.00
Phonograph Records ....39¢
Movie Camera...........................$89.00
Movie Projector.........................$54.00
Box Camera................................$2.29
Film, 24 exposures ....38¢
Folding Pocket Camera.............$16.15
Film, 6 exposures ....50¢
Developer Kit $4.95

Lodging & Dining

Hotels (per night)
Fleabag Hotel ....75¢
Average Hotel..............................$4.50
    per week (with service)..........$24.00
Good Hotel $9.00

House (rent per year).............$1000.00
Flat (rent per week)...................$12.50
Apartment (rent per week)........$10.00

Meals
Breakfast..45¢
Lunck..65¢
Dinner..$1.25

Medical Equipment

Medical Case $10.45
Forceps $3.59
Scalpel Set...................................$1.39
Hypodermic Syringes................$12.50
Atomizer......................................$1.39
Gauze Bandages (ten yards)...........39¢
Clinical Thermometer $1.39
Alcohol (half gallon)......................20¢
Hard Rubber Syringe ....29¢
Bed Pan $2.48
Wheel Chair $33.30
Metal Crutches $1.69

Outdoor & Travel Gear

Camping Equipment
Cooking Kit.................................$8.48
Camp Stove $5.85
Folding Bathtub..........................$6.45

Waterproof Blanket $1.79
Folding Camp Bed $5.95
Carbide Lamp..............................$2.59
Searchlight...................................$5.95
Gasoline Lantern $6.59
Binoculars....................................$28.00
Jeweled Compass $2.45
Hunting Knife...............................$2.65
Pocket Knife................................$1.98
Hand Axe.....................................$1.59
Small Live Animal Trap..............$2.48
Coil Spring Animal Trap.............$5.98
Fishing Tackle $16.00
Hemp Twine (2 rolls) ....27¢

Luggage
Handle Bag (8 lbs.) $7.45
Suitcase (15 lbs.)..........................$9.95
Steamer Trunk (55 lbs.)..............$13.95
Wardrobe (95 lbs.).......................$41.95

Tents
7 x 7 foot Tent $11.25
12 x 16 foot Tent $24.85
16 x 24 foot Tent $55.45
24 x 36 foot Tarpaulin................$39.35

Canteen (1 quart)..........................$1.69
Insulated Tank (5 gallons)............$3.98
Water Bag (1 gallon)......................89¢

Tools

Tool Outfit (20 tools) $12.90
Hand Drill (plus bits) $5.98
Large Steel Pulley $1.75
Padlock..95¢
Rope (50 feet)...............................$8.60
Light Chain (per foot) ....65¢
Watchmaker's Tool Kit $14.38
Crowbar..$2.25
Hand Saw $2.80
Gasoline Blowtorch......................$4.45

Transport

Motor Vehicles
Ford Model T ....$385.00+
Ford Model A..........................$560.00+
Chevrolet Superior.................$600.00+
Mercedes-Benz SSK ....$8,000.00+
Packard 626...........................$2,400.00+
Buick 121 ....$1,400.00+
Norton Motorcycle $95.00
Tire (with rim)...........................$10.95
Auto Battery $8.35
Radiator $8.69
Replacement Headlamp $3.95
Auto Luggage Carrier $1.25
Socket Wrench Set $6.95

Illegal Weapons for the 1920s

Rare things or illegal things can be obtained on the black market. Stages for a purchase include finding a seller, negotiating a price, exchanging cash for goods, and getting away safely. Police may intervene, or the seller may try to rob or murder the purchaser. The following prices are nominal for the 1920s. For fresh military ammunition, if it can be found at all, double the pertinent price below and wait one month.

- Thompson SMG — 1D6 x $50 for one weapon.
- .30 caliber MG — D100 x $50 for one weapon.
- .30 caliber AP ammo — $25 per 500 WWI rounds.
- .50 caliber watercooled MG — D100 x $30 + $300 for one weapon.
- .50 caliber AP ammo — $45 per 500 WWI rounds
- 60mm field mortar — 1D6 x $200.
- 60mm HE round — $2 per round (4D6 3-yard radius, 30% duds).
- 60mm illumination round — 100,000 candlepower, 25-second suspension.
- 75mm field gun — D100 x $100 + $800 per weapon. Those costing less than $3,000 are accurate at 200 yards or less.
- 75mm HE or AP ammunition — $10 per WWI round, 50% duds.
- hand grenade — $50 per crate of 24 WWI grenades, 50% duds.

Air Travel
Av. ticket price (per 10 miles)......$2.00
International (per 100 miles)......$18.00
Surplus Trainer Biplane $300.00
Travelair 2000 Biplane...........$3000.00

Train Fares
50 miles $2.00
100 miles $3.00
500 miles $6.00

Sea Voyage (U.S. / England)
First Class (one way) $120.00
First Class (round trip).............$200.00
Steerage $35.00

4-man Hot Air Balloon ....$1800.00+
Streetcar Fare ....10¢
Bus Fare ....5¢

Ammunition & Weapons

Firearm Ammunition
For firearm prices, see the Weapons Table, pp. 58-59.
.22 Long Rifle (box of 100)............48¢
.22 Hollow Point (box of 100)........53¢
.25 Rim Fire (box of 100) $1.08
.30-06 Gov't (box of 100) $7.63
.32 Special (box of 100)...............$5.26
.32-20 Repeater (box of 100) $2.56
.38 Short Round (box of 100) $2.07
.38-55 Repeater (box of 100) $5.58
.44 Hi-Power (box of 100)...........$4.49
.45 Automatic (box of 100)..........$8.60

Rapier $12.50
Bayonet..$3.75
Dagger $2.50
Straight Razor.................................35¢
Brass Knuckles.............................$1.00
Billy Club......................................85¢
Horsewhip $1.25
Handcuffs $3.00

Miscellaneous

College Tuition (semester).....$480.00+
Wrist Watch $5.95
Gold Pocket Watch.....................$32.50
Self-filling Fountain Pen.............$1.25
Writing Tablet................................20¢
Straightjacket...............................$9.50
Complete Diving Suit.............$1200.00
Remington Typewriter...............$40.00
250-power Microscope..............$11.98
Umbrella.......................................$1.79
Turkish Water Pipe.........................99¢
Playing Cards ....75¢
Ouija Board ....95¢
Cigarettes (per pack) ....10¢
Mah Jong Board $1.80
Coca-Cola (12 oz.) ....5¢
Make-up Kit $4.98
Unabridged Dictionary................$6.75
10-volume Encyclopedia............$49.00
Men's Toilet Set (10 pieces).........$9.98
Women's Toilet Set (15 pieces)..$22.95

Present-Day Costs & Equipment

Clothing

Men's Clothing
Tailored Silk Suit ....$800+
Wool Pinstripe Suit $279.95
Rayon-blend 2-piece Suit.........$149.95
Baggy Jogging Suit 59.95
Leather Bomber Jacket.............$249.95
Good Trenchcoat $299.95
Oversized Twill Shirt $24.95
Double-pleated Pants $39.95
Crew Neck Cotton Sweater........$32.95
Jeans $49.95
Leather Docksider Shoes $49.95
Cross-trainer Shoes $109.95
Silk Tie $33.95
Thermal Underwear $12.95
Nylon Swim Trunks $14.95
Pocket Vest $89.95
Good Hiking Boots $249.95

Women's Clothing
Designer Dress, worn once $399
Fine Silk Side-drape Dress.......$389.95
Acrylic 2-piece Dress...............$169.95
Woven Rayon Coat Dress $89.95
Dacron Pleat-front Pants $39.95
Stonewashed Jeans $49.95

Leather Motorcycle Jacket $289.95
Wool-blend Swing Coat $149.95
Button Polo Sweater..................$39.95
Fashion Print Challis Skirt $44.95
Fashion Pumps $89.95
Fashion Boots..........................$159.95
Good Hiking Boots $249.95
Silk Chemise Nightgown $109.95
Matte Black Hoop Earrings $15.95
Gucci Shoulder Bag $249.95
Spandex Bicycle Shorts $29.95
Pocket Vest $99.95

Communication

Local Telephone Service $18.00
Cordless Phone..........................$89.95
Car Phone $299.95
Cell Phone ..in service sign-up package
Plain-paper Fax / Photocopier /
Scanner $449.95
Digital Answering Machine $99.95
Beeper/Pager $89.95
Basic Pager Service ....$6.00 monthly

Computers
Server Computer $5000
Cheap PC System....................$999.95

Cheap Laptop $1,199.95
Good PC System $2,499.95
Good Laptop..........................$2,399.95
Palmtop PC.............................$499.95
Internet Service Provider (month)...$20
T-1 Line (month) $999.95
56k Modem $139.95
8″ x12″ Flat-Bed Scanner $249.95
Portable Storage Disk Drive $149.95
Portable Storage Disk (100M) ...$19.95
CD Writers...............................$599.95
Quick Cam (color) $219.95

CB Radio w/ Police Scanner....$299.95
Three-band Walkie Talkie $139.95
Radar Scanner $169.95
News Magazine $3.95
Newspaper.....................................50¢

Entertainment

Electronics & Mass Media
35″ Stereo PiP Television $1299.95
27″ Stereo PiP Television $499.95
20″ Color Television.................$199.95
Mini Satellite Dish and Two Receivers
....$459.95
Av. Monthly DB Service $50.00
DVD Playback $595.95
200-watt Music System............$459.95
Stereo CD Player.....................$109.95
CD $11.95
Cassette/CD Boom Box $89.95
Aiwa Personal CD.....................$79.95
4-head VCR.............................$139.95
VHS-C Stabilized Camcorder 549.95

First-run Movie Ticket $8.50
Popular Concert Ticket...............$35.00
Pro Football Ticket (bad seat) ...$55.00
Ballet Ticket (bad seat) $75.00

Spirits
Liquor (shot)...............................$2.50
Cocktail $3.00
Wine (glass)................................$3.50
Beer (glass).................................$2.50

Electric Guitar $699.95
Excellent 5-piece Drum Kit ...$2999.95

35mm SLR Camera..................$499.95
Basic Zoom Lens, 35mm $259.95
Film, 36 exposures, 35mm...........$8.95

Digital Camera (w/software)....$359.95
Basic Polaroid Camera...............$49.95
Polaroid Film, 12 exposures $12.95
Pocket One-use Camera.............$14.95
Photo Enlarger..........................$399.95
90mm Scope, 1 Eyepiece, Case
....$599.95
Tripod, 3 Eyepieces, Adapt. $289.95

Lodging & Dining

Hotels (per night)
Econo Motel................................$29.95
Average Motel............................$89.95
per week (with service)............$400.00
Good Hotel............................$159.00+
Grand Hotel............................$490.00+

House (rent per year)...........$16,000.00
Apartment (rent per week).......$240.00
One-Room Apt. W/kitchen ..$200 / wk.

Decent Meals, with tip
Breakfast......................................$8.95
Lunch..$10.95
Dinner...$24.95

Medical Equipment

Medical Case...............................$69.95
Adhesive Bandages (per 100)......$4.95
Instant Cold Packs (per 12)........$12.95
Disposable Respirator $24.95
Complete First Aid Kit..............$79.95
Centrifuge..................................$429.95
EMT Kit $299.95
Foam Pad Splint.........................$19.95
Electronic Thermometer.............$34.95
Stretch-gauze Bandage.................$3.95
Emergency Burn Kit $124.95
Aluminized Blanket $8.95
Folding Pole Stretcher.............$149.95
Portable Oxygen Unit...............$289.95
SPF-64 Sunscreen $8.95
Insect Repellent (large) $10.95

Outdoor & Travel Gear

Camping Equipment
4-person Cook Set......................$19.95
Propane Camp Stove..................$69.95
Portable Chem Toilet..................$79.95
Poly/Cotton Sleeping Bag..........$39.95
Polar Sleeping Bag...................$749.95
Nylon Air Mattress.....................$29.95
Aluminum Folding Cot $69.95
6-watt Fluorescent Lamp $34.95
Thermoelectric Cooler $139.95
Stabilized 8x45 Binoculars $259.95
"Survival" Knife........................$59.95

Swiss Army Knife $39.95
Cheap Machete...........................$13.95
Whetstone....................................$6.95
10.5mm Dry Rope (50m).........$128.95
Asst. Climbing Gear (1 person) .$1,500
Touring Kayak (1 person) $624.95

Luggage
Good Book Bag (15 oz.) $59.95
Carry-on Upright (5 lbs.) $74.95
Duffel Bag (5 lbs.) $39.95
Attache Case (3 lbs.)...............$149.95
Large EZ-Cart (6 lbs.)..............$129.95
Hanging Bag (6 lbs.) $69.95
26" Samsonite Hardside (7 lbs.) ..94.95

Tents and Campers
3-room Family Tent...................$159.95
2 person Geodesic Tent $249.95
4 person Geodesic Tent $379.95
Winnebago RV $48,000
Thermal Canteen (1 quart).........$10.95
Nylon Water Bag (5 gallons) $10.95
Electrical Generator (1500 watts)
....459.95

Tools

G.P.S. Receiver.........................$395.95
60-gallon Air Compressor, $399.95
Socket and Bit Set (90 piece).....$89.95
Mechanic's Tool Chest (812 pc.) ....
....$2,199.95
Welder's Kit $3,100
6-volt Cordless Drill...................$33.95
2 1/2 HP Circular Saw $67.95
7/8″ Rotary Hammer $229.95
Digital AC/DC Multi-Meter.......$19.95
18V Cordless Reciprocating Saw Kit ...
....$296.95
Triple Beam Balance..................$99.95
Scientific Calculator..................$19.95

Transport

Motor Vehicles
Ford Escort Wagon...................$13,999
Explorer 4DR XLT 4x4............$29,988
Honda Accord...........................$20,899
BMW 3 series...........................$45,000
Plymouth Voyager $24,699
Chev. Town & Country $30,899
Cheap Harley-Davidson $9,999.95
Cheap Mercedes-Benz $35,999

12-Ton Hydraulic Jack $44.95
Radial Tire...................................$64.95
Auto Battery $59.95
Muffler, installation...................$74.95
Small Steel Frame Trailer $359.95

Airline Fares, Coach
7-10 cents per mile, medium to long
distance.

Train Fares, Coach
100 miles $24
500 miles $119
1,000 miles $165

Small Used Helicopter $120,000
Small Used Single-prop Plane .$60,000
Auto Rental (day)......................$44.95
Mountain Bike $479.95
Inline Skates............................$219.95

Ammunition & Weapons

Ammunition Prices
*For firearms Prices. see the Weapons
Table, pp. 58-59.*
.22 Long Rifle (box of 500).......$18.50
.220 Swift (box of 50)...............$23.95
.25 Automatic (box of 500)........$54.95
.30 Carbine (box of 50).............$27.25
.30-06 Rifle (box of 50) $18.50
.357 Magnum (box of 50) $36.50
.38 Special (box of 100).............$48.95
5.56mm (box of 50) $23.90
9mm Parabellum (box of 50) $11.95
.44 Magnum (box of 100) $67.95
.45 Automatic (box of 100)........$36.50
12-gauge Shell (box of 25) $27.00
Illegal Suppressor (pistol)...........$800+
Laser Gunsight $259.95
Hand-held Taser $219.95
Aluminum Knuckles $6.95
Self-cocking Crossbow $529.95
12 Crossbow Quarrels...............$34.95
Blowdart Pen (with darts) $19.95
Bandolier $64.95
Nunchaku $19.95

Miscellaneous

College Tuition (Semester) $6,000
Passive Night Goggles...........$394.95+
Lockpicking Tools.....................$79.95
Bunsen Burner...........................$15.95
Bulletproof Vest........................$345.95
Signal Gun.................................$99.95
Stereo Microscope....................$269.95
Metal Detector..........................$229.95
Fireproof Safe...........................$389.95
Geiger Counter $269.95
Good Scuba Gear ....$1,999.95+
Motion Detector Alarm Set......$279.95
Wireless Perimeter Alarm $229.95
Document Shredder..................$199.95
Telephonic Voice Changer 189.95
False Identity Kit.......................$59.95

References for Keepers & Players

Here are books we've found of use. Someday someone will create a web site with thousands of annotated titles contributed by hundreds of people, but these will have to do for now. For more references, see the Resources pages near the front of this book, pp. 32-33.

General

Almanacs. These are published annually, just after the turn of the year. *World Almanac* or *Information Please Almanac* are very similar in coverage and of much the same size. The *New York Times Alamanac* is more thoughtful than either, but also foregoes some of the froth of life. Larger, older libraries keep full sequences of almanacs. They are good sources for earlier game eras.

Atlases, Highway. These offer good small-scale coverage of a state, province, or whole country for the price of a good lunch. Atlases of any sort are of interest and use.

Encyclopedia Britannica. Most of the routine historical or geographical information needed for roleplaying can be found in an encyclopedia. The *Britannicas* have been consistently the best in English for more than a century. The earlier editions cited can be found at main libraries. Branch libraries of any significance will have the latest edition of the *Britannica*.

> —*For the 1890s, use the Eleventh Edition (1908). Superbly written, opinionated, often cited as the best encyclopedia ever published. Represents the last time in English that an encyclopedia was thought of in part as a how-to manual. Take a look, for instance, at the entry for shipbuilding.*

> —*For the 1920s, use the Fourteenth Edition (1929). Grayer and more business-like than its predecessor but with more city maps and photos, too.*

> —*For the present day, especially for technical subjects, use the newest edition you can find.*

Mail-order Catalogues. Though catalogues offering a complete selection of personal and household goods are no longer published, reprints of earlier Montgomery Ward or Sears Roebuck catalogues are issued episodically. They are gold mines of period information.

Travel Guides. There are many series of these books, and new editions of each book are published annually. As with almanacs, being out of date by a year renders such books almost worthless commercially, but they are still loaded with great background for roleplaying.

Books

*Bintliff, Russell. *Police Procedural: A Writer's Guide to the Police and How They Work.* 1993.

*Blyth, Sweet, and Landreth. *Private Eyes: A Writer's Guide to Private Investigators.* 1993.

Cahill, Robert Ellis. *Witches and Wizards, Ghostly Haunts, Strange Sea Sagas,* etc. Small books recounting the lore and legends of New England. Old Saltbox Publishing House, 40 Felt Str., Salem MA 01970.

Cannon, Peter. *The Chronology Out of Time: Dates in the Fiction of H. P. Lovecraft.* Necronomicon Press, 1997.

*Chase, Elaine Raco, & Wingate, Anne. *Amateur Detectives: A Writer's Guide to How Private Citizens Solve Criminal Cases.* 1996.

Collier, J. A. B., and Longmore, J. M. *Oxford Handbook of Clinical Specialties.* A quick reference for all sorts of hospital emergencies and procedures. Clear, practical, witty. 1987.

Cookbridge, E. H. *Orient Express: The Life and Times of the World's Most Famous Train.* 1979. History, photos, anecdotes; well worth browsing.

*Corvasce, Mauro V., and Paglino, Jospeh R. *Modus Operandi: A Writer's Guide to How Criminals Work.* 1995.

Darling, Harold. *Bon Voyage: Souvenirs from the Golden Age of Travel.* 1990. Luggage stickers, posters, baggage tags, etc., from the 1920s and 1930s. Full color throughout.

De Camp, L. Sprague. *Lovecraft: A Biography.* 1975. Decades old, but a worthwhile if intrusive vision of Lovecraft. Paper edition also includes the photos.

Fagam, Brian M., ed. *The Oxford Companion to Archaeology.* Oxford University Press, 1996. Lengthy survey in alphabetical form; good worldwide coverage of sites. Significant essays on topics like "Speech and Language" introduce more concepts. Maps and timelines.

*Faron, Fay. *Missing Persons: A Writer's Guide to Finding the Lost, the Abducted and the Escaped.* 1997.

Flayderman. *Flayderman's Guide to Antique American Firearms,* various editions.

Fort, Charles. *The Books of Charles Fort.* Dover. His tongue-in-cheek compilations from early in the century have founded a cynical media genre today. Perhaps the joke is on Fort.

Gardner, Martin. *Fads and Fallacies in the Name of Science.* Dover, 1957. Believing is a self-hypnotic state, coincidentally true or not true case by case. Essays describe the development of pyramidology, Lysenkoism, the notion of the master race, much more.

Georgano, G. N. *New Encyclopedia of Motorcars, 1885 to the Present.* 1982. Alphabetical entries, hundreds of file photos. What was the Duck, and who made it? Find out here.

Gould and Pyle. *Anomalies and Curiosities of Medicine.* Original ed. 1896. Many photos of malformed individuals and strange episodes of use in plotting adventures. See for instance the case of snake bite on p. 717.

Grun, Bernard. *The Timetables of History.* 1988. Three thousand years of world events and occurrences, the last 1,500 years on a more or less yearly basis.

Guinness Book of World Records. New edition published yearly. Setting a new record for some stunt or endeavor is always a good way to draw in players and investigators.

Grzimek, Dr.Dr. h.c. Bernhard, ed. *Animal Life Encyclopedia*, in 13 volumes. Covers nearly everything that moves; excellent information and amazing anecdotes.

Harms, Daniel. *Encyclopedia Cthulhiana* 2nd ed. Chaosium, 1998. Much enlarged entries defining the myriad threads of the Cthulhu Mythos: entities, characters, places, books, and several appendices. Indispensable.

Harris, Marvin. *Cows, Pigs, Wars, and Witches: The Riddles of Culture.* Useful anthropological eye on human conventions. 1974.

Hartley, Dorothy. *Lost Country Life.* Pantheon, 1979. Practical procedures before the Machine Age.

Held, Robert. *Inquisition: A Bi-lingual Guide to the Exhibition of Torture Instruments from the Middle Ages to the Industral Era.* Evocative modern photos, period woodcuts, and text descriptions of seventy or so devices and procedures designed to break the human will.

How-Dunnit Series: for individual volumes, see asterisked titles. From Writers Digest, in Cincinnati, Ohio, comes a marvelous series of books designed for writers of murder mysteries and thrillers, and consequently also well shaped to the needs of roleplaying keepers and players. These concise books are written by experts in their fields and contain a wealth of explanation, authoratative judgment, bibliographies, canny observation, and sometimes sample forms or diagrams. There is nothing else like them. Well worth collecting. No volume treats how to create a Mythos cult—yet. Writer's Digest publishes many other useful books as well, including books summarizing previous historical periods.

Jane's Weapon Systems, Fighting Aircraft, Infantry Weapons, etc., etc., appear annually in fat, expensive, very detailed editions. They are as near to bibles as the armaments industry is likely to approach.

Joshi, S. T. *H. P. Lovecraft: A Life.* Necronomicon Press, 1996. Joshi's detailed, lengthy, authoritative biography of the most influential horror writer in the United States in the twentieth century. Regretfully, no photos.

Joshi, S. T. *Index to the Fiction and Poetry of H. P. Lovecraft.* Necronomicon Press, 1992.

Joshi, S. T. *Index to the Selected Letters of H. P. Lovecraft.* Necronomicon Press, 1991. An index to the Arkham five volume edition of the letters.

Lehner, Ernst. *Symbols, Signs & Signets.* Dover, 1969. Graphics from dead and living religions, alchemy, heraldry, cattle brands, etc. Over a thousand marks.

Luttwak, Edward. *Coup d'Etat: A Practical Handbook.* 1968. Old but sound analysis of the factors vital to toppling vulnerable regimes. Cultists, synch your watches.

*Mactire, Sean. *Malicious Intent: A Writer's Guide to How Murderers, Robbers, Rapists and Other Criminals Think.* 1995.

Manguel and Guadalupi. *The Dictionary of Imaginary Places.* 1988. Earthly places in literature and popular fantasy, from Pellucidar to Dunwich to Gormenghast to Atlantis. Large pages, small print. Many maps and incidental drawings.

Maniguet, Xavier. *Survival: How to Prevail in Hostile Environments.* 1988. Shipwrecks, snakes, cold, deserts, orientation, food, symptoms, emergency treatment, etc.

McNeill, William H. *Plagues and Peoples.* 1976. First popularization of the notion of disease as a function of human trade and migration.

Miller, William H., Jr. *The Fabulous Interiors of the Great Ocean Liners: in historic photographs.* Dover, 1985. Excellent photos and concise, informative text evoke classic vessels like the *Mauretania*, the *Rex*, and the brilliant *Normandie*.

National Geographic Magazine. Ubiquitous bound volumes found in older libraries across the U.S. Reliable picture source well indexed by topic.

*Newton, Michael. *Armed and Dangerous: A Writer's Guide to Weapons.* 1990.

*Page, David W., MD. *Body Trauma: A Writer's Guide to Wounds and Injuries.* 1996.

Page One: Major Events 1920-1983. Times Books, 1983. Some 300 reproductions of the front pages of the *Times*, large enough that body text can be read.

Scarre, Chris, ec. *Past Worlds: The* Times *Atlas of Archaeology.* 1988. Many maps and artifacts, systematically located and dated.

Schlesinger, Arthur M. *Almanac of American History.* Bison, 1983. Yearly chronologies, personalities, special topics.

Shooter's Bible. New edition published yearly. Annual compendium of personal firearms and ammunition, ballistics table, weapon prices, etc.

Stanley, Joan C. *Ex Libris Miskatonici: A Catalogue of Selected Items from the Special Collections.* Necronomicon Press, 1993. Fine short study of M.U.'s unique holdings.

*Stevens, Serita Deborah, and Klarner, Anne: *Deadly Doses: A Writer's Guide to Poisons.* 1990.

Sturtevant, William C., ed. *Handbook of North American Indians.* In 20 volumes. Exhaustive survey of customs, history of relations, artifacts, languages, territories, etc.

Sullivan, Jack, ed. *The Penguin Encyclopedia of Horror and the Supernatural.* 1986. Authoritative and insightful entries on authors, personalities, books, films, directors, and topics. International coverage, very well written.

Theroux, Paul. *The Great Railway Bazaar: By Train Through Asia.* 1975. Read anything by this writer.

*Wingate, Anne. *Scene of the Crime: A Writer's Guide to Crime-scene Investigations.* 1992.

*Wilson, Keith D., M.D. *Cause of Death: A Writer's Guide to Death, Murder and Forensic Medicine.* 1992. ■

Cthulhu Supplements

The following Cthulhu supplements were in print at the time this rulebook was originally published. Please see our web site for the most current list of in-print items, at www.chaosium.com. The entire line of Call of Cthulhu® supplements is order-ready at Wizard's Attic, www.wizards-attic.com.

CORE RULEBOOKS

1920s Investigator's Companion. A sourcebook of the 1920s, containing background, equipment, and more. Complete player's reference. CH2370.

The Creature Companion. A sourcebook full of monsters, also featuring the notebooks of Sir Hansen Poplan. CH2375.

The Keeper's Companion. Tomes, cults, and lots of other background material for the keeper. *In 2000.*

1890s BOOKS

Dark Designs. Three independent adventures set in Victorian England, with a fold-out map of England. CH2332.

1920s BOOKS

Adventures in Arkham Country. Five adventures set in Lovecraft Country, including spotlights on Arkham, Innsmouth, and Kingsport. A Lovecraft Country release. CH2342.

Before the Fall. A group of adventures set in Innsmouth prior to the government raid of 1928. A Lovecraft Country release. CH2377.

Compact Arkham Unveiled. A reprint of the classic Arkham sourcebook, featuring background material on the town of Arkham. A Lovecraft Country release. CH2356.

Arkham Sanitarium Kit. A set of handouts related to the Arkham asylum. A Lovecraft Country release. CH2366.

Day of the Beast. An epic campaign taking investigators to South America, Europe, Asia, and even to the stars. Battle the Brotherhood of the Beast. CH2374.

Dead Reckonings. Walking corpses, the granddaughter of Shub-Niggurath, and a battle between witches and ghouls. Three adventures in all. A Lovecraft Country release. CH2373

Escape from Innsmouth. The second edition of the classic sourcebook on Innsmouth, featuring a new adventure and an expansion of the "Raid on Innsmouth" scenario. A Lovecraft Country Release. CH2371.

Miskatonic University Antarctic Expedition Pack: items for CH2380 *Beyond the Mountains* campaign—cloth expedition patch, special Antarctica map, much more. CH2381.

Horror's Heart. A short mini-campaign, set in Montreal. Two cults collide. CH2359.

King of Chicago. Two independent adventures, set in Chicago and Marseilles. Gangsters and the Mythos. CH2347.

Minions. A set of fifteen short encounters. CH2365.

The New Orleans Guidebook. Detailing the Crescent City for the 1920s. Includes one adventure. CH2369.

Beyond the Mountains of Madness. A worthy sequel to Lovecraft's classic adventure, a long campaign unveiling the secrets of the Antarctic to daring investigators. CH2380.

1990s BOOKS

The Bermuda Triangle. Background material on the Devil's Triangle and the Caribbean. Also featuring a short adventure. CH2373.

Last Rites. Four New England adventures against unusually dangerous foes. Witty. CH2379.

Unseen Masters. Wild NYC adventures with drugs, perception, madness, the Mythos. Detailed, dense. CH2378.

A Resection of Time. A mini-campaign taking investigators from a seedy modern Arkham to Central America. CH2364.

Secrets. Four short adventures. Ghouls, organ donors, and more. A Fright Night release. CH2367.

THE DREAMLANDS

The Complete Dreamlands. A sourcebook detailing the lands beyond the wall of sleep. CH2363.

The Dreaming Stone. The first-ever Dreamlands campaign. Against the Crawling Chaos! CH2368.

OTHER ERAS

Blood Brothers 2. Non-mythos Call of Cthulhu adventures, based on your favorite movies. CH2340.

No Man's Land. Terrifying Mythos adventure amid the front-line horrors of World War I. Excellent background and wartime character generation. CH2385.

Strange Aeons. Call of Cthulhu in other eras—from the Spanish Inquisition to the U.N. moon base. CH2353.

Taint of Madness. Insanities and asylums for Call of Cthulhu, including three adventures. CH2354.

MYTHOS CARD GAME

Chaosium also publishes the Mythos collectible card game, in which two or more players take on the roles of Cthulhu investigators combatting the horrors of the Mythos. Players should begin with the Standard Edition. Expansions explore Miskatonic University, the world in the 1920's, the Dreamlands (delving beyond the Wall of Sleep), and New Aeon (emphasizing the Mythos in the present day). ■

Disasters, Natural and Man-Made

A roll of unrelieved awfulness for the years 1890 to the present, establishing a scale of newsworthiness as well as recording what actually happened.

1890 British cruiser *Serpent* wrecked in storm off the coast of Spain; 167 lost.

1891 Devastating quake levels 20,000 structures and kills 25,000 people in Japan.

1892 Fire and flood create a human hell at Oil City, Pennsylvania, 130 dead.

1893 Floods pushed by hurricane winds devastate U.S. South Atlantic coast, 2000 dead.

1894 Steamer *Walraro* wrecked off coast of New Zealand, 134 lost; Minnesota forest fire kills 480.

1895 Building collapses in Ireland, killing 14.

1896 Railway collision kills 60, Reading PA; earthquake and tidal wave kill 27,000 at Sanriku, Japan.

1897 Three sampans collide off Sarawak, 138 die.

1898 Tropical cyclone hits southern U.S., hundreds die; 2446 U.S. dead in Spanish-American War.

1899 Windsor Hotel in New York goes up in flames; millions in damage and 14 killed.

1900 Pier fire, steamer *Rio de Janeiro* wrecked in San Francisco harbor, 128 lost; great Galveston hurricane kills 6,000; mine explosion kills 200 in Utah.

1901 Two serious typhoid outbreaks in U.S.

1902 Steamer *Primus* sunk in collision with steamer *Hansa* on the Elbe River, 112 lost; Mt. Pelée eruption kills 40,000 on Martinique; Roland Molineux, the "Knickerbocker Murderer", is acquitted.

1903 Fire at Iroquois Theater, Chicago, worst theater fire in U.S. history (602 dead); disaster prompts fire codes across the nation.

1904 Steamship *General Slocum* catches fire near Manhattan, 1000 dead; Eden CO train derailed into flood, 96 killed.

1905 Japanese warship *Mikasa* sunk by explosion, 599 lost.

1906 Earthquake and fire devastate San Francisco, 28,818 houses destroyed and 700 announced killed; typhoon and tidal surge kill 10,000 in Hong Kong.

1907 Explosion on French battleship *Jena* kills 117 persons; West Virginian coal mine explosion kills 361.

1908 Steamer *Ying King* founders off Hong Kong, 300 lost; massive earthquake kills 150,000 in southern Italy.

1909 Steamer *Seyne* sunk in collision with steamer *Onda* off Singapore, 100 lost; hurricane in Louisiana and Mississippi kills 350.

1910 Landslide buries workers in the Norman open-pit mine, in Virginia MN; Wellington WA trains swept away by avalanche, killing 96.

1911 Forty tons of dynamite explode at Communipaw terminal, NJ, killing 30; Triangle Shirtwaist Factory fire in New York City leaves 145 dead.

1912 *Titanic* rams iceberg, 1517 passengers and crew are lost.

1913 British steamer *Calvadas* lost in blizzard in the Sea of Marmora, 200 lost.

1914 Canadian Pacific steamship *Empress of India* sunk in collision with the *Storstad* in the St. Lawrence River, 1024 lost.

1915 *Lusitania* sunk by German submarine, 1199 lost; Avezzano, Italy, quake leaves 30,000 dead; central Gulf Coast hurricane leaves 275 dead; three-train collision in Scotland kills 227.

1916 French auxiliary cruiser *Provence* sunk in the Mediterranean, 3100 die; some 700,000 die in the battle of Verdun; some one million die in the battle of the Somme; U.S. polio epidemic kills 7000 and leaves 27,000 youngsters paralyzed.

1917 Steamer *Castalia* wrecked on Lake Superior, 22 men lost; Pennsylvania munitions plant explosion kills 133; 1600 dead in ship collision and explosion in Halifax, Nova Scotia; derailment in France leaves 550 dead.

1918 U.S.S. *Cyclops* leaves Barbados and is never heard of again. U.S. dead total 116,516 in WWI; Austria-Hungary 1.2 million; Bulgaria 1.3 million; France 1.3 million; British Empire 900,000; Italy 650,000; Germany 1.8 million; Rumania 335,000; Russian 1.7 million; Turkey 325,000. Train collision near Nashville TN kills 101.

1919 French steamer *Chaonia* lost in Straits of Messina, 460 lost; hurricane along Gulf Coast kills 570 on land and 330 at sea.

1920 Earthquake in Gansu province, China, kills 200,000.

1921 Bridge collapses in Chester PA, 21 die.

1922 British steamer *Egypt* in collision off France, 98 people dead, five million in gold and several million in banknotes lost; British dirigible *AR-2* breaks in two, killing 62.

1923 Big fire in Berkeley CA destroys 600 buildings, causes $10 million in damage, and 60 persons killed; great earthquake and fires in Japan kill more than 140,000.

1924 Ward Line steamship *Santiago* sunk by storm off Cape Hatteras, 25 lost;

1925 Italian sub sinks during naval maneuvers off Sicily, 50 lost; in U.S. Midwest, 792 die from tornadoes in one day; U.S. dirigible *Shenandoah* breaks apart, killing 14.

1926 Lightning starts a massive explosion at the U.S. Naval ammunition dump, Lake Denmark NJ—85 million in damages and 30 dead; hurricane through Florida and Alabama leaves 243 dead; Cuban dead in hurricane reportedly 650.

1927 British Indian steamer *Tukaram* sunk in

storm in Bay of Arauco, 291 lost;

1928 Dam collapses at Santa Paula CA leaving 450 dead; southern Florida hurricane kills 1836.

1929 Russian passenger steamer *Volga* struck by remnant WWI mine in the Black Sea, 31 lost.

1930 Fire at the Ohio State Penitentiary traps and kills 322 in locked cells; cigarette sales rise 10% to 11 billion smoked; hurricane kills 2,000 in Santo Domingo; British dirigible *R-101* crashes, killing 47.

1931 Earthquake in Managua kills 1,100; 200,000 die in Yangtze floods; tens of thousands die as Japanese offensive in Manchuria accelerates.

1932 British submarine goes down in English Channel; quake kills 1,500 in Santiago; tens of thousands die in encirclement campaigns in central China; hurricane claims 1,000 in Cuba; Chinese quake kills 70,000; 268 die from tornadoes in a single day from Arkansas to South Carolina; millions believed dead in Soviet kulak purges.

1933 Many die in continued Japanese encroachments in China; Long Beach quake kills 123; hundreds die in Cuban rebellion; 400,000 Germans to be sterilized as defective; 73 die as U.S. dirigible *Akron* crashes.

1934 Economic depression deepens as starvation and unrest spread in U.S.; drought extends from New York State to California; Chaco War deaths now in the thousands; *Morro Castle* burns off New Jersey as a hundred thousand watch; hurricane at Honshu, Japan, kills 4,000.

1935 Increasingly severe dust storms batter the High Plains and Midwest of the U.S.; quake off Taiwan kills 2000; 26,000 die in Pakistan earthquake; 1000 die as dam collapses near Turin; hurricane kills 200 in Florida; second Florida hurricane kills 408; Italian bombing in Ethiopia kills 1700; lynchings continue in the South.

1936 Floods in Midwest kill 134; clashes in Palestine leave 11 dead; U.S. heat wave kills 3,000; dust-bowl conditions continue; revolt in Madrid leaves 25,000 dead; 498 die in two days from a series of tornadoes in U.S.

1937 Gas explosion kills 294 in Texas school; *Hindenburg* dirigible explodes with loss of 36; 8 Soviet generals die in Stalinist purges; 109 die in U.S. heat wave; two blacks lynched in Florida; Cairo riots continue.

1938 *Endymion* torpedoed in Mediterranean; floods in California leave 144 dead; Bukharin and 17 more die in Stalinist purges; major battles between Chinese and Japanese; bomb at Arab market kills 21 in Palestine; New York-New England hurricane kills 600.

1939 A victorious Franco arrests 100,000+ Spanish; liner *Simon Bolivar* sunk by mine; U.S. submarine *Squalus* sinks with loss of 26 hands; French submarine *Phoenix* sinks with loss of 63;

continued next page

Disasters, Natural and Man-made, cont.

Chilean quake kills 30,000; 26 die as Italy expels foreigners from Tyrol; two IRA bombs in London; 250,000 casualties in Polish invasion; as WWII begins, many warships and civil craft lost at sea; Turkish earthquake kills 11,000.

1940 Mine explosion kills 92 in West Virginia; thousands die in Russo-Finnish War; German blitzkrieg to Channel; bombings in Germany and England kill tens of thousands.

1941 Thousands die in Bucharest riots; war rages in Africa, at sea, and in the air; tens of thousands shipped to concentration camps in Occupied Europe; Red Army estimates more than a million casualties thus far from German invasion; about 2,500 die in Japanese raid on Pearl Harbor; Coconut Grove (Boston) nightclub fire kills 491.

1942 German casualties in the East reach 1.5 million, and Soviet losses estimated at nearly 5 million. The carnage in this theater of war will by 1945 amount to some 32 million deaths: it is the greatest disaster visited upon humanity. Cyclone devastates Bengal, killing 40,000.

1943 Some 190,000 Germans and greater numbers of Soviet soldiers and civilians die at Stalingrad; Warsaw ghetto falls; 29 die in Detroit race riots; heavy fighting in the Central Pacific.

1944 Enormous aerial bombings of Germany; leap-frog attacks across Pacific; Normandy landings; Warsaw rebellion alone leaves 200,000 dead; hurricane kills 46 along East Coast, and 344 more at sea; Ringling Bros. tent fire kills 168; ammunition explosion kills 322 at Port Chicago CA.

1945 Some 130,000 die in Dresden fire-bombing; 60,000 die from nuclear blast at Nagasaki, and other mass bombings kill hundreds of thousands more in Japan. Total casualties of WWII are estimated at 50 million people. Europe and Japan need 15 years to effect significant recovery. U.S. war-related dead total 405,399.

1946 Starvation and disease endemic in war areas; Chicago hotel fire kills 58; Irgun kills 100+ in Jerusalem bombing; Calcutta riots kill 90; worst U.S. air crash kills 39.

1947 Illinois mine explosion traps 119; tornadoes kill 132 in Texas and Oklahoma; Soviets still hold 892,000 German prisoners; 150,000 die in Indian religious riots; starvation and hunger persist in Europe and China; 516 dead in Texas City TX explosion; passenger ship *Kiangya* hits mine and sinks off Shanghai, killing 3,000.

1948 Carnage in India after the Gandhi assassination; daily bloodshed in Palestine; war in French Indo-China; Greeks execute 213 communists; chemical plant blast in Germany kills 250; war in Israel and Transjordan; guerilla war in Indonesia.

1949 Hundreds dead in Bolivian labor unrest; massive floods in China; quake in Ecuador kills 4600; 207 perish in the *Noronic* liner fire; 4,000 Guatemalans die in flood; 55 die in worst U.S. plane disaster; 2,700 deaths and 42,000 paralyzed in U.S. polio epidemic.

1950 Iranian earthquakes kill 1,500; 51 die in weather-ship collision with mine; 25,000 die from Assam earthquake; U.S. blizzards kill hundreds;

thousands die as Korean War begins.

1951 New Jersey train crash kills 84; El Salvador quake kills 100+; 50 die in U.S. place crash; 9 die in Tehran oil-dispute riots; 12 die in British-Egyptian clash near Suez.

1952 Iranian tribal clash kills 50; 108 dead in Brazil train wreck; tornadoes kill 343 in U.S. mid-section; 176 die in U.S. naval collision; vast crop failures in India; worst U.S. bus crash kills 28; French submarine *La Sybille* disappears in Mediterranean with 49 aboard; U.S. polio epidemic kills 3,300 and affects 57,000 children.

1953 Storms off North Sea kill 200 in Britain; Turkish earthquake leaves 1,000 dead and 50,000 homeless; tornadoes around Waco TX and Flint MI kill 124 and 116, respectively; Netherlands storm-floods kill 1,794; Nigerian independence riots leave 32; 37 dead in carrier *Leyte* dock fire; total U.S. dead in Korea war 54,246.

1954 Avalanches bury 198 in Alps; first H-bomb exploded; Pakistani labor riots; two hurricanes kill 155 along U.S. east coast;

1955 Navy plane crashes in Hawaii, killing 66; 300+ die in train crash near Guadalajara; tornadoes scourge South, 121 dead; floods in northeastern U.S. kill 179; thousands die in North African nationalist struggles; Hurricane Diane kills 184.

1956 Over 10,000 Mau-Mau rebels killed in 4 years; Poznan riots; earthquake in India leaves 117 dead and 800 missing; typhoon kills about 2,000 in China; Hungarian uprising; *Andrea Doria* collision kills 52.

1957 Earthquakes in Iran kill about 2,000; 42 Algerian rebels killed by French; Hurricane Audrey wipes out Cameron, LA, killing 390.

1958 California midair collision claims 47; Nike base explosion in New Jersey kills ten; Soviet weapons-plant explosion spews radioactivity across southern Urals, hundreds apparently dying; 96 miners trapped in Nova Scotia; 90 die in Chicago school fire.

1959 Milan Airliner crash kills 68; Algerian fighting continues; 1,000+ die in Japan from typhoon; Kilauea Ike crater erupts on Hawaii; dam collapse leaves 412 dead in France.

1960 In South Africa, 50 protesters are shot to death; Agadir, Morocco, leveled by earthquake, and 10,000-12,000 die; first smog-control bill passes in California; Iranian quake kills 1,500; 200 die in Guatemalan asylum fire; Hurricane Donna devastates U.S. East Coast and Puerto Rico, claiming ,165 lives; tidal waves kill 7000 in East Pakistan.

1961 78 die in plane crash near Chicago; Hurricane Carla kills 46 along Gulf Coast.

1962 Huge landslide wipes out Peruvian town of 3,100 people; mine explosion in Germany kills 249, with 146 missing; murderous fighting in Algiers; 110 die in west African airliner crash; U.S. national debt exceeds $300 billion; Iranian quake kills 20,000.

1963 Cold wave in U.S. kills 150; quake kills 300 in Libya; landslide kills 300 in Peru; eruption on Bali kills 11,000; racial violence continues in U.S. South; U.S. submarine *Thresher* goes down with

129 hands; 1,000+ die in Yugoslav quake; hurricane kills 5,000 in Haiti and Cuba; landslide into Italian dam kills 2,000; Japanese mine blast kills 327; Canadian jetliner crash kills 119; 22,000 die in East Pakistan cyclone; Hurricane Flora kills 7,000 in Haiti and Cuba.

1964 Religious riots in Calcutta kill 200; Alaskan quake kills 117; U.S. accidentally releases a kilo of plutonium into atmosphere; munitions blast in Algiers kills 100; major and continuous fighting in Vietnam; burst reservoir kills 1,000 in India; dozens of hostages die in Congo rescue; hurricane kills 7,000 in Madras and Ceylon.

1965 Cyclone kills 5,000 and leaves 5 million homeless in Pakistan; missile silo fire kills 53 workers in Arkansas; 650 U.S. citizens dead in Vietnam since 1961; Hurricane Betsy kills 75; cyclones kill 47,000 in East Pakistan; liner *Yarmouth Castle* sinks with loss of 91; tornadoes across Midwest kill 256 in one day.

1966 Airliner crashes in Alps with 117 lost; airliner crashes in Tokyo Bay with 133 dead; flood devastates the art treasures of Florence; Aberfan (Wales) avalanche kills 144.

1967 3 astronauts die in Apollo fire; U.S. loses 500th plane over Vietnam; Newark race riots leave 26 dead in four days; 31 deaths in Detroit race riots; soccer riot in Turkey kills 42 and injures 600; 250 die in Portugal floods.

1968 B-52 carrying four H-bombs crashes in a Greenland bay; 31 die in violence following the King assassination; earthquake in Iran kills 8000+.

1969 Biafran market bombed, killing 300; snow-storm of the decade closes New York City; clash on Chinese border kills 31 Soviets; Hurricane Camille kills 256; Venezuelan airline crash kills 150; U.S. deaths in Vietnam now total 33,641; Egyptian attack leaves 40 Israeli casualties; Mylai massacre of 567 villagers reported; floods kill 100+ in southern California.

1970 French submarine *Eurydice* sinks with 57 lost; earthquake in Turkey kills 600; six blacks shot dead in back in Georgia; Kent State killings; enormous quake kills 30,000 in Peru; 46 shot in Asbury Park riots; PLO mass-hijacking; cyclone and tidal wave kill 200,000 in East Pakistan.

1971 Quake in Los Angeles kills 51; Turkish earthquake kills 600; civil war in East Pakistan causes 2 million refugees; worst airliner crash on record kills 162 in Japan; hurricane and tidal wave kill 6000 in India.

1972 Airline antihijacking procedures established in U.S.; airline crash kills 118 in Britain; 11 Israeli Olympians massacred; 147 die and 700 injured in Mexican train disaster; 170 die at Moscow in worst jetliner crash; Hurricane Agnes leaves 117 dead; jetliner crash kills 155 in Canary Islands; 10,000 die in Nicaragua quake; 5,000 dead in Iranian earthquake; 237 dead in South Dakota flash floods;

Interlude: from 1961-1973, approximately 57,000 Americans died in Vietnam; South Vietnamese armed forces deaths are listed at 183,000; communist militia and North Viet-namese regulars losses estimated at one million; civilian deaths are thought to be at least 500,000 and perhaps more than four million.

1973 Thousands die in Yom Kippur War; 100 die in Japanese department store fire.

1974 In Sao Paulo, 170 die in office building fire; Iran-Iraq border clash leaves 70 dead; In Bali, jetliner crashes with loss of 107; 30+ die in shootout in Israeli school; smallpox sweeps India, killing 10,000; hurricane Fifi kills 10,000 in Honduras; IRA bomb kills 22 in England; Darwin, Australia, leveled and 50 killed; quakes kill 4700 in Pakistan; tornadoes kill 315 in two days in U.S.

1975 Drought in Ethiopia; thousands die in Beirut as fighting spreads; quake in Turkey takes 1,000+; 26 die in guerilla attack in Buenos Aires.

1976 Guatemalan quake kills 23,000; world arms spending reaches 300 billion dollars yearly; strong quake kills 100+ in Italy; New Guinea earthquake takes 9,000; Colorado flash flood kills 139; 20 die from what will be identified as Legionnaires disease; 46 Argentineans die in political mass murders; airliner deaths total 146 in Turkish crash; Hurricane Lizzie leaves 2,500 dead in Mexico; Turkish quake kills 3,000; Cairo riots kill 44; Tangshan (China) earthquake leaves 242,000 dead; quake and tidal wave kill 8,000 in Mindanao.

1977 Canary Islands jetliner collision kills 574; May Day clash in Istanbul kills 39; Kentucky nightclub fire kills 160; cyclone kills 10,000 in India; Rumanian earthquake leaves 1,600 dead.

1978 Airliner carrying 213 explodes over Arabian sea; 30 die as Palestinians seize bus; Rhodesian attacks in Zambia kill 38; 40 Iranians die in antigovernment riots; air collision over San Diego kills 150; 30 die in Guatemalan general strike; 909 die in Jonestown mass suicide; 25,000 dead in Iranian quake.

1979 3-Mile Island nuclear power plant leak; 100 Vietnamese boat-people drown off Malaysia; Hurricane David kills 1,200 in Dominican Republic; 275 die in Chicago air accident; Spanish hotel fire claims 71; 257 killed in Antarctic airliner crash; exploratory oil well in the Gulf of Mexico spills 140 million gallons of oil into the sea, the largest known oil spill.

1980 18 die in Miami race riots; Mt. St. Helens WN eruption kills 50+; explosion at Italian train station kills 80+; Iran-Iraq War begins; 25 dead from toxic-shock syndrome; Hurricane Allen leaves 228 dead in Caribbean and Texas Gulf; 3,000 die in Italian earthquake; 20 slain in El Salvadorean violence; 80 die in MGM Grand Hotel fire in Las Vegas.

1981 In two years, GM has posted more than a billion dollars in losses; Chrysler reports a loss of $1.7 billion for 1980 alone; quake near Naples kills 2916; fighting continues around Beirut; 72 die in Tehran bombing; riots across England; 123 die in Israeli attacks on PLO; 111 die in Kansas City hotel lobby collapse; South African incursion into Angola kills 240; Iranians execute 149 leftists; bomb in PLO offices kills 50; bomb in Syria kills 64.

1982 Airliner smashes into Potomac bridge, kills 78; 84 die as Newfoundland oil rig sinks; New Orleans airliner crash kills 149; 20,000 reported dead in Lebanon fighting between June and August; 60 die in Tehran bomb blast; remains of 1,000 "disappeared" located in Argentina.

1983 Nicaraguan fighting continues; 600 die in Indian religious strife; Iran-Iraq War continues; ANC bomb kills 16 South African military; 100 die in Volga River ship collision; Soviets down jetliner, killing 269; 64 die in South African coal mine explosion; 216 U.S. Marines die in Beirut bombing; in Spain, 176 die in airliner crash.

1984 Iran-Iraq war now involves oil tankers in Persian Gulf; Indonesian death squads reportedly kill some 4,000 people; homeless in U.S. officially at up to 350,000; Indian troops seize Sikh Golden Temple, 308 die; Bhopal insecticide plant accident kills 2,100+ people.

1985 Rail accident in Ethiopia kills 392; blast at Shiite mosque in Lebanon kills 15; Beirut car-bomb kills 62; 59 die in Sikh attacks in India; another Beirut car-bomb kills 50; prisoners in Brazil kill 13 by lottery to protest conditions; soccer violence and deaths continue; 10,000 die in Bangladesh storm; Air-India jet explodes, killing 329; Nicaragua's war with Contras said to have killed 12,000 so far; Beirut car-bomb kills 50 more; 122 die in Dallas airliner crash; 50 die in Malta hijacking; 250 U.S. soldiers die in air crash at Gander; quake devastates Mexico City leaving 25,000 dead.

1986 Jetliner crashes in Guatemala, killing 90; 500 die as Bangladesh ferry sinks; 40 die in Ceylon from Tamil bombs; bomb in Tehran kills 20; at Chernobyl, dozens of heroes sacrifice themselves to contain the disaster and in the years to come, experts expect 24,000 deaths to be influenced by the released atomic cloud; 1,200 die from toxic cloud in Cameroon; Soviet ship sinks, 398 lost; 177 die in South African gold mine fire; 21 die in Istanbul synagogue assassinations; tunnel collapse kills 2000+ in Afghanistan; Karachi riots kill 54; San Juan hotel arson fire kills 96.

1987 Deaths in Iran-Iraq War said to total 1 million; widespread civil unrest in Korea; South Africans kill 190 in Namibia; sinking ferry *Dona Paz* in Philippines kills 1500.

1988 U.S. Navy downs Iranian airliner, 290 die; Pan-Am jetliner explodes over Lockerbie, Scotland, 259 aboard; Armenian earthquake kills 25,000 and leaves 400,000 homeless; Bangladesh monsoons kill 1,300 and leave 30 million homeless; Hurricane Gilbert devastates northeastern Mexico, leaving 260 dead.

1989 U.S.S. *Iowa*'s turret explodes, killing 42; Hurricane Hugo leaves 71 dead; Loma Prieta quake cause widespread destruction and 67 deaths in northern California; in Ural Mts., liquefied gas leak and explosion kills 500.

1990 Iranian earthquake kills 50,000; Luzon quake kills 1,600; a puzzling panic leaves 1,426 pilgrims dead at Mecca.

1991 Gulf War kills at least 50,000 Iraqis; Iraq releases 40 million gallons of crude oil into the Persian Gulf, and leaves some 600 oil wells aflame. Oakland Hills fire burns some 3,000 homes and leaves dozens dead; massive eruptions of Mt. Pinatubo on Luzon; Bangladesh cyclone kills 125,000 and leaves 9 million homeless; all Kuwait oil fires put out.

1992 Tens of thousands massacred during "ethnic cleansing" in former Yugoslavia; hurricanes in

Florida, Louisiana, and Hawaii kill dozens and leaving thousands homeless; major earthquakes in Southern California and Egypt cause extensive damage. Estimated 13 million people now infected with HIV virus.

1993 Terrorists bomb NY World Trade Center; storm kills 2,000 in Eastern U.S.; resurgence of neo-Nazi violence in Germany; a "thousand-year flood" inundates Mississippi Valley; IRA bomb devastates London financial district.

1994 Northridge CA quake kills 61; Mexico's president assassinated; serial tornadoes across Alabama to S. Carolina kill 52; Bangkok toy factory fire leaves 213 dead; 6.8 quake in Columbia kills 1,000+; hundreds of thousands massacred in Rwanda; Estonian ferry sinks with 900 people; Bosnians, Serbs, and Croats continue savage fighting.

1995 Kobe, Japan earthquake kills more than 5,000 people; Fighting in former Yugoslavia quiets after Croat land offensive and NATO air strikes; large quakes rattle Mexico's Pacific coast, leaving scores dead; Shoemaker-Levi comet cluster hurtles into Jupiter; terrorist bomb smashes Oklahoma City federal building, killing 161.

1996 Earth's recent average surface temperature rises to new high; coldest winter in Minnesota in nearly a hundred years; huge oil spill off Welsh coast; 22 die in Hurricane Fran; world-wide, 28 million are estimated to be HIV+; world population at 5.789 billion.

1997 Guam airliner crash 228 lost; Haitan ferry *Pride of la Gonave* sinks with 200+ dead; 7.5 mag. Iran quake kills 1,500+;hurricane Pauline scours southwestern Mexico, killing over 200; new AIDS infections estimated at more than 3 million; approximately 5.8 million now have died from the disease; North Korean famine intensifies.

1998 El Nino soddens California and sends violent storms across the Midwest; storms in Europe; tornadoes in Alabama kill 34; drought plagues southern Asia where fires rage unchecked for weeks. U.S. aircraft severs gondola cable in Italy, and 20 die; embassy bombing in Nairobi kills 224, and U.S. retaliattion aims at Osama bin Laden; Swissair jet crashes, killing 229; North Korean famine unabated; Algerian civil war toll estimated at 26,000; hurricane Mitch leaves more than 10,000 dead in Central America.

1999 1000 die in earthquake in Columbia; Kosovar deaths at hands of Serbians estimated at 10,000; NATO air strikes halt the ethnic cleansing; NATO missile hits Chinese embassy and kills 3; NATO occupies Kosovo. 15 people took advantage of Oregon's legally-sanctioned assisted suicide law; 15 die in school shooting in Littleton, CO; world-wide AIDS infections estimated at 32 million; within days, earthquakes kill 10,000 in Turkey and 1100 in Taiwan. ■

Events Occult, Criminal & Futurist

For the credulous many, the far-sighted few, and the infallible of hindsight: a selection of the bizarre, the Fortean, the fiendish, and the long-term by year, 1890 on.

1890 Alaskans see image of mysterious sky-borne city (16 March); Hagenbeck's agents have found no evidence of Congo dinosaurs.

1891 Fresh snows inexplicably covered by layers of worms in Valley Bend district, Virginia; in Michigan, a seven-foot wild man covered with hair is seen.

1892 Unexplained explosions occur along the English Channel for several years; no evidence, damage, or explanation is ever found.

1893 A great luminous body passes over Virginia and North and South Carolina; visible 15-20 minutes; Smith demonstrates that parasites can be vectors for disease; Lizzie Borden acquitted of murder at Fall River, MA; the ghost of Admiral Tyrone is observed and seen to vanish at a large and exclusive dinner party in London.

1894 Pickering at Lowell Observatory sees conspicuous light floating above Mars (Nov. 14); marine saurian seen at mouth of Red Sea.

1895 Peasants near Odessa, Russia, attacked by strange beast; Roentgen announces the discovery of X-rays; at his 100-room Chicago hotel, H. H. Holmes maintained basement rooms with acid baths, torture devices, and dissection theaters, and he was tried and hung for the murders of 27 women.

1896 In the summer, hundreds of dead birds fall from the sky near Baton Rouge, Louisiana; Becquerel rays discovered.

1897 Giant illuminated airship passes over Kansas City, Chicago, Texas, and W. Virginia (April); the "Jig-Saw Murder" in which pieces of a corpse were found scattered around New York harbor.

1898 Phosphorescent strands of an asbestos-like substance fall on Montgomery, Alabama (Nov. 21); Olof Ohman digs up a Viking runic stone at Kensington MN.

1899 Strange yellow worms found strewn across an Alaskan glacier.

1900 A trickle of people appear across the world who speak no known language; many living and dead sea monsters reported.

1901 Alaskan Indians repeatedly report visions of a great airborne city; thousands of tiny snakes appear overnight in Canton MN; two credible English-women report a brief visit to Versailles of 1789.

1902 The *Freya* is discovered dismasted but otherwise undamaged; her crew is never found; mutineers aboard the *Veronica* kill seven; the ghost of Marie Laveau, the voodoo queen of New Orleans, commonly appears hereafter.

1903 Mud, ash, and fireballs fall across southeast Asia; a box of arrowheads is found in a coal seam

some 300 million years old; many animal mutilations in Staffordshire, England.

1904 At Wimbledon, England, an intense and inexplicable darkness occurs for 10 minutes (Apr. 17); in Virginia, ghost-like dogs exhume pottersfield corpses and eat them.

1905 Sheep are killed and their blood sucked from them (Badminton, Gloucester, Nov. 1); renewed Druid solstice ceremonies at Stonehenge.

1906 "Typhoid Mary" is found; playboy Harry Kendall Thaw kills noted architect Stanford White.

1907 Balls of light fall from sky and explode near Burlington VT (2 July); automatic writing received from monkish spirits at Glastonbury Abbey.

1908 A woman burns to death in her bed without the bed sheets being damaged or scorched (Blythe, England, in March); Belle Gunness of Laporte IN either killed 13 men and successfully escaped with their money, or was killed herself by her 14th victim, Ray Lamphere; enormous explosion in Siberia flattens 100 square miles of forest.

1909 Globules of hot metal fall from skies in Santa Cruz, CA; the information relayed by his ghost causes Lt. Sutton's body to be exhumed from Arlington National Cemetery; lighted airship repeatedly seen across New England (14-23 Dec.).

1910 Fresh blood falls from sky in South America; tales persist of the secret rooms in Glamis Castle, Scotland.

1911 Ground found covered with masses of jellies "the size of peas [and] contained eggs of numerous species from which the larvae soon emerged" (Eton, Bucks., England, 24 June); "Ax-Man of New Orleans" murders continue until 1919.

1912 An intensely black object is seen upon the Moon, estimated to be 250 miles long by 50 miles wide (27 Jan.).

1913 Ambrose Bierce prepares for Mexico; the spirit of Patience Worth begins to communicate through Pearl Curren's ouija board.

1914 Manchester, England, reports a spindle-shaped object transiting the Sun (10 Oct.); "Ruahine Ax Murders" of New Zealand.

1915 Bright spots appear upon the Moon in December; U-boat torpedo claimed to have blown sea-serpent-like animal out of the water; Alfred Wegener expresses the theory of continental drift; Henri Landru (Gambais, France) murders at least 11 people into the year 1919.

1916 Red tides along the U.S. coasts; a ghostly biplane appears at Montrose, Scotland; Bela Kiss of Czinkota, Hungary, is shown to have killed at least 24 young women, but is believed to have escaped during the confusion of the Great War.

1917 Luminous objects seen moving on the Moon; 70,000+ witness the miracle of Fatima; Amy Archer-Gilligan convicted of multiple murders at her Home for Elderly People.

1918 Unusual weather in many parts of the world; Shapley correctly discerns the relative size and shape of our galaxy; the jinxed German U-65 submarine is destroyed with all hands by a mysterious explosion.

1919 Captain James and his aircraft disappear over New York; Castlerigg (Cumbria) lights phenomena noted; Eddington verifies the curvature of light; Toronto millionaire Ambrose J. Small disappears without a trace.

1920 Shafts of light project from the Moon; furry humanoid killed and photographed on Columbia-Venezuelan border.

1921 Millions of tiny frogs suddenly appear in north London; more than a dozen ships disappear without a trace during the year; Alfred Watkins invents ley lines; crew of schooner *Carroll A. Deering* disappears.

1922 Rocks mysteriously fall from the sky for weeks at Chico CA (March); Evanek natives of Siberia report several encounters with mammoths; Sarah Winchester dies, her San Jose home having 160 rooms and 10,000 windows.

1923 Three large mounds discovered in Archimedes crater, Moon.

1924 The footprints of Day and Stewart end abruptly 40 yards from their intact aircraft; the intrepid pilots are never found; the Matthews death-ray has all London talking; Leopold and Loeb attempt and fail to perpetrate the perfect murder; Mina Crandon's claim to the *Scientific American*'s mediumship prize is disputed by Harry Houdini.

1925 Edale, Derbyshire, England, terrorized by many evidences of a werewolf; SS *Watertown* haunting reported, and a corroborative photo is displayed in the Cities Service Company's New York office.

1926 No trace of the Percy Expedition, seemingly swallowed by the northern Brazilian jungles; Heisenberg and Schroedinger lay the foundations of quantum theory.

1927 Black rain in Ireland; Lemaitre introduces the notion of the expanding universe; Muller successfully uses X-rays to induce mutations in fruit flies; Bible-quoting Earle Nelson is hanged at Winnipeg for the international murderers of at least 22 landladies; publication of *An Experiment with Time*.

1928 Danish training ship *Kobenhoven* disappears without trace after sailing from Montevideo.

1929 The infamous "Vampire of Düsseldorf" terrorizes the city; St. Valentine's Day massacre in Chicago; by now, 11 people associated with the opening of King Tut's tomb have died.

1930 Scores die and 300 are stricken by a poisonous fog in Belgium (Dec. 5); Peter Kürten (Düsseldorf) sadistically murders at least nine people before being caught and executed in 1931; mysterious explosions heard near Charleston SC.

1931 Lawrence invents the cyclotron.

1932 In the next five years, Dr. Morris Bolber and associates successfully murder and collect the insurance money for more than 30 victims.

1933 Mystery lights, presumably from aircraft, are seen over Scandinavia all winter.

1934 A 30-foot-long serpent is seen swimming in waters near Battle River, Alberta; first expedition organized to photograph the Loch Ness monster; Dr. Langoria of Cleveland OH destroys his death-ray for the good of humanity; Bonnie and Clyde die in a police ambush.

1935 Beaumont TX *Enterprise* reports that the U.S. government now possesses an invisibility ray; Domagk opens the way to sulfa drugs, which save hundreds of thousands of lives in WWII; Ma Barker dies in Florida shoot-out; a human arm disgorged by a shark in an Australian aquarium leads to acquittal of Patrick Brady for murder.

1936 First printed reference to the Lubaantun crystal skull; the "Mad Butcher of Kingsbury Run" terrorizes Cleveland OH for several years, and into the 1940s the total number of unsolved decapitations in the area number 28; last reported haunting of the Brown Lady of Raynham Hall, when the Lady is dimly photographed.

1937 Joe Ball is believed to have fed at least five waitresses to his alligators, but commits suicide before he can be arrested; Amelia Earhart disappears over the Central Pacific.

1938 Sudden increase in hot spring and geyser activity in Oregon and California; *War of the Worlds* broadcast leads to nation-wide panic.

1939 Nuclear fission achieved; Borley Rectory, "the most haunted spot in England", burns to the ground.

1940 U.S. government said to possess the Mohr ray, which explodes gunpowder at a distance.

1941 Many stories this year of pets finding their ways home after traveling long distances.

1942 Fermi and associates build the first controllable nuclear reactor; in Melbourne, the "Singing Strangler" kills three women to "get their voices;" Nazis dispatch an expedition to a Baltic island to take infrared photos of the British fleet (hypothesized to be visible at those wave lengths across the inside of the hollow Earth).

1943 U.S murder rate drops.

1944 Moth-man of Maryland in Hollywood, MD.

1945 Dr. Marcel Petiot of Paris kills 27 wartime escapees to profit from their wealth, estimated to total four million dollars; 5 TBF Avengers disappear in the Bermuda Triangle.

1946 ENIAC is the first high-speed electronic calculator; radiocarbon dating techniques developed.

1947 Pilot Kenneth Arnold compares the 9 objects he saw to "saucers;" near Roswell NM, four dead aliens are believed recovered by the U.S. government; Diebold and Harder coin the word "automation"; the Black Dahlia murder near Los Angeles goes unsolved; the ancient Antikythera astronomical computer is recognized for what it is.

1948 Ball lightning plagues Svaneke, Denmark; the ghost of psychic investigator Harry Price

appears repeatedly; the ghost of Charles II appears at the Drury Lane Theatre apparently to watch *Oklahoma!*; Captain Mantell dies chasing a UFO.

1949 Deliberate *War of the Worlds* hoax broadcast in Quito, Ecuador, and in the resulting riot the radio station is burnt to the ground with 20 dead inside; residents of Thorntown IN report a hairy bipedal creature; the case of possession which inspired *The Exorcist* occurs.

1950 Two photos made of a UFO made near McMinnville OR.

1951 Nazca Desert lines and glyphs publicized; Mrs. Reeser (St. Petersburg FL) is consumed by fire in a room mostly untouched by flame.

1952 Huge locust plague in Middle East; first atomic submarine *Nautilus* dedicated; Christine Jorgenson is first announced sex change; top of Mt. Everest reached; reports of flying saucers reach maximum in this year.

1953 DNA described as double helix; archaeologists find Ice Age artifacts thought oldest known; the Düsseldorf Doubles Killer attacks young couples until the year 1956.

1954 French bathyscaphe descends to record 13,284 feet; "Big Bang" theory; more than 40 visits of humanoid aliens reported this year; an epidemic of scratched and pitted auto windshields plagues Seattle; Ed Gein, necrophile and cannibal, commits his first murder; Eisenhower is rumored to have viewed alien remains in Hangar 18.

1955 Atomic clock developed; frog-like humanoids seen near Loveland, Ohio; Evansville IN woman almost pulled into river by greenish clawed hand.

1956 Lakenheath, England, UFO sighting confirmed visually and by radar; *Joyita* found adrift in the Samoan Islands, her 25 passengers and crew are missing.

1957 Artificial diamonds; *Sputnik*, first artificial satellite, is launched; mysterious white object hovers near Westville, Illinois; 200 reports in from Upper Marlboro, MD, of a hairy, gorilla-like creature; UFO sightings greatly increase.

1958 World's deepest oil well reaches 25,340 feet before being abandoned; ape-man seen in the Argentinean Corderilla; scale-covered humanoid jumps on car near Riverside CA; Starkweather-Fugate killings leave a trail of corpses across mid-America.

1959 *Lunik II* is first man-made object to reach Moon; *Lunik III* photographs back side of the Moon; Ocean City MD sea serpent hoax; luminous, green-eyed monsters leave tracks near Mansfield OH; hundreds of fishes fall on Lismore, N.S.W.

1960 Remains of man 30,000 years old found in Mexico; X-15 rocket plane reach 2,550 mph; small humanoid alien with glowing eyes seen in Arizona; tiny frogs fall from the sky in Columbia; Pope John is rumored to have cried for three days upon reading the terrible Fatima prophecy.

1961 Gagarin is first man into space; X-15 reaches 4,070 mph and 40+ miles of altitude; Betty and Barney Hill abducted by aliens; Hess develops new version of continental drift; career of international criminal Jacques Mesrine begins and con-

tinues until dying in a shootout in 1979, including murders, multiple escapes from prison, and fabulously successful robberies.

1962 X-15 reaches 59 miles; London smog kills 55; Loch Ness Investigation formed; *Mariner 2* sends back first close-up data of another planet, Venus; two brothers report a succession of bizarre apparitions in Scotland.

1963 New land speed-record is 407+ mph; Viking ruins in Newfoundland 500 years older than Columbus; in Greece, live frogs fall in a downpour.

1964 Socorro NM UFO landing; world population increasing at 63 million per year; new land speed-record is 434+ mph; Selbyville MD swamp-man hoax; the Boston Strangler operates until 1964, killing 13 women.

1965 Four UFOs in a diamond formation are tracked from Oklahoma to New Mexico; new land speed record of 576+ mph; sea serpent seen in South River, near Annapolis MD; Vinland Map authenticated by scholars.

1966 Vatican abolishes index of banned books; Richard Speck murders eight nurses in Chicago; Charles Whitman shoots 46 people from the observation tower on the U. Texas (Austin) campus (17, including Whitman, die); surge in UFO sightings leads to establishment of the Condon Committee.

1967 Humanoid remains found 2.5 million years old; world's first white gorilla located; Canadian touches UFO and is hospitalized with symptomatic radiation poisoning; first human is placed in cryonic storage.

1968 First heart-transplant; *Apollo 8* astronauts orbit the Moon; hooded figure floating over the altar seen at Newby Church, England; a ghostly black cat at Killakee, Ireland, defies exorcism.

1969 Barnard college women seek co-ed dormitories; *Apollo 11* astronauts land on the Moon; *Apollo 11* team reportedly sees flying saucers on the Moon; Jimmy Carter sees a UFO; Condon Report closes the Air Force's door to UFOs; Tate-LaBianca murders committed by the Mansons; the five Zodiac murders in the San Francisco area are never solved; the Silver Cliff CO spook lights are summarized in *National Geographic*.

1970 "Champ" the sea-serpent of Lake Champlain, is seen again; Dale Merle Nelson (British Columbia) alleges that his multiple murders were provoked by LSD.

1971 An article details more than 80 cases in which short-wave messages were received hours or days after transmission.

1972 Gill man seen at Lake Thetis, British Columbia; another frog-like humanoid seen near Loveland OH; *Mariner 9* orbits Mars; Herbert Mullin commits at least 13 murders as blood sacrifices to save California from a great earthquake; the thallium poisonings in Hertfordshire affect more than 70; after Flight 401 crashes, the ghosts of the captain and flight engineer are seen repeatedly on other Eastern airline flights.

1973 Public Health Service links smoking to fetal and infant risks; Sykesville MD monster repeatedly

continued next page

Events Occult, Criminal and Futurist, *cont.*

observed; *Pioneer 10* reports on Jupiter's magnetic field and sends back first close pictures; giant man-like alligator seen near Newton NJ; upsurge in UFO reports continues into 1975; the Zebra race-killings leave 15 dead in San Francisco, and arrests are made the following year.

1974 Sextuplets born in U.S.; *Mariner 10* gets first close-up images of planet Mercury; *Soyuz 15* links with *Salyut* space station; Green Revolution technology raises crop yields; *Pioneer II* transmits close-up pictures of Jupiter; Vinland map denounced as modern fraud; many cattle mutilations recorded in Nebraska and South Dakota; De Feo family murders (the beginning of the Amityville Horror) leave six dead.

1975 Chinese uncover some 6000 life-size pottery warriors; new proto-human remains dated at 3.75 million years; giant biped lizard seen near Milton KT; Viking 1 detects no positive signs of life on Mars; handsome young Ted Bundy begins killing about one woman monthly until caught in early 1978; Yorkshire Ripper begins slayings for the next five years.

1976 Foul-smelling humanoids repeatedly seen in Baltimore County, MD; India plans penalties for more than two children per family; "Cornish sea serpent" photos; ship with 37 aboard vanishes in Bermuda Triangle; Son of Sam killer terrorizes young lovers in New York City.

1977 Cellular fossils 3.4 billion years old found in Africa; cigar and pipe-smoking banned on U.S. airliners; first black woman joins Presidential cabinet; the spirit of Teresita Basa apparently contacts a woman in the Philippines to name her murderer.

1978 Humanoid footprints 3.5 million years old found; Proposition 13 wins in California; first test-tube baby born in London; tall alien seen in Palpala, Argentina; 21 bodies discovered buried at John Gacy's home; megalithic remains demonstrated on and around Bimini; Northamptonshire, England, UFO multiple-abduction incident; the Hillside Strangler leaves a dozen or more women dead in the Los Angeles area.

1979 Gold prices in U.S. continue to soar; new sightings of frog-like humanoids around Loveland OH; Rudy Warner UFO sighting near San Antonio TX; Lake City MN saucer-site discovery.

1980 Indian satellite in orbit; many witness the Huffman TX UFO contact; *Voyager I* discovers 15th Saturnian moon; very tall humanoids met near Santa Rosa, Argentina; Mackal and Powell lead an expedition into the Congo to find a sauropod-like creature; the Scarsdale Diet Murder.

1981 32-bit CPU; serial murders of 18 black youths in Atlanta; apparitions of the Blessed Virgin Mary reported from Medugorje, Yugoslavia; space shuttle *Columbia* in orbit; Jack Sutton (the Yorkshire Ripper) sentenced to life; French TGV "bullet-train" inaugurated; Wayne B. Williams arrested for the 28 victims in the Atlanta murders, but unpublicized at that time are 38 more murders, all females.

1982 Scientists find first land animal fossils in Antarctica; life found at volcanic vents in Pacific, 8600 feet below surface; Greenpeace boats block dumping of radioactive waste off Spain; Tudor flagship *Mary Rose* raised mostly intact; first artificial heart recipient; Arnfinn Nesset of Oarkdal, Norway, admits killing 27 elderly people in order to accumulate money for charities.

1983 Pioneer 10 passes beyond orbit of Pluto; world population estimated at 4.72 billion; Dennis Nilsen of London, the "creative psychopath", admits to killing and dismembering 15 people.

1984 First human free-float in space; gunman kills 20 in San Ysidro CA McDonald's; hepatitis virus identified.

1985 Nuclear-equipped vessels banned from New Zealand waters; divers recover millions in treasure from the Spanish galleon *Nuestra Señora de Atocha* off Florida; hackers begin to tap Pentagon computers; Richard Ramirez charged with 14 "night-stalker" murders; wreck of *Titanic* located; CD-ROM.

1986 *Voyager 2* gives first good views of Uranus; severed human finger falls from sky onto auto in Berlin; *Vega I* returns close-ups of Halley's comet; African AIDS cases number at least 50,000; very tall humanoids again reported near Santa Rosa, Argentina; super-light plane circles the world non-stop.

1987 Galaxy seen 12 billion light years distant; systematic sonar search made of Loch Ness; superconducting compound discovered; Atlanta, Georgia, home plagued by traces and pools of human blood throughout it; U.S patent office allows patenting of animals created by genetic engineering; new analysis shows Vinland Map may be genuine.

1988 Horicon WI poltergeist; geneticists postulate common ancestress of all humanity; defying the odds, several meteorites fall directly on houses in central Europe; evidence found of planet-like bodies circling other stars; the "lizard man" confounds South Carolina; unrelated ice falls in Weistropp and Poing, Germany; saucer-like craft seen in Haywards Heath, Sussex; "George" haunts the U.S.S. *Forrestal*; Soviet orbital endurance flight of 366 days.

1989 Mysterious large designs ("crop circles") are found impressed in English wheat fields; on 27 June, aerial lights and explosions are reported all over Greece; giant octopus reportedly capsizes a small vessel; large greenish mass overflies Los Angeles; three enormous inscribed stone tables found in Peru; *Galileo* probe launched; *Magellan* orbiter begins radar mapping of Venus.

1990 Bushels of hay fall from sky in Bottmingen, Switzerland; I Am movement indicates that dismayingly negative karma will be abroad in the world for about the next 12 years; Shroud of Turin dated as approx. 700 years old; some 600 crop-circles appear on four continents; Kharkhov Radio-Astronomical Institute detects mysterious radio transmissions from the vicinity of Altair.

1991 Crop-circle phenomenon a fraud, perpetrators claim, but they are not believed; sacred serpent of Yig shoots trespassing human; theory of a plasma-generated steady-state universe gains adherents; grounded electrical fields create bizarre bovine behaviors on New Zealand dairy farms.

1992 Eight towers discovered in Oman believed the remnants of Ubar, the Atlantis of the sands; an enormous spreading fungus spawned some ten thousand years ago weighing over 100 tons and extending more than 30 acres near Crystal Falls, MI; UFO scare continues in Russia.

1993 CD-ROM is a household term; nearing Mars, the *Mars Observer* spacecraft ceases all communication; the Biosphere 2 experiment is in its second year; *Jurassic Park* stomps its way to filmdom box-office records.

1994 Mass suicide by Order of the Solar Temple believers; Andrei Chikatilo, serial killer of 55 people, executed in Russia; radiation and biological mass experiments made on unsuspecting U.S. citizens in the 1950s.

1995 Poison gas attacks in Tokyo subways lead to investigation and arrests of Japanese religious cult; renewed paranormal activity along Maryland's Route 40 "abduction corridor"; *Galileo* spacecraft to Jupiter reactivated, probe lasts 57 minutes in the atmosphere while another portion of the mission makes flybys of the moons.

1996 appearance of Comet Hayatuke; enigmatic crop-circles continue to mutilate grain fields across Europe; prosecutions of satanic child molestations collapse as U.S. juries begin to ask for evidence; evidence of extrasolar planets becomes routine; perceived conspiracies of every variety titillate the far Left and Right in the U.S. as marketers learn how to penetrate these trend-setting demographics.

1997 appearance of Comet Hale-Bopp; impressive photos continue to flow from Hubble; the lost library of Ivan the Terrible is "nearly located" under the Kremlin; alien abduction accounts continue to reap millions for writers and producers; Clyde Tombaugh, discoverer of Pluto, dies; 39 members of the Heaven's Gate cult commit mass suicide in order to transmit themselves to a flying saucer near Hale-Bopp; *Pathfinder* lands on Mars.

1998 God does not appear on channel 18, and his prophet admits he was wrong, two remarkable events in one day. Evidence accumulates for the open expansion of the universe; the male impotence drug Viagra is introduced and becomes a best seller; India and Pakistan conduct multiple nuclear tests; great effort to update computer chips as the millennium approaches--the problem is termed "Y2K".

1999 Researchers fashion computer chip elements which are one molecule thin; first successful around-the-world balloon flight; splendid total solar eclipse delights Europe and Middle East; despite widespread naysaying, biological cloning experiments continue unabated. ∎

A Hundred Years & More

Important events and commercial curiosities from 1890 on.

1890 First entirely steel-framed building erected in Chicago; first electric tube railway in London; Sitting Bull killed in Sioux uprising; first ice-cream sundae; U.S. resident population is 62.9 million.

1891 First practical hydroelectric station; electric torch adopted in England.

1892 Cholera vaccine; Cape-Johannesburg railroad completed; crown top for bottles developed; diesel engine patented.

1893 World Exposition in Chicago; first practical roll film; shredded wheat cereal.

1894 War between China and Japan; Captain Dreyfus exiled to Devil's Island; first wireless.

1895 Roentgen discovers X-rays; cigarette-making machine invented; the Lumieres open their Cinematographie.

1896 Klondike gold rush begins; Addressograph patents confirmed; Ford's first motorcar; periscopes for submarines; first modern Olympic Games held in Athens.

1897 Mimeo stencils are invented; first cathode-ray tube.

1898 Spanish-American War; disk recordings become practical; commercial aspirin appears; Kellogg's Corn Flakes; tubular flashlight.

1899 Rutherford discovers alpha and beta rays; general adoption of typewriters underway.

1900 Boxer Rebellion in China; Kodak "Brownie" camera; Count Zeppelin launches 420-foot airship; U.S. public debt is $1.263 billion; U.S. resident population is 76 million.

1901 President McKinley assassinated; Queen Victoria dies; human blood groups classified; first trans-Atlantic wireless.

1902 Boer War; first steam-turbine-driven passenger ship; modern macadam developed; first alum-dried powdered milk; puffed cereals; first Teddy bear; first Caruso gramophone recording; economical hydrogenated fats make fats for soap and cooking plentiful.

1903 Wright Bros. fly first heavier-than-air powered aircraft; first fluorescent light; postal meter developed; center-frame motorcycle engine.

1904 Broadway subway opens in NYC; thermos flask patented; tracks (as opposed to wheels) first appear on farm machinery; kapok life belts; Russo-Japanese War.

1905 Cullinan diamond (3,000 carats) found, largest to that date; steam turbines standard for British navy; abortive revolution in Russia; electric motor horn; chemical foam fire extinguisher; Special Theory of Relativity.

1906 U.S. troops occupy Cuba till 1909; *Lusitania* and *Mauretania* launched; the juke box; mass-production oef marine outboard motors.

1907 Rasputin great influence in Czarist Russia; animated cartoons; electric washing machine; household detergent; upright vacuum cleaner.

1908 Minkowski formulates his 4-dimensional geometry; paper cups for drinking.

1909 Robert E. Peary reaches the North Pole; first powered flight across the English Channel; double-decker buses in U.K.

1910 Murray and Hjort undertake the first deep-sea research expedition; radio-direction finder; spring-operated mouse trap; incorporation of the Boy Scouts of America; U.S. resident population is 92 million.

1911 Zapata arrives in Mexico City, but the battles have just begun; revolution in China leads to the republic under Sun Yat-sen; the electric frying pan; Norwegian explorer Roald Amundsen reaches South Pole.

1912 Wilson's cloud chamber leads to the detection of protons, electrons; cellophane patented; Saville Row creates what will be named the "trench coat" in WWI; Cadillac shows first electric self-starter for automobiles; two self-service grocery stores in California.

1913 The Balkan War begins; Wilson inaugurated; electric starters for motorcycles; vitamin A; income tax and popular election of senators added to U.S. Constitution.

1914 The Great War begins; first air raids; first use of the Panama Canal.

1915 The *Lusitania* is sunk, and consternation and anger follow in the United States; enormous and unprecedented casualties in the Great War; cereal flakes are marketed; chlorine gas used as weapon; gas mask; the zipper is patented.

1916 Gallipoli; Verdun; Easter uprising; Jutland; the Somme; mechanical windshield wipers; General Theory of Relativity; Pershing's raid in Mexico.

1917 United States enters WWI; the Russian Revolution unfolds and the Bolsheviks seize power; mustard gas; Ford mass-produces tractors.

1918 WWI ends; Russian Civil War; regular U.S. airmail service; world influenza epidemic kills 21.6 million; powered flight reaches 150+ mph and 30,000+ feet; electric clocks.

1919 Prohibition enacted in U.S.; first trans-Atlantic flight (1,880 miles in 16:12 hours); grease-guns; parachutes.

1920 Prohibition in effect in U.S.; the Bolsheviks win Russia; first radio broadcasting station on the air; teabags; U.S. public debt is $24.3 billion; women's suffrage ratified; U.S. resident population is 105.7 million.

1921 Rorschach devises his inkblot tests; inflation of the German mark begins; KDKA broadcasts sports; Capek coins the word "robot."

1922 Revival and growth of Ku Klux Klan; insulin is isolated; first practical postal franking machine;

Soviet May Day slogans omit "world revolution"; water-skiing; Mussolini marches on Rome.

1923 Teapot Dome scandal rocks Harding administration; German mark stabilized; continuing Klan violence in Georgia; Nazi *putsch* in Munich fails; King Tut's tomb opened; whooping-cough vaccine.

1924 Leopold and Loeb convicted of the kidnap-slaying of Bobby Franks; paper egg cartons developed; Kleenex.

1925 W. Pauli formulates Exclusion Principle; I.G. Farben formed; Sun Yat-sen dies; German SS formed; Scopes "Monkey Trial"; aerial commercial crop-dusting.

1926 Dr. Goddard fires his first liquid-fuel rocket; Chiang stages coup in Canton; Trotsky expelled from Politburo; Rolex waterproof watch.

1927 Charles A. Lindbergh flies solo and non-stop between NYC-Paris; the *Jazz Singer* first feature-length sound film; first remote juke box; pop-up toaster; Sacco and Vanzetti executed, later cleared by proclamation in 1977.

1928 Television experiments; Byrd expedition sails to Antarctica; teletypes come into use; waterproof cellophane developed; Geiger counter; vitamin C.

1929 Great stockmarket crash, 24 Oct.; *Graf Zeppelin* circles the world; 16mm color film developed; Scotch tape; tune-playing automobile horn.

1930 Technocracy movement at its highest; flash bulb ends flash powder explosions at press conferences; first frozen foods marketed; bathysphere; cyclotron; Pluto discovered; telescopic umbrella; U.S. public debt now $16.18 billion; U.S. resident population now 122.8 million.

1931 German millionaire support builds for Nazi Party; British Navy mutiny at Invergordon; Empire State Building formally opens; Al Capone imprisoned; Alka-Seltzer; electric razor; George Washington Bridge (3,500 feet) completed.

1932 Gandhi arrested; Roosevelt elected President in landslide; Mussolini drains Pontine Marshes; Lindbergh baby kidnapped; first car radios; first Gallup Poll; Mars Bars; invention of zoom lens; Zippo lighter introduced.

1933 Hitler named Chancellor of Germany; Japan withdraws from League of Nations; U.S. abandons gold standard; freed Gandhi weighs 90 pounds; first German concentration camp (Dachau) established; day-glo pigments; the game *Monopoly* published; fluorescent lights introduced commercially.

1934 Sandino assassinated by Somoza supporters; San Francisco general strike ends; Huey Long assumes dictatorship of Louisiana; first commercial launderette.

1935 Dust storms in high plains; first Pan-Am Clipper departs San Francisco for China; Social

continued next page

A Hundred Years & More, cont.

Security system enacted; Huey Long assassinated; Mao's Long March concludes in Yenan; first passenger flight for the DC-3; mass-market paperback books; Richter earthquake scale; tape recorder is retailed.

1936 Nazis enter Rhineland; Italy conquers Ethiopia; Spanish Civil War; Jesse Owens wins 4 gold medals at Berlin Olympics; Axis powers sign pact; Boulder Dam in operation; first Volkswagen.

1937 Purges continue in Soviet Union; DuPont patents nylon; dirigible *Hindenburg* destroyed by fire; Japanese sink U.S. gunboat *Panay*; Golden Gate Bridge (4,200 feet) completed; first supermarket carts; Buchenwald concentration camp opens.

1938 Mexico appropriates all foreign oil holdings; Germans enter Austria unopposed; Kristallnacht; electric steam iron with thermostat; instant coffee; nylon; ball-point pen is patented; prototype of photocopy machine; major German-American Bund rally at Madison Square Garden; arrests of Jews throughout Germany and Austria.

1939 Germany annexes the Czechs; Madrid falls to Franco; cellophane wrappers first appear in stores; annexation of Baltic states; Germany invades Poland, and France and Britain declare war; Rockefeller Center opens; DDT; yellow-fever vaccine; radar.

1940 Finland surrenders to Soviets; Nazis strike at Denmark and Norway; Churchill becomes Prime Minister; Holland and Belgium fall; Dunkirk evacuation; Roosevelt elected for third term; fall of France; automatic gearbox for automobiles; inflatable life vests; radar operational and deployed in Britain; artificial insemination developed; penicillin produced in quantity; U.S. public debt now $42.97 billion; U.S. resident population is now 131.7 million.

1941 Aerial battle of Britain joined; Lend-Lease; U.S. institutes military draft; the Jeep adopted as general-purpose military vehicle; Germans invade Soviet Union; Japan attacks in Far East and at Pearl Harbor.

1942 Singapore, Philippines fall; major carrier battle off Midway Island; German siege of Leningrad continues; Crimea falls; Doolittle raid on Tokyo; battle of Stalingrad joined; U.S. lands on Guadalcanal; Allies land in North Africa; atomic fission succeeds; bazooka; napalm.

1943 Germans surrender at Stalingrad; Warsaw Ghetto uprising; Germany defeated in the biggest tank battle (Kursk) in history; Allies land in Sicily; Mussolini deposed then reseated by Germans; Allies invade Italy; Soviets crack Dnieper River line; Marshall Islands fall; ball-point pens gain first acceptance; aqualung; LSD.

1944 De Gaulle is Free-French commander-in-chief; continuing massive air raids on Germany; Crimea freed; Allies take Rome; D-Day landings in Normandy; Marianas under attack; Paris falls to Allies; Roosevelt re-elected for fourth term; mass killings in Nazi concentration camps revealed; V-1 and V-2 missiles hit London; MacArthur returns to Philippines; Battle of the Bulge; nerve gas.

1945 Auschwitz liberated; Yalta conference; Iwo Jima falls; Remagen Bridge taken; Roosevelt dies; Mussolini executed; Hitler commits suicide; full extent of Nazi death camps revealed; Berlin falls; Churchill resigns; battle of Okinawa; United Nations formed; Potsdam conference; atomic attacks on Hiroshima and Nagasaki; Japan surrenders; Korea partitioned; Jackie Robinson first modern African-American major leaguer; Nuremberg war-crime trials; Tupperware.

1946 ENIAC computer unveiled by War Department; Churchill proclaims Iron Curtain; violence continues in Palestine; labor strikes dot U.S.; Chinese Civil War renewed; smoking said to cause lung cancer; uprising in Vietnam; Chester F. Carlson unveils "xerography"; bikini swimsuits; espresso coffee machines.

1947 U.S. gives up attempts to broker a peace in China; religious strife in India; Marshall Plan advanced; last New York streetcar retired; India and Pakistan independent; Polaroid Land Camera; House committee looks for subversives in films.

1948 Gandhi assassinated; Communist coup in Czechoslovakia; civil war continues in the Palestine Mandate; Berlin airlift starts; state of Israel recognized and war continues; 200-inch telescope at Mt. Palomar; New York subway fare doubles to ten cents; Kinsey Report on sex; Scrabble; solid-body electric guitar; Velcro invented; transistor developed at Bell Labs; 33 1/3 long-playing records introduced.

1949 Chinese Communists take Peking; NATO organized; Berlin blockade concludes; German Federal Republic created; Red scare continues in U.S.; USSR explodes nuclear device; Nationalist Chinese forces retreat to Taiwan; Indonesia achieves independence; cable television; color television tube; key-starting auto ignitions.

1950 One-piece windshield for Cadillacs; RCA announces color television; French appeal for aid against the Viet Minh; South Korea invaded; Inchon landings; China enters the Korean War; Gussie Moran sports lace underwear at Wimbledon; Diners' Club card; Xerox 914 commercial copier; U.S. public debt now $256 billion; U.S. resident population is now 150.7 million.

1951 MacArthur stripped of all commands; color television transmitted from Empire State Building; hydrogen bomb tests at Eniwetok; truce talks in Korea; Cinerama; Chrysler introduces power steering; 3-color stoplights for autos introduced.

1952 Queen Elizabeth II accedes to British throne; Walk/Don't Walk lighted pedestrian signs in New York City; GM offers built-in airconditioning in some 1953 cars; Eva Peron dies; transistorized hearing aid; hydrogen bomb announced; videotape.

1953 Joseph Stalin dies; DNA described as double-helix in form; Pius XII approves of psychoanalysis in therapy; Rosenbergs executed; East Berlin uprising quashed; Korean armistice; U.S. flight to suburbs noted; Kennedy-Bouvier marriage; expedition searches for yeti; measles vaccine.

1954 Nautilus is first atomic-powered submarine; Army-McCarthy hearings; Murrow takes on McCarthy; Dien Bien Phu falls; Supreme Court orders school integration; North and South Vietnam established; retractable ball-point pen; silicon transistor.

1955 Missile with atomic warhead exploded in Nevada test; Albert Einstein dies; Warsaw Pact treaty signed; rebellion in Algeria; Mickey Mouse Club debuts on television; air-to-air guided missile; Disneyland opens.

1956 Bus boycott in Montgomery; suburbs boom in U.S.; Khrushchev denounces Stalin; Nassir seizes Suez Canal; Hungarian Revolt; Teflon Company formed; go-karts.

1957 Smoking shown to promote cancer; Nike Hercules atomic warheads to defend U.S. cities from enemy aircraft; Sputnik shocks U.S.; Mackinac Straits Bridge (3,800 feet) completed.

1958 Elvis Presley drafted; *Nautilus* sails across North Pole under the ice; Faubus closes Little Rock's high schools; Pan Am inaugurates first 707 jet service to Paris; Sabin polio vaccine; communications satellite; hula-hoop.

1959 Castro gains power in Cuba; Ford's Edsel judged a failure; Volvo introduces safety belts.

1960 Unrest continues in Algeria; artificial kidney introduced; lunch counter sit-ins begin; Brasilia (the first public-relations city) is open for business; birth control pill goes on sale in U.S.; first weather satellite; popularity of portable transistor radios begins; U.S. public debt now $284 billion; U.S. resident population is now 179.3 million.

1961 Eisenhower warns against military-industrial complex; the Leakeys find earliest human remains; Berlin Wall; Peace Corps established; Bay of Pigs landing in Cuba; Valium.

1962 Cuban missile crisis nearly brings nuclear war; gallium-arsenide semiconductor laser; Polaroid color film .

1963 Enormous civil rights demonstration in Washington; Kennedy assassinated; coup in Vietnam removes Diem; mob actions increasingly common in the South.

1964 Aswan dam in service; satellite transmissions link Europe and North America; Beatles enormously popular; Nehru dies; Verrazano-Narrows Bridge (4,260 feet) completed; LBJ signs Civil Rights Act; Tonkin Gulf resolution; 3-D laser-holography; Moog synthesizer; FTC requires health warning on cigarettes.

1965 Malcolm X assassinated; race riots in Watts; Pope disassociates Jews from guilt for the crucifixion of Jesus; great Northeastern states' electrical black-out; Kevlar; radial tires; IBM word processor.

1966 Cultural Revolution in China; opposition to Vietnam War increases; sniper kills 12 at U. Texas; miniskirts; first black Senator elected by popular vote; Dolby-A; skateboards; body counts.

1967 The Six-Day War; the Summer of Love; first black Supreme Court justice; antiwar protests accelerate; body count now a regular feature of Vietnam reports; Satellite transmissions link Europe and North America; 209 pounds of heroin seized in Georgia; bell bottoms.

1968 Tet Offensive stuns civilian United States; Martin Luther King assassinated; black riots; student revolt in Paris; Robert Kennedy assassinated; Soviets quash liberalizing Czech government; Spain voids 1492 law banning Jews; Democrats' convention in Chicago battles protesters; *Apollo 8* astronauts orbit the Moon.

1969 Skyjackings to Cuba continue; Barnard women integrate men's dorm; first artificial heart implant; anti-Vietnam War demonstrations in more than 40 cities on same weekend; Woodstock; 250,000 protesters march on capital; *Apollo 11* lands on the Moon; Mylai massacre; Boeing 747 jumbo jet; oil spill fouls Santa Barbara beaches; first flight of Concorde Mach 2 jetliner.

1970 Radical chic; Palestinian group hijacks five planes; De Gaulle dies; "Weathermen" arrested for bomb plot; tuna recalled as mercury-contaminated; bar codes; floppy disks; windsurfing; U.S. public debt now $370 billion; U.S. resident population is now 203.3 million.

1971 Reaction against drug use in armed forces at full tide; hot pants; Pentagon Papers printed; liquid-crystal displays.

1972 Ten members in European Common Market; Nixon in China; burglars caught in Democrats' Watergate headquarters; 11 Israelis massacred at Olympics; electronic pocket calculators; *Pong* video game.

1973 Last trip to Moon; oil embargo; Bosporus Bridge (3,524 feet) completed; recombinant DNA.

1974 Patty Hearst is kidnapped by Symbionese Liberation "Army"; widespread gasoline shortage in U.S.; Nixon resigns from Presidency; Green Revolution agricultural technology.

1975 South Vietnam falls; Cambodia falls; civil war in Beirut; Atari video games.

1976 Extinction of animal species a public concern; Mao Tse-tung dies; Cray I supercomputer.

1977 Trans-Alaskan oil pipeline in operation; three Israeli settlements approved on West Bank; optical fiber telephone line; last trip of Orient Express; protesters try to stop Seabrook nuclear power plant.

1978 Panama Canal to be controlled by Panama; Proposition 13 wins in California, heralding decline of capital expenditures across the nation; 1 U.S. dollar equals 175 Japanese yen; first test-tube baby born in London.

1979 The Shah flees Iran; 3 Mile Island nuclear leak; Somoza ousted in Nicaragua; U.S. embassy in Tehran seized and hostages held; Soviets enter Afghanistan; Rubik's cube; Sony Walkman.

1980 An ounce of gold reaches $802 U.S.; U.S. inflation rate highest in 33 years; banking deregulated; hostage rescue fails in Iran; Solidarity recognized in Poland; gold rush in the Amazon; Dolby-C; U.S. public debt now $908 billion; U.S. resident population is now 226.5 million.

1981 Iran releases embassy hostages; millions in Poland on strike; U.S. budget deficit reaches one trillion dollars; Israeli raid destroys Iraqi nuclear reactor; Humber Bridge (4,626 feet) completed; widespread marches and rallies against nuclear weapons and arms in Europe; strange immune-system disease noted by CDC.

1982 Worldwide oil glut; war for Falkland Islands; 800,000 march against nuclear weapons in New York City; Israeli incursion reaches Beirut; PLO moves to Tunisia.

1983 Aquino assassinated upon arriving in Manila; widespread missile protests in Europe;

world population estimated at 4.7 billion.

1984 VCR taping legalized in U.S.; battles in Beirut continue; AIDS virus isolated; federal estimate of 350,000 homeless in U.S.; passive inhalation of cigarette smoke held to cause disease; 900,000 march in Manila; President Reagan asks if you've ever had it so good.

1985 Kidnappings continue in Beirut; Gorbachev chosen as USSR chairman; Rock Hudson hospitalized for AIDS; France sinks Greenpeace vessel; U.S. trade balance now negative; terrorism becomes widespread tactic of splinter groups; *Achille Lauro* hijacking and murders; massive federal spending continues to fuel economic expansion; U.S. public debt now $1.82 trillion, doubled since 1980.

1986 *Challenger* shuttle explosion effectively shuts down NASA manned program for several years; English Channel tunnel project okayed; Chernobyl nuclear disaster; crack cocaine epidemic in U.S.

1987 One million dead in Iran-Iraq War; Dow average loses 508 points in one day; this year 13,468 AIDS deaths in U.S.; Arabs within Israel begin general resistance; 50 million VCRs in U.S.

1988 The term "Greenhouse effect" is widely used; RU-486; widespread drought in U.S.; U.S. AIDS cases top 60,000; U.S. estimated to have spent $51.6 billion on illegal drugs this year.

1989 The U.S. "war on drugs"; political stress in Soviet Union; Salman Rushdie affair begins; Panama invasion topples Noriega; Tiananmen Square demonstrations in Beijing; federally insured bank losses in U.S. estimated at $500 billion dollars; U.S. citizens spent $49.8 billion on illegal drugs last year; CDs become dominant playback medium in United States.

1990 Iraq invades Kuwait, and U.S. organizes expeditionary force in opposition; South African government lifts emergency decrees; U.S. public debt at $3.23 trillion; Hubble telescope fiasco; U.S. estimated to have spent $40 billion on illegal drugs this year; U.S. resident population now 248.7 million.

1991 The Gulf War; coup foiled in USSR; Arab-Israeli talks; at the end of May, AIDS deaths in U.S. total 113,426; import auto sales now account for 1/3 of U.S. market; USSR dissolves into constituent republics; Gorbachev resigns; one fifth of sub-Saharan college graduates believed to be HIV+.

1992 Economic recession in industrial nations, homelessness and mass layoffs widely reported; rioting in Los Angeles and other U.S. cities over Rodney King verdict, 52 killed and damages over $1 billion; U.S. military deployed to aid against famine amid Somalia civil war; vicious ethnic warfare intensifies in former Yugoslavia; Czechs and Slovaks separate.

1993 FBI lays siege to Branch Davidians near Waco, and 80 finally die; Clinton first Democratic President since Carter; strife continues in Bosnia; North Korea withdraws from nuclear nonproliferation treaty; U.S. troops withdrawn from Somalia; Congress votes over 130 U.S. military bases closed; U.S. unemployment declines; U.S. national debt $4.35 trillion.

1994 NAFTA agreement ratified by all parties; CIA's Aldrich Ames found to be Russian spy; Anglican church ordains first female priests; first universal-suffrage election in South Africa signals end of white dominance; Israel and PLO sign self-rule accord; O.J. Simpson charged in 2 murders; fifty years since WWII Normandy landings; professional baseball strike marks the decline of that sport; U.S. lands in Haiti and successfully returns Aristide to presidency.

1995 In the U.S., about one in ten are wired into theInternet; O.J. Simpson acquitted of murder; peace progresses in Northern Ireland, Bosnia, and Middle East; Rabin assassinated in Israel; Colin Powell declines to run for U.S. presidency; U.S. federal debt at $5 trillion.

1996 U.S. federal workers return to work after budget crisis; one killed when bomb explodes at Atlanta Olympic Games; Mt. Everest climbing deaths rise steadily; Islamic rebels capture Kabul; abortion struggle continues in Senate; copyright piracy continues friction between U.S. and China; U.S. national debt at $5.2 trillion; prosperity reigns in U.S.; ill-conceived attempts to control immigration and drug-addiction; McVeigh held in Oklahoma City bombing; Kaczinski indicted as Unabomber suspect.

1997 Approx. 275 million residents of U.S.; 40% of the U.S. now connected to the Internet. Clinton under heavy pressure concerning sexual conduct; Dow-Jones average breaks 8,000 in July; tobacco companies admit that tobacco is addictive; comet Hale-Bopp passes nearby in March; Hong Kong reverts to China; Ames Research Center to have department of astrobiology; Diana, Princess of Wales, dead in auto crash; Ted Turner gives $1 billion to United Nations.

1998 Pres. Clinton under cloud from possible perjury and obstruction of justice; U.S. economic expansion shows signs of slowing; Kaczinski pleads guilty to unabombings; U.S. federal budget shows small surplus for the first time in 30 years; Rwanda executes 22 for genocide; Iraq wages apparently successful end to UN weapons inspections; economic and social turmoil continue in Russia; passenger arrivals and departures at Chicago O'Hare number 70 million in 1997.

1999 Pres. Clinton impeached by the House, but the Senate acquits him; U.S. economy surges; Dow Jones average finishes above 11,000 for first time in history; very large balance of payment deficits for U.S.; violent crime in U.S. has not been lower since 1973; AMA approves a union for medical doctors. ■

Artist: Tim Callender

reprinted from *Space Gamer/Fantasy Gamer*

CALL OF CTHULHU IS THE ONLY ROLE-PLAYING GAME WHERE...

BY RICHARD FICHERA

...the gamemaster says, "you see a large cave ahead", and the characters respond with, "I think my mother's calling me."

...the gamemaster puts a miniature figure of an encounter monster on the table and players haven't the faintest idea what it is.

...combat skills are the weakest abilities on every character sheet in the party.

...the most experienced characters have the highest movement rates.

...the big treasure of the adventure is a musty old book that eliminates your character from the next scenario just by looking at the pictures.

...there are no thieves in the party (by profession or otherwise).

Lady Jane Simpson Age 32, Priveleged Dilettante 1890s

STR 9 CON 13 SIZ 8 INT 13 POW 15 Idea 65% Luck 75% Know 85%
DEX 15 APP 14 SAN 75 EDU 17
99-Cthulhu Mythos ____ HP 11 Damage Bonus: none.

HIT POINTS

Dead -2	-1	0	+1	+2
3	4	5	6	7	8
9	10	(11)	12	13	14
15	16	17	18	19	20

MAGIC POINTS

Unc. 0	1	2	3
4	5	6	7	8
9	10	11	12	13
14	(15)	16	17	18

SANITY POINTS

Insanity 0 1 2 3 4 5 6 7 8 9 10 11 12 13 14
15 16 17 18 19 20 21 22 23 24 25 26 27 28 29 30 31
32 33 34 35 36 37 38 39 40 41 42 43 44 45 46 47 48
49 50 51 52 53 54 55 56 57 58 59 60 61 62 63 64 65
66 67 68 69 70 71 72 73 74 (75) 76 77 78 79 80 81 82
83 84 85 86 87 88 89 90 91 92 93 94 95 96 97 98 99

WEAPONS

Weapon	Skill%	Damage	Range	Shots/Rnd
Fencing Foil	60%	1D6+1	touch	1

INVESTIGATOR POINTS

- Accounting ....(10) ___
- Anthropology ....(01) ___
- Archaeology ....(01) ___
- Art (Painting) ....(45) ___
- Astronomy ....(01) ___
- Bargain ....(40) ___
- Biology ....(25) ___
- Conceal ....(25) ___
- Chemistry ....(01) ___
- Craft (_____) ...(05) ___
- Credit Rating ....(95) ___
- Cthulhu Mythos .....(00) ___
- Disguise ....(01) ___
- Dodge ....(50) ___

- Drive (Carriage) ....(20) ___
- Fast Talk ....(35) ___
- Fencing ....(60) ___
- First Aid ....(30) ___
- Geology ....(01) ___
- Hide ....(10) ___
- History ....(45) ___
- Jump ....(55) ___
- Law ....(30) ___
- Library Use ....(25) ___
- Listen ....(25) ___
- Locksmith ....(01) ___
- Mech. Repair ....(20) ___
- Medicine ....(05) ___

- Natural History ......(60) ___
- Occult ....(40) ___
- Own L. (English) ....(65) ___
- Oth.L. (French) ......(50) ___
- Persuade ....(45) ___
- Pharmacy ....(01) ___
- Physics ....(01) ___
- Photography ....(30) ___
- Psychoanalysis .....(01) ___
- Psychology ....(45) ___
- Ride ....(75) ___
- Sneak ....(10) ___
- Spot Hidden ....(50) ___
- Swim ....(55) ___

- Track ....(10) ___
- .... ___
- .... ___
- .... ___
- .... ___
- .... ___
- .... ___
- .... ___
- .... ___

Firearms
- Handgun ....(20) ___
- Rifle ....(25) ___
- Shotgun ....(30) ___

Present skill percentages are in parentheses; distribute 60 points among skills to customize investigator

Stephen St. John Age 38, Wealthy Solicitor (Lawyer) 1890s

STR 13 CON 12 SIZ 11 INT 16 POW 14 Idea 80% Luck 70% Know 99%
DEX 10 APP 13 SAN 70 EDU 23
99-Cthulhu Mythos ____ HP 12 Damage Bonus: none.

HIT POINTS

Dead -2	-1	0	+1	+2
3	4	5	6	7	8
9	10	11	(12)	13	14
15	16	17	18	19	20

MAGIC POINTS

Unc. 0	1	2	3
4	5	6	7	8
9	10	11	12	13
(14)	15	16	17	18

SANITY POINTS

Insanity 0 1 2 3 4 5 6 7 8 9 10 11 12 13 14
15 16 17 18 19 20 21 22 23 24 25 26 27 28 29 30 31
32 33 34 35 36 37 38 39 40 41 42 43 44 45 46 47 48
49 50 51 52 53 54 55 56 57 58 59 60 61 62 63 64 65
66 67 68 69 (70) 71 72 73 74 75 76 77 78 79 80 81 82
83 84 85 86 87 88 89 90 91 92 93 94 95 96 97 98 99

WEAPONS

Weapon	Skill%	Damage	Range	Shots/Rnd
.30 Carbine	55%	2D6	50 yds.	1

INVESTIGATOR POINTS

- Accounting ....(10) ___
- Anthropology ....(01) ___
- Archaeology ....(01) ___
- Art (Lecture) ....(45) ___
- Astronomy ....(01) ___
- Bargain ....(75) ___
- Biology ....(01) ___
- Conceal ....(25) ___
- Chemistry ....(01) ___
- Craft (_____) ...(05) ___
- Credit Rating ....(80) ___
- Cthulhu Mythos .....(00) ___
- Disguise ....(01) ___
- Dodge ....(50) ___

- Drive (Carriage) ....(40) ___
- Fast Talk ....(75) ___
- First Aid ....(30) ___
- Geology ....(01) ___
- Hide ....(10) ___
- History ....(20) ___
- Jump ....(25) ___
- Law ....(75) ___
- Library Use ....(55) ___
- Listen ....(25) ___
- Locksmith ....(01) ___
- Mech. Repair ....(20) ___
- Medicine ....(05) ___
- Natural History ......(25) ___

- Occult ....(05) ___
- Own L. (English) ....(80) ___
- Oth.L. (French) ......(30) ___
- Oth.L. (Latin) ....(20) ___
- Persuade ....(55) ___
- Pharmacy ....(01) ___
- Physics ....(01) ___
- Photography ....(10) ___
- Psychoanalysis .....(01) ___
- Psychology ....(65) ___
- Ride ....(30) ___
- Sneak ....(40) ___
- Spot Hidden ....(50) ___
- Swim ....(25) ___

- Track ....(10) ___
- .... ___
- .... ___
- .... ___
- .... ___
- .... ___
- .... ___
- .... ___
- .... ___

Firearms
- Handgun ....(20) ___
- Rifle ....(55) ___
- Shotgun ....(30) ___

Present skill percentages are in parentheses; distribute 60 points among skills to customize investigator

Dr. Warren Bedford — Age 56, Prof. of European History — 1920s

STR 10   CON 9   SIZ 10   INT 17   POW 16   Idea 85%   Luck 80%   Know 99%
DEX 7   APP 9   SAN 80   EDU 23
99-Cthulhu Mythos ____   HP 10   Damage Bonus: none.

HIT POINTS
Dead -2   -1   0   +1   +2
3   4   5   6   7   8
9   (10)   11   12   13   14
15   16   17   18   19   20

MAGIC POINTS
Unc. 0   1   2   3
4   5   6   7   8
9   10   11   12   (13)
14   15   16   17   18

SANITY POINTS
Insanity 0 1 2 3 4 5 6 7 8 9 10 11 12 13 14
15 16 17 18 19 20 21 22 23 24 25 26 27 28 29 30 31
32 33 34 35 36 37 38 39 40 41 42 43 44 45 46 47 48
49 50 51 52 53 54 55 56 57 58 59 60 61 62 63 64 65
66 67 68 69 70 71 72 73 74 75 76 77 78 79 (80) 81 82
83 84 85 86 87 88 89 90 91 92 93 94 95 96 97 98 99

WEAPONS
Weapon	Skill%	Damage	Range	Shots/Rnd
.30 Carbine	40%	2D6	50 yds.	1

INVESTIGATOR POINTS

- Accounting ....(10) ___
- Anthropology ....(25) ___
- Archaeology ....(50) ___
- Art (Painting) ....(25) ___
- Astronomy ....(20) ___
- Bargain................(01) ___
- Biology ....(01) ___
- Conceal................(25) ___
- Chemistry..............(01) ___
- Craft (_____) ...(05) ___
- Credit Rating ....(75) ___
- Cthulhu Mythos .....(00) ___
- Disguise ....(01) ___
- Dodge..................(14) ___

- Drive (Auto) ....(50) ___
- Fast Talk ....(05) ___
- First Aid ....(30) ___
- Geology ....(01) ___
- Hide....................(10) ___
- History.................(85) ___
- Jump ....(25) ___
- Law.....................(30) ___
- Library Use............(75) ___
- Listen..................(25) ___
- Locksmith ....(01) ___
- Mech. Repair.........(20) ___
- Medicine...............(05) ___
- Natural History ......(35) ___

- Occult.................(55) ___
- Own L. (English)....(85) ___
- Oth.L. (French) ....(45) ___
- Oth.L. (German) ....(30) ___
- Oth.L. (Italian) .....(25) ___
- Oth.L. (Latin) ....(55) ___
- Persuade ....(15) ___
- Pharmacy..............(01) ___
- Physics ....(01) ___
- Photography ....(10) ___
- Psychoanalysis .....(01) ___
- Psychology............(55) ___
- Ride....................(30) ___
- Sneak..................(10) ___

- Spot Hidden ....(25) ___
- Swim ....(25) ___
- Track....................(10) ___
- .... ___
- .... ___
- .... ___
- .... ___
- .... ___
- .... ___
- **Firearms**
- Handgun...............(20) ___
- Rifle ....(40) ___
- Shotgun.................(30) ___

Present skill percentages are in parentheses; distribute 60 points among skills to customize investigator

Rachel Hemingway — Age 32, Journalist & Writer — 1920s

STR 8   CON 11   SIZ 9   INT 16   POW 13   Idea 85%   Luck 65%   Know 80%
DEX 12   APP 14   SAN 65   EDU 17
99-Cthulhu Mythos ____   HP 10   Damage Bonus: none.

HIT POINTS
Dead -2   -1   0   +1   +2
3   4   5   6   7   8
9   (10)   11   12   13   14
15   16   17   18   19   20

MAGIC POINTS
Unc. 0   1   2   3
4   5   6   7   8
9   10   11   12   (13)
14   15   16   17   18

SANITY POINTS
Insanity 0 1 2 3 4 5 6 7 8 9 10 11 12 13 14
15 16 17 18 19 20 21 22 23 24 25 26 27 28 29 30 31
32 33 34 35 36 37 38 39 40 41 42 43 44 45 46 47 48
49 50 51 52 53 54 55 56 57 58 59 60 61 62 63 64 (65)
66 67 68 69 70 71 72 73 74 75 76 77 78 79 80 81 82
83 84 85 86 87 88 89 90 91 92 93 94 95 96 97 98 99

WEAPONS
Weapon	Skill%	Damage	Range	Shots/Rnd
.38 Revolver	40%	1D10	15 yds.	2

INVESTIGATOR POINTS

- Accounting ....(10) ___
- Anthropology ....(40) ___
- Archaeology ....(01) ___
- Art (Piano).............(05) ___
- Astronomy ....(01) ___
- Bargain................(01) ___
- Biology ....(01) ___
- Conceal................(25) ___
- Chemistry..............(01) ___
- Craft (_____) ...(05) ___
- Credit Rating ....(40) ___
- Cthulhu Mythos .....(00) ___
- Disguise ....(10) ___
- Dodge..................(24) ___

- Drive (Auto) ....(35) ___
- Fast Talk ....(45) ___
- First Aid ....(30) ___
- Geology ....(01) ___
- Hide....................(35) ___
- History.................(65) ___
- Jump ....(25) ___
- Law.....................(45) ___
- Library Use............(75) ___
- Listen..................(25) ___
- Locksmith ....(01) ___
- Mech. Repair.........(20) ___
- Medicine...............(05) ___
- Natural History ......(25) ___

- Occult.................(40) ___
- Own L. (English)....(80) ___
- Oth.L. (French) .....(55) ___
- Persuade ....(25) ___
- Pharmacy..............(01) ___
- Physics ....(01) ___
- Photography ....(10) ___
- Psychoanalysis .....(01) ___
- Psychology............(45) ___
- Ride....................(05) ___
- Sneak..................(35) ___
- Spot Hidden ....(25) ___
- Swim ....(40) ___
- Track....................(10) ___

- .... ___
- .... ___
- .... ___
- .... ___
- .... ___
- .... ___
- .... ___
- .... ___
- **Firearms**
- Handgun...............(40) ___
- Rifle ....(25) ___
- Shotgun.................(30) ___

Present skill percentages are in parentheses; distribute 60 points among skills to customize investigator

Anna Vixen   Age 27, Torch Singer & Actress   1920s

STR 8   CON 14   SIZ 11   INT 10   POW 15   Idea 50%   Luck 75%   Know 60%

DEX 14   APP 17   SAN 75   EDU 12

99-Cthulhu Mythos ____   HP 13   Damage Bonus: none.

HIT POINTS

Dead -2	-1	0	+1	+2
3	4	5	6	7	8
9	10	11	12	(13)	14
15	16	17	18	19	20

MAGIC POINTS

Unc. 0	1	2	3
4	5	6	7	8
9	10	11	12	13
14	(15)	16	17	18

SANITY POINTS

Insanity 0 1 2 3 4 5 6 7 8 9 10 11 12 13 14
15 16 17 18 19 20 21 22 23 24 25 26 27 28 29 30 31
32 33 34 35 36 37 38 39 40 41 42 43 44 45 46 47 48
49 50 51 52 53 54 55 56 57 58 59 60 61 62 63 64 65
66 67 68 69 70 71 72 73 74 (75) 76 77 78 79 80 81 82
83 84 85 86 87 88 89 90 91 92 93 94 95 96 97 98 99

WEAPONS

Weapon	Skill%	Damage	Range	Shots/Rnd

INVESTIGATOR POINTS

- ❑ Accounting ....(10) ___
- ❑ Anthropology.........(01) ___
- ❑ Archaeology ....(01) ___
- ❑ Art (Acting)............(75) ___
- ❑ Art (Singing).........(75) ___
- ❑ Astronomy.............(01) ___
- ❑ Bargain.................(50) ___
- ❑ Biology ....(01) ___
- ❑ Conceal................(25) ___
- ❑ Chemistry..............(01) ___
- ❑ Craft (_____)...(05) ___
- ❑ Credit Rating ....(55) ___
-    Cthulhu Mythos .....(00) ___
- ❑ Disguise ....(01) ___

- ❑ Dodge...................(28) ___
- ❑ Drive (Auto)...........(20) ___
- ❑ Fast Talk ....(35) ___
- ❑ First Aid.................(30) ___
- ❑ Geology.................(01) ___
- ❑ Hide......................(10) ___
- ❑ History...................(20) ___
- ❑ Jump ....(25) ___
- ❑ Law.......................(05) ___
- ❑ Library Use............(25) ___
- ❑ Listen....................(55) ___
- ❑ Locksmith ....(01) ___
- ❑ Mech. Repair.........(20) ___
- ❑ Medicine................(05) ___

- ❑ Natural History ......(10) ___
- ❑ Occult...................(05) ___
- ❑ Own L. (English)....(50) ___
- ❑ Oth.L. (Spanish) ....(30) ___
- ❑ Persuade...............(75) ___
- ❑ Pharmacy..............(01) ___
- ❑ Physics..................(01) ___
- ❑ Photography..........(10) ___
- ❑ Psychoanalysis .....(01) ___
- ❑ Psychology............(45) ___
- ❑ Ride......................(05) ___
- ❑ Sneak...................(10) ___
- ❑ Spot Hidden ....(45) ___
- ❑ Swim ....(25) ___

- ❑ Track.....................(10) ___
- ❑ .... ___
- ❑ .... ___
- ❑ .... ___
- ❑ .... ___
- ❑ .... ___
- ❑ .... ___
- ❑ .... ___
- ❑ .... ___
- **Firearms**
- ❑ Handgun................(20) ___
- ❑ Rifle......................(25) ___
- ❑ Shotgun................(30) ___

Present skill percentages are in parentheses; distribute 60 points among skills to customize investigator

---

Artie Gumshoe   Age 36, Tough Private Investigator   1920s

STR 15   CON 16   SIZ 12   INT 11   POW 12   Idea 55%   Luck 60%   Know 70%

DEX 14   APP 12   SAN 60   EDU 14

99-Cthulhu Mythos ____   HP 14   Damage Bonus: +1D4.

HIT POINTS

Dead -2	-1	0	+1	+2
3	4	5	6	7	8
9	10	11	12	13	(14)
15	16	17	18	19	20

MAGIC POINTS

Unc. 0	1	2	3
4	5	6	7	8
9	10	11	(12)	13
14	15	16	17	18

SANITY POINTS

Insanity 0 1 2 3 4 5 6 7 8 9 10 11 12 13 14
15 16 17 18 19 20 21 22 23 24 25 26 27 28 29 30 31
32 33 34 35 36 37 38 39 40 41 42 43 44 45 46 47 48
49 50 51 52 53 54 55 56 57 58 59 (60) 61 62 63 64 65
66 67 68 69 70 71 72 73 74 75 76 77 78 79 80 81 82
83 84 85 86 87 88 89 90 91 92 93 94 95 96 97 98 99

WEAPONS

Weapon	Skill%	Damage	Range	Shots/Rnd
Fist/Punch	60%	1D3+db	touch	1
.45 Auto	65%	1D10+2	15 yds.	1

INVESTIGATOR POINTS

- ❑ Accounting ....(10) ___
- ❑ Anthropology.........(01) ___
- ❑ Archaeology ....(01) ___
- ❑ Art (Harmonica) ....(05) ___
- ❑ Astronomy.............(01) ___
- ❑ Bargain.................(75) ___
- ❑ Biology ....(01) ___
- ❑ Conceal................(25) ___
- ❑ Chemistry..............(01) ___
- ❑ Craft (_____)...(05) ___
- ❑ Credit Rating ....(15) ___
-    Cthulhu Mythos .....(00) ___
- ❑ Disguise ....(20) ___
- ❑ Dodge...................(28) ___

- ❑ Drive (Auto)...........(40) ___
- ❑ Fast Talk ....(55) ___
- ❑ First Aid.................(30) ___
- ❑ Geology.................(01) ___
- ❑ Hide......................(40) ___
- ❑ History...................(20) ___
- ❑ Jump ....(25) ___
- ❑ Law.......................(55) ___
- ❑ Library Use............(25) ___
- ❑ Listen....................(25) ___
- ❑ Locksmith ....(40) ___
- ❑ Mech. Repair.........(20) ___
- ❑ Medicine................(05) ___
- ❑ Natural History ......(10) ___

- ❑ Occult...................(05) ___
- ❑ Own L. (English)....(55) ___
- ❑ Persuade...............(35) ___
- ❑ Pharmacy..............(01) ___
- ❑ Physics..................(01) ___
- ❑ Photography..........(45) ___
- ❑ Psychoanalysis .....(01) ___
- ❑ Psychology............(45) ___
- ❑ Ride......................(05) ___
- ❑ Sneak...................(40) ___
- ❑ Spot Hidden ....(25) ___
- ❑ Swim ....(25) ___
- ❑ Track.....................(10) ___
-    .... ___

- ❑ .... ___
- ❑ .... ___
- ❑ .... ___
- ❑ .... ___
- ❑ .... ___
- ❑ .... ___
- ❑ .... ___
- ❑ .... ___
- **Firearms**
- ❑ Handgun................(65) ___
- ❑ Rifle......................(25) ___
- ❑ Shotgun................(30) ___

Present skill percentages are in parentheses; distribute 60 points among skills to customize investigator

Dr. Elliot Jurgens — Age 48, Dedicated Surgeon — 1990s

STR 11   CON 13   SIZ 10   INT 17   POW 13   Idea 85%   Luck 65%   Know 99%
DEX 16   APP 11   SAN 65   EDU 24
99-Cthulhu Mythos _____   HP 12   Damage Bonus: none.

HIT POINTS

Dead -2	-1	0	+1	+2
3	4	5	6	7	8
9	10	11	(12)	13	14
15	16	17	18	19	20

MAGIC POINTS

Unc. 0	1	2	3
4	5	6	7	8
9	10	11	12	(13)
14	15	16	17	18

SANITY POINTS

Insanity	0	1	2	3	4	5	6	7	8	9	10	11	12	13	14
	15	16	17	18	19	20	21	22	23	24	25	26	27	28	29	30	31
	32	33	34	35	36	37	38	39	40	41	42	43	44	45	46	47	48
	49	50	51	52	53	54	55	56	57	58	59	60	61	62	63	64	(65)
	66	67	68	69	70	71	72	73	74	75	76	77	78	79	80	81	82
	83	84	85	86	87	88	89	90	91	92	93	94	95	96	97	98	99

WEAPONS

Weapon	Skill%	Damage	Range	Shots/Rnd
9mm Auto	45%	1D10	20 yds.	3

INVESTIGATOR POINTS

- ❑ Accounting ....(10) ___
- ❑ Anthropology ....(01) ___
- ❑ Archaeology ....(01) ___
- ❑ Art (Violin) ....(30) ___
- ❑ Astronomy ....(01) ___
- ❑ Bargain ....(50) ___
- ❑ Biology ....(60) ___
- ❑ Conceal ....(25) ___
- ❑ Chemistry ....(40) ___
- ❑ Craft (_____)...(05) ___
- ❑ Credit Rating ....(75) ___
- Cthulhu Mythos .....(00) ___
- ❑ Disguise ....(01) ___
- ❑ Dodge...................(32) ___

- ❑ Drive (Auto)...........(45) ___
- ❑ Fast Talk ....(45) ___
- ❑ First Aid ....(50) ___
- ❑ Geology ....(01) ___
- ❑ Hide......................(10) ___
- ❑ History ....(30) ___
- ❑ Jump ....(25) ___
- ❑ Law......................(30) ___
- ❑ Library Use............(65) ___
- ❑ Listen...................(35) ___
- ❑ Locksmith ....(01) ___
- ❑ Mech. Repair.........(20) ___
- ❑ Medicine...............(80) ___
- ❑ Natural History ......(10) ___

- ❑ Occult ....(05) ___
- ❑ Own L. (English)....(85) ___
- ❑ Oth.L. (Latin) ....(45) ___
- ❑ Persuade ....(25) ___
- ❑ Pharmacy ....(35) ___
- ❑ Physics ....(01) ___
- ❑ Photography ....(10) ___
- ❑ Psychoanalysis .....(01) ___
- ❑ Psychology............(60) ___
- ❑ Ride......................(05) ___
- ❑ Sneak...................(10) ___
- ❑ Spot Hidden ....(75) ___
- ❑ Swim ....(45) ___
- ❑ Track....................(10) ___

- ❑ .... ___
- ❑ .... ___
- ❑ .... ___
- ❑ .... ___
- ❑ .... ___
- ❑ .... ___
- ❑ .... ___
- ❑ .... ___
- ❑ .... ___
- ❑ .... ___
- **Firearms**
- ❑ Handgun...............(45) ___
- ❑ Rifle......................(25) ___
- ❑ Shotgun................(30) ___

Present skill percentages are in parentheses; distribute 60 points among skills to customize investigator

Shirley Bath — Age 37, New Age Author & Lecturer — 1990s

STR 9   CON 16   SIZ 9   INT 12   POW 17   Idea 60%   Luck 85%   Know 95%
DEX 13   APP 12   SAN 85   EDU 19
99-Cthulhu Mythos _____   HP 13   Damage Bonus: none.

HIT POINTS

Dead -2	-1	0	+1	+2
3	4	5	6	7	8
9	10	11	12	(13)	14
15	16	17	18	19	20

MAGIC POINTS

Unc. 0	1	2	3
4	5	6	7	8
9	10	11	12	13
14	15	16	(17)	18

SANITY POINTS

Insanity	0	1	2	3	4	5	6	7	8	9	10	11	12	13	14
	15	16	17	18	19	20	21	22	23	24	25	26	27	28	29	30	31
	32	33	34	35	36	37	38	39	40	41	42	43	44	45	46	47	48
	49	50	51	52	53	54	55	56	57	58	59	60	61	62	63	64	65
	66	67	68	69	70	71	72	73	74	75	76	77	78	79	80	81	82
	83	84	(85)	86	87	88	89	90	91	92	93	94	95	96	97	98	99

WEAPONS

Weapon	Skill%	Damage	Range	Shots/Rnd

INVESTIGATOR POINTS

- ❑ Accounting ....(10) ___
- ❑ Anthropology ....(40) ___
- ❑ Archaeology ....(01) ___
- ❑ Art (Painting) ....(25) ___
- ❑ Astronomy ....(01) ___
- ❑ Bargain.................(30) ___
- ❑ Biology ....(01) ___
- ❑ Conceal ....(25) ___
- ❑ Chemistry ....(01) ___
- ❑ Craft (_____)...(05) ___
- ❑ Credit Rating ....(65) ___
- Cthulhu Mythos .....(00) ___
- ❑ Disguise ....(01) ___
- ❑ Dodge...................(24) ___

- ❑ Drive (Auto)...........(45) ___
- ❑ Fast Talk ....(45) ___
- ❑ First Aid ....(30) ___
- ❑ Geology ....(01) ___
- ❑ Hide......................(10) ___
- ❑ History ....(45) ___
- ❑ Jump ....(25) ___
- ❑ Law......................(15) ___
- ❑ Library Use............(65) ___
- ❑ Listen...................(25) ___
- ❑ Locksmith ....(01) ___
- ❑ Mech. Repair.........(20) ___
- ❑ Medicine...............(05) ___
- ❑ Meditation.............(40) ___

- ❑ Natural History ......(25) ___
- ❑ Occult ....(75) ___
- ❑ Own L. (English)....(80) ___
- ❑ Oth.L. (Sanskrit) ....(25) ___
- ❑ Persuade ....(75) ___
- ❑ Pharmacy ....(01) ___
- ❑ Physics ....(01) ___
- ❑ Photography ....(10) ___
- ❑ Psychoanalysis .....(01) ___
- ❑ Psychology............(75) ___
- ❑ Ride......................(05) ___
- ❑ Sneak...................(35) ___
- ❑ Spot Hidden ....(25) ___
- ❑ Swim ....(40) ___

- ❑ Track....................(10) ___
- ❑ .... ___
- ❑ .... ___
- ❑ .... ___
- ❑ .... ___
- ❑ .... ___
- ❑ .... ___
- ❑ .... ___
- ❑ .... ___
- **Firearms**
- ❑ Handgun...............(20S) ___
- ❑ Rifle......................(25) ___
- ❑ Shotgun................(30) ___

Present skill percentages are in parentheses; distribute 60 points among skills to customize investigator

Call of Cthulhu Monster Master

Name _____

Desc _____
_____
_____
_____
_____

SAN Loss _____

STR _____ INT _____ APP _____
CON _____ POW _____ EDU _____
SIZ _____ DEX _____ MOV _____

HIT POINTS   DEAD =0 1 2 3 4 5
6   7   8   9   10 11 12 13 14 15 16 17 18
19 20 21 22 23 24 25 26 27 28 29 30 31
32 33 34 35 36 37 38 39 40 41 42 43 44
45 46 47 48 49 50 51 52 53 54 55 56 57
58 59 60 61 62 63 64 65 66 67 68 69 70
71 72 73 74 75 76 77 78 79 80 81 82 83
84 85 86 87 88 89 90 91 92 93 94 95 96
97 98 99 100

Skills _____
_____
_____
_____
_____

Spells _____
_____
_____
_____
_____
_____
_____
_____

MAGIC PTS   UNCN =0 1 2 3 4 5
6   7   8   9   10 11 12 13 14 15 16 17 18
19 20 21 22 23 24 25 26 27 28 29 30 31
32 33 34 35 36 37 38 39 40 41 42 43 44
45 46 47 48 49 50 51 52 53 54 55 56 57
58 59 60 61 62 63 64 65 66 67 68 69 70
71 72 73 74 75 76 77 78 79 80 81 82 83
84 85 86 87 88 89 90 91 92 93 94 95 96
97 98 99 100

Damage Bonus _____

	weapon	skill	damage
Fist/Claw		____%	_____
_____		____%	_____
_____		____%	_____
_____		____%	_____
_____		____%	_____
_____		____%	_____

Armor _____

Possessions _____
_____
_____
_____
_____
_____
_____
_____
_____

MINION ONE

Name _____
Desc _____
SAN Loss _____

STR _____ INT _____ APP _____
CON _____ POW _____ EDU _____
SIZ _____ DEX _____ MOV _____

HIT POINTS   DEAD =0 1 2 3 4
5   6   7   8   9   10 11 12 13 14 15 16
17 18 19 20 21 22 23 24 25 26 27 28
29 30 31 32 33 34 35 36 37 38 39 40
41 42 43 44 45 46 47 48 49 50 51 52
53 54 55 56 57 58 59 60 61 62 63 64
65 66 67 68 69 70 71 72 73 74 75 76
77 78 79 80 81 82 83 84 85 86 87 88

Damage Bonus _____

	weapon	skill	damage
Fist/Claw		____%	_____
_____		____%	_____
_____		____%	_____
_____		____%	_____
_____		____%	_____

Armor _____

Skills _____
_____

Magic Points _____
Spells _____
_____
_____

Possessions _____

MINION TWO

Name _____
Desc _____
SAN Loss _____

STR _____ INT _____ APP _____
CON _____ POW _____ EDU _____
SIZ _____ DEX _____ MOV _____

HIT POINTS   DEAD =0 1 2 3 4
5   6   7   8   9   10 11 12 13 14 15 16
17 18 19 20 21 22 23 24 25 26 27 28
29 30 31 32 33 34 35 36 37 38 39 40
41 42 43 44 45 46 47 48 49 50 51 52
53 54 55 56 57 58 59 60 61 62 63 64
65 66 67 68 69 70 71 72 73 74 75 76
77 78 79 80 81 82 83 84 85 86 87 88

Damage Bonus _____

	weapon	skill	damage
Fist/Claw		____%	_____
_____		____%	_____
_____		____%	_____
_____		____%	_____
_____		____%	_____

Armor _____

Skills _____
_____

Magic Points _____
Spells _____
_____
_____

Possessions _____

MINION THREE

Name _____
Desc _____
SAN Loss _____

STR _____ INT _____ APP _____
CON _____ POW _____ EDU _____
SIZ _____ DEX _____ MOV _____

HIT POINTS   DEAD =0 1 2 3 4
5   6   7   8   9   10 11 12 13 14 15 16
17 18 19 20 21 22 23 24 25 26 27 28
29 30 31 32 33 34 35 36 37 38 39 40
41 42 43 44 45 46 47 48 49 50 51 52
53 54 55 56 57 58 59 60 61 62 63 64
65 66 67 68 69 70 71 72 73 74 75 76
77 78 79 80 81 82 83 84 85 86 87 88

Damage Bonus _____

	weapon	skill	damage
Fist/Claw		____%	_____
_____		____%	_____
_____		____%	_____
_____		____%	_____
_____		____%	_____

Armor _____

Skills _____
_____

Magic Points _____
Spells _____
_____
_____

Possessions _____

1920s

Investigator Name _____
Occupation _____
Colleges, Degrees _____
Birthplace _____
Mental Disorders _____
Sex _____ Age _____

Characteristics & Rolls

STR ____	DEX ____	INT ____	Idea ____
CON ____	APP ____	POW ____	Luck ____
SIZ ____	SAN ____	EDU ____	Know ____

99-Cthulhu Mythos _____   Damage Bonus _____

1920s Investigator's Sheet

Player's Name _____

CALL OF CTHULHU
Horror Role-Playing

Sanity Points

Insane 0 1 2 3 4 5 6 7 8 9 10 11 12 13 14
15 16 17 18 19 20 21 22 23 24 25 26 27 28 29 30 31
32 33 34 35 36 37 38 39 40 41 42 43 44 45 46 47 48
49 50 51 52 53 54 55 56 57 58 59 60 61 62 63 64 65
66 67 68 69 70 71 72 73 74 75 76 77 78 79 80 81 82
83 84 85 86 87 88 89 90 91 92 93 94 95 96 97 98 99

Magic Points

Unconscious 0 1 2 3
4 5 6 7 8 9 10 11
12 13 14 15 16 17 18 19
20 21 22 23 24 25 26 27
28 29 30 31 32 33 34 35
36 37 38 39 40 41 42 43

Hit Points

Dead -2 -1 0 1 2 3
4 5 6 7 8 9 10 11
12 13 14 15 16 17 18 19
20 21 22 23 24 25 26 27
28 29 30 31 32 33 34 35
36 37 38 39 40 41 42 43

Investigator Skills

- Accounting (10%) ____
- Anthropology (01%) ____
- Archaeology (01%) ____
- Art (05%):
- ____
- ____
- Astronomy (01%) ____
- Bargain (05%) ____
- Biology (01%) ____
- Chemistry (01%) ____
- Climb (40%) ____
- Conceal (15%) ____
- Craft (05%):
- ____
- ____
- Credit Rating (15%) ____
- Cthulhu Mythos (00) ____
- Disguise (01%) ____
- Dodge (DEX x2%) ____
- Drive Auto (20%) ____
- Electr. Repair (10%) ____
- Fast Talk (05%) ____
- First Aid (30%) ____
- Geology (01%) ____
- Hide (10%) ____
- History (20%) ____
- Jump (25%) ____

- Law (05%) ____
- Library Use (25%) ____
- Listen (25%) ____
- Locksmith (01%) ____
- Martial Arts (01%) ____
- Mech. Repair (20%) ____
- Medicine (05%) ____
- Natural History (10%) ____
- Navigate (10%) ____
- Occult (05%) ____
- Opr. Hvy. Mch. (01%) ____
- Other Language (01%):
- ____
- ____
- ____
- Own Language (EDUx5%):
- ____
- Persuade (15%) ____
- Pharmacy (01%) ____
- Photography (10%) ____
- Physics (01%) ____
- Pilot (01%):
- ____
- ____
- Psychoanalysis (01%) ____
- Psychology (05%) ____
- Ride (05%) ____

- Sneak (10%) ____
- Spot Hidden (25%) ____
- Swim (25%) ____
- Throw (25%) ____
- Track (10%) ____
- ____
- ____
- ____
- ____
- ____
- ____

Firearms
- Handgun (20%) ____
- Machine Gun (15%) ____
- Rifle (25%) ____
- Shotgun (30%) ____
- SMG (15%) ____

Weapons

	melee	%	damage	hnd	rng	#att	hp
❑	Fist (50%)	____	1D3+db	1	touch	1	n/a
❑	Grapple (25%)	____	special	2	touch	1	n/a
❑	Head (10%)	____	1D4+db	0	touch	1	n/a
❑	Kick (25%)	____	1D6+db	0	touch	1	n/a
❑	____						
❑	____						

	firearm	%	damage	malf	rng	#att	shots	hp
❑	____							
❑	____							
❑	____							
❑	____							
❑	____							
❑	____							

Personal Data

Investigator Name _____

Residence _____

Personal Description _____

_____

_____

Family & Friends _____

_____

_____

_____

Episodes of Insanity _____

_____

Wounds & Injuries _____

_____

Marks & Scars _____

_____

Investigator History

_____   _____

_____   _____

_____   _____

_____   _____

_____   _____

_____   _____

_____   _____

Income & Savings

Income _____

Cash on Hand _____

Savings _____

Personal Property _____

_____

_____

Real Estate _____

_____

Adventuring Gear & Possessions

_____ _____ _____

_____ _____ _____

_____ _____ _____

_____ _____ _____

_____ _____ _____

_____ _____ _____

_____ _____ _____

_____ _____ _____

_____ _____ _____

_____ _____ _____

Mythos Tomes Read

_____ _____

_____ _____

_____ _____

_____ _____

Entities Encountered

_____ _____

_____ _____

_____ _____

_____ _____

_____ _____

_____ _____

_____ _____

Magical Artifacts / Spells Known

Artifacts _____   Spells _____

_____   _____

_____   _____

_____   _____

1890s

Investigator Name _____
Occupation _____
Colleges, Degrees _____
Birthplace _____
Mental Disorders _____
Sex _____ **Age** _____

Characteristics & Rolls

STR ____	**DEX** ____	**INT** ____	**Idea** ____
CON ____	**APP** ____	**POW** ____	**Luck** ____
SIZ ____	**SAN** ____	**EDU** ____	**Know** ____

99-Cthulhu Mythos _____   Damage Bonus _____

1890s Investigator's Sheet

Player's Name _____

CALL OF CTHULHU
Horror Role-Playing

Sanity Points

Insane 0 1 2 3 4 5 6 7 8 9 10 11 12 13 14
15 16 17 18 19 20 21 22 23 24 25 26 27 28 29 30 31
32 33 34 35 36 37 38 39 40 41 42 43 44 45 46 47 48
49 50 51 52 53 54 55 56 57 58 59 60 61 62 63 64 65
66 67 68 69 70 71 72 73 74 75 76 77 78 79 80 81 82
83 84 85 86 87 88 89 90 91 92 93 94 95 96 97 98 99

Magic Points

Unconscious 0 1 2 3
4 5 6 7 8 9 10 11
12 13 14 15 16 17 18 19
20 21 22 23 24 25 26 27
28 29 30 31 32 33 34 35
36 37 38 39 40 41 42 43

Hit Points

Dead -2 -1 0 1 2 3
4 5 6 7 8 9 10 11
12 13 14 15 16 17 18 19
20 21 22 23 24 25 26 27
28 29 30 31 32 33 34 35
36 37 38 39 40 41 42 43

Investigator Skills

☐ Accounting (10%) _____
☐ Anthropology (01%) _____
☐ Archaeology (01%) _____
Art (05%):
☐ _____ _____
☐ _____ _____
☐ Astronomy (01%) _____
☐ Bargain (05%) _____
☐ Biology (01%) _____
☐ Chemistry (01%) _____
☐ Climb (40%) _____
☐ Conceal (15%) _____
Craft (05%):
☐ _____ _____
☐ _____ _____
☐ Credit Rating (15%) _____
Cthulhu Mythos (00)
☐ Disguise (01%) _____
☐ Dodge (DEX x2%) _____
☐ Drive Carriage (20%) _____
☐ Electr. Repair (10%) _____
☐ Fast Talk (05%) _____
☐ First Aid (30%) _____
☐ Geology (01%) _____
☐ Hide (10%) _____
☐ History (20%) _____
☐ Jump (25%) _____

☐ Law (05%) _____
☐ Library Use (25%) _____
☐ Listen (25%) _____
☐ Locksmith (01%) _____
☐ Martial Arts (01%) _____
☐ Mech. Repair (20%) _____
☐ Medicine (05%) _____
☐ Natural History (10%) _____
☐ Navigate (10%) _____
☐ Occult (05%) _____
☐ Opr. Hvy. Mch. (01%) _____
Other Language (01%):
☐ _____ _____
☐ _____ _____
☐ _____ _____
Own Language (EDUx5%):
☐ _____ _____
☐ Persuade (15%) _____
☐ Pharmacy (01%) _____
☐ Photography (10%) _____
☐ Physics (01%) _____
☐ Pilot Balloon (01%) _____
☐ Pilot Boat (01%) _____
☐ Psychology (05%) _____
☐ Ride (05%) _____
☐ Sneak (10%) _____
☐ Spot Hidden (25%) _____

☐ Swim (25%) _____
☐ Throw (25%) _____
☐ Track (10%) _____
☐ _____ _____
☐ _____ _____
☐ _____ _____
☐ _____ _____
☐ _____ _____
☐ _____ _____
☐ _____ _____
☐ _____ _____
☐ _____ _____

Firearms
☐ Handgun (20%) _____
☐ Machine Gun (15%) _____
☐ Rifle (25%) _____
☐ Shotgun (30%) _____

Weapons

	melee	%	damage	hnd	rng	#att	hp
☐	Fist (50%)	____	1D3+db	1	touch	1	n/a
☐	Grapple (25%)	____	special	2	touch	1	n/a
☐	Head (10%)	____	1D4+db	0	touch	1	n/a
☐	Kick (25%)	____	1D6+db	0	touch	1	n/a
☐	_____						
☐	_____						

	firearm	%	damage	malf	rng	#att	shots	hp
☐	_____							
☐	_____							
☐	_____							
☐	_____							
☐	_____							
☐	_____							

Investigator Name _____
Occupation _____
Colleges, Degrees _____
Birthplace _____
Mental Disorders _____
Sex _____ Age_____

Characteristics & Rolls

STR _____ DEX _____ INT_____ Idea_____
CON_____ APP _____ POW ___ Luck_____
SIZ_____ SAN_____ EDU ___ Know_____
99-Cthulhu Mythos _____ Damage Bonus _____

Present Day Investigator's Sheet

Player's Name _____

CALL OF CTHULHU
Horror Role-Playing

Sanity Points

Insane 0	1	2	3	4	5	6	7	8	9	10	11	12	13	14

15 16 17 18 19 20 21 22 23 24 25 26 27 28 29 30 31
32 33 34 35 36 37 38 39 40 41 42 43 44 45 46 47 48
49 50 51 52 53 54 55 56 57 58 59 60 61 62 63 64 65
66 67 68 69 70 71 72 73 74 75 76 77 78 79 80 81 82
83 84 85 86 87 88 89 90 91 92 93 94 95 96 97 98 99

Magic Points

Unconscious 0 1 2 3
4 5 6 7 8 9 10 11
12 13 14 15 16 17 18 19
20 21 22 23 24 25 26 27
28 29 30 31 32 33 34 35
36 37 38 39 40 41 42 43

Hit Points

Dead -2 -1 0 1 2 3
4 5 6 7 8 9 10 11
12 13 14 15 16 17 18 19
20 21 22 23 24 25 26 27
28 29 30 31 32 33 34 35
36 37 38 39 40 41 42 43

Investigator Skills

- ❑ Accounting (10%) _____
- ❑ Anthropology (01%) _____
- ❑ Archaeology (01%) _____
- Art (05%):
- ❑ _____ _____
- ❑ _____ _____
- ❑ Astronomy (01%) _____
- ❑ Bargain (05%) _____
- ❑ Biology (01%) _____
- ❑ Chemistry (01%) _____
- ❑ Climb (40%) _____
- ❑ Computer Use (01%) _____
- ❑ Conceal (15%) _____
- Craft (05%):
- ❑ _____ _____
- ❑ _____ _____
- ❑ Credit Rating (15%) _____
- Cthulhu Mythos (00) _____
- ❑ Disguise (01%) _____
- ❑ Dodge (DEX x2%) _____
- ❑ Drive Auto (20%) _____
- ❑ Electr. Repair (10%) _____
- ❑ Electronics (01%) _____
- ❑ Fast Talk (05%) _____
- ❑ First Aid (30%) _____
- ❑ Geology (01%) _____
- ❑ Hide (10%) _____

- ❑ History (20%) _____
- ❑ Jump (25%) _____
- ❑ Law (05%) _____
- ❑ Library Use (25%) _____
- ❑ Listen (25%) _____
- ❑ Locksmith (01%) _____
- ❑ Martial Arts (01%) _____
- ❑ Mech. Repair (20%) _____
- ❑ Medicine (05%) _____
- ❑ Natural History (10%) _____
- ❑ Navigate (10%) _____
- ❑ Occult (05%) _____
- ❑ Opr. Hvy. Mch. (01%) _____
- Other Language (01%):
- ❑ _____ _____
- ❑ _____ _____
- ❑ _____ _____
- Own Language (EDUx5%):
- ❑ _____ _____
- ❑ Persuade (15%) _____
- ❑ Pharmacy (01%) _____
- ❑ Photography (10%) _____
- ❑ Physics (01%) _____
- Pilot (01%):
- ❑ _____ _____
- ❑ _____ _____
- ❑ Psychoanalysis (01%) _____

- ❑ Psychology (05%) _____
- ❑ Ride (05%) _____
- ❑ Sneak (10%) _____
- ❑ Spot Hidden (25%) _____
- ❑ Swim (25%) _____
- ❑ Throw (25%) _____
- ❑ Track (10%) _____
- ❑ _____ _____
- ❑ _____ _____
- ❑ _____ _____
- ❑ _____ _____

Firearms
- ❑ Handgun (20%) _____
- ❑ Machine Gun (15%) _____
- ❑ Rifle (25%)_____ _____
- ❑ Shotgun (30%) _____
- ❑ SMG (15%) _____

Weapons

	melee	%	damage	hnd	rng	#att	hp		firearm	%	damage	malf	rng	#att	shots	hp
❑	Fist (50%)	___	1D3+db	1	touch	1	n/a	❑								
❑	Grapple (25%)	___	special	2	touch	1	n/a	❑								
❑	Head (10%)	___	1D4+db	0	touch	1	n/a	❑								
❑	Kick (25%)	___	1D6+db	0	touch	1	n/a	❑								
❑								❑								
❑								❑								

Name _____ **Age** _____ **Occupation** _____

STR ____ CON ____ SIZ ____ INT ____ POW ____ Idea ____% Luck ____% Know ____%
DEX ____ APP ____ SAN ____ EDU ____
99-Cthulhu Mythos ____ HP ____ Damage Bonus _____

HIT POINTS

Dead -2	-1	0	+1	+2
3	4	5	6	7	8
9	10	11	12	13	14
15	16	17	18	19	20

MAGIC POINTS

Unc. 0	1	2	3
4	5	6	7	8
9	10	11	12	13
14	15	16	17	18

SANITY POINTS

Insanity	0	1	2	3	4	5	6	7	8	9	10	11	12	13	14
	15	16	17	18	19	20	21	22	23	24	25	26	27	28	29	30	31
	32	33	34	35	36	37	38	39	40	41	42	43	44	45	46	47	48
	49	50	51	52	53	54	55	56	57	58	59	60	61	62	63	64	65
	66	67	68	69	70	71	72	73	74	75	76	77	78	79	80	81	82
	83	84	85	86	87	88	89	90	91	92	93	94	95	96	97	98	99

WEAPONS

Weapon	Skill%	Damage	Range	Shots/Rnd

INVESTIGATOR SKILLS

- ❏ Accounting ....(10) ___
- ❏ Anthropology.........(01) ___
- ❏ Archaeology ....(01) ___
- ❏ Art (_____).....(05) ___
- ❏ Art (_____).....(05) ___
- ❏ Astronomy ....(01) ___
- ❏ Bargain.................(05) ___
- ❏ Biology ....(01) ___
- ❏ Conceal................(15) ___
- ❏ Chemistry.............(01) ___
- ❏ Craft (_____)...(05) ___
- ❏ Craft (_____)...(05) ___
- ❏ Credit Rating ....(15) ___
- Cthulhu Mythos .....(00) ___

- ❏ Disguise ....(01) ___
- ❏ Dodge..........(DEX x2) ___
- ❏ Drive (_____)..(20) ___
- ❏ Fast Talk...............(05) ___
- ❏ First Aid................(30) ___
- ❏ Geology................(01) ___
- ❏ Hide....................(10) ___
- ❏ History ....(20) ___
- ❏ Jump ....(25) ___
- ❏ Law......................(05) ___
- ❏ Library Use............(25) ___
- ❏ Listen...................(25) ___
- ❏ Locksmith ....(01) ___
- ❏ Mech. Repair........(20) ___

- ❏ Medicine...............(05) ___
- ❏ Natural History ......(10) ___
- ❏ Occult...................(05) ___
- ❏ Own L. (_____)...(01) ___
- ❏ Oth.L. (_____)...(01) ___
- ❏ Oth.L. (_____)...(01) ___
- ❏ Own L. (_____)...(01) ___
- ❏ Persuade ....(15) ___
- ❏ Pharmacy..............(01) ___
- ❏ Physics ....(01) ___
- ❏ Photography ....(10) ___
- ❏ Psychoanalysis .....(01) ___
- ❏ Psychology............(05) ___
- ❏ Ride.....................(05) ___

- ❏ Sneak...................(10) ___
- ❏ Spot Hidden ....(25) ___
- ❏ Swim ....(10) ___
- ❏ Track....................(10) ___
- ❏ ....
- ❏ ....
- ❏ ....
- ❏ ....
- ❏ ....

Firearms
- ❏ Handgun...............(20) ___
- ❏ Rifle.....................(25) ___
- ❏ Shotgun................(30) ___
- ❏ SMG ....(15) ___

Following each skill name is the investigator base chance in parentheses

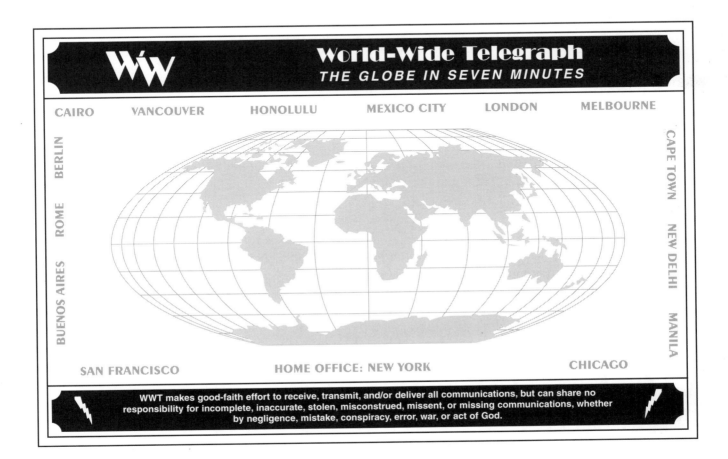

WW — **World-Wide Telegraph**
THE GLOBE IN SEVEN MINUTES

CAIRO   VANCOUVER   HONOLULU   MEXICO CITY   LONDON   MELBOURNE

BERLIN   ROME   BUENOS AIRES

CAPE TOWN   NEW DELHI   MANILA

SAN FRANCISCO   HOME OFFICE: NEW YORK   CHICAGO

WWT makes good-faith effort to receive, transmit, and/or deliver all communications, but can share no responsibility for incomplete, inaccurate, stolen, misconstrued, missent, or missing communications, whether by negligence, mistake, conspiracy, error, war, or act of God.

Character Generation
pp. 34-35

Play Aids

Resistance Table
p. 50

PHYSICAL INJURIES

ACID CONTACT
- Weak acids: 1D3-1 damage per round.
- Strong acids: 1D4 damage per round.
- Very strong acids: 1D6 damage per round.

DROWNING, SUFFOCATION
- Roll CON x10 or less on D100 in the first round; CON x9 or less in the second; CON x8 or less in the third; and so on, to CON x1 per round.
- Failure costs 1D6 damage plus 1D6 each additional round until rescue. No further CON rolls need be made.

EXPLOSION
- Calculate effect in terms of the strength of the blast and the radius of effect in yards. Example: a stick of dynamite does 5D6 damage in the first two yards, 4D6 in the third yard, 3D6 in the fourth, and so on. Each victim takes separate full damage. Doubling a charge increases damage by half.

FALLING
- Per 10 feet or fraction over first 10 feet: +1D6 points of damage. With a successful Jump roll first, lose 1D6 fewer hit points.

FIRE DAMAGE
Serious burns (total exceeding half hit points) cost APP, CON, or DEX as well as hit points.
- Small fire: 1D6 damage per round. Luck roll to prevent flaming clothes or hair. Luck roll or First Aid roll to put out fire on person.
- Large bonfire: 1D6+2 damage per round. Hair and clothes aflame.
- Room in flames: 1D6+2 damage per round. Luck roll each round or begin suffocating.
- Conflagrations: deadly, each a special case.

POISONING
Match poison's POT vs. target's CON on Resistance Table. See Sample Poisons, on facing page.
- If POT wins, poison takes effect, usually doing damage equal to full POT.
- If CON wins, damage equals half POT or less.

INVESTIGATOR INCOME

For the 1890s, roll 1D10: 1 = $500 + room & board, 2 = $1,000, 3 = $1,500, 4 = $2,000, 5 = $2,500, 6 = $3,000, 7 = $4,000, 8 = $5,000, 9 = $5,000, 10 = $10,000.

For the 1920s, roll 1D10: 1 = $1500 + room & board, 2 = $2,500, 3 + 4 = $3,500, 5 = $4,500, $6 = 5,500, 7 = $6,500, 8 = $7,500, 9 = $10,000, 10 = $20,000.

For the Present, roll 1D10: 1 = $15,000, 2 = $25,000, 3 = $35,000, 4 = $45,000, 5 = $55,000, 6 = $75,000, 7 = $100,000, 8 = $200,000, 9 = $300,000, 10 = $500,000.

The investigator also has property and other assets of value equal to five times yearly income: an investigator in the Present who makes $55,000 has $225,000 in assets. One tenth of that is banked as cash. Another one tenth is in stocks and bonds, convertible in 30 days. The remainder is in old books, a house, or whatever seems appropriate to the character.

INVESTIGATOR SKILL CATEGORIES

Some skills are in more than one category.

COMMUNICATION—Art, Bargain, Craft, Credit Rating, Disguise, Fast Talk, Other Language, Own Language, Persuade, Psychology.

MANIPULATION—Art, Conceal, Craft, Disguise, Drive Auto, Electrical Repair, First Aid, Handgun, Locksmith, Mechanical Repair, Photography, Pilot, Rifle, Shotgun, Submachine Gun.

PERCEPTION—Art, Listen, Spot Hidden, Track.

EXERTION—Art, Climb, Dodge, Hide, Jump, Machine Gun, Martial Arts, Operate Heavy Machine, Ride, Sneak, Swim, Throw.

THOUGHT—Accounting, Anthropology, Archaeology, Art, Astronomy, Biology, Cthulhu Mythos, Geology, History, Law, Library Use, Medicine, Natural History, Navigate, Occult, Pharmacy, Physics, Psychoanalysis.

SIGNS AND SIGILS

ELDER SIGN

YELLOW SIGN

PNAKOTIC PENTAGON

SIGN OF THE DARK MOTHER

SIGN OF KOTH

SIGN OF EIBON

INSANITY

TEMPORARY INSANITY—5 or more Sanity points lost in a single roll. See below tables for possible insanities. *Short-term lasts for 1D10+4 combat rounds. Longer-term lasts for 1D10x10 game hours. Player must roll D100. If result is INT x5 or less, consult Temporary Insanity Tables.*

INDEFINITE INSANITY—20% or more of current Sanity points lost in one game hour. *Effects last for 1D6 months, or as arranged. Keeper and player consult to choose an appropriate mental disorder.*

PERMANENT INSANITY—zero Sanity points reached. *Effects last for years, if not forever. Keeper and player consult to choose an appropriate mental disorder.*

SHORT TEMPORARY INSANITY
roll 1D10

1 fainting or screaming fit
2 flees in panic
3 physical hysterics or emotional outburst (laughing, crying, etc.)
4 babbling, incoherent, rapid speech, or logorrhea (a torrent of coherent speech)
5 intense phobia, perhaps rooting investigator to the spot
6 homicidal or suicidal mania
7 hallucinations or delusions
8 echopraxia or echolalia (investigator does/says what others around him do/say)
9 strange eating desire (dirt, slime, cannibalism, etc.)
10 stupor (assumes foetal position, oblivious to events) or catatonia (can stand but has no will or interest; may be led or forced to simple actions but takes no independent action)

SAMPLE SANITY LOSSES

SAN Loss	Prompting Situation
0/1D2	surprised to find mangled animal carcass
0/1D3	surprised to find corpse
0/1D3	surprised to find body part
0/1D4	see a stream flow with blood
1/1D4+1	find mangled human corpse
0/1D6	awake trapped in a coffin
0/1D6	witness a friend's violent death
1/1D6+1	meet someone you know to be dead
0/1D10	undergo severe torture
1/1D10	see a corpse rise from its grave
2/2D10+1	see gigantic severed head fall from sky

LONGER TEMPORARY INSANITY
roll 1D10

1 amnesia *or* stupor/catatonia
2 severe phobia (can flee, but sees object of obsession everywhere)
3 hallucinations
4 strange sexual desires (exhibitionism, nymphomania or satyriasis, teratophilia, etc.)
5 fetish (investigator latches onto some object, type of object, or person as a safety blanket)
6 uncontrollable tics, tremors, or inability to communicate via speech or writing
7 psychosomatic blindness, deafness, or loss of the use of a limb or limbs
8 brief reactive psychosis (incoherence, delusions, aberrant behavior, and/or hallucinations)
9 temporary paranoia
10 compulsive rituals (washing hands constantly, praying, walking in a particular rhythm, never stepping on cracks, checking one's gun constantly, etc.)

SAMPLE POISONS

poison	speed of effect	POT	symptoms
amanita	6-24 hours	15	violent stomach pains, vomiting, jaundice
arsenic	1/2 to 24 hours	16	burning pain, vomiting, violent diarrhea
belladonna	2 hours-2 days	16	rapid heartbeat, impaired vision, convulsions
black widow	2-8 hours	7	chills, sweating, nausea
chloral hydrate	1-3 minutes	17	unconsciousness for 1 hour; each added dose increases effect by 1 hour plus a 10% chance of respiratory failure
chloroform	1 round	15	unconsciousness, depressed respiration
cobra	15-60 minutes	16	convulsions, respiratory failure
curare	1 round	25	muscular paralysis, respiratory failure
cyanide	1-15 minutes	20	dizziness, convulsions, fainting
rattlesnake	15-60 minutes	10	vomiting, violent spasms, yellowish vision
Rohypnal, etc.	15-30 minutes	18	odorless, tasteless; unconsciousness or memory loss for 4-8 hours
scorpion	24-48 hours	9	intense pain, weakness, hemorrhaging
sleeping pills	10-30 minutes	6	normal sleep; each additional dose increases the chance for respiratory failure by 5%
strychnine	10-20 minutes	20	violent muscle contractions, asphyxiation

Index

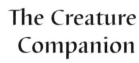